Thomas Francis Wade, Great Britain Foreign Office, Henry Kellett

Despatches from Mr. Wade and Vice-admiral Kellett Respecting the State of Affairs in China

presented to both houses of Parliament by command of Her Majesty, 1871

Thomas Francis Wade, Great Britain Foreign Office, Henry Kellett

Despatches from Mr. Wade and Vice-admiral Kellett Respecting the State of Affairs in China

presented to both houses of Parliament by command of Her Majesty, 1871

ISBN/EAN: 9783337735111

Printed in Europe, USA, Canada, Australia, Japan

Cover: Foto ©Andreas Hilbeck / pixelio.de

More available books at **www.hansebooks.com**

BRITISH

PARLIAMENTARY PAPERS

STATE OF

AFFAIRS IN CHINA

1871 - 1913

CLEVELAND

1915

CONTENTS

CHINA. No. 4 (1871).

DESPATCHES

FROM

MR. WADE AND VICE-ADMIRAL KELLETT

RESPECTING THE

STATE OF AFFAIRS

IN

CHINA.

Presented to both Houses of Parliament by Command of Her Majesty.
1871.

LONDON:
PRINTED BY HARRISON AND SONS.

[C.—367.] Price 1d.

LIST OF PAPERS.

Despatches from Mr. Wade and Vice-Admiral Kellett, respecting the State of Affairs in China.

No. 1.

Mr. Wade to Earl Granville.—(Received June 3.)

(Extract.)   *Peking, March 29, 1871.*

M. DE ROCHECHOUART has more than once assured me that, since his arrival in Peking, he remembers no time when there were so few complaints from the missionaries scattered throughout the Empire, and I have not had, since the winter commenced, a single alarm from any one of the Consular ports. Before he had been at Newchwang a month, Mr. Adkins wrote to say that, even without a gun-boat, he considered the place perfectly safe.

On the condition of Tien-tsin I inclose an extract from a letter published in the "North China Herald" of the 16th instant, and I beg attention not only to the writer's account of the attitude of the people at Tien-tsin, but to his mention of the medical missionary's reception in various parts of the interior of this province (Chih-li). He "was everywhere treated with civility."

At Che-foo, after the first alarm of peril last year, I have heard no rumour of disquiet. The American missionaries who had fled from Teng-chow returned to their station within a few weeks.

I forwarded your Lordship Mr. Medhurst's despatch of the 3rd of December.

Up the river all has been quiet. At Hankow there is an immense population of Chinese from all provinces. There are large Romish establishments. There was, last year, a demonstration against a picnic party (of whom the Consul was one) occasioned by the belief that the foreigners were about to eat their own little children. Lastly, at Wu Chang, the provincial capital, on the other side of the river, foreigners have been continually insulted or assaulted any time these ten years. Hankow, therefore, was the one place about which I felt some anxiety. The community have not been in any way disturbed there. Neither have they at Chin-kiang or Kiu-kiang, although in Kiang-si, the province in which the latter port lies, two Romish establishment have been destroyed.

Ningpo has been perfectly quiet from first to last. So has Foo-chow, a port of known hostility, and at which the authorities, on the only occasion on which appeal to them became necessary, appear to have shown unusual activity, in the interests, too, of missionaries. Within the last few days Mr. Sinclair reports the publication at Foo-chow of the Proclamation of which I induced the Prince of Kung to direct the issue by the Provincial Governments.

Your Lordship has my reports of the state of things at Amoy, the alarm caused by apparent preparations for war, and the restoration of confidence even before the steps authorized by me were made known. Let me add that the only section of the Amoy population from which danger was apprehended, was the section which always has been, and will be, dangerous. There is no ground for stating that the demeanour of the people at Amoy is changed any more than at Swatow, Canton, Taiwan, or Tamsuy, which four ports complete our list of places where we have communities to protect.

I have not failed to expose the slackness of the Chinese Government in the matter of the Tien-tsin massacre, the ineptitude which has distinguished its proceedings both before and since the event. The penalty of these may indeed yet be to be inflicted by the Power most outraged ; and it is impossible to predict, if France decide upon hostile action, the extent to which foreign interests, those of France included, may be compromised. We can certainly not afford to diminish our naval force in these seas; but, this precaution observed, I think I am justified in maintaining that, so far as the temper of the people is concerned, Her Majesty's Government will be safely guided by my official telegrams.

                                                            B 2

If the assumption be correct that the people heretofore well disposed are everywhere becoming hostile to the foreigner, the foreigner must shortly elect either to conquer the country or to leave it ; to my eye there is no indication of such a change.

Inclosure in No. 1.

Extract from the " North China Herald" of March 16, 1871.

TIEN-TSIN.—THE past winter has been remarkable for its fine clear weather and for few windy days. Up to nearly the Chinese new year we had only five windy days from the closing of the river. During the new year holiday time we had our coldest weather, the thermometer falling to two degrees below zero. In addition to the usual amusements of former winters, such as fox and hare hunting and skating, we added that of paper hunts ; and what with our pleasant weather, and our several amusements, the winter has passed over very rapidly. The sporting members of the community had a meeting a few days back, and elected race stewards for the current year; and as we hear of several wonderful fast ponies having been bought, we are led to suppose we shall see a brilliant race meeting next May. Our letters, thanks to the admirable system established by the Inspector-General of Customs, have been received with extraordinary regularity; and as we have also been receiving regular weekly news from Europe by the Russian telegraph, we have assuredly had no cause to complain of any lack of intelligence regarding the great events which have been taking place there. In respect to the conduct of the Chinese people at Tien-tsin towards foreigners, I have only to say that I have observed no difference from any of the previous winters during the last ten years, since the opening of this port to foreign trade. We have gone up to town as we used to do, and did not meet with abuse or molestation in the slightest degree. Several of the residents have been up the country, and returned sound and safe, having had no complaint against the people of the interior. Dr. Treat, an American medical missionary, has just arrived here ; and we learn he has been in various parts of the interior of the province during the last few months, and was everywhere treated with civility by the people. In the interior of the North of China, north of this to Mongolia, and west of this to Shanse, all has been tranquil and no bands of robbers have appeared. The Viceroy of this province, Li-hung Chang, has resided during all the winter at Tien-tsin, as the Edict stated he would do which mentioned his appointment to the post, instead of at Paou-ting-foo. He removed into the Yamên formerly occupied by Chung-how, just before the setting in of the cold weather.

Despatch referred to in Mr. Wade's despatch of March 29, 1871.

Mr. Wade to Earl Granville.

(Extract.) Peking, December 19, 1870.
I NOW beg to inclose a despatch from Mr. Medhurst to the effect that the Proclamation has been issued at Shanghae.
There is nothing remarkable, as Mr. Medhurst seems to think, in its appearing merely under the seal of the Taoutae. Had that officer put it forth as from himself, he might have been charged with taking from its importance. As it is, he publishes it as coming from his immediate superior in foreign business, namely, the Minister Superintendent of Trade, who sends it him under instructions from the Yamên of Foreign Affairs. This Superintendent of Trade, as I have before explained, acts as a sort of Consul-General between the Maritime Customs of the Southern Ports and the Yamên. The Taoutae's proceeding is perfectly *en règle.* I beg particular attention to the second paragraph of Mr. Medhurst's despatch, in which, speaking of the effect of the Proclamation upon the native public in his vicinity, he observes that " their demeanour towards foreigners has, as a rule, been always so exemplary that it could not well be improved upon." I have

myself been in the habit of regarding the population of Shanghae and its vicinity as the last from which anything like aggressive action was to be looked for.

Consul Medhurst to Mr. Wade.

Sir,   *Shanghae, December* 3, 1870.

THE Proclamation, a translation of which was inclosed in your despatch dated the 26th October last, has been issued here, but merely under the seal of the Taoutae, who quotes the Proclamation as having been forwarded to him by the Officiating Superintendent of Commercial Affairs under instructions from the Tsung-li Yamên.

I have not been able so far to detect any effects which the issue of the Proclamation has had upon the people within this immediate neighbourhood. Indeed, their demeanour towards foreigners has, as a rule, been always so exemplary that it could not well be improved upon.

An instance occurred a short time ago in which a shooting party visiting Su-chow received some annoyance whilst walking through the city, and I availed myself of the opportunity to address the Futae Ting, and suggested that the Proclamation might, if issued there, have a beneficial effect. His reply, which is courteous and to the point, is inclosed herewith for your information.

From Chin-kiang, Mr. Interpreter Gardner reports that he has as yet seen nothing of the Proclamation, but that the people are friendly and quiet.

Your, &c.
(Signed)   W. M. MEDHURST.

Ting, Futae, to Consul Medhurst.

(Translation.)

TING, Governor of Kiang-su, &c., &c., makes a communication in reply.

On the 27th day of the 10th moon (19th November, 1870) the writer received a despatch from the Consul, to the effect that four foreigners who had returned to Shanghae from a shooting excursion reported that wherever they went they were kindly treated by the Chinese, but on the 14th November, when passing down the main street of Su-chow, the people pelted and hooted them, and, on reaching the pagoda, the priests treated them with rudeness, and used threatening language, with a view to extorting money. The Consul cannot understand how such a disturbance could have occurred in Su-chow, a city the people of which have hitherto been so orderly, and in which his Excellency the Governor resides.

He is perfectly aware that his Excellency always governs justly, and he is sure that after reporting this case such a disturbance is never likely to arise again. (The Consul goes on to state that) a proclamation has been issued by the Tsung-li Yamên relative to the Tien-tsin outrage, which was sent to Mr. Wade, Her Britannic Majesty's Chargé d'Affaires resident at Peking, with the promise that it should be circulated throughout the provinces. The proclamation Mr. Wade has transmitted to the Consul, who forwards it to his Excellency for his information, with the request that it may be extensively promulgated (within his jurisdiction) so as to prevent any recurrence of such disturbance. The Consul then begs for an answer.

The Governor has received the above quoted despatch, and knows that all trade (and intercourse) between foreigners and Chinese ought to be protected, as provided for by the Treaty. It appears, however, that Englishmen, whilst on a shooting excursion, have been pelted in Su-chow, and the priests in the pagoda have used threatening language to them, in order to extort money, and these priests are greatly to blame, and this ill-treatment is much to be deplored. His Excellency does not know whether the priests did get anything out of the Englishmen, but if they did they must be severely punished, so as to prevent any recurrence of the same annoyance. His Excellency has therefore ordered the magistrate (of Su-chow) to institute a strict inquiry, and get at the root of the case.

With reference to the Tien-tsin outrage, so soon as the writer reached that place he, in conjunction with (the authorities on the spot) took most stringent measures for arresting (the criminals) and moreover employed detectives in the cities and provinces beyond, who seized and brought up (to Tien-tsin) all the ringleaders and accomplices.

The Proclamation of the Tsung-li Yamên was received by the Governor some days ago from the Acting Superintendent of Trade Kwei, and it was immediately forwarded to

the Superintendent of Customs to be published. The Governor is now writing to the Acting Superintendent of Trade on this subject, and will besides order the Superintendents of Customs to post up copies of it at once, so as to prevent all disturbances hereafter.
A necessary communication addressed to Mr. Consul Medhurst.
T'ung Chih, 9th year, 10th month, 29th day (21 November, 1870).

No. 2.

The Secretary to the Admiralty to Mr. Hammond.—(Received May 31.)

(Extract.) *Admiralty, May 30, 1871.*
I AM commanded by my Lords Commissioners of the Admiralty to transmit to you, for the information of Earl Granville, the inclosed extract from a letter of Vice-Admiral Sir Henry Kellett, dated Yokohama, the 8th ultimo, reporting on the state of affairs in China and Japan.

Inclosure in No. 2.

Vice-Admiral Sir H. Kellett to the Secretary to the Admiralty.

(Extract.) *Yokohama, April 8, 1871.*
SINCE the despatch of my last letter of proceedings on the 28th ultimo, I have visited Shanghae, Hiogo, and Osaka, on my way to this port, and have found everything perfectly quiet and satisfactory both in China and Japan.
The River Peiho is again open to navigation. The city of Tien-tsin is now perfectly safe for foreigners, and the greatest order continues to prevail amongst the inhabitants.

No. 3.

The Secretary to the Admiralty to Mr. Hammond.—(Received June 5.)

(Extract.) *Admiralty, June 3, 1871.*
I AM commanded by my Lords Commissioners of the Admiralty to transmit herewith, for the information of Earl Granville, extracts of a general letter of Vice-Admiral Sir Henry Kellett, dated the 24th of March.

Inclosure in No. 3.

Vice-Admiral Sir H. Kellett to the Secretary to the Admiralty.

(Extract.) *Foo-chow, March 24, 1871.*
SINCE the date of my last general letter, nothing of importance has occurred in China or Japan.
From here I go to Ningpo, Shanghae, and Yokohama.

CHINA. No. 4 (1871).

DESPATCHES from Mr. Wade and Vice-Admiral Kellett, respecting the State of Affairs in China.

Presented to both Houses of Parliament by Command of Her Majesty. 1871.

CHINA. No. 1 (1885).   *no. 2*

CORRESPONDENCE

RESPECTING THE

STATE OF AFFAIRS IN CHINA.

Presented to both Houses of Parliament by Command of Her Majesty.
1885.

LONDON:
PRINTED BY HARRISON AND SONS.

To be purchased, either directly or through any Bookseller, from any of the following Agents, viz.,
Messrs. HANSARD, 32, Abingdon Street, Westminster, and 6, Great Turnstile, Holborn;
Messrs. EYRE and SPOTTISWOODE, East Harding Street, Fleet Street, and Sale Office, House of Lords
Messrs. ADAM and CHARLES BLACK, of Edinburgh;
Messrs. ALEXANDER THOM and Co. (Limited), or Messrs. HODGES, FIGGIS, and Co., of Dublin.

[C.--4245.]   *Price 10½d,*

TABLE OF CONTENTS.

[561]

TABLE OF CONTENTS.

Correspondence respecting the State of Affairs in China.

No. 1.

Earl Granville to Lord Ampthill.[*][†][‡]

My Lord,   *Foreign Office, November* 21, 1883.

IN view of the crisis which appears to be imminent in China, I have to request your Excellency to propose, confidentially, to the German Government, that the British and German Admirals should be instructed to concert together in case of necessity for the protection of their respective nationals.

I have instructed Her Majesty's Minister at Washington in a similar sense.

I am, &c.
(Signed)   GRANVILLE.

No. 2.

Mr. West to Earl Granville.[‡]—*(Received November* 24.)

(Telegraphic.)   *Washington, November* 24, 1883.

INSTRUCTIONS will be sent to the American Admiral on China Station to act in concert with the vessels of England and other neutral Powers in protecting their respective subjects in China.

No. 3.

Lord Ampthill to Earl Granville.[§]—*(Received November* 26, 12·30 P.M.)

(Telegraphic.)   *Berlin, November* 26, 1883, 11 A.M.

YOUR Lordship's telegram of the 21st instant.

Minister for Foreign Affairs informs me that instructions have been sent to German Admiral in China seas to concert measures with British Admiral for protection of our respective subjects.

One or two more German men-of-war will be ordered to reinforce the squadron on the China Station.

No. 4.

The Secretary to the Admiralty to Sir J. Pauncefote.—*(Received November* 27.)

Sir,   *Admiralty, November* 26, 1883.

I AM commanded by my Lords Commissioners of the Admiralty to transmit, for the information of the Secretary of State for Foreign Affairs, a copy of a telegram which has been sent to the Commander-in-chief on the China Station at Shanghae, desiring him to act in concert with the German Admiral if the necessity should arise.

I am, &c.
(Signed)   G. TRYON.

---

[*] Also to Mr. West.   [†] Substance telegraphed.   [‡] Copy to Admiralty.
                               [§] Substance to Admiralty.

Inclosure in No. 4.

The Secretary to the Admiralty to Vice-Admiral Willes.

(Telegraphic.)   *Admiralty, November* 26, 1883.
INSTRUCTIONS sent to German Admiral, China, to concert measures with British Admiral for protection of British and German subjects against possible outbreak of population. One or two more German ships of war will be ordered to reinforce squadron.
You are to concert with German Admiral in event of any necessity arising.
Similar arrangement has been proposed to United States' Government.

No. 5.

The Secretary to the Admiralty to Sir J. Pauncefote.—(Received November 28.)

Sir,   *Admiralty, November* 27, 1883.
WITH reference to my letter of the 26th instant, stating that Vice-Admiral Willes had been directed to concert with the German Admiral on the China Station for the protection of British and German subjects should the necessity arise, I am commanded by my Lords Commissioners of the Admiralty to request that you will state to Earl Granville that Vice-Admiral Willes has been informed that the United States' Government have sent similar instructions to their Admiral commanding in the China seas.
                                                        I am, &c.
                                      (Signed)   G. TRYON.

No. 6.

*Earl Granville to Lord Ampthill.**

My Lord,   *Foreign Office, November* 29, 1883.
WITH reference to your telegram of the 26th instant, in which you report the steps taken by the German Government, with a view to the protection of British and German subjects in China, I am informed by Her Majesty's Minister at Washington that the answer received from the United States' Government is to the effect that they will instruct their Admiral in the China seas to act in concert with the vessels of Great Britain and other neutral Powers.
    I have to request that, under these circumstances, your Excellency will ascertain whether the German Government does not consider it desirable that the instructions on this point which have been issued to the British and German Admirals should be similarly extended.
    I have communicated the substance of this despatch to your Excellency to-day by telegraph.
                                                        I am, &c.
                                      (Signed)   GRANVILLE.

No. 7.

Lord Ampthill to Earl Granville.—(Received December 1.)

(Telegraphic.)   *Berlin, December* 1, 1883.
MINISTER of Foreign Affairs agrees to instruct German Admiral on China Station to act in concert with ships of England and America, and other neutral Powers, for protection of respective subjects in China.

---

* Copy to Admiralty

3

No. 8.

Sir J. Pauncefote to the Secretary to the Admiralty.

THE Under-Secretary of State presents his compliments to the Secretary to the Admiralty, and is directed by Earl Granville to request that he will inform the Lords Commissioners of the Admiralty that a telegram has been received from Her Majesty's Ambassador at Berlin, to the effect that the German Government agree to instruct their Admiral in the Chinese seas to act in concert with the ships of England, America, and other neutral Powers for the protection of their respective subjects.
Foreign Office, December 1, 1883.

No. 9.

Lord Ampthill to Earl Granville.—(*Received December 3.*)

My Lord,   *Berlin, November 26, 1883.*
WITH reference to your Lordship's telegram of the 21st instant, I have the honour to state that the Acting Minister for Foreign Affairs, in the absence of Count Hatzfeldt, called to say that the German Government had determined to send instructions to the German Admiral on the Chinese Station to concert measures with the British Admiral in the sense suggested by Her Majesty's Government for the protection of our respective subjects.
I understood his Excellency to say that other German ships would probably be sent to reinforce the German squadron in the China seas.
I have, &c.
(Signed)   AMPTHILL.

No. 10.

Lord Ampthill to Earl Granville.—(*Received December 3.*)

My Lord,   *Berlin, December 1, 1883.*
IN obedience to your Lordship's telegraphic instruction of the 29th ultimo, I asked the German Minister for Foreign Affairs whether, considering that the United States' Government had instructed the American Admiral on the China Station to act in concert with the English and German Admirals, as well as with the ships of neutral Powers, his Excellency did not think that it would be desirable to instruct our Admirals similarly for the protection of our respective subjects.
Count Hatzfeldt replied that he saw no objection to the course proposed, and that he would speak in that sense to the Minister of Marine, General Caprivi.
I have, &c.
(Signed)   AMPTHILL.

No. 11.

Earl Granville to Mr. Fraser.†

Sir,   *Foreign Office, December 5, 1883.*
THE German and United States' Governments have agreed with Her Majesty's Government to instruct their Admirals in the China seas to concert with the Commanders of the men-of-war of Great Britain and the other neutral Powers for the protection of neutral subjects.
I have to request that you will confidentially invite the Italian Government to issue similar instructions to its naval Commander on the China Station, as a crisis seems unfortunately to be impending.
I am, &c.
(Signed)   GRANVILLE.

* Substance telegraphed.
† Also to Sir E. Thornton, Sir C. Wyke, and Mr. Le Poer Trench.
[561]   B 2

4

No. 12.

Earl Granville to Viscount Lyons.

My Lord,   *Foreign Office, December 5, 1883.*
   I HAVE to inform your Excellency that, after sounding the German and United States' Governments, Her Majesty's Government have proposed to all the neutral Powers who have men-of-war on the China Station to concert, if war should unfortunately break out between France and China, for the protection of neutrals.
                                              I am, &c.
                              (Signed)   GRANVILLE.

No. 13.

Sir J. Pauncefote to the Secretary to the Admiralty.

Sir,   *Foreign Office, December 5, 1883.*
   WITH reference to the letter from this Office of the 1st instant, I am directed by Earl Granville to transmit to you herewith, to be laid before the Lords Commissioners of the Admiralty, copy of a telegram which his Lordship is about to address to Her Majesty's Representatives at Rome, St. Petersburgh, Lisbon, and in Japan, inviting the Italian, Russian, Portuguese, and Japanese Governments to instruct their naval Commander in the China seas to concert with the Commanders of the British and other neutral ships of war for the protection of neutral subjects;* and I am to request that you will move their Lordships to cause instructions in this sense to be addressed to the British Admiral.
                                              I am, &c.
                              (Signed)   JULIAN PAUNCEFOTE.

No. 14.

The Secretary to the Admiralty to Sir J. Pauncefote.†—(Received December 6.)

Sir,   *Admiralty, December 5, 1883.*
   I HAVE received and laid before my Lords Commissioners of the Admiralty your letter of the 5th instant, sending a copy of a telegram which the Secretary of State is about to dispatch, inviting the Italian, Russian, Portuguese, and Japanese Governments to instruct their naval Commanders in the China seas to concert with the Commanders of British and other neutral ships of war for the protection of neutral subjects, and requesting that instructions in this sense may be addressed to the British Admiral.
   2. My Lords desire me to request that you will state to Earl Granville that the telegram of which a copy is attached has been this day sent to Vice-Admiral Willes.
                                              I am, &c.
                              (Signed)   G. TRYON.

Inclosure in No. 14.

The Secretary to the Admiralty to Vice-Admiral Willes.

(Telegraphic.)   *Admiralty, December 5, 1883.*
   THE Governments of Italy, Russia, Portugal, and Japan have been invited to instruct their naval Commanders in China seas to concert with you and Commanders of other neutral men-of-war for protection of neutral subjects.
   Governments of Germany and United States will send instructions in this sense to their Admirals.

---

* See No. 11.
† Copy to Viscount Lyons, Mr. Fraser, Lord Ampthill, Sir E. Thornton, Mr. West, Mr. P. Le Poer Trench, C. Wyke, and Sir H. Parkes.

No. 15.

*Earl Granville to Mr. West.**

Sir, *Foreign Office, December 6,* 1883.

WITH reference to your telegram of the 24th ultimo, I have to request that you will inform the Government of the United States that an invitation has been addressed to the Governments of Italy, Russia, Portugal, and Japan, on the part of Her Majesty's Government, to issue instructions to the Commanders of their respective naval forces in the China seas to concert measures with the officers in command of the British and other ships of war belonging to neutral Powers for the protection of the subjects of those Powers, should such measures become necessary in consequence of the differences between France and China.

I am, &c.
(Signed) GRANVILLE.

No. 16.

Mr. Fraser to Earl Granville.†—(Received December 7.)

(Telegraphic.) *Rome, December 7,* 1883.

IN reply to your Lordship's telegram of the 5th instant, Italian Government is sending out two ships to the China seas, and will instruct the Senior Officer to act in conformity with your Lordship's suggestion for the protection of neutral subjects.

No. 17.

Mr. Le Poer Trench to Earl Granville.‡—(Received December 9.)

(Telegraphic.) *Tôkiô, December 9,* 1883.

IN reply to your Lordship's telegram of the 5th instant Japanese Government entirely concur in proposal, and, if thought necessary, will send ships of war to China seas, and instruct Commander-in-chief in sense desired as to protection of neutral subjects.

No. 18.

Mr. West to Earl Granville.—(Received December 10.)

My Lord, *Washington, November 25,* 1883.

WITH reference to your Lordship's telegram of the 21st instant, and to my reply thereto, I have the honour to inclose to your Lordship herewith copy of a note which I have received from the Secretary of State, informing me that the President has directed instructions to be sent to the Admiral commanding the Asiatic squadron of the United States to act in concert with the vessels of England and other neutral European or American Powers in protecting the lives and property of their citizens.

I have, &c.
(Signed) L. S. SACKVILLE WEST.

---

* Substance telegraphed.
† Communicated to Admiralty, Viscount Lyons, Sir H. Parkes, Lord Ampthill, Mr. West, Mr. P. Le Poer Trench, Sir C. Wyke, and Sir E. Thornton.
‡ Communicated to Admiralty, copy to Viscount Lyons, Sir H. Parkes, Mr. Fraser, Lord Ampthill, Sir E. Thornton, Mr. West, Sir C. Wyke, and Mr. P. Le Poer Trench.

Inclosure in No. 18.

Mr. Frelinghuysen to Mr. West.

Sir,   *Department of State, Washington, November* 24, 1883.
I HAVE the honour to acknowledge the receipt of your note of the 22nd instant, in which you state that Earl Granville has instructed you to propose confidentially to the Government of the United States that orders be sent to the American and British Admirals in relation to the apparently impending crisis in China.

In reply, I have the honour, confidentially, to inform you that the President has directed instructions to be sent to the Admiral commanding the Asiatic squadron of the United States to act in concert with the vessels of England and other neutral European or American Powers in protecting the lives and property of our and their citizens, taking care to observe the strict neutrality of this Government.

I have, &c.
(Signed)   FREDERICK T. FRELINGHUYSEN.

No. 19.

Sir C. Wyke to Earl Granville.—(Received December 10.)

(Telegraphic.)   *Lisbon, December* 10, 1883.
PORTUGUESE Government accept with much satisfaction proposal of Her Majesty's Government, and will telegraph instructions to naval Commander at Macao as to protection of neutral subjects.

No. 20.

Earl Granville to Sir R. Morier.†‡

Sir,   *Foreign Office, December* 11, 1883.
THE German and United States' Governments have agreed with Her Majesty's Government to instruct their Admirals in the China seas to concert with the Commanders of the men-of-war of Great Britain and the other neutral Powers for the protection of neutral subjects.

I have to request that you will confidentially invite the Spanish Government to issue similar instructions to their naval Commanders on the China Station, as a crisis seems unfortunately to be impending.

I am, &c.
(Signed)   GRANVILLE.

No. 21.

Mr. Fraser to Earl Granville.—(Received December 13.)

My Lord,   *Rome, December* 7, 1883.
I HAVE the honour to transmit herewith to your Lordship, in reference to your telegram of the 5th and to my reply of the 7th instant, the copy of a Confidential note from the Italian Ministry for Foreign Affairs, to the effect that two Italian ships of war, the "Cristoforo Colombo" and the "Caracciolo," are on their way to Singapore for the China seas, and that their Senior Naval Officer will be directed to concert with the Commanders of Her Majesty's ships, and those of other neutral vessels, for the protection of neutrals in the event of hostilities.

I have, &c.
(Signed)   HUGH FRASER.

---

* Communicated to Admiralty, copy to Viscount Lyons, Sir H. Parkes, Mr. Fraser, Lord Ampthill, Sir E. Thornton, Mr. West, Sir C. Wyke, and Mr. P. Le Poer Trench.
† Substance telegraphed.
‡ Communicated to Admiralty.

Inclosure in No. 21.

M. Mancini to Mr. Fraser.

M. le Chargé d'Affaires,   *Rome, le 6 Décembre,* 1883.

VOUS êtes venu, aujourd'hui, nous demander au nom de votre Gouvernement, si des navires Italiens vont se trouver dans les eaux Chinoises, nous proposant, pour le cas où il en serait ainsi, de donner instruction à notre Commandant Supérieur de s'associer à l'œuvre commune de protection des intérêts des neutres pour laquelle un accord existe déjà, en vue de l'éventualité où des hostilités éclateraient entre la France et la Chine, entre l'Angleterre, l'Allemagne, et les États-Unis.

Deux navires Italiens, le "Cristoforo Colombo" et le "Caracciolo" ne tarderont pas à paraître dans les parages de la Chine. Le "Cristoforo Colombo" a dépassé Aden depuis quelques jours et le "Caracciolo" doit, venant d'Australie, se joindre au "Cristoforo Colombo" à Singapore pour continuer ensemble leur route directement vers le nord. Ainsi nous sommes heureux d'être en mesure d'accepter l'offre du Gouvernement de la Reine.

Notre Commandant Supérieur va recevoir instruction de se concerter, à cet effet, avec les Commandants des trois escadres.

Vous priant de porter ce qui précède à la connaissance de votre Gouvernement, je saisis, &c.

           (Signé)   P. S. MANCINI.

(Translation.)

M. le Chargé d'Affaires,   *Rome, December* 6, 1883.

YOU inquired to-day in the name of your Government whether Italian ships of war will be sent to the China seas, inviting us, in the event of such being the case, to issue instructions to our Senior Commanding Officer to act in concert for the common object of protecting the interests of neutral subjects for which, in the eventuality of hostilities breaking out between France and China, an agreement already exists between England, Germany, and the United States.

It will not be long before two Italian vessels of war, the "Cristoforo Colombo" and the "Caracciolo," will arrive in Chinese waters. The "Cristoforo Colombo" passed Aden some days since, and the "Caracciolo" is under orders on its way from Australia to join the "Cristoforo Colombo" at Singapore, in order to proceed in company in a due northerly direction. Thus we are gratified at being in a position to accept the proposal of Her Majesty's Government.

Our Senior Commanding Officer will be instructed to act accordingly in concert with the Commanders of the three naval squadrons.

Requesting you to convey the above to the knowledge of your Government, I avail, &c.

           (Signed)   P. S. MANCINI.

No. 22.

Sir E. Thornton to Earl Granville.*—(Received December 13.)

(Telegraphic.)   *St. Petersburgh, December* 13, 1883.

I HAVE communicated invitation contained in your telegram of the 5th instant to the Russian Government. They adhere to your Lordship's proposal within the limits in which such an arrangement was made in the waters of Egypt in 1882.

No. 23.

Viscount Lyons to Earl Granville.—(Received December 14.)

My Lord,   *Paris, December* 13, 1883.

M. JULES FERRY said to me yesterday that it appeared that some understanding, with a view to joint action on the part of their naval forces in China, had been proposed by Great Britain to other Powers. Could I, he asked, give him any definite information on the subject.

           * Communicated to Admiralty.

I answered that Her Majesty's Government had in fact proposed to all the neutral Powers who had men-of-war on the China Station to concert for the protection of neutrals if war should unfortunately break out between France and China.

M. Jules Ferry went on to say that some little time ago Prince Hohenlohe, the German Ambassador, had come to him with a suggestion from Germany, that in consequence of the then recent outbreak at Canton the several Powers, France included, should send gun-boats to that place for the protection of their subjects, and should agree that the command of the united force should be taken by the officer of highest rank, to whatever nation he might belong. M. Jules Ferry had, he told me, agreed to the suggestion. The command would, he supposed, devolve upon Great Britain, and he was quite willing that this should be the case. He would, however, ask me whether there was any connection between the suggestion brought to him by Prince Hohenlohe and the proposal made by Great Britain to the neutral Powers.

I said that the English proposal did not appear to refer to the past outbreak at Canton, but to the contingency (I hoped a very improbable one) of war between France and China; and I added that I conceived that it had been made in general terms, and that it did not contain any suggestions as to the command or other details.

I have, &c.
(Signed) LYONS.

No. 24.

Sir R. Morier to Earl Granville.—(*Received December* 14.)

(Telegraphic.) *Madrid, December* 14, 1883.
THE Admiralty has been instructed to send orders to the Spanish Commanders in Chinese waters in the sense of your Lordship's telegram of the 11th instant.†

No. 25.

Sir C. Wyke to Earl Granville.—(*Received December* 15.)

My Lord, *Lisbon, December* 6, 1883.
IMMEDIATELY upon the receipt of your Lordship's telegram of yesterday I addressed a note to Senhor du Bocage, copy of which I have the honour to inclose, proposing, confidentially, in view of the impending crisis in China, that the Portuguese Government should send instructions to their naval Commanders in Chinese waters to concert with the Commanders of the British and other neutral ships of war for the protection of neutral subjects, and informing him that the German and United States' Governments would instruct their Admirals in this sense.

I have, &c.
(Signed) CHARLES LENNOX WYKE.

Inclosure in No. 25.

Sir C. Wyke to Senhor du Bocage.

M. le Ministre, *Lisbon, December* 5, 1883.
I HAVE just been instructed by Earl Granville to propose, confidentially, to the King's Government, that, in view of the crisis which is impending in China, they should cause instructions to be sent to the Portuguese naval Commanders in Chinese waters to concert measures with the officers commanding British and other neutral vessels of war for the purpose of protecting the subjects of neutral nations.

I may add that both the German and United States' Governments are about to instruct their Admirals to this effect.

Your Excellency will greatly oblige me by informing me, at your earliest

* Communicated to Admiralty, Viscount Lyons, Lord Ampthill, Mr. West, Mr. P. Le Poer Trench, Sir C. Wyke, Mr. Fraser, Sir H. Parkes, and Sir E. Thornton.
† See No. 20.

convenience, whether the Government of His Most Faithful Majesty are inclined to accede to this proposal from Her Majesty's Government.

I avail, &c.

(Signed)　　CHARLES LENNOX WYKE.

No. 26.

*Earl Granville to Sir E. Thornton.**

Sir,　　　　　　　　　　　　　*Foreign Office, December 15, 1883.*

I HAVE to request that your Excellency will furnish me with full explanations of the conditions which appear, from your telegram of the 13th instant, to be attached by the Russian Government to their acceptance of the proposal, that the neutral Powers having ships in the China seas should co-operate for the protection of their subjects in the event of war between France and China.

I am, &c.

(Signed)　　GRANVILLE.

No. 27.

Sir C. Wyke to Earl Granville.†—(Received December 17.

My Lord,　　　　　　　　　　　*Lisbon, December 10, 1883.*

I HAVE the honour to inclose herewith translation of a note which I have just received from the Minister for Foreign Affairs, stating that the Portuguese Government have much satisfaction in accepting the proposal of Her Majesty's Government, which I conveyed to them in compliance with your Lordship's telegram of the 5th instant, that they should send instructions to their naval Commander in the Chinese seas to concert with the Commanders of the British and other neutral ships of war for the protection of neutral subjects.

Senhor du Bocage adds that orders in this sense will be transmitted by telegraph to the Commander of the Portuguese naval forces at Macao.

I have, &c.

(Signed)　　CHARLES LENNOX WYKE.

Inclosure in No. 27.

Senhor du Bocage to Sir C. Wyke.

(Translation.)

Your Excellency,　　　　　　*Foreign Department, Lisbon, December 7, 1883.*

I HAVE before me the note which your Excellency did me the honour to address to me on the 5th instant, proposing, in the name of your Government to that of His Majesty, that, in view of the impending crisis in China, instructions should be sent to the officer in command of the Portuguese naval forces in Chinese waters for him to concert with the commanding officers of the ships of war of Great Britain and of other neutral nations the necessary measures for the protection of their respective subjects.

His Majesty's Government, acknowledging as they do the advantages of the agreement referred to, gladly accept the proposal made by Her Britannic Majesty's Government; and, being anxious to carry the same into effect as soon as possible, will telegraph the necessary instructions to the commanding officer of the Portuguese naval forces at Macao.

I avail, &c.

(Signed)　　JOSÉ V. B. DU BOCAGE.

---

* Substance telegraphed.
† Copy to Admiralty, Viscount Lyons, Lord Ampthill, Mr. Fraser, and Sir R. Morier.

10

No. 28.

Sir E. Thornton to Earl Granville.*—(Received December 17.)

My Lord,   *St. Petersburgh, December 13, 1883.*

ON the receipt of your Lordship's telegram of the 5th instant I called upon M. Vlangaly and submitted to him, confidentially, the proposal made by Her Majesty's Government that instructions should be sent to the Russian naval Commander in the China seas to concert with the Commanders of the British and other neutral ships of war for the protection of neutral subjects.

I also informed his Excellency that the Governments of Germany and of the United States had agreed to instruct their Admirals in this sense.

M. Vlangaly replied that he would consult with the Navy Department upon the subject, and would take the orders of His Imperial Majesty. He, at the same time, expressed his opinion that the naval Commanders would have to exercise great caution in approaching Chinese ports with a view to affording protection to foreigners residing there; for he did not doubt that if war were declared, and even in anticipation of its declaration, torpedoes would be laid down by the Chinese authorities, but in so careless a manner that even they might themselves be ignorant of their exact position. He pointed out, also, that Canton could only be approached by vessels of light draught.

I called again upon his Excellency on the 12th instant, when he informed me that he had not yet had an opportunity of taking the Emperor's orders, and again yesterday, but still he said that he was not able to give me an answer; inquiries were, however, being made as to the course which had been pursued on previous similar occasions, and particularly last year at Alexandria, but that he would soon send me an answer.

I conjecture, however, that the Imperial Government intend to assent to your Lordship's proposal, because M. Vlangaly observed, in the course of conversation, that it might be well to establish it as a principle, that when there were disturbances in Eastern countries like China, involving danger to foreigners, it should be a matter of course that foreign ships of war should combine for their protection, whether the vessels belonged to the nation of those who were exposed to danger or not.

I replied that the oftener the instances of such concert were repeated the more likely it would be that it would become an established custom; and I trusted that if it should be needed this would be one of those instances.

I have, &c.
(Signed)   EDWD. THORNTON.

No. 29.

Sir E. Thornton to Earl Granville.*—(Received December 17.)

My Lord,   *St. Petersburgh, December 13, 1883.*

WITH reference to my despatch of to-day's date, I have the honour to inclose copy of a private note which I have just received from M. Vlangaly, in which his Excellency states that the Imperial Government adhere to your Lordship's proposal within the same limits in which a similar arrangement was made in the waters of Egypt.

I have, &c.
(Signed)   EDWD. THORNTON.

Inclosure in No. 29.

M. Vlangaly to Sir E. Thornton.

Mon cher Sir Edward,   *St. Pétersbourg, le 1 (13) Décembre, 1883.*

JE m'empresse de vous faire part que notre Gouvernement adhère à la proposition de Lord Granville dans les mêmes limites que cela a été fait dans les eaux de l'Égypte.

Votre, &c.
(Signé)   A. VLANGALY.

* Copy to Admiralty, Lord Lyons, Lord Ampthill, Mr. Fraser, Sir R. Morier, and Sir C. Wyke.

(Translation.)

My dear Sir Edward,   *St. Petersburgh, December* 1 (13), 1883.
   I HASTEN to inform you that our Government adhere to Lord Granville's proposal within the same limits in which a similar arrangement was made in Egyptian waters.

Yours, &c.
(Signed)   A. VLANGALY.

No. 30.

*Earl Granville to Sir H. Elliot.**

Sir,   *Foreign Office, December* 21, 1883.
   IT is stated in the newspapers that the Austro-Hungarian Government contemplate sending a man-of-war to the coast of China.
   I have to-day requested your Excellency, by telegraph, to ascertain whether this is the case, and I have requested you, if it should be so, to ask Count Kálnoky whether the Government of His Imperial and Royal Majesty are disposed to authorize the officer in command of their naval force in the China seas to concert with the Commanders of the men-of-war of Great Britain and the other neutral Powers for the protection of neutrals.

I am, &c.
(Signed)   GRANVILLE.

No. 31.

Sir E. Thornton to Earl Granville.†—(Received December 22.)

My Lord,   *St. Petersburgh, December* 17, 1883.
   WITH reference to your Lordship's telegram of the 15th instant, concerning the proposed concert between the different Commanders of naval forces in the China seas, I had this afternoon an interview with M. Vlangaly, and begged him to let me know the exact conditions which he intended to signify in stating that the Imperial Government would adhere to the proposal within the limits of what had been done in Egypt. His Excellency replied that he had perhaps expressed himself ill, but that he meant nothing more than that the object of the concert would be entirely humanitarian, and that it should not go beyond the protection, as far as possible, of neutral subjects and their property, without taking any part ("sans s'ingérer") in questions which might arise between France and China. M. Vlangaly considered that such a concert would be very desirable, in order that the ships of war might be distributed amongst the different ports at which there might be apprehension of danger to neutrals.
   I told his Excellency that if war should unhappily ensue between those two Powers, I was convinced that it would be the wish of Her Majesty's Government that Her Majesty's naval forces should observe the strictest neutrality.

I have, &c.
(Signed)   EDWD. THORNTON.

No. 32.

Sir H. Elliot to Earl Granville.—(Received December 23.)

(Telegraphic.)   *Vienna, December* 23, 1883.
   IN reply to your telegram of the 21st instant, there is no intention of sending an Austrian ship of war to the China seas.

---

* Substance telegraphed.
† Copy to Lord Lyons, Sir S. Lumley, Lord Ampthill, Sir R. Morier, and Sir C. Wyke.
[561]   C 2

12

No. 33.

Earl Granville to Sir E. Thornton.

Sir, *Foreign Office, January* 3, 1884.
HER Majesty's Government approve the language which your Excellency held to M. Vlangaly on the 17th ultimo, upon the subject of the proposed concert for the protection of neutral subjects in China, as reported in your despatch of the same date.

I am, &c.
(Signed) GRANVILLE.

No. 34.

The Secretary to the Admiralty to Sir J. Pauncefote.—(Received January 11.)

Sir, *Admiralty, January* 9, 1884.
I AM commanded by my Lords Commissioners of the Admiralty to transmit, for the information of the Secretary of State for Foreign Affairs, the inclosed extract of a letter, dated the 20th November, from the Commander-in-chief on the China Station.

I am, &c.
(Signed) G. TRYON.

Inclosure in No. 34.

(Extract.)
THE "Swift" is now at Pakhoi, and I have directed the Commodore to dispatch the "Linnet" to cruize between the Treaty ports of Hoihow and Pakhoi, in the Gulf of Tonquin, for the protection of British interests.

The French ship of war "Triomphante" has just left Chefoo for the south; and the "Villars," which quitted Shanghae on the 15th instant, to communicate with her off the river, returned to Woosung, where she now remains.

The "Audacious" was in dock at Nagasaki. I thought it prudent to undock her immediately and hold her in readiness to proceed to any part of the station where her presence might be required.

I purpose remaining at Shanghae for the present, keeping a vigilant watch on events.
"*Vigilant,*" *Shanghae, November* 20, 1883.

No. 35.

Mr. Grosvenor to Earl Granville.—(Received January 16, 1884.)

My Lord, *Peking, November* 19, 1883.
I HAVE the honour to report that on receiving a despatch from the Tsung-li Yâmen on the Tonquin question, the arrival of which I had been led to expect from a conversation with the Ministers some days before, I noticed that no mention was made therein of the intention of the Chinese Government to protect foreigners resident in China.

I took the earliest opportunity of pointing out to their Excellencies this omission in the text of their despatch. They said that whilst adhering to the policy of protecting foreigners resident in China under all circumstances, they deemed the insertion of such an assurance in their note on the Tonquin question to be premature, and had determined, on reflection, not to insert it, although they admitted having told me that it should be inserted. I then said that I thought your Lordship would be somewhat surprised at so important an omission, unless some explanation were given. That, in fact, it would inevitably point to the conclusion that China had changed her policy in this respect.

The Ministers then promised to write me a semi-official explanatory note, translation of which I have the honour to inclose.

13

I had the honour to acquaint your Lordship with the substance of this despatch by telegram this day.

I have, &c.
(Signed) T. G. GROSVENOR.

Inclosure in No. 35.

Letter from Tsung-li Yamén explaining Omission of Assurance of Protection in recent Despatch.

(Translation.)

THE Ministers present their compliments, and beg to refer Mr. Grosvenor to the inquiry which he made personally a few days ago, during the course of an interview at the Yámen, regarding the omission, in the despatch on the Tonquin question, of an assurance of protection to the merchants of every nationality resident in China.

The Ministers would now beg to state that ever since the establishment of Treaty relations between China and foreign Governments, over twenty years ago, China has always acted in accordance with Treaty, and protected the subjects and merchants of every nationality.

As regards the question of protection in the present instance, as China has no wish whatever for any rupture with France, China will, as a matter of duty, continue as hitherto to afford protection to foreign residents in China. The Yámen, therefore, did not insert this assurance in the despatch which they recently sent on the Tonquin question.

The Ministers now beg to forward the present letter, specially explaining this.

No. 36.

Mr. West to Earl Granville.—(Received January 19, 1884.)

My Lord, Washington, December 31, 1883.

I HAVE the honour to acknowledge the receipt of your Lordship's despatch of the 6th instant, and to inform your Lordship that I have duly notified the United States' Government that an invitation has been addressed to the Governments of Italy, Russia, Portugal, and Japan, on the part of Her Majesty's Government, to concert measures for the protection of their subjects in consequence of the difference between France and China.

I have, &c.
(Signed) L. S. SACKVILLE WEST.

No. 37.

Mr. Trench to Earl Granville.—(Received February 1, 1884.)

My Lord, Tôkiô, December 14, 1883.

ON the receipt, on the afternoon of the 6th instant, of your Lordship's telegram of the previous day, I repaired immediately to the private residence of the Minister for Foreign Affairs, and informed his Excellency that I had received instructions from your Lordship directing me, in view of the impending crisis in China, to propose confidentially to the Japanese Government that they should send instructions to their naval Commander in the Chinese seas to concert with the Commanders of the British and other neutral ships of war for the protection of neutral subjects, and I added that the German and United States' Governments would instruct their Admirals in the same sense.

Mr. Inouyé replied that he fully concurred in the wisdom of your Lordship's proposal and that his Government would not fail to adopt the measures suggested, but at present the Japanese Government had no ships of war in the Chinese seas. There was, however, one at Nagasaki, which would be ready to proceed to China at any moment, and there were three or four at Yokohama and at Yokosuka which would be available on short notice; these, in the event of its being deemed necessary, would be dispatched to the Chinese seas, and orders, in harmony with your Lordship's proposal, would be given to the Japanese Commander-in-chief. His Excellency begged me, however, to address him

14

a confidential note embodying your Lordship's proposal so that he might lay the same
before the Cabinet, and promised me an early answer, giving the views of the Japanese
Government on the subject. I have the honour to inclose a copy of the note which I
addressed to Mr. Inouyé on the 7th, as well as a copy of the answer which his Excellency
favoured me with on the following day; and it was on the receipt of the latter that I had
the honour to forward to your Lordship my telegram of the 9th instant.

Count Dönhoff, the German Minister, told me last night that orders, in the sense
desired, had already been given to the German naval Commanders in the Chinese seas,
but Mr. Bingham says he is not aware that similar orders have as yet been sent to
Commanders of United States' ships of war. He stated, however, that the flag-ship
"Richmond," lately stationed at Kôbé, had received orders to proceed at once to
China.

I have, &c.
(Signed) P. LE POER TRENCH.

Inclosure 1 in No. 37.

Mr. Trench to Inouyé Kaoru.

M. le Ministre, *Tôkiô, December 7, 1883.*
I HAVE the honour to inform your Excellency that I have received telegraphic
instructions from Her Majesty's Principal Secretary of State for Foreign Affairs directing
me, in view of the impending crisis in the relations between China and France, to propose,
confidentially, through your Excellency, that the Japanese Government should send
instructions to their naval Commanders in the China seas to concert with the Commanders
of the British and other neutral ships of war, for the protection of neutral subjects.

In communicating to your Excellency the proposal of my Government, which has
for its object the establishment of joint and concerted action on the part of the naval
Commanders of the ships of war of neutral Powers in Chinese waters, with a view to the
adoption of identical measures for the protection of the subjects and property of those
Powers in case of emergencies arising which might call for such joint co-operation, I beg
to request that your Excellency will favour me at your earliest convenience with the
views of your Government on this subject, and communicate to me, for the information
of Her Majesty's Government, the nature of the orders which the Japanese Government
may think fit to issue to the Japanese naval Commander-in-chief in the Chinese seas,
with the object of securing the concerted action which is desired.

I have the honour to add that the Governments of Germany and of the United
States are in accord with Her Majesty's Government in regard to this matter, and that
instructions will be issued to the German and American Admirals on the China Station
in the sense of my present communication to your Excellency.

I take, &c.
(Signed) P. LE POER TRENCH.

Inclosure 2 in No. 37.

Inouyé Kaoru to Mr. Trench.

Sir, *Foreign Office, Tôkiô, December 8, 1883.*
I HAVE the honour to acknowledge the receipt of your note of the 7th instant, in
which you inform me that you have received telegraphic instructions from Her Majesty's
Principal Secretary of State for Foreign Affairs, to propose, confidentially, that the
Japanese Government should, in view of the impending crisis in the relations between
China and France, send to their Commanders in the China seas, instructions to concert
with the Commanders of British and other neutral ships of war for the protection of
neutral subjects, and request me to favour you with the views of my Government on the
subject, and to communicate to you, for the information of Her Britannic Majesty's
Government, the nature of the orders which His Imperial Majesty's Government may
think fit to issue to the Japanese Commander-in-chief in the China seas with the object
of securing the concerted action desired.

In reply, I hasten to acquaint you that His Imperial Majesty's Government are in
full accord and sympathy with the measures which Her Britannic Majesty's Government
have wisely suggested for the joint protection of neutrals in China, and that in the event

it is deemed necessary to dispatch vessels of war to the China seas, orders in harmony with the proposals contained in your note will be given to the Commander-in-chief, and in this sense I beg that you will have the goodness to communicate confidentially to your Government the views entertained by His Imperial Majesty's Government on the subject.

Accept, &c.
(Signed)   INOUYÉ KAORU.

No. 38.

The Secretary to the Admiralty to Sir J. Pauncefote.—(Received February 4.)

Sir,   *Admiralty, February 2, 1884.*
MY Lords Commissioners of the Admiralty desire me to forward herewith, for the perusal of Earl Granville, a copy of a letter from Vice-Admiral Willes, dated the 25th December, in which he reports the steps he has taken for the protection of neutrals at the Treaty ports of China, and the result of his communications with the naval officers of foreign Powers inviting their co-operation for that purpose.

I am, &c.
(Signed)   G. TRYON.

Inclosure in No. 38.

Vice-Admiral Willes to the Secretary to the Admiralty.

Sir,   *"Audacious," at Hong Kong, December 25, 1883.*
IN reference to previous telegrams from their Lordships concerning the protection of neutral subjects at the Treaty ports, and co-operation with the naval Commanders of neutral Powers in case of need, I have the honour to report that I have placed myself in communication with the German Admiral and with the Senior Naval Officer of the United States' squadron on this station.

2. From the latter officer I have not yet received any reply, but Baron Von der Goltz, the Commander-in-chief on this station of the German squadron, has lost no time in assuring me of his willing co-operation, and I expect shortly to receive similar assurances from Commodore Davis, who has only just arrived to command the United States' squadron, and has hardly yet had time to address me.

3. The German Admiral has brought all his ships to Hong Kong for inspection. I have suggested to him that it would be convenient and desirable that the nations of Great Britain, Germany, and the United States should be represented at Canton and Shanghae by one of the vessels of each country, and I have made a similar proposal to Commodore Davis. I also hope to induce Admiral Von der Goltz to attach a ship to one of the ports in the Yang-tse-kiang.

4. As the interests of Japanese subjects are larger in Shanghae than elsewhere, I have requested the British Representative at Tôkiô to endeavour to induce the Japanese Government to station a vessel of war at Shanghae.

5. On the 19th the Portuguese gun-vessel "Tamega" arrived from Macao, having been dispatched by the Governor of that dependency to communicate with me on the question of protection which his Government had directed him to do. Commander Cabral, an intelligent officer who spoke perfect English, gave me to understand that two Portuguese vessels of war were coming to reinforce the China squadron, which at present only consisted of the "Tamega." I recommended that the "Tamega" should visit Canton occasionally.

If I can induce the German and United States' Commanders to station a vessel as I have described, and the Japanese to attach one to Shanghae, I shall find the task of providing for the wants of the other Treaty ports an easy one, and I can rely, I think, on cordial assistance from the naval officers of the different nationalities on this station.

I have, &c.
(Signed)   GEORGE O. WILLES.

No. 39.

Earl Granville to Sir H. Parkes.

Sir,   *Foreign Office, February* 11, 1884.

I REFERRED to the Lords Commissioners of the Admiralty your telegram of the 20th December last, relative to the strengthening of the China squadron; and I have to acquaint you that a reply has been received, stating that Vice-Admiral Willes has reported that he considers a reinforcement unnecessary in view of the international arrangement which has been concluded for the protection of the subjects of neutral Powers.

I have this day communicated to you the substance of the foregoing by telegraph.

I am, &c.

(Signed)   GRANVILLE.

No. 40.

Sir H. Parkes to Earl Granville.—(Received February 14, 1884.)

My Lord,   *Peking, December* 15, 1883.

I HAVE the honour to inclose a copy of a despatch which I received from Vice-Admiral Willes, informing me of the distribution he had made of Her Majesty's vessels on this station with a view to the protection of British residents at the various Treaty ports.

I also beg to add a copy of my reply, in which I stated to the Commander-in-chief that the arrangements he had made appeared to me to be perfectly satisfactory.

I have, &c.

(Signed)   HARRY S. PARKES.

Inclosure 1 in No. 40.

Vice-Admiral Willes to Sir H. Parkes.

Sir,   " *Vigilant,*" *at Shanghae, November* 21, 1883.

I HAVE the honour to inform your Excellency that in view of the present state of affairs in China and the possibility of the services of Her Majesty's ships being required at the Treaty ports for the protection of the British residents, I have made the following arrangements to provide for that contingency.

The " Kestrel," in accordance with the instructions of the Lords Commissioners of the Admiralty, will winter at Tien-tsin, but in the event of her not being released from her duties in Corea before the river is closed with ice, the " Cockchafer " will be stationed there. The latter vessel has orders to remain at Chefoo if the " Kestrel " takes up the duty assigned to her.

I have considered that matters are sufficiently urgent to justify me in departing from their Lordships' instructions, and have dispatched the " Albatross " to Hankow, to remain there until the river rises in the ensuing year.

The other Treaty ports in the Yang tse will be visited by the " Espoir," which vessel is now on her way to Shanghae from Hong Kong, calling at the Formosa ports.

The " Curaçao " remains at Shanghae with Captain Anstruther in charge of the North China Division.

The " Foxhound " is now at Pagoda anchorage with orders to proceed to Foochow when the town is free from cholera, or under any circumstances if her presence is required off the Settlement.

The ships which will be at Hong Kong during the winter will be available for Amoy and Swatow, should circumstances render the presence of a man-of-war necessary at these ports. They will be visited from time to time by one of Her Majesty's ships.

The " Linnet " is at Canton where she remains until relieved by " Fly," she then proceeds to the Gulf of Tonquin to cruize between Pakhoi and Hoihow.

These two ports are now being visited by Her Majesty's ship " Swift," which is expected to return to Hong Kong at the end of the month.

I have, &c.

(Signed)   GEORGE O. WILLES.

Inclosure 2 in No. 40.

Sir H. Parkes to Vice-Admiral Willes.

Sir, *Chefoo, December* 1, 1883.
I HAVE the honour to acknowledge the receipt, this day, of your Excellency's despatch of the 21st ultimo, informing mo of the distribution you have been so good as to make of Her Majesty's vessels on this station with a view to the protection of British residents at the various Treaty ports.
It appears to me that these arrangements are entirely satisfactory, and I should not omit to thank your Excellency for the careful consideration they denote. As, however, I have been absent more than five weeks from China it is possible that on my return to Peking I may receive representations affecting the condition of one or other of the ports which may have some bearing on these arrangements, and in that case I shall not omit to submit to your Excellency's notice as promptly as possible such further recommendations as may thus be suggested.
I have, &c.
(Signed) HARRY S. PARKES.

No. 41.

Sir H. Parkes to Earl Granville.—(*Received February* 14, 1884.)

My Lord, *Peking, December* 15, 1883.
I BEG to forward to your Lordship a copy of a despatch, in which Vice-Admiral Willes informs me of the arrangements he proposed to submit to the Lords Commissioners of the Admiralty, in reply to their instruction to report upon the best way of distributing the squadron on this station, in order to protect British subjects at the Treaty ports against risings on the part of the Chinese.
In the reply, of which I inclose a copy, I stated to the Commander-in-chief that I believed the object in view would be secured by the plan he proposed, but as I was travelling when I received his Excellency's despatch I reserved the opinion which his Excellency invited me to furnish on the subject generally until I returned to Peking.
I have, &c.
(Signed) HARRY S. PARKES.

Inclosure 1 in No. 41.

Vice-Admiral Willes to Sir H. Parkes.

Sir, "*Vigilant*," *at Shanghae, November* 21, 1883.
I HAVE the honour to inform your Excellency that the Lords Commissioners of the Admiralty have directed me to report how I would distribute the squadron if it became necessary to protect merchants at Treaty ports, in the event of a rising by Chinamen.
It is within my power to provide a ship for every Treaty port except Wenchow, Takau, and Tamsui, and I would ask your Excellency whether, in making provision for the contingency alluded to, you would consider it necessary that a vessel of war should be detailed for each of those ports, as it appears to me that the duty of protecting them might be assigned to ships stationed at near ports on the mainland.
I propose to allot a corvette for the protection of Chinkiang Foo and Wuhu, and a large sloop for Pakhoi and Hoihow. At every other port a ship might be stationed. I should be glad if your Excellency will inform me whether or not you consider these arrangements would be sufficient, and I would invite your Excellency's opinion on the subject generally.
In replying to the Admiralty I feel bound to express my opinion that the simultaneous rising of Chinamen at all Treaty ports is an event highly improbable.
I have, &c.
(Signed) GEORGE O. WILLES.

D

18

Inclosure 2 in No. 41.

Sir H. Parkes to Vice-Admiral Willes.

Sir, *Chefoo, December* 1, 1883.

I HAVE the honour to acknowledge your Excellency's despatch of the 21st ultimo, on the subject of the instructions received by your Excellency from the Lords Commissioners of the Admiralty, requiring you to report on the way in which the squadron under your command may best be distributed, in order to protect British subjects at the various ports against risings on the part of Chinese.

The arrangements which your Excellency proposes to make would enable you to station a ship at every Treaty port, by treating the contiguous ports of Pakhoi and Hoihow as one station, and Chinkiang and Wuhu as another. According to this plan the Formosan ports of Takau and Tamsui, and the single port of Wenchow on the mainland would alone remain unprotected, and your Excellency asks me whether I think it necessary that a vessel should also be stationed at each of those ports.

As the above plan would provide a vessel at Swatow, Amoy, and Foochow, all of which are in the vicinity of Takau, Tamsui and Wenchow, and as the number of British residents at the latter port is very limited, I am of opinion that it would not be necessary to station a vessel at each of the three ports last named, as in the event of trouble occurring at any of those ports assistance might be rendered by the vessels stationed at one or other of the three ports first mentioned.

I am unable to enter into considerations of a general nature bearing on this important subject by the present opportunity, but I shall respond to your Excellency's invitation to do so shortly after my arrival at Peking.

I have, &c.
(Signed) HARRY S. PARKES.

No. 42.

The Secretary to the Admiralty to Sir J. Pauncefote.—(*Received February* 19.)

Sir, *Admiralty, February* 16, 1884.

MY Lords Commissioners of the Admiralty desire me to forward herewith, for the perusal of the Secretary of State for Foreign Affairs, extracts from a letter of the Commander-in-chief in China dated the 8th January, reporting the state of affairs at the Treaty ports, and the steps that have been taken to protect Europeans in case of necessity.

I am, &c.
(Signed) G. TRYON.

Inclosure in No. 42.

Vice-Admiral Willes to the Secretary to the Admiralty.

(Extract.) "*Audacious," at Hong Kong, January* 8, 1884.

THE "Zephyr" left Hong Kong on the 27th December for Singapore to relieve the "Merlin." I ordered her to call at the Treaty ports of [Pakhoi and Hoihow in the Gulf of Tonquin on her way, remaining two days at each place.

The "Champion" sailed on the 29th December for Shanghae.

The "Cleopatra" left Hong Kong on the 30th December to be stationed at Amoy, where she arrived on the 2nd January. The French iron-clad "Triomphante" was also in port on the 4th at Amoy.

I dispatched the "Esk" (manned by part of the crew of the "Flying Fish") to Swatow to remain for the present, under the command of Lieutenant Rooper.

The "Midge" left Hong Kong on the 4th January. She visits Amoy, the Min River, Tamsui (in Formosa), Wenchow, and finally Ningpo, where she will remain for the present protection of British interests.

The "Fly" is now stationed at Canton and the "Linnet" and "Swift" remain at Hong Kong for general service. I have manned the "Wivern" with the officers and crew of the "Swift" to work her turrets and perform the usual annual exercise.

* Copy to Viscount Lyons.

On the morning of the 31st December I transferred my flag to the "Vigilant" and proceeded to Canton. I found affairs generally quiet.

I feel satisfied that the Residents on the Shamien are now more than adequately protected by vessels of war of Great Britain, Germany, the United States, and France which are at anchor off the Settlement; and there is, moreover, a guard of 600 Chinese troops encamped on the Shamien itself between the European houses and the approaches from the city.

I hope to dispatch the "Daring" on the 14th or 15th to the Gulf of Tonquin, stationing her alternately at Pakhoi and Hoihow for the protection of British residents.

North China.—All reports received from the north are satisfactory. There may be some uneasiness on the part of native Chinese merchants in view of the complications with France, and trade is certainly not brisk amongst them at this juncture; but I have as yet received no expressions of alarm or suspicion from any of the Treaty ports.

There is no change of feeling noticeable at present in any part of the station.

No. 43.

Mr. Trench to Earl Granville.--*(Received March 11.)*

My Lord,   *Tōkiō, January 25,* 1884.

WITH reference to my despatch of the 14th ultimo, I have the honour to transmit to your Lordship herewith copy of a despatch which I received from Vice-Admiral Willes in regard to the proposed joint action for the protection of neutral subjects at the Treaty ports of China, and of a note which I addressed to the Acting Minister for Foreign Affairs on the 31st ultimo on the above subject; also copy of a despatch I sent to Admiral Willes on the 11th instant.

After allowing more than a week to elapse, during which Mr. Ito informed me he had been in consultation with the other members of the Cabinet, his Excellency favoured me with an answer, copy of which I have the honour to inclose.

Your Lordship will perceive that Mr. Ito in his reply states that the Japanese Government are determined to make preparations for the dispatch of one or more vessels of war to Shanghae under proper instructions, but reserve to themselves the discretion of deciding, upon information they may receive, as to the proper time for carrying Admiral Willes' proposal into effect, and requests to be informed of the nature and scope of the instructions issued to his Excellency with a view to making those to be given to the Japanese Commanders identical, and also to learn what steps the Governments of Germany and the United States have actually taken in regard to the proposal referred to.

On the receipt of Mr. Ito's note I telegraphed to Admiral Willes that, before deciding to dispatch a vessel to Shanghae, the Japanese Government desired to learn the nature of the instructions issued to him by Her Majesty's Government in regard to the proposed joint action, and asked whether he could supply me with a copy of the same, and his Excellency telegraphed to me yesterday that his reply to my telegram had been sent by a steamer shortly due at Yokohama.

I also forwarded to his Excellency a copy of Mr. Ito's note in a despatch, of which copy is inclosed.

At the same time, I took an early opportunity of calling on the Ministers of Germany and of the United States, who informed me that they had not been made acquainted with the nature of the instructions issued to their respective Admirals, but that they believed that their Admirals had been ordered to act in concert with Admiral Willes in protecting neutral subjects at the Treaty ports of China.

In spite, however, of the desire shown by Mr. Inouyé and by Mr. Ito to meet the wishes of Her Majesty's Government in regard to the proposed joint action for the protection of neutrals, I am of opinion that unless they learn that Japanese subjects at Shanghae are in great danger, or that war has actually been declared, the Japanese Government will not dispatch vessels to the Chinese seas, for fear that such a step might be regarded as a menace against China.

I have the honour to add that I have forwarded to Her Majesty's Minister at Peking copies of the correspondence inclosed in this despatch.

I have, &c.
(Signed)   P. LE POER TRENCH.

Inclosure 1 in No. 43.

Vice-Admiral Willes to Mr. Trench.

Sir,   "*Audacious*," *at Hong Kong, December* 17, 1883.

AS you are doubtless aware, Her Majesty's Government has solicited the Japanese to assist neutral Powers in protecting neutral subjects at the Treaty ports of China in the event of occasion arising.

I have recently received a telegram, informing me that Japan is willing to send ships to the China seas if necessary.

In view of the state of public feeling in China, and the strained relations which are well known to exist between one foreign Power and that of China, which are supposed to engender hostile feelings towards foreigners at the Treaty ports, and also bearing in mind that Japan has special interests on account of the number of her subjects domiciled at Shanghae, I would ask you to be so good as to inform the Japanese Government that I propose that a German, United States, and British ship of war should be stationed at Shanghae for the present, and hope that it may be considered desirable to station a Japanese vessel at the same port to act in concert with the vessels of other Powers in protecting their respective subjects.

I have, &c.
(Signed)   GEORGE O. WILLES.

Inclosure 2 in No. 43.

Mr. Trench to Ito Hirobumi.

M. le Ministre,   *Tôkiô, December* 31, 1883.

WITH reference to my confidential note of the 7th instant on the subject of the proposed concerted action on the part of the naval Commanders of neutral Powers for the protection of neutral subjects and property in the event of exigencies arising in connection with the impending crisis in the relations between China and France, I beg to inform your Excellency that I have now received a confidential despatch from the Admiral in command of Her Majesty's fleet on the China and Japan Station.

In this despatch Admiral Willes, after stating that he has been apprized by Her Majesty's Government of Japan's willingness to send ships of war to the China seas, if necessary, begs me to acquaint your Excellency, for the information of your Excellency's Government, that in view of the state of public feeling in China, and the animosity towards foreigners which is supposed to have been excited at the open ports by the strained relations known to exist between China and France, he proposes that a German, United States, and British ship of war should be stationed at Shanghae for the present, and that, bearing in mind the number of Japanese subjects resident at that place, he hopes that it may be considered desirable to station a Japanese vessel at the same port, to act in concert with the vessels of other Powers in protecting their respective subjects.

I shall be glad to hear from your Excellency, at your early convenience, whether the Japanese Government are prepared to dispatch a ship of war to Shanghae for the purpose of carrying out the object indicated in Admiral Willes' proposal.

I take, &c.
(Signed)   P. LE POER TRENCH.

Inclosure 3 in No. 43.

Mr. Trench to Vice-Admiral Willes.

Sir,   *Tôkiô, January* 11, 1884.

I HAVE the honour to inform your Excellency that on the receipt of your Confidential despatch of the 17th ultimo I immediately called upon the Acting Minister for Foreign Affairs, and informed him that you proposed, in view of the impending crisis in the relations between China and France, that a German, United States, and British ship of war should be stationed at Shanghae for the present, and that you considered it would likewise be desirable to station a Japanese vessel at the same port to act in concert with the vessels of other Powers in protecting their respective subjects.

Mr. Ito replied that Japan was willing to send a vessel of war to the China seas, if deemed necessary, but that, as war had not yet been declared, he did not consider that the occasion for doing so had arrived, and it was evident to me that he was afraid that the sending a Japanese man-of-war to Shanghae might be interpreted as a menace against China. I pointed out to his Excellency that when danger to foreigners was most to be apprehended would be immediately on the outbreak of war, and that it was therefore of the utmost importance to have ships actually on the spot to protect neutrals.

His Excellency, admitting the force of what I said, then asked me to address him a confidential note on the subject, a copy of which is inclosed herewith, and promised to consult with his colleagues, and let me know, as soon as possible, what decision might be arrived at by the Cabinet; but though it is now more than a week since I sent in my note, I have as yet been unable to obtain the promised reply to it.

I have, &c.
(Signed)   P. LE POER TRENCH.

Inclosure 4 in No. 43.

Ito Hirobumi to Mr. Trench.

Sir,   *Foreign Office, Tôkiô, January* 11, 1884.

I HAVE had the honour to receive your confidential note dated the 31st ultimo, in which you were good enough to communicate to me, for the information of my Government, the proposal made by the Admiral in command of Her Britannic Majesty's fleet on the Asiatic Station with reference to the proposed concerted action on the part of the Governments of Great Britain, Germany, the United States and Japan for the protection of neutral subjects and property in China in the event of emergencies arising which should render such action desirable.

The proposal of Admiral Willes contemplates the stationing of a vessel of war by each of the Powers named at Shanghae, in view of the state of public feeling in China, and the animosity towards foreigners which is supposed to have been excited by the strained relations existing between China and France, and you express the desire to learn whether His Imperial Majesty's Government are prepared to dispatch a ship of war to Shanghae for the purpose indicated.

The telegraphic reports received from our Consular officers in China tend to encourage the belief that no immediate danger need be apprehended; nevertheless, desiring to co-operate with Her Britannic Majesty's Government in such measures as may be deemed essential, and bearing in mind that the object of the Powers named, in agreeing to the proposed joint and concerted action, was none other than the protection of the lives and property of neutrals in China in case of necessity, His Imperial Majesty's Government have determined to proceed at once to make preparations to dispatch one or more vessels of war to Shanghae under proper instructions.

In taking these preliminary measures, however, His Imperial Majesty's Government are persuaded that they should, in view of the reassuring nature of the reports to which I have adverted, reserve to themselves the discretion of deciding, upon information which they may receive, when the moment arrives for carrying the suggestion of Admiral Willes into effect.

Under any circumstances, it seems very desirable that the instructions in the premises to the several naval Commanders should, so far as practicable, be identical, and I beg to request, therefore, that you will have the kindness to inform me as fully as possible regarding the nature and scope of the orders which Her Britannic Majesty's Government have issued to their Commander-in-chief upon the subject of the proposed concerted action, and, at the same time, they are anxious to be informed as to what steps the Governments of Germany and the United States have actually taken in pursuance of the proposal referred to.

I avail, &c.
(Signed)   ITO HIROBUMI,
His Imperial Majesty's Acting Minister for Foreign Affairs.

Inclosure 5 in No. 43.

Mr. Trench to Vice-Admiral Willes.

Sir, *Tökiö, January* 18, 1884.

WITH reference to my Confidential despatch of the 11th instant, I have the honour to transmit to your Excellency herewith copy of the reply which I have received from the Acting Minister for Foreign Affairs to the note which I addressed to his Excellency on the 31st ultimo, expressing your hope that the Government of the Mikado would see fit to dispatch a Japanese ship of war to Shanghae to act in concert with the vessels of other Powers in protecting neutral subjects at that port.

In this note Mr. Ito states that, before deciding to dispatch a vessel to Shanghae, the Japanese Government desired to learn the nature and scope of the instructions issued to the several naval Commanders. I therefore telegraphed to your Excellency on the 12th instant to inquire whether you could supply me with a copy of those which you have received from Her Majesty's Government, in order that I might communicate their tenour to the Acting Minister for Foreign Affairs, but I have not yet received a reply from your Excellency.

The Ministers of Germany and of the United States have informed me that they have not been furnished with copies of the instructions issued to their respective Admirals, but that they believe their Admirals have been instructed to act in concert with your Excellency in protecting neutral subjects at the Treaty ports of China.

I have, &c.

(Signed) P. LE POER TRENCH.

No. 44.

The Secretary to the Admiralty to Sir J. Pauncefote.—(Received March 13.)

Sir, *Admiralty, March* 12, 1884.

WITH reference to my letter of the 7th ultimo,* forwarding a copy of a telegram from Vice-Admiral Willes, the Commander-in-chief on the China Station, stating that, in his opinion, reinforcements of the naval force on the station were not required, my Lords Commissioners of the Admiralty desire me to forward herewith, for the perusal of Earl Granville, a copy of a letter dated the 5th ultimo, confirming the telegram alluded to.

I am, &c.

(Signed) G. TRYON.

Inclosure in No. 44.

Vice-Admiral Willes to the Secretary to the Admiralty.

Sir, *"Audacious," at Hong Kong, February* 5, 1884.

IN reply to your letter dated the 4th December, 1883, in which you forward me a copy of a telegram from Sir Henry Parkes to the Foreign Office on the position of affairs in China, and convey their Lordships' directions to me to report whether I consider any reinforcements necessary, I have the honour to request that you will inform the Lords Commissioners of the Admiralty that I yesterday telegraphed that, in view of the present international arrangements, I do not consider it necessary to increase our force in China.

2. I might add that I adhere to the opinions which I expressed in my letter dated the 24th November, 1883,* relative to the protection of British interests in China.

I have, &c.

(Signed) GEORGE O. WILLES.

No. 45.

Mr. Trench to Earl Granville.—(Received March 25.)

(Extract.) *Tökiö, February* 8, 1884.

IN continuation of my despatch of the 25th ultimo, I have the honour to inform your Lordship that I received, on the 31st of last month, from Admiral Willes,

* Not printed.

a letter dated the 12th January, inclosing, for the information of the Japanese Government, a copy of the instructions given by him to the officers commanding Her Majesty's ships, relative to the protection of neutral subjects at the Chinese Treaty ports. I lost no time in forwarding the copy of these instructions to the Acting Minister for Foreign Affairs, though they were not those issued by Her Majesty's Government to the Admiral, the nature and scope of which his Excellency desired to learn, in order to make the instructions to be given to the Japanese Commander identical. I called upon Mr. Ito the following day, and also on Saturday, and on both occasions urged his Excellency to hasten the dispatch to Shanghae of at least one vessel of war. I referred him to the instructions given to the officers in command of Her Majesty's ships, from which he would see that the Governments of Germany, Spain, Portugal, Italy, and the United States, had already agreed to instruct the Commanders of their ships of war to concert measures with the British Admiral for the protection of neutral subjects at the Treaty ports in the event of an outbreak of the populace, and I pointed out to him the desirability of united action on the part of all neutral Governments.

From what Mr. Ito said I gathered that the Japanese Government were inclined to abandon the idea of sending several vessels under the command of an Admiral to the Chinese seas, but his Excellency, after reminding me that I had not furnished him with a copy of the instructions he had asked for, viz., those issued by Her Majesty's Government to Admiral Willes, still assured me that the Japanese Government would send one ship to Shanghae.

P.S.—I have the honour to inclose copy of a confidential note just received from the Acting Minister for Foreign Affairs, a copy of which I am likewise forwarding to Admiral Willes.

Inclosure in No. 45.

Ito Hirobumi to Mr. Trench.

Sir, *Foreign Office, Tôkiô, February* 8, 1884.
I HAVE the honour to acknowledge the receipt of your note of the 31st January last, inclosing copy of the instruction issued by Admiral Willes to the officers commanding Her Britannic Majesty's ships in the China seas relative to the protection of neutral subjects at the Chinese Treaty ports.

I beg to tender you my cordial thanks for the goodness you have shown in thus far complying with my request. Should you hereafter find yourself in possession of the orders of Her Britannic Majesty's Government to their naval Commander-in-chief, to which my previous note more especially related, I would thank you to furnish me a copy of them.

I avail, &c.
(Signed) ITO HIROBUMI.

No. 46.

Mr. Trench to Earl Granville.—(Received April 22.)

My Lord, *Tôkiô, March* 7, 1884.
WITH reference to my despatch of the 8th ultimo, I have the honour to transmit to your Lordship herewith copy of a letter from Admiral Willes, in answer to one which I addressed to him on the 8th of last month, in which I asked to be furnished, for the information of the Japanese Government, with a copy of the instructions issued to him by Her Majesty's Government relative to the proposed joint action for the protection of neutrals at the Chinese Treaty ports.

Mr. Inouyé told me this morning that the Japanese Government were quite prepared to dispatch vessels of war to the Chinese seas when the necessity for doing so should arise; that would not, however, be till war had been actually declared, when Japan would be found ready to join with the other Powers in protecting neutral subjects and property at the Treaty ports in China.

I have, &c.
(Signed) P. LE POER TRENCH.

24

Inclosure in No. 46.

Vice-Admiral Willes to Mr. Trench.

Sir,   "*Audacious*," *at Hong Kong, February* 20, 1884.
    WITH reference to your letter of the 8th instant, inclosing a copy of a note from
the Japanese Acting Minister for Foreign Affairs, asking to be furnished with a copy of
the instructions issued to me by Her Majesty's Government relative to proposed joint
action for the protection of neutrals at the Chinese Treaty ports, I have the honour to
inform you that the instructions are similar to those issued by me to the officers in
command of Her Majesty's ships, a copy of which was forwarded in my letter of the 12th
January, 1884, and there are no further details in them to communicate.
                                             I have, &c.
                            (Signed)   GEORGE O. WILLES.

No. 47.

Mr. Plunkett to Earl Granville.—(Received May 30.)

My Lord,   *Tōkiō, April* 26, 1884.
    WITH reference to Mr. Trench's despatch of the 14th December last, and to
subsequent correspondence, I have the honour to inclose copy of a confidential note
which I received yesterday from the Japanese Minister for Foreign Affairs, stating that
Rear-Admiral Matsumura Junzo had received orders to proceed on the 1st proximo to the
China seas with two men-of-war, for the purpose of taking part, if necessary, in the
concerted action on the part of neutral Powers proposed by Her Majesty's Government
for the protection of neutral subjects and property, in view of possible difficulties between
France and China.
    I have forwarded a copy of Mr. Inouyé's note to Vice-Admiral Sir William
Dowell.
    Mr. Inouyé, whom I met yesterday afternoon at the Mikado's garden party, told me
that the Cabinet had now come to the decision of sending these vessels in consequence
of the grave nature of their latest telegrams from Peking, which show that the war party
has obtained a dangerous ascendency, and that a regular declaration of war against France
is not impossible.
                                             I have, &c.
                            (Signed)   F. R. PLUNKETT.

Inclosure in No. 47.

Mr. Inouyé to Mr. Plunkett.

Sir,   *Foreign Office, Tōkiō, April* 25, 1884.
    WITH reference to the confidential correspondence passed on the subject of the
concerted action on the part of the Naval Commanders of neutral Powers, which was
proposed by Her Britannic Majesty's Government through the Honourable P. Le Poer
Trench, and agreed to by His Imperial Majesty's Government, for the protection of
neutral subjects and property in the event of emergencies arising in connection with the
impending crisis in the relations between China and France, I have the honour to inform
your Excellency that His Imperial Majesty's Government have ordered Rear-Admiral
Matsumura Junzo to proceed to China seas on the 1st May next with the men-of-war the
"Fuso Kan," and the "Amagi Kan" under his command for the purpose above
indicated.
    I therefore beg that your Excellency will have the goodness to communicate to
that effect to the Admiral in command of Her Britannic Majesty's fleet on Asiatic
Station.
                                             I avail, &c.
                            (Signed)   INOUYÉ KAORU.

No. 48.

Viscount Lyons to Earl Granville.—(Received July 5.)

(Extract.)   *Paris, July 4,* 1884.

I HAVE the honour to inform your Lordship that an announcement appeared in the "Temps" last evening, stating that the President of the Council of Ministers had informed his colleagues that the Tsung-li Yamên had not disavowed the conduct of the troops who attacked the French on their way to Langson, but, on the contrary, had refused to recognize as binding some of the stipulations of the Treaty of Tien-tsin.

No. 49.

Viscount Lyons to Earl Granville.—(Received July 9.)

Extract.)   *Paris, July 8,* 1884.

WITH reference to my despatch of the 4th instant, I have the honour to inform your Lordship that M. Jules Ferry made yesterday in the Chamber of Deputies a statement respecting the attack by the Chinese on French troops on their way to Langson.

M. Jules Ferry declared that the French Government considered that the Treaty of Tien-tsin had been formally violated, and that this violation made reparation necessary.

No. 50.

Earl Granville to Mr. West.†

Sir,   *Foreign Office, July* 16, 1884.

I HAVE requested you by telegram this day to state to the Government to which you are accredited that, in view of the possibility that the recent occurrence at Langson may lead to hostilities between France and China, Her Majesty's Government presume that the joint arrangement which was made last year by the neutral Powers for the protection of their subjects at the Treaty ports will still be carried out, and that the necessary instructions in this sense will be telegraphed to their Naval Commanders in the China seas.

I am, &c.
(Signed)   GRANVILLE.

No. 51.

Sir J. Pauncefote to the Secretary to the Admiralty.

Sir,   *Foreign Office, July* 16, 1884.

I AM directed by Earl Granville to state to you, confidentially, for the information of the Lords Commissioners of the Admiralty, that in view of the possibility that the recent attack at Langson by the Chinese on the French troops under General Millot may lead to hostilities between France and China, Lord Granville has directed Her Majesty's Representatives at Berlin, Washington, Rome, St. Petersburgh, Madrid, Lisbon, and Tôkiô to inform the Governments to which they are accredited that it is presumed by Her Majesty's Government that, if necessary, the joint arrangement will be carried out which was made last year by the neutral Powers for the protection of their subjects at the Treaty ports in China, and that instructions will be telegraphed accordingly to their naval Commanders in the East.

I am to request that you will move the Lords Commissioners of the Admiralty to cause instructions in this sense to be telegraphed to the British Admiral in the China seas.

I am, &c.
(Signed)   JULIAN PAUNCEFOTE.

---

* Also to Mr. Plunkett, Sir E. Thornton, Mr. de Bunsen, Mr. Petre, Sir J. S. Lumley, and Lord Ampthill.
† Substance to Viscount Lyons and Sir H. Parkes.

No. 52.

Sir E. Thornton to Earl Granville.—(*Received July* 17.)

(Telegraphic.) *St. Petersburgh, July* 17, 1884.

I AM assured that proper instructions were sent to Russian naval officers in Chinese waters in December last, and are still in force.

No. 53.

Sir J. S. Lumley to Earl Granville.—(*Received July* 17.)

(Telegraphic.) *Rome, July* 17, 1884.

IN reply to your telegram of yesterday, Italian Government consider joint arrangement made last year by neutral Powers for protection of their subjects in China Treaty ports as in vigour.

They will shortly have two vessels in Chinese waters, and, should necessity arise, will communicate with them by telegraph.

No. 54.

The Secretary to the Admiralty to Sir J. Pauncefote.—(*Received July* 19.)

Sir, *Admiralty, July* 18, 1884.

I HAVE laid before my Lords Commissioners of the Admiralty your letter of the 16th instant, stating that, in view of the relations between France and China, Her Majesty's Representatives at Berlin, Washington, Rome, St. Petersburgh, Madrid, Lisbon, and Tôkiô have been directed to inform the Governments to which they are accredited that it is presumed by Her Majesty's Government that, if necessary, the arrangements made last year by the neutral Powers for the protection of their subjects will be carried out.

My Lords desire me to forward herewith, for the perusal of Earl Granville, copies of two telegrams which have been sent to Vice-Admiral Sir W. Dowell on the subject.

I am, &c.

(Signed) EVAN MACGREGOR.

Inclosure 1 in No. 54.

The Secretary to the Admiralty to Vice-Admiral Sir W. Dowell.

(Telegraphic.) *Admiralty, July* 16, 1884.

HER Majesty's Government consider that, in view of present relations between France and China, you should be prepared to afford assistance to Europeans at Treaty ports if required, in concert with officers of neutral Powers. You should cruize in southern part of China sea.

Inclosure 2 in No. 54.

The Secretary to the Admiralty to Vice-Admiral Sir W. Dowell.

(Telegraphic.) *Admiralty, July* 18, 1884.

INSTRUCTIONS have been sent to Her Majesty's Representatives at Berlin, Washington, Rome, St. Petersburgh, Madrid, Lisbon, and Tôkiô to state that Her Majesty's Government presume that, if necessary, joint arrangements of last year by neutral Powers for protection of their subjects at Chinese Treaty ports will be carried out, and that the naval Commanders in the East will be instructed accordingly by telegraph.

---

* Copy to Admiralty.

No. 55.

Mr. Plunkett to Earl Granville.—(*Received July* 19.)

(Telegraphic.) *Tôkiô, July* 19, 1884.

WITH reference to your Lordship's telegram of 16th instant, Japanese Government is ready to co-operate for protection of neutrals as arranged last year.

Japanese Admiral, with two frigates, is now at Shanghae, and has been instructed by telegraph to ascertain what steps will be taken by English and other Admirals.

No. 56.

Sir J. S. Lumley to Earl Granville.—(*Received July* 21.)

My Lord, *Rome, July* 17, 1884.

I HAVE the honour to inclose copy of a private letter I have received from M. Mancini in reply to a verbal communication I made to his Excellency of the substance of your Lordship's telegram of the 16th instant.

While expressing the hope that hostilities between France and China may be averted, his Excellency says that the Italian Government are disposed, should the occasion arise, to consider as valid the joint agreement come to last year between the neutral Powers for the protection of their subjects in the Treaty ports of China.

M. Mancini adds that the Italian cruizer "Cristoforo Colombo" is still in Chinese waters, and will shortly be joined by the "Vittor Pisani."

I have, &c.

(Signed) J. SAVILE LUMLEY.

Inclosure in No. 56.

M. Mancini to Sir J. S. Lumley.

M. l'Ambassadeur, *Rome, le* 17 *Juillet*, 1884.

VOTRE Excellence a bien voulu me faire part d'un télégramme par lequel Lord Granville, dans la prévision où, contrairement à l'attente générale, les hostilités éclateraient entre la France et la Chine, vous prie de nous demander si nous sommes disposés à considérer comme étant toujours en vigueur l'accord entre les différentes Puissances pour la protection collective des intérêts des neutres dans les mers de la Chine.

Je prie votre Excellence de vouloir bien remercier Lord Granville de sa communication. Nous espérons et souhaitons que la préoccupation dont sa demande s'inspire puisse se dissiper. Mais nous sommes disposés, si cela devenait opportun, à considérer, en ce qui nous concerne, comme valable, l'arrangement qu'on avait pris entre les Puissances au début des difficultés entre la France et la Chine. Je puis ajouter à toute bonne fin, que le croiseur "Cristoforo Colombo" est maintenant encore dans les eaux Chinoises, où il ne tardera pas à être rejoint par le "Vittor Pisani."

Je suis, &c.

(Signé) MANCINI.

(Translation.)

M. l'Ambassadeur, *Rome, July* 17, 1884.

YOUR Excellency has been good enough to communicate to me a telegram from Lord Granville requesting you to inquire whether, if contrary to general expectation, hostilities should be declared between France and China, we are willing to consider that the agreement between the different Powers for the joint protection of the interests of neutral subjects in Chinese waters remains still in force.

I request your Excellency will be good enough to thank Lord Granville for his communication. We hope and trust that the eventuality alluded to in his proposal may not occur. But we are disposed, should the occasion arise, to consider, so far as we are concerned, that the joint agreement entered into between the Powers at the commencement of the differences between France and China is still in force. Finally,

* Copy to Admiralty and Sir H. Parkes.

E 2

I may add that the cruizer "Cristoforo Colombo" is at this moment still in Chinese
waters, where it will not be long before she is joined by the "Vittor Pisani."

I am, &c.
(Signed) MANCINI.

No. 57.

Lord Ampthill to Earl Granville.°—(Received July 21.)

My Lord, Berlin, July 19, 1884.

IN reply to your Lordship's telegraphic query of the 16th instant, respecting the
joint arrangement made by the neutral Powers for the protection of their subjects in
the event of hostilities between France and China, the Minister for Foreign Affairs told
me to-day that the instructions sent to the German Naval Commanders were still in force,
and would not require to be renewed.

I have, &c.
(Signed) AMPTHILL.

No. 58.

Mr. de Bunsen to Earl Granville.—(Received July 21.)

(Telegraphic.) Madrid, July 20, 1884.

I HAVE received your Lordship's telegram of the 16th instant.

Spanish Government considers that instructions sent last year to their Commander
in Chinese waters are still in force. Spanish Minister for Foreign Affairs offers to
telegraph fresh instructions should your Lordship think it desirable.

No. 59.

Earl Granville to Mr. de Bunsen.

Sir, Foreign Office, July 21, 1884.

WITH reference to your telegram of the 20th instant, I have to state to you that I
think it will be unnecessary for the Spanish Government to telegraph fresh instructions to
their naval Commanders in Chinese waters, unless news is received of any difficulty
arising.

I am, &c.
(Signed) GRANVILLE.

No. 60.

The Secretary to the Admiralty to Sir J. Pauncefote.—(Received July 23.)

Sir, Admiralty, July 21, 1884.

I AM commanded by my Lords Commissioners of the Admiralty to transmit, for
the information of the Secretary of State for Foreign Affairs, two telegrams, dated 19th
and 20th instant, from Vice-Admiral Dowell, relative to his movements, and the movements of ships of war on the China Station.

I am, &c.
(Signed) EVAN MACGREGOR.

Inclosure 1 in No. 60.

Vice-Admiral Sir W. Dowell to the Secretary to the Admiralty.

(Telegraphic.) Taku, July 20, 1884.

I HAVE to report that squadron sails to-day for Chefoo and the south. Propose
leaving one corvette, two gun-vessels, protect Europeans, Pechili ports, one corvette,
two sloops, and Italian corvette Yang-tse-Kiang River; three French ships at Chefoo.
Telegraph Taku until 21st, then Shanghae.

---

* Copy to Admiralty and Sir H. Parkes.

Inclosure 2 in No. 60.

Vice-Admiral Sir W. Dowell to the Secretary to the Admiralty.

(Telegraphic.)   *Taku, July 20, 1884.*
I AM leaving direct for Amoy.

No. 61.

Mr. Petre to Earl Granville.†—(Received July 30.)*

My Lord,   *Lisbon, July 24, 1884.*
WITH reference to my despatch of the 17th instant,‡ I have the honour to
inclose a translation of a note I have to-day received from the Minister for Foreign
Affairs, in which he informs me that he has requested the Minister of Marine to send
instructions to the Portuguese Naval Commanders in Chinese waters to concert measures
with the officers in command of British and other neutral ships of war, for the protection
of foreign subjects residing in the Treaty ports of China.
I have, &c.
(Signed)   GEORGE G. PETRE.

Inclosure in No. 61.

Senhor du Bocage to Mr. Petre.

(Translation.)
Your Excellency,   *Foreign Department, Lisbon, July 21, 1884.*
I HAVE the honour to acknowledge the receipt of the note which you were pleased
to address to me on the 17th instant, in which you request that instructions should be
sent to the Commanders of the Portuguese naval forces in Chinese waters with a view to
their concerting with the Commanders of the naval forces of Great Britain and of the
other neutral Powers, the steps which it may be necessary to adopt in order to afford
protection to their respective subjects.
I beg to inform you that I have already made the application to my colleague in
the Marine Department, that the requisite orders should be sent in compliance with the
wish expressed by your Excellency.
I avail, &c.
(Signed)   J. V. BARBOZA DU BOCAGE.

No. 62.

The Secretary to the Admiralty to Sir J. Pauncefote.—(Received August 2.)

Sir,   *Admiralty, August 1, 1884.*
I AM commanded by my Lords Commissioners of the Admiralty to transmit, for
the information of the Secretary of State for Foreign Affairs, copy of a telegram dated
the 31st ultimo, from Vice-Admiral Sir William Dowell, at Amoy.
I am, &c.
(Signed)   EVAN MACGREGOR.

Inclosure in No. 62.

Vice-Admiral Sir W. Dowell to the Secretary to the Admiralty.

(Telegraphic.)   *Amoy, July 31, 1884.*
I HAVE made arrangements for the safety of Settlement at Foochow-foo. Both
French Admirals there with eight ships and two torpedo-boats.

---

* Substance telegraphed.   † Copy to Admiralty.
‡ Not printed.

30

No. 63.

Mr. West to Earl Granville.*—(Received August 5.)

My Lord,   *Washington, July 19, 1884.*
WITH reference to your Lordship's telegram of the 16th instant, I have the honour to inclose herewith copy of a note which I have received from the Secretary of State, informing me that the arrangement made last year by the neutral Powers for the protection of their subjects at the Treaty ports in China is receiving consideration.

I have, &c.
(Signed)   L. S. SACKVILLE WEST.

Inclosure in No. 63.

Mr. Frelinghuysen to Mr. West.

Sir,   *Department of State, Washington, July 17, 1884.*
I HAVE the honour to acknowledge the receipt of your note of yesterday, inquiring whether the arrangement made last year by the neutral Powers for the protection of their subjects at the Treaty ports in China, will now be carried out by the American Government in case the war now threatened between China and France shall break out.

In reply, I have to inform you that the matter is receiving consideration, and that I shall take pleasure in promptly advising you of any action which may be taken by this Government in reference thereto.

I have, &c.
(Signed)   FREDK. T. FRELINGHUYSEN.

No. 64.

Mr. West to Earl Granville.*—(Received August 5.)

My Lord,   *Washington, July 24, 1884.*
WITH reference to my despatch of the 19th instant, I have the honour to inclose herewith to your Lordship copy of a note which I have received from the Secretary of State, together with copies of the inclosures, stating that the instructions of the 24th November last, respecting the protection of the citizens of neutral Powers at the Treaty ports of China in case of war, have been renewed to the Commander-in-chief of the American naval force on the Asiatic Station.

I have, &c.
(Signed)   L. S. SACKVILLE WEST.

Inclosure 1 in No. 64.

Mr. Frelinghuysen to Mr. West.

Sir,   *Department of State, Washington, July 23, 1884.*
WITH reference to my reply of the 17th instant to your note of the 16th of the present month, in regard to making arrangements the for protection of the citizens of neutral Powers at the Treaty ports of China in case of war, I now have the honour to inclose herewith, for your information, a copy of a letter to this Department from the Acting Secretary of the Navy, stating that the instructions of the 24th November last have been renewed to the Commander-in-chief of the American naval force on the Asiatic Station.

I have, &c.
(Signed)   FREDK. T. FRELINGHUYSEN.

---

* Copy to Viscount Lyons.

31

Inclosure 2 in No. 64.

Mr. Nichols to Mr. Frelinghuysen.

Sir, *Navy Department, Washington, July* 21, 1884.
I HAVE the honour to acknowledge the receipt of your letter of the 17th instant, inclosing a copy of a note from the British Minister at Washington inquiring whether the arrangements made last year by neutral Powers for the protection of their citizens at the Treaty ports in China will now be carried out in the event of war between China and France.

In reply, I beg leave to inform you that instructions have been cabled to the Commanders-in-chief of the United States' naval force on the Asiatic Station, renewing the instructions of the 24th November last, in the event of war between the Powers above mentioned.

I am, &c.
(Signed)   ED. T. NICHOLS.
Acting Secretary of the Navy.

Inclosure 3 in No. 64.

Mr. Chandler to the Admiral commanding the Asiatic Squadron.

(Telegraphic.) *November* 24, 1883.
IN view of the possible conflict between China and France, you are instructed to act in concert with the vessels of England and other neutral European or American Powers in protecting lives and property of our and their citizens.

You will observe the strict neutrality of the United States.

No. 65.

The Secretary to the Admiralty to Sir J. Pauncefote.—(Received August 7.)

Sir, *Admiralty, August* 6, 1884.
I AM commanded by my Lords Commissioners of the Admiralty to transmit, for the information of the Secretary of State for Foreign Affairs, copy of a telegram dated the 5th August, from the Commander-in-chief on the China Station.

I am, &c.
(Signed)   EVAN MACGREGOR.

Inclosure in No. 65.

Vice-Admiral Sir W. Dowell to the Secretary to the Admiralty.

(Telegraphic.) *Foochow, August* 5, 1884, 6·30 A.M.
ALL quiet at Foochow. I shall remain, as Chinese preparations continue.

No. 66.

Sir J. Pauncefote to the Secretary to the Admiralty. *

Sir, *Foreign Office, August* 8, 1884.
I AM directed by Earl Granville to acquaint you, for the information of the Lords Commissioners of the Admiralty, that the English Secretary to the Chinese Legation in London called at this Office on the 7th instant, by desire of the Chinese Minister, to state that the Marquis Tsêng had received a telegram to the effect that the greatest alarm had been created among the Chinese at Foochow by the report that British marines were about to be landed there for the protection of the British Settlement; that an Imperial Edict had been issued enjoining on the Chinese authorities,

* Copy to Viscount Lyons.

civil and military, at that port, to use the utmost care and to take every precaution for the safety of all foreigners; and under these circumstances the Minister was instructed to express the hope that Her Majesty's Government would give directions that no marines or troops should be landed.

Dr. Macartney was informed, in reply, that it was extremely difficult and dangerous to fetter the discretion of the British naval officers at such a moment and in such a matter, especially as the ships of war of neutral Powers were acting in concert by agreement, for the protection of the foreign communities in the Treaty Ports, but that in view of the precautions taken by the Chinese Government, and also of the hopes now entertained of a friendly settlement, it was probable that the necessity would not arise of landing any force on the Foreign Concession.

I am to request that in laying this letter before their Lordships you will move them to take steps to ascertain by telegraph whether there is any probability of marines being required on shore at Foochow for the protection of Her Majesty's Consulate.

I am, &c.

(Signed) JULIAN PAUNCEFOTE.

No. 67.

The Secretary to the Admiralty to Sir J. Pauncefote.—(Received August 9.)

Sir, *Admiralty, August 9, 1884.*

I HAVE laid before my Lords Commissioners of the Admiralty your letter of the 8th August, requesting that the Commander-in-chief in China may be asked by telegraph whether there is any probability of marines being required on shore at Foochow for the protection of Her Majesty's Consulate, as the Chinese at Foochow are alarmed at a report that marines were about to be landed to protect the British Settlement there.

2. My Lords request that you will state to Earl Granville that the last telegram received from the Commander-in-chief in China was dated the 5th August, and ran as follows :—

" All quiet at Foochow. I shall remain, as Chinese preparations continue."

3. Their Lordships would be glad to be informed whether, under these circumstances, the Secretary of State considers it desirable to send any fresh orders to the Commander-in-chief who is now at Foochow.

4. I am to add that it does not appear to their Lordships to be probable that there is any foundation for the report that the Commander-in-chief intended to land Royal Marines at Foochow, and their Lordships do not consider it desirable to fetter his discretion with respect to any measures which he, in conjunction with the officers in command of the squadrons of our allies, may think it necessary to take if any occasion should arise.

I am, &c.

(Signed) EVAN MACGREGOR.

No. 68.

Sir H. Parkes to Earl Granville.—(Received August 11.)

My Lord, *Peking, June 20, 1884.*

I HAVE the honour to forward copy of a letter I have received from Vice-Admiral Sir William Dowell, informing me that he was about to form a portion of the naval force under his orders into an evolutionary squadron, but would still leave seven vessels to be distributed in the manner named for the protection of the Treaty ports in China.

According to the Admiral's programme, the cruize he is about to undertake will occupy rather more than three months, and the squadron will be absent from Chinese waters for more than two months. It appears to me that the arrangements which his Excellency has made for the protection of the China Treaty ports during that interval are sufficient to meet all ordinary contingencies, and I have accordingly expressed that opinion to the Admiral in the inclosed letter.

Having referred in this letter to two recent Reports from Her Majesty's Consuls,

* Copy to Sir J. Walsham.

howing how easily mob riots may occur in China, I add an extract from one of these in which Mr. Mansfield reports an incident which had occasioned some temporary excitement at Canton, but which was fortunately at once repressed.

I have, &c.

(Signed) HARRY S. PARKES.

Inclosure 1 in No. 68.

Vice-Admiral Sir W. Dowell to Sir H. Parkes.

Sir, *" Vigilant," at Chinkiang, June 4,* 1884.

I HAVE the honour to inform your Excellency that in view of the peaceable settlement of the difficulty between France and China, and the generally tranquil state of affairs at the Treaty ports, I have given directions for a portion of the naval force under my orders to join my flag at Woosung about the 20th instant, to cruize as an evolutionary squadron, and the " Midge " and " Cockchafer," now stationed in the Gulf of Pechili, will join the squadron at Chefoo on the 1st proximo. I beg to inclose for your information copy of the programme I purpose carrying out.

Your Excellency will observe that I have arranged for the squadron to reach Taku on the 13th proximo. I intend coming up to Tien-tsin in the " Vigilant " the following day, and I hope to have the pleasure of meeting your Excellency whilst there.

The protection of our interests at the Treaty ports will be provided for, whilst the squadron is cruizing, by a corvette and a gun-vessel for Shanghae, and the Yangtse ports, whilst in the neighbourhood of Hong Kong there will be, for the southern ports, one corvette (at Amoy), one sloop (at Canton), one gun-vessel (at Hong Kong), and two gun-boats (one at Foochow with orders to visit the Formosan ports monthly, and one in the Gulf of Tonquin).

I have ordered the " Cockchafer " to proceed from Chefoo on the 20th instant to Chemulpho, to communicate with Her Majesty's Consul-General, returning to Chefoo by the 1st proximo.

I have, &c.

(Signed) W. M. DOWELL.

Inclosure 2 in No. 68.

PROGRAMME of Cruize.

Leave—			Arrive—		
Woosung ..	..	July 1	Chefoo ..	..	July 4
Chefoo ..	..	,, 10	Taku, for Tien-tsin	..	,, 13
Taku ..	..	,, 17	Ning-Hai ..	..	,, 20
Ning-Hai ..	..	,, 25	Chefoo ..	..	,, 29
Chefoo ..	..	August 7	Port Hamilton	..	August 13
Port Hamilton	..	,, 16	Nagasaki ..	..	,, 18
Nagasaki ..	..	,, 28	Fusan ..	..	,, 31
Fusan ..	..	September 3	Port Lazareff	..	September 9
Port Lazareff	..	,, 13	Hakodate ..	..	,, 19
Hakodate ..	..	,, 27	Yamada Harbour	..	,, 30
Yamada Harbour	..	October 4	Yokohama ..	..	October 8

I may possibly leave Woosung with the squadron after the departure of the homeward mail of the 24th instant, but this alteration will not affect the date of my arrival at Tien-tsin.

(Initialled) W. M. D.

Inclosure 3 in No. 68.

Sir H. Parkes to Vice-Admiral Sir W. Dowell.

Sir, *Peking, June 13,* 1884.

I HAVE the honour to acknowledge the receipt of your Excellency's letter of the 4th instant, informing me of your intention to cruize with a portion of the naval force under your ordérs as an evolutioñary squadron, and of the arrangements you have made when that squadron is cruizing for the protection of British interests at the Treaty ports of China.

In thanking your Excellency for this information, I beg to observe that the force you have assigned for the protection of the ports appears· to me to be adapted to the existing state of affairs. The settlement of the difference between France and China removes a special cause of disturbance, and ih ordinary times danger in this country is mainly attributable, as your Excellency is aware, to Chinese mobs, who are generally careful to refrain from excesses when they see that a coercive force is at hand.

I inclose copies of two Reports which I received yesterday from Her Majesty's Consuls at Amoy and Canton, which serve to show how easily popular commotions may arise.

I have, &c.
(Signed)   HARRY S. PARKES.

Inclosure 4 in No. 68.

Mr. Mansfield to Sir H. Parkes.

(Extract.)   *Canton, June 3, 1884.*

ON Sunday the 1st instant, Mr. Lo Kee, Commander of the Shameen Chinese guard, sent word that a foreigner had got into trouble near the lower steamer wharf, and that he had sent 100 soldiers to quell the disturbance. As it was stated that the soldiers were still on the spot, and that the crowd was quiet, I sent the Consular constable to the spot to bring up the foreigner. In the meantime the Commissioner of Customs received a report from the Custom-house that there was a riot, and that the rumour was current that a foreigner had killed a Chinaman. A little later the constable returned by river with a man called Thomas Ide Bowles, who made the following statement. He said he was lodging in a Chinese inn, where he had been about three days. (This inn is situated almost between the two steamer wharves, and the neighbourhood is a nest of gambling dens and a resort of rowdies.) That being indisposed he was lying on the bed, when a boy of 15 or 16 came to the grated window opposite him, and began to call him names. After submitting to the abuse for some time, he got up and ran out into the street to catch the boy, but the latter ran away. A crowd began to collect, and he remained arguing with the people. In a narrow and populous thorough-fare the way is soon blocked. A large mass of people quickly formed, and Bowles hearing one or two shouts of "Ta! Ta!" thought it prudent to retire into the inn, and send word to Mr. Lo Kee, who at once sent soldiers to the spot. It was nearly two hours, however, before the crowd dispersed, and, though no violence was attempted, the occurrence shows what a mere trifle may begin a disturbance, and the false rumours that are circulated on the smallest excuse by the evil-disposed.

The locality where the present disturbance occurred is close to the old factory site, and is said to be inhabited almost entirely by persons who live by smuggling carried on in the river steamers, and it was by this class, doubtless, that the initiative in the Shameen riots was taken.

I have told Mr. Bowles that he must either make arrangements to live on the Concession or return to Hong Kong. The number of gun-boats in port is well kept up, and there are indications that arrangements have been come to on this point between the Admirals of the respective flags.

No. 69.

Sir J. Pauncefote to the Secretary to the Admiralty.

Sir,   *Foreign Office, August 11, 1884.*

YOUR letter of the 9th instant has been laid before Earl Granville, and, in reply, I am to request that you will inform the Lords Commissioners of the Admiralty that his Lordship entirely concurs in their opinion that it is undesirable that the action of the Commander-in-chief of Her Majesty's naval forces in Chinese waters should be fettered in regard to the measures in which he may, in concert with the Commanders

* Copy to Sir J. Walsham.

of the squadrons of the neutral Maritime Powers, consider it necessary to adopt under certain eventualities.

I am, however, to state that Lord Granville considers that it would be advantageous that inquiry should be made of the Commander-in-chief by telegraph whether it is likely to be necessary to land any British force for the protection of Her Majesty's Consulate at Foochow, adding at the same time that it is not desired to restrict his discretion, and I am to request that you will move the Lords Commissioners of the Admiralty to give directions in this sense.

I am, &c.
(Signed) JULIAN PAUNCEFOTE.

No. 70.

The Secretary to the Admiralty to Sir J. Pauncefote.*—(Received August 13.)

Sir, Admiralty, August 13, 1884.
WITH reference to your letter of the 11th instant, I am commanded by my Lords Commissioners of the Admiralty to transmit, for the information of the Secretary of State for Foreign Affairs, a copy of a telegram, dated the 11th August, which was sent to the Commander-in-chief on the China Station, relative to the question of landing men from Her Majesty's ships at Foochow in case of need.

A reply which has been received from the Vice-Admiral, dated the 13th August, is also attached.

I am, &c.
(Signed) EVAN MACGREGOR.

Inclosure 1 in No. 70.

The Secretary to the Admiralty to Vice-Admiral Sir W. Dowell.

(Telegraphic.) Admiralty, August 11, 1884, 5·30 P.M.
REPORT your opinion whether it is likely to be necessary to land any British force to protect British Consulate, Foochow. It is not desired to restrict your discretion.

Inclosure 2 in No. 70.

Vice-Admiral Sir W. Dowell to the Secretary to the Admiralty.

(Telegraphic.) August 13, 1884, 10·10 A.M.
SHALL probably have to land [for] protection Settlement if French attack Arsenal. Captain [of] "Champion" with men on board "Merlin" ready; will not land unless necessary. Tranquil at present. United States' Admiral co-operating. French attack appears imminent.

No. 71.

Earl Granville to the Marquis Tsêng.

M. le Ministre, Foreign Office, August 16, 1884.
REFERRING to your communication of the 7th instant,† relative to the measures taken by the Chinese Government to insure the safety of all foreigners at Foochow, and to their hope that no marines or troops would be landed from Her Majesty's ships at that port, I have the honour to state that it is extremely difficult and dangerous to fetter the discretion of the British naval officers at such a moment and in such a matter, especially as the ships of war of neutral Powers are acting in concert, by agreement, for the protection of neutrals in the Treaty ports.

In view, however, of the precautions taken by the Chinese Government, it may be

* Copy to Sir J. Walsham. † This was verbal.

[561] F 2

hoped that the necessity will not arise of landing any force on the foreign Concession' Indeed I immediately requested the Lords of the Admiralty to cause inquiries to be addressed by telegraph to the Commander of Her Majesty's naval forces on the station, desiring him to report whether there is any probability of any British force being required on shore at Foochow for the protection of Her Majesty's Consulate, and I have the honour to inform you that a reply has been received from the Vice-Admiral, who is now at Foochow, in which he states that he will not land any men unless necessary, and that matters there are at present tranquil.

I have, &c.
(Signed)   GRANVILLE.

No. 72.

The Marquis Tséng to Earl Granville.—(Received August 30.)

My Lord,   *Chinese Legation, August 28, 1884.*
I BEG to acknowledge receipt of your Lordship's letter of the 16th instant, and on the part of the Imperial Government, to offer to Her Majesty's Government their best thanks for the measure of compliance which they have been able to give to the request of the Chinese Government, that no men should be landed from the British ships of war now lying in the port of Foochow.

I have, &c.
(Signed)   TSÉNG.

No. 73.

Earl Granville to Sir H. Parkes.

Sir,   *Foreign Office, September 3, 1884.*
A TELEGRAM has been received from Vice-Admiral Sir William Dowell, dated from Foochow on the 30th ultimo, in which he reports that the city is in a disturbed state, that the Mandarins have hardly any authority there, that the soldiers at Pagoda Island are under no control, that it is not safe for foreigners to land, and that he has applied for the presence of a Mandarin of authority.

I have, in consequence, sent you instructions by telegraph this afternoon to support the Admiral's application, and to urge the Chinese Government to take every precaution at the ports in question, and at other places, for the safety of foreigners.

I am, &c.
(Signed)   GRANVILLE.

No. 74.

Sir H. Parkes to Earl Granville.—(Received September 7, 10·15 A.M.)

(Telegraphic.)   *Peking, September 6, 1884, 6·35 P.M.*
IN reply to your telegram of 3rd instant, I have the honour to state that having received similar information from Admiral on 1st, I at once obtained orders for control of troops at Pagoda. I have repeatedly urged on Government the necessity of ensuring safety of foreigners everywhere, and full protection was commanded by Imperial Decree issued on the 26th ultimo.

No. 75.

Mr. Plunkett to Earl Granville.—(Received September 8.)

(Extract.)   *Tōkiō, July 19, 1884.*
ON the receipt of your Lordship's telegram of the 16th instant, which reached me only next day, I requested Mr. Trench to be so good as to call at the Foreign Department and to inquire of Count Inouyé whether, in case of hostilities unfortunately

breaking out between France and China, Japan was still prepared to adhere to the arrangement made by the neutral Powers last year for the protection of their subjects at the Treaty ports, and whether any instructions had been as yet telegraphed to the Japanese Admiral on the Chinese coast.

Count Inouyé being out of town, Mr. Yoshida at once came to me to show the last telegrams which had reached the Japanese Government from their Agents in China.

Mr. Yoshida, having reported our conversation to Count Inouyé, called on me this morning, and with him I drew up the telegram which I had the honour of sending to your Lordship to-day, stating that:—

Japanese Government is ready to co-operate for protection of neutrals as arranged last year.

Japanese Admiral with two frigates is now at Shanghae, and has been instructed by telegraph to ascertain what steps will be taken by English and other Admirals.

No. 76.

Mr. Scott to Earl Granville.—(Received September 8.)

My Lord,   Berlin, September 4, 1884.

I HAVE the honour to report that, according to the semi-official "Nord-Deutsche-Allgemeine Zeitung" of this morning, the French Ambassador at this Court has communicated to the Ministry for Foreign Affairs the following steps taken by the French authorities for the protection of foreigners in China:—

1. The Commander of the French Squadron in Chinese waters has, from the outbreak of hostilities, been requested to take every step, compatible with the nature of his operations, to insure the safety of foreigners and the protection of their interests.

2. The plan of operations has been drawn up with the object of keeping open towns and foreign quarters as much as possible outside the sphere of action of the French fleet.

3. The bombardment of Foo-choo by Admiral Courbet was directed exclusively against the fleet, the Arsenal, and the Min River forts. The city itself, lying apart from the fortified points, has not suffered any damage.

Lastly, the Chinese Governor of Shanghae, "after coming to an arrangement with the French Consul," has issued a Proclamation to allay the fears of the inhabitants, in which he threatens disturbers of the peace with severe punishment.

I have, &c.
(Signed)   CHARLES S. SCOTT.

No. 77.

Sir H. Parkes to Earl Granville.—(Received September 12.)

(Extract.)   Peking, July 24, 1884.

I HAVE the honour to inclose copies of various letters I have addressed to the Naval Commander-in-chief, Sir William Dowell, on the present disturbed state of affairs.

In my letter of the 18th I stated, with reference to your Lordship's telegram of the 16th relative to the naval co-operation of the neutral Powers for the protection of the Treaty ports, that the places where popular commotion was most likely to occur were Tien-tsin, Hankow, Shanghae, Foochow, and Canton; and of these I particularly begged his Excellency to give special consideration to the three last ports; to Shanghae on account of the magnitude of the foreign interests, and to Foochow and Canton because the people of those two cities are particularly ill-disposed towards foreigners.

In a third letter of the same date I informed his Excellency of the movements of the German Commodore, Paschen, who commands the German squadron in Chinese and Japanese waters.

On the 19th I heard from his Excellency that he had ordered the squadron to cruize in the southern part of the station, and I expressed the opinion that this arrangement was exceedingly well suited to the present condition of affairs.

I should add that Sir William Dowell visited Tien-tsin on the 16th and 17th instant, and on hearing there that the French Commander-in-chief, Vice-Admiral Courbet, had proceeded from Shanghae with the bulk of his squadron to Foochow, he at once determined to go south with the British squadron.

38

Inclosure 1 in No. 77.

Sir H. Parkes to Vice-Admiral Sir W. Dowell.

Sir,   *Peking, July* 18, 1884.

I HAVE the honour to inform your Excellency that I received this morning the following telegram from Earl Granville :—

"Her Majesty's Representatives at Berlin, Washington, Rome, St. Petersburgh, Madrid, Lisbon, and Tôkiô, have been directed to intimate to the Governments to which they are accredited that Her Majesty's Government assume that joint arrangement of last year for protection of their subjects at Treaty ports will be carried out, and requested that necessary instructions may be given to naval Commanders by telegraph."

The ports where popular commotion is most likely to be directed against foreigners are Tien-tsin, Hankow, Shanghae, Foochow, and Canton, and of these five ports I consider the population of the two latter to be the most ill-disposed. I beg, therefore, to recommend the security of British subjects at these two ports, and at the great central port of Shanghae, to your Excellency's special consideration.

By a telegram received last night from Her Majesty's Consul-General at Shanghae, I learn that Rear-Admiral Lespès has been directed to proceed to Foochow. I am afraid that the object of this movement may be the seizure of the arsenal at that port. I fear that, if this step should be taken, it will occasion great local excitement among the Chinese population of the city.

I have, &c.
(Signed)   H. S. PARKES.

Inclosure 2 in No. 77.

Sir H. Parkes to Vice-Admiral Sir W. Dowell.

Sir,   *Peking, July* 18, 1884.

HIS Excellency Herr von Brandt, the German Minister here, has just informed me that in view of the telegram from Earl Granville which I have communicated to your Excellency in another letter of this date, he is requesting by telegraph Commodore Paschen, who is now at Yokohama, to come to China and make such arrangements for the protection of the Treaty ports as the means at his disposal will permit.

Herr von Brandt added that he leaves Commodore Paschen entirely at liberty to make such distribution of the vessels of the German squadron as he, in connection with your Excellency, may see fit.

I have, &c.
(Signed)   H. S. PARKES.

Inclosure 3 in No. 77.

Sir H. Parkes to Vice-Admiral Sir W. Dowell.

Sir,   *Peking, July* 19, 1884.

I HAVE the honour to acknowledge the receipt this morning of the following telegram, dated Taku, 18th :—

"Have ordered cruize on southern part of station. Shall leave one corvette, 'Midge' and 'Espoir' in Pechili (Gulf), for protection of Europeans at Treaty ports."

I have to thank your Excellency for having communicated to me this determination, and I beg to add that I consider it to be exceedingly well suited to the present condition of affairs.

I have, &c.
(Signed)   H. S. PARKES.

Inclosure 4 in No. 77.

Sir H. Parkes to Vice-Admiral Sir W. Dowell.

(Extract.)   *Peking, July* 24, 1884.

AS you were so good as to inform me in your private letter of the 19th instant that you then intended to proceed from Taku to Amoy, I sent this morning the following

message to Her Majesty's Consul at that port for communication to your Excellency on your arrival :—
" Hope Foochow is safe."
I well know how difficult it is to protect the foreign community in that city, but I am perfectly confident that as the matter is in your Excellency's hands, and as you will be near to the spot, the best possible measures will be taken to secure the safety of British subjects at that port.

No. 78.

Sir H. Parkes to Earl Granville.--(Received September 12.)

(Extract.)   *Peking, July* 24, 1884.
IN a note communicated by the Tsung-li Yamên to all the foreign Representatives at Peking on the 19th instant, of which I inclose an extract, the Prince and Ministers state that they will protect all the foreigners living at the Treaty ports, and also all French officials, merchants, and missionaries; but they add that if France should disturb the peace of the ports, and thereby occasion stoppage of trade, or loss or damage to property, France alone must be held responsible. All Governments, they add, should prohibit their subjects from assisting the enemy with supplies.

Inclosure in No. 78.

The Prince and Ministers of the Yamên to Sir H. Parkes.

(Extract.)   *July* 19, 1884.
THE merchants and subjects of every nationality are congregated at every Treaty port of China, and it is the duty of the Chinese Government to protect them all—French officials, merchants, missionaries, and citizens being equally included in the category of those who are entitled to protection. Should France, however, on account of the indemnity which she claims, go so far as to disturb the peace of any of the ports with her ships of war, thereby causing stoppage of trade or loss and damage to property, she alone will have to admit the responsibility of making good all losses whatsoever; these will not concern the Chinese Government in the very slightest degree. All Governments ought, moreover, to prohibit their merchants and subjects at every place from clandestinely assisting the foe with war stores, provisions, or any supplies whatsoever, that international law may be duly observed.

No. 79.

Sir H. Parkes to Earl Granville.—(Received September 12.)

My Lord,   *Peking, July* 24, 1884·
I HAVE the honour to inclose copy of the reply which I addressed to the Tsung-li Yamên in reply to their Circular note inclosed in my previous despatch of this date.
That note contains the observation that " should France, on account of the indemnity which she claims, go so far as to disturb the peace of the ports with her ships of war, thereby causing stoppage of trade or loss and damage to property, she alone will have to admit the responsibility of making good all losses whatsoever; these will not concern the Chinese Government in the very slightest degree."
Believing that the Chinese Government might at some future date appeal to this declaration to acquit them from responsibility for attacks on foreigners or for damages occasioned by popular tumult, which they might attribute to the action of the French, I thought it desirable to point out in my reply that the Chinese Government must be held responsible for any aggression committed on foreigners by Chinese subjects, and I therefore urged them to take effective measures for keeping the ill-disposed classes of their people under proper restraint. I added that whether responsibility would attach to the Chinese Government for stoppage of trade must depend upon the circumstances of the case.
I have, &c.
(Signed)   HARRY S. PARKES.

Inclosure in No. 79.

Sir H. Parkes to Prince Yi-Kuang.

Peking, July 23, 1884.

HER Britannic Majesty's Minister has the honour to acknowledge the receipt of the note of the Prince and Ministers of the 19th instant, informing him of the misunderstanding which has arisen between China and France on the Langson affair.

Her Britannic Majesty's Minister deeply regrets to hear of the occurrence of a misunderstanding between China and a friendly Power, but he sincerely trusts that the negotiations, which he understands are still being carried on between the Chinese and French Governments, will eventually result in an amicable adjustment of the present difficulty.

Her Britannic Majesty's Minister fully appreciates the assurance given by the Prince and Ministers in the note under acknowledgment, that it is the duty of the Chinese Government to protect the merchants and subjects of every nationality who are congregated at the Treaty ports of China. But he observes that they also state that "should France, on account of the indemnity which she claims, go so far as to disturb the peace of any of the ports with her ships of war, thereby causing stoppage of trade or loss and damage to property, she alone will have to admit the responsibility of making good all losses whatsoever; these will not concern the Chinese Government in the very slightest degree."

Her Britannic Majesty's Minister therefore considers it incumbent upon him to remark that should a collision unfortunately occur between the two Powers, there can be no question that the Chinese Government will be responsible for affording complete protection to all foreigners, being subjects or citizens of friendly Powers, resident within their territory, either at the ports or in the interior of the country, against any aggression on the part of Chinese subjects. He therefore strongly urges them, in the interest even of their own Government, to take immediate and effective measures to keep under proper restraint the ill-disposed classes of their people, and prevent their attacking British subjects and injuring either their lives or their property. Whether any responsibility will attach to the Chinese Government for the stoppage of trade must depend upon the circumstances under which such an event occurs.

Her Britannic Majesty's Minister takes this opportunity, &c.

No. 80.

Earl Granville to Sir J. Walsham.

Sir,
Foreign Office, September 12, 1884.

I TRANSMIT to you herewith a copy of a despatch from Her Majesty's Chargé d'Affaires at Berlin, reporting that the "Nord-Deutsche Allgemeine Zeitung" of the 4th instant stated that the French Ambassador at the Imperial Court had communicated to the Ministry for Foreign Affairs the steps which had been taken by the French authorities for the protection of foreigners and of their interests in China during the present hostilities;* and I have to request you to suggest that, if a similar communication were made to Her Majesty's Government, it would have a good effect in allaying the apprehensions felt by the commercial community in this country as to the possible effects of the hostilities between France and China.

I am, &c.
(Signed)   GRANVILLE.

No. 81.

Earl Granville to Sir H. Parkes.

Sir,
Foreign Office, September 17, 1884.

I HAVE received and laid before the Queen your despatch of the 24th July, and I have to convey to you the approval by Her Majesty's Government of the communication, a copy of which you inclose, which you addressed to the Tsung-li Yamên, in reply to their Circular note of the 19th of the same month, disclaiming responsibility for any

* No. 76.

injury or loss which may occur to foreigners, in consequence of the difficulties which have arisen between France and China.

I am, &c.
(Signed)   GRANVILLE.

No. 82.

Sir J. Walsham to Earl Granville.—(Received September 20.)

My Lord,   *Paris, September* 19, 1884.

AS M. Jules Ferry is still absent from Paris, and unlikely to return at present, I called this morning by appointment upon M. Billot, the Political Under-Secretary for Foreign Affairs, and, with reference to your Lordship's despatch of the 12th instant, which reached me yesterday by the messenger, spoke to him in the sense of that despatch in regard to the statement made in the "Nord-Deutsche Allgemeine Zeitung" of the 4th instant, that the French Ambassador at Berlin had communicated to the German Government the steps which had been taken by the French authorities for the protection of foreigners, and of their interests in China during the present hostilities. After reading to M. Billot the extract from the German paper which contained the statement, I asked him whether it was correct; and he at once gave me the following explanation:—

Count Hatzfeldt had, he said, spoken a short time ago to their Ambassador on the subject of the position of foreigners and their interests in China at the present time, and Baron de Courcel having requested M. Jules Ferry to let him know what answer he should return to Count Hatzfeldt, if the latter again alluded to the matter, was instructed to give the assurances mentioned in the "Nord-Deutsche Allgemeine Zeitung."

Baron de Courcel soon after receiving this instruction had occasion to see Count Hatzfeldt, and verbally communicated to him the measures which had been adopted for the protection of foreign interests in China. Thereupon, Count Hatzfeldt expressed a wish that he might have the assurances in writing, and be authorized to publish them, with a view to allaying the apprehensions felt by the Representatives of German commerce.

Baron de Courcel readily acceded to this suggestion, and wrote accordingly to Count Hatzfeldt. This would account therefore for the statement having found its way into the newspapers.

As regards the Proclamation said by the papers to have been issued by the Governor of Shanghae, "after coming to an arrangement with the French Consul," for the purpose of calming the fears of the inhabitants, and notifying that disturbers of the peace would be severely punished, M. Billot told me that the Proclamation had been drawn up in the terms and in the manner described, but that on the Governor asking for permission from Peking to promulgate it his request had been refused.

I then begged M. Billot to inform me whether there would be any objection to Her Majesty's Government receiving the same assurances from the French Government as the German Government had received, and for the same purpose.

He considered that there would be none, and promised to lay the matter at once before M. Jules Ferry. He thought, however, that it might perhaps be well if I addressed a note in the meantime to his Excellency, and I assured M. Billot that I should have much pleasure in doing so.

I have, &c.
(Signed)   JOHN WALSHAM.

No. 83.

Sir H. Parkes to Earl Granville.—(Received September 22.)

My Lord,   *Peking, July* 31, 1884.

WITH reference to my despatch of the 24th instant, inclosing a copy of the note I had addressed to the Tsung-li Yamên in reply to that passage in their Circular letter of the 19th instant which disclaimed all responsibility for damage to property occasioned by the proceedings of the French, and which might be held to cover losses caused by popular commotion, I have now the honour to inclose copies of the notes addressed to the Yamên on the same subject by my colleagues, the Ministers of Germany,

Russia, and the United States, the tenour of which your Lordship will perceive is similar to that of my communication.*

I have, &c.

(Signed)   HARRY S. PARKES.

No. 84.

Sir H. Parkes to Earl Granville.—(Received September 22.)

My Lord,   *Peking, July* 31, 1884.

WITH reference to my other despatch of this date,† I venture to suggest that the advantage of affording encouragement to the Shanghae volunteers is illustrated by the inclosed despatch from Her Majesty's Consul-General, reporting that the Taotai of Shanghae had requested the Consuls in writing to call upon the Commanders of the foreign men-of-war in port to land men to co-operate with the Chinese troops in restoring order in the event of popular disturbance.

It appears to me singular that such a request should have been made at a time when, in consequence of the unfavourable aspect of the question between China and France, a considerable Chinese force has been concentrated at Shanghae or in its neighbourhood. A local paper speaks of 8,000 Chinese troops being stationed between Shanghae and Woosung, and of more than 6,000 at the Kiangnan Arsenal near the city, in addition to the garrison within the walls, and of the considerable escort which was expected to arrive with the Viceroy Tsêng Kuo-chuan.

The foreign naval force will be ample for the protection of the foreign Settlement, as, in addition to several vessels which were already stationed at Shanghae, the German Commodore, with two ships, and the United States' Admiral, with three, have proceeded there from Yokohama, on the recommendation of the German and American Ministers at Peking.

I also inclose an earlier despatch from Mr. Hughes, showing that preparations had been made by the naval authorities for the defence of the Settlement before the application of the Taotai had been received, and that the volunteers had been called on to take part in the arrangements.

I have, &c.

(Signed)   HARRY S. PARKES.

Inclosure 1 in No. 84.

Consul-General Hughes to Sir H. Parkes.

Sir,   *Shanghae, July* 21, 1884.

THE senior Consul called a meeting of his colleagues last Saturday to consider a matter of grave importance. On assembling, we learned that the Taotai had made a verbal request to the senior Consul that, in case of disturbance in the city or suburbs, the Commanders of the men-of-war in harbour be called upon to assist Chinese troops in restoring order. It was deemed advisable that in a question of this importance the Taotai should be asked to put his request in writing, more especially as, so far as our information went, there was no reason to apprehend an immediate outbreak. The letter, of which copy is inclosed, was accordingly sent to the senior Consul. It will be observed that it is written in English, and that it is signed for the Taotai by his interpreter, Mr. Kwong Ki-chiu. The senior Consul sent round a notice this morning convening a meeting of his colleagues for this afternoon at half-past 3 o'clock.

At this meeting it was agreed, in accordance with a proposition made by me, that an answer should be sent substantially to the following effect :—

The duty of protecting all foreigners as well as natives rests with the Taotai and the other Chinese authorities. We are sure that the officers commanding the men-of-war in port, to whom copy of Taotai's letter will be communicated, will do all that is possible in case of need for the protection of life and property. We request that in the event of actual or imminent danger the Taotai will have the goodness to com-

---

municate at once with the senior Consul and the other Consular Representatives at this port, &c.

I have, &c.
(Signed) P. J. HUGHES.

P.S.—The officers commanding men-of-war will not, of course, be able to furnish any assistance beyond the limits fixed by the plan of defence already arranged.

P. J. H.

Inclosure 2 in No. 84.

Shao Yu-liu, Taotai, to Dr. Lührsen.

Sir, *Shanghae City, July 19, 1884.*
I BEG to state that as Shanghae is inhabited by the people of the different places of China, there are many homeless persons. At present the dispute between China and France is not yet settled, and the inhabitants are feeling uneasy, fearing that some rascals may find opportunity to be riotous, and to do harm to this port. I therefore write you, with the request that yourself and the Consuls of all different countries will communicate to the Commanders of all men-of-war in the harbour that in future, if there will be rascals disturbing either in the foreign Settlements or in other places which are close to this city any of the Consuls or I myself inform you of this, and the soldiers should be sent on shore from all the men-of-war immediately to join the Chinese troops to suppress the disturbance and to protect the property of the people.

By so doing you will oblige, yours, &c.
(Per Kuong Ki-chui, Deputy of the Local Bureau
of Foreign Affairs),
(Signed) SHAO YU-LIU, *Taotai of Shanghae.*

Inclosure 3 in No. 84.

Consul-General Hughes to Sir H. Parkes.

Sir, *Shanghae, July 16, 1884.*
I HAVE the honour to report that the officers commanding the British, Italian, and American ships of war in port, viz., Her Majesty's "Cleopatra," His Imperial Majesty's "Cristoforo Colombo," United States' ship "Monocacy," have, in consultation with the Major commanding the local volunteers, arranged a plan for the defence of the Settlement in the event of local disturbance.

The plan, which is based on the one drawn up last year, with which you are acquainted, provides, like the former plan, for the effective defence of portions only of the Settlement.

The Japanese Admiral has promised to render assistance, and provision is made for the co-operation of a Spanish man-of-war shortly expected. The present arrangements are to be carried out under the superintendence of Captain Accini, of the Royal Italian Navy, as Senior Officer.

I have, &c.
(Signed) P. J. HUGHES.

No. 85.

Sir H. Parkes to Earl Granville.—(Received September 23.)

(Extract.) *Peking, August 7, 1884.*
ON the 26th ultimo the Prince and Ministers wrote a note, of which I inclose an extract, acknowledging the letter I had addressed them on the 23rd (inclosed in my despatch to your Lordship of the 24th ultimo) relative to the responsibility which would devolve upon the Chinese Government for acts of aggression upon foreigners committed by their own people.

Inclosure in No. 85.

The Prince and Ministers of the Tsung-li Yamén to Sir H. Parkes.

(Translation.) *July 26, 1884.*

THE Prince and Ministers have the honour to acknowledge the receipt on the 23rd instant of the British Minister's note, stating, with regard to the differences that have arisen between France and China in connection with the affair at Langson, that should hostilities unfortunately occur the Chinese Government would, of course, be responsible for the safety of all foreign residents.

They will inform the local authorities along the coast that they must keep the native population under restraint, giving them emphatically to understand that they must not make a season of trouble the occasion for disturbance of the peace.

No. 86.

Sir J. Walsham to Earl Granville.—(Received September 24.)

My Lord, *Paris, September 22, 1884.*

IN continuation of my despatch of the 19th instant, I have the honour to transmit herewith to your Lordship a copy of a note which I have addressed to M. Jules Ferry, with the object of suggesting to his Excellency whether it would not have a beneficial effect as regards the apprehensions of the mercantile community in England with respect to the possible results of the hostile relations between France and China if the French Government were disposed to make to the Government of Her Majesty a communication as to the steps which have been taken by the French authorities for the protection of foreigners and their interests similar to the statement upon this subject which, according to the "Nord-Deutsche Allgemeine Zeitung" of the 14th instant, the French Ambassador at Berlin had been permitted to make to the German Government on a recent occasion.

I have, &c.

(Signed) JOHN WALSHAM.

Inclosure in No. 86.

Sir J. Walsham to M. Ferry.

M. le Président du Conseil, *Paris, September 22, 1884.*

IN the "Nord-Deutsche Allgemeine Zeitung" of the 14th instant a statement was made to the effect that the French Ambassador at Berlin had informed the German Government that the following measures had been adopted by the French authorities for the protection of foreigners and of their interests in China during present events:—

1. The Commander-in-chief of the French fleet had from the commencement taken every step compatible with the nature of the operations to be undertaken to insure the safety of foreigners and the protection of their interests.

2. The plan of operations had been drawn up with the object of keeping open towns and foreign quarters as much as possible outside the sphere of action of the French fleet.

3. The bombardment of Fouchow had been directed exclusively against the fleet, the arsenal, and the forts of the Min River, while the city itself had not suffered damage.

4. The Governor of Shanghae, after coming to an arrangement with the French Consul, had issued a Proclamation with the view of allaying the apprehensions of the inhabitants, and of letting it be known that those who might attempt to disturb the peace would be severely punished.

Her Majesty's Government cannot help feeling that, supposing the statement in the German paper to be correct, and the French Government to be willing to address a similar communication to them for publication, it would have a beneficial effect in calming the fears of the British mercantile community as to the possible results of what is occurring in China, and they would, therefore, gladly learn that the suggestion which they venture to make had met with your Excellency's concurrence.

I have, &c.

(Signed) J. WALSHAM.

45

No. 87.

Earl Granville to Sir J. Walsham.

Sir, *Foreign Office, September* 24, 1884.
1 APPROVE your language to M. Billot, as reported in your despatch of the 15th instant, in regard to the assurances given to the German Government with reference to the measures taken by the French authorities for the protection of foreigners and of their interests in China during the present hostilities; and I authorize you to address a note to the French Government, as suggested by M. Billot, requesting to be furnished with similar assurances in writing.

I am, &c.
(Signed) GRANVILLE.

No. 88.

Sir H. Parkes to Earl Granville.—(Received September 26, 11 P.M.)

(Telegraphic.) *Peking, September* 26, 1884, 7·30 P.M.
I HEAR by telegraph from Consul at Canton and Governor of Singapore high authorities at Canton have issued Proclamation calling on Chinese to destroy French ships and poison French at Singapore, Penang, and elsewhere.
I have denounced this grave offence against law, humanity, and British sovereignty, and have told them only remedy is Imperial Decree recalling Proclamation, and censuring the authorities. They still disavow knowledge of Proclamation, although they called for Report a week ago.

No. 89.

Earl Granville to Sir H. Parkes.

Sir, *Foreign Office, September* 27, 1884.
I HAVE received your telegraphic despatch of the 26th instant, in regard to a Proclamation issued by the Canton authorities inciting the Chinese at Singapore and elsewhere to destroy French ships and to poison French citizens.
I have to convey to you the approval of Her Majesty's Government of the language which you used to the Tsung-li Yamên, and to request you to continue to press for the issue of an Imperial Decree annulling the Proclamation in question and censuring the provincial authorities.
I have this day communicated to you by telegraph the substance of the foregoing.

I am, &c.
(Signed) GRANVILLE.

No. 90.

Earl Granville to Sir J. Walsham.

Sir, *Foreign Office, September* 27, 1884.
I TRANSMIT to you the accompanying copy of a telegram from Her Majesty's Minister at Peking in regard to a Proclamation issued by the Canton authorities, inciting the Chinese at Singapore and elsewhere to destroy French ships and to poison French citizens.*
I have to request you to communicate confidentially to the French Government the substance of Sir H. Parkes' telegram, and to state that his proceedings have been approved by telegraph, and that he has been further instructed to continue to press the Chinese Government to issue an Imperial Decree annulling the Proclamation, and censuring the Canton authorities.

* No. 88.

I have this day communicated to you the substance of the foregoing by telegraph.

I am, &c.
(Signed)   GRANVILLE.

No. 91.

Mr. Currie to Sir R. Herbert.

Sir,   *Foreign Office, September* 27, 1884.

I AM directed by Earl Granville to acquaint you that Her Majesty's Minister at Peking has reported, by telegraph, that the Acting Consul at Canton and the Governor of the Straits Settlements have telegraphed to him to say that the high authorities of Canton have issued a Proclamation calling on the Chinese at Singapore, Penang, and elsewhere to destroy French ships and to poison French citizens.

Sir H. Parkes states that he has denounced to the Chinese Government this grave offence against law, humanity, and British sovereignty, and has informed them that the only remedy for it is to issue an Imperial Decree annulling the Proclamation and censuring the provincial authorities. He adds that the Chinese Government still disavow any knowledge of this Proclamation, although they called for a Report a week ago.

I am to request that, in laying this letter before Her Majesty's Secretary of State for the Colonies, you will suggest to his Lordship the desirability of telegraphing this intelligence to the Governor of Hong Kong, and to state that it is proposed, with Lord Derby's concurrence, to instruct Sir H. Parkes to keep the Colonies likely to be concerned informed in matters of this kind.

I am to add that Sir H. Parkes' action has been approved, and that he has been instructed to continue to press for an Imperial Decree. The Marquis Tsêng also, at Lord Granville's request, has undertaken to telegraph at once to his Government in a similar sense.

Her Majesty's Minister in Paris has been instructed to communicate the substance of Sir H. Parkes' telegram to the French Government, and to inform them of the steps which have been taken in the matter.

I am, &c.
(Signed)   P. CURRIE.

No. 92.

Sir J. Walsham to Earl Granville.—(Received September 29.)

My Lord,   *Paris, September* 28, 1884.

I HAVE the honour to inform your Lordship that I have this day addressed a note to the French Government in the terms of your Lordship's telegram of yesterday, relative to a Proclamation recently issued by the Chinese authorities at Canton.

I have, &c.
(Signed)   JOHN WALSHAM.

No. 93.

Sir H. Parkes to Earl Granville.—(*Received September* 30.)

(Telegraphic.)   *Peking, September* 30, 1884.

IN reply to your telegram of the 27th instant, the "Peking Gazette" published to-day a very satisfactory Imperial Decree, issued yesterday, censuring the high authorities, and disapproving the Proclamation.

* Substance to Colonial Office.

47

No. 94.

Sir J. Walsham to Earl Granville.—(Received October 1.)

My Lord,   *Paris, September 28, 1884.*
I HAVE the honour to forward to your Lordship herewith a copy of a note which, in obedience to your Lordship's telegraphic instructions of yesterday afternoon, I have this morning addressed to the French Government, explaining to them the action which Sir H. Parkes, with the approval of Her Majesty's Government, has taken for the purpose of denouncing to the Chinese Government a recent Proclamation of the authorities at Canton, calling upon Chinese subjects to kill Frenchmen and destroy their ships at Singapore, Penang, and elsewhere.

I have, &c.
(Signed)   JOHN WALSHAM.

Inclosure in No. 94.

Sir J. Walsham to M. Ferry.

(Confidential.)
M. le Président du Conseil,   *Paris, September 28, 1884.*
THE British Representative at Peking, Sir H. Parkes, has informed Her Majesty's Government by telegraph that, in consequence of having learnt, also by telegraph, from the Governor of Singapore and Her Majesty's Consul at Canton, that a Proclamation had been issued by the Chinese high authorities at the latter port, calling upon the subjects of the Emperor to destroy French ships, and to poison Frenchmen at Singapore, Penang, and elsewhere, he had immediately taken steps for denouncing to the Tsung-li Yamên so grave an offence against law, humanity, and His Majesty's sovereignty, and had also pointed out to the Yamên that, under the circumstances, the only possible remedy would be the immediate promulgation of an Imperial Decree severely censuring the Canton authorities, and recalling the Proclamation.
Sir H. Parkes adds that the Tsung-li Yamên continued to disavow all knowledge of the Proclamation in question, although they had some days ago ordered the authorities at Canton to report on the subject.
In having the honour of making this confidential communication to your Excellency, in consequence of an instruction which I have received from Her Majesty's Government, I hasten to state that they have sent a telegram to Sir H. Parkes approving the action taken by him, and instructing him to continue to urge upon the Chinese Government the necessity of an Imperial Decree being published in the terms already mentioned.

I have, &c.
(Signed)   JOHN WALSHAM.

No. 95.

Sir J. Walsham to Earl Granville.—(Received October 1.)

My Lord,   *Paris, September 28, 1884.*
I HAVE the honour to transmit herewith to your Lordship a copy of a note I have to-day received from M. Jules Ferry, in which, with reference to a suggestion I had made on the part of Her Majesty's Government, his Excellency assures me that the French Government have no objection to publicity being given in England to the measures which have been adopted by the French authorities with a view to the protection of the lives and interests of foreigners during the present operations in China ; and after enumerating these measures, M. Ferry expresses his satisfaction that they should appear to Her Majesty's Government to be of a nature calculated to allay any apprehensions which might exist amongst the representatives of commerce in the United Kingdom.

I have, &c.
(Signed)   JOHN WALSHAM.

48

Inclosure in No. 95.

M. Ferry to Sir J. Walsham.

Monsieur,   *Paris, le 25 Septembre,* 1884.

VOUS avez bien voulu, par votre lettre du 22 de ce mois, m'entretenir des informations publiées, le 4 Septembre dernier, dans la "Gazette de l'Allemagne du Nord," et d'après lesquelles l'Ambassadeur de la République à Berlin a fait part à la Chancellerie Impériale des mesures prises par les autorités Françaises en faveur des résidents étrangers dans les ports de Chine.

Vous m'avez en même temps fait connaître le désir du Gouvernement de la Reine de se trouver en mesure de rassurer au moyen d'un avis analogue les commerçants Britanniques.

Dès le 31 Août dernier, le Chargé d'Affaires de France à Londres a été autorisé à répondre aux questions qui pouvaient lui être faites à cet égard par le Cabinet Anglais, en le tenant au courant des dispositions que nous nous étions empressés de prendre pour préserver les Européens en général, et les résidents Britanniques en particulier, contre les sévices de la population Chinoise.

Nous n'avons d'ailleurs pas d'objection à ce que l'on sache en Angleterre :—

1. Que le Commandant-en-chef de la flotte Française dans les mers de Chine a, dès le début de ses opérations, été spécialement invité à aviser, dans la mesure du possible, à la sécurité des étrangers résidant dans les ports, et à la protection de leurs intérêts.

2. Qu'afin de préserver les villes et les Concessions étrangères de tout contre-coup, le plan des opérations a été combiné de façon à les laisser, autant que possible, en dehors de l'action directe des forces Françaises.

C'est ainsi qu'à Fou-tcheou le bombardement exécuté par l'Amiral Courbet a été exclusivement dirigé sur la flotte, l'arsenal, et les fortifications de la Rivière Ming, et que la ville même, séparée des points fortifiés, n'a subi aucune atteinte. De même à Shang-haï le Gouverneur Chinois avait publié, à la suite d'une entente avec le Consul de France, une Proclamation destinée à rassurer les habitants, et menaçant de peines sévères les fauteurs de désordre.

Il convient toutefois d'ajouter que, d'après des renseignements récents, la Cour de Pékin se serait refusée à sanctionner cet arrangement favorable au commerce Européen.

Je vous serai obligé de transmettre ces indications au Comte Granville. Nous avons été heureux d'apprendre qu'elles paraissaient à sa Seigneurie de nature à produire une bonne impression dans le public Anglais, en l'édifiant sur la sollicitude dont les intérêts du commerce Britannique ont de notre part été l'objet.

Agréez, &c.
(Signé)   JULES FERRY.

(Translation.)

Sir,   *Paris, September 25, 1884.*

IN your letter of the 22nd instant you were good enough to address me on the subject of the information published on the 4th September last in the "North German Gazette," according to which the Ambassador of the Republic at Berlin had communicated to the Imperial Chancery the measures taken by the French authorities for the protection of foreign residents in the Chinese ports.

At the same time you informed me of the desire of Her Majesty's Government to be enabled to reassure British traders by means of a similar notification.

On the 31st August last the Chargé d'Affaires of France in London was authorized to reply to questions which might be addressed to him on this subject by the English Cabinet, by recounting the measures which we had hastened to take to protect Europeans in general, and British residents in particular, against ill-usage on the part of the Chinese populace.

We have, further, no objection that it should be known in England :—

1. That the Commander-in-chief of the French fleet in the Chinese seas has from the very outset of his operations been especially desired to take all possible measures for the security of foreigners residing in the ports, and for the protection of their interests.

2. That, in order to guarantee the towns and the foreign Concessions against injury, the plan of operations has been combined in such a way as to leave them, as far as possible, outside the direct action of the French forces.

Thus at Foochow, the bombardment carried out by Admiral Courbet was exclusively directed against the fleet, the arsenal, and the fortifications of the Ming River, and the town itself, being situated apart from the fortified points, suffered no damage. Also at Shanghae the Chinese Governor, after an agreement with the French Consul, published a Proclamation intended to reassure the inhabitants and threatening with severe penalties the promoters of disorder.

It should, however, be added that, according to recent information, the Court of Peking has refused to sanction this arrangement, which would have been favourable to European commerce.

I shall be obliged by your transmitting this information to Earl Granville. We were glad to learn that, in his Lordship's opinion, a good impression would be produced on the British public by its publication, as proving the solicitude which we have shown for the interests of British commerce.

Accept, &c.
(Signed)   JULES FERRY.

No. 96.

Mr. Bramston to Mr. Currie.—(Received October 1.)

Sir,   *Downing Street, September 30, 1884.*
I AM directed by the Earl of Derby to acknowledge the receipt of your letter of the 27th instant, reporting the substance of information received from Her Majesty's Minister at Peking in regard to a Proclamation alleged to have been issued at Canton, inciting to the destruction of French ships and citizens at Singapore and elsewhere.

2. In reply, I am to acquaint you, for the information of Earl Granville, that in accordance with his Lordship's suggestion the intelligence received from Sir H. Parkes on this subject was telegraphed to the Officer administering the Government of Hong Kong on the 27th instant, and I am to state that a reply was received from that Officer on the 29th instant, reporting that Hong Kong native newspapers which had published the Proclamation were being criminally prosecuted.

3. I am to add that Lord Derby concurs in Lord Granville's proposal to instruct Sir H. Parkes to keep the Colonies likely to be concerned informed in matters of this kind.

I am, &c.
(Signed)   JOHN BRAMSTON.

No. 97.

Earl Granville to Sir J. Walsham.

Sir,   *Foreign Office, October 1, 1884.*
I HAVE received your despatch of the 22nd ultimo, and I have to convey to you my approval of the terms of the note which you addressed to M. Jules Ferry, a copy of which you inclose, relative to the adoption of measures for allaying the apprehensions of foreigners in China in the existing state of affairs.

I am, &c.
(Signed)   GRANVILLE.

No. 98.

Earl Granville to Sir H. Parkes.

Sir,   *Foreign Office, October 2, 1884.*
I HAVE to request you to keep the authorities of British Colonies likely to be interested informed of such matters as the recent Proclamation issued by the Canton officials.

I have this day sent you by telegraph the substance of the foregoing.

I am, &c.
(Signed)   GRANVILLE.

No. 99.

Mr. Plunkett to Earl Granville.*—*(Received October 3.)*

(Extract.) *Tôkiô, August* 30, 1884.

WITH reference to my despatch of the 26th April last, I have the honour to transmit to your Lordship herewith an extract of a confidential note received yesterday from the Japanese Minister for Foreign Affairs, stating that, in view of the very critical state of relations between China and France, the naval force of His Imperial Majesty's Government in Chinese waters has been increased by the addition of another man-of-war, the "Iwaki Kan," which left Nagasaki on the 23rd instant for Shanghae. Count Inouyé says that the Government will also be prepared, in case of necessity, to further strengthen the fleet under Admiral Matsumura's command, and I learned to-day from a trustworthy source that orders have already been issued to get the "Riujo," wooden armour-clad, and the "Kasuga," ready for sea immediately. I have the honour to add that I am forwarding to Vice-Admiral Sir William Dowell a copy of Count Inouyé's note.

Inclosure in No. 99.

Count Inouyé to Mr. Plunkett.

(Extract.) *Foreign Office, Tôkiô, August* 28, 1884.

REFERRING to my confidential note of the 25th April last to his Excellency the Honourable F. R. Plunkett, informing him of the departure for China seas of Admiral Matsumura with His Imperial Majesty's men-of-war the "Fuso Kan" and the "Amagi Kan" under his command, for the protection of neutral subjects and property in the event of emergencies, as agreed upon by Japan with Great Britain and other Powers, I have the honour to state, for your information, that, in view of the increasingly critical state of relations between China and France, the naval force so dispatched by His Imperial Majesty's Government to China seas for the purpose above mentioned has been added to by another man-of-war, the "Iwaki Kan," which left Nagasaki on the 23rd instant for Shanghae.

Should it happen that future events render any addition to the naval force of His Imperial Majesty already dispatched either desirable or necessary, I have the honour to inform you that this Government will be prepared to send one more vessel to the same destination.

No. 100.

Sir J. Walsham to Earl Granville.†—*(Received October 4.)*

My Lord, *Paris, October* 2, 1884.

IN continuation of my despatch of the 28th instant, I have the honour to transmit herewith to your Lordship a copy of a note from M. Jules Ferry in reply to the communications which, by your Lordship's instructions, I made to his Excellency on the above-mentioned dates upon the subject of a Proclamation which had recently been issued by the authorities at Canton inciting Chinese subjects to acts of hostility against the French at Singapore and Penang, and the withdrawal of which had been urged upon the Chinese Government by Sir H. Parkes, with the approval of the Government of Her Majesty.

In acknowledging the receipt of these two communications, M. Ferry says that the French Government know with what energy Her Majesty's Government would act under the circumstances in affirming the principles of humanity, and they also feel assured that the steps taken with the approval of Her Majesty's Government will prove sufficient to guarantee that complete security which Frenchmen are in the habit of finding in British possessions.

On both grounds, therefore, M. Ferry is desirous of conveying to Her Majesty's Government the satisfaction with which the Government of the Republic has received the confidential communications which I have addressed to him.

I have, &c.

(Signed) JOHN WALSHAM.

---

* Copy to Admiralty. † Copy to Colonial Office.

Inclosure in No. 100.

M. Ferry to Sir J. Walsham.

Monsieur,   *Paris, le 30 Septembre,* 1884.

VOUS m'avez fait l'honneur de m'annoncer, par vos lettres Confidentielles du 28 et du 29 de ce mois, que le Ministre de la Reine à Pékin a reçu de Singapour et de Canton l'avis que les autorités Chinoises de ce dernier port avaient publié une Proclamation invitant les sujets du Céleste Empire à détruire les navires Français et à empoisonner nos nationaux dans les établissements Anglais du Détroit de Malacca.

Vous m'apprenez, en outre, que Sir Harry Parkes a immédiatement dénoncé au Tsung-li Yamên ces provocations, aussi outrageantes pour les lois de l'humanité qu'offensantes à l'égard des droits souverains de Sa Majesté Britannique, en faisant observer au Cabinet de Pékin qu'il n'avait d'autre parti à prendre que de promulguer sans retard un Décret Impérial, censurant les autorités de Canton et annulant leur Proclamation. Le Tsung-li Yamên n'avait encore répondu au Représentant Britannique qu'en excipant de l'ignorance où il se trouverait des procédés des autorités de Canton.

Vos communications m'informent également de l'approbation que le Comte Granville a donnée à l'initiative de Sir Harry Parkes. Des représentations analogues, directement adressées au Ministre de Chine à Londres, ont amené ce dernier à envoyer par le télégraphe à Pékin une dépêche qui ne peut laisser aucune incertitude au Tsung-li Yamên sur le prix que le Gouvernement de la Reine attache au succès des démarches de son Représentant.

Nous ne pouvions douter un instant de l'énergie que le Gouvernement de la Reine mettrait, dans une pareille circonstance, à affirmer les principes d'humanité que les nations civilisées tiennent à honneur de faire prévaloir, et nous nous plaisons à penser que ses démarches suffiront pour garantir la complète sécurité que nos nationaux sont habitués à trouver dans les établissements Britanniques. A ce double point de vue je vous serai reconnaissant de vouloir bien remercier de ma part le Comte Granville, et de lui exprimer la satisfaction avec laquelle le Gouvernement de la République a reçu les communications confidentielles dont vous étiez chargé.

Agréez, &c.
(Signé)   JULES FERRY.

(Translation.)

Sir,   *Paris, September 30, 1884.*

YOU did me the honour to inform me, in your Confidential letters of the 28th and 29th instant, that Her Majesty's Minister at Peking had received intelligence from Singapore and Canton that the Chinese authorities at the latter port had published a Proclamation inviting subjects of the Celestial Empire to destroy French ships and to poison French subjects in the English possessions of the Straits of Malacca.

You acquainted me further that Sir H. Parkes had immediately denounced to the Tsung-li Yamên these incitements, outrageous alike to the laws of humanity and offensive to the sovereign rights of Her Britannic Majesty, and had informed the Cabinet of Peking that there was no other course open to them than to publish without delay an Imperial Decree censuring the authorities at Canton, and annulling their Proclamation. The Tsung-li Yamên had as yet only replied by pleading ignorance of the action of the authorities at Canton.

I further learn from your communications that Lord Granville has approved the initiative taken by Sir H. Parkes; and that similar representations, addressed directly to the Chinese Minister in London, induced him to dispatch a telegram to Peking which can leave no doubt to the Tsung-li Yamên as to the importance which Her Majesty's Government attach to the success of the measures taken by their Representative.

We did not for a moment doubt the energy which Her Majesty's Government would show under such circumstances in affirming those principles of humanity which civilized nations desire should prevail, and we are pleased to believe that their proceedings will suffice to guarantee to our citizens that complete security which they are accustomed to enjoy in British possessions. On both grounds I shall be obliged if you will thank Lord Granville on my behalf, and express to him the satisfaction with which the Government of the Republic have received the confidential information which you were instructed to communicate.

Accept, &c.
(Signed)   JULES FERRY.

No. 101.

Sir J. Walsham to Earl Granville.—(Received October 4.)

My Lord,   *Paris, October 3, 1884.*

WITH reference to my despatch of the 2nd instant, I have the honour to state that owing to my having received on the 1st instant a copy of Sir H. Parkes' telegram of the 30th ultimo, I had the satisfaction of being enabled to inform M. Jules Ferry, when I saw his Excellency in the afternoon at his usual weekly reception, that in consequence of the representations which had been made to the Chinese Government by Sir H. Parkes with the approval of Her Majesty's Government, an Imperial Decree had been issued and published in the Peking Gazette of the 30th September, by the terms of which the Proclamation recently promulgated by the Canton authorities for the purpose of inciting Chinese subjects to acts of hostility against the French at Singapore and Penang, was disapproved and its authors censured.

I have, &c.

(Signed)   JOHN WALSHAM.

No. 102.

Sir H. Parkes to Earl Granville.—(Received October 6.)

(Extract.)   *Peking, August 14, 1884.*

I INCLOSE an extract of a Report from Mr. Consul Sinclair to myself, describing the position of affairs at Foochow during the continuation of the hostile demonstration of the French.

The prompt arrival of Vice-Admiral Sir William Dowell at that port and the arrangements he made for the protection of the Settlement, immediately restored to the foreign community a feeling of comparative security.

After visiting Foochow on the 29th ultimo, Sir William Dowell proceeded to Amoy, but left again on the 2nd for Foochow, as he felt satisfied that in the event of hostilities breaking out the arsenal at that port would be the object of French attack.

Inclosure in No. 102.

Consul Sinclair to Sir H. Parkes.

(Extract.)   *Foochow-foo, August 5, 1884.*

A STEAMER is clearing to-day for Shanghae, and I avail myself of the opportunity to forward to you what scanty intelligence there is respecting the Franco-Chinese business since my despatch to you of the 26th ultimo.

Admiral Dowell was in here on the 29th of last month for the day, and is back again to-day from Amoy.

There are of Her Majesty's ships at the anchorage, the corvettes "Champion," "Sapphire," and the Admiral's tender, the "Vigilant;" and off the Settlement the gun-boat "Merlin," and the United States' gun-vessel, the "Monocacy."

From the "Champion" there are sixty-five men with officers, to be in readiness in the event of a declaration of war to land for the protection of the foreign Settlement.

Their landing has the sanction of the Governor-General when it becomes actually necessary; meanwhile, the "Champion" men are kept afloat in a cargo-boat off Jardine's jetty.

I think that with this force to defend our position, we may consider ourselves safe from the rabble and pillagers.

All the ladies but three or four of the community have left with their children, some for Amoy, others for Hong Kong, and a few for Sharp Peak Island, where are situated the missionary seaside retreats.

No. 103.

Sir H. Parkes to Earl Granville.—(Received October 6.)

My Lord,   *Peking, August* 14, 1884.
I HAVE the honour to inclose a translation of a note which I received from the Ministers of the Tsung-li Yamên, requesting that a naval force should not be landed at Foochow. According to their information this had already been done, and they feared that it would add to the alarm of the people.

I replied that I believed their Excellencies were under some misapprehension as to a force having actually been landed, as this would only be done in the face of serious emergency, in accordance with an understanding already arrived at with the local authorities. I added that, as Vice-Admiral Sir William Dowell was at Foochow, I had perfect confidence in the arrangements which his Excellency would make for the protection of the foreign residents, and was satisfied that they would only be such as the circumstances of the case rendered absolutely necessary.

On reverting to the subject at a subsequent interview with the Ministers, they explained that their only fear in regard to the landing of our men was that they might be mistaken for the French, and they concurred with me that it must be left to the responsible officers on the spot to determine when men should be landed from the ships; they quite approved of the latter being stationed off the Settlement, and they particularly desired that if war should unfortunately break out between France and China the ships should remain there, as then their services would be most needed.

I beg to add a copy of a letter, in which I forwarded this correspondence to Vice-Admiral Sir William Dowell, and communicated to him the subsequent explanations of the Chinese Ministers.

I have, &c.
(Signed)   HARRY S. PARKES.

Inclosure 1 in No. 103.

The Tsung-li Yamên to Sir H. Parkes.

(Translation.)   *August* 7, 1884.
THE Prince and Ministers of the Tsung-li Yamên have the honour to inform the British Minister that they have recently received a telegraphic Report from the Tartar General, Governor-General and Governor of Fuhkien, stating that the British Consul wished to land some troops at Foochow. His Excellency the Minister Superintendent of Trade for the North has also received a foreign telegram, in which it is stated that, in consequence of the unsatisfactory state of the French question, the native population of Foochow was much excited, and the British Government had already landed a military force there.

On the occasion of his visit the other day, the British Minister was requested to inform the Consul at Foochow that a naval force must not land, when his Excellency replied that a note should be written to the foreign Representatives on the subject.

The Yamên have to observe that a number of French vessels of war being now congregated at the port of Foochow, the people there are just in that state of suspicion and apprehension, that if foreign soldiers were to land there is reason to fear that the ignorant folk might possibly create disturbance.

If there are any British vessels of war at Foochow for the protection of British merchants and subjects, it is earnestly hoped that the British Minister will promptly instruct the Consul to call upon them to take up their usual stations, and not allow men to land.

This is a matter of the utmost importance.

Inclosure 2 in No. 103.

Sir H. Parkes to the Tsung-li Yamên.

Peking, August 8, 1884.
HER Britannic Majesty's Minister has the honour to acknowledge the note of His Highness the Prince and their Excellencies the Ministers of yesterday's date on the

subject of two telegrams which they have received, one from the Tartar General, Governor-General and Governor of Fuhkien, stating that the British Consul wished to land troops at Foochow; the other from the Minister Superintendent of Trade for the North, stating that the British Government had already landed a military force at that port.

Her Britannic Majesty's Minister thinks that there must be some mistake in these Reports, as when the subject was mentioned to him at the interview of the 5th instant, to which the Prince and Minister refer, he telegraphed to Her Majesty's Consul at Foochow for information, and he has received this morning a reply stating that all is quiet at the Pagoda anchorage, that the French Squadron and the British Admiral are there, and that the Viceroy will permit men to be landed for the protection of foreign residents in case of emergency. Now, if any force had been landed from the British ships, or if Her Majesty's Consul had wished that a force should be landed, he would certainly have said so in his message, but, on the contrary, he states that all is quiet.

Her Britannic Majesty's Minister is fully sensible that in consequence of the excitement caused at Foochow by the presence there of a large number of French ships of war, it is specially incumbent on the British authorities to take every precaution in their power to prevent the spread of alarm among the people. The Prince and Ministers may therefore feel assured that the British vessels of war at that port will remain in their usual stations, and that their commanders will not land men unless absolutely compelled to do so, in order to protect the lives and property of British subjects or other foreign residents who may appeal to them for assistance.

Her Britannic Majesty's Minister is very glad that at this juncture the British Naval Commander-in-chief, Vice-Admiral Dowell, is present at Foochow. His Excellency is an officer of very high rank and great experience, and he may be fully relied on to take only such steps for the security of British subjects as the circumstances of the moment may render necessary. The foreign residents at Foochow should, indeed, be protected by the high Chinese authorities of that city against any violence on the part of the Chinese people, and it is only in the event of those authorities failing to fulfil their duty in this respect that the British naval authorities will be obliged, greatly against their wish, to interfere for the protection of their countrymen.

Her Britannic Majesty's Minister begs his Highness and their Excellencies to assure the Viceroy and other high authorities of Foochow that Admiral Dowell's visit to that port is entirely of a friendly character, and that his presence there is intended to afford support to rather than to add to the difficulties of the Chinese Government.

Her Britannic Majesty's Minister takes, &c.

(Signed)   HARRY S. PARKES.

Inclosure 3 in No. 103.

Sir H. Parkes to Vice-Admiral Sir W. Dowell.

Sir,   *Peking, August 12, 1884.*

I BEG to forward, for your Excellency's information, a translation of a note addressed to me by the Prince and Ministers of the Tsung-li Yamên, objecting to the landing of a British naval force at Foochow, and also a copy of my reply, in which I pointed out to their Excellencies that the representations upon which they wrote were possibly based upon some misapprehension. I explained to them that the commanders of Her Majesty's ships would only land men in the face of so serious an emergency as would render it absolutely incumbent on them to do so, in order to protect the lives and property of British subjects or other foreign residents whenever the Chinese Government failed to ensure their safety. I also added that I was glad to know that your Excellency was present at Foochow, as I was satisfied that whatever steps might be taken under your direction would be such as the circumstances of the moment rendered indispensable.

I have since seen their Excellencies the Ministers, who concurred with me that when British subjects are attacked or are in danger the commanders of Her Majesty's ships would be perfectly justified in landing men to protect them, that it must be left to the officers on the spot to determine whether such a step was necessary or not, and that in adopting it they would of course come to an understanding, and would co-operate with the local Chinese authorities whenever they could do so.

Your Excellency was so good as to telegraph to me on the 31st ultimo from Amoy that you had visited Foochow and made arrangements for the safety of the Settlement.

There has not yet been time for me to receive from Her Majesty's Consul at Foochow a report of these arrangements, but I have heard that two of Her Majesty's ships, the "Linnet" and "Merlin," and also the United States' ship "Monocacy," are off the Settlement (Nantai), and I feel satisfied therefore that the safety of the foreign residents is well secured. I observed to the Chinese Ministers that the proper and usual station or a British ship of war is where she is needed, and in justice to the Ministers I should add that they expressed gratification on hearing that the three ships above named were at Nantai, and added that the objections they had expressed as to the landing of their men was only attributable to apprehension that they might be mistaken for the French.

I have, &c.
(Signed)   HARRY S. PARKES.

No. 104.

Sir H. Parkes to Earl Granville.—(Received October 6.)

My Lord,   *Peking, August 15, 1884.*

I INCLOSE a copy of a note which I addressed to the Prince and Ministers of the Tsung-li Yamên on receiving an unfavourable Report from Her Majesty's Acting Consul at Canton relative to the disposition of the populace of that city after the collision between the French and Chinese at Langson became known. This occurrence seemed to have revived much ill-will against foreigners, and also a strong desire for war with France, and the officials appeared indisposed to check either of these feelings. Foreigners were now frequently insulted in the streets, and Mr. Butler, the Assistant of the Consulate, felt it unsafe to travel daily between the Canton office at Shamien and his residence within the city.

I therefore thought it desirable to use this Report in order to emphasize in a note the representations I had made verbally to the Ministers on the previous day as to the urgent necessity of the Chinese Government doing all in their power to keep under control the unruly population of Canton and Foochow, and prevent abuse and ill-treatment of foreigners. I thought I perceived—as I pointed out in my despatch of the 24th ultimo—a disposition on the part of the Chinese Government to attach responsibility to the French for the turbulence of their own people, and I therefore considered it desirable to repeat in this note, as I had already stated to the Ministers in my note to them of the 23rd (inclosed in the above-mentioned despatch), that the Chinese Government were directly responsible for any aggression against foreigners committted by the Chinese people. I also added that the incendiary disposition of the Canton populace was directed against foreigners generally, irrespective of nationality, but that the exhibition of popular ill-feeling against France, in particular, might precipitate fresh collisions, and seriously complicate the relations between the two countries.

The Ministers have since assured me that they telegraphed instructions in the sense I desired to the new Viceroy of the Two Kwang, Chang Chih-tung, who arrived there about the middle of the month. This Viceroy has hitherto evinced a decided bias against foreigners in all the State Papers he has written on foreign questions. He is, however, a resolute and highly capable man, and now that he is face to face with responsibility in the conduct of foreign affairs, he may evince a different disposition. Her Majesty's Acting Consul has already reported the issue of fresh Proclamations, enjoining friendly behaviour on the part of the people, which have been followed by some improvement in their demeanour towards foreigners in the streets.

I have, &c.
(Signed)   HARRY S. PARKES.

Inclosure in No. 104.

Sir H. Parkes to the Tsung-li Yamên.

Peking, July 24, 1884.

HER Britannic Majesty's Minister has the honour to recall to the recollection of his Highness and their Excellencies the remarks he made at yesterday's interview with reference to the turbulent character of the native population at Canton and Foochow, and the necessity of taking prompt and energetic measures for keeping them under due control.

The justice of these remarks is forcibly sustained by a Report which has just been received from Her Majesty's Acting Consul at Canton. In a despatch dated the 10th instant he states that popular feeling in Canton seems lately to have undergone a considerable change for the worse. Foreigners passing through the streets of the city are insulted at almost every step, and it is a noticeable fact that whereas, until recently, it was children or youths who chiefly made use of insulting language, this bad practice is now commonly resorted to by grown-up people. One of the officers employed in Her Majesty's Consulate, who has been living in the official residence within the city occupied by Her Majesty's Consul for many years past, finds that he is so frequently threatened and insulted in his daily journeys to and from the Consulate offices on Shamien, that he has thought it prudent to remove his residence to the foreign Settlement in order to avoid encountering personal violence.

Her Majesty's Acting Consul attributes the growth of this hostile feeling to the rumours of impending hostilities with the French, an eventuality, he adds, that appears to be eagerly looked forward to by a large section of the population, while the authorities show no desire to repress the exhibition of this feeling.

In view of the above Report, Her Britannic Majesty's Minister cannot too strongly impress upon his Highness and their Excellencies the necessity not only of causing active measures to be taken to repress the incendiary disposition of the Canton population, who have already shown, by the destruction of the foreign residences at Shamien, that they make no distinction between foreigners of this or that nationality whenever their latent hostility finds vent in acts of open violence, but he would also venture to suggest that the exhibition of popular hostile feeling towards France may precipitate at any moment a fresh collision, which would seriously complicate the relations between the two countries.

(Signed)   HARRY S. PARKES.

No. 105.

Acting Consul Frater to Earl Granville.—(Received October 6.)

My Lord,   *Tamsuy, August 15, 1884.*

I HAVE the honour to inclose, for your Lordship's information, copies of despatches from me to Her Majesty's Minister at Peking about the state of affairs at Kelung and Tamsuy.

I have, &c.

(Signed)   A. FRATER.

Inclosure 1 in No. 105.

Acting Consul Frater to Sir H. Parkes.

Sir,   *Tamsuy, August 11, 1884.*

I HAVE the honour to inclose copies of a correspondence between the Rear-Admiral in command of the French naval forces at Kelung and myself about the protection of British subjects returning to Kelung, and as to whether Chinese law is still in force there.

I have issued a Circular, acquainting British subjects that if they return to or remain at Kelung they do so at their own risk. I have taken advantage of a Customs courier leaving for Kelung this morning to send it in the first instance to the British subjects that have elected to remain there.

Yours, &c.

(Signed)   A. FRATER.

P.S.—I shall send a copy of this despatch to the Foreign Office direct.

A. F.

57

Inclosure 2 in No 105.

Acting Consul Frater to Rear-Admiral Lespès.

Sir,   *Tamsuy, August* 7, 1884.
I HAVE the honour to request that you will kindly inform me whether British
subjects can now return to Kelung to reside there with safety, or when this will be
possible, and whether such as return to live on shore will be under the protection of the
French naval authorities.
I beg also to be informed whether the Chinese authorities are permitted by you to
administer their own laws in Kelung, and whether you are in military possession of
the whole town and its immediate neighbourhood.
I have, &c.
(Signed)   A. FRATER.

Inclosure 3 in No. 105.

Rear-Admiral Lespès to Acting Consul Frater.

A bord de " La Galissonnière," Rade de Kélung,
M. le Consul,   *le* 9 *Août*, 1884.
J'AI l'honneur de vous accuser réception de votre lettre datée de Tamsui,
le 7 Août.
Je n'occupe actuellement aucun point à terre, il ne m'est donc pas possible de
protéger les sujets Britanniques. S'ils reviennent à Kélung avant que nos affaires ne
soient réglées, ce sera, par conséquent, à leurs risques et périls.
Je ne vois d'ailleurs aucun inconvénient à ce que les autorités Chinoises continuent,
dans tous les cas, même si je venais à l'occuper, à administrer la ville de Kélung et à
y exercer la police.
Veuillez, &c.
Le Contre-Amiral Commandant-en-chef la Division
Navale des Mers de Chine et du Japon,
(Signé)   J. LESPÈS.

(Translation.)

On board " La Galissonnière," Kelung Roadstead,
M. le Consul,   *August* 9, 1884.
I HAVE the honour to acknowledge the receipt of your letter dated Tamsuy, the
7th August.
As I do not at the present moment occupy any point on land, I am not in a
position to protect British subjects. If they return to Kelung before our affairs are
settled, they will, consequently, do so at their own risk and peril.
I do not, moreover, see any inconvenience in the Chinese authorities continuing,
in any case, to conduct the administration of Kelung and to preserve order there, even
if I were to occupy the town.
I have, &c.
(Signed)   J. LESPÈS,
*Commander-in-chief of the Naval Division of the
China and Japan Seas.*

Inclosure 4 in No. 105.

Acting Consul Frater to Sir H. Parkes.

(Extract.)   *Tamsuy, August* 15, 1884.
I OBSERVE to-day in the streets a Proclamation by General Sun, warning his
soldiers against ill-treatment of non-French foreigners (the whole foreign community
here) if the French visit this port.
Yesterday, Dr. Mackay, the agent of the Presbyterian Mission of Canada,
informed me that reports had reached him from many quarters in North Formosa,
that if there is to be war the Mission chapels are to be destroyed, and the converts
[561]   I

attacked by rowdies. Though not placing entire credence in these Reports (from Chinese sources), I thought it prudent to bring the matter officially to the knowledge of the Prefect.

This district is, all things considered, remarkably quiet. Numbers of people have removed, and I have hinted to the authorities that they should try to prevent a scare. Trade is going on but languidly, and for ready money only.

No. 106.

Earl Granville to Sir J. Walsham.

Sir,   Foreign Office, October 6, 1884.
I HAVE received your despatch of the 28th ultimo, inclosing copy of a note addressed to you by M. Ferry in regard to the measures which have been adopted by the French authorities with a view to the protection of the lives and interests of foreigners during the present operations in China, and I have to state to you that Her Majesty's Government have received his Excellency's assurances with satisfaction, and will avail themselves of his permission to make them public.
I am, &c.
(Signed)   GRANVILLE.

No. 107.

Sir H. Parkes to Earl Granville.—(Received October 9.)

My Lord,   Peking, August 19, 1884.
WITH reference to my despatch of the 14th instant, relative to the landing of men from Her Majesty's ships for the protection of British subjects and other foreign residents at Foochow in the event of it being necessary to do so, I beg to inclose a copy of the instruction which I addressed to Mr. Consul Sinclair on this subject.
I have, &c.
(Signed)   HARRY S. PARKES.

Inclosure in No. 107.

Sir H. Parkes to Consul Sinclair.

Sir,   Peking, August 14, 1884.
WITH reference to my telegram of the 6th instant, which was based upon a verbal representation made to me by the Ministers of the Yamên on the previous day, I inclose, for your information and guidance, copies of two notes,* together with their respective translations, which I have exchanged with the Yamên on the subject of landing a force for the protection of foreign residents at Foochow.

It is clear that in this case, as in other instances, the responsible officers on the spot must determine when it may become necessary to land men from the ships of war. Such a step would of course only be adopted in the face of absolute necessity; it should be taken, whenever possible, in concurrence with the Chinese authorities, and when the arrangements of the latter are considered insufficient to insure the safety of the lives and property of the foreign residents.

The Ministers of the Yamên have since explained to me that their only anxiety in regard to the landing of our men was that they might be mistaken for the French, and regarded therefore as an enemy; but of course it will not be difficult to prevent the occurrence of such a mistake by giving timely information as to how our men or other friendly force may be distinguished.

The Ministers welcome the presence of neutral ships of war off Nantai, and have observed to me that their presence there would be most needed if war should unfortunately break out.
I am, &c.
(Signed)   HARRY S. PARKES.

* See No. 103.

No. 108.

Sir H. Parkes to Earl Granville.—(Received October 9.)

My Lord,   Peking, August 19, 1884.

WITH reference to my despatch of the 14th instant, relative to the disturbed state of affairs at Foochow, I beg to inclose an extract of a despatch which I wrote to Mr. Consul Sinclair in acknowledgment of his reports, and in which I informed him that I considered it unadvisable that Her Majesty's ship "Merlin" should be withdrawn from her station off the foreign Settlement.

I have, &c.
(Signed)   HARRY S. PARKES.

Inclosure in No. 108.

Sir H. Parkes to Consul Sinclair.

(Extract.)   Peking, August 14, 1884.

I HAVE read with great interest your despatches reporting the serious state of alarm which prevailed at Foochow in consequence of the apparently hostile character of the naval demonstration made by the French squadron at that port, and I fully approve of your proceedings as reported in those despatches.

I was glad to learn that the timely arrival of a British naval force and the arrangements made by Vice-Admiral Sir William Dowell for the protection of the Settlement had quickly relieved the foreign residents of the apprehensions they entertained as to their personal safety.

I consider it undesirable that Her Majesty's ship "Merlin" should be withdrawn from her station off Nantai.

No. 109.

Sir H. Parkes to Earl Granville.—(Received October 9.)

My Lord,   Peking, August 20, 1884.

IN continuation of my despatch of the 15th instant, I have the honour to report that I have since received a despatch, of which I inclose an extract, from Her Majesty's Acting Consul at Canton, reporting that quiet has been restored in the streets of Canton, and that foreigners going through them now enjoy comparative immunity from insult. Her Majesty's Consul attributes this improvement to the energetic character of the new Viceroy Chang Chih-tung.

I mentioned in the above-named despatch that the Ministers of the Tsung-li Yamên had assured me that they would instruct the Viceroy, by telegraph, to take measures to keep the unruly populace of Canton under effective restraint, and the Proclamation which Mr. Hance incloses in his despatch, and which was issued a week after I received that assurance, may partly be attributable thereto. The appearance of the incendiary placard, which Mr. Hance also incloses, and which had been posted three days before the publication of the Proclamation, proved the necessity of fresh injunctions to check the very malevolent feeling which the placard denotes.

It is satisfactory to see from Mr. Hance's despatch that he considers the safety of the foreign settlement at Canton (Shamien) to be effectually secured

I have, &c.
(Signed)   HARRY S. PARKES.

Inclosure 1 in No. 109.

Acting Consul Hance to Sir H. Parkes.

(Extract.)   Canton, August 7, 1884.

IN continuation of my despatch of the 30th ultimo, I have the honour to report that on the 31st ultimo I went, at the invitation of Mr. Travers, to the German Consulate, where I met Mr. Seymour, and the Commanders of the vessels of war at present stationed here, the object of our assembling being to ascertain what course the latter officers would follow, in the event of the Chinese authorities deciding altogether to block up the river—a measure not unlikely, I apprehend, should hostilities between France and China break out.

Mr. Travers having briefly explained the object of the meeting, Commander Ching, of Her Majesty's ship "Daring," stated that the vessel under his command would remain here whether the river was blocked or not. Captain Rötger, of the Imperial German gun-vessel "Iltis," said that, in the event of the closing of the river being notified, it would be his duty to leave with his vessel, unless he received a written requisition to remain from Mr. Travers, which the latter stated he should not feel justified in making. The First Lieutenant of the United States' ship "Palos," representing Commander Glidden, who is indisposed, explained that his vessel would remain here, under all circumstances, until orders had been received from the Admiral. I am informed this morning that Captain Rötger received telegraphic instructions on the day following the meeting reported above, to consult with the Commanders of the other vessels of war as to the necessity or otherwise of staying here, in the event of the river being blocked.

The Chinese officer, Mr. Lo Kee, who has command of the guard stationed on Shamien, reports that he has under him close upon 600 troops well armed, without counting 130 picked men of the "An-yung," who are on guard at the gates, and the whole body has instructions, in the event of a disturbance, to co-operate with the landing-parties from the men-of-war. It may therefore be said that the safety of Shamien is effectually secured. British subjects living outside the settlement have been advised to come in at once at the first sign of a disturbance. The streets, however, appear very quiet, and the usual insults and abuse are conspicuously absent. It is to be hoped that this is owing to the well-known character of the new Governor-General, Chang Chih-tung, for meting out vigorous and unsparing justice to evil-doers.

I also inclose translation of an anti-foreign placard which was posted on the wall of the native hospital. There were rumours of anti-foreign placards and hand-bills being posted up and circulated in the city, but I believe there was no foundation for the report, for I have tried in vain to get a copy of anything of the kind.

I also inclose translations of a Proclamation issued by the magistrates, under instructions from the Governor-General. It appears to be of a very satisfactory nature, and has doubtless contributed largely towards the comparative immunity from insult now enjoyed by foreigners going through the streets.

Matters continue quiet here, and we have still the three gun-boats, "Daring," "Iltis," and "Palos" in port.

Inclosure 2 in No. 109.

A further strictly prohibitory Proclamation by the Magistrate of the Pan Yü District and the Acting Magistrate of the Namhoi District.

(Translation.)

FOREIGNERS of all nations carrying on business in China in accordance with the provisions of the Treaties, or unobtrusively preaching their religion, ought to be treated in a friendly manner by you all.

That they should be in any way intimidated, insulted, or disturbed is inexcusable. Lately foreigners, passing to and fro the streets and roads, have been followed and abused by quarrelsome scoundrels.

We received instructions from the late Governor-General Chang to take stringent repressive measures, and we issued a Proclamation prohibiting such conduct. All the people ought to respond to the desire of the high authorities to keep the peace between Chinese and foreigners, as it has hitherto existed, and to carry on trade in peace. The least resistance to the law will not be tolerated.

We have heard that of late reckless rowdies have invented lying rumours, posted up anonymous placards, and acted with a view to producing excitement. Such persons may truly be said to be regardless of the law. We have issued orders to the police to make rigorous search for and arrest them. We also issued this further Proclamation, that all of you who live in our districts, and all artizans, may clearly understand and act accordingly. In future you must attend peacefully to your duties, and must not again circulate lying rumours or post up anonymous placards to excite men's minds, or recklessly raise disturbances against foreigners. But if you dare to follow your old courses and try to resist lawful rule, your leader will assuredly be diligently searched for and punished. The Tipao of the place, whose preventive regulations were not sufficiently strict, will be at once brought before the Tribunal, and be first punished with the utmost rigour of law.

Let each one, trembling, obey this special Proclamation.

11th day of 6th moon, 10th year K.S. (1st August, 1884).

Inclosure 3 in No. 109.

Anonymous Placard posted on the night of July 29 [on the walls of the Native Hospital].

(Translation.)

ALL dealings with foreigners are detestable.
These men have no father or mother.
Their offspring are beasts.
Jesus is their ancestor.
Of your males they make catamites.
And of your females devils' wives.
Our country has a sacred religion.
Why should we imitate foreign devils?
Our country has powerful gods,
And it is our bounden duty to reverence Shangti.
Under pretence of establishing hospitals,
They in reality develop their fiendish designs.
We have our own native doctors.
Why ask for favours from the foreign devils?
By distributing medicine they entice you to come,
With a view to making your wives their own.
A certain class of degraded women
Become converts and disgrace their homes.
In one month are four Sundays,
When women come from all parts;
And, no sooner do they see the barbarian's face,
Than they throw both arms round the foreign devil.
My words are of little weight,
But are destined to arouse you in some degree.
He who defaces or tears down this [placard]
Is certainly a friend of the foreign devils.

No. 110.

Sir H. Parkes to Earl Granville.—(Received October 9.)

My Lord,   *Peking, August 20, 1884.*

MR. HANCE, in the Report which I inclosed in my despatch of this date, reports that a meeting had been held by the Commanders of the vessels of war stationed off Shamien, to consider whether they should remain there if the river were entirely closed by the Chinese authorities. The British and American Commanders declared that they would stay under all circumstances, while the German Commander considered that it would be his duty to withdraw.

I was very glad to find that the instructions of the British and American Commanders admitted of such a satisfactory resolution, but in order that the Commander-in-chief might be acquainted with my views on the subject, I at once telegraphed to his Excellency: "I beg you to allow Her Majesty's ships to remain off Settlements in the event of river being closed at Foochow or Canton. This is also considered necessary by Chinese Government." I also explained the grounds of my telegram in a letter to his Excellency, of which I inclose a copy.

Sir William Dowell was so good as to send me, in reply, the following message, which I received yesterday: "I will comply with your request."

On communicating with my colleague, the German Minister, on the subject, he informed me that he had telegraphed to the German Commodore to leave the German gun-vessel at Canton, even if the river were closed.

I have, &c.

(Signed)   HARRY S. PARKES.

62

Inclosure in No. 110.

Sir H. Parkes to Vice-Admiral Sir W. Dowell.

Sir,   *Peking, August* 17, 1884.
I BEG to inclose extract from a despatch which I received last evening from
Her Majesty's Consul at Canton, reporting a meeting held by the British, German,
and American Consuls with their respective naval Commanders, in order to ascertain
what course those officers would take in the event of the river being completely closed
by the Chinese authorities.
Commander Ching stated that he would remain for the protection of the foreign
Settlement, whether the river was blocked or not, and the Lieutenant representing
Commander Glidden, of the United States' ship " Palos," also said that his Commander
would follow the same course. The Commander of the German gun-vessel " Iltis "
considered, however, that it would be his duty to leave, though he afterwards received
a telegram instructing him to confer with the other Commanders.
I am very glad that the instructions of Commanders Ching and Glidden admitted
of their taking such a decisive and satisfactory determination. I feel certain that no
request from me is needed to persuade your Excellency to keep Her Majesty's vessels
off the Settlements of Canton and Foochow, if war should unfortunately render it
necessary for the Chinese authorities to completely close the barriers they have
constructed in the Canton and Min Rivers. The Chinese Ministers stated to me a
few days ago, that in that event the presence of neutral ships of war would be more
than ever needed for the protection of those Settlements.
In order, however, that your Excellency may at once be acquainted with my
views on this point, I have sent you to-day the following telegram :—
" I beg you to allow Her Majesty's ships to remain off Settlements in event of
river being closed at Foochow or Canton. This is also considered necessary by
Chinese Government."
I have, &c.
(Signed)   HARRY S. PARKES.

No. 111.

Sir H. Parkes to Earl Granville.—(Received October 9.)

(Extract.)   *Peking, August* 21, 1884.
I HAVE the honour to inclose a further Report from Mr. Consul Sinclair on the
state of affairs at Foochow. It shows that the Tsung-li Yamên had been misinformed
as to the reported landing of a British naval force at that port, and that I was correct
in the assumption, which I expressed to the Chinese Ministers, and reported in
my despatch of the 14th instant, namely, that our men would only be landed
under circumstances of sufficient gravity to render such a step absolutely necessary.
Mr. Sinclair also shows that he had been in communication with the high authorities
with regard to all the precautionary measures that had been adopted, and that the
latter had stated to him in their note of the 3rd instant (Inclosure No. 7) that " it
would be a distinctly satisfactory arrangement if, in the event of an emergency, they
(the Chinese Guards) were to co-operate with the officers and men of your British force,
and exert themselves for the preservation of order."
It is satisfactory to see that Mr. Sinclair considers that adequate arrangements
have been made for the protection of the foreign residents by Vice-Admiral Sir
William Dowell and the Chinese authorities.

Inclosure 1 in No. 111.

Consul Sinclair to Sir H. Parkes.

(Extract.)   *Foochow, August* 11, 1884.
ON the morning of the 7th instant I received a telegram from you, which
reads as follows :—
" Viceroy telegraphs to Yamên that naval authorities propose landing men in
opposition to his wishes, and that you declined to interfere. Send explanations by

telegraph in this case, and report by telegram state of affairs at present. Order Vice-Consul to send full particulars from date of arrival of French fleet as to occurrences at Pagoda."

The same forenoon I wired the following reply to your telegram :—

"Viceroy will permit landing men in case of emergency. British Admiral and French fleet all quiet at Pagoda. Nothing new. Have told Vice-Consul to send particulars."

What possessed the Viceroy to telegraph what he did to the Yamên is beyond my comprehension. All along I have told the Taotai and the other emissaries of the Viceroy that in accordance with his wishes the blue-jackets would not be landed until the last extremity.

The inclosed copies of correspondence with the English naval authorities show most clearly the rôle I have taken in the landing of the men.

Should blue-jackets be landed without my being first consulted, to enable me to communicate with the Chinese authorities, it would be on the sole responsibility of the officer in command of the naval detachment.

I embrace this opportunity for forwarding, for your information, a series of correspondence between myself and the high authorities on the present situation of affairs, as embodied in the following copies, namely :—

1. Despatch dated the 24th July from the three high authorities (Tsiang-keun, Tsung-Tuh, and Footai) defining, on the inquiry of the Acting Russian Consul, the steps taken for the preservation of peace at the foreign Settlement.

2. A despatch from myself, dated 31st July, in reply to their communication of the 24th of that month, expressing thanks for the steps adopted by their Excellencies for the protection of the Settlement against plunder, and informing them of the receipt of a letter from Captain Powlett, R.N., that in the event of hostilities between China and France he proposed sending up a naval force of 100 men to co-operate in preserving order, and, at Captain Powlett's request, inquiring whether their Excellencies would not stop ingress and egress by the bridge, for the greater security of the Settlement.

3. A despatch, dated 2nd August, in reply to mine of the 31st July, from the high authorities, stating that fresh orders would be given to the Swatow irregulars to attend properly to their duty; that as for stopping the bridge up, as proposed by Captain Powlett, this could not well be done, for it would lead to disturbances; that with regard to the British seamen helping to keep order on shore, they had commissioned Lew Taotai to write and ask me to delay doing so, and that I had replied in that sense to the Taotai by private note; further, that they put a body of Kueichow (Hoonan) irregulars over at Nantai, under the orders of Choo Taotai, to maintain order and protect the foreign community, who need not be alarmed.

4. A despatch from myself, dated 1st August, to the high authorities, in which, while referring to my reply to them of the 31st July, I stated that, accompanied by a naval officer, I had visited the Swatow irregulars at their various stations, and had found them rather like common coolies than soldiers fit for the work of defence, and that they were badly armed and ill disciplined, &c., and I proposed that their Excellencies should give us, instead of these irregulars, some 400 soldiers of the regular army, with an officer of the army in command. I added, in conclusion, that there were four nations doing trade at Foochow, and that if any harm come to their persons or their property, through neglect of the provincial authorities to afford protection, it might happen that these four nations would put in claims for compensation of losses sustained.

5. A reply, dated 3rd August, from the high authorities to the above, informing me that the Swatow "yuugs," or irregulars, had been selected by Fang Taotai; that they had an officer of the rank of Too-sze (? Major) over them, who was competent; remarking on the passage in my despatch as to the irregulars looking like common coolies, that I must not expect irregulars to look otherwise than common, and that elegant men were not the proper persons for such employment—a remark which, I suppose, their Excellencies thought would strike me as excessively witty and clever. These high authorities have evidently looked into Wheaton's "International Law," put into Chinese by Dr. Martin, for in this reply of theirs they say they know all about the usages, and request me not to trouble myself on their account.

Translations of these Chinese inclosures will be faithfully forwarded so soon as received from Mr. Allen, who is engaged on them.

Every precaution has been taken inside and outside the city to arrest pillage; there is scarcely a street without one or two postern gates of great strength, and these are closed at 11 o'clock and are guarded at night. Committees of public safety have been organized, under the directions of the high authorities, and the streets and wards are gay with flags of every colour and dimension.

As far as our security goes at Foochow I am glad to be able to reassure you on this point. With Her Majesty's ship "Merlin" and the United States' gun-vessel "Monocacy" off the Settlement, and a detachment of blue-jackets from Her Majesty's ship "Champion," and further reinforcements, if necessary, to stop plunder, I think that with the Chinese men in addition we run no great danger.

I beg to inclose copy of a despatch received on the 10th instant from Vice-Admiral Sir William Dowell, who, as you will see, is seeing to our safety.

The Cantonese, under instructions from the authorities, have formed themselves into companies for the protection of the hongs at the east end of the foreign Settlement.

Inclosure 2 in No. 111.

Captain Powlett to Consul Sinclair.

Sir, "*Champion*," *Pagoda Anchorage, July* 30, 1884.

I HAVE to acquaint you that this morning I met some gentlemen at Messrs. Jardine's hong, and arranged with them that, in the event of an attack on the Settlement being imminent, they would assemble for mutual defence at Her Britannic Majesty's Consulate, where I also propose to send a detachment of men from the ship. I intend also to occupy the bridge across the creek, and to have a third detachment on board Her Majesty's ship "Merlin" in reserve, which vessel will be moved into a more commanding position than that which she at present occupies.

2. Should it become necessary to land men as suggested in paragraph 1, I have to request you will inform the Chinese authorities that the men in question are sent to prevent unlawful acts, and to preserve order in the European Settlement, and that any Chinese subject found offending will be handed over to the Chinese authorities to be dealt with, and, moreover, request that you will call upon his Excellency the Viceroy to close the bridge and other means of ingress to the Settlement until quiet is restored.

I have, &c.
(Signed) ARMAND T. POWLETT.

Inclosure 3 in No. 111.

Consul Sinclair to Captain Powlett.

Sir, *Foochowfoo, July* 31, 1884.

I HAVE received your despatch of yesterday's date, marked duplicate.

In it you acquaint me that yesterday morning you had met some gentlemen at Messrs. Jardine's hong, and had arranged with them that in the event of an attack on the Settlement being imminent they would assemble for mutual defence at this Consulate, where you also propose to send a detachment of men from your ship.

You further inform me that you intend also to occupy the bridge across the creek, and to have a third detachment on board Her Majesty's ship "Merlin" in reserve, which vessel will be moved into a more commanding position than that which she at present occupies.

You also request that, should it become necessary to land men, I would then inform the Chinese authorities that the men in question are sent to prevent unlawful acts, and to preserve order in the European Settlement, and that I would call upon the Viceroy to close the bridge.

In reply, I have to state that I apprehend nothing in the shape of "an attack on the Settlement." This is a dream of a few of the timid members of the community.

What may happen is that some rowdies may take it into their heads to pillage, and possibly foreign residences might be threatened.

But precautions have been taken in all directions by the local authorities to put down misrule and plunder.

It may be that the means at hand may be inadequate, and it is there that the naval detachment you speak of placing up here would become useful, simply to prevent plunder, and to aid in arresting the pillagers for punishment by their own authorities.

For the special protection of the foreign Settlement a force of 250 Swatow men, well accoutred, is posted in various temples in and round the residences of foreigners.

And I think they would be able to render the service required of these militia.

I believe I may trust to your prudence in not sending the men up or landing them until there is real necessity, and in instructing the officers who will be placed in command of the naval detachment to be cautious in restraining the men from interfering with the people needlessly.

I should hope that he would be instructed to consult from time to time with myself as senior Consul.

I would request you to delay as much as possible occupying with an armed force the small bridge, as such a measure would be certain to create excitement among the surrounding villages which still remain quiet, but which would resent any stopping of their daily traffic with the centre islet and suburbs beyond on the city side of the long bridge.

It has been said that a Gatling gun is to be placed by your orders on the small bridge to stop passage along it.

I would beg you to reconsider this order before it be given, because I believe the placing of a gun in that position would lead to trouble.

Already this morning there is additional excitement among the people round about, in consequence of the meeting yesterday at Jardine's; the previous meeting at the club; the fatal talkings of the merchants before their Chinese servants of what they have decided on doing on the war breaking out, viz., rushing up in a body to the Consulate; the inspection yesterday by a naval officer of the precincts of the small bridge, and the intended placing of a gun there; all these things have become known to the Chinese population, and must do an infinity of harm.

But I am certain I may place entire confidence in your discretion, convinced that you will do nothing that is likely to aggravate the situation by precipitate or premature measures.

I am indeed pleased to find that it is only "in the event of an attack on the Settlement being imminent," that you would propose landing a detachment of men from Her Majesty's ship "Champion."

In conclusion, I beg to inform you that I will communicate on the subject of your despatch with his Excellency the Viceroy this day.

I have, &c.

(Signed)   CHARLES A. SINCLAIR.

Inclosure 4 in No. 111.

Captain Powlett to Consul Sinclair.

(Extract.)   *"Champion," at Pagoda Anchorage, August* 1, 1884.

I BEG to acknowledge the receipt of your letter dated the 31st July, 1884, in which I understand you to deprecate any precautionary measures being taken by me for the protection of the Settlement, as you consider its safety assured by the presence of Chinese troops.

I trust that your view of the situation is the correct one, and that it may not be necessary to land men from Her Majesty's ship "Champion;" but being intrusted with the protection of the Settlement, I have deemed it my duty to place men on board Her Majesty's ship "Merlin" to be in readiness.

Inclosure 5 in No. 111.

Mu, Manchu General-in-chief, Ho, Governor-General, and Chang, Governor, to Consul Sinclair.

(Translation.)

Sir,   *Foochow, July* 24, 1884.

WE are in receipt of a representation from the Grain Intendant, Lin, informing us that he has received from His Imperial Russian Majesty's Consul, M. Shcoisky, a request that, in view of the entrance of French men-of-war into the port, protection may be given to the officials and merchants of his nationality. We beg to state that, on account of the fact that the population of the localities about Nantai contained good and bad alike, a battalion of men from Ch'ao-chou and P'u-zŭan was, on a former occasion, detached to remain on duty in and about the T'ien-an Temple, so as to afford a means of keeping order.

In addition to this, the system of mutual security among the wards has now been revised anew, and volunteers from among the people have been enrolled.

A change has at the same time been made in the disposition of the irregulars of the Ch'ao P'u battalion, who have been variously posted at the following important points, viz., the (jetty road) end on the T'ien-an Pu Road, the New Temple at Chêng Pu-t'ou, the Ming-chên Temple on Mei-wu Shan, the Tsung-kuan Temple at Tung-zao, and the Shê-jên Temple in Hung Street. They have been thus placed for the protection of the foreign mercantile community, to the end that the precautions may be complete and minute.

For the present, indeed, no cessation of friendly relations has taken place between China and France.

Although French ships (of war) have entered the port, China will certainly not of her own accord provoke a quarrel. Should a quarrel be suddenly picked with her by France, and should China, from the inadequacy of her defences to that which she has to defend, lack the power as she has the wish (to protect foreign interests), then, this not being a matter in which mere good-will or calculation are of much avail, public opinion will assuredly be there to pronounce (whose is the blame).

There is no need for us to enlarge upon it.

We have, &c.

Inclosure 6 in No. 111.

Mu, Manchu General-in-chief, Ho, Governor-General, and Chang, Governor, to Consul Sinclair.

(Translation.)

Sir,   *Foochow, August 2, 1884.*

WE have received within the last few days your reply to our despatch, in which you request that it may be impressed upon the irregulars of the Ch'ao-p'u battalion that they are legally to do their duty as a defensive force, and that there must be no negligence on their part.

You ask also whether, in the case of trouble abruptly taking place, arrangements could not be made for closing the road over the South River Bridge.

We shall be happy to accede to your wishes so far as to have orders sent anew to the irregulars of the Ch'ao-p'u battalion to do their duty legally in defence. For the rest, we have already communicated what we had to say on this head in a former despatch.

With regard to the South River Bridge Road, it is a main thoroughfare, and, therefore, in the case of trouble abruptly arising, it would be practically impossible to close it. It is to be feared, indeed, that to shut it off by forcible means would rather hasten the outbreak of trouble.

You, Sir, from your many years' residence at Foochow, are thoroughly conversant with the temper of the local population, and we think that you cannot but acknowledge our view to be the just one.

Again, as to the question of 100 of your Marines co-operating with [our troops] to preserve order, we beg to state that we took occasion to instruct the Grain Inten-dant, Lin, to consult you by letter as to delaying such action, and that we were verbally informed by the latter that he had received a note from you in reply, agreeing so to do.

We, the undersigned authorities, are now detaching an additional force, con-sisting of a battalion of Kuci-zang irregulars, under Chu Taotai, to proceed to Nantai for the purpose of keeping order. This measure is taken solely with a view to the protection of the various foreign merchants, and ought still further to quiet anxiety.

We have to request that the purport of our present reply may be communicated to the foreign mercantile community [and that the latter may be warned], to carefully avoid originating alarms of their own accord, and so causing trouble.

We have, &c.

67

Inclosure 7 in No. 111.

Mu, Manchu General-in-chief, Ho, Governor-General, and Chang, Governor, to Consul Sinclair.

(Translation.)

Sir,   *Foochow, August 3, 1884.*

WE are in receipt of your despatch, in which you request that 400 properly drilled soldiers may be specially detached from the [force at the] Southern Parade Ground, under the command of a *bonâ fide* officer, and posted at the T'ien-an Temple, and that the Ch'ao-p'u left battalion may be transferred to some other post.

We beg to state that the irregulars of the Ch'ao-p'u battalion are a force formed and drilled under the selection and care of Fang Taotai, and that their commanding officer, Captain Huang-zú, is a *bonâ fide* officer, and a conscientious and capable man to boot.

With regard to the statement in your despatch, that these irregulars whom you have seen are all a rough and unsoldierly set of men, you probably say so on account of their not being well versed in the ways of politeness ; but as a matter of fact, the material of which irregular troops are made is a rough article by rights ; culture and refinement are not wanted of them. It is sturdy power of defence rather than an ornamental exterior.

When the Captain of your gun-vessel visited the places where they were posted, these irregulars, not being skilled in the mandarin dialect, and also not well versed in politeness, appeared, on account of [this ignorance of theirs], without either swords or muskets. Nevertheless, these men have now been stationed at Nantai for a considerable time, and have behaved themselves very quietly. It would be a distinctly satisfactory arrangement if, in the event of an emergency, they were to co-operate with the officers and men of your British force, and exert themselves for the preservation of order ; and thus there is no need to transfer them to some other place.

The troops at the Southern Parade Ground have all got their duty to do in the different defensive posts allotted to them, and cannot be detached therefrom.

With regard to Nantai and its neighbourhood, a further force has now been told off to assist in keeping order there, consisting of the battalion of Kwei-zang irregulars, under Chu Taotai. This, it is considered, is an exceptional measure of defence, and should speak for the strictness of the precautions taken.

As to the reference made in your despatch to compensation to be exacted in case of looting, we must beg you to be under no apprehension, lest, in whatever course be adopted, there should be any departure from the principles of the Treaty and of the law of nations.

We have, &c.

Inclosure 8 in No. 111.

Vice-Admiral Sir W. Dowell to Consul Sinclair.

Sir,   *"Sapphire," at Pagoda Anchorage, August 10, 1884.*

HAVING received authentic information from the Commodore at Hong Kong that the French have occupied Kelung, I have thought it desirable, as a precautionary measure, to send Captain Powlett, of the "Champion," with a party of sixty men, to reinforce the English and United States' vessels now at Foochow.

Captain Powlett will place himself in communication with you and the other Consuls, and act in concert with the United States' Commander for the protection of neutrals in the Settlement.

I have left it to Captain Powlett's discretion to land the men or not, but they will be kept afloat unless their services are required on shore.

If necessary, a further force of about 150 men will be sent up.

I have, &c.

(Signed)   W. M. DOWELL.

P.S.—I request that you will point out to the Viceroy that the men are only sent to strengthen the hands of the police in the event of emergency arising, and I desire you will be good enough to keep Captain Powlett constantly informed of what is happening.

W. M. D.

68

No. 112.

Acting Consul Frater to Earl Granville.—(Received October 9.)

My Lord,   *Tamsuy, August 25, 1884.*
WITH reference to previous communications from me, I have now the honour to inclose an extract of a despatch to Her Majesty's Minister at Peking relative to the state of affairs.

I have, &c.
(Signed)   A. FRATER.

Inclosure in No. 112.

Acting Consul Frater to Sir H. Parkes.

(Extract.)   *Tamsuy, August 18, 1884.*
THE Prefect of North Formosa, whom I visited in T'aipei city yesterday, has taken, by means of proclamations and orders to his subordinates, measures for preventing attacks on missionary chapels and converts in the country, or on the foreign hongs, and either resident or travelling foreigners. In a letter acquainting me with what be has done, he has requested me to warn British subjects against making trips into the country. This I have done. He also recommends that the chapels should be closed, and services not held in public for the present. Dr. Mackay is to act on the recommendation. The Prefect has been provided with 500 suddenly-enlisted braves for the defence of the district against robbers, &c.

No. 113.

Consul-General Hughes to Earl Granville.—(Received October 9.)*

My Lord,   *Shanghae, August 29, 1884.*
I HAVE the honour to forward to your Lordship copy of a despatch which I have addressed to Her Majesty's Minister at Peking relative to announcements made by French and Chinese officials at this port that Shanghae and Woosung are intended to be outside the range of hostilities during the existing conflict between France and China.

I have, &c.
(Signed)   P. J. HUGHES.

Inclosure 1 in No. 113.

Consul-General Hughes to Sir H. Parkes.

Sir,   *Shanghae, August 27, 1884.*
I HAVE the honour to inclose translation of a Notification published in Chinese by the French Consul-General, announcing that no action will be taken by France at Shanghae or Woosung, but that these places shall be protected and left unmolested.

I beg also to inclose copy of a letter addressed by the French Consul-General to the German Consul-General, who is the Senior Consul at this port. This letter was circulated yesterday evening for the information of the Consular Body. It confirms the statements in the Notification, pointing out, however, that the advantage of freedom from the range of hostilities would cease in the event of neutrality being violated by the act of China at Shanghae or Woosung, or of the safety of French subjects being endangered. The French Consul-General therefore expresses his approval of a proposal made by the Taotai to join with the Consular Body in issuing a Proclamation, informing the people that they need not apprehend any hostile attack in this neighbourhood.

The proposal of a joint Proclamation was, however, not carried into effect, owing, I believe, to some objection made by the German Consul-General.

To-day Mr. Chên, late magistrate of the Mixed Court, called on behalf of the Taotai and handed to me copy of a Proclamation just issued, which he begged me to have translated and published at once. The principal object of the Taotai was, Mr. Chên said, to set

* Published in " London Gazette " of October 17.

the minds of the people at case, and allay the fears said to be entertained of acts of pillage by native marauders. No doubt, also, the Taotai is anxious that trade be not interrupted, so that he may be able to collect the revenue as usual. The document will most interest our merchants as a formal Declaration, based on the assurances of the French authorities that Shanghae and Woosung are, to all intents and purposes, to be regarded as neutral ground during the continuance of the existing conflict between France and China. In accordance, therefore, with the wishes of the Taotai, and in the interest of trade at this port, I issued the Notification, copy of which I inclose, and have arranged for its publication in to-morrow's issue of the "North China Daily News."

I propose sending copy of this letter and of its inclosures by the outgoing mail to Her Majesty's Secretary of State for Foreign Affairs.

I have, &c.
(Signed)   P. J. HUGHES.

Inclosure 2 in No. 113.

Proclamation by M. Lemaire, Consul-General for France, &c.

(Translation from the Chinese.)
SHANGHAE has long been a port open to the commerce of all nations, and Chinese and foreigners have lived here in peace and comfort for many years.

I have heard that on account of the state of affairs between France and China the people living in the city and its suburbs and in the foreign settlements have been much disturbed in their minds of late, and have been leaving the place in crowds. Their reason for doing this is, that on account of false reports which are circulated, or on the strength of statements in the Chinese newspapers, they have come to consider Shanghae a dangerous place. Now, these reports rest upon no foundation whatever, and the stories in the newspapers of peace, of war, constantly changing and growing more vivid, and frightening those who hear them; these all arise from the desire of the publishers to extend the sale of their papers, regardless of the fright they may cause. Although a difficulty has risen between France and China, peaceful relations will certainly be resumed.

In reply to an inquiry made by the proprietor of the "North China Daily News," whether, in the event of hostilities between France and China, there was any cause for anxiety in the neighbourhood of Shanghae and Woosung, I, the Consul-General, stated explicitly that there was no cause for anxiety, as no action would be taken by France at Shanghae or Woosung. It having thus been agreed that these places should be protected and left unmolested, boats which are in the habit of plying between Shanghae and Woosung can continue to do so, as before, without feeling any anxiety.

Lest the above facts should be unknown to Chinese and foreigners, I now issue this Proclamation for the information of the inhabitants of the city, suburbs, and settlements, bidding them continue to live in peace and comfort·as at other times, and not cause themselves trouble by listening to false reports and newspaper stories.

August 25, 1884.

Inclosure 3 in No. 113.

M. Lemaire to M. Lührsen.

M. et cher Doyen,   *Shanghae, le 26 Août,* 1884.
ME référant à l'entretien que j'ai eu ce matin avec vous au sujet de la Proclamation que le Taotai de Shanghae se propose de faire paraître d'accord avec le Corps Consulaire, je suis heureux de pouvoir vous confirmer, après en avoir referé à M. Patenôtre, les renseignements que j'ai déjà eu l'honneur de vous donner de vive voix. Ainsi que j'ai eu récemment l'occasion d'informer le public par la voix de la presse, le Gouvernement Français, désireux de sauvegarder autant qu'il lui sera possible les intérêts du commerce international qui sont ici si largement représentés, est résolu de s'abstenir de tout ce qui pourrait porter atteinte à la tranquillité du port et de la ville de Shanghae.

Quelles que·soient les mesures que la France puisse être amenée à prendre sur d'autres points du territoire Chinois pour arriver à la solution des difficultés existante

Shangbae et Woosung resteront donc en dehors du conflit. Il va sans dire qu'il n'en serait pas de même si la neutralité était violée à Shanghae ou à Woosung du fait de la Chine, et si la sécurité de nos nationaux se trouvait mise en péril. Il dépend donc des autorités locales d'assurer le maintien de la paix et de dissiper les inquiétudes de la population, et dans ces conditions je ne puis que m'associer à la proposition faite par le Taotai.

Veuillez, &c.
(Signé)   G. LEMAIRE.

(Translation.)

Sir,   Shanghae, August 26, 1884.
WITH reference to the conversation I had with you this morning on the subject of the Proclamation which the Taotai of Shanghae proposes to issue with the con-currence of the Consular Body, I am happy to be able, after communication with M. Patenôtre on the subject, to confirm the information I have already had the honour to give you verbally. As I lately had occasion to inform the public through the medium of the press, the French Government, being anxious to protect as much as possible the interests of international commerce which are so extensively repre-sented here, are resolved to avoid anything which might disturb the peace of the port and town of Shanghae.

Accordingly, whatever measures France may have to take in other parts of the Chinese territory in order to arrive at a solution of the present difficulties, Shanghae and Woosung will remain outside the region of hostilities. Of course, this arrange-ment would not hold good if the neutrality were violated at either Shanghae or Woosung by the Chinese, and if the safety of our fellow-subjects were threatened. It rests, then, with the local authorities to insure the preservation of order and to allay the fears of the natives, and under these conditions I am willing to give my adhesion to the Taotai's proposal.

I have, &c.
(Signed)   G. LEMAIRE.

Inclosure 4 in No. 113.

Notification.

HER Britannic Majesty's Consul-General publishes herewith, for the information of British subjects, the accompanying translation of a Proclamation issued this day by the Taotai, announcing that arrangements have been made for maintaining neutrality at Shanghae and Woosung during the existing conflict between France and China.
Shanghae, August 27, 1884.

Proclamation.

Shanghae is a town where people congregate from all quarters, and contains large numbers of homeless vagrants. At the end of last July the failure to arrange the difficulty between China and France caused a general feeling of anxiety, it being feared that the dangerous classes might avail themselves of the opportunity to commit excesses. I therefore addressed the German Consul-General as Senior Consul, and requested him to call a meeting of Consuls for the purpose of arranging a general plan of defence, and employing troops for the repression of rioters in the settlements, city, and adjoining districts. During the month that has elapsed since then perfect tranquillity has prevailed. Now again, however, false reports have arisen of the probability of warlike operations at Woosung. In consequence there has been much anxiety, an exodus of many inhabitants, and a slackness of trade. These alarming reports are all the work of lawless ruffians, who hope thereby to terrify the public and find opportunities for the commission of robberies.

But Shanghae is the general emporium of foreign commerce in China, and the only approach to it is through Woosung. Should there be an actual conflict between China and France there will certainly be no fighting in such a place. The Senior Consul has now sent to me, for the information of the public, a letter from the Consul-General for France, who says that the inhabitants of Shanghae have no cause for alarm, as France will certainly commit no act of war at Shanghae, Woosung, or their neighbourhood, but will treat the same as neutral ground. At the present moment the Chinese Government has stationed troops at the most important points in the above-mentioned districts. The troops will patrol the country, and at once arrest any bad characters who disturb the public peace. The Taotai has also arranged with the Senior Consul and the other Consuls that Woosung and Shanghae, with the settlements, city, suburbs, and surrounding districts, shall all continue to be protected by a military force. The troops will at once arrest all rioters, and hand them over to the authorities, who will punish them with the utmost rigour. As a further measure for the preservation of tranquillity, all persons found spreading false reports will also be arrested and punished.

This Notification is therefore issued to inform the inhabitants of Shanghae that they have no cause for alarm, but may continue to live in peace and comfort.

No. 114.

The Secretary to the Admiralty to Mr. Currie.—(Received October 13.)

(Extract). Admiralty. October 10, 1884.
I AM commanded by my Lords Commissioners of the Admiralty to transmit, for the information of the Secretary of State for Foreign Affairs, the inclosed from Vice-Admiral Sir William Dowell relative to recent affairs in China.

Inclosure in No. 114.

Vice-Admiral Sir W. Dowell to the Secretary to the Admiralty.

(Extract.) *"Vigilant," at Pagoda Anchorage, August 30, 1884.*
ON the 27th I received your telegram of the 25th instant, informing me that the Eastern Telegraph Company feared a piratical attack on the telegraph-ship at Sharp Peak. Both the "Sapphire" and "Champion" being shorthanded, with their boats at Foochow, I decided upon proceeding to Sharp Peak in the "Vigilant," and ascertaining myself the position of affairs and the extent of the danger to which the telegraph people were exposed. I found, however, that the French squadron were still on this side of the Kinpai Pass, in which were the heaviest batteries in the river, and where a boom had been prepared, which would probably have been placed across the river, and I therefore decided not to attempt the passage, and requested Admiral Courbet to send protection to the telegraph station when he got through, which he most courteously promised to do. I will here add that in all my relations with Admiral Courbet I have invariably found him most courteous and friendly.

I telegraphed to the Commodore at Hong Kong to send either "Midge" or "Zephyr" to Sharp Peak.

To-day I shifted my flag to the "Sapphire," and sent the "Vigilant" to communicate with Sharp Peak. She has just returned. He found at anchor below the Kinpai Pass the "Duguay-Trouin," bearing the flag of Vice-Admiral Courbet, "La Galissonnière," with the flag of Rear-Admiral Lespès, "Triomphante," "Vipère," "Lynx," and "Aspic," the latter anchored about a cable from the telegraph-vessel. The other vessels of the squadron are believed to be off Matson Island. Captain Fullerton called upon Admiral Courbet, who informed him that he was about to leave the river shortly, and Captain Fullerton understood him to mean that he should leave when the bar was practicable for the two iron-clads. In a note I have just received from the Vice-Admiral, he tells me that he will leave a gun-boat to protect the telegraph station until I can send a vessel there.

The telegraph-vessel at Sharp Peak is simply a house boat, anchored in Woga Channel, in the bay in Sharp Peak Island, and the establishment consists of two operators, English, who remain on board the boat during the day to send or receive telegrams, sleeping on shore. These gentlemen said that the natives of the village off which the boat is moored were perfectly friendly, but they feared attack from the junks which had lately been seen in the neighbourhood, and which the natives warned them were piratical vessels.

Since the appearance of the French squadron in the river, ordinary communication with the telegraph station at Sharp Peak has been more or less interrupted, and we have only maintained desultory communication by ship's boats. I do not anticipate that it will be possible to re-establish the regular land courier service for some time to come.

The troops at this place appear to be under no control whatever, and the Government service of the province seems to have lapsed into utter confusion. On the 25th, after the departure of the French squadron, the Vice-Consul landed and went up to his house, only to find it in possession of Chinese soldiers who had looted it, destroying the things they could not take away. They moved out of the house, but their attitude being very threatening, the Vice-Consul returned to the "Vigilant," where he has since remained. At my desire, Her Majesty's Consul at Foochow represented the state of affairs to the Viceroy, urging upon him the imperative necessity for taking immediate measures for restoring order, and suggesting that some military officer of authority should be sent here. The Viceroy promised that he would take steps to bring the soldiery under discipline, and that he would appoint an officer to take command. He has not done so yet, and it is not safe to land. During the 26th and 27th the soldiers, scattered about in small parties, fired indiscriminately at passing steam-launches and boats; but since then they have abstained from doing so, and although frequent rifle shots are heard, I imagine they are fired at native craft approaching the arsenal for looting purposes.

On the 27th instant Her Majesty's Consul at Foochow, Mr. Sinclair, called on the Viceroy, to urge him to take the steps referred to in paragraph 7 of this letter; whilst engaged with the Viceroy the Yamên was surrounded by a mob, and the Consul had a narrow escape. His own words will describe the incident, and serve to show the state of affairs at Foochow. He writes :—

" With regard to the temper of the people within the city walls, I am able, from personal observation yesterday, to say that it is perfectly unsafe for a foreigner to put his foot within the city gates; for certain, he would not come out alive. I myself have been concealed all night in the Viceroy's Yamên, not expecting to come out alive. The Yamên was besieged by a furious mob of several thousands, who, with spears and bamboos, battered at the gates half the night, yelling like wild beasts. They broke their way into the inner court, and it was expected they would set to to pull down the Yamên. The Viceroy, the Taotai, and the Prefect were all of them very anxious on my account. At last the crowd dispersed towards midnight, overcome by fatigue. This early morning I was smuggled out of the city in a closed sedan, disguised in the costume of a Chinaman, or I should not be here to write this despatch to you."

To-day Mr. Sinclair came down from Foochow and attempted to land at the arsenal, but was prevented from doing so by the Chinese, who told him that it would be perfectly unsafe.

The Settlement at Foochow continues quiet, and trade has, to a certain extent, been recommenced, the tea for the cargo of the steam-ship " Glenfinlas " having been sent down from Foochow on the 28th instant without molestation. Rear-Admiral Davis, commanding the United States' squadron, remains there in the " Monocacy," and is prepared to co-operate with our force in the event of its becoming necessary to land for the protection of neutral life and property.

The Senior Officer of Her Majesty's ships at Shanghae, telegraphing on the 26th instant, reports all quiet there, at Ningpo, and in the Yang-tse ports; that the " Midge " left Chefoo on the 18th instant for Hong Kong, my orders directing her to proceed to Ningpo not having reached Chefoo until after she had left ; that the " Daring " arrived on the 25th from Hong Kong, and would leave on the 27th for Ningpo ; and that the " Albatross " was to proceed from Chinkiang to Hankow on the 26th instant.

From Chefoo I learn than a Russian squadron, consisting of the " Minine," " Skoboleff," and " Nayedznik," under Rear-Admiral Krow, arrived there on the 14th instant from Nagasaki, and that the Admiral had expressed his intention of remaining about ten days.

No. 115.

The Secretary to the Admiralty to Mr. Currie.—(Received October 13.)

Sir,   *Admiralty, October 10, 1884.*

I AM commanded by my Lords Commissioners of the Admiralty to transmit, for Earl Granville's perusal, copy of a letter, dated the 30th August, from Vice-Admiral Sir William Dowell, Commander-in-chief in China, relative to the plundering of

73

the British Vice-Consulate at Pagoda Island by Chinese soldiers during the absence of the Vice-Consul.

2. My Lords desire me to add that they propose to approve of Sir W. Dowell's action in the matter, if Lord Granville sees no objection.

I am, &c.
(Signed)   EVAN MACGREGOR.

Inclosure in No. 115.

Vice-Admiral Sir W. Dowell to the Secretary to the Admiralty.

Sir,   *" Vigilant," at Pagoda Anchorage, August* 30, 1884.

IN my general letter of this date I reported that Her Majesty's Vice-Consulate at this place has been looted, and the furniture removed or destroyed by Chinese soldiers during the absence of the Vice-Consul, who had been received on board the "Vigilant" whilst hostilities were being carried on at the anchorage between the French and Chinese.

2. It was suggested to me to-day by Her Majesty's Consul at Foochow that men should be landed from Her Majesty's ships for the protection of the Vice-Consulate and the houses of the four Englishmen who compose the foreign community at Pagoda, but I had decided not to do so. The houses had already been looted before the conclusion of the French operations, European life was not in danger, the amount of property involved was inconsiderable ; over 200 men from the "Sapphire" and "Champion" being off Foochow leaves but very few men available in those ships, and I felt sure that to land a small body of men would almost necessarily lead to collision with the Chinese troops, infuriated as they are against all foreigners, and would probably end in our having to clear the heights with our ships' guns.

3. My endeavour has been to maintain an attitude of strict neutrality, and I could not expect the Chinese to understand this if I landed men to drive their troops (however ill-behaved) out of the place, and subsequently resorted to artillery fire to dislodge them from the hills. I consider that such a course of action on my part would inevitably be followed by an attack on the settlement at Foochow, and I determined on waiting, in the hope that the officers would soon regain their authority over the troops, and the Commissioner in charge of the arsenal would return to his post. In the meantime, the few English residents at Pagoda will be temporarily inconvenienced, but that will be a small matter compared with the evils which would occur if the foreign settlement at Foochow were attacked.

I have, &c.
(Signed)   W. M. DOWELL.

No. 116.

Earl Granville to Sir H. Parkes.

Sir,   *Foreign Office, October* 14, 1884.

I HAVE received your despatch of the 14th August, and I have to convey to you my approval of the note which you addressed to the Tsung-li Yamên, a copy of which accompanies your despatch, in regard to the landing of a naval force for the protection of the foreign community at Foochow.

I am, &c.
(Signed)   GRANVILLE.

No. 117.

Earl Granville to Sir H. Parkes.

Sir,   *Foreign Office, October* 14, 1884.

I HAVE received your despatch of the 15th August, and I have to convey to you my approval of the terms of the note, a copy of which accompanies your
[561]   L

74

despatch, which you addressed to the Tsung-li Yamên in regard to the demeanour of the populace of Canton in the existing state of affairs.

I am, &c.
(Signed)   GRANVILLE,

No. 118.

Earl Granville to Sir H. Parkes.

Sir,   *Foreign Office, October 14, 1884.*
I HAVE received your despatch of the 19th August, and I have to convey to you my approval of the instruction which you have addressed to Her Majesty's Consul at Foochow in regard to the steps to be taken for the protection of the foreign community at that port during the existing disturbed state of affairs.

I am, &c.
(Signed)   GRANVILLE.

No. 119.

Mr. Lister to the Secretary to the Admiralty.

Sir,   *Foreign Office, October 14, 1884.*
I AM directed by Earl Granville to transmit to you the accompanying copy of a despatch from Her Majesty's Minister at Peking in regard to the desirability of retaining Her Majesty's ship "Merlin" at Foochow, for the protection of the foreign community at that port during the present disturbed state of affairs;* and I am to request that, in laying this letter before the Lords Commissioners of the Admiralty, you will state to their Lordships that Lord Granville proposes, with their concurrence, to approve Sir H. Parkes' proceedings.

I am, &c.
(Signed)   T. V. LISTER.

No. 120.

Sir H. Parkes to Earl Granville.—(Received November 18.)

My Lord,   *Peking, October 1, 1884.*
IN the afternoon of the 18th ultimo I received a telegram from Her Majesty's Acting Consul at Canton, stating :—
"Proclamation issued by high authorities inciting Chinese in Tonquin, Saigon, Singapore, and Penang to damage French ships and poison Frenchmen."
I, therefore, wrote a note to the Tsung-li Yamên, denouncing this act as a gross offence both against international law and humanity, and asking for an interview with the Prince and Ministers at the earliest hour they could name.
His Highness and their Excellencies received me on the 19th, when I forcibly impressed upon them the gravity of the matter, the injury it would occasion to the reputation of the Chinese Government, and the serious consequences that might ensue unless the evil effects of such a publication were promptly remedied.
The Prince and Ministers disavowed all knowledge of the Proclamation, and declared that if it had been issued it would certainly be disapproved. They said they would immediately telegraph to Canton for information, and would communicate with me again on receiving a Report.
A week passed without my hearing from them. In this interval Her Majesty's Acting Consul at Canton had assured me that he was certain of the authenticity of the Proclamation, and on the morning of the 26th I received the following telegram from the Governor of Singapore :—
"Proclamation, issued by high authorities, Canton, 15th September, published here, calling on Chinese in Singapore and Penang to destroy French vessels and poison French subjects. Suggest you should request its immediate cancellation."
I at once demanded another interview, and saw the Prince and Ministers the same day.
Having expressed disappointment at having received no communication from them on

* No. 108.

the subject, they assured me that the Report they had called for had not yet reached them I then told them that the telegrams I had received from the Consul and Governor clearly proved the publication of the Proclamation, and also that it was the act of a high provincial Government, and not of a subordinate local official, whose wrong-doing could be easily disavowed. The mode of correction, therefore, I said, must be as exemplary as the offence. I had well considered the matter since our last interview, and had formed the conclusion that nothing less than an Imperial Decree annulling the Proclamation and censuring the high authorities for issuing it would adequately serve to remedy the ill-effects of such an ill-advised measure.

The Prince and Ministers evinced a degree of concern which I think they would scarcely have shown if they had not been satisfied from their own information that the charge I made was well founded. They appeared to acquiesce in my view, that the wrong done should be corrected by an Imperial Decree, but they maintained that they could not address the Throne on the subject until they were in possession of the terms of the Proclamation.

I agreed to wait for two or three days longer, but addressed them on the following morning the inclosed note, in which I renewed the language I had used at the two interviews, and which, as it is given in this note, I feel need not be repeated at length in this despatch.

At the close of the interview of the 26th, I also telegraphed to your Lordship begging that I might be authorized to insist upon the publication of an Imperial Decree. I gratefully thank your Lordship for your reply, which I received on the afternoon of the 28th, approving of my language to the Yamên.

The next day I sent Mr. Hillier to the Yamên to inform the Ministers that I had been authorized by your Lordship to insist on the publication of an Imperial Decree, but before making a formal demand on this point, I wished to know whether the Chinese Government were prepared to take this step of their own motion, as I preferred that it should appear to be a spontaneous act of their own. The Ministers told Mr. Hillier that they could spare me the necessity of making such a demand, as an Imperial Decree had already been issued, and would be communicated to me in the course of the day. They alleged that they had only received their Report from Canton the previous evening, but that in the meantime, the publication of the offensive Proclamation had come to the knowledge of the Empress from another source, and that Her Majesty had at once ordered the issue of a Decree disapproving of the employment of such underhand means of attack, censuring the high authorities who issued the Proclamation, and proclaiming the inviolability of foreign jurisdiction. They added that the Decree would be published in the "Peking Gazette," as I had desired.

In the evening I received from the Yamên the note, of which I inclose a translation, communicating to me the Decree, which appears to me to be quite satisfactory, and I trust it will be so regarded by your Lordship. It appeared yesterday morning in the "Peking Gazette." I add a copy of my reply to the Yamên, acknowledging its receipt, and expressing my high appreciation of the promptness with which His Majesty the Emperor had marked his high disapproval of an act which constituted an aggression on the sovereignty of Great Britain, and was calculated by its inhuman character to bring grave reproach upon the Chinese Government.

In conclusion, I venture to observe that the publication of an Imperial Decree censuring two High Imperial Commissioners, the Governor-General of two provinces and the Governor of the province in which Canton is situated, in less than three days from the time when I first intimated that I considered such a step necessary, furnishes very acceptable evidence of the desire of this Government to maintain friendly relations with ourselves, and of a disposition to comply with the just requirements of Her Majesty's Representative.

I have, &c.
(Signed)   HARRY S. PARKES.

Inclosure 1 in No. 120.

Sir H. Parkes to the Tsung-li Yamên.

Peking, September 27, 1884.

WITH a view to prevent misunderstanding, Sir H. Parkes thinks it desirable to place on record the representations which he made to the Prince and Ministers at the two interviews he has held with them relative to the Proclamation issued by the high authorities at Canton on the 15th instant, and in which they call on the Chinese in

Tonquin, Saigon, Singapore, and Penang to destroy French vessels and poison Frenchmen.

Sir H. Parkes first saw the Prince and Ministers on this subject on the 19th instant, immediately on receiving a telegram from Her Majesty's Consul at Canton, informing him of the publication of the Proclamation. He pointed out to the Prince and Ministers that such a Proclamation was a grave infraction of international law and a gross offence against humanity; that it would most seriously injure the reputation of China in the estimation of all nations, and that for any Chinese authority to issue Proclamations to the Chinese in British territory was a serious affront to the Government of Great Britain. It also seemed to him that this Proclamation was wholly opposed to the spirit and injunctions of the Imperial Decree of the 26th ultimo, the liberal tone of which had elicited general admiration.

The Prince and Ministers disavowed all knowledge of the Proclamation, and declared that such a publication would never be permitted by the Government, if only for the reason mentioned by Sir H. Parkes, namely, that it was altogether adverse to the Imperial Decree of the 26th August. They assured Sir H. Parkes that they would at once call upon the high authorities at Canton for an explanation by telegraph, and would communicate with Sir H. Parkes immediately on receiving a reply.

Pending this reference, Sir H. Parkes also telegraphed to Her Majesty's Consul at Canton to ask whether he was quite sure that the Proclamation had been issued, and the Consul reported in answer that he was certain of its authenticity. Yesterday morning Sir H. Parkes also received a telegram from his Excellency the Governor of Singapore, stating that the Proclamation had been published at Singapore, and demanding that immediate steps should be taken to rectify the serious evils it would create.

Seven days having elapsed since the first interview, Sir H. Parkes considered that the Prince and Ministers would surely have received the telegraphic Report they had called for, and when he visited them again yesterday he expected to find them fully informed on the subject. He was therefore surprised to learn from them that they had yet received no reply from the high authorities at Canton.

Sir H. Parkes then stated to his Highness and their Excellencies that having carefully thought over the subject during the interval which had elapsed between his two visits, and being now assured by the telegrams he had received, both from the Consul at Canton and the Governor of Singapore, that the publication of the Proclamation was an undoubted fact, he had formed the conclusion that the only adequate remedy for an act which would be universally regarded with abhorrence, and which was an offence against the dignity of the Chinese Government, as well as against the sovereignty of Great Britain, was the issue of an Imperial Decree, to be published in the "Peking Gazette," denouncing the adoption of such barbarous measures of retaliation, enunciating the impropriety of invading the sovereign rights of other Powers, and censuring the authorities who had issued the Proclamation.

He understood the Prince and Ministers to say that they acquiesced in this view, but that they could not frame a Report to the Throne and pray for the issue of such a Decree until they were in possession of the terms of the Proclamation, which they were momentarily expecting. If the representations of Sir H. Parkes were confirmed by their Report, they were certain that the Proclamation would be entirely disapproved by the Emperor, as it was opposed to His Majesty's previous Decree.

Sir H. Parkes expressed his appreciation of these assurances, though he felt compelled to regret the unaccountable delay shown by the high authorities of Canton in reporting on the subject. He would continue to wait two or three days, by which time he trusted these Reports would have arrived.

Sir H. Parkes has to add that having telegraphed at the close of yesterday's interview Her Majesty's Consul at Canton, to ask him to name the high authorities who had issued the Proclamation, he has just received a reply from the Consul stating that they are the Governor-General and Governor with the Imperial Commissioners, P'êng and Chang.

With, &c.

(Signed) HARRY S. PARKES.

Inclosure 2 in No. 120.

The Tsung-li Yamén to Sir H. Parkes.

(Translation.) Peking, September 29, 1884.

THE Prince and Ministers of the Tsung-li Yamén have the honour to inform the British Minister that on the 29th September, 1884, the Grand Secretariat were honoured by the receipt of the following Imperial Decree:—

" In consequence of the infringement of Treaty and breach of good faith of which the French were guilty some time since, and the hostilities which were commenced by them, we called upon the high officers in command of troops along the coast, with the Governors-General and Governors concerned, to combine in a united attack upon the French troops with their armies of defence, ordering them to continue, as heretofore, to extend their protection in an equal degree to the merchants and subjects of every nationality, even French officials, merchants, missionaries, and citizens, who pursued their avocations in an orderly manner, being included in the category of those entitled to protection.

" The Court was guided in the dignified line of action thus assumed by no other considerations than sincerity in the treatment [of the subjects of other Powers].

" It has lately come to our knowledge that the Governor-General, Governor, and others at Canton have issued a Proclamation calling upon the inhabitants of the sea-coast to show their loyalty and patriotism by piloting French ships upon the sea into shallow waters where they will take ground, and placing poison in the food [of the French]. They further extended this mandate to Chinese in Singapore, Penang, and other places.

" In posting such Proclamations on Chinese soil the Governor-General, Governor, and those associated with them were animated by a desire to arouse a strong feeling of patriotism. There was nothing objectionable in such a course, but the employment of such expressions as ' the placing of poison in food ' is a departure from uprightness and dignity, while the reference to Singapore, Penang, and other places which are not under our jurisdiction is likely, when it becomes noised abroad, to be misinterpreted, and to be distorted in process of transmission from one to another, possibly giving rise to trouble.

" As this reference is not in accordance with the spirit of our Decree of the 26th August, we hereby command that our censure be conveyed to P'êng Yü-lin, Chang Chih-tung, Chang Shu-shêng, and Ni Wên-wei.

" The French have broken their compact, and have acted in an unprincipled manner, and all our Chinese subjects are naturally capable, with that unity of purpose which will overcome any obstacle, to make common cause against the enemy of their Sovereign, and it is for this very reason that it is unnecessary to depend upon underhand devices or treacherous schemes which prejudice the object of China in moving her armies in support of a righteous cause.

" As regards Chinese dwelling in the islands of the outer seas, we command them to refrain from concerning themselves with hostilities, that mistakes and complications may be avoided."

As in duty bound, the Prince and Ministers beg to forward a copy of this Decree, which they have reverently prepared, for the information of the British Minister.

Inclosure 3 in No. 120.

Sir H. Parkes to the Tsung-li Yamén.

Peking, September 30, 1884.

HER Britannic Majesty's Minister has the honour to acknowledge the receipt of the note of the Prince and Ministers of yesterday's date, communicating to him an Imperial Decree censuring the Imperial Commissioners, P'êng Yü-lin and Chang Shu-shêng, the Viceroy of the Two Kuang, Chang Chih-tung, and the Governor of Kuang-tung,. Ni Wên-wei, for having issued a Proclamation calling on Chinese in the British Colonies of Singapore and Penang to poison Frenchmen and destroy French vessels.

Her Britannic Majesty's Minister begs to express his high appreciation of the promptness with which His Majesty has been pleased to mark his high disapproval of the above-mentioned act of the said high authorities, which constituted an aggression on the sovereignty of Great Britain, and was calculated by its inhuman character to bring grave reproach upon the Chinese Government.

Her Majesty's Minister avails himself, &c.

(Signed)   HARRY S. PARKES.

CHINA. No. 1 (1912).

CORRESPONDENCE

AFFAIRS OF CHINA.

Presented to both Houses of Parliament by Command of His Majesty.
May 1912.

LONDON:
PUBLISHED BY HIS MAJESTY'S STATIONERY OFFICE.
To be purchased, either directly or through any Bookseller, from
WYMAN AND SONS, LTD., FETTER LANE, E.C., and 32, ABINGDON STREET, S.W.; or
OLIVER AND BOYD, TWEEDDALE COURT, EDINBURGH; or
E. PONSONBY, LTD., 116, GRAFTON STREET, DUBLIN.

PRINTED BY
HARRISON AND SONS, PRINTERS IN ORDINARY TO HIS MAJESTY,
45–47, ST. MARTIN'S LANE, W.C.

[Cd. 6148.] *Price 1s. 1d.*

b

Correspondence respecting the Affairs of China.

No. 1.

Sir J. Jordan to Sir Edward Grey.—(Received October 10.)

(Telegraphic.) *Peking, October 10, 1911.*
REVOLUTIONARIES have been arrested in Russian concession at Hankow and in Wuchang. Three or four were executed this morning. Trial of remainder is proceeding.

No. 2.

Sir J. Jordan to Sir Edward Grey.—(Received October 11.)

(Telegraphic.) *Peking, October 11, 1911.*
MY telegram of 10th October.
The acting British consul-general at Hankow reports that Wuchang is in full revolution and yamêns have been burnt. Viceroy, who is on board Chinese cruiser astern of British gun-boat, has informed consul-general that he cannot protect British concession, and has asked His Majesty's ships to prevent mutinous troops from crossing river to Hankow.
I am requesting commander-in-chief to send all the assistance he can.

No. 3.

Sir J. Jordan to Sir Edward Grey.—(Received October 12.)

(Telegraphic.) *Peking, October 12, 1911.*
WUCHANG is entirely in the hands of the revolutionaries. Firing continued throughout the night. One thousand Honan troops expected there to-day. Police force in Hankow city has disappeared. All is quiet in concessions, which were guarded by bluejackets and volunteers last night.

No. 4.

Sir J. Jordan to Sir Edward Grey.—(Received October 12.)

(Telegraphic.) *Peking, October 12, 1911.*
REVOLUTION at Hankow.
The acting British consul-general reports by telegram to-night that rebels have taken possession of Hankow and Hanyang, that they promise protection to foreigners, and are maintaining order.
An Imperial edict appeared to-day ordering the Minister of War, with two divisions of troops, to proceed to Hankow. Admiral Sah is commanded to move ships there and to co-operate in the recovery of Wuchang and the restoration of order.

B

2

No. 5.

Sir J. Jordan to Sir Edward Grey.—(Received October 13.)

(Telegraphic.)   *Peking, October* 13, 1911.
REVOLUTION at Hankow.
Further telegram received from the acting British consul-general at Hankow as follows:—

" Concessions are well guarded, Japanese admiral being in command, and rebels are preserving order. Food and finance are the pressing questions. Nearly all missionaries are in concession, and foreign life and property is unmolested.
" A despatch has reached me from the rebel commander. It states that a Government has been constituted by which foreign treaties and previous, but not subsequent, loans and indemnities will be respected, and that, so long as they do not assist the Manchu Government, protection will be afforded to foreigners. I await your instructions in regard to the matter. On the subject of the restoration of order and credit, I am in indirect communication with the rebel leaders."

The following reply has been telegraphed to Mr. Goffe to-day :—

" I am requesting the instructions of the Secretary of State in respect of your telegram, which has been repeated to him. In the meantime, beyond what is absolutely indispensable for the security of British life and property, you should not hold any communication with the rebel commander.

No. 6.

Sir J. Jordan to Sir Edward Grey.—(Received October 14.)

(Telegraphic.)   *Peking, October* 14, 1911.
REVOLUTION at Hankow.
I have telegraphed to-day to Admiral Winsloe as follows :—

" The foreign representatives have received a request from the consular body at Hankow to make urgent representations to the Chinese Government with a view to the issue of instructions to Admiral Sah, who has been ordered to retake Wuchang, to avoid exposing the foreign concessions to the risk of fire during the operations. A similar request will be made to Admiral Sah by the Japanese admiral on his arrival. It would be necessary in the alternative event to evacuate the concessions, and Admiral Sah should then be asked to allow time to effect this before his operations are begun.
" The situation will become one of great gravity to the concessions, and a meeting of the diplomatic body is being held to-day to consider it. We are required by the nature of our interests at Hankow to do our utmost to protect them, and I feel sure that there is no one to whom Admiral Sah would listen more readily than to you, both in view of his former close connection with His Majesty's navy, and of his high respect for yourself. In the circumstances, I venture to suggest the desirability of your presence at some spot where, in the event of danger to the concessions, you would be able to offer suggestions to Admiral Sah."

No. 7.

Sir J. Jordan to Sir Edward Grey.—(Received October 14.)

(Telegraphic.)   *Peking, October* 14, 1911.
MY telegram of 14th October.
Following sent to Hankow to-day :—

" Wai-wu Pu informed me that they would at once consult Board of Admiralty and ask whether Admiral Sah could be instructed by telegraph to conduct bombardment in such a way as to avoid as far as possible any risk to the concessions."

3

No. 8.

Sir J. Jordan to Sir Edward Grey.—(Received October 14.)

(Telegraphic.) *Peking, October 14, 1911.*
YUAN SHI-KAI has been appointed Viceroy of Hu-kwang, with command of the
provincial troops, and the forces under the Minister of War and Admiral Sah are to
co-operate with him. This appointment will probably ensure loyalty of the northern
troops, which was doubtful, and will materially strengthen the hands of the Government in dealing with this crisis.

No. 9.

Sir Edward Grey to Sir J. Jordan.

(Telegraphic.) *Foreign Office, October 16, 1911.*
YOUR telegram of 13th October.
I approve what you have said to the acting consul-general. We must do what is
in our power to protect British life and property when in danger, but any action we
take should be strictly limited to this purpose. Protection of foreign life and property
would also, of course, be included in protection of British when possible and when
not otherwise protected.

No. 10.

Sir J. Jordan to Sir Edward Grey.—(Received October 17.)

(Telegraphic.) *Peking, October 17, 1911.*
MY telegram of 14th October.
Admiral Sah arrived at Hankow yesterday, but will probably do nothing until
arrival of military reinforcements. He has assured Japanese admiral that concessions
will not be endangered.
Revolutionaries are maintaining order in three cities.
Railway is still held by Imperialists.
Admiral Winsloe is due at Hankow to-day.

No. 11.

Sir J. Jordan to Sir Edward Grey.—(Received October 21.)

(Telegraphic.) *Peking, October 21, 1911.*
INNISKILLING Fusiliers.
The Inniskillings are to be relieved by the Somerset regiment, due to reach
Tien-tsin on the 24th October.
Until the situation becomes more clearly defined I venture to suggest that the
postponement of the departure of the outgoing Inniskilling Fusiliers for a week or ten
days might be a prudent precaution, since, although no cause for anxiety has as yet
arisen out of the situation here, the issue of events at Hankow is still doubtful.

No. 12.

Foreign Office to War Office.

Sir, *Foreign Office, October 23, 1911.*
I AM directed by Secretary Sir E. Grey to transmit to you herewith a copy of a
telegram* from His Majesty's Minister at Peking, suggesting the desirability, in view of
the political situation, of retaining the Royal Inniskilling Fusiliers at Tien-tsin for a

* No. 11.

[335] B 2

week or ten days after the arrival of the Somersetshire Light Infantry to relieve them. Sir E. Grey will be glad to learn that the Army Council are able to comply with Sir J. Jordan's suggestion.

I am, &c.
F. A. CAMPBELL.

No. 13.

War Office to Foreign Office.—(Received October 24.)

Sir, Whitehall, *October* 24, 1911.
I AM commanded by the Army Council to acknowledge the receipt of your letter dated the 23rd instant, transmitting a copy of a telegraphic despatch from His Majesty's Minister at Peking, recommending that the departure of the Royal Inniskilling Fusiliers from Tien-tsin be postponed for a period of seven to ten days.
In reply, I am to say that the Council will issue orders postponing the move of this regiment for the present.

I am, &c.
E. W. D. WARD.

No. 14.

Sir J. Jordan to Sir Edward Grey.—(Received October 24.)

(Telegraphic.) Peking, *October* 24, 1911.
FOLLOWING from His Majesty's consul-general at Shanghai to-day :—

"Chinese telegraph administration inform me that revolutionaries burnt taotai's yamên at Kiukiang about 11·30 last night. Communication with Kiukiang at present through Wuhu, thence by steamer. Senior naval officer informed."

No. 15.

Sir J. Jordan to Sir Edward Grey.—(Received October 26.)

(Telegraphic.) Peking, *October* 26, 1911.
THE Commissioner of Customs at Changsha having been notified by the rebel Government that he may, under their orders, continue to exercise his functions, telegraphic instructions have, after consultation with the inspector-general, to-day been sent to His Majesty's consul at that port as follows :—

"The rebel Government should be induced to allow the customs revenue to be held by the inspector-general or the consular body in deposit for the time being, and you should do your utmost to this end, acting in co-operation with the Commissioner of Customs.

"The money rightfully belongs to the foreign bondholders, and serious complications with foreign Powers may ensue in the event of its appropriation by the rebels. This you should point out to the rebel Government."

No. 16.

Sir J. Jordan to Sir Edward Grey.—(Received October 26.)

(Telegraphic.) Peking, *October* 26, 1911.
FOLLOWING on impeachment by Senate yesterday, decree has been issued to-night cashiering Shêng for misdirecting Government's railway policy. He is never to be re-employed, and Tong Shao-Yi is appointed Minister of Communications in his place.

5

No. 17.

Admiralty to Foreign Office.—(Received October 27.)

Sir, *Admiralty, October 27, 1911.*

I AM commanded by my Lords Commissioners of the Admiralty to transmit, for the information of the Secretary of State for Foreign Affairs, copy of a telegram dated the 27th instant from the commander-in-chief on the China station relative to the situation in China.

I am, &c.
W. GRAHAM GREENE.

Enclosure in No. 17.

Commander-in-chief in China to Admiralty.

(Telegraphic.) *Shanghai, October 27, 1911.*

THE situation at Hankow is unchanged. The bridge at Seven-Mile Creek is held by the Imperial troops, but no other large force shows signs of coming. The rebels probably number at Kilometre Ten from 6,000 to 8,000 men; they have received large reinforcements.

Thirty Italians from the Peking guard are expected, and 100 Japanese sailors have arrived. A report that German troops are coming is denied by the German admiral. The Chinese ships are not in sight.

The rebels are preserving good order everywhere; they have taken Kiu-kiang and Changsha-fu.

Large ships will be obliged to leave about the 1st November, as the river is falling fast.

No. 18.

Sir J. Jordan to Sir Edward Grey.—(Received October 28.)

(Telegraphic.) *Peking, October 28, 1911.*

A RESOLUTION having been proposed in the Senate yesterday praying the Throne to order the execution of Shêng, the Ministers of the four Powers called upon Prince Ch'ing and obtained assurances that no harm would befall him. Shêng left late last night for Tien-tsin with an escort of ten men from four legations, and will proceed, in the first instance, to Tsing-tau.

Although Government state positively that Yuan Shih-kai will start to-day for Hankow as High Commissioner, and build high hopes upon appointment, public are still very sceptical on the subject, and great uneasiness prevails here, large numbers of people leaving by every train for the south.

No. 19.

Sir J. Jordan to Sir Edward Grey.—(Received October 29.)

(Telegraphic.) *Peking, October 29, 1911.*

MUTINOUS troops at Lanchow.

The reported refusal of troops of the 20th Division now at Lanchow to entrain for Hankow has, in reply to an enquiry from me, been to-day confirmed by the chief of the general staff, Prince Tsai Tao; his Highness stated that when ordered to move the general in command of this division had memorialised the Throne urging that a constitution be immediately granted.

Before deciding on their course of action the general staff will await the result of their negotiations with the general.

Lanchow lies on the Peking–Mukden Railway, 100 miles to the north of Tien-tsin.

[335] B 3

6

No. 20.

Sir J. Jordan to Sir Edward Grey.—(Received October 30.)

(Telegraphic.) *Peking, October* 29, 1911.
FOLLOWING from commander-in-chief, dated 28th October:—

"All day there has been heavy fighting at the back of the concession at Hankow. This morning rebels in strong force held position on railway and rifle range. They retired about 2 P.M., since which most of them have crossed in sampans and junks to Wuchang. Chinese ships were fired on at 7 A.M. and 3 P.M. by batteries of field guns on south bank some 5 miles below Wuchang. Firing lasted under an hour. Each time reply fire from ships was very inaccurate. There has been no bombardment of Wuchang or Hanyang. Merchant-vessels and hulks are at anchor some 10 miles down the river. Rebel losses in two days heavy. Hankow is full of wounded."

No. 21.

Sir J. Jordan to Sir Edward Grey—(Received October 29.)

(Telegraphic.) *Peking, October* 29, 1911.
REVOLUTIONARY movement appears to be spreading.

At Shanghai, taotai confesses his inability to hold city, and says that rebels can take it at any moment.

Canton has practically declared its autonomy.

Reports from consul at Nanking show that situation there is very critical.

Tai-yuen-fu has passed into the hands of the rebels, and Tien-tsin is wavering.

It looks as if the authority of the Manchus could be re-established only after a protracted campaign, for which Government is ill prepared.

No. 22.

Sir J. Jordan to Sir Edward Grey.—(Received October 30.)

Sir, *Peking, October* 13, 1911.
I HAVE the honour to enclose copy of a despatch from Mr. Consul Brown at Chungking, giving an interesting account, as furnished to him by a member of the Chengtu gentry, of the outbreak in the province of Szechuan and of the causes which led to it. This version, though evidently coloured by party feeling, may be taken to represent the views and beliefs of a large section of the population whose ignorance has converted them into the tools of the shareholders' representatives and of the provincial assembly in the resistance offered to Government authority.

It is satisfactory to learn from the enclosed despatches from His Majesty's consul-general at Chengtu, of Mr. Wilkinson's and Mr. Teichman's safety, and also of the absence of any attacks upon foreigners, with the one exception of the assault on Mr. Manly, of the American Methodist Episcopal Mission. Mr. Wilkinson acted wisely in conveying a timely warning to missionaries in the outlying districts whose isolation would undoubtedly have constituted a source of danger had the movement assumed an anti-foreign character.

From recent telegrams received from Chengtu there appears to have been no further fighting in the city, but it is evident that the issue is still in doubt. No reinforcements have arrived yet, whilst the Government troops are being seriously depleted by desertions and by constant engagements with the rebels in the districts south and west of the capital.

I have, &c.
J. N. JORDAN.

7

Acting Consul Brown to Sir J. Jordan.

Sir,   *Chungking, September 22*, 1911.
THE following account of the disturbance in Chengtu and the causes which led up to it, as seen from the Railway League's point of view, has been furnished me by a member of the gentry who left Chengtu on the 9th September.
The present trouble has its origin in the—

1. Friction between the provincial assembly and the authorities on the subject of finaucial control. The Assembly has, for instance, endeavoured to cut down the salaries of the Governor-General and other high officials.
Further, the frequent complaints of the assembly against district officials for corruption and illegal torture, and the requests for their dismissal have irritated the provincial authorities.
2. Resentment of the provincial assembly and the gentry at the corrupt and conservative nature of the Cabinet. Prince Ch'ing and Na Tung are both Manchus and Hsu Shih-ch'ang, although a Chinese, is a weak man. Prince Ch'ing's demands for money are endless, and nothing can be done unless he has first been paid. All the provincial assemblies are indignant, and wish to curtail Prince Ch'ing's evil influence.
This was the state of affairs before the railway question came to the front. When it was found that the loan had been contracted without the consent of the people, the Chengtu Railway League was formed to oppose the Government's policy. The league realised that its strength was insufficient unless the support of the province were obtained, and branches were started in each district. The opinion of all was that the matter must be taken up by the shareholders.
A general meeting of shareholders was fixed for the 4th August at Chengtu, to which each district sent its accredited representative. The first two sessions were secret, and it was decided—

(*a.*) That the question of the loan was immaterial.
(*b.*) That the revenues pledged for repayment of the loan were immaterial, as money would not be lent without guarantee of repayment.
(*c.*) That the commission allowed the banks was immaterial.

These decisions were not made public, and as the shareholders could not expect their demands to be granted in full, it was resolved to aim high in order to get as much conceded as possible. The Government was therefore asked to cancel the loan and hand the railway back to the province. This was put forward as a basis of compromise, and Acting Governor-General Wang Jen-wen was persuaded to memorialise the Throne in this sense.
Peking's reply was that no compromise could be made. The shareholders then asked for the return of their capital, if the Government insisted on taking over the line. In reply, they were informed that there was no available capital in Szechuan, the major portion of the railway funds having been lost or embezzled. If their capital were to be repaid the Government would be obliged to borrow from abroad, and national railway bonds at 6 per cent. would be issued to cover the actual capital and assets in the hands of the company. This decision of Peking caused great dissatisfaction, as it was held that the Government, as represented by the Shanghai Taotai and the Ta Ch'ing Bank were mainly responsible for the loss of Szechuan capital in the Shanghai rubber slump of 1910.
The shareholders meeting drew up a lengthy statement in which they pointed out that there were 70,000,000 people in Szechuan. Deducting 20,000,000 who were too poor or unwilling to subscribe, 30,000,000 for people on the borderland and hill districts who were uninterested in the railway, there remained 20,000,000, all of whom would subscribe 1 cash a-day to the railway fund. This would give 20,000 tiao a-day, or, approximately, 7,000,000 dollars a-year. With this sum they would be able to construct the Ichang–Kuei Chou line, and their schemes had this advantage that it was Chinese money and would be expended in China. If this were explained to the loan-contracting Powers it was hoped that they would allow the loan money to be diverted to other uses. The representatives were unanimous on this point, and the statement was signed by all.
The provincial assembly declined to take part in the discussion, although they were prepared to move should they consider the shareholders' proceedings irregular. The

[335]   B 4

president, Mr. P'u Tien-chun, did not attend the shareholders' meeting, nor did he address them or intervene in any way. He was nevertheless associated with the movement by Prince Ch'ing, whose bitter enmity he had incurred by his action in inducing the provincial assemblies of Szechuan, Hupei, Hunan, and Kuangtung to send representatives to Peking to protest against the conservative nature of the Cabinet.

A telegram was subsequently received by Governor-General Chao Erh-feng, ordering the execution of P'u Tien-chu, Teng Hsiao-k'a, and Lo Lun. If these men were killed the agitation would cease.

To this telegram the provincial authorities replied that the executions were impossible, and that they would rather resign than obey.

The Peking officials then contrived to have Li Chi-hsun appointed railway manager at Ichang, and the strike was declared.

At about this time a censor memorialised the Throne denouncing Wang Jen-wen and Chao Erh-feng as abettors of the railway agitation. Tuan Fang was then ordered to examine into the matter, and it was secretly resolved in Peking to disgrace Chao Erh-feng. An edict was issued to warn him of his responsibility should he mismanage the affair.

In the meantime the shareholders continued their discussion of the situation. They had no belief in the National Railway bonds, and quoted, in support of their view, the still unpaid " good faith bonds " issued by the Government some twenty years ago. There is, they said, interest amounting to 960,000 taels on our capital of 16,000,000 taels. Most of this capital has been produced by rent shares. The Throne has, in an Imperial edict, promised us interest at 6 per cent. per annum on our capital. Now the land tax of Szechuan produces an annual sum of about 700,000 taels. The Government insists on taking over the railway. They may have it and our capital with it, but the interest at 6 per cent. has been promised us by this edict, and this we will stop from the land tax. This will save the authorities the trouble of paying us and we shall be acting in accordance with the Imperial wishes. The Government must further refund the remaining 260,000 taels, but part of this sum can be recovered by refraining from dealing in real property and so saving the fees.

As for the " benevolences " (" chuan shu "), the Government declares that we are very poor. So we are ! Far too poor to pay special subscriptions for campaigns that are now past history.

A long report embodying these resolutions was submitted by the meeting to the provincial assembly, who were requested to transmit it to the Governor-General. Should he deem their action in order, he was asked to memorialise the Throne. If irregular, he was urged to discuss the matter and state his views.

The report was duly forwarded to the Governor-General by the president of the assembly, who added a note to the effect that if no reply were received from his Excellency within fifteen days it would be considered that the report was in order.

To this report the Governor-General did not reply in any way, but he telegraphed to Peking that the people of Szechuan had refused to pay the land tax and benevolences, and that there was a state of rebellion. It is believed that he forwarded the shareholders' report by the slow and not the fast route to Peking.

A second telegram followed close on the heels of the first to report the destruction of the tax offices and the looting of the official salt depôts by smugglers in the Hsin Ching and Hsin Fan districts.

A reply from Peking was received, which informed Chao that the responsibility rested on him, as he should have crushed the movement long before.

The shareholders' representatives, fearing that the people would not understand their policy, had pamphlets printed in popular language for distribution everywhere in the province. The fifteen days allowed the Governor-General for his decision expired on the 2nd September, and on the 4th the Railway League and the shareholders decided to hand these pamphlets to their representatives, who should distribute them in every district. The question was then raised as to the league's action should the authorities attempt to repress them, and it was decided to call out the militia, most of whom were country people and dependent on the large landholders, who in their turn were the largest shareholders. If force were resorted to, it would be met with force ; 4,000 dollars would be paid to the family of any of the gentry who should be killed, and lesser sums granted to the poorer people. The sons of such men would be exempt from payment of school fees. General mourning would be observed for all who died for the cause, and their portraits would be placed in the provincial assembly chamber.

Lo Lun and the other marked men now felt that they could afford to disregard the telegram ordering their execution.

On the 6th September an edict was received ordering Chao to seize the ringleaders, dissolve the league, punish all who refuse to pay taxes, and crush all resistance. The Governor-General, aware of the storm his action must excite, had no option but to obey, and he made his preparations. Patrols were sent round the town and soldiers stationed at the street corners.

The same day a telegram had been received by the league from a censor named Chao Hsi in Peking, who informed them that Sheng Hsuan-huai and Tuan Fang insisted that the league should be suppressed ; that Prince Ch'ing and Na T'ung were of the same opinion, but that Hsu Shih-Ch'ang alone had refused to sign the order.

Rumours were current in Chengtu that Chao would be assassinated if any attempt were made on the leaders of the league. It was also said that the city would be set on fire. Chao Erh-feng was very nervous at the report of these rumours.

On the 7th September there was to be a general meeting of the railway shareholders. On its conclusion each representative was to return to his district with the bundle of pamphlets regarding non-payment of taxes, &c. At 9 A.M. a telephone message was received from the Governor-General informing the heads of the meeting that a telegram had been received from Peking and that a way out of the railway *impasse* had been found. Would they come round and discuss the matter with him? The five men in question immediately repaired to the Governor-General's office.

Some 600 of the shareholders waited outside the railway bureau for their return. When 11 o'clock had passed they telephoned to the yamên to ask when they might be expected as they were anxious to begin their meeting. A police officer replied that there were still some matters to be discussed and the meeting began to suspect that all was not well. Their suspicion was confirmed by the arrival of 200 to 300 soldiers, who surrounded the building and refused to allow anyone to enter. The arrival of the troops alarmed the shareholders, who enquired the reason of their coming. They were told that houses had been set on fire in the city and that there were disturbances in the streets. " We are here to protect you." The officer did not know why so many troops had been sent, but everyone must wait for the Governor-General's permission before leaving.

Someone then went to the top of the building and saw a large fire in the Pei Ta Chin Kai. This stopped at 2 o'clock. At a later hour a military officer arrived bearing the Governor-General's card, and said " His Excellency informs you that he has sent troops to the doors of the railway office on account of the rumours that he was to be assassinated if any attempt were made on your leaders. This morning he invited Lo Lun and others to his office and a fire broke out immediately on their arrival. His Excellency has ordered the troops to stop all traffic in order that the fire may be the easier extinguished and pillage prevented. The fire has now stopped, but passage along the streets is impossible. If you leave you will be in danger. You must wait until his Excellency tells you to return." This was not correct, as a proclamation, prepared previously, had been posted warning everyone that the ringleaders had been arrested and that all were to attend to their own affairs.

On hearing of the arrests, the president of the provincial assembly, Mr. P'u Tien-chun, called on the acting judge, Chou Shan-pei, to protest against the illegal act. The principals of the shareholders' meeting were, he said, law-abiding persons who would not take part in any disturbance. Chou suggested that P'u should accompany him to the Governor-General and discuss the matter. The two men left together but, on arrival at the yamên, P'u was also placed under arrest. Jen K'ai, another of the prominent league men, who had returned to his home to perform the customary fifteenth day religious ceremonies, was seized in his country house by a squad of soldiers and taken to the Governor-General's yamên. Hu Jung, ex-director of telegraphs, was also arrested, but lodged in another yamên. In all ten persons were taken.

Troops had now been posted in front of the Governor-General's yamên, where a procession of 2,000 or 3,000 persons soon appeared. The late Emperor Kuang Hsü's tablet was placed in the front of the crowd, some of whom were respectable people, others of the lower class. All begged the Governor-General to release the prisoners, and they promised that, if this were done, the shops would open and the agitation cease. Suddenly a red notice was exhibited from the yamên warning all that anyone entering the inner gates would be shot. No attempt had been made to enter the yamên, but on seeing the notice an expectant taotai, one Wang by name, ordered the troops to fire and some fifteen of the crowd were killed and wounded. Many more were injured in the wild stampede that followed the volley.

The only other incident in the city occurred in the Ta Chin Street. Here a police officer, unable to force his way through the crowd, drew a revolver and fired, wounding two or three persons.

Great excitement prevailed in the city, and it was decided that men with lanterns should form a cordon round the yamên to prevent their friends from being brought out for execution. If they were to die, all would die with them.

Slight rain fell that evening and quiet was restored.

The railway shareholders had now been told that they were at liberty to return home, but this they declined to do until they knew the fate of their friends. Instructions were then received that five members could go to the yamên and interview the prisoners. Five men accordingly proceeded to the yamên and saw the leaders. Three returned and reported that they were safe and that the remaining two had elected to stop with the others in the yamên. Everyone now returned home. The railway office was then entered by the soldiers, who seized all books, papers, &c., and sealed the doors. The troops also visited the railway school and took away all papers, &c.

It should be mentioned that the railway students had, in imitation of the official Vigilance Society, started one of their own called the Szechuan Self-Defence Society, and had issued numerous copies of a bombastic notice, full of absurdities, termed the " Declaration of Self-Defence Szechuanese Rights." This notice was treated as a huge joke by everyone except the Governor-General, who telegraphed to Peking that Szechuan was declaring a republic ! To find out where the notice had been printed, a raid was made on the offices of the three newspapers, and all documents found were impounded.

On the 8th September heavy rain fell from early morning until late at night, and all was quiet.

On the morning of the 9th, the north, east, and south gates of Chengtu were surrounded by armed bands of peasants. A body of the Hsun Fang, or reserve troops, issued from the east gate, and demanded to know why these bands had gathered. The answer was, that they had come to see the Governor-General. When asked why they were armed, they retorted that unarmed people had been shot down in front of the yamên the previous day. The officer in command of the troops then promised the leaders that, if all arms were piled, he would take them to see the Governor-General. The mob then laid down their arms, and the troops at once fired on them, killing and wounding several. The remainder fled. The troops then returned in triumph with the arms, and reported that a victory had been gained.

The same day the militia cut up a small body of cavalry, very few of whom returned alive. Horse flesh, I am informed by a correspondent, was selling at 15 cash a catty on the local markets ! Several other small detachments of troops were defeated in other places, that in Hsin Ching Hsien was reported to be exterminated.

My informant left Chengtu at noon on the 9th September. On his way down he was stopped at no less than three bridges by the militia, who had poised boulders on the arches of the bridges, and threatened to drop them on any boat that refused to stop. His boat was searched for Government despatches, officials, soldiers, and foreigners. The militia professed themselves as anxious to secure foreign subjects in order that they might induce them to lay their case before the Powers that had entered into the loan contract, in the hope that the latter would realise the reasonableness of their contention.

From missionary and other sources, I learn that the insurgents established a large camp some 20 miles from Chengtu, where not only men but food and supplies of all sorts were sent from the neighbouring districts by the branch leagues. In spite of the reverses in front of Chengtu, large bodies of militia and robber bands were still passing Chiating on the 19th September. Writing from Chiating on the 19th September, Lieutenant Commander Brooke, of His Majesty's ship " Widgeon," states that the local situation appears to be getting worse. It is reported that the yamêns in many smaller Hsien cities have been attacked, and well-to-do Chinese are leaving the city, while others are arriving from the neighbouring country for safety.

Mr. Barham at P'en Shan was ordered to leave by the official, who informed him that he could no longer protect him. The entire town was in the hands of the league, and even Mr. Barham's church members talked of uniting with the league to capture and hold him as a hostage. On his way down river, Mr. Barham tied up alongside a Chinese gun-boat for protection. During the night a band of several hundred men boarded the gun-boat, removed all arms and ammunition, and seized the boat. Most of the Chinese gun-boats in the neighbourhood of Chengtu are in the hands of the league, who also control many of the smaller Hsien cities and towns, although in some instances they allow the magistrates to co-operate with them in maintaining order in the town. No *li-kin* is paid on the river, and most of the recent unpopular taxes have been

abolished by the league. It is reported that the league is collecting the older established taxes, and diverting the proceeds to their war-chest, but the truth of this cannot be ascertained. In many towns the officials have been forced to place their police and dependents on half-pay, as they have no funds from which to pay them. When the half-pay ceases, the police and soldiers will probably help themselves.
This appears to be the situation to the south-east of Cheng-tu as far as Chiating. The Government troops are now reported to be at Shuang Liu Hsien, and the insurgents to be falling back on the Hsin Ching and Ch'iung Chou districts, a region bearing an evil name for robbery and piracy. A messenger from His Majesty's ship "Widgeon," who left Chiating on the 16th September with a telegram overland to Suifu, was stopped and the telegram taken from him. The man considers that he is lucky to have returned alive. None of the couriers to Chengtu, dispatched by the "Widgeon" at my request, have been able to get within 50 *li* of the city, and the letters have been returned to Captain Brooke. Messengers sent through the French mission and the Japanese have also failed to reach Mr. Wilkinson. On the 21st September the taotai reported the receipt of a telegram from the Governor-General, viâ Tzuchou, stating that the rebels had been defeated, and that the road to Chengtu was now clear. No direct messages have yet arrived from the city, but on the east absolute quiet is reported from Suining and Shun Ching Fu.

I have, &c.
W. R. BROWN.

P.S.—With regard to the attitude of the Lu Chun or territorial army force and the police towards the railway agitation, my informant states that, on the cessation of business, General Chu held a review of these men, when he asked that all who were members of the Railway League should stand up, as he wished to expel them from the ranks. All stood up! General Chu withdrew, and the men subsequently refused to drill. On hearing of the conditions in their ranks the Viceroy made a surprise visit to their camp at Feng Huang Shan, 5 miles outside the city, and with the aid of soldiers of the reserve he removed the cannon and all cartridges, saying that he proposed to serve out a fresh supply of the latter.
The bolts of the police rifles were removed at an early date, and they were permitted to carry the useless rifles for a few days, when they were withdrawn and sticks issued to them.
The police and territorial army troops were mainly educated Szechuanese in sympathy with the league, and they had proclaimed their intention of refusing to fire on their fellow provincials.

W. R. B.

Enclosure 2 in No. 22.

Consul-General Wilkinson to Sir J. Jordan.

Sir,   *Chengtu, September* 16, 1911.
ON the 7th instant I telegraphed to you to report that the Governor-General had arrested the ringleaders of the Railway League, that the city gates of Chengtu were closed, and that the issue of the conflict was not yet certain. Receipt of this telegram was acknowledged by you on the following day.
These are the last telegrams to and from the legation that have reached their respective destinations. On the afternoon of the 7th I sent to the telegraph office a message for His Majesty's vice-consul at Chungking. This was twice refused by the operating clerks, or by the guards who were now surrounding the office; and I accordingly wrote to the Governor-General requesting that orders might be given for its transmission. To this request his Excellency acceded, but asked me to send future telegrams through him. When, however, on the following day I asked that a long telegram might be forwarded to you, his Excellency replied that the wire between Chengtu and Tzu-Chou—the mid-station of the line to Chungking—had been cut, but that my message would be sent on to Tzu-Chou by mounted courier. Last night he wrote again to say that the courier to whom this telegram and that of the 7th to Chungking were entrusted had been seized by the insurgents at Ch'a-tien-tzu, a market town a third of the way down the road. There is therefore no likelihood that either message has got through, or that a still later one of the 11th can have reached you.

I am endeavouring to get news down to Chungking by a native transport agency, but I cannot be certain of success. The Imperial Chinese Post Office has practically ceased to function here. For the first few days after the Governor-General's coup a few mails were received and distributed, but no outgoing mails were made up; Ch'engtu is, in short, in a state of siege, and I can form no conjecture as to when and how my present despatch will be transmitted. In the hope, however, that some opportunity may offer, I have prepared the following accounts of events here since the date of my last despatch.

The Railway League, emboldened by success, had passed resolutions that all the so-called benevolences or voluntary levies ("chüan-shu") should cease, and that the "scutage" (poll and land-tax) should be collected by the administration chambers ("pan-shih ch'u") which they were about to establish. The regulations for these last had been drafted, but not yet published, though a "compact," prescribing the course of conduct to the branch chambers, had appeared in the form of a printed poster. Of this "compact" I have the honour to enclose a translation, which serves to show the revolutionary character of the movement.

Meanwhile the Governor-General had received from the Central Government peremptory orders to arrest the ringleader, and had—as he has since affirmed in more than one proclamation—discovered clear proof that these men were plotting treason. About noon on the 7th instant, while the league was in session, his Excellency invited several of the agitators to a conference at his yamên. These were, first and foremost, Lo Lun, vice-president of the provincial assembly; P'u Tien-Chün, president; Chang Lan, vice-chairman of the shareholders' extraordinary general meeting; Teng Hsiao-k'o, clerk in one of the Peking Ministries; Hu Jung, brother of the first general manager of the Ch'uan-Han Railway, and—until he resigned as a protest against orders to refuse telegrams to and from the agitators—director of telegraphs in Szechuan; Chiang San-Ch'eng, a member of the provincial assembly; P'eng Lan-Fen, a "weiyuan" of the Education Office; and Meng Ts'ai-Ch'eng, superintendent of one of the local schools. Yen K'ai, chairman of the shareholders' meeting, was at the Ch'ing Yang Kung, the famous temple outside the city, where the annual fair is held, and a force of twenty troopers was dispatched to bring him in.

Once assembled at the yamên, the ringleaders were curtly informed by the Governor-General that they were under arrest as rebels, whilst a guard, partly of "lu-chün" (modern-drilled troops), partly of "Hsün-fang Tui" (patrol men), was placed over the shareholders still at the railway office. Chao Chih-t'ai's dispositions had indeed been skilfully taken. For some days the only soldiers seen in the streets were a few of the "lu-chün," apparently strolling aimlessly up and down, armed with a small sword-bayonet. These men were, however, reporting from time to time to larger bodies quartered unostentatiously in private houses, police stations, temples, and other points of vantage. When the blow was struck (the signal for which was the ringing of the fire bell) the streets were found to be everywhere in occupation of the military.

That fact did not prevent a demonstration being made by some of the populace. According to a proclamation by the Governor-General, published in the official "Chengtu Jih-pao" of the 11th, but subsequently suppressed, rushes were made on his yamên with a view to the release by force of the imprisoned agitators. His Excellency was compelled to order the guards to fire, and a number of the rioters were killed. According to the story of those who sympathise with the league, "the rioters" were peaceable folk who had approached the yamên gates as suppliants, and were humbly kneeling in front of them. Whatever their true attitude may have been, it is certain that thirteen at least of them were shot dead; for that number of corpses were counted the next day lying where they had fallen. I may here say that the bodies were encoffined on the 9th September, and removed at the dead of night to the Hsiao-kuan Miao. It is declared that the Governor-General gave to the family of each man killed the sum of 40 taels as blood-money ("ming chia"), taking in exchange an acquittance.

In the Tung Ta Kai a mob formed, which broke and fled when the soldiers fired in the air. Several persons were injured and some were trampled to death. Opposite the Ta Ch'ing bank a man was shot dead because he was carrying incense sticks and bewailing the arrest of Lo Lun. The shops, which had been doing some business behind half-closed shutters, now fastened their doors, and the streets were deserted except by the armed patrols.

The Governor-General posted a metrical proclamation to the effect that the ring-leaders alone were to be arrested, and had been arrested; the league was dissolved, and

13

business must now be resumed. As at the same time the city gates were barred and closely guarded, this proclamation had little effect in reassuring the public; the less so that the patrols were reported to be firing at random in the streets and to have already killed or wounded some of the passers-by.

Rain fell heavily all night of the 7th, and lasted throughout the 8th. Numbers of "min-t'uan," or trained bands, nevertheless assembled outside the east and south gates, clamouring for the release of the agitators. Their presence at those places and on this date renders credible the assertion which the Governor-General has recently so often made, that a conspiracy to seize the city was arranged for the 8th September. The plans of the conspirators were, it is said, betrayed by a youth, who handed a copy of the programme to his Excellency, who, it is further declared, is about to print and publish this document.

However that may be, attacks certainly were made on the city gates this day, but were repulsed without difficulty, as the assailants were only armed with matchlocks and tridents.

Another brief metrical notification repeated that the ringleaders now arrested were fomenters of disorder. As for the railway question, a proposal had been submitted by memorial that would save the Szechuanese from loss; the people, therefore, must not listen to idle rumours, and so bring disaster on their persons. A third notification, still shorter, was issued on the 9th:—

" It is the will of the court that only a few should be arrested, and these are all ringleaders. Honest people will not be troubled, but if crowds gather and enter the yamêns they may be killed at sight and nothing said."

The opportunity was taken to close two of the newspaper offices, those of the "Hsi-ku Pao" and the "Ch'i-chih Hua-pao," "for breach of the press law." Since the 7th instant, the only journal to appear is the official organ, the "Ch'engtu Jihpao."

On the 10th instant the public granaries were opened for the sale of rice, after consultation between the financial commissioner and the chamber of commerce. There has, however, been no sustained complaint of shortage of provisions in the city. The gates were after the 7th opened from time to time to allow the market folk to enter and leave; and as the insurgents have been gradually forced back, so has the period of entry been extended. At the present date (16th September) the north, south, and east gates are open to their full extent (inner and outer doors, and both wings of each door) from 8 A.M. to 6 P.M.; while the west gate, which is under the control of the Tartar general, was opened yesterday (for the first time) from 2 to 6 P.M. On the other hand, the walls are more closely guarded, and idlers are not allowed so ascend them, even in the daytime.

On the 12th instant an attempt was made to recruit men in the city for the Governor-General; this, it is said, was a failure, not a tenth of the required number joining. It is rumoured that secret meetings of the league are being held inside the city; but so far the Governor-General appears to control the situation within the walls, and to be able to enforce order and discipline.

Outside the city, more particularly along the west, south, and south-east roads, there has been a succession of encounters between the Government troops and insurgents. It is difficult to give a connected story of these operations. As far as I can judge, at the present moment the insurgents have been forced back to beyond Shuang-liu, Chung-ho Ch'ang, and Ch'a-tien-tzu, on those respective lines. The town of Shuang-liu is reported to have been completely gutted; there was a story that the magistrate had committed suicide, but this is not confirmed. The insurgents have made use of bamboo cannon, bound round with wire torn from the telegraph-lines, and loaded with scrap-iron. With these rude weapons they have done some execution, but not more than a score or two of wounded Government soldiers have been brought into Chengtu. On the other hand, as might be expected, the losses of the "min-t'uan" have been heavy. Some prisoners were taken, but these the Governor-General has (at least in some instances) released, going indeed, so far in his clemency as to give them food and money.

The rebels repulsed along the Shuang-liu road appear to have retreated northward through Wenchiang towards P'i Hsien, where also there has been fighting. Those advancing down the north road, instead of engaging the troops sent to oppose them consented to parley, and in the end laid down their arms and dispersed to their homes. Along the line of the eastern hills, by Lung Ch'üan Yi, the resistance has been most stubborn; while on the river route, towards Chiang-k'ou, the insurgents are still holding up all boats. Thus, as far as I can judge, the country for 15 miles or so around the capital has been cleared, but the routes east, west, and south are blocked, that at the north alone remains open.

The blockade, however, is curiously intermittent. Two days ago a consignment of groceries reached me from Chungking, having passed without hindrance through what, if they were organised, would be described as the rebel lines; while the Governor-General's courier with outgoing telegrams was, as I have said, held up. As I write, I have received through the telegraph office Mr. Brown's telegrams of the 8th September and 9th September, Mr. Ritchie receiving at the same time a message from Peking dated the 11th September. All these had been forwarded from Tzu-chou by courier. I have taken advantage of both opportunities (the Transport Agency and the courier) to endeavour to get replies through to Mr. Brown, who would forward them to you.

On the morning of the day of the Governor-General's coup, the 7th September, a party of foreigners left Chengtu by boat for Chungking. This consisted of Dr. Davidson, his wife and three children; Mr. H. Silcock, his wife and child; Mrs. Simkin (all the above are members of the Friends' Mission); Mrs. Ritchie and her three children; Mr. and Mrs. Vale of the China Inland Mission with one child; and the Hon. and Rev. O. St. M. Forester, of the Church Hostel. Preparations had been made for the departure on that afternoon of three employés of the British and American Tobacco Company (Messrs. England, Rowntree, and Steriker), and on the following morning of all the remaining British and American missionaries, with the exception of Dr. Kilborn, and Messrs. Neave and J. L. Stewart. It was expected that Dr. and Mme. Mouillac, their child and French maid, and M. and Mme. Triffaut (his dispenser) and their children would also leave, and in all probability the three American teachers at the high school.

The seizure of the ringleaders, and the closure of the gates prevented this prudent design from being carried out, and the foreign residents here to-day are those of three weeks ago, except for Dr. Davidson's party, above enumerated, and the Rev. J. R. Stewart, of the Church Hostel, who left for Mien-Chou on the 7th September to see to the safety of his sister at Chung-pa. (They are, I may add, the children of the mission-aries murdered at Kutien, Fukien province, in 1895.) My German colleague, M. Fischer, returned to Chengtu on the 3rd instant; M. Bons d'Anty, the French consul-general, is still in the wilds north of Ta chien-lu, and in all probability ignorant of our plight.

My telegrams up to and including that of the 7th instant will have told you of the steps I have taken to secure the safety of British residents here and else-where in my district. On the 28th August, at the request of the Provincial Department for Foreign Affairs, I sent round a circular warning foreigners to go about the streets as little as possible, and then not on horseback, but preferably in closed native chairs. On the 1st September, this time at the request of the Governor-General himself, I issued another circular suggesting that foreigners should, if the necessity arise, remove to the extensive premises of the Canadian Methodist Mission in the north-east of the city and contiguous to the Eastern Parade Ground, the head-quarters of Commandant Chu. On the 6th September the Governor-General wrote to say, in effect, that the necessity had arisen, and asked me to tell all my people to withdraw to the Canadian Mission. Copy of this note I at once sent to M. Fischer and M. Leurquin, while I embodied its contents in a third circular.

On the morning of the 7th, as I have already stated, Dr. Davidson and sixteen men women, and children left by boat. The great majority of the British and American missionaries had already moved over to the Canadian Mission premises, and were occupying the hospital which is just approaching completion. Here they had been joined by the Canadian missionaries from P'eng-hsien (Dr. and Mrs. Barter and their two children, Mr. and Mrs. Sibley and child, and Mr. and Mrs. Irish). The few missionaries still at their homes inside the city were easily and safely transferred to the hospital during the 7th; but Mr. and Mrs. Taylor and Mr. Williams, American missionaries, and Mr. Carscallen, Canadian, who had gone out to the "Union Christian University," outside the south gate, had to be hauled over the wall. Mr. Ritchie, the provincial postmaster, came to reside with me, and was joined here by Mr. Brian Bates, a gentleman to whose services I have been greatly indebted. In short, the only British or American residents not either at the Szu-Sheng Tz'u or at this consulate (ten minutes' walk away) are Miss Loveday and Mr. Teichman.

Miss Loveday was asked to go to the Szu-Sheng Tz'u, but replied that she felt safe where she was. To Mr. Teichman, who had been suffering from too close confinement during the summer in this malodorous city, I have given leave to recruit his health in the mountains beyond Li-fan T'ing, and he was not due to return till the 13th September. He is now at Kwan Hsien (some 35 miles away to the west), but the Governor-General does not consider that it would be safe as yet for him to come on to Chengtu.

The'French sisters from outside the north gate have been called in to the orphanage at P'ing-an Ch'ian, in the west of this city, adjacent to the Evêché. The few French laymen (already enumerated), including M. Chaudoin, of the Imperial Chinese Post Office, are lodged at the French consulate. The Germans (M. Fischer, acting consul; M. Sperlein, teacher of German; M. Fabig, agent of Messrs. Schuchardt and Schuette; and the three arsenal employés, Messrs. Janks, Zang, and Spitzewski) are at the German consulate.

No sort of ill-will has so far been shown to the foreigners here by anyone. The danger lies, not in the hostility of the officials or of the agitators, but in the confusion and rioting that would follow a successful irruption of the insurgents into Chengtu, or a rising of their friends within the city. Such rising and such irruption become daily less probable, and the entrance yesterday of some 1,500 veteran troops from Tachienlu still further strengthens the hands of the Governor-General.

With regard to the out-stations of the various British and American missionaries, I am without news of any that lie south-west and south from Chengtu (Ch'iung-Chou, P'ingshan, Chiating, Yachou, Jenshou, Jung Hsien), and can get no messengers through. With Kwan Hsien I have got into touch, but have advised Mr. Hutson, Mr. Teichman's present host, and Mr. and Mrs. Muir, who arrived there a few days ago on their way home, to remain at the town for the present. At Sintu Mr. Hamilton appears to be quite secure, and my latest letters from Mien-Chou (September 11th) and Teyang (September 12th) tell me that all is quiet. A similar report comes from T'ung-Ch'uan. I have, however, advised the missionaries to concentrate quietly at Mien-Chou and T'ung-Ch'uan, both of which have direct connection by river with Chungking, and to prepare to leave as unostentatiously as possible, should the situation become more alarming. They will have passed on my advice, and a brief account of occurrences here up to the 9th instant with which I accompanied it, to their colleagues at Paoning and the stations beyond.

One copy of my present despatch I am endeavouring to send down to Chungking viâ T'ung-Ch'uan, retaining other copies until the mail service recommences.

I have, &c.
W. H. WILKINSON.

P.S. 5 P.M.—Mr. Teichman, Mr. and Mrs. Muir and child, and Mr. Hutson with his child and wife, have been escorted into Chengtu by the 100 "luchün" that formed the Kuan Hsien garrison.

W. H. W.

Enclosure 3 in No. 22.

Compact for the Administration Chambers of the Branch Shareholders' Associations in the Departments, Sub-departments, and Districts.

(Translation.)

THE Branch Administration Chambers in the departments, sub-departments, and districts are to be set up by the Branch Shareholders' Associations, in accordance with a resolution of the extraordinary general meeting of shareholders by means of a letter of appointment. They will deal solely with the refusal to pay benevolences, the expropriation for interest charges of the land tax and additional levy, and the abstention from purchase of land and houses, now voted by the said general meeting.

2. A branch administration office shall be composed of the following officials :—

(*a.*) Two general officers, whose duty shall be to have general control over all things. They shall be elected by the Branch Shareholders' Association of the locality and shall be men of credit and repute fully qualified to undertake complete reponsibility for the management of the affairs of their office.

(*b.*) A number of lecturers, to be appointed by the general officers. Their duty will be to lecture on the bearings, for good or ill, and the reasons of the action to be taken by their office.

(*c.*) A number of intelligent officers, to be appointed by the general officers. Their duty will be to ascertain whether the attitude of the officials and gentry of the locality is opposed to the action of their office.

3. The officials of a branch administrative office shall all be honorary. Any charges for maintenance or contingencies shall be defrayed by the general officers after verification of the work done, but the total to be expended must not exceed in a large district 300 taels, or in a small 200 taels.

4. Should the gentry of the locality, by way of falling in with the view of the local authorities, raise obstacles or do damage, they must be resisted with all one's strength, thus :—

(a.) By publication of their criminal attitude.
(b.) By limitation of their voting power and of their communal privileges.
(c.) By removal of their names from the local register, and by making residence impossible for them.
(d.) By an attitude of indifference should their lives and property be endangered.

5. Should the officials of the locality arrest any of the well-disposed, wrongfully stigmatising them as criminals, or unlawfully imprison them, the members of their chamber must resist with their whole strength thus :—

(a.) By strong protest.
(b.) By themselves as a body assuming the guilt.
(c.) By reporting to the head chamber at Chengtu, who will at once negotiate with the executive.
(d.) By petitioning the yamêns of the higher authorities, and asking for an enquiry.
(e.) By bringing the matter to the notice of (1) the national, (2) the provincial assembly.
(f.) By a refusal on the part of the local government officers to undertake any duty laid on them by the State.

6. Should any member of the chamber get into trouble by acts done for his chamber, he must be aided as follows :—

(a.) By suitable payments.
(b.) In the case of the poor and helpless, by payments for the support of their families.
(c.) By efforts on the part of the chamber to get the man acquitted.

7. Should any member of the chamber be involved in such serious trouble by acts done for his chamber as to lose his life, the facts shall be published throughout the Empire, and the following signal marks of compassion shall be shown :—

(a.) A public funeral.
(b.) An entry in the local annals.
(c.) Where the results of his deed are great, a subscription for a bronze statue.
(d.) In addition to subscriptions from the capital and country districts in aid of his family, a sum of 1,000 taels from benevolences or railway fund shall, if approved by a majority of the head chamber, be bestowed on his family.
(e.) The school expenses of his children and young brothers shall be paid.
(f.) These last shall not be called in to discharge any onerous duty.

8. Bye-laws may be made by a branch chamber, provided that they are not inconsistent with the present compact or the regulations.

Enclosure 4 in No. 22.

Consul-General Wilkinson to Sir J. Jordan.

Sir,   *Chengtu, September* 18, 1911.
    A SPECIAL courier from the Imperial Chinese Post Office at Chien-Chou arrived in the late afternoon of yesterday, bringing to Mr. Ritchie a letter from M. von Strauch (commissioner of customs at Chungking), dated Chungking, the 12th September. The courier reported that he had met with no obstacles on the road, and from the dates we gather that the post-office service from Chien-Chou viâ Tz'u Chou to

Chungking is in working order. I am therefore sending this brief despatch and a copy of my preceding despatch by the returning courier this morning.

Mr. Teichman, Mr. and Mrs. Muir, and their child, and Mr. Hutson, with his child and wife, were escorted from Kuan Hsien by the garrison of 100 "luchün," who had received orders to fall back on Chengtu. As their route was by way of Ch'ung-ning and Hsin-fan, it is evident that the direct road through P'i Hsien was then blocked. Mr. Teichman reports :—

"I arrived at Kuan Hsien on the 11th September, from the mountains, where the wildest and most absurd rumours were current, among others that the capital was in the hands of the insurgents and the head of his Excellency Chao Erh-feng hanging over the city walls. At Kuan Hsien I found Messrs. Muir and Hutson, with their families, anxiously awaiting the course of events on the premises of the China Island Mission, having been cut off from all communication with Chengtu for some days. On the following morning I called on the Hsien magistrate, a courteous and agreeable man, who was most anxious to do all in his power to protect the foreigners, but was as much in the dark as we were as to the true course events had taken in the capital ; he said, however, that it was impossible for us to attempt to approach Chengtu at present, as fighting was going on around P'i Hsien. Kuan Hsien itself, he said, was now quiet, 18 "t'u-fei," or banditti, having just been decapitated in his yamên, where the garrison of 100 "luchün" troops, who had arrived a few days before from Chengtu, were stationed. Soon after daybreak on the following morning he called on me at the mission to inform me that a despatch had just got through ordering the immediate retirement of the troops on Chengtu, as all the garrisons in the outlying Hsien cities were being withdrawn to the capital, and that they were going to march viâ Ch'ung-ning Hsien and Hsin-fan Hsien to avoid a collision with the insurgents. He suggested that our party should take advantage of this escort to return to Chengtu, and begged me to urge Mr. Hutson, the resident China Inland Mission missionary, to leave Kuan Hsien, since after the withdrawal of the troops he would be powerless to protect him. This course having been decided on, a new difficulty arose, as it appeared impossible to get chair-bearers and porters at any price ; refugees were flocking up into the mountains from the Chengtu plain, and chair-bearers were getting 4, 5, and 6 dollars a-day instead of 30 or 40 cents. The official, however, very kindly came to the rescue again, and procured porters and chair-bearers of a kind, so that we at length left Kuan Hsien at 2 o'clock in the afternoon, the troops, who were under imperative orders to march immediately, waiting more than six hours for us to start. Owing to the bad state of the roads through recent rain, we were only able to travel 10 miles that afternoon before being overtaken by darkness.

"On the following day we marched viâ Ch'ung-ning Hsien to Hsin-fan Hsien. In both these towns the shops, except those that sold food, were for the most part closed, and the situation was the same as at Kuan Hsien. The 'luchün' troops had been withdrawn to Chengtu, the magistrates were still in their yamêns, but without any knowledge of what was going on, and the city gates and walls were being guarded by the local 't'uan,' or popular militia, armed with spears, swords, tridents, and matchlocks ; but, unlike the village 't'uans,' they were upholding law and order, and showed no signs of hostility to the troops as we passed through. The day's march was without incident, save that the porters and chair-bearers were constantly endeavouring to put down their loads and bolt, and that one of the officer's servants, lagging behind, was attacked and wounded by some banditti, and, though brought in, died during the night from want of proper medical assistance ; it was also rumoured that two of the soldiers were cut off, but that the insurgents, on finding that they were 'luchün' troops (Szechuanese) and not the hated 'hsünfang' (a corps recruited from Anhui and other provinces), let them go again. The next day we reached the large military camp at Fenghuangshan outside the North Gate of Chengtu, where we were most hospitably received by the commandant and other officers, and whence a new force was deputed to escort us to the capital. I was much impressed during our journey by the excellent conduct of the 'luchün' troops, both officers and men, who took the greatest pains to look after our party, and the friendly attitude of all the local officials, who rendered us every assistance in their power. In appearance the country seemed quiet enough, and the rice crop was being harvested ; the people looked anxious and alarmed, rather than sullen or aggressive ; but during the journey our commanding officer received three despatches ordering him to hasten, as his men were urgently needed, and at Fenghuangshang firing was audible to the west. The Kuang Hsü posters are still much in evidence outside the capital."

C

The calling in of the garrisons at Kuan Hsien and elsewhere would seem to show that the Governor-General intends to concentrate his forces at Chengtu in anticipation of a general attack on the capital by " min-t'uan " and brigands. It cannot mean that all danger on the west has passed away; for to the south of Chengtu Kuan Hsien line, on the Yachou road between Shuangliu and Hsingching, severe fighting is reported, and as late as yesterday mountain-guns were being sent to the scene of action. On the south-east the high road to Chien-Chou would now appear to have been cleared by the victory of the Government troops at Lung-ch'üan Li; but the train bands and marauders if they are easily dispersed (as has not always been the case), easily re-form, and a road open to-day may be closed to-morrow. On the southern road towards Chiang-k'ou it is said that the Government troops are burning Chung Ho Ch'ang, the winter port of Chengtu and a stronghold of the league.

Fifteen hundred troops from Tachienlu, presumably veterans of the marches, arrived at Chengtu on the 16th. The number of killed and wounded on either side is hard to estimate; it is put at 3,000 for the insurgents and about a tenth of that number for the Government troops. Few prisoners are made, and these only in the hope of extracting information.

More stringent precautions are being taken in Chengtu city itself. No one is allowed on the walls, which are patrolled day and night. The beating of drums and gongs and the firing of crackers are forbidden; the makers of fireworks may on no account sell gunpowder to anyone.

No sort of hostility has so far been shown to foreigners by anyone, but on my advice the refugees at the Szu-sheng-tz'u keep as far as possible to their present quarters, which are very extensive and, all things considered, not devoid of comfort. They should suffer no great hardship, even if circumstances compel them to remain there a few weeks longer.

I have, &c.
W. H. WILKINSON.

Enclosure 5 in No. 22.

Consul-General Wilkinson to Sir J. Jordan.

Sir,   *Chengtu, September* 19, 1911.
YESTERDAY'S issue of the semi-official " Chengtu Jihpao " gives an account of the repulse at Lung-ch'üan-yi, on the south-east road, of " upwards of a myriad banditti " by the Government troops on the 9th instant. The rebels re-formed after their defeat, but were again attacked in the neighbourhood of Chien-Chou and completely routed. " Several of their leaders were taken prisoner, and the road from the capital to Chien-Chou is now, in consequence, open and unobstructed."

This explains why the postal courier, of whom mention was made in my immediately preceding despatch, sent by M. von Strauch (commissioner of customs at Chungking) to Mr. Ritchie, was able to get through, and it encourages me to hope that the mail service between Chengtu and Chungking may shortly be re-established.

The courier in question brought me a note from Mr. Brown, His Majesty's vice-consul at Chungking, dated the 12th September, but as this was sent under cover to Père Bayon, a Catholic missionary outside the East Gate, I did not receive it in time to acknowledge it in my despatch of yesterday. In this note Mr. Brown told me that " the Chengtu party is coming down the river in sections." I took this—and rightly, as it now appears—to refer to Dr. Davidson's party of seventeen men, women, and children, who (as I reported in my despatch of the 16th September) left Chengtu on the morning of the 7th September.

Persistent rumours had declared that this party was being held up by the rebels as hostages for the lives of Lo Lun and his fellow conspirators. The latest news we had received of them was that they had passed Ch'iang-k'ou (where the Chengtu River rejoins the Min) on the morning of the 8th. At noon yesterday the two sergeants of the " luchün," whom General Chu had detailed to escort Mrs. Ritchie, returned, bringing a letter from her to her husband, and one from Dr. Davidson to Mr. Simkin, both dated Sui Fu, the 10th September.

Mr. Brown will doubtless have reported to you the condition of affairs at Sui Fu, where an attack was being made by a mob, headed by the students, on the yamên of the prefect, just as Dr. Davidson's party came alongside His Majesty's ship " Widgeon."

Neither in Mrs. Ritchie's nor in Dr. Davidson's letter is any mention made of P'ing-shan Hsien, where a married missionary of the China Inland Mission (Mr. Barham) is stationed. As regards Chiating their information is vague :—

" We arrived at Chiating on the 9th September about 2 P.M. and found all quiet, but could not get telegrams through to Chengtu, and also heard that communication between Chungking and Chengtu was cut. Our communication was open to Chungking, but we did not use it. . . . . Although we stayed at Chiating until 6 o'clock there was no word of the Canadians. . . . . The Chiating post-office clerk said no mail had arrived."

I do not know, therefore, whether the missionaries at Chiating have left that city. Some of these are Canadians ; but I am inclined to believe that the Canadians of whom Dr. Davidson said "there was no word" are the large party that was to have followed them from Chengtu down river, and not the residents of Chiating.

Of other situations, south of Chengtu, in my district I have no news. As regards Jenshou it is rumoured that the " t'uan " decided to stand by the magistrate, and maintain order ; but nothing has reached us from Dr. Allan or any other of the resident missionaries. It would seem probable, however, that they have kept in touch with Chiating, and, through Chiating, with Chungking. The same remark applies, I trust, to Jung Hsien ; while Tzuliuching is on the telegraph line.

I have reported the arrival at Chengtu of all the Protestant missionaries from P'eng Hsien and Kuan Hsien. The Catholics at Ho-pa-ch'ang, the seminary in the hills north of P'eng Hsien, have not come in ; nor, as far as I am aware, have any other Catholic missionaries, with the exception of the sisters of mercy outside the North Gate.

At Wei-chou, on the Min valley, north of Kuan Hsien, is a station of the China Inland Mission, occupied by Mr. Coates, with his wife and infant. Mr. Teichman, who passed through this place on the 4th September, reports that all was quite at that time, and that if the insurrectionary movement spread up the Min valley, Mr. Coates would probably retreat northwards towards Sungpanting, and so on to Kansu, or else take refuge with a neighbouring Thibetan chief, who is a trustworthy friend to all foreigners, and in whose mountain fastnesses he would be perfectly safe.

From certain of the stations of the Church Missionary Society, north and north-east of Chengtu, and from the Friends' Mission at T'ung Ch'uan Fu, I have during the past fortnight received letters, a précis of which (by Mr. Teichman) I have the honour to enclose.

The attack on Mr. Whiteside at Lung-an was, I think, unconnected, or only very indirectly connected, with the present disturbances. It took place during church service, and the assailant, who was arrested, was evidently a lunatic, or, at the least, a fanatic. Matters seem to have been otherwise at Lung-ch'ang (on the Chungking Tzuliuching road), where Mr. Manly, of the American Methodist Episcopal Mission, was assaulted on or about the 4th instant. As this is the only instance in which, as far as I am aware, foreigners have been molested, I give my authority (a note to me from Mr. Beach, dated Chengtu, the 18th September) :—

" Our preacher from Chien-Chou, who arrived on Saturday, reported the road all clear to Tzuchou. He also said that Mr. Manly was hooted at by a crowd as he passed through the city of Lung-ch'ang. He endeavoured to remonstrate, but as the crowd became more unruly he made his escape by the help of the police and the officials, who came on to the street. A letter from Miss Brethorst, dated the 7th, adds the item that he was attacked, and escaped through a ' pi-t'ou ' (partition). She adds no other particulars. I judge the incident happened on the 4th or 5th."

I have, &c.

W. H. WILKINSON.

Enclosure 6 in No. 22.

Summary of Letters received from surrounding Districts.

Sintu, September 2.—Influential members of the local gentry met Mr. Hamilton and assured him that he was in no danger. The city was being garrisoned by the local militia. Shops were still shut. Most of the local people are members of the T'ung-

C 2

chih-hui. The leaders announce that their intentions are peaceful, though it is doubtful whether they would be able to keep the peace in the event of trouble.

Sintu, September 4.—The son of a man named Liu, the local head of the T'ung-chih-hui, called on Mr. Hamilton and assured him that he had nothing to fear.

Chung-chiang Hsien, September 4.—On the night of the 3rd September a small riot took place, during which the police and tax offices were wrecked, but the mission premises not touched. On the following day the shops and the city gates were closed, and the police all went into the magistrate's yamên.

T'ung-ch'uan Fu, September 4.—On this date the shops will still open, though the agitators were urging their closure; both Fu and Hsien magistrates were most solicitous for foreigners' safety.

Kuan Hsien, September 5.—A riot took place here during which the police and *li-kin* offices and the tea school were wrecked, but the mission station was not attacked; the missionary ascribing his immunity to the good-will of the local residents. Soon after a garrison of 100 "luchün" troops arrived and matters quieted down, a good number of rioters and bad characters being apprehended and executed. This neighbourhood has for long been a favourite haunt of the revolutionaries, who carry on their propaganda on the Chengtu plain and retreat to the mountains when things get too warm for them. The attitude of the students and merchants at the present time is sullen and determined, and their placards breathe a spirit of resistance to the death.

Mienchou, September 6.—All quiet and no great interest taken in political affairs locally.

Mienchu Hsien, September 6.—Shops closed on the 3rd September, but subsequently opened on official's request.

Tehyang, September 6.—Shops closed on the 2nd September, much anti-foreign talk, and the local official says he has no power left to protect foreigners.

Chung-chiang Hsien, September 6.—Riot on the 3rd September, but mission untouched.

Lungan Fu, September 6.—A missionary injured by a fanatic, but no general disturbance.

Chung-pa; September 6.—Missionaries withdrawn, but no trouble.

T'ung-ch'uan Fu, September 11.—Communications with Chengtu cut off; shops still closed, rumours of all kinds, but no riots; T'ung-chih-hui rule the city; their public pronouncements are peaceful, but they do not allow the shopkeepers to pay the usual taxes; both Fu and Hsien magistrates working well.

Tehyang, September 12.—Business recommenced on the 11th after eleven days of suspension; the city much agitated, and open war advocated; all kinds of wild rumours are current, such as that the officials have given the province to the British as security for the railway loan.

Sintu, September 12.—City still quiet, and Hsien magistrate most energetic; shops still closed; all kinds of wild rumours; the neighbouring city of Hanchou is reported to be in a turmoil, and in the hands of the insurgents.

Sintu, September 16.—On the 13th there was a sudden commotion in the city as it was reported that the Hanchou insurgents were coming to punish the Sintu people for the apathy; the gates were promptly closed, guards placed on the walls, and baskets of lime prepared to throw on the heads of the attacking party; fortunately it began to rain heavily, and no attacking party arrived; at T'ang-chia-szu and Hsiang-yang-ch'ang, 17 and 15 *li* to the north, skirmishes have taken place between the insurgents and the troops, in which thirty-eight soldiers were killed and several wounded; five insurrectionary leaders were captured, who were offered their lives for information about the movement; they are reported members of the Ko-lao-hui.

No. 23.

Sir J. Jordan to Sir Edward Grey.—(*Received October 30.*)

Sir,   *Peking, October 16, 1911.*

MY telegrams during the last few days will have made you acquainted with the serious developments which have arisen at Wuchang and the measures which have been taken by the Government to deal with the gravest crisis which has confronted them in recent years.

The prospect of trouble at Hankow had been foreseen for some time past. It was known that the 8th division of the army which was stationed there was in a

21

very unsatisfactory state of discipline, and that considerable disaffection existed in its ranks. Two regiments, comprising some 2,000 men, had been sent to Szechuan, and there had been frequent desertions and acts of insubordination amongst the remainder. On the 30th September the acting British consul-general telegraphed, on the authority of the American mission at Wuchang, a report of an impending mutiny amongst the troops, but no confirmation of the rumour was apparently obtainable. Nevertheless on the 3rd October, Mr. Goffe addressed a despatch to the senior naval officer at Shanghai stating the reasons which, in his opinion, rendered it desirable that Hankow should be provided with naval assistance for some time to come, and his representations were, I understand, favourably entertained by the commander-in-chief.

As I learn from Mr. Goffe, revolutionaries were discovered at work in the Russian concession at Hankow on the afternoon of the 9th instant, and three or four men were executed in front of the Viceroy's yamên on the following morning. This was followed on the 11th by the news that Wuchang was in full revolution; that the yamêns had been burnt; and that the Viceroy, who had taken refuge on a Chinese cruiser which was anchored close to a British gun-boat, had notified the consuls that he was unable to protect foreigners, and had asked the assistance of His Majesty's ships in preventing the mutinous troops from crossing the river.

On the receipt of this news I at once asked the naval commander-in-chief to send all available assistance to Hankow, and his Excellency readily responded to the request.

The receipt of these alarming reports caused much consternation in Peking, where a series of decrees, copies of which are enclosed, were issued reflecting the feelings of the court at the successive phases of the movement. Jui Ch'êng, the Viceroy at Wuchang, and the ablest Manchu holding office in the provinces, was at first complimented on his promptitude and success in "nipping the revolution in the bud," only to find himself a day later severely censured and degraded for his remissness and gross neglect of duty.

Two divisions of the northern army were ordered to Hupei under the command of Yin Ch'ang, the Minister of War, who gained his military experience in Germany and Austria.

Admiral Sah, who served in the British navy, was at the same time directed to co-operate with all the naval forces at his disposal in the recapture of the revolted city. It soon became evident that the task before the Imperialists was one of increasing difficulty, as the revolution spread to the adjoining cities of Hanyang and Hankow, and the capture of the arsenal and the ironworks placed the rebels in possession of a large supply of war material. The orderly manner in which the movement is being conducted and the marked consideration shown for foreign interests distinguish it from all previous risings of this kind, and has enlisted for it a measure of sympathy amongst the Chinese which the Manchu dynasty can no longer claim to command.

The rebel generalissimo, Li Yuan-Hung, is reported to be a man of considerable intelligence, who speaks English and has had some experience abroad. He has notified the consuls in Hankow that he has constituted a Government which will respect existing treaties and engagements with foreign Powers, and will guarantee efficient protection to all foreigners so long as they refrain from rendering assistance to the Manchu Government. No notice has been taken of this announcement by the acting British consul-general, who has been instructed to hold no communication with the insurgents further than what is absolutely necessary to safeguard British life and property.

The instructions which were given to Admiral Sah to bombard Wuchang appear to have caused considerable uneasiness at Hankow, and the senior consul telegraphed to the diplomatic body suggesting that the admiral should be directed to conduct his operations in such a way as to involve a minimum risk to the foreign concessions. If this were impracticable the only alternative would be to evacuate the concessions, and in that event, the consuls asked that sufficient notice should be given beforehand. At a meeting held at this legation on the 14th instant I was authorised by my colleagues to approach the Wai-wu Pu on the subject, and the result was that I received an assurance from the Ministers in the sense suggested by the consuls.

In my telegram of the 14th October, I have explained at length the reasons which, in my opinion, rendered it very desirable that the commander-in-chief should be present at Hankow during the proposed bombardment of Wuchang, and I am glad to report that I have received a telegram from Vice-Admiral Winsloe stating that he expects to reach Hankow about noon to-morrow, the 17th October.

[335]   C 3

In the meantime the autumn manœuvres, which were to have been held on the 17th October and three following days, and for which all preparations were completed, were cancelled, and arrangements were hurriedly made for the dispatch of the two divisions to Hankow. One of these divisions, the 6th, was not altogether beyond suspicion, and responsible officials like Shêng Hsuan-Huai did not hesitate to express their doubts as to its willingness to engage in a civil conflict. And then a dramatic incident occurred which illustrates the extremities to which the Prince Regent and his Government are reduced, and which exposes their weakness to a discontented Empire. Yuan Shih-K'ai, who was unceremoniously dismissed from office two years ago and who had practically to flee for his life, was recalled to power, and requested in so many words to save the Empire. The decree embodying this humiliating decision is enclosed herewith.

I gather from the Wai-wu Pu that Yuan's consent was obtained before this step was taken, and he has confidence, presumably, in his ability to carry out the thankless task with which he has been entrusted. His name will carry great weight with the troops, especially with the 6th division, which still treasures his portrait, and his loyalty is not in question, but the Government is badly equipped for military operations of any magnitude. It is believed that there is a shortage of ammunition for the troops, and desperate efforts have been made during the last few days to raise funds for the campaign.

As a significant commentary on the value of China's modern army it may be mentioned that the foreign-drilled troops at Nanking have all been disarmed, and their place taken by 8,000 troops of the old régime.

The general opinion is that the present revolt will be suppressed, but the prospect which faces the Manchu dynasty is a gloomy one. It is largely discredited amongst its own people, and its recent treatment of several questions affecting foreigners shows a narrowness of view and a jealousy of encroachment upon its so-called sovereign rights which blocks all enterprise.

Fully half the Empire is threatened with a partial failure of the crops, and the Yang-tsze valley is overrun with swarms of homeless and starving people.

I have, &c.

J. N. JORDAN.

Enclosure 1 in No. 23.

Imperial Decree of October 11, 1911.

(Translation.)

JUI CH'ENG has telegraphically memorialised us to the effect that, having ascertained that the revolutionaries hiding in Wuchang had fixed the night of the 19th for rising in revolt, he gave instructions to have them arrested. Subsequently, Chi Yao-Shan reported by telegram that he had arrested a notorious outlaw in Hankow named Liu Yao-chang, and also seized many false seals, seditious notifications, and despatches. Thereupon the memorialist and General Chang Piao and other officers sent out troops and arrested, in the provincial capital, thirty-two ringleaders and rebels, and also captured a large quantity of ammunition and bombs. Among the prisoners were one Liu Ju-Kuei, who resisted capture by firing a revolver at the police ; one Yang Hung-Sheng, who secretly stored fire-arms ; and one Peng Chu-Fan, who used the most revolutionary language. These three prisoners were summarily tried and executed on the spot.

These revolutionaries, by planning a great rising in Hupei, have indeed despised the law. The said Viceroy, in nipping the trouble in the bud and suppressing the disturbance in a moment, has acted with great promptitude. The civil and military officials engaged in the affair have shown bravery worthy of praise.

We hereby command that the rebels who have been arrested, with the exception of the three prisoners, Liu Ju-Kuei, &c., who have been executed, be at once rigorously examined and punished with the full penalty of the law. At the same time, the local, civil, and military officials should make a strict search for, arrest, and bring to trial the rebels who are at large. Further, a notification shall be issued to the effect that those who have been forced to join the rebels are allowed to repent and mend their ways. The police, as well as the local, civil, and military officials, who have failed to detect the uprising, are graciously exonerated from punishment, since they have taken concerted actiou in securing the arrest of the rebels. The more deserving officers who have rendered valuable services in this connection may be recommended for reward, but no recommendations on a lavish scale can be allowed. The other suggestions in the memorial are sanctioned.

Enclosure 2 in No. 23.

Imperial Decree of October 12, 1911.

(Translation.)

ON the 12th October the Cabinet received the following edict :—

Jui Ch'eng has memorialised us to the effect that on the night of the 9th instant, when the rebels, who had been arrested in connection with the first disturbance, were being brought up for trial, the remaining revolutionaries won over to their cause the Engineer and Transport Corps. Suddenly, at 8 o'clock on the evening of the 10th, the Engineer Corps, on a signal, made a desperate attack on the Chu-Wang-T'ai arsenal, while the Transport Corps set fire to their barracks and forced their way into the city. Memorialist co-operated with Chang Piao, T'ieh Chung, and Wang Li-Kang in dispatching troops and police to various points, and himself led a force of police to withstand the rebels. The latter, unfortunately, advanced to the attack by numerous routes, and, appalled by their numbers and formidable aspect, Jui Ch'eng retreated, and embarked on the gun-boat "Chu Yü," which brought him to Hankow. He had telegraphed to Hunan and Hupei, calling for the dispatch to Hupei of patrol forces to assist in the work of suppression. At the same time, he begs for the appointment of a number of high officials who should proceed to Hupei with well-trained troops to punish the rebels.

This memorial has filled us with great surprise. Though the troops and the rebels had been plotting for so long a time Jui Ch'eng took no precautionary measures, with the result that there has been a sudden uprising, and the provincial capital has fallen into the hands of the rebels. Thus has he ill-requited our bounty and has neglected the duties of his office, and his punishment must be severe. We hereby order that Jui Ch'eng, Viceroy of Hukuang, be at once deprived of rank, but that he be allowed to atone for his error by meritorious deeds. We therefore order that he act temporarily as Hukuang Viceroy, that we may watch his behaviour in the future. The said Acting Viceroy is commanded to recapture the city immediately, and in case of failure or immoderate delay he will be very severely punished.

The general staff and the Ministry of War are also commanded to detail at once two divisions of troops to proceed to Hupei for the suppression of the revolt. At the same time, the Admiralty should dispatch additional gun-boats, under the command of Sah Chen-ping, while Ch'eng Yün-Ho should be instructed to take the Yang-tsze squadron to the rescue without delay. The Minister of War, Yin Ch'ang, is hereby commanded to proceed to Hupei at once with troops. All the troops in the province, as well as the reinforcements, will be placed under his command. Jui Ch'eng is instructed to co-operate with him in devising methods for the early suppression of the rebels. The movement must not be allowed to spread.

Enclosure 3 in No. 23.

Imperial Decree of October 13, 1911.

(Translation.)

ON the 13th October the Cabinet received the following edict :—

Jui Ch'eng has presented two telegraphic memorials reporting the course of the joint revolt of the troops and the rebels. Chang Piao has been in command of the Hupei troops for many years, and the fact that the troops have joined with the rebels in revolt and the loss of the provincial capital are enough to show that his methods of discipline are faulty. Before the revolt broke out he took no precautions, and, when it broke out, he was slow beyond belief in taking action. He failed to win the loyalty of the army, and actually dared to abandon his garrison hurriedly and flee. This is a serious breach of discipline and cannot go unpunished. We hereby order that Commander-in-chief Chang Piao be forthwith deprived of rank, and we further order Jui Ch'eng to instruct him to suppress immediately and mercilessly the revolutionaries and recapture the provincial capital. Measures must be taken to pacify those soldiers who have been coerced, and have not joined the revolt of their free will. If Chang Piao still hesitates he will be yet more severely punished.

[335]   C 4

The troops under the command of Yin Ch'ang have to-day left by special trains. On their arrival in Hupei, we order that Jui Ch'eng co-operate with them in devising means for dealing promptly with the situation.

We further order the Ministry of Finance to appropriate speedily a sum for military purposes, as requested by the memorialist.

Enclosure 4 in No. 23.

Imperial Decrees of October 14, 1911.

(1.)

(Translation.)

YUAN SHIH-KAI is hereby appointed Viceroy of Hukuang, and commanded to direct the suppression and pacification of the rebels.

Ts'en Ch'un-Hsuan is hereby appointed Viceroy of Szechuan, and commanded to direct the suppression and pacification of the rebels.

They are both ordered to proceed immediately to their posts, and there is no need for them to come to Peking for Imperial audience. At the present critical state of affairs, the said Viceroys who have for generations received the Imperial bounty should be most solicitous for the welfare of the whole Empire, and should use their utmost efforts to perform their difficult tasks without persistent refusal. Thus will they act up to their commission.

When Yuan Shih-kai and Ts'en Ch'un-Hsuan have arrived at their posts, Jui Ch'eng and Chao Erh-Feng will hand over their duties.

(2.)

Yuan Shih-kai having now been appointed Viceroy of Hukuang, we hereby command that the military forces of the said provinces as well as the reinforcements from various points be placed under his control and at his disposal.

Yuan Shih-kai is further ordered to co-operate in dispatching military and naval forces under the command of Yin Ch'ang and Sah Chen-Ping, and in taking immediate action to cope with the situation with a view to the restoration of peace at an early date.

(3.)

Ts'en Ch'un-Hsuan having been appointed Viceroy of Szechuan, we hereby command that the military forces of the said province as well as reinforcements from various points be placed under his control and at his disposal.

No. 24.

Admiralty to Foreign Office.—(Received October 30.)

Sir, *Admiralty, October* 30, 1911.

I AM commanded by my Lords Commissioners of the Admiralty to transmit, for the information of the Secretary of State for Foreign Affairs, copy of a telegram of the 30th instant from the commander-in-chief on the China station relative to the situation in China.

I am, &c.

W. GRAHAM GREENE.

Enclosure in No. 24.

Commander-in-chief, China, to Admiralty.

(Telegraphic.) Viâ *Shanghai, October* 30, 1911.
THE Imperial troops entered Hankow at 2 P.M. to-day, and are burning the city after clearing out the rebels. Nothing was done by the Chinese men-of-war.

A good deal of fighting has been going on to-day amongst the Chinese houses in the western end of the British concession.

No. 25.

Sir J. Jordan to Sir Edward Grey.—(Received October 30.)

(Telegraphic.) *Peking, October* 30, 1911.
DECREES issued this evening, substance of which will appear in newspapers to-morrow, read like despairing effort to save throne and the dynasty, and may possibly effect their object unless country insists on expulsion of Manchus. They constitute such a complete surrender to the demands of the Nationalists, and so entirely exonerate rebels, as to suggest that they have been drafted in consultation with leaders of the Nationalist movement in the Senate, who may influence provinces in favour of their acceptance under adequate guarantees for their fulfilment.

If they fail and the rebellion continues, issue is likely to be the downfall of dynasty.

No. 26.

Sir J. Jordan to Sir Edward Grey.—(Received October 31.)

(Telegraphic.) *Peking, October* 31, 1911.
REVOLUTION. Peking–Tien-tsin line.
In order to keep open communication with the sea, it may at any moment become necessary to guard the railway, as the situation both here and at Tien-tsin becomes more critical daily. We should, I think, be justified in using British troops for this purpose, and I trust that you concur.

No. 27.

Sir Edward Grey to Sir J. Jordan.

(Telegraphic.) *Foreign Office, November* 1, 1911.
YOUR telegram of 31st October: China revolution.
I concur, but I assume that you would act in concert with your colleagues representing nations who have troops in North China.

No. 28.

Admiralty to Foreign Office.—(Received November 2.)

Sir, *Admiralty, November* 2, 1911.
I AM commanded by my Lords Commissioners of the Admiralty to transmit, for the information of the Secretary of State for Foreign Affairs, copy of a telegram, dated the 1st instant, from the commander-in-chief on the China station, relative to the state of affairs in China.

I am, &c.
W. GRAHAM GREENE.

Enclosure in No. 28.

Commander-in-Chief, China, to Admiralty.

(Telegraphic.)   *November* 1, 1911.
NOTHING of importance occurred to-day.
The Imperialists are shelling Hanyang, and their troops are clearing Hankow city.
British vessels at Wuchang and below Kiukiang have been occasionally fired on by
rebels. Consular officer, who was sent in man-of-war to interview the rebel leader,
reports that the latter explained that he merely desired to prevent the passage of
Chinese vessels carrying coal, ammunition, &c., for the use of the Imperialists, and
added that British vessels should not attempt to pass places in the hands of the
revolutionaries after nightfall. It is reported that the Imperialists intend to bombard
Hanyang fort, but are awaiting the arrival of larger howitzers. The arrival of the new
Viceroy is reported from the camp at Niekow.

No. 29.

Sir J. Jordan to Sir Edward Grey.—(Received November 2.)

(Telegraphic.)   *Peking, November* 2, 1911.
MY telegram of 29th October.
To-night decree commits the drafting of constitution to National Assembly in
compliance with demand of mutinous troops at Lanchou.
Yuan Shih-kai is ordered to come to Peking at once.

No. 30.

Foreign Office to War Office.

Sir,   *Foreign Office, November* 2, 1911.
I AM directed by Secretary Sir E. Grey to transmit to you herewith, to be laid
before the Army Council, a copy of a telegram* from His Majesty's Minister at Peking
on the subject of the present situation at that place.
The Council will observe from a perusal of Sir J. Jordan's telegram that the
position of affairs in the Chinese capital is becoming daily more critical, and
that it is possible that British troops may be required to guard the railway line
between Peking and the sea. Until the situation develops somewhat further,
Sir E. Grey regrets that it is impossible to say for how long the detention of the Royal
Inniskilling Fusiliers in North China may be necessary.
                                                                    I am, &c.
                                                              F. A. CAMPBELL.

No. 31.

Admiralty to Foreign Office.—(Received November 3.)

Sir,   *Admiralty, November* 3, 1911.
I AM commanded by my Lords Commissioners of the Admiralty to transmit, for
the information of the Secretary of State for Foreign Affairs, copy of a telegram,
dated the 3rd instant, from the commander-in-chief on the China station, relative to
the state of affairs in China.
                                                                    I am, &c.
                                                              W. GRAHAM GREENE.

* No. 26.

Enclosure in No. 31.

Commander-in-Chief, China, to Admiralty.

(Telegraphic.)   *November* 3, 1911.
IT is reported that the situation at Shanghai is critical.
Ships cannot be spared from the other ports on the river for the protection of the foreign settlements, which, in any case, are so large that it would be impossible to land a force large enough for the purpose, and it would be extremely unfortunate if the city were to be burnt and looted.
I would suggest that the other Governments concerned—American, Japanese, German, and French—should be consulted on the subject. The safety of the city could be assured by the dispatch of a small number of troops by each.
Should the rebels here be suppressed, the unrest in the surrounding country may be expected to continue for some months.
It is suggested that each Power should send 1,500 infantry with some small guns.
Similar communications are being made by telegraph to their respective Governments by the Japanese and German admirals.

No. 32.

Admiralty to Foreign Office.—(Received November 4.)

Sir,   *Admiralty, November* 4, 1911.
I AM commanded by my Lords Commissioners of the Admiralty to transmit, for the information of the Secretary of State for Foreign Affairs, copy of a telegram dated the 3rd instant from the commander-in-chief on the China station relative to the situation in China.
I am, &c.
W. GRAHAM GREENE.

Enclosure in No. 32.

Commander-in-chief, China, to Admiralty.

(Telegraphic.)   [*Viâ Shanghai*], *November* 3, 1911.
HANKOW city is still burning. No fighting worth mentioning has taken place for several days. Viceroy and rebel leaders are, I understand, now in communication with one another.

No. 33.

Sir J. Jordan to Sir Edward Grey.—(Received November 4.)

(Telegraphic.)   *Peking, November* 4, 1911.
REBEL Government notified His Majesty's consul-general yesterday that they had taken over Shanghai, and asked him to co-operate in maintaining order in the settlement. There has been no disturbance so far, but in afternoon thirty or forty rebel troops entered Shanghai–Nanking Railway station, which abuts on district of settlement inclined to disorder. At the request of the general manager the consul-general has authorised the occupation of the station by the volunteers.
I have telegraphed to him as follows :—
"I approve your action in authorising occupation of railway station.
"Railway being mortgaged to British bondholders, you are, in my opinion, justified in insisting, so far as means at your disposal admit, upon its being run as a purely commercial undertaking on neutral lines. I do not think, for instance, that it should be used for the conveyance of troops or munitions of war by either side.
"Agent of British and Chinese Corporation has, at my request, instructed the general manager to act under your orders for the time being, and you should explain

to both sides that our action is entirely impartial, and is merely intended to safeguard an enterprise in which there is a large amount of British capital involved, and to protect British lives and property in the adjoining international settlement."

No. 34.

Sir J. Jordan to Sir Edward Grey.—(Received November 5.)

(Telegraphic.) *Peking, November 5,* 1911.
MY telegram of 4th November.
Consul-general Shanghai reported yesterday that Wusung forts and Shanghai city passed peacefully into the hands of the rebels, also arsenal after some resistance. Settlements quiet. Volunteers will evacuate railway station as soon as revolutionary leaders produce an apparently organised body to protect it. Latter undertake not to interfere with working and receipts of railway so long as it carries troops and munitions of war for neither side. Viceroy of Nanking is rumoured to be entraining troops to recover Shanghai.
At my request Wai-wu Pu telegraphed urgent instructions to Viceroy of Nanking not to use railway for conveyance of troops or to take any action which may result in hostilities in Shanghai or neighbourhood. Consul at Nanking has been instructed to make pressing representations in this sense to his Excellency.
I have told consul-general that question of prohibition over whole line of conveyance of troops, &c., is being considered, but that for this purpose we should have to exercise effective supervision, and that in my opinion station should continue to be occupied—in any case until Viceroy's intentions become known—either by volunteers or by British naval force.

No. 35.

Sir J. Jordan to Sir Edward Grey.—(Received November 6.)

Sir, *Peking, October 20,* 1911.
I HAVE the honour to report, with reference to my telegram of the 14th instant, that on the night of the 13th instant a telegram reached me from the senior consul at Hankow requesting the diplomatic body to make urgent representations to the Wai-wu Pu with a view to their instructing Admiral Sah, the Chinese naval commander-in-chief at Hankow, to conduct the bombardment of Wuchang in such a way as to avoid all risk to the foreign concessions. The Japanese admiral would, it was stated, address a demand in this sense to Admiral Sah on the latter's arrival. In the event of the request being refused the consular body suggested, as a last alternative, that time should be given to evacuate the concessions.
In pursuance of the authority granted me by my colleagues, whom I convened on the 14th, I submitted to the Ministers of the Wai-wu Pu the recommendation above referred to as regards the conduct of the bombardment. Their Excellencies replied that Admiral Sah would naturally use the utmost precaution, but that they would request the Admiralty to send instructions to him in the sense desired by the diplomatic body. I was informed on the 17th October that the instructions had been duly telegraphed, but on his arrival, and before hearing from Peking, Admiral Sah assured the Japanese admiral that he was ready to take into consideration the wishes of the consular body.
I have, &c.
J. N. JORDAN.

No. 36.

Admiralty to Foreign Office.—(Received November 6.)

Sir, *Admiralty, November 6,* 1911.
I AM commanded by my Lords Commissioners of the Admiralty to transmit, for the information of the Secretary of State for Foreign Affairs, copy of a telegram dated the 5th instant from the commander-in-chief on the China station relative to the situation in China.
I am, &c.
W. GRAHAM GREENE.

Enclosure in No. 36.

Commander-in-chief, China, to Admiralty.

(Telegraphic.) [*Viâ Shanghai*], November 5, 1911.
CONSUL-GENERAL at Shanghai has received letter stating that the rebels are taking over government of Shanghai, and that they will protect foreigners. The letter proceeds to enquire whether, as settlements are so large, consul-general will take measures for their safety.

Rioting is reported to have taken place last night in the native city, and police yamên to have been burnt. Kiangnan arsenal is said to have been captured.

The rebels have established a battery on the south bank of the river, 5 miles below Hankow. They also hold Kiukiang and Matunua forts. They fire upon every vessel passing along the river at night, and a Japauese ship has been fired upon because it was suspected that Chinese officials were being carried.

Applications for presence of war-ship are being received from consuls at all the treaty ports along the coast. It is, however, impossible to accede to applications during continuance of trouble at Hankow.

No. 37.

Sir J. Jordan to Sir Edward Grey.—(Received November 6.)

(Telegraphic.) Peking, November 6, 1911.
REVOLUTION.
A satisfactory guarantee for the protection of the settlements seems to be afforded by the fact that Shanghai is evidently the head-quarters of the central machinery of the rebel Government, office under which has been accepted by several prominent officials and influential Chinese residents, and an opportunity of influencing the movement may thus eventually be offered to the foreign Powers.

City after city passes quietly into the hands of the rebels, and the country seems unwilling for the present to endorse the attempts of the Senate to mediate between the throne and the people.

It is not apparently a very hopeful task that has been committed to Yuan Shih-kai.

No. 38.

Sir Edward Grey to Sir J. Jordan.

(Telegraphic.) Foreign Office, November 6, 1911.
YOUR telegram of 4th November.
I entirely approve if you can arrange for neutralisation of Shanghai–Nanking Railway in manner proposed.

No. 39.

Admiralty to Foreign Office.—(Received November 7.)

Sir, Admiralty, November 7, 1911.
I AM commanded by my Lords Commissioners of the Admiralty to transmit herewith, for the information of the Secretary of State for Foreign Affairs, a copy of a telegram of to-day's date received from the Commander-in-chief, China, in continuation of his telegram of the 3rd instant, forwarded to you on the same date, respecting the suggested dispatch of troops to Shanghai. My Lords consider that in view of the Commander-in-chief's telegrams troops should be ordered to be in readiness at Hong Kong and transport provided, in order that they may be sent instantly to Shanghai to take the place of any men it is found necessary to land from the fleet, who would thus only be landed in case of urgent necessity pending the arrival of the troops. My Lords would be glad to be informed if Sir Edward Grey concurs in this proposal.

I am, &c.
W. GRAHAM GREENE.

Enclosure in No. 39.

Commander-in-chief, China, to Admiralty.

(Telegraphic.)   *November* 7, 1911.

WUSUNG fort at Shanghai has been taken by rebels, who have distributed arms and ammunition from the arsenal to their adherents. This will certainly lead to trouble. I am convinced that a request will soon be made for men to be landed, and parties have already been disembarked from United States and French ships. If men are landed from our cruisers the fleet will be disabled. I should be glad to be informed of Admiralty's wishes on this point, and, pending the receipt of a reply, have ordered the "Monmouth" to remain at Wusung. Revolution is apparently spreading rapidly.

No. 40.

Sir J. Jordan to Sir Edward Grey.—(Received November 7.)

(Telegraphic.)   *Peking, November* 7, 1911.

MY telegram of the 5th November.

Situation at Shanghai.

Railway station had already been handed back to rebels, and a larger force than is available would be required to reoccupy and hold it. Chinese Government are anxious to maintain neutrality, but require guarantee that it will not be used by rebels for the carriage of troops or munitions of war. Assurances are impracticable, but general manager is doing his best to prevent contravention of neutrality.

Taotai has left his residence in the native city, and desires to carry on his duties under the protection afforded by the foreign settlement. I think the consuls must now treat with the revolutionaries as the *de facto* masters of the situation, but the substitution of the rebel for the Imperial Government must not be allowed to affect in any way the status of the international settlement as regards freedom of interference by any native authority, and we should stipulate that any funds, such as customs revenue, which are ear-marked for meeting foreign obligations, should not be touched by the rebel Government. I have instructed His Britannic Majesty's consul-general in the above sense pending the decision of the diplomatic body.

Though I hope that no occasion for such a step will arise, any forcible attempt to modify the administration of the settlement as it now exists should, in my personal opinion, be met by foreign military occupation.

No. 41.

Sir Edward Grey to Sir J. Jordan.

(Telegraphic.)   *Foreign Office, November* 7, 1911.

AS commander-in-chief from his telegrams evidently considers that a demand for the landing of men at Shanghai will soon be made, and as the landing of men from the fleet would disable it, the Admiralty consider that troops should be held in readiness in Hong Kong to replace the bluejackets who would be landed temporarily in case of urgent necessity. I have concurred in this proposal as the matter is pressing, but should be glad to have your views.

No. 42.

Foreign Office to Admiralty.

Sir,   *Foreign Office, November* 8, 1911.

I AM directed by Secretary Sir E. Grey to acknowledge the receipt of your letter of the 7th instant, and to state, for the information of the Lords Commissioners of the Admiralty, that he concurs in the proposal that troops should be ordered to be in readiness at Hong Kong and transport provided in order that they may be sent instantly to Shanghai to take the place of any men it is found necessary to land from the fleet, who would only be landed in case of urgent necessity pending the arrival of the troops.

His Majesty's Minister at Peking has been informed by telegraph that Sir E. Grey has expressed his concurrence owing to the urgency of the matter, but has been requested to furnish his views.

I am, &c.
F. A. CAMPBELL.

No. 43.

Sir Edward Grey to Sir J. Jordan.

(Telegraphic.) *Foreign Office, November 8, 1911.*
SITUATION at Shanghai.
Your telegram of the 7th November.
Your action and policy have my entire approval.

No. 44.

Admiralty to Foreign Office.—(Received November 9.)

Sir, *Admiralty, November 9, 1911.*
I AM commanded by my Lords Commissioners of the Admiralty to transmit, for the information of the Secretary of State for Foreign Affairs, copy of a telegram, dated the 9th instant, from the commander-in-chief on the China Station relative to the Chinese rebellion.

I am, &c.
W. GRAHAM GREENE.

Enclosure in No. 44.

Commander-in-chief, China, to Admiralty.

(Telegraphic.) *November 9, 1911.*
REVOLUTIONARIES are everywhere successful. Their leader has been offered peace and pardon on his own terms. Peking Government has given instructions that Nanking shall be surrendered to the rebels.

As no serious fighting has taken place for the last ten days and the business houses are being reopened, there appears to be no necessity for me to remain here any longer.

I am proposing therefore, with the concurrence of Sir J. Jordan, to leave on the 11th November. The German admiral has also decided to leave on that date.

No. 45.

Sir J. Jordan to Sir Edward Grey.—(Received November 9.)

(Telegraphic.) *Peking, November 9, 1911.*
THERE has been indecisive fighting at Nanking, and foreigners have left. Canton has declared for the new Government. Viceroy fled to consulate-general and left for Hong Kong in His Majesty's ship "Handy." No fighting.

Fuchow regained this morning after sharp fighting.

Rebel troops are in possession of junction of Tai-yuen-fu and Peking and Hankow lines, thus cutting communications of Yuan Shi-kai's troops with Peking. All foreigners in Tai-yuen-fu are safe.

Imperial troops have been allowed to occupy temporarily space within radius of 20 *li* of foreign settlements of Tien-tsin for protection of city. Chang, commander of mutinous troops at Lanchou, has requested similar privilege, but has been refused by consular body. Ministry of Communications forbade railway directors to supply trains for his troops, and they are reported to be marching to Peking.
Tien-tsin expected to go over at any moment.

No. 46.

Sir J. Jordan to Sir Edward Grey.—(Received November 9.)

(Telegraphic.)   *Peking, November 9,* 1911.
BRITISH, Japanese, and French commanders at Tien-tsin arranged on 7th instant a scheme for maintaining communications between Peking and Tien-tsin until river freezes. In view of development of events at Tien-tsin, the three representatives to-day instructed commanders to put scheme into immediate operation as soon as they had reason to believe that any overt attempt was being made to break line. The scheme does not involve foreign occupation, and Ministers of Russia, Germany, America, and Italy have been consulted and kept informed.

No. 47.

Sir J. Jordan to Sir Edward Grey.—(Received November 10.)

Sir,   *Peking, October 23,* 1911.
OWING to the irregular working of the telegraph wires, the interruption of the mail service, and consequent absence of despatches from the acting consul-general at Hankow, it is difficult to form a clear idea of the course of events there during the week which has elapsed since I wrote my despatch of the 16th instant. Until to-day no official news of the operations had been given to the public, but a brief paragraph appears in this morning's Peking "Daily News," according to which hostilities opened on the 18th October between the Imperialist troops under the command of General Yin Ch'ang and rebel forces on the railway some few miles out of Hankow, and after three days' skirmishing, in which Admiral Sah's gun-boats appear to have taken part, resulted in what is described as a great victory for the Government troops. This report is, however, largely discounted by advices from other sources. A telegraphic report from the Viceroy Jui Cheng and Admiral Sah shows that the Government troops were in a precarious position at the close of the engagement. As it transpired, they were forced to retire the following day on a position further up the railway, and simultaneously the Chinese flotilla dropped down the river. This news, which reached me from Hankow through wireless telegraphy established at my suggestion by Sir Alfred Winsloe with Kiukiang, has naturally created much elation in the rebel camp. A serious factor in the situation was the refusal of the northern troops to fight, and unless the *moral* of the reinforcements now on their way is better than that of the advance regiments, the task before the Imperial forces will not be the light one which their superior numbers should have made it.
Colonel Willoughby and Captain Sir Douglas Brownrigg, who is on a brief visit to China from Tokyo, recently made an attempt to reach Hankow, but were unable to proceed beyond Sinyang, in Honan, a place on the line about 133 miles from Hankow. They have now left for the Yang-tsze by sea.
In the meantime, the news from other provinces is less satisfactory.
At Nanking the situation was saved just in the nick of time by the complete disarmament of the modern-drilled troops, but the feeling there, as elsewhere in the central and southern provinces, is entirely on the side of the rebellion, which is regarded as a popular movement against misrule and oppression.
Anhui is quiet at present, but His Majesty's consul at Wuhu reports that there is local apprehension of rioting by the famine refugees, and sympathy with the revolution is felt by the local officials, who are probably awaiting the turn of events before declaring themselves. On the 22nd October, Mr. Goffe reported that Changsha and Ichang were in the hands of the revolutionaries. This has been confirmed by information received through the Imperial Maritime Customs. There has been no violence at either port, but I understand that in the event of disturbances the foreign

community would concentrate in the Commissioner of Customs' premises. Mr. Goffe also stated very briefly that the revolutionary leader had "notified the consuls regarding contraband of war," and enquired whether he might communicate with him on such matters. I replied that, in my opinion, Mr. Goffe would be justified in giving such assurances to the rebel leader as his *de facto* government of the city enabled him for the moment to exact if the security or legitimate interests of British subjects might be imperilled by failure to notice the communication.

Imperial decrees, two of which are enclosed, have succeeded one another with bewildering rapidity, but they betray a weakness and nervousness which are not calculated to inspire confidence in the Government. Although Yuan Shih-kai has been appointed Viceroy of Hukwang, and the naval and military forces in the region of the Yang-tsze have been placed temporarily under his control, it is evident that the ruling Manchu clique is fearful of giving him the free hand which alone would enable him to deal with the situation promptly.

I have the honour to transmit to you a translation of Yuan Shih-kai's memorial to the Throne, in which he pleads for time to recover his health before taking up his new appointment.

I have, &c.

J. N. JORDAN.

P.S. *October* 25.—I have to-day received the accompanying despatch with its enclosure from the acting consul-general at Hankow. I am not forwarding the press accounts enclosed by Mr. Goffe, but the notification issued by Li Yuan Lung, who styles himself the Commander-in-chief of the Army of Hupei of the Military Government of the Republic of China, contains an interesting *exposé* of the aims and policy of the rebels.

J. N. J

Enclosure 1 in No. 47.

Imperial Decree of October 19, 1911.

(Translation.)

DURING the last two months disturbances have broken out successively in the two provinces of Szechuan and Hupei, which have been secretly planned by the revolutionaries with the object of disturbing the peace of the country. The Throne has hitherto conducted the Government in a lenient spirit, and favourable treatment has been dealt out in equal measure to all its subjects. There is no instance of anyone having been exceptionally harshly treated. Without any reason rebels have at this time incited a revolution, seized a city and offered resistance. They have devastated districts, thus causing unexpected misery and distress to innocent and law-abiding people. The ringleaders are guilty and wicked in the extreme, and cannot be exonerated from punishment by the law. But considering that some soldiers and people have been forced to join the rebels, and that their case is somewhat excusable, we cannot refrain from showing some leniency. We hereby order that those who have been compelled to join the rebels, if they personally surrender at an early date, will be allowed to repent without being punished for their past errors, no matter whether they are soldiers or common people. Any person who shall achieve merit by killing the rebels or by arresting them for presentation to the authorities shall receive a special reward. If the roll of names of the revolutionaries is found it shall be destroyed at once, for people must not be in any way involved in trouble. The regions of the two provinces of Szechuan and Hupei have undoubtedly suffered an intolerable calamity through the sudden disturbance of peace, and even in places where the rebels have not appeared there are inevitable alarms causing the people the hardship of fleeing and emigrating.

We hereby order Yin Ch'ang, Yuan Shih-kai, Ts'en Ch'un-hsuan, and Tuan Fang to comply with our wishes by proclaiming along their route the intention of pacifying the people. They should also issue earnest proclamations to the soldiers and people, exhorting them not to be led away by seditious statements, and not to act in a panic through being deceived by mere rumours.

After this decree has been issued you, soldiers and people, should understand that advantage and disadvantage lies in the distinguishing or otherwise of the right from the wrong. You should all observe your own duties in order to meet our wish in suppressing the rebellion and showing kindness to the people.

[335]   D

Enclosure 2 in No. 47.

Extract from "Gazette" of October 21, 1911.

(Translation.)

MEMORIAL by the Ministry of Finance recommending that, in view of the urgency of providing Military Supplies, all other Treasury Payments should be temporarily discontinued.

OWING to a revolution among the troops having suddenly broken out in Hupei, large issues of funds have been made in connection with the movement of troops and the issue of pay for them. On the 11th October our Ministry was instructed by Imperial decree to prepare funds immediately for the pay of the troops. We accordingly on two occasions made a grant in cash of 1,000,000 taels, which was handed over for the use of the Ministry of War. Subsequently, when large bodies of troops started out (for the south) large supplies of funds were required. The Treasury is therefore empty, and our position is really very difficult. Now Hupei province is a rich district for revenue purposes, and has large sums to provide for foreign loans and the indemnity, as well as having to supply funds to Peking and contributions to other provinces. A state of war having arisen, it is impossible for the province to forward any money. In Szechuan, moreover, the agitation has not yet subsided, and remittances from that quarter cannot arrive at due date. In addition to this the eastern and southern provinces have important, defensive preparations to make, and they are equally short of supplies. There is not much money in the Treasury, and the source of supply is easily dried up. We have considered ways and means, and are worried to an extraordinary degree. At the present as regards the use of funds military supplies naturally are the first consideration, and, further, the payment of foreign loans, involving as they do international relations, must not in any way be delayed. Apart from these, although much money is required for other purposes, yet when compared with the former there can be no question but that discrimination must be shown and payment delayed.

We have considered the matter in concert, and we are of opinion that all our resources should be devoted to providing military supplies and to the payment of foreign loans. The Treasury will, as the only course to adopt temporarily, defer payment of any other sums, and will devote special attention to pressing needs. We propose also to telegraph to all Viceroys and governors that they consider the question of temporarily suspending the carrying out of any matters which are not urgent so as to retain some little surplus to provide against unforeseen dangers. In the event of the Imperial sanction being received our Ministry will take the necessary action.

On the 18th October the Imperial decree was received, "Let it be as proposed."

Enclosure 3 in No. 47.

Memorial from Yuan Shih-kai to the Throne, published in the "Gazette" of Saturday, October 21, 1911.

(Translation.)

YOUR memorialist begs the sacred glance on his memorial thanking the Throne for the favour shown to him, and reporting in detail the bad state of his health, which renders it temporarily necessary to hasten on with his cure. Your memorialist has respectfully perused a copy of the decree of the 21st October, which was sent him by the Cabinet, and which ran as follows :—

"Yuan Shih-kai is hereby appointed Viceroy of Hukuang, and will also superintend the measures for suppression of the rebels. He should proceed at once to his post, and he need not come to Peking for audience."

He has also perused the decree of the same day, namely :—

"Yuan Shih-kai having been appointed Viceroy of Hukuang, the troops of these provinces as well as the reinforcements sent from other provinces are all placed under the control of and at the disposal of the said Viceroy."

I am much ashamed at being the recipient of the Imperial commands, and, in view of the favour shown for generations, I feel remorse that I have done nothing to requite it. After the accession of your Imperial Majesty to the Throne, I again received very great favours, in which affection and honours were equally predominant. In the interval I have not been serving the Throne, owing to my being away at my native place on account of the state of my health. On receipt of the Imperial commands I was filled with the deepest gratitude. At this time of crisis in the Empire I ought to comply with the Imperial decree and proceed immediately to deal with the situation. But my old trouble with my foot is not yet thoroughly set right, and last winter my left arm became affected, and frequently caused me great pain. A habitual complaint of some years can hardly be expected to be cured immediately. Although my breathing and my body showed weakness yet my energy remained unimpaired. Recently, however, it suddenly becoming cold in the beginning of autumn, asthma and fever, which I used to suffer from, again attacked me. In addition to this I suffer from giddiness and nervousness, and when reflecting on a matter my mind wanders. Although these symptoms cannot be cured in a day they are merely external complaints, which are much easier to cure than my old illness. At this time of crisis in military affairs I do not venture to make a hasty application for leave. But my loss of energy makes it really difficult for me to struggle along. I have called in a doctor to effect a cure as quickly as possible, and at the same time I am making all necessary arrangements. As soon as I am somewhat able to struggle along I will at once proceed on the way, thus taking the opportunity to requite in an infinitesimal degree the great kindness shown to me. This memorial containing my gratitude for the Imperial favour and reporting in detail the bad state of my health is hereby presented for the Imperial glance and commands.

This memorial has been sealed with the seal of the Prefect of Chang Te-fu.

On the 18th October a rescript in the vermilion pencil was received :—

"The above has been noted. Matters at Wuchang and Hankow are very critical, and the said Viceroy in the past has always been a just and loyal officer, and zealous in performing service. Let him immediately cure himself, and in spite of his illness let him proceed, thus requiting the extraordinary confidence placed in him by the Throne."

Enclosure 4 in No. 47.

Acting Consul-General Goffe to Sir J. Jordan.

Sir,   *Hankow, October* 16, 1911.

MY telegrams will have kept you informed of the progress of the revolutionary movement here, and I enclose copies of the local papers which give full accounts of the whole affair. I enclose also translation of a despatch which I received from the revolutionary leader, notifying me of the establishment of a republic.

The revolutionaries are maintaining order in the three cities, but outside there is practically mob law. The Chinese are panic-stricken, and are fleeing in all directions; steamers are being chartered at fabulous rates for Shanghai; trade is practically at a standstill owing to lack of coolies; and the foreign firms are finding the greatest difficulty in inducing their native staffs to remain. The financial situation, which was at first most acute, has to some extent been relieved by the foreign banks obtaining large supplies of silver dollars from Shanghai, the first shipment of which has been received. Hupeh Government notes and Tach'ing bank notes are now being taken, but no silver will be given in exchange; the revolutionary commander has also sent over from Wuchang a supply of 10-cash pieces.

The revolutionaries are recruiting fast, but they have, I learn on good authority, only 5,000 trained soldiers; these latter are, I am informed, well equipped, and have good officers. The loyal troops, to the number of some 400, together with some soldiers recently arrived from Changsha, are entrenched at Kilometre 10, where they are to some extent supported by Admiral Sah's gun-boats. General Chang Piao is with these men. Loyal troops from Honan are said to have arrived in considerable numbers this afternoon, and as the revolutionaries are known to have moved out from Hankow, fighting may be expected there in the near future.

We have had considerable trouble with the revolutionaries coming armed into the concession, but this matter is in process of being arranged indirectly with the revolutionary leader, who, in the five or six despatches he has sent me, discoursed at some length on the subject of neutrality. Yesterday one man was shot on the bund by the revolutionaries close to the custom-house, and not strictly in the concession; and to-day the revolutionary leader has addressed me a despatch expressing his regret for this occurrence.

The Viceroy and his staff occupy a gun-boat anchored near Kilometre 10, and Admiral Sah complained that he is in this way deprived of the services of one of his ships. The revolutionaries are in possession of the telegraph office, and most of the operators have fled ; the foreign superintendent has, however, arranged for the transmission of all consular messages, but he asks that they should be as brief as possible. Telegraphic communication with Shanghai is interrupted, but the men-of-war can get Tsingtau and Hong Kong by wireless.

No foreigners have been molested, and nearly all the missionaries have come into the concession. A few insist on remaining at their posts to look after their property and reassure the Chinese.

The following men-of-war are in port :—

Great Britain.--His Majesty's ships " Thistle," " Britomart," " Woodlark," " Woodcock," " Nightingale."

United States.—" Helena," " Elcano," " Villalobos."

France.—" Décidée."

Germany.—" Tiger," " Vaterland."

Japan.—" Tsushima," " Sumida."

The " Alacrity " and " Leipzig " are expected to-morrow.

I have, &c.

H. GOFFE.

Enclosure 5 in No. 47.

Revolutionary Commander to Acting Consul-General Goffe.

(Translation.)

NOTIFICATION by Li Yuan Lung, Commander-in-chief of the Army of Hupei of the Military Government of the Republic of China.

ON the defeat of the republican forces at Canton the Military Government was moved to the west, and was subsequently successfully established in Szechuan. In view of the fact that the republican party, although it possessed both adherents and power had no territorial jurisdiction, foreign Governments have hitherto refused to recognise it. Now that the territory within the province of Szechuan has been occupied, however, the three necessary constituents of a nation have been secured. The Military Government is inspired with an ardent desire to recover the land of our ancestors and with hatred of the wrong doing of the Manchu oppressors.

I have now been instructed to raise forces at Wuchang, and it has been unanimously decided to exterminate the enemy in the hope of preserving international peace, of furthering the happiness of the human race, and of strengthening the good relations existing between us and friendly Powers.

The line of action to be pursued by the Military Government is now communicated to you in order that any misunderstanding may be avoided—

1. All treaties contracted by foreign Powers with the Imperial Government will continue to be observed.

2. All property of the subjects of foreign Powers situated within territory occupied by the Military Government will be recognised and protected.

3. All privileges already granted to foreign Powers will also be recognised and protected.

4. All payments due from the various provinces on account of indemnities or loans will be made in full at the proper dates as hitherto.

5. All munitions of war supplied by any foreign Power for the assistance of the Imperial Government will be confiscated.

6. Any foreign Power assisting the Imperial Government to resist the Military Government will be regarded as an enemy.

7. No treaties whatsoever made subsequent to the date of this notification between foreign Powers and the Imperial Government will be recognised by the Military Government.

The above seven articles are now communicated to you for your information, in order that you may be assured that the troops are acting in the public interests, and that there is no anti-foreign feeling whatever in the movement.

I therefore have the honour to request that you will communicate the contents of this notification to your Government for their information.

(Seal of the Commander-in-chief of the Army of Hupei of the Military Government of the Republic of China.)

21st day of 8th moon of 4609th year of Huang Ti (October 12, 1911).

*

No. 48.

Admiralty to Foreign Office.—(Received November 10.)

Sir, *Admiralty, November 10, 1911.*

I AM commanded by my Lords Commissioners of the Admiralty to forward herewith, for the information of the Secretary of State for Foreign Affairs, a copy of a telegram which has been sent to the senior naval officer, Hong Kong, and repeated to the commander-in-chief, China, respecting the holding of troops in readiness at Hong Kong for dispatch to Shanghai in case of necessity.

I am, &c.
W. GRAHAM GREENE.

Enclosure in No. 48.

Admiralty to Senior Naval Officer, Hong Kong.

(Telegraphic.) *Admiralty, November 9, 1911.*

THE military authorities are holding the following troops ready at Hong Kong to be sent to Shanghai immediately if they are required :—

Engineers..	40
Artillery ..	80
British infantry	350
Native infantry	150

with four Maxims and the same number of mountain guns.

Concert with military authorities to make arrangements to dispatch them at short notice if required and to provide the transport necessary.

No. 49.

Sir J. Jordan to Sir Edward Grey.—(Received November 10.)

(Telegraphic.) *Peking, November 10, 1911.*

PROTECTION of Shanghai settlements.

Your telegram of 7th November.

I concur in views expressed in following telegram from His Majesty's consul-general at Shanghai, whom I have consulted :—

" Deliberate interference with the settlements by the revolutionary leaders is, in my opinion, unlikely.

" The landing of foreign forces to occupy the settlements would cause greater irritation to Chinese than the presence of one or more men-of-war, which would have a considerable overawing effect.

" I do not regard the former step as necessary, at any rate immediately, but it is most desirable to send a ship, which should be as large as possible, or ships at once.

" I have repeated this telegram to Admiral Winsloe."

38

No. 50.

Sir Edward Grey to Sir J. Jordan.

(Telegraphic.)   *Foreign Office, November* 10, 1911.

MY telegram of 7th November.

Following troops are being held in readiness at Hong Kong for immediate dispatch to Shanghai if required : British infantry 350, Indian native infantry 150, artillery 80, engineers 40, with four mountain guns and four Maxims.

The commodore at Hong Kong has been instructed to arrange for transport at short notice.

Two companies of Indian native infantry are held ready at Hong Kong for dispatch to Canton if required.

No. 51.

Sir J. Jordan to Sir Edward Grey.—(Received November 12.)

(Telegraphic.)   *Peking, November* 12, 1911.

A REASSURING effect has been produced on the situation here by the prospect of the arrival early to-morrow morning of Yuan Shih-kai. In the provinces however, the Imperial authority has almost ceased to run, and a severe blow has been dealt at the Manchus by the news that the Mukden Provincial Assembly is preparing to declare for a republic. The only hope of the Manchus now lies in the ability of Yuan Shih-kai and the Senate to convince the provinces that rather than have a number of political entities deprived of any common bond of union, it is preferable to retain the Manchu dynasty as a figurehead. I understand that the delegates who have been sent from the Senate to Hankow, Shanghai, and other revolutionary centres have not met with a very cordial reception.

In Peking, I am assured by the Manchu princes and dignitaries, there will in no case be any massacre, but the assurance must be accepted with reserve in view of what has occured at Nanking, and I presume that, in the event of the necessity arising, the intervention of the diplomatic body to prevent such deplorable outrages would be justified.

No. 52.

Sir J. Jordan to Sir Edward Grey.—(Received November 13.)

(Telegraphic.)   *Peking, November* 13, 1911.

SHANGHAI–NANKING Railway.

Consul-general at Shanghai telegraphed yesterday as follows :—

"The revolutionaries now hold undisputed possession of the whole length of country through which railway runs. The Imperialist authorities, who are under the domination of the general commanding the old style troops, are shut up in Nanking, and I venture to suggest that it would be favouring them to continue the prohibition of the use of the line by the revolutionaries for the transport of troops and munitions of war. Is it not possible to limit the prohibition, which in similar circumstances would not be observed by the Imperialists, to the terminus at Shanghai, and to permit entraining from Naziang and beyond, the avoidance of complications being sufficiently guaranteed by neutralising the ten miles adjoining the settlement? Serious friction may otherwise result if, as is possible, the prohibition is ignored by the militant section of the revolutionaries."

39

No. 53.

Sir J. Jordan to Sir Edward Grey.—(Received November 13.)

(Telegraphic.) *Peking, November 13, 1911.*
SHANGHAI-NANKING Railway.
My telegram of to-day's date.
I have to-day sent the following reply to Mr. Fraser's telegram :—

" As the revolutionaries are in undisputed possession of the country, you are authorised to agree to their using the line with the limitation suggested in your telegram under reply. It would however, I think, be advisable for the fact that he is acting under *force majeure* to be recorded in a formal protest by the general manager, and all rebel transport should continue to be treated on a purely commercial basis by him.

" I understand that, for the benefit of the bond-holders, a special account has been opened at the Hong Kong and Shanghai bank into which the earnings of the railway are being paid."

No. 54.

Consul Tours to Sir Edward Grey.—(Received November 14.)

(Telegraphic.) *Swatow, November 14, 1911.*
SWATOW and Chaochow were taken without resistance by revolutionaries from Canton on the 10th and 11th November respectively.
A United States citizen, of Chinese extraction, is at the head of the local revolutionary organisation, and as representative of the Republican Government of China, has announced his assumption of the government of Swatow.

No. 55.

Sir Edward Grey to Sir J. Jordan.

(Telegraphic.) *Foreign Office, November 15, 1911.*
YOUR telegram of 13th November: Shanghai-Nanking Railway.
I approve your instructions to consul-general.

No. 56.

India Office to Foreign Office.—(Received November 15.)

THE Under-Secretary of State for India presents his compliments to the Under-Secretary of State for Foreign Affairs, and forwards herewith, for the information of the Secretary of State, copies of telegrams from the Viceroy, dated the 3rd and 14th November, 1911, relative to the revolution in Yünnan.

India Office, November 15, 1911.

Enclosure 1 in No. 56.

Government of India to Secretary of State for India.

(Telegraphic.) *November 3, 1911.*
CHINESE revolution.
We repeat for information following telegram, dated the 2nd instant, from Burmah Government :—

"Capture of Tengyueh by rebels is reported by consul-general, Yünnan-fu. Chinese traders of Bhamo confirm report. When he left Tengyueh, Mr. Smith, consul at Tengyueh, who has arrived at Maymyo, had no information of revolution and anticipated no disturbance. He is returning at once viâ Bhamo to Tengyueh."

[335] D 4

Enclosure 2 in No. 56.

Government of India to Secretary of State for India.

(Telegraphic.)   *November* 14, 1911.
REVOLUTION in Yünnan.
We have received from Burmah Government the two following telegrams, dated
13th instant:—

1. "We have received two telegrams sent viâ Hanoi from consul-general
Yünnan-fu, dated 7th instant. Telegrams sent from Bhamo on 30th ultimo and 3rd
instant do not appear to have reached him. Consul-general states in his first telegram
that news has reached Provisional Government that Puerh has given in allegiance to
Government, and he says that revolutionaries are masters of practically the whole of
Yünnan. Following are the terms of his second telegram :—

"'Rumour is current here that Tengyueh Consulate has been looted and destroyed,
and that an advance on Tengyueh is being made by British troops. Please say if this
is true. Owing to highly insecure position of foreigners here, it is important to know.
The new Government is anxious for the internment of refugees escaping from Yünnan
into Burmah, whether military or others.'

"We are informing consul-general that no advance is being made on Tengyueh
by British troops ; that consul is now returning to Tengyueh from Bhamo ; that a
state of anarchy prevails at the former place ; and that all foreigners have come to
Burmah."

2. "Bhamo has received news that revolutionaries captured Lon Lin and Yon
Chuan on the 30th ultimo and the 3rd instant. It is stated by Howell, commissioner
of customs at Tengyueh, who arrived on 11th November at Bhamo and intends to go
back at once to Tengyueh, that the latter place is in a state of anarchy, and that
refugees are coming in to Bhamo by hundreds. Howell reports that all the banks
in Tengyueh are closed, and that the funds of the revolutionaries have come to an
end. Only paper money, which no one will accept, is being issued for pay.
Howell anticipates that further disturbances will soon take place, the man in
authority having no hold on the people."

No. 57.

Sir J. Jordan to Sir Edward Grey.—(Received November 15.)

(Telegraphic.)   *Peking, November* 15, 1911.
MY telegram of 12th November.
The diplomatic body are to-morrow making strong representations to Chinese
Government in regard to barbarities committed by the Imperial troops, and the
consuls at Shanghai and Hankow are being instructed to address similar protest
against conduct of rebel forces.
Yuan Shih-kai has confirmed Manchu princes' assurances that there will be no
massacre in Peking.

No. 58.

Sir Edward Grey to Sir J. Jordan.

(Telegraphic.)   *Foreign Office, November* 15, 1911.
YOUR telegram of 12th November.
We have conceived very friendly feelings and respect for Yuan Shih-kai. We
should wish to see a Government sufficiently strong to deal impartially with foreign
countries and to maintain internal order and favourable conditions for the progress
of trade established in China as a consequence of the revolution. Such a Government
would receive all the diplomatic support which we could give it.

No. 59.

Sir J. Jordan to Sir Edward Grey.—(Received November 17.)

Sir,   *Peking, October 28, 1911.*
WITH reference to my telegram of the 26th instant, I have the honour
to transmit to you herewith copy of a decree by the Prince Regent cashiering
Shêng Hsüan-huai, and ordering that he shall never again be employed in the
public service. The memorial from the Senate which elicited this decree is also
enclosed, and its perusal leaves little doubt about the attitude of its authors
towards the railway policy of the Government. The Senate claims that, as a matter of
constitutional procedure, the matter should have been submitted to it, and doubtless it
should, but the result would have been a continuance of the existing chaos.
    The decree is signed by Prince Ch'ing, Na T'ung, and Hsü Shih-ch'ang, who, while
condemning their colleague to perpetual exclusion from the public service, assign to
themselves the nominal penalty of having their action examined by the boards
concerned. For the last year or so Shêng-kung-pao has stood out head and shoulders
above all the members of the effete Government of Peking as the champion of the
railway policy, which was deliberately adopted as an essential condition of national
existence, and he has met the storm of provincial opposition with a courage and
resolution which would have done honour to a man of his age and frail health in any
country.
    Shêng does not seem to have had the least conception that the impeachment,
which formed the subject of a noisy and ill-informed debate in the Senate, would result
in his downfall, but he received the blow with Oriental composure, and spent the night
in arranging his papers preparatory to departure. On the next day, however, things
took a more serious turn, and a printed resolution was circulated in the Senate asking that
the Throne should be moved to order the immediate execution of the aged Minister. This
was brought to my notice by the American chargé d'affaires, who said that Shêng looked to
the Ministers of the four Powers for protection in his hour of need, and suggested that,
as dean, I should at once convene a meeting to consider the question. This I lost no
time in doing, with the result that we unanimously decided to see Prince Ch'ing and
inform him that we viewed the incident with grave concern, and could not permit the
Government to do any harm to Shêng.
    The Prince, on reading over the resolution, remarked that a memorial making a
similar demand had been presented to the Throne that morning by a censor, but that
the Prince Regent thought that Shêng had been sufficiently punished already, and
refused to consider it. He assured us that no further punishment would be inflicted
upon Shêng, and undertook to send a message to the President of the Senate to have
the resolution withdrawn.
    The Prince showed an anxiety during the course of the conversation to impress upon
us that the Government's policy in the railway question remained unaltered, but he
must have seen that the statement taxed our credulity.
    We told his Highness that the readiness with which the Government had
accepted the recommendation of the Senate for the degradation of Shêng had made
us apprehensive lest they might endorse the suggestion for his execution, and we
expressed our feelings of relief at learning that there was no intention of perpetrating
such a barbarity.
    Shêng decided to proceed at once to Shanghai viâ Tsingtau, and as he was
apprehensive of an attack by revolutionaries, he was furnished with a guard of two
soldiers from each of the four legations, and accompanied to Tien-tsin by Dr. Tenney
and Mr. Barton, the Chinese Secretaries of the American and British Legations
respectively.

                                                        I have, &c.
                                                            J. N. JORDAN.

Enclosure 1 in No. 59.

Decree dated October 26, 1911.

(Translation.)

ON the 26th October the Cabinet received the following decree by the Prince Regent:—

The Senate has memorialised alleging illegal usurpation of authority on the part of a Minister of State, which has caused an outbreak of rebellion, and showing cause for the infliction of a penalty for his offence.

This memorial states that the origin of the present revolution is to be ascribed to the Minister of Communications, Shêng Hsüan-huai, who deceived the Throne and stirred up hatred by his illegal actions. The said Minister, being in control of the system of communications, did not scruple to obstinately act on his own authority, and, failing to distinguish between matters great and small, no heed was paid by him to consulting the Senate or referring to the Cabinet for decision in cases where this should have been done. No sooner had the Cabinet announced a policy than he would at once proceed to spoil it, memorialising in his own name to the deception of the Throne and people alike, and besmirching the schemes of the Government, thus gradually bringing about calamities.

The present trouble in Szechuan is principally due to the Ministry's decision only to allow the funds actually expended on work and materials to rank for repayment in guaranteed Government bonds, and not to repay in accordance with the actual capital subscribed, as was done in the case of the mercantile shares of the Hupei Railway, and, further, the decision to treat the millions lost through Shih Tien-chang's fault as non-existent, caused great hatred and grief—governors and governed were estranged, and the outbreak in Szechuan was the result, men's minds were disturbed, and revolutionaries and mutinous soldiery seized the opportunity to create disturbance. Verily this Minister is a principal enemy of the State.

We find that the nationalisation of the railways was in its inception a policy based on our compassion for our merchants and people, but Shêng Hsüan-huai failed to carry out our virtuous intention, and dealt ill in many respects. Shêng Hsüan-huai has enjoyed many favours from the Throne, and his conduct in presuming to illegally act on his own authority to the detriment of the public interest displays an utter lack of sense of gratitude and of duty.

Let the Minister of Communications, Shêng Hsüan-huai, be forthwith cashiered never to be re-employed. The Premier, Prince Ch'ing, and the associate Premiers, the Grand Secretaries Na T'ung and Hsü Shih-ch'ang, in that they joined with Shêng Hsüan-huai in adding their names to misleading memorials also did wrong, let them be handed over to the boards concerned for the determination of a penalty.

In future these Ministers should see to it that in employing men and conducting the affairs of State they avoid stirring up hatred, so that they may loyally assist us in safeguarding the public weal and render help in this time of crisis.

(Signed by Prince Ch'ing, Na T'ung, and Hsü Shih-ch'ang.)

Enclosure 2 in No. 59.

Memorial by the Senate impeaching a certain Minister for violating the Law, usurping Power and having been instrumental in bringing about Revolution.

(Translation.)

YOUR memorialists humbly present their respectful memorial for the Imperial inspection in which they impeach a certain Minister for breaking the law, risking the welfare of the State and harassing the people. It is requested that an Imperial decree may be issued meting out severe punishment so that we may cut at the root of the trouble. In our opinion it is most essential for the administration of the Empire to pacify the minds of the people, and to effect this it is most essential to remove the author of the trouble.

At this critical period of the State's existence the one person who is abhorred on all sides as being the author of the trouble is indeed the Minister of Posts and Communications, Shêng Hsüan-huai. He kept special power in his own hands and recklessly followed his own inclinations deceiving his superiors and oppressing the people. He has brought misfortune on the State and has indeed merited punishment.

We have received the clear decree instructing your memorialists to display their loyalty, and we hope that the Throne will make a fresh start with the masses by studying their likes and dislikes. We have set forth below seriatim the offences of this Minister. The cause of the present trouble can be set down to the Government policy of State-owned railways which was adopted by the Throne in order to show sympathy for the people's hardships. Because, however, the Throne followed the proposals of the Ministry of Posts and Communications great indignation filled the whole Empire, a result quite different to what was expected. All this is entirely due to the Minister of Posts and Communications, who has deceived the Throne, broken the law, and heaped odium on himself. This Minister's principal object has been to employ the policy of State-owned railways for the completion of the preliminary agreement for the Szechuan, Canton, and Hankow railways which had formerly been definitely agreed upon by the late Grand Secretary Chang Chih-tung as a matter of international relations. He does not appear to know that the whole Empire quite appreciates the fact that questions affecting foreign relations present difficulties. The Throne being unable to allow relations with four countries to be impaired on account of one affair had no option but to conclude the matter. What therefore was there against making a clear statement to the people and so dispelling all abuse. But recklessly adopting a scheme under the name of State-owned railways this Minister alarmed the whole Empire causing the present disturbance. Let this Minister be asked what kind of funds he has in hand, what uniform scheme he has decided on as regards main lines which will suffice for the taking over of the various lines operated by merchants throughout the Empire. The lines taken over are only four in all, how then can it be said to be a fixed policy, and, seeing that merchants and people have capital in these railways which amounts to co-operation between officials and merchants, how can they be said to be State-owned?

The people naturally are suspicious of the actions of Shêng Hsüan-huai in this matter. Moreover, if his policy is adopted the decree of the late Emperor Kuang Hsü permitting the merchants to construct the line is cancelled. Further the matter ought to have been submitted to the Senate in accordance with their regulations, and should also have been submitted to the Cabinet. But Shêng entirely ignored the Senate and the Cabinet. He has no respect for constitutional procedure. We cannot understand why the Prime Minister and the associate Prime Ministers lightly attached their names to the decrees on the subject which have called forth so much adverse criticism. Their action has involved the Throne in odium. Shêng has also shown differential treatment towards the provinces of Szechuan, Hunan, and Canton. The trouble in Szechuan is mainly due to the Ministry of Communications only offering to pay for materials already expended, and to their refusal to recognise the several million taels lost by Shih Tien-chang. This has caused the outbreak, and the revolutionaries have seized the opportunity to capture Wuchang and Hanyang. The author of this great calamity is Shêng Hsüan-huai. He prohibited the dispatch of telegrams from Szechuan, and in this way prevented free communication between Sovereign and subject. He has indeed usurped authority to an unparalleled extent in the history of the country.

No one can understand the reason for his borrowing 10,000,000 dollars from Japan. Further he borrowed from the Japanese funds for the Hanyang Arsenal and the P'ing Hsiang mines. We do not know what connection this 10,000,000-dollar loan has with the former loans. The security for this last loan was to be the Peking-Hankow Railway which is equivalent to selling the country. This Shêng is of a crafty nature, and is always prevaricating with the people by saying that he is acting under Imperial instructions.

To sum up, from the closing of last session the situation has been fraught with difficulties owing to the maladministration of the officials both high and low. Since Shêng took charge of the Ministry of Posts and Communications he has ignored constitutional procedure, and injured the machinery for registering the popular opinion, i.e., the Senate.

We realise that he is not the only one who has brought misfortune on the country, but he is the chief author of the trouble. If he is put away, popular resentment will be somewhat appeased, and the difficulties of the State lessened. If any leniency is shown him, and he is kept in office, it will be difficult to foresee what may happen. We are very distressed and melancholy over the state of affairs, and in accordance with article 21 of the original regulations of the Senate we present this memorial of impeachment begging that an Imperial decree may be issued meting out severe punishment to him.

No. 60.

Sir J. Jordan to Sir Edward Grey.—(Received November 17.)

Sir, *Peking, October* 30, 1911.
WITH reference to my telegram of the 14th instant, I have the honour to transmit to you herewith a translation of the Imperial decree of the 27th instant, appointing Yuan Shih-kai Imperial Commissioner to deal with the revolutionary crisis. By separate edicts of the same date the Minister for War, Yin Ch'ang, is recalled to Peking, and the command of the first army is given to General Feng Kuo-chang, while that of the second army is conferred upon General Tuan Chi-jui, both of whom were closely associated with Yuan in former years.

Nothing definite is known here of Yuan's movements, but the general impression is that he will now start for Hankow in a few days. His mission, though bearing a military character, is understood to be rather one of conciliation, and it is possible that his prestige may enable him to arrange some compromise which will save the Throne and satisfy the demands of the insurgents. The movement has assumed such widespread dimensions that any attempt to repress it by force will probably not appeal to a man of Yuan's practical common sense as affording much prospect of success.

No man could be better fitted to play the rôle of mediator between the Chinese people, of whom he is the most trusted living representative, and the Manchu dynasty, whom he and his family have served for several generations.

I have, &c.
J. N. JORDAN.

Enclosure in No. 60.

Decree of October 27, 1911.
(Translation.)
THE Viceroy of Hukwang, Yuan Shih-kai, is hereby appointed Imperial High Commissioner. All the auxiliary land and sea forces, the Yang-tsze flotilla, as well as the troops actually dispatched are placed under his control and at his disposal.

The Viceroys and governors of neighbouring provinces should take part in concert with him in elaborating the necessary measures. As regards questions which concern the re-establishment of order and tranquillity in the said provinces, Yuan Shih-kai should, according to circumstances, take action as quickly as possible.

As military affairs may undergo many changes in a short space of time, the General Staff and the Ministry of War shall cease to exercise control at such a great distance over the campaign in Hupei. This is in order to place the responsibility on one person, in the hope that speedy success may be attained.

No. 61.

Sir J. Jordan to Sir Edward Grey.—(Received November 17.)

Sir, *Peking, October* 30, 1911.
I HAVE the honour to transmit to you herewith, with reference to my despatch of the 23rd instant, copy of a despatch from the acting British consul-general at Hankow, giving an account of the revolutionary movement up to the 20th of this month, upon which it is unnecessary for me to enlarge.

The evacuation by the Imperial forces of their position at Kilometre 10 and the withdrawal of Admiral Sah with his flotilla down the river put heart into the revolutionaries, and no doubt contributed to the subsequent defection of other Yang-tsze ports.

After the 20th, a lull seems to have ensued in the hostilities. The rebels maintained themselves at Kilometre 10, while the Imperialists occupied Niekow and the bridges over Seven Mile Creek. In the three cities order and quiet prevailed, and the rebels secured a number of recruits. On the 26th there were some signs of an advance from the Imperialist side, and on the following day they re-captured Kilometre 10, together with guns and camp equipment abandoned by the defenders. Admiral Sah reappeared on the scene simultaneously, and announced his intention of bombarding Wuchang and Hanyang the following afternoon. This threat was not carried out, but, as reported in my telegram of the 29th October, more heavy fighting took place on the 28th, close to the concessions, with the result that the majority of the rebels were driven across the river to Wuchang unmolested by the Chinese flotilla, whose fire was apparently held in check by batteries posted on the southern bank.

At Changsha a rising was planned for the 18th, but miscarried owing to the precautions taken by the authorities, who deprived the regular troops of their ammunition, believing them to be in sympathy with the revolution. On the 25th, however, the troops forcibly recovered their ammunition, joined hands with the revolutionaries, and got control of the city without firing a shot. The gendarmerie, who had been regarded as loyal, joined the movement. This is the only port where the rebels have as yet interfered with the working of the foreign customs. They gave the commissioner of customs to understand that he could continue to function under their orders, but, as mentioned in my telegram of the 26th October, they have been warned that this procedure may bring them into collision with foreign Powers, and advised to allow the customs duties to be placed in deposit with the inspector-general of customs or the consular body, pending the issue of the present struggle. Whether this warning has had any effect is unknown to me, as I can get no replies to telegrams to Changsha.

On the 23rd Kiukiang went over ; the taotai's yamên was partly destroyed by fire, though he himself escaped, and, as elsewhere, the revolutionaries maintained good order and refrained from molesting the concessions.

At Nanking everything remained quiet until the 28th, when His Majesty's consul reported that the situation was becoming more uncertain. The authorities believed that trouble was imminent ; the Manchus were desperate and might precipitate an outbreak ; while the new troops, fearful of being massacred by the old ones, were clamouring for ammunition, which the Viceroy refused, and disobeyed his orders to move outside the city. Two regiments were subsequently induced to go, but a reported threat of the Tartar general to bombard the city and kill all Chinese had greatly increased the panic, and numbers were fleeing.

At Canton, on the 25th October, a bomb was thrown at the newly-arrived Tartar general. He was killed by the explosion, and there were many others killed and injured. His Majesty's consul-general reported that the bulk of the population, both in the city and province, were anti-dynastic, but were awaiting developments in the north.

On the same afternoon a series of resolutions, to which the Viceroy is said to have adhered, were passed by a meeting of merchants and gentry in Canton. The principal one was that, in view of the province's financial straits, Canton should not assist other provinces with money, arms, or troops.

Hsian Fu, in Shensi, is admitted by the Imperial Government to be in the hands of rebels. At Tai Yuan-fu the troops have mutinied, and are moving down the railway to its junction with the Peking–Hankow line, with the evident intention of cutting the communications of the main Imperialist forces under General Yin Chang, unless forestalled by troops who have been ordered hastily from Paoting-fu.

At Lanchow, on the Imperial railways of North China, some 5,000 troops of the XXth Division, who were under orders to proceed to Hupei, refused to entrain, and have since demanded of the Government at Peking certain conditions as the price of their advance to the front. The upshot of this act of mutiny is not yet known.

Ichang passed peacefully into the hands of the revolutionaries about the 21st October and I have to-day received a telegram from His Majesty's consul at Chungking, stating that a rising is expected to take place there any day, and that Chengtu is believed to be surrounded.

Shanghai has remained politically undisturbed, but I understand from Mr. Fraser that the revolutionaries are able to take possession at any moment that may suit them, and that the authorities admit their inability to offer any resistance.

Numerous applications have been made to the commander-in-chief by consular officers at the various Yang-tsze ports for the dispatch of a gun-boat. Admiral Winsloe found himself able to detach a vessel to proceed to Ichang and thence to Changsha, but pointed out on the 23rd October that until the trouble at Hankow was over it was impracticable to send ships to other ports. He added that in the case of cities going over to the rebels there was no fighting or danger to foreigners, whereas at Hankow, until the restoration of order in the native city, there might be some danger if the Imperial troops attacked and forced the revolutionaries back.

I have, &c.

J. N. JORDAN.

Enclosure in No. 61.

Acting Consul-General Goffe to Sir J. Jordan.

Sir,   *Hankow, October* 20, 1911.

IN continuation of my despatch of the 16th instant, I have the honour to report as follows respecting the progress of the revolutionary movement here :—

On the morning of the 18th instant the revolutionary troops moved out from Hankow to attack the Imperialists at Kilometre 10, but only some slight skirmishing ensued. In the afternoon the attack was renewed, and Admiral Sah's gun-boats opened fire on the rebels; neither side achieved any advantage, the net result, as far as could be seen, being one field gun abandoned by the rebels. During the night trains with troops arrived from the north, and the following morning (19th) the rebels again moved out to the attack, and succeeded in taking the railway station at Kilometre 10. By the evening the Imperialist troops were in full retreat, and are now reported to be encamped at Kilometre 17. They left everything behind them, and the rebels captured a lot of ammunition, rifles, foodstuffs, and various impedimenta. Some of the northern troops are reported to have gone over to the rebels, but this is not confirmed from any authentic source. The shooting on both sides was exceedingly poor.

The reason for the departure of Admiral Sah's fleet is not known, but one of his officers, who has been in France, told the commander of the "Décidée" that Admiral Sah was short of ammunition and was not sure of his men. The river steamers report the gun-boats anchored at various places between here and Kiukiang, the nearest being 10 miles below Hankow. It is possible that they are waiting for coal, as they were unable to obtain any here.

The rebel troops are behaving extremely well, and show the utmost respect for foreign property; they made the racecourse a base of operations yesterday, but the property has not sustained the slightest damage. This contrasts very markedly with the behaviour of the Imperial troops, who, on the evening of the 18th, entered the Asiatic Petroleum Company's premises and demanded food, and, on this being refused, shot three of the coolies. The rebel soldiers now do not even enter the concession. I authorised the council to write to General Li, pointing out to him that the concession regulations did not permit armed men to enter the concessions, and, in reply, he sent a dozen proclamations directing his men to respect our regulations.

I have authorised Mr. Langeback, the foreign superintendent of the Telegraph Administration, to establish an office in the concession, General Li having agreed to such a step. I have also given permission for the Chinese Customs staff to sleep in the concession, as Mr. Sugden feared that, without such protection as would be afforded them in this way, they would desert. I trust that my action in these matters will meet with your approval.

Trade is at a standstill and the concession almost deserted. There are frequent fires in the city, but good order is maintained and everything is perfectly quiet.

The revolutionaries wished to censor all correspondence passing through the Chinese post-office, and the postal commissioner was inclined to close the offices. He came to see me, and I advised him to remain and carry on his duties under protest. This morning he saw General Li, and it has been arranged that there shall be no interference with the post-office at all, the commissioner undertaking not to allow the Imperial authorities to establish any censorate.

The rebels have made no attempt to interfere with the custom-house. Owing to lack of ready money, Mr. Sugden is allowing respectable firms to ship under guarantee of payment of duty, and such moneys as he receives he is paying into a special account with the Hong Kong and Shanghai Banking Corporation.

General Li has addressed a despatch to the senior consul thanking the consuls for their neutrality, and he has also sent a despatch to each consul requesting that no munitions of war, foodstuffs, &c., be supplied to the enemy.

All telegraphic communication is now stopped owing to some of the posts having been set on fire during the fighting yesterday, but it is expected that the line to Peking will be in order by to-morrow.

There is considerable anxiety at Ichang owing to there being no funds to pay the railway coolies, who number some 15,000. There are, however, two gun-boats there as well as a British steamer. Telegraphic communication with Ichang has been interrupted for the last three days.

There is no telegraphic communication with Changsha, as the line passes through Wuchang ; but the steamers report all quiet, and I have no news from Mr. Giles.

The German admiral arrived last evening, and the following men-of-war are in port :—

" Alacrity," " Cadmus," " Thistle," " Woodlark," " Woodcock," " Nightingale," " Helena," " Elcano," " Villalobos," " Leipzig," " torpedo-boat S 90," " Iltis Tiger," " Tiger," " Décidée," " Tsushima," " Sumida."

I have, &c.
H. GOFFE.

P.S.—" Woodlark " leaves to-morrow for Ichang.

H. G.

No. 62.

Admiralty to Foreign Office.—(Received November 18.)

Sir,   *Admiralty, November* 17, 1911.
I AM commanded by my Lords Commissioners of the Admiralty to forward herewith, for the information of the Secretary of State for Foreign Affairs, a copy of a telegram of to-day's date received from the commander-in-chief, China, and to enquire whether the proposal that forty military should be sent from Tien-tsin to Hankow for policing duties is concurred in.

A copy of the telegram has also been sent to the War Office.
I am, &c.
W. GRAHAM GREENE.

Enclosure in No. 62.

Commander-in-chief, China, to Admiralty.

(Telegraphic.)   *November* 17, 1911.
THE men of the " Thistle " and " Cadmus," now at Hankow, should, in my opinion, be relieved, as they have been on shore for over a month, and the ships are consequently getting into bad order. The British concession will need police for some time as it adjoins the native city, and I would therefore suggest that forty soldiers should be sent to Hankow from Tien-tsin, and that they should be prepared to remain there as long as necessary.

Some ship would, of course, remain there also.

No. 63.

Sir J. Jordan to Sir Edward Grey.—(Received November 18.)

(Telegraphic.)   *Peking, November* 18, 1911.
MY telegram of 15th November.
I spoke strongly to Yuan Shih-kai to-day about the outrages which have been perpetrated at Nanking, and told him that he ought to do all in his power to have them stopped at once.

He ordered Minister for Foreign Affairs, who was present, to give immediate attention to the matter.

No. 64.

Sir Edward Grey to Sir J. Jordan.

(Telegraphic.)   *Foreign Office, November* 18, 1911.
ADMIRAL WINSLOE suggests that forty military should be sent from Tien-tsin to Hankow for policing duties, and thus relieve sailors, who have been landed over a month.

No. 65.

India Office to Foreign Office.—(Received November 20.)

THE Under-Secretary of State for India presents his compliments to the Under-Secretary of State for Foreign Affairs, and forwards herewith, for the information of the Secretary of State, copy of a telegram from the Viceroy, dated the 19th November, 1911, relative to the revolution in Yünnan.

India Office, November 20, 1911.

Enclosure in No. 65.

Government of India to Secretary of State for India.

(Telegraphic.) *November 19, 1911.*
YÜNNAN revolution. Please refer to my telegram, dated the 14th instant. Burmah Government telegraphed to following effect on the 18th instant:—

First telegram.—" We have received on the 17th instant telegram from consul-general, Yünnan-fu, dated the 14th instant, to following effect:—

" ' *Yünnan-fu, November 14.*
" ' In order to maintain order, Lu-chun troops are being sent to Tengyueh from Tali by the new Government. Complete order is maintained under new régime at Yünnan-fu, which is perfectly safe. Please say whether any news of Tengyueh missionary Ser has reached you. Telegrams should be sent, care of resident superior, Hanoi.'

" We have already repeated to address now given information which had previously been sent to consul-general by telegram."

Second telegram.—" Deputy-commissioner, Bhamo, received a telegram on the 15th instant from Consul Smith, who has returned to Tengyueh, saying that he was sending his writer's family to Burmah. Agent of Chinese Shan State of Santa, who arrived on the 15th instant at Myitkyina, states that the State has been taken possession of by young Sawbwa Hung Sheng. Captain Ma Shao An, commander of Chinese post, Kuyan, south-east of Sadon, has arrived at Myitkyina, and reports that his men have joined revolutionaries and marched to Tengyueh."

No. 66.

Consul-General O'Brien-Butler to Sir J. Jordan.—(Received at Foreign Office, November 20.)

(Telegraphic.) *Yünnan-fu, November 20, 1911.*
IN Szechuan everything is in chaos, and war has been started on the Chinese by the independent Lolos and by brigands. In the Ningyuan prefecture a French missionary has been killed, and in the same region there was an attack on the Legendre Mission on the 25th October. One Annamite was killed. Two French officers were wounded. A third had already left for Chengtu. The French consul is convinced that they are all dead.

I am afraid that the British and American missionaries in the city of Ningyuan are exposed to the gravest danger. It is also to be feared that the trouble will spread to Yünnan. Latter already assumes to be an independent republic and even intends to send troops to annex part of Szechuan. The idea of Yünnan for the Yünnanese is dominant, and there are in consequence dissensions among the leaders. The head of the Government is a Hunan man and is losing power owing to scarcity of money in the Treasury. Depreciation of paper currency probable. Brigandage increasing. The French consul and myself have strongly recommended the missionaries in outlying parts to concentrate at Yünnan-fu and all foreigners here who can to withdraw gradually to Tonquin.

No. 67.

Admiralty to Foreign Office.—(Received November 22.)

Sir,   *Admiralty, November 22, 1911.*
    I AM commanded by my Lords Commissioners of the Admiralty to transmit, for the information of the Secretary of State for Foreign Affairs, copy of a telegram, dated 22nd instant, from the Commander-in-chief, China, relative to the Chinese rebellion.
I am, &c.
W. GRAHAM GREENE.

Enclosure in No. 67.

Commander-in-chief, China, to Admiralty.

(Telegraphic.)   *Shanghai, November 22, 1911.*
    THE rebels are now attacking Nanking. There is no danger of trouble here for the present if they capture the place, but trouble is certain, and all revolutionary leaders here will disappear if the rebels are defeated by the Imperial troops, and if the latter advance to Chinkiang and Suchau. The rebels are keeping good order at Shanghai, which is quiet. At Hankow fighting is still in progress. The rebel flag has been hoisted on all the Chinese ships in the river.

No. 68.

Colonial Office to Foreign Office.—(Received November 23.)

Sir,   *Downing Street, November 22, 1911.*
    I AM directed by the Secretary of State for the Colonies to transmit to you copy of a telegram to the Commissioner of Wei-hai Wei on the subject of the revolt in China.
I am, &c.
JOHN ANDERSON.

Enclosure in No. 68.

Mr. Harcourt to the Commissioner of Wei-hai Wei.

(Telegraphic.)   *Downing Street, November 20, 1911.*
    YOU should communicate with the revolutionary authorities only so far as is strictly necessary, and should avoid any action implying formal recognition of the revolutionary Government.

No. 69.

Vice-Consul Brown to Sir Edward Grey.—(Received November 23.)

(Telegraphic.)   *Chungking, November 23, 1911*
    REVOLUTION proclaimed. All foreigners safe.

No. 70.

Sir J. Jordan to Sir Edward Grey.—(Received November 24.)

Sir, *Peking, November 6, 1911.*

WITH reference to previous despatches on the subject of the revolt in Szechuan, I have the honour to report that Tuan Fang, director-general of railways, after he arrived in Szechuan and had had an opportunity to investigate into the causes of the outbreak, addressed a telegraphic memorial to the Throne on the subject.

In this memorial Tuan Fang blames the Acting Viceroy, Chao Erh-feng, for having first sympathised with the popular movement and then suddenly proceeding to the drastic step of imprisoning the chief agitators, among whom was the president of the provincial assembly. Tuan Fang goes on to recommend that certain of the Chengtu local officials should be cashiered, and that the chief agitators should be released on the ground that they had no connection with the revolutionary movement.

In response to this memorial the Throne issued a decree on the 26th October awarding punishment to the various officials adversely reported on by Tuan Fang, and ordering the release of the chief agitators. Chao Erh-feng and Wang Jen-wen, the former Acting Viceroy, are ordered to be handed over to the Cabinet for determination of a penalty. Chao Erh-feng and Wang Jen-wen, moreover, have already experienced the Imperial displeasure at their conduct, for on the 14th October a decree was issued transferring Chao to his old post of High Commissioner for the frontier affairs of Szechuan and Yünnan, which Wang Jen-wen was ordered to vacate. The latter was at the same time deprived of his brevet rank of a vice-president of a board. Chao Erh-feng, however, continues to act as Viceroy of Szechuan pending the arrival of the new Viceroy Ts'en Ch'un-hsuan.

Ts'en Ch'un-hsuan has not yet started for his post, although in a decree dated the 28th October he was ordered to proceed to Szechuan with all speed. He has been granted permission to raise eight more battalions in addition to the two battalions from Kwangtung which were to accompany him in the first instance. 1,000,000 taels will also be provided by the Ministry of Finance for the payment of his troops.

Owing to the interruption of telegraphic communication little authentic news is reaching Peking regarding the situation in Szechuan, which has, however, been eclipsed by events in other parts of the Empire.

I have, &c.
J. N. JORDAN.

No. 71.

Admiralty to Foreign Office.—(Received November 24.)

Sir, *Admiralty, November 24, 1911.*

I AM commanded by my Lords Commissioners of the Admiralty to transmit, for the information of the Secretary of State for Foreign Affairs, copy of a telegram dated the 24th instant, from the commander-in-chief on the China Station, relative to the protection of the British concession at Hankow by British troops.

I am, &c.
W. GRAHAM GREENE.

Enclosure in No. 71.

Commander-in-chief, China, to Admiralty.

(Telegraphic.) *Shanghai, November 24, 1911.*

THE British volunteers, to the number of about sixty, have been on night duty since the 27th October. They have applied for relief, and I suggest that 100 troops should be sent to Hankow. The British are on duty every night because their concession is separated only by a narrow street from the native city. The other concessions are able to do without volunteers as they are further off the city.

51

No. 72.

Sir J. Jordan to Sir Edward Grey.—(Received November 24.)

(Telegraphic.)   *Peking, November 24, 1911.*

AT a diplomatic meeting yesterday it was agreed that present situation, which some Ministers regard as very critical, required that legation guards should be raised to full strength at which they stood in year following 1900.

No. 73.

Sir C. MacDonald to Sir Edward Grey.—(Received November 24.)

(Telegraphic.)   *Tokyo, November 24, 1911.*

AS a result of diplomatic meeting held on 23rd instant in Peking, Japanese Government propose increasing legation guard to 300 men. They have at present only 530 men in North China, including above. Should they find it necessary further to increase garrison, His Majesty's Government will at once be informed. Troops are in readiness to proceed at a moment's notice.

No. 74.

Sir Edward Grey to Sir F. Bertie.

Sir,   *Foreign Office, November 24, 1911.*

WITH reference to the telegram of the 20th instant from His Majesty's consul-general at Yünnan-fu relative to the revolutionary disturbances in Yünnan, of which a copy was sent to you on the same day, I should be glad if you would request the French Government to keep us informed of any news which they may receive from China.

When so doing you might add that the intention of His Majesty's Government is to restrict their own action to the protection of the lives and property of British subjects, and of foreign subjects who may be unprotected, and not to impair the integrity of China, which they wish to see preserved.

I am, &c.
E. GREY.

No. 75.

India Office to Foreign Office.—(Received November 25.)

THE Under-Secretary of State for India present his compliments to the Under-Secretary of State for Foreign Affairs, and forwards herewith, for the information of the Secretary of State, copy of a telegram from the Viceroy, dated the 24th November, 1911, relative to the Yünnan revolution.

India Office, November 25, 1911.

Enclosure in No. 75.

Government of India to Secretary of State for India.

(Telegraphic.)   *November 24, 1911.*

SEE our telegram, dated the 19th instant, regarding revolution in Yünnan. Following telegram, dated the 21st instant, received from Burmah Government :—

"Message from Smith at Tengyueh has reached deputy commissioner, Bhamo, to the effect that all is quiet at Tengyueh, and that, so far as Smith has heard, country round Tengyueh is also quiet. For the present Smith is not returning to Bhamo."

52

No. 76.

Sir J. Jordan to Sir Edward Grey.—(Received November 25.)

(Telegraphic.)   *Peking, November* 25, 1911.
TELEGRAM from His Majesty's consul-general at Chengtu, dated 18th November, and received to-day through Ichang, states that Tuan-fang was expected to arrive at Chengtu on 19th November. Rebel ringleaders released. Fighting continued a few miles away. Government still held out in city.

No. 77.

Sir C. MacDonald to Sir Edward Grey.—(Received November 25.)

(Telegraphic.)   *Tokyo, November* 25, 1911.
MY telegram of 24th November.·
Japanese Government are raising their total establishment in North China to 1,250 men. Reinforcements are due at Tien-tsin about the 2nd December and consist of six machine guns and 500 men.

No. 78.

Sir J. Jordan to Sir Edward Grey.—(Received November 26.)

(Telegraphic.)   *Peking, November* 26, 1911.
AFFAIRS at Hankow.
Acting consul-general at Hankow telegraphed yesterday as follows :—

" There is still severe fighting going on, but I am unable to ascertain result. The revolutionaries, for whom reinforcements left Kiukiang yesterday to the extent of 4,000 men and 10 guns, are landing below Kilometre Ten in force.
" Further representations as regards shells, which are fired from the Hanyang batteries, falling in the British and Russian concessions, are to be made by Japanese flag captain and commander of ' Cadmus,' who proceed to Wuchang to-day for that purpose."

I have to-day sent the following reply by telegraph :—

" Your telegram of yesterday.
" I impressed on Yuan Shih-kai, whom I saw to-day, the danger and anxiety to which the continuance of hostilities exposes the British community at Hankow.
" Yuan replied that the attitude of the Imperial troops was entirely defensive, and assured me, in proof of his sincerity, that if an armistice on mutually satisfactory terms could be arranged, he would gladly give orders to suspend hostilities, and he gave me liberty to convey through you an intimation to that effect.
" This might take the form of an unofficial and verbal message in the above sense from yourself to General Li Yuan-hung, and you should be at pains to explain that the only object we have in view is that the dangerous situation in which the British community has now for some six weeks been placed should not be prolonged, and that useless bloodshed be averted."

No. 79.

Sir J. Jordan to Sir Edward Grey.—(Received November 27.)

Sir,   *Peking, November* 5, 1911.
WITH reference to my despatch of the 30th ultimo, I have the honour to submit a further report on the progress of the present revolutionary movement in China.
At Hankow fighting was resumed on the 30th October among Chinese houses on the west side of the British concession. The Imperial troops, after clearing out the rebels, entered Hankow city and set fire to it. Since that date, with the exception of

53

some desultory shelling of Hanyang on the 1st November, little has been done, though Hankow city remained ablaze, and there were fires also in Hanyang. In consequence of a British ship having been fired on by the rebels near Wuchang, and also below Kiukiang, a consular officer was sent to Wuchang on a man-of-war to interview the revolutionary leader. The latter explained that all he wanted was to prevent the carriage of coal, ammunition, &c., for the use of the Imperialists by Chinese vessels ; he promised that British ships should not be fired on at Wuchang or Kiukiang, but said that they should not pass places held by the revolutionary forces between nightfall and 7 A.M. It was known on the 3rd November that communications were passing between Yuan Shih-kai and the rebel leader, but that the latter showed no alacrity to respond to the overtures that had been made to him.

The outbreak of dissensions among the Republican party the very day after its secession caused considerable anxiety at Changsha, especially in view of the presence of numerous bad characters likely to take advantage of any relaxation of authority in the event of the factions coming to blows. The arrival of a German gun-boat on the 27th October exercised a calming influence, and arrangements were made for concentrating foreigners on an island should need arise. On the 31st the situation again became critical owing to the murder of the military and deputy governors by the troops. On the 2nd November His Majesty's consul reported that the Provisional Government had requested the withdrawal of all foreign residents to the island, the outbreak of faction fighting being momentarily expected.

Mr. King reports from Kiukiang that he has it on good authority that the rebels have possession of Nanchang ; that the rebel batteries have frequently fired on shipping, including one Japanese torpedo-boat destroyer ; and that 1,000 men with six guns have arrived from Wucheng, on the Poyang Lake, to join the rebels.

Nanking still remains in the hands of the Imperialists, and on the 30th October His Majesty's consul reported an improvement in the situation owing to the withdrawal from the city of the new troops. I enclose copy of a despatch from His Majesty's consul describing the situation at his post up to the 27th October.

Wuhu was reported yesterday as quiet, but ready to secede at any moment.

As a result of the meeting of which mention was made in my despatch above referred to, the guilds, Manchus and Bannermen, at Canton agreed to combine for the maintenance of law and order. Having regard to the uncertainty of developments elsewhere in the Empire, it was resolved to declare Kwangtung a self-governing entity, disclaiming any connection with the revolutionaries. It does not appear that the Viceroy, whose position was obviously embarrassing, took up any definite attitude. The hoisting of an Independence flag on the 29th October brought about some sporadic disturbances, and there were reports of a revolutionary advance on Canton under the leadership of an ex-bandit.

On the evening of the 30th His Majesty's consul-general reported that the Imperial flags which had disappeared from shipping were all rehoisted, that the city was quiet, and would, in his opinion, remain so.

His Majesty's consul at Swatow reported by telegraph on the 30th October that a meeting of local Chinese had been held and had decided upon a scheme of independent government on the Canton model. It was also proposed to appropriate customs receipts and *li-kin* dues for revenue purposes, and I accordingly furnished Mr. Tours with the same instructions as were sent to His Majesty's consul at Changsha, where a similar situation had previously arisen (see my despatch of the 30th October).

As regards the mutinous troops at Lanchow and Tai Yuan-fu, reliable information has been difficult to obtain, and I venture to draw your attention to the remarks made in this connection by the acting military attaché in the accompanying report.

Briefly, the mutinous troops from Tai Yuan-fu, 3,000 strong, are holding the branch line near Ching-hsin-hsien, at the point where it pierces the Great Wall, while Imperialist troops are in possession of its junction with the main Peking–Hankow line at Shih-Chia-Chuang.

At Lanchow there are assembled 8,000 troops, who are not under the control of the Imperial Government nor have they definitely pronounced themselves as in sympathy with the revolutionary cause. Their aim has apparently been to extort guarantees for constitutional reform from the Throne, and they are understood to be acting with the approval, if not at the instigation of Yuan Shi-k'ai, who has been in close communication with them.

On the 30th ultimo His Majesty's consul-general at Yünnan-fu telegraphed that Tengyueh had been occupied by rebels, and two days later Mr. Smith wired from Maymyo confirming this, and adding that the development was totally unexpected, and

[335]   E 3

that he was returning to his post at Tengyueh immediately. No danger to foreigners was anticipated.

On the night of the 30th Yünnan-fu followed suit, but its capture was not effected without some fighting, The mutinous modern troops joined forces outside the east city and developed a simultaneous attack on the east and west gates, which were defended by guns mounted on the wall. The resistance was overcome, the yamên occupied, and a partially successful search for fugitive officials ensued; the defending general was killed during the engagement. Telegraphing on the 4th November Mr. O'Brien Butler announced that the city was quiet under military law, that the rebel organisation had been perfect throughout, that the consulates were guarded, and foreigners respected.

On the 4th instant a Chefoo native paper published an open appeal from Li Yuan Hung to the people of Shantung calling upon them to help Hupeh by the occupation of strategic points for an advance on the capital. Chefoo has hitherto remained remained passive, but some excitement was caused by the news of revolutionary successes in Shanghai. If Shantung goes, the only loyal province left, except Manchuria, will be Honan, which is occupied by the Imperialist forces.

Events in Shanghai, and the special situation which has arisen in Tien-tsin, will form the subject of separate despatches.

I have, &c.

J. N. JORDAN.

Enclosure 1 in No. 79.

Consul Wilkinson to Sir J. Jordan.

Sir, *Nanking, October 27, 1911.*

I HAVE the honour to report that it is estimated that since the news of the Hankow outbreak was received in Nanking some 40,000 people, mostly students, women, and children, have left the port; the first to flee or to send their families away being some of the highly placed officials of Nanking. The Viceroy, the financial treasurer, the commissioner for foreign affairs, and the customs taotai are almost the only high officials whose families still remain here.

The financial stringency which prevailed in Nanking has, on the other hand, been somewhat relieved by the issue, partly in payment of the troops and partly through the banks, of 500,000 of the Imperial dollars coined at the local mint. Many of the banks have been able, in consequence, to reopen and cash their notes, which, through lack of silver, they were unable for a time to do, but they still refuse to pay depositors on the ground that, in the present condition of affairs, they are unable to realise their assets. They promise, however, to pay everyone as soon as the situation becomes normal again. As the Imperial dollars which have been put into circulation are looked at somewhat askance by the public, the mint has ceased for the time being to coin them, and is again turning out the old Kiangnan dollars.

From a military point of view, there is little change in the situation to report, but I have been able to obtain accurate details of the number of troops in the city. Of new or modern troops there are quartered here two infantry regiments, in all about 3,000 men, 600 cavalry, 900 artillery, 500 engineers, and a commissariat corps about 500 strong, making a total force of 5,500 men. Of old troops there are fourteen battalions in all; the average strength of a battalion being between 300 and 400 men. Six of these battalions were quartered in the city before the outbreak, and eight have been moved into it from Pukow since. The Chinese here appear to have a poor opinion of the former, but are in terror of the troops lately brought over from Pukow, who belong to the Yang-tsze defence army, under the command of General Chang Hsün. They are reputed to be men of fierce disposition, who, in the event of trouble, are not in the least likely to spare either their foes or the population generally. In addition to the above, there are at least 400 men garrisoning the various forts, &c., of whose leanings little is known, and, of course, the Manchu garrison, estimated at about 1,500 men.

Last week the modern troops, who are well known to be disaffected, were, as a matter of precaution, deprived of the bolts of their rifles, and their ammunition was also taken from them. I am now informed that, with the permission of the Viceroy, a certain number of bolts have been returned to each company, together with fifty rounds of ammunition for each complete rifle, the reason being that the men had become almost dangerously restive at the idea that in the event of trouble in Nanking they would be in a defenceless condition, and might be massacred by their enemies, the old troops. The commander of the division, General Hsü Shao Cheng, appears to have guaranteed the loyalty, or, at any rate, the neutrality of his men. Both infantry regiments stationed here have now received orders to move out of the city, the one to Pukow and the other to a camp south of Nanking. Whether they will obey orders or not appears to be a moot point.

As far as the future is concerned, I am still of opinion that there is no danger of a serious rising at this port, though the loafer element may possibly give some trouble. I must admit, however, that my views on the situation have not been shared by all my colleagues here.

With regard to the Chinese officials, the Viceroy still professes to be as optimistic as ever both as to the local situation and that of Hankow, but his staff, who have caught the general panic, are less confident, and I am told he greatly exasperates them by his coolness and refusal to believe the numerous reports that are brought to him. His Excellency made an excellent impression, I should mention, by attending the opening of the provincial assembly on the 22nd instant.

The men-of-war stationed here have been increased by the arrival of the United States steamer "New Orleans" and the Japanese cruiser "Akitsushima." No Europeans have left the port, a fact which has given some confidence to the Chinese who are unable to get away.

I have, &c.

F. E. WILKINSON.

Enclosure 2 in No. 79.

Report by Captain Otter-Barry respecting the Rising in Hupei.

FROM a strategical point of view the position of the Imperial Government at the present time would appear almost desperate seeing that :—

(*a.*) The 1st army (southern expeditionary forces) is fully occupied at Hankow.

(*b.*) The 2nd army at Lanchow, Mukden, Ch'angchun, &c., is in a state of partial mutiny.

(*c.*) The troops most likely to remain loyal are being kept for the protection of Peking.

(*d.*) Such towns as Ch'angsha, Wuch'ang, Hanyang, Ch'ungking, Yünnan-fu, Anching, Kiukiang, Nanch'ang, Ichang, Hsian-fu, Ch'êngtu, T'ai-yuan-fu, Têngyueh, Canton, and Swatow, are either in open revolt or in a state of great unrest and the Luchün in them, therefore, cannot be brought to restore order elsewhere.

(*e.*) The mixed brigade at T'ai-yuan-fu has revolted, and the lines of communication between the 1st army and Peking are, therefore, threatened.

(*f.*) The loyalty of many of the Luchün is of uncertain quality.

To further particularise as regards the position of affairs at various places, there seems, no doubt, that the southern expeditionary force (1st army), has gained, after a stubborn resistance on the part of the rebels, a victory at Hankow, but this was only after a disastrous delay, which gave the rebels some of that time they apparently required for organisation, and this delay was, also no doubt, the spark that set fire to the revolt in other towns. The rebels have now fallen back upon what must have been their main position at Hanyang and Wuchang, and a position further down the Yang-tsze on the southern bank. with the Han River and the Yang-tsze to their front, and although Hankow is now reported clear of rebels, the Imperials' positions is still no easy one. They have the gun-boats it is true, but they do not, up to the present, appear to have been of much use, and it would seem that with no lines of communication to hold, if the rebels have any heart in them at all they should be able to keep the Imperial force, the whole of the 1st army, well engaged for some time.

Passing up the line to the north we find the mixed brigade (consisting of 2 infantry regiments, 1 cavalry ying, 1 artillery ying, 1 company of engineers, and 1 company of transport) stationed at T'ai-yuen-fu (at the head of that branch line, which leaves the main Peking–Hankow line at Shih–Chia-Chuang) in open revolt—a fact in itself, perhaps, not very serious, but from the point of view of tactics and morale of considerable importance insomuch as :—

(*a.*) These troops are holding a strong position at the Great Wall on this branch line, and are threatening the lines of communication of the 1st army at Hankow, a move which would naturally have a great moral effect on the 1st army at Hankow, more especially in a case such as this, when distance serves to magnify any rumour of danger to one's rear.

(b.) This force in revolt is drawing Imperial troops from other parts of Chihli, &c., which can ill be spared to oppose them.

(c.) The very fact of Luchün having revolted would naturally try the wavering loyalty of neighbouring troops.

That this force at T'ai-yuan-fu has seized the railway and rolling-stock and closed T'ai-yuan-fu there seems no doubt.

Again, we have to touch on the very doubtful loyalty of the remainder of the 6th division left at Paoting-fu, and now at the junction at Shih-Chia-Chuang, another added danger.

Turning one's attention to the north of Chihli at Lanchow, and to Mukden in Manchuria, we find the 20th division (and, it is also said, the 2nd mixed brigade and the 3rd division at Ch'angchun in sympathy with them) actually putting conditions to the Government before they will consent to entrain to the south. It is even said that the action of these troops was the final cause of that humiliating edict published by the Government on the night of the 30th October, and even up to the present time no definite settlement seems to have been arrived at.

Yuan Shih-kai, who, by an edict issued last night, has now been appointed Premier of the Cabinet, but has still the control of the military and naval forces that have been dispatched to Hupei as well as the Yang-tsze squadron, may perhaps carry out successful negotiations with the rebel leaders Li Yuan Hung, &c.; but it seems doubtful, now that the rising is so general, and, from a strategical point of view, the balance of favour on the side of the rebels, whether the rebel leaders will accept anything less than the abolition of the Manchu dynasty.

General Yin-Chang, in an edict to-day, has been appointed chief of the General Staff and temporarily in charge of the Board of War; and General Teng Kuo-Chang has relieved General Ying-Chang of the command of the 1st army.

It may be of interest at the present time to know the various positions of troops in the north. They are naturally approximate, but they will give some idea as to the recent moves, &c., during this rebellion.

1st Army (Southern Expeditionary Force).

6th Division: Less three yings infantry reported to be at junction Shih-Chia-Chuang to oppose the T'ai-yuan-fu rebels.

2nd Division: With the exception of details at Paoting-fu, and about half ying at Shih-Chia-Chuang.

4th Division: With the exception of 500 infantry at Mach'ang, 100 cavalry and 600 infantry at Hsiao-chan, and a few further details left at Paoting-fu.

1st Division: Two battalions at front in addition to three train-loads dispatched on the 31st instant, strength 1,500 to 2,000, destination or units not yet known.

29th Mixed Brigade: Consisting of about six infantry yings, two cavalry yings, two artillery yings, &c.

21st Mixed Brigade: One and a-half yings of 42nd Regiment and two yings of the 41st Regiment reported to have remained loyal at Wuchang.

Peking.

Imperial Guards: Less one ying artillery dispatched to the south.

1st Division: 3rd and 4th Infantry Regiments, 2 yings 2nd Regiment at Summer Palace, 1 ying P'ei-yuan, engineers, 1 company; transport, 1 company; 1 company commissariat at F'engtai, and a few men of the 1st Regiment, less those troops reported to have been dispatched by three trains on 31st, units unknown.

Police: Strength on paper 7,000; actual estimated available strength, 5,000.

P'uchun: 1,500 men.

H'uchun Guards, &c: About 1,000 men, but almost impossible to estimate.

T'ungchow Provincial Troops: About 3,600 infantry and cavalry remaining at T'ungchow.

57

Tien-tsin.

4th Division; 500 infantry (Mach'ang); 100 cavalry, 600 infantry (Hsiao-chow); 500 infantry, Provincial troops (Han-Chia-Hsu); 1 ying Huaichün Infantry; 1 ying Huaichün Cavalry.

Langhow.

Two yings of the 77th Regiment.
Two yings of the 78th Regiment.
79th Regiment.
80th Regiment.
Three yings of the 20th Regiment (cavalry).
One ying of the 20th Artillery Regiment.
20th Company Engineers.
One company commissariat.
Two and a-half companies of transport.

Mukden and Hsin-nin-Tun.

The remainder of the 29th Division (3rd, 5th, 6th, 7th, 2nd, 9th, and 10th yings of Hauichün), under orders to be prepared to transport to the south of Chihli. Of these Huaichün, it has been possible to trace 280 men and 108 horses dispatched to a station near Peitaiho; 260 men and 70 horses to Tien-tsin; 210 men and 110 horses to Tien-tsin–Pukow Railway; 150 men and 109 horses to the south (destination unknown). The remainder of the Huaichün are present at Mukden.

The Huaichün are a force originally trained by Li Huang Chang, formerly Viceroy of Chihli. Physically these men are very fine. They are, it is reported, to be now brought for garrison duty in Chihli. It is reported from Mukden that the latest idea is to garrison Manchuria by the formation of Hsün-fang-tui to replace the Luchün, which are to be brought to Chihli.

Changchun.

3rd division, of which the 11th Infantry Regiment has already passed Mukden for the south.

Tsinan-fu.

5th division.

T'ai Yuan-fu.

Mixed Brigade mentioned above, which have now revolted.

It is reported that any movement of troops by sea is now cancelled.
(For Military Attaché, absent on tours),
M. OTTER-BARRY, Captain,
Royal Sussex Regiment.

November 2, 1911

No. 80.

Sir J. Jordan to Sir Edward Grey.—(Received November 24.)

Sir,   Peking, November 6, 1911.
WITH reference to my telegrams of the 30th October and the 2nd November, I have the honour to transmit herewith translations of the more important edicts issued between those dates. These documents embody the complete surrender of the Throne to popular pressure. From the beginning of the Regency the Imperial utterances have gradually degenerated with the increasing weakness of the Government until they have ceased to carry much weight with the people. In the prosperous days of the dynasty, and even down to the death of the late Empress-Dowager, decrees were issued sparingly and in very dignified language, and were appreciated accordingly. It was an unwritten law that no decree could be recalled. Now they are poured forth in volumes and follow each other in bewildering confusion and often in contradictory terms. The more the Throne takes the people into its confidence the colder the response with which its overtures are met.

The edict of the 30th October is perhaps the most humiliating one which was ever issued by the Throne in China, and is said to surpass in pathos even the despairing appeals issued by the last Emperor of the Mings. This penitential edict, in which the Imperial House stands self-condemned for the trouble brought upon the country, is immediately followed by an edict excluding Princes of the Blood from holding offices of State. Members of the reigning House have attained an ascendency under the Regent which they have acquired during no previous reign. Prince Kung, the brother of the Emperor Tao Kuang was, it is true, Foreign Minister of China for many years after the war of 1860, and Prince Ch'ing, a collateral member of the Imperial Family, has acted in the same capacity ever since. But these were exceptions, and it is only during the last three years that Princes and members of the Imperial clan have monopolised office. The Regent's two brothers, Tsai-hsün and Tsai Tao, took charge of the navy and army respectively. Prince Yü-lang, who had never held any post of importance before, was made chief of the general staff. Prince Pu-lun was given a variety of posts, and since Yuan Shih-kai's removal in January 1909, Manchus have been advanced to nearly all the highest offices in the capital.

The next steps were to order the draft of the constitution to be handed over to the Senate for deliberation, and to grant a pardon to political offenders.

The decree of the 1st November accepts the resignation of all the Ministers of State and appoints Yuan Shih-kai Premier, with powers to form a new Cabinet. The vacillation of the Imperial will is shown in the issue of two decrees on succeeding days, the first ordering Yuan to retain control of the forces on the Yang-tsze and remain there for a time, and the second instructing him to come to Peking at once.

The next concession made by the Regent was to request the Assembly to draft a constitution. There is no doubt that the strong position held by the mutinous 20th division at Lanchow and the pourparlers with the divisional commander had a very important bearing on the political situation, and forced the Throne to issue the panacea of a constitution which, as now drafted by the Senate in an abbreviated form, circumscribes the powers of the Sovereign to a far greater degree than did the constitution of 1908. The framework of the new constitution, modelled upon the British one, appears to have been drafted over night, and great hopes are now built upon its efficacy in appeasing a discontented Empire and saving the Throne. It has undoubtedly had a tranquillising effect in Peking and the neighbourhood, but there are indications that it may fail to satisfy the aspirations of the more advanced sections of the revolutionary parties elsewhere. The Throne's hopes rest upon Yuan and the National Assembly being able to convince the country that it is better to keep the Manchu dynasty in position, shorn of all its power, than to face the prospect of probable confusion and disorder.

Yuan's task is a stupendous one. In his favour are the innate stability and desire for peace at any price which characterise the masses of the Chinese people in ordinary times, and also the fact that there is no other constructive programme before the nation. On the other hand, the widespread nature of the movement, and the success which has everywhere attended it, put all attempt to recover the country by force out of the question, and the rebels may prefer to risk establishing a Government of their own, which, indeed, they have already done in some provincial centres, rather than trust Manchu promises given under compulsion.

I have, &c.

J. N. JORDAN.

Enclosure 1 in No. 80.

Extract from "Gazette" of October 30, 1911.

PENITENTIAL EDICT.

(Translation.)
IT is now three years since with much trepidation and misgiving we took up the arduous task of government, and it has ever been our object to promote the best interests of all classes of our subjects. But we have employed incompetent Ministers and have in our conduct of affairs of State displayed all too little statesmanship. We have filled the executive departments with Princes of the Blood, thus offending the canons of constitutional government; in railway matters we have allowed ourselves to be blinded and have acted contrary to the wishes of the country; when we hurried on measures of reform, the officials and gentry used them for their own ends; when we

changed old institutions the powerful turned the occasion to their own profit. Much of the people's wealth has already been taken, and not a single measure beneficial to the people given in return. Edicts dealing with the reform of the judiciary have been issued time and again, but not a person has obeyed them. By degrees it has come to this, that when the people were seething with discontent, we knew it not; when danger was imminent we were kept in ignorance. As a result, a rising broke out in Szechuan, closely followed by one in Hupei, while now Shensi and Honan are disturbed and grave news comes from Kuangtung and Kiangsi. In short, the whole Empire is in a ferment and men's minds on fire, the spirits of past Emperors are disturbed, and the people all reduced to utter misery. The fault lies solely with us, and we hereby declare to all the world that we swear an oath with our subjects to bring about a general reform for the establishment of a full constitution. On all the good and bad points in the laws, on all the changes to be made, we will consult public opinion, and all in the old system that is inconsistent with the constitution shall be abolished.

As regards putting an end to the distinction between Manchus and Chinese, the several edicts issued by the late Emperor must be put into immediate execution. The rising in Hupei and Honan, though troops are involved, is due actually to the mismanagement of Jui Ch'eng and others, who forced the people into rebellion and the troops to mutiny, and is no meaningless revolt. We take on ourself the blame for having appointed Jui Ch'eng to this post and we hold the troops and people blameless, so let them but return to their allegiance, and past offences shall be forgiven.

We are but a weak body to be set above all you Ministers and people, and the result is the outbreak of such a revolt as will destroy all the good performed by our ancestors. We are grieved at our failure, and filled with remorse, and we rely entirely on the support of our people and troops to restore prosperity to the millions of our subjects and to strengthen the foundations of our Throne. That peace may succeed disorder and peril and yield to safety depends entirely on the loyalty of our people, on whom we rely implicitly. At the present time the financial and foreign situations are both desperate, and even if prince and people work in harmony the condition of the country may still be critical. But if the people disregard the national safety and allow themselves to be led away by counsels of revolt, some overwhelming calamity will befall them, and then will China's future be dark indeed. Therefore is our mind filled with anxiety and apprehension day and night. We earnestly hope that all our people will understand our meaning.

Let this be known to all.

Enclosure 2 in No. 80.

Extract from " Gazette " of October 30, 1911.

EDICT: EXCLUSION OF IMPERIAL FAMILY FROM CABINET.

(Translation.)

THE Senate has presented a memorial to the effect that the Cabinet should be actually a responsible body, and that members of the Imperial Family should not be appointed Ministers of State. The appointment of members of the Imperial Family to discharge administrative functions is at variance with the practice of constitutional countries. By the established laws of our dynasty Princes of the Blood are not allowed to interfere with affairs of State, a principle which is expressly laid down in the rescripts of our ancestors, and which fulfils all the requirements of a constitutional State.

From the time of T'ung Chih the country has been whelmed in a sea of trouble, and it was then first that a Prince Regent was appointed to share the burden of Government, a practice which has been continued down to the present day. With the formation of a Cabinet this year, princes and other nobles were appointed Ministers of State, but this has only been a temporary expedient, and is not the avowed policy of the Throne. The Senate's memorial states that a Cabinet composed of members of the Imperial clan is absolutely irreconcilable with a constitutional régime, and requests that the provincial regulations of the Cabinet be annulled, that a Cabinet with proper powers be formed, and that Princes of the Blood be not appointed Ministers of State. This has for its object the showing of due respect to the Imperial House and the consolidation of the foundations of the State, and as such we fully agree with its terms. As soon as matters have become somewhat quieter we will select able and deserving men to form a responsible Cabinet. Princes of the Blood shall not again be appointed Ministers of State, and the provisional regulations of the Cabinet shall be abolished, so as to conform with constitutional principles and strengthen the State.

Enclosure 3 in No. 80.

Extract from " Gazette " of October 30, 1911.

EDICT : DRAFT CONSTITUTION TO BE HASTENED AND SUBMITTED TO SENATE.

(Translation.)
THE Senate has presented a memorial requesting the promulgation of an edict ordering that the constitutional laws of the Empire be handed over to the Senate for its deliberation.

Successive Emperors of our dynasty have ruled the country with humanity and benevolence for some 300 years. The late Empress Dowager and the late Emperor, seeing the difficulties of the times, took a drastic measure of reform, and issued a number of edicts determining the formation of a constitutional monarchy, and promulgating a programme of constitutional preparation which laid down the progress to be made year by year.

We were but a child when we took up the reins of government, and it is with the utmost trepidation that we strive to follow in the footsteps of our glorious forbears.

In the 10th moon of last year the Senate presented a memorial requesting the speedy opening of Parliament, and we issued an edict naming the 5th year of Hsüan T'ung (1913) as the time for the assembly of Parliament, and specially appointed P'u Lun and others to draft a constitution with all speed and await our approval. The Senate states that the constitutional laws are for the purpose of bringing about a more perfect harmony and understanding between the Throne and the people, and that they ought to be laid before the Ministers and people for discussion as soon as they are drawn up. Also that deliberation by the Senate on these laws after their first draft, and before their promulgation, would be in no way at variance with the declared wishes of the late Emperors.

We hereby order P'u Lun and others, in accordance with the general scheme of the constitutional laws as already sanctioned, to hand over the draft of the constitution as soon as it is completed to the Senate for careful deliberation. On obtaining our sanction it will be promulgated, in order to give confidence to the people and meet their wishes for reform.

Enclosure 4 in No. 80.

Extract from " Gazette " of October 30, 1911.

EDICT : AMNESTY FOR POLITICAL OFFENDERS.
(Translation.)
THE Senate has presented a memorial praying for the speedy removal of the ban on political offenders, so as to exercise clemency and win the hearts of the people. From earliest times a ban on political offenders has been regarded as an evil to be avoided, for not only does it smother talent and crush a manly spirit, but political theories change from day to day, and utterances which were regarded as criminal in other times may become the accepted views of to-day. If, while drooping in exile abroad, such offenders may have uttered incendiary speeches, this is but a negligible fault, born of their political ardour, which caused them to overstep the bounds. Their feelings, therefore, are pardonable.

We hereby issue a special proclamation making known our gracious desire to make a new beginning with our people. All political offenders since 1898 ; all men who, on account of revolution against the Government, have gone into exile in order to avoid punishment ; and all those who, involved in the present disturbances against their will, voluntarily return to their allegiance, will be forgiven for their past offences and be regarded as loyal subjects. In future, all subjects of the Chinese Empire who do not actually transgress the law will be entitled to the protection of the Government, and no person shall be arrested on suspicion and without due process of law. All those to whom this amnesty will apply should endeavour to improve their ways and manifest their loyalty, eagerly awaiting the completion of the constitution. Thus does the Throne declare its earnest desire for reform.

Enclosure 5 in No. 80.

Extract from " Gazette " of November 1, 1911.

EDICT: RESIGNATION OF CABINET AND APPOINTMENT OF YUAN SHIH-KAI AS PREMIER.

('Translation.)

ON the 1st November the Cabinet received the following edict by the Prince Regent :—

Prince Ch'ing and others (*i.e.*, Na Tung and Hsü Shih-chang) have memorialised us, stating that they have failed in the discharge of their duties, and praying for their immediate dismissals.

Tsai Tse and others (probably the other princely Ministers) have memorialised us, stating that matters of State are of extreme importance, and praying that capable men may be appointed in their place in accordance with constitutional principles and for the better governing of the country.

Tsou Chia-lai and others (probably the other non-princely Ministers) have memorialised us, stating that in the present time of crisis matters of government are of extreme importance, and praying that they may be allowed to resign in the interests of the State and of the public tranquillity.

These memorials are most proper : let the requests be granted ; let Prince Ch'ing vacate the office of Premier ; let the Grand Secretaries Na Tung and Hsü Shih-chang vacate their offices of Associate Premiers ; let Duke Tsai Tse and others and Tsou Chia-lai and others vacate their offices as Ministers of State.

Yuan Shih-kai is hereby appointed Premier ; as he has already left for Hupeh to take command there, let him perform the outlines of his task, and then proceed forthwith to Peking, form a complete Cabinet, and devise speedy measures for the reform of the Government, &c. During the few days that must elapse before Yuan Shih-kai's return, let Prince Ch'ing and others perform their duties as before, and, pending the completion of the Cabinet, let Tsai Tse and others and Tsou Chia-lai and others continue to function as hitherto, and let none seek to evade his responsibility.

Tsai T'ao resigns the general staff and Yin Chang succeeds him, retaining the Ministry of War temporarily.

Pince Ch'ing is appointed President and Na Tung and Hsü Shih-chang advisers of the Privy Council.

Wei Kuang-tao is appointed Viceroy of Hukuang, and ordered to proceed to his post forthwith.

[*Note.*—Formerly Viceroy at Yünnan, at Nanking and at Foochow ; retired 1907.]

Yuan Shih-kai is to retain control of all naval and military forces in Hupeh and of all naval forces on the Yang-tsze.

Enclosure 6 in No. 80.

Extract from " Gazette " of November 2, 1911.

EDICT: YUAN SHIH-KAI SUMMONED TO PEKING.

(Translation.) ·

LET Yuan Shih-kai come to Peking forthwith, and, pending the arrival of Wei Kuang-tao, let Wang Shih-chen* act as Viceroy of Hukuang.

[*Note.*—*Formerly commander-in-chief, Kiangpei ; retired for illness April 1910.]

Enclosure 7 in No. 80.

Extract from "Gazette" of November 2, 1911.

EDICT: CONSTITUTION TO BE DRAFTED BY THE SENATE.

(Translation.)

THE Commander of the 20th Division, Chang Shao-tseng and others, have presented a telegraphic memorial stating that the decree of the 31st ultimo, making clear the intention of the Throne to give effect to the constitution for the reform of the country, has been received by the troops with tears of gratitude. But they state the Cabinet cannot be formed in a day nor the disturbances quelled at once, and, moreover, the constitution should be settled by the Parliament.

The object of the memorialists is to protect the dynasty and suppress disorder and evinces great loyalty, which is most praiseworthy.

The Premier and all the Ministers of State yesterday tendered their resignations, which were accepted, and Yuan Shih-kai has been appointed Premier to form a complete Cabinet.

As for the constitution of China, let it be for the Senate to at once submit a draft for our consideration, in order to make clear the common interest, which unites Throne and people, and that we seek the good of all and not our own.

Enclosure 8 in No. 80.

Extract from "Gazette" of November 3, 1911.

EDICT.

(Translation.)

MEMORIAL by the Senate reporting their choice of a Constitutional Monarchy, submitting in the first place a Protocol of nineteen important articles, and requesting the Emperor to take the Oath and publish the Constitution for the benefit of the People.

YOUR servants would humbly venture to point out that the revolutionary movement has spread in every direction, having gradually extended to Szechuan, Kuangtung, Hunan, Kiangsi, Shensi, Shansi, and Hupei. The Empire is tottering already, and conditions become daily worse. The one means to save the situation, the one remedy for the national ills, may be summed up in the words, "Look to it that the constitution is sound."

Edicts have just been issued promising reform to the people, while the points put forward by General Chang Chao-tseng and his fellow officers have all been conceded by the Throne, so now the whole Empire knows that it is the Emperor's fixed determination to set up such an excellent constitutional monarchy as shall satisfy the universal longing for good government. Now we are gratified beyond measure by the receipt of another edict, ordering that the drafting of the constitution be left to the Senate, and we cannot but try with all sincerity to put into effect the Imperial will.

In every nation which has a constitutional monarchy, the British constitution has been taken as the model, and in the present instance, in drafting our constitution, we cannot do better than follow its principles. But the task of alteration and arrangement of the text is enormous, and will take a considerable time to complete. If the people surmise as to the forces influencing the Throne, they may perhaps suspect that the Ministers round the Emperor are whispering in his ear that once the danger past he can go back on his words. Just so did Napoleon III of France prove unfaithful after the danger was over. But if a short scheme of the constitution be first of all proclaimed to the people, then the whole nation will rejoice, saying, "Our Emperor is indeed listening to his people's prayer, meeting us with all fairness and sincerity." This report will spread abroad, and will do more good than a million soldiers. We have now respectfully prepared a preliminary draft of nineteen important articles of constitution, which are all recognised by the constitutions of all constitutional countries, and we present them in the present abbreviated condition. As soon as the full draft is prepared it will be again discussed.

These articles having been repeatedly deliberated by the Senate, which has voted in their favour, we hereby respectfully present a list of them for the Throne's perusal, requesting that the Throne may give its decision, accept the articles boldly, take the oath in the Imperial ancestral temple, and proclaim the articles to the people, so as to strengthen the State and defend the Imperial House. We do not deliberately use such terrifying language, but any delay will be too late. If the Throne does not proclaim the constitution at once, we fear the Imperial favour will never reach the people, and the revolution will reach unspeakable lengths. Moved by our devoted loyalty as well as by the sight of the present troubles, we cannot refrain from speaking thus plainly to the Emperor's face, and we await the Throne's commands with fear and trembling.

The constitutional laws are an unchangeable ordinance, which it is of the utmost importance that both ruler and people should observe. This Senate received the Imperial commands to draft the constitution with great misgiving, and we dare not act without taking the opinion of the whole nation, so as to secure the best results. We have therefore telegraphed to the various provincial assemblies to collect their views, and we propose that in all matters of importance at present, the troops be allowed temporarily to give their opinion in order to satisfy the wishes of the people.

The Nineteen Articles of Constitution.

Article 1. The Imperial line of the Chinese Empire can continue perpetually unchanged.

Art. 2. The person of the Emperor is sacred and inviolable.

Art. 3. The powers of the Emperor shall be limited by the constitution.

Art. 4. Succession to the Throne shall be determined by the constitution.

Art. 5. The constitution shall be drafted and passed by the Senate and promulgated by the Throne.

Art. 6. Amendments in the constitution shall be originated by the national Parliament.

Art. 7. The members of the Upper House shall be elected by the people, the electorate being limited to those who have certain qualifications required by law.

Art. 8. The Prime Minister shall be elected by the national Parliament, and his appointment ratified by the Emperor. Ministers of State shall be recommended by the Prime Minister and appointed by the Emperor. No member of the Imperial House shall act as Prime Minister, Minister of State, or high officer in the provinces.

Art. 9. If the Prime Minister is denounced by the national Parliament, either the latter shall dissolve or the former resign ; but there shall be no dissolution of two successive Parliaments during the same Cabinet.

Art. 10. The Emperor shall be the commander-in-chief of the army and navy ; but no military or naval force shall be employed within the Empire except in accordance with the rules expressly provided therefor by the national Parliament.

Art. 11. No ordinance shall set aside the laws or anything settled by law, except in the case of an emergency ordinance, for which special rules shall be drafted.

Art. 12. No treaty shall be concluded without the approval of the national Parliament, but in case of a declaration of war or of the conclusion of peace when Parliament is not in session, approval may be given at a subsequent session.

Art. 13. The official system and the rules governing it shall be decided by law.

Art. 14. In case the budget of any year is not passed by the national Parliament, that of the preceding year shall not hold good for that year. There shall be no fixed annual expenditure, and there shall be no extraordinary excess of expenditure beyond the budget.

Art. 15. The amount of the expenditure for the Imperial household, and any increase or decrease therein, shall be voted by the national Parliament.

Art. 16. No ceremony of the Imperial House shall be contrary to the constitution.

Art. 17. Administrative courts shall be established by both Houses of Parliament.

Art. 18. All Acts passed by the national Parliament shall be promulgated by the Emperor.

Art. 19. For the purposes of articles 8, 9, 10, 12, 13, 14, 15, and 18 the Senate shall be deemed to occupy the position of the Parliament until the latter shall have been convoked.

No. 81.

Sir J. Jordan to Sir Edward Grey.—(Received November 27.)

Sir,   *Peking, November* 8, 1911.

YOU are aware from my despatch of the 23rd October that circumstances have obliged the consular body at Hankow to enter to a certain extent into relations with the rebel leaders.

On the 22nd October the consular body at Hankow telegraphed that the commander-in-chief of the rebel army had communicated to the consuls a list of goods which would be considered as contraband, and which, if discovered, would be confiscated together with the ship carrying them. The consuls stated that questions daily arose which required discussion with the revolutionary authorities, and that it seemed impossible to avoid official relations with them, although it was understood that the question of recognising the Military Government should not be raised. They proposed to take note of General Li's communication regarding contraband, and to say that they had referred it to their Ministers at Peking. In circulating this telegram, I expressed to my colleagues my personal opinion that the rebel general had no power whatever to confiscate foreign ships carrying such articles, and that all goods the import of which was not prohibited by treaty could be conveyed freely in foreign vessels to Hankow.

At a meeting held by the foreign representatives on the 28th October the general feeling was that the first duty of the consular body was to safeguard the tranquillity of the concessions, and that if, with this object in view, the consular body considered that they were obliged to enter into relations with the rebels, the diplomatic body could certainly not disapprove that proceeding. The consuls, however, could alone decide whether it was indispensable. A telegram in this sense was accordingly dispatched to the senior consul the following day.

I have since received from the acting consul-general a despatch covering copies of correspondence with the rebel general on the subject. The latter encloses a somewhat extensive list of the articles which he holds to be contraband of war. His presumption that the consuls have accorded his forces the status of belligerents is not, so far as I know, warranted by the facts, and I have informed Mr. Goffe that it does not appear to me desirable to recognise it at present, since such recognition would justify a protest from the Chinese Government.

Another matter which caused some concern was the position in which the concessions would be placed when hostilities reached the city of Hankow itself. The senior consul reported by telegraph that Vice-Admiral Sir A. L. Winsloe was of opinion that it was absolutely necessary for the safety of the concessions that they should be extended to the railway line, and that the Chinese living on the intervening land should be evicted. He added that the consular body unanimously endorsed this opinion. The question of demanding the extension from the Wai-wu Pu was discussed at a meeting of the diplomatic body on the 28th October, but it was pointed out that as the Imperial troops had recovered the city the matter was no longer one of urgency.

It was inevitable, when once the movement had developed into a state of war, that difficulties should arise in regard to the rights of the subjects of the treaty Powers. There has been some firing, probably both intentional and unintentional, on foreign shipping by rebel guns, and a British tug, which was towing two barges loaded with military stores for the Imperialists, was interfered with, but I have so far only received very brief telegraphic reports of these occurrences. Our principal object has been to guard as far as possible against any restriction of the normal trading business of foreign shipping firms. and it was with this object in view that we have refused a request of the Wai-wu Pu that foreign ships should only be allowed at present to call at the larger ports on the river, in order, apparently, that the movements of the revolutionaries might be the better controlled. Copies of the correspondence on this subject are enclosed herewith.

A despatch from His Majesty's consul-general at Shanghai warned me that it was not impossible that certain British subjects might take an opportunity of indulging their taste for military adventure, and, by my instructions, a notification has been issued, both there and at Tien-tsin, calling attention to article 71 of the order in council of 1904.

I have, &c.

J. N. JORDAN.

Enclosure 1 in No. 81.

Acting Consul-General Goffe to Sir J. Jordan.

Sir, *Hankow, October* 21, 1911.
I HAVE the honour to transmit herewith translations of two despatches
which I have received from the revolutionary general on the subject of contraband. The
matter was discussed at a meeting of the consular body this afternoon, and, as we heard
that the general was somewhat annoyed at our continued refusal to recognise him in
any way, it was decided that the senior consul should acknowledge the receipt of these
two despatches on behalf of the consular body. I enclose a copy of the communication
sent by the senior consul, which was written only in English, and accompanied by his
foreign visiting card.
The revolutionary leader is establishing his position more firmly every day, and it
is becoming increasingly difficult to ignore him.

I have, &c.
H. GOFFE.

Enclosure 2 in No. 81.

The Revolutionary General to Acting Consul-General Goffe.

(Translation.)
Sir, *October* 18, 1911.
I HAVE the honour to inform you that our soldiers have driven back the Manchu
army which was encamped at Liu Chia Miao. I have now the honour to request you
to strictly forbid British officials, merchants, and people to sell to the enemy, in contravention of international law, any of the articles mentioned in the attached list, which
are hereby declared contraband.

I have, &c.
(Seal of Li, General of the Hupeh army of the Military
Government of the Chinese Republic.)

List of Contraband Articles.

Military arms, ammunition, shell, and material for making same, such as lead,
saltpetre, sulphur, &c., materials for fortifications, and cement, clothes and accoutre-
ments for soldiers and sailors, armour plate, materials for building or repairing ships,
food and drink, bedding, and like material, horses, saddlery, fodder, carts, lime and
similar materials, timber, telegraph and telephone apparatus, and materials for railway
building.

Enclosure 3 in No. 81.

The Revolutionary General to Acting Consul-General Goffe.

(Translation.)
Sir, *Wuchang, October* 20, 1911.
I HAVE the honour to convey to you the expression of the deep sense of gratitude
entertained towards you by the Military Government for the impartial attitude adopted
by you during hostilities existing between the Military and Manchu Governments in
recognising us as belligerents, and in proclaiming your neutrality.
I have already had the honour to request you to prevent your nationals of all ranks
from selling to the enemy articles regarded as contraband of war, and I have no doubt
that you will assent to this request.
In the arrangements which have already taken place my forces have invariably
been successful, and the Manchu army has already beaten a retreat. It may therefore
be expected that the foreign concessions will remain undamaged, a fact which, I think,
cannot fail to relieve you of all anxiety. If, however, the rendering of assistance to the
enemy by means of persons or letters is not strictly forbidden, the Manchu army may
take advantage of the circumstances to renew disturbances, which, under present
conditions, would be a source of inconvenience both to you and my Government.
[335] F

I have the honour, therefore, to request that you will issue stringent instructions that no British steamers, men-of-war, or any of your nationals shall, in any circumstances, send or carry men or letters for the use of the enemy, in accordance with the rules of international law, otherwise my forces will have no alternative but to seize such persons sent and confiscate any letters so carried as a means of self-defence.

I avail, &c.
(Seal of the Commander-in-chief of the Army of
Hupeh of the Republic of China.)

Enclosure 4 in No. 81.

Senior Consul at Hankow to the Revolutionary General.

THE senior consul presents his compliments to the general officer commanding at Wuchang, and begs to acknowledge, on behalf of the consular body, the receipt of his letters of the 18th and the 20th, on the subject of contraband. The requests contained therein have been brought to the knowledge of the subjects of the treaty Powers resident in Hankow, and the matter will be referred to the Foreign Ministers in Peking for their consideration.

The senior consul trusts that the general officer commanding in Wuchang will use his best endeavours to have telegraphic communication with Peking and Shanghai restored, so that the consuls of the treaty Powers can communicate with their respective Governments.

October 21, 1911.

Enclosure 5 in No. 81.

Prince Ch'ing to Sir J. Jordan.

Sir,   *Peking, October* 28, 1911.
ON the 26th instant I received a despatch from the Ministry of Posts and Communications as follows :—

"I have received the following telegram from the Governor-General of Liang Kiang and the Governor of Kiangsi :—

"'The Hupei revolt is very widespread, and the utmost precautions must be taken with respect to the carriage of passengers on steamers between Shanghai and Hankow."

"All steam-ship firms should be informed that steamers may only stop at the larger ports of Kiukiang, Nganking, Wuhu, Nanking, Chinkiang, and Shanghai, and that they may not take on either passengers or goods at any of the smaller ports on the route. The China Merchants' Steam Navigation Company must also be instructed to comply with these rules. I accordingly request that the dean of the diplomatic body at Peking be invited to enforce obedience to these instructions."

This proposal of the Ministry of Posts and Communications is due to the present disturbances, in view of which the above plan should most assuredly be put into execution as a temporary measure to facilitate the work of inspection.

I have therefore the honour to request your Excellency to bring these rules to the notice of your honourable colleagues that they may give the necessary instructions for compliance therewith, and so strengthen the bonds of friendship between our respective nations.

I have, &c.
Prince CH'ING.

67

Enclosure 6 in No. 81.

Sir J. Jordan to Prince Ch'ing.

Your Highness, November 7, 1911.

I HAVE the honour to acknowledge the receipt of your Highness's note of the 28th October, requesting that, in accordance with rules proposed by the Viceroy of the Liang Kiang and the Governor of Kiangsi, all steam-ship firms should be informed that, in view of the widespread nature of the Hupei rebellion, steamers may only stop at the larger ports of Kiukiang, Wuhu, Nanking, Chinkiang, and Shanghai, and that they may not take on either passengers or goods at any of the smaller ports *en route.* Your Highness added that the China Merchants' Steam Navigation Company was being instructed to comply with these rules, and you requested that I would bring the same to the notice of my honourable colleagues.

I have the honour to inform your Highness that the above request has been carefully considered by the diplomatic body, who have charged me to reply that the representatives of the Powers regret that they are unable to forbid the steam-ship companies calling at ports where the right is recognised by the treaties, but that they are willing to recommend the companies to take every possible precaution to avoid any intervention in the actual conflict.

I avail, &c.
J. N. JORDAN.

No. 82.

Sir J. Jordan to Sir Edward Grey.—(Received November 27.)

Sir, Peking, November 10, 1911.

I HAVE the honour to transmit herewith a copy of a report of to-day's date which I have received from Captain Otter-Barry, acting military attaché to His Majesty's Legation, on the movements and present disposition of the Imperial troops.

I have, &c.
J. N. JORDAN.

Enclosure in No. 82.

Report by Captain Otter-Barry respecting the Chinese Revolution.

SINCE my report of the 2nd instant events have been following with so much rapidity that it has been almost impossible to come to any logical conclusion as to the plans of the Government.

No fresh news has been received of any fighting at Hankow, and presumably the position of the southern expeditionary force and the rebels at that place remains much the same.

The revolt of the troops at Taiyuan-fu, in Shansi, has, after a small skirmish, resulted in an affair at the junction at Shih-chia-chuang, when General Wu Lu Chen (the late commander of the 6th division, sent to pacify the Shansi rebels) was murdered.

There are several reports regarding this affair, but I am unable to give at the present any authentic account, as the reports differ in essential details.

The effect of this affair was temporarily to suspend the traffic on the line, and therefore, during this period, from a strategical point of view, the lines of communication of the southern expeditionary force were temporarily cut.

The murder took place on the 7th, and traffic was not resumed until the 10th, when, strategically, the position looked more hopeful for the Imperials.

From reports received last night Paoting-fu still appears to be in a very unsettled state, and during the last few days troops of the 3rd division, 1st division, and Huaichun

[335] F 2

(provincial troops) have further been dispatched in order to help cope with the unsettled state of affairs at Shih-chia-chuang and district.

I estimate that approximately at Shih-chia-chuang and district there should be now from 5,000 to 6,000 men from the 6th division, the 2nd division, the 4th division, the 1st division, and the 5th division, but it appears that some of these troops are divided into factions, and are somewhat disorganised.

The 20th division at Lanchow have, up to the present, not moved from that place, although most of their conditions were complied with; still their behaviour and the behaviour of their commander, Chang-hsao-tseng, makes it appear that they are still in an unsettled condition, and they can hardly be called loyal.

There are at Lanchow about 8,000 to 9,000 men of this division, of which about 1,000 are believed to be Manchus.

General Chang-hsao-tseng, shortly after the edict of the 30th, was given orders to go to the south and take in hand the pacification of some of these rebel towns along the Yang-tsze. He excused himself from going. Lanchow is practically "held up" by the men of the 20th division, that is to say, the telegraph offices are under the general's censorship, and he has to a great extent taken control of the trains passing that place, although he has permitted all trains, with the exception of two trains of ammunition, to pass through.

The general asked for cars to rail his men to Peking, and these were refused by the General Staff, on the plea of shortage of railway stock, and he was told that his division was to remain at Lanchow. I understand that he has now applied, and obtained, sick leave, and temporarily the command of the division has devolved on General Pan.

What the actual movements of this division will be seems uncertain, but it would appear that, although the general's political opinions are in favour of a constitution, he does not at present go to the length of the rebels.

The Mukden Mixed Brigade seem to be in sympathy with him, although so far they have not shown their hand. Up to the present no definite information of the 20th's departure has come to hand, but this half-disloyal body, led by a strong man, in their present position is a matter of considerable importance from a strategical point of view, and may lead to further trouble.

The 11th regiment of the 3rd division, with a battalion of artillery and companies of engineers and transport, have been railed from Chang-chun to Paoting-fu for Shih-chia-chuang (these troops are included in the estimate given above of troops at Shih-chia-chuang). The 10th regiment of the 3rd division arrived from Chengte-fu to Hsin-min-fu by road yesterday. This regiment's eventual destination would appear to be Fengtai, where they are to await further orders.

The Mukden Mixed Brigade is also shortly to be railed south. As regards the force at Peking, there are practically no alterations (with the exception of two battalions already mentioned at Shih-chia-chuang of the 1st division) in the troops mentioned in my previous report.

The troops at Tungchow, under the command of Kiang-kuei-ti, have been increased by some 2,000 recruits, and the detachment brought in from Liang-ko-chuang, and so there are at Tungchow approximately 6,000 men.

A new force of Hsin-fang-tui (these men can be classed considerably below the Luchun) are now being raised in Manchuria to take the place of the Luchun moving from Manchuria.

The Huaichun have now been practically all railed south from Manchuria to stations in Chih-li.

The Luchun Reserve up to ten yings is now being called out, of which three yings are already formed. But, unarmed and without uniforms, they can as yet hardly be seriously considered.

I have no further information regarding the garrison at Tien-tsin. Reports have daily been coming in of towns fallen into the hands of the rebels. In short, the Government itself appears surrounded by dangers, though yesterday and to-day the general position appears a little less critical. Orders for the movement of troops seem to be issued in a somewhat panic-stricken way and without much thought.

Yuan Shih-kai still delays his return to Peking. Some of the Manchu officials have already dispatched their families away from Peking for safety, others are making arrangements for their own safety or successful flight. It appears probable that there is some intention of the Imperial troops holding a position on the railway between here and Paoting-fu, but the unsettled state of the loyalty of the troops places the Government in a dangerous position. Perhaps the most extraordinary side of the whole revolution is the fact that this Luchun, on whom much money has been spent, and upon whom great confidence has been placed, has now proved the instrument for the partial undoing of the Government.

(For Military Attaché, absent on tour),

R. B. OTTER-BARRY, *Captain,*

November 11, 1911. *Royal Sussex Regiment.*

No. 83.

Sir J. Jordan to Sir Edward Grey.—(Received November 27.)

Sir, *Peking, November* 10, 1911.

I HAVE the honour to report that on the 28th ultimo, I received a telegram from His Majesty's consul-general at Tien-tsin, stating that the Viceroy of the metropolitan province wished to obtain the consent of the foreign representatives to a temporary revocation of the agreement made in 1902 on the occasion of the dissolution of the Tien-tsin Provisional Government, in respect of the stipulation that Chinese troops should not be stationed within 20 *li* of Tien-tsin. The Viceroy's grounds for making this request were that he required troops for the maintenance of order in possible contingencies; as an alternative he suggested that foreign troops should assist him.

With the concurrence of the foreign representatives here instructions were sent to the senior consul, who had sent a similar report, that a revocation of the agreement might be agreed to for such period as the consular body considered necessary.

On the 2nd November, the question having been raised by the senior consul, the consular body were authorised to make such reasonable conditions as local circumstances seemed to them to require in regard to the number and nature of the Chinese troops who were to occupy temporarily the area round the foreign concessions, and as to the manner of their employment.

These conditions were embodied in a note addressed to the Viceroy by the senior consul, copy of which I have the honour to enclose. They were, subsequently, circulated among the heads of missions, and met with no dissent from any quarter.

I have, &c.

J. N. JORDAN.

Enclosure in No. 83.

Senior Consul to Viceroy.

Your Excellency, *Tien-tsin, November* 4, 1911.

I HAVE the honour to acknowledge the receipt of your note of the 30th ultimo, asking for the consent of the consular body for temporarily bringing in Chinese soldiers within the limits of 20 *li* of Tien-tsin, in contradiction to the provisions of the agreement of 1902.

I am instructed by the consular body to reply to you that, with the sanction of the diplomatic body, they agree to the temporary removal of the agreement in question, and authorise the Chinese troops to be stationed within the said limits under the following conditions :—

1. No Chinese soldiers shall be admitted into the foreign concessions.
2. No artillery or quick-firing guns shall be brought in.
3. The consular body have been informed by Mr. Wang, commissioner for foreign affairs, that two companies of Hwai Chün have been already stationed within the limits and they approve it. In case, however, the Chinese authorities wish to bring in more soldiers, consent of the consular body shall be first obtained, and the consular body will agree only to a reasonable number.

The consular body further instruct me to state that it is understood that the soldiers so brought in shall be employed simply for police purpose, and also that this authorisation of temporarily bringing in soldiers shall be rescinded as soon as the consular body consider it shall be no longer necessary.

Compliments, &c.

Senior Consul.

No. 84.

Admiralty to Foreign Office.—(Received November 27.)

Sir,   *Admiralty, November 25, 1911.*

I AM commanded by my Lords Commissioners of the Admiralty to acquaint you, for the information of the Secretary of State for Foreign Affairs, that His Majesty's ships " Prometheus " and " Pegasus," ordered to China from the Australia station, are due to arrive at Hong Kong on the 13th December. The consent of the Government of the Commonwealth of Australia has been obtained locally to their departure from Australian waters.

I am, &c.

W. GRAHAM GREENE.

No. 85.

Sir J. Jordan to Sir Edward Grey.—(Received November 27.)

(Telegraphic.)   *Peking, November 27, 1911.*

REVOLUTION in Hupei.

Please see my telegram of yesterday.

Acting consul-general at Hankow telegraphs to-day as follows :—

"Imperialists have retaken Hanyang. The revolutionary forces are fleeing to Wuchang, and are demoralised. General Li Yuan-Hung is prepared to accept constitutional Government, and has sent a message to that effect.

" I will telegraph you Li's terms for an armistice if I can obtain them."

No. 86.

Mr. Jerome to Sir Edward Grey.—(Received November 28.)

Sir,   *Lima, October 20, 1911.*

THERE is a considerable Chinese colony in Peru, estimated as being some 14,000 or 15,000, many of whom are Christians and who intermarry with the Peruvians. I am told that the most important business house here, even including the large English, American, and German firms, is a firm of Chinese merchants and bankers, which, presumably, is allied to one of the four great trading hongs.

One or more newspapers in Chinese characters are published here.

The recent news of a revolution in China has excited much interest among the Chinese of Lima, and a considerable propaganda in favour of the Chinese rebels is taking place. As an instance, my Chinese servant has given over two months' wages as his subscription to the movement. A large and enthusiastic meeting took place in the Chinese theatre last night, speeches being made by Lee-Kay-Pen. The subscriptions are being received by the firm of L. Yun Knam.

I enclose, for your information, a specimen of an advertisement which for some days has been appearing in the Lima daily papers.

I learn that the amount actually subscribed by the Chinese in Lima, Iquique, and Guayaquil already is, within a few hundreds, a million pounds, and that arrangements are being made to at once place by telegraph 500,000l. at the disposal of the revolutionary finance committee, which is located apparently at Honolulu.

The Chinese revolutionary committee here are in telegraphic communication with the rebels in the field at Hankow.

I have, &c.

LUCIEN J. JEROME.

Enclosure in No. 86.

Advertisement appearing in Principal Lima Newspapers.

CHINESE PATRIOTIC SOCIETY.

(Translation.)
THE undersigned announces to his compatriots that from this date has been opened in Billinghurst Street, No. 331, an office where donations are received to protect the republicans of China.
The office works from 8 to 11 A.M., from 1 to 5 P.M., and from 7 to 11 of the night.

THE SECRETARY.

No. 87.

Admiralty to Foreign Office.—(Received November 29.)

Sir, Admiralty, November 28, 1911.
I AM commanded by my Lords Commissioners of the Admiralty to transmit, for the information of the Secretary of State for Foreign Affairs, a telegram, dated to-day, from the commander-in-chief, China. ·

I am, &c.
W. GRAHAM GREENE.

Enclosure in No. 87.

Commander-in-chief, China, to Admiralty.

(Telegraphic.) November 28, 1911.
HANYANG was reoccupied by Imperial troops yesterday; rebels having abandoned guns, &c., fled to Wuchang-fu. The rebels have driven Imperialists into city at Nanking, having taken all outer forts, and are now presumably bombarding city from eight ships and with guns posted on Tiger Hill. It appears fairly certain that Nanking will be taken during the week, in which case there should be no trouble at Hankow for the present.
The Russians have sent 100 and the Germans fifty troops, to guard their concessions at Hankow.

No. 88.

Sir J. Jordan to Sir Edward Grey.—(Received November 29.)

(Telegraphic.) Peking, November 28, 1911.
ARMISTICE at Hankow.
Acting consul-general at Hankow telegraphed yesterday as follows :—

" My telegram of the 27th November and your telegram of the 26th November.
" Terms as follows suggested by General Li Yuan-hung :—

" 1. Fifteen days' armistice, during which territory at present occupied shall be held by each side.
" 2. Assembly in Shanghai of representatives from all the provinces that have joined the revolutionary party ; these will elect plenipotentiaries to negotiate with representatives appointed by Yuan Shih-kai.
" 3. If necessary, extension of armistice for a further fifteen days.

" I have not approached General Feng, but much bloodshed would be saved if he were instructed to accept these terms."

No. 89.

Sir J. Jordan to Sir Edward Grey.—(Received November 29.)

(Telegraphic.) *Peking, November 29, 1911.*
REVIVAL of piracy on West River.
Consul-general at Canton has, with my approval, arranged with British naval authorities for patrol of river by one torpedo-boat destroyer, three torpedo-boats, and usual river flotilla, which should enable British steam-ship services to be resumed.

No. 90.

India Office to Foreign Office.—(Received November 30.)

THE Under-Secretary of State for India presents his compliments to the Under-Secretary of State for Foreign Affairs, and forwards herewith, for the information of the Secretary of State, copy of a telegram from the Viceroy, dated the 29th November, 1911, relative to the Chinese revolution.

India Office, November 30, 1911.

Enclosure in No. 90.

Government of India to Secretary of State for India.

(Telegraphic.) *November 29, 1911.*
FOLLOWING telegram, dated the 27th instant, has been received from Govern-of Burmah and repeated to Peking :—

"Deputy commissioner, Bhamo, has received letter from Chang, revolutionary general, in which he gives history of the rebellion. Our neutrality is asked for, and undertaking is given that frontier cases will be settled as before. Chang states that orders have been given to chiefs of Chinese Shan States to prevent trouble on the frontier, and encloses copy of a proclamation to foreign nations promising that foreigners will be protected, debts paid, and agreements respected, provided that no recognition will be accorded to loans raised or agreements executed by Manchu Government after date of proclamation. Formal acknowledgment of letter has been sent by deputy commissioner, and we will forward a copy of it to Government of India as soon as we receive it. Tengyueh postmaster, according to deputy commissioner, returned to Tengyueh on the 24th. Customs commissioner is communicating with Peking about returning and reorganising customs, and caravans have started again."

No. 91.

Sir J. Jordan to Sir Edward Grey.—(Received November 30.)

(Telegraphic.) *Peking, November 30, 1911.*
HIS Majesty's consul-general at Yünnan-fu reports that rebels were defeated with great loss at Ningyuan-fu. Missionaries safe 21st November.

No. 92.

Sir J. Jordan to Sir Edward Grey.—(Received December 1.)

Sir,   *Peking, November 12, 1911.*

THE progress of the revolutionary movement in so many important provincial
centres; the constant reports of the imminent secession of Tien-tsin ; the risk of the
capital being isolated in the possible event of the mutinous troops at Lanchow and, as
has been commonly thought, at Shih-chia-chuang on the Peking–Hankow line, throwing
in their lot with the revolutionaries ; the anxious tension which evidently exists between
the Chinese and Manchu population of this city ; and the complete and humiliating
demoralisation of the Central Government, have combined to induce a not unnatural
sense of uneasiness among European residents here.

Until it became necessary I was reluctant to issue any instructions or warning,
being apprehensive lest any such step should intensify rather than allay the feeling of
insecurity, and possibly be misinterpreted as a confirmation of the many wild rumours
which daily obtained currency.

At the same time it appeared desirable to make some provision for any emergency
that might dictate the concentration within its precincts of British subjects residing
outside the legation quarter, and I accordingly authorised the formation of a committee,
composed of Lieutenant-Colonel Koe and four members of my staff, to study the question
of bringing in, accommodating, and provisioning outside residents should need arise.

Upon this work the committee are still engaged and the organisation is rapidly
approaching completion. In order to secure the co-operation of British residents in the
native city and to keep them informed of what was being done, a circular, copy of which
I have the honour to enclose herewith, was issued to each householder. So far as I am
able to judge, the circular has been well received and has succeeded in its primary object
of assuring the recipients that their interests are being cared for by His Majesty's
Legation.

I have, &c.
J. N. JORDAN.

Enclosure in No. 92.

Circular to British Residents outside the Legation Quarter.

SEVERAL letters having been received by His Majesty's Minister asking for advice
as to the course to be pursued in the event of disorder breaking out at Peking, a
committee of members of the staff has been formed under Sir John Jordan's instructions,
to consider the questions of accommodation, provisioning, &c., which may arise in case of
emergency.

2. It should be distinctly understood that the Minister sees no necessity at present
to advise residents to move into the legation quarter and that the arrangements
suggested now are only precautionary. A further circular will be issued if circumstances
seem to render it advisable that residents should move into the legation quarter.

3. It will assist the committee if residents will as soon as possible notify the
undersigned where they propose to go in the event of such a further circular being
issued. It is recommended that residents should if possible make their own arrangements to go to houses of friends or hotels within the quarter. If this is not possible,
arrangements will be made to provide some accommodation in the limited space available
in the legation. No such accommodation will in any case be available for Chinese
servants, &c., of British residents outside the legation quarter.

4. Portable valuables such as jewellery, plate, furs, may be sent now, if desired,
into the legation for safer custody. Such packages must be clearly marked outside with
the name of the sender, and may be delivered to Mr. A. E. Eastes, His Majesty's vice-
consul.

5. British residents are advised to pack ready for immediate transport, in case of
emergency, blankets, bedding, linen, clothing, and stores, sufficient for, say, a fortnight's
use.

6. The residences of all persons to whom this circular is addressed have been located
and are known to the legation. In the event of an emergency, the committee will send
out special messengers and arrangements will be made for escorting persons into the
legation quarter. This can only be done effectively with the prompt co-operation of
the persons themselves.

7. Residents with telephone numbers are requested to communicate them to the undersigned.

8. Any recipient of this circular who knows any British householder resident outside the quarter who has not received a copy will please move such British householder to apply at once to the legation for a copy, and at the same time to communicate the address, in full detail, of his residence.

9. Any communications, especially those called for under paragraph 9 above, should be addressed to the second secretary of the legation, Mr. P. L. Loraine, who is secretary of the committee above mentioned.

P. L. LORAINE.

Peking, November 4, 1911.

No. 93.

Sir J. Jordan to Sir Edward Grey.—(Received December 1.)

Sir,   *Peking, November 13, 1911.*

I HAVE the honour to report briefly the circumstances which led me to ask your authority by telegraph to employ His Majesty's troops to keep the lines of communication open between Peking and the sea, in terms of article 9 of the final protocol of the 7th September, 1901, in case they should be threatened, and, by way of preliminary explanation, I may point out, what is perhaps sufficiently obvious, that to effect this, the sole object I had in view, it is enough to protect the section of the Imperial railways of North China between the capital and Tien-tsin until the Pei-ho connecting the latter port with the gulf freezes over.

In sending you my telegram of the 31st October, I had the following considerations in mind. A mixed brigade of the 20th Division, under General Chang Chao-tseng, had been assembled at Lanchow, originally for the purpose of the autumn manœuvres in Chihli. When the revolution broke out the Chinese Government delayed railing these troops, some 5,000 men, to the south, as the general was suspected of revolutionary leaning. They were therefore left temporarily at Lanchow, and, meanwhile, they were reinforced by additional troops of the same division, which brought their numbers up to 9,000 men. The position on the Yang-tsze now made it desirable that they should be sent to support the first army, but when the order came they refused to entrain, and through the intermediary of General Chang, who is credited with being a capable and influential leader, put forward certain political demands, and, as mentioned in my despatch of the 6th instant, morally forced the Throne to promise a full constitution at an early date.

In spite of this indulgence the troops remained at Lanchow with their commander, and the strength and independence of their position now became doubly evident. If they decided to throw in their lot openly with the revolutionaries, there would have been nothing to prevent them from advancing on Tien-tsin and Peking and cutting the line behind them, to hinder the pursuit of a force from Manchuria. The railway might equally have been broken by the Imperialists to intercept their advance from Lanchow.

On the 4th November the general officer commanding at Tien-tsin telegraphed to me that Mr. Ricketts, the chief engineer, expected to receive orders from the Viceroy to cut the line. I therefore lost no time in acting on the authority conveyed to me in your telegram of the 1st November. I warned the Chinese Government of the right secured to the Powers by the final protocol, and of the grave consequences which would ensue from any tampering with the line, and I instructed His Majesty's consul-general at Tien-tsin to use similar language to the Viceroy and to the Chinese director of the railway through Mr. Ricketts. At the same time, I consulted the representatives of France and Japan, who are the only other Powers besides ourselves having troops for the purpose at Tien-tsin.

The Viceroy denied any intention of the kind attributed to him, but it was thought necessary to take precautions, and a consultation between the British, French, and Japanese commanders at Tien-tsin resulted in the scheme, copy of which I beg to enclose, together with General Cooper's covering letter of the 7th November.

In conclusion, I may add that the British employés on the railway have been instructed, should the line be taken over by the revolutionaries, to do their utmost to continue working the service as a commercial concern in the interests of the British bondholders. The line is still running freely without any interference, and the knowledge that we are prepared to protect it may, it is hoped, enable it to continue running under the direction of the British staff.

I have, &c.
                                                               · J. N. JORDAN.

Enclosure 1 in No. 93.

General Officer Commanding, Tien-tsin, to Sir J. Jordan.

Sir,   *Tien-tsin, November 7,* 1911.
    I HAVE the honour to inform your Excellency that, in accordance with your instructions, I arranged a meeting of the French and Japanese commanders.
    I laid before them a scheme I had drawn up for maintaining communication between Peking and Tien-tsin until the river freezes, and they expressed to me, verbally, their complete agreement.
    We propose having our posts reconnoitred, so as to know the buildings, &c., we require, and to be ready to move out the troops at short notice should we receive instructions to do so.
    A copy of the scheme referred to is attached.
                        I have, &c.
                                E. J. COOPER, *Brigadier-General,*
                                        Commanding North China Command.

Enclosure 2 in No. 93.

Scheme for maintaining Communication between Peking and Tien-tsin until the River freezes.

The British.—To take from Peking to 6 kilom. south of Wan-chuang (71 kilom.).
To maintain posts at Feng-t'ai, Huang-tsun, An-t'ing, and Wan-chuang.

The Japanese.—To take from 5 kilom. north of Lang-fang to 5 kilom. south of Chang-chuang (35 kilom.).
To maintain posts at Lang-fang, Lofa, and Chang-chuang.

The French.—To take from 6 kilom. north of Yang-ts'un to Tien-tsin east (35 kilom.).
To maintain posts at Yang-ts'un and Tangku.

Each nation to arrange that its section is properly patrolled and the bridges protected.

The British propose putting 200 men at Feng-t'ai; at Huang-tsun, 30; An-t'ing, 30; and Wan-chuang, 30; say, 300 men. They are also sending 120 men to Tongshan.

No. 94.

Sir J. Jordan to Sir Edward Grey.—(Received December 1.)

(Telegraphic.)   *Peking, December 1,* 1911.
    ARMISTICE negotiations at Hankow.
    Please see my telegram of the 28th ultimo.
    I have to-day telegraphed to acting consul-general at Hankow as follows :—

    " Following are the terms of armistice which Yuan Shih-kai has offered :—

    "(1.) Ground as at present occupied to be held by each side. No reconnoitring to be done in secret.
    "(2.) Three days fixed as duration of armistice.
    "(3.) Advantage must not be taken of the armistice by men-of-war during the period mentioned to anchor at Wuchang or Hankow up against the south and north banks, and so acquire a more favourable position. Until the expiration of the armistice the ships must drop down river some distance below Wuchang.

" (4.) During the armistice neither side to get reinforcements, erect fortifications, or otherwise increase their military strength.
" (5.) In order that any infringement of the conditions may be obviated, British consul-general to sign armistice agreement as witness."

I trust that last condition may meet with your approval : I had no time to consult you in regard to it.

No. 95.

Sir Edward Grey to Sir J. Jordan.

(Telegraphic.)   *Foreign Office, December* 1, 1911.
YOUR telegram of 1st December : Signature of armistice.
Your action entirely approved.

No. 96.

Admiralty to Foreign Office.—(Received December 2.)

Sir,   *Admiralty, December* 2, 1911.
I AM commanded by my Lords Commissioners of the Admiralty to transmit, for the information of the Secretary of State for Foreign Affairs, copy of a telegram, dated to-day, from the Commander-in-chief, China.
I am, &c.
W. GRAHAM GREENE.

Enclosure in No. 96.

Commander-in-Chief, China, to Admiralty.
(Telegraphic.)   *December* 2, 1911.
REBELS have captured Nanking. They state that they will attempt to send their troops and ship up the river to Hankow.
I shall go on 4th December to Nanking, and can proceed later, if necessary, to Hankow.
Sir J. Jordan has concurred in this proposal.

No. 97.

Sir Edward Grey to Sir J. Jordan.

(Telegraphic.)   *Foreign Office, December* 2, 1911.
MY telegram of 18th November.
Orders were telegraphed to Hong Kong yesterday to send at once 100 infantry with, if possible, two guns to Hankow, also small detachment of engineers, medical corps, &c., in order to relieve sailors and volunteers in guarding concession.

No. 98.

Sir J. Jordan to Sir Edward Grey.—(Received December 3.)

(Telegraphic.)   *Peking, December* 3, 1911.
ARMISTICE and peace negotiations.
Telegram of to-day's date received from acting consul-general at Hankow as follows :—

"Through my intermediary truce for three days without terms has been agreed to by both sides. The present conditions are practically identical with what Yuan Shih-kai demanded.
" Revolutionaries will doubtless gain confidence from the fall of Nanking and negotiations thus become more difficult to conduct."

I have instructed His Majesty's consul-general to use his good offices between now and the expiration of the truce on the 6th December at 8 A.M. to bring about a meeting at Wuchang of provincial representatives to discuss terms. Yuan Shih-kai is anxious that arrangements should be made for such a meeting.

No. 99.

Sir J. Jordan to Sir Edward Grey.—(Received December 4.)

Sir,   *Peking, November* 15, 1911.

IN continuation of my despatch of the 5th instant, recording the progress of the present revolutionary movement in China, I have the honour to submit a report on the course of events in Shanghai, which I venture to think merit separate treatment in view of the diversity and magnitude of foreign interests grouped in that city.

As early as the 18th October I had received a request from the senior consul to sanction the issue of a proclamation declaring the neutrality of Shanghai, a request to which the diplomatic body was unable to accede.

On the 27th October His Majesty's consul-general telegraphed a report of an interview between himself and the taotai, which entirely corroborated information already supplied to the senior consul from other sources. The taotai admitted that the revolutionaries were ready to assume possession of Shanghai whenever it suited them, and that lacking both men and money he could offer no resistance. He urged Mr. Fraser to move the consular body to declare a neutral zone of 30 to 50 *li* round the settlements, since any disturbance would endanger the peace of the port, which he was powerless to guarantee. Mr. Fraser stated that the matter was one for decision by the diplomatic body, but expressed his opinion to me that neutralisation of the port had become advisable, since he believed that any outbreak in a place crowded with refugees, and in the midst of a financial crisis, would have disastrous consequences.

I accordingly brought the matter again to the attention of my colleagues, and as a result a telegram in the following sense was dispatched to the senior consul :—

" We regard it as entirely impracticable to maintain effective neutrality within a radius of 30 miles from Shanghai, and think it very unlikely that our Governments would consent to such a proposal. In the event of the anticipations of the consular body being realised, we think it would be justified in making such arrangements for the protection of life and property, and for the safety of the settlements, as the circumstances may seem to demand."

Meanwhile a delegate of the taotai was pressing the consular body for neutralisation, but was informed that a definite proposal should be laid before the diplomatic body by the Wai-wu Pu, and that in the meantime the Chinese authorities could not be absolved of their responsibility for protecting foreign lives and property.

On the 3rd November Admiral Winsloe was so good as to repeat to me a telegram he had addressed to the Admiralty suggesting that in view of the critical situation at Shanghai, it might be advisable to consult with the other Powers principally interested, Germany, America, France, and Japan, and that each should send about 1,500 infantry, with some small guns, to afford the protection for which the existing naval forces were, owing to their necessary dispersal among Yangtse ports, inadequate. It was also thought that such a step would exercise a restraining influence in the Yangtse valley generally. Similar telegrams were dispatched by the German and Japanese naval commanders.

I telegraphed to the admiral for fuller information as to the nature of the emergency for which it was thought necessary to provide, and as to the scope of the proposed measure. This telegram crossed one from His Majesty's consul-general at Shanghai, in which Mr. Fraser stated that he had no reason to believe that an attack on the settlements would follow a revolutionary rising in the native city, which was then quiet; nor that any trouble was likely to arise with which the police and volunteers, possibly aided by naval guards over the consulates and banks, could not cope.

An hour or two after this telegram had been sent a despatch, bearing the seal of the Military Government of the Chinese Republic, was handed in at His Majesty's consulate-general announcing that Shanghai had been taken over, and requesting the consul-general to co-operate in the maintenance of order in the settlement. The revolutionaries had, in fact, taken possession of Shanghai city and the Woosung forts peacefully, and of the Kiangnan arsenal after a little fighting.

A difficulty arose, however, in connection with the Shanghai-Nanking Railway. On the 3rd November, thirty or forty rebels entered the station and left one of their number in the telephone office, who started tampering with the instruments, and was arrested by the general manager, Mr. Pope. At the latter's request, and with the concurrence of the senior consul, Mr. Fraser authorised the occupation of the station by volunteers, his grounds for doing so being that the station was adjacent to a district of disorderly tendencies, and that the railway, although a Chinese Government line, was constructed by British capital and managed under British superintendence.

In reporting the fall of the Woosung forts, the native city and the Kiangnan arsenal, His Majesty's consul-general stated that the volunteers would evacuate the railway station as soon as the revolutionary leaders produced an organised body to protect it, and that these leaders had undertaken not to interfere with the working and receipts of the railway so long as it was not used for the carriage of troops and munitions of war for either side. He added that it was rumoured that the Viceroy at Nanking was entraining troops to recover Shanghai. On receipt of this report I at once urged the Wai-wu Pu to send immediate instructions to the Viceroy to refrain from using the railway for the conveyance of troops, or taking any action which might result in hostilities at or in the neighbourhood of Shanghai, and I instructed His Majesty's consul at Nanking to make urgent representations to his Excellency in the same sense. In informing Mr. Fraser of my action, I stated that it might be advisable for the volunteers to defer the evacuation of the railway station until the Viceroy's intentions were known, but my telegram did not reach him till next morning, when he informed me that the station had already been handed over to a uniformed revolutionary guard, which the general manager considered most satisfactory. The general manager also reported that all was quiet along the line, and that he had learned from the station-master at Soochow that six soldiers had arrived to guard the station. On the 6th instant I received a telegram from His Majesty's consul at Nanking stating that the Viceroy had assured him that in view of the foreign interests involved he would not for the present send troops to recover Shanghai, but could not bind himself not to do so in the event of Shanghai being made a base for revolutionary activity.

I had in the meantime ascertained that the Chinese Government, while anxious to maintain the neutrality of the line, could not undertake to do so without an absolute guarantee that it would not be used by the rebels for the carriage of troops or munitions of war. To ensure this they considered that the Shanghai station should either be in foreign occupation or under effective foreign supervision, and information had already reached them that rebel recruits not in uniform had passed along the line to Soochow. To my telegraphic enquiry whether in these circumstances the desired assurances could be given, His Majesty's consul-general replied on the 7th instant that in response to a similar request from the revolutionary leader, the general manager had stated that the instructions issued to station-masters precluded them from accepting troops or munitions of war for transport. Mr. Fraser, however, pointed out that no force was available to enforce these instructions ; that the general manager was doing all he could to prevent any infringement of neutrality, but that it was impracticable to give the assurances asked for. A notice was also issued at Shanghai declaring the line to be a purely commercial undertaking, and declining to accept suspicious persons or packages. The occupation of the station was, Mr. Fraser added, disliked by some of his colleagues and by a large part of the community, and reoccupation would be opposed especially as the rebels had been prepared to attack the volunteers on the night of the 4th November in the event of non-evacuation.

In a later telegram of the 12th November, which I had the honour to repeat to you in my telegram of the following day, Mr. Fraser pointed out that the situation in respect of the Shanghai-Nanking Railway had materially changed in that the line had passed, throughout its entire length, into the possession of the revolutionaries. He suggested that to confine the operation of the prohibition to transport troops and munitions of war to a distance of 10 miles from the Shanghai terminus would suffice to prevent complications and obviate the risk of serious friction, should the militant section of the revolutionaries ignore the prohibition, which they were undoubtedly in a position to do without effective opposition.

In my reply, repeated to you in my telegram of the 13th instant, I authorised Mr. Fraser, so long as the rebels retained undisputed possession of the country, to agree to the proposed limitation. But I thought that a formal protest that he was acting under *force majeure* should be recorded by the general manager, and that all rebel transport should continue to be treated on a purely commercial basis. The earnings of the railway were, I presumed, for the benefit of the bondholders, being placed to a special account at the Hongkong and Shanghai Bank.

On the 14th instant His Majesty's consul-general received a formal protest from Wu Ting-Fang, the newly appointed Secretary of State for Foreign Affairs of the republican Government, against the prohibition to transport troops, &c., being further maintained. Mr. Fraser replied in the sense of the above instructions. The general manager, however, urged the inconvenience of Naziang, the 10-mile point outside Shanghai, for entraining operations on any extended scale, and Mr. Fraser has accordingly consented to the use of the terminus subject to the consent of Mr. Pope and to due notice being given.

In reporting this by telegram Mr. Fraser added that the working of the line was not to be affected, full fares and freight being payable in advance, and that my assumption as regards the banking of the railway earnings was correct.

On the 4th instant Mr. Fraser informed me by telegraph that the taotai had written to the senior consul applying for police protection for the Bureau of Foreign Affairs within the international settlement, where he has been forced by the rising to transact his business as customs superintendent, and as the question of the taotai's carrying on his official duties from within the settlement was to be considered at a meeting of the consular body on the 6th instant, requested my instructions on the point, and at the same time referred to the possibility of interference with the mixed court. In my telegraphic reply of the 5th instant I informed Mr. Fraser that the taotai could not be allowed to turn the bureau in the settlement into a yamên or exercise any official functions, under cover of settlement protection, to which the rebel Government might object, as the foreign community of Shanghai could not be expected to expose itself to the risk of retaliation by the rebels for harbouring the representative of a Government that had lost control of the place.

My colleagues proved to be in agreement with this view, and instructions in the above sense were telegraphed to the senior consul four days later, it being clearly understood, of course, that the taotai might continue to reside in the settlement as a private gentleman.

As regards the mixed court and other established institutions of the international settlement, I trusted that so long as we maintained a strict impartiality the rebels would refrain from all interference. In communicating this view to His Majesty's consul-general, I stated that personally, far rather than submit to any modification of the system under which the government of the settlement had been conducted in the past, I should be prepared to recommend the occupation of Shanghai by a military force, and I authorised him, if necessary, to make this known to all concerned.

The instructions which the foreign representatives agreed to send enjoined the observance of strict impartiality, and authorised the consular body to transact with the rebel authorities, as the *de facto* rulers of the place, all business which the protection of foreign life and property and the maintenance of the status of the international settlement might require.

On the 8th instant I received a note from the Wai-wu Pu, stating the receipt of information that the revolutionaries abroad had purchased fortress and machine guns, which were to be imported through Shanghai some five days later, and requesting that the diplomatic body would telegraph immediately to the consular body at Shanghai instructing them to detain any such munitions of war if imported into Shanghai. The request appeared to be one which might legitimately be complied with, and as the other foreign representatives shared this view, authorisation was telegraphed to the consular body to take such steps as were open to them, in co-operation with the customs authorities, to meet the wishes of the board. I communicated these instructions to the inspector-general of customs, who informed me in his reply that orders had already been given to the Shanghai customs commissioner to retain all munitions of war imported into that port under customs control, and if necessary to apply for the support of the consular body.

I have, &c.
J. N. JORDAN.

No. 100.

Sir J. Jordan to Sir Edward Grey.—(Received December 8.)

Sir,   *Peking, November* 16, 1911.
    IN continuation of my despatch of the 5th instant, I have the honour to enclose
copies of two despatches from the acting British consul-general at Hankow respecting the
situation at that port.
    In acknowledging Mr. Goffe's despatch of the 26th ultimo, I have expressed my
entire approval of his action in sheltering the Manchu refugees.
    Hupeh.—Since the date of Mr. Goffe's despatch of the 29th October matters
have evidently quieted down at Hankow. Vice-Admiral Sir A. L. Winsloe telegraphed
on the 7th November that fighting had practically ceased, the concessions were
fairly safe, and there were no rebel forces left in Hankow city. Two days later his
Excellency asked me if I could suggest that the Central Government should recall the
Imperial troops, since further fighting seemed useless and prevented a resumption of
trade. I had previously seen Prince Ch'ing, who assured me that, as far as the Government could control the situation, further fighting would be discontinued. I hope to
have an opportunity of mentioning the matter to Yuan Shih-kai, though I have no
doubt the question has not escaped his attention, for the problem of maintaining the
army on the Yangtsze in pay and provisions must make itself felt before long. Moreover,
there seems to be some risk of the troops degenerating into bands of looters if they
are not properly supplied.
    Admiral Sah's squadron appears throughout to have given but lukewarm support
to the Imperialist cause, and I confess I was not greatly surprised to hear that his three
cruisers went down the river on the 12th November flying the revolutionary flag.
They are now anchored off Kiukiang. The gun-boats followed later, but it is not yet
known under what colours.
    Hunan.—I enclose an interesting despatch from His Majesty's consul at Changsha,
describing the surrender of the city to the rebel flag. The transfer was not effected
without causing considerable alarm, but no damage appears to have been sustained by
foreigners. Telegrams from Mr. Giles as late as the 7th November report the presence
of a Japanese and an American gun-boat, as well as the German gun-boat previously
reported. Mr. Giles also states that the general situation has improved for the time
being; that most of the women and children have left, and the other foreign residents
are remaining on the island.
    Kiangsi.—Telegraphic reports from His Majesty's consul at Kiukiang state that
Nanchang, Jaochow, Wucheng, Nankang, and other ports on the Poyang Lake are in
the hands of the rebels. The governor of the province committed suicide at Kiukiang
by taking a dose of opium.
    Anhui.—Wuhu passed quietly into revolutionary hands on the 9th November, but
His Majesty's consul reports that there may be partisan fighting at any time. He adds
that there are three foreign ships of war in port, and he has no apprehension for the
safety of the residents. Anking and most of Northern Anhui are reported to have
also seceded.
    Kwangtung (Canton, Swatow).—At Canton events moved rapidly. The new Tartar
general, Feng Shan, who had only arrived on the 25th October, was literally blown to
pieces by a bomb on the 26th October. On the previous day the affairs of the
province had been discussed at a large meeting of merchants and gentry. On the
9th November the senior consul received a communication from one Hu Han-min,
stating that Kwangtung had delared its independence under the jurisdiction of the
military Government of the Chinese Republic and that he himself had been elected
Governor-General, with the title of Tu Tu. He promised to hold himself responsible
for the protection of foreigners and their property, and requested that intercourse
should be conducted in the manner similar to that which obtains in Hupei. The
city so far remains peaceful, but the treasury is empty, and it is therefore as well
that two companies of Indian infantry are being held ready at Hong Kong for dispatch
to Canton if necessary.
    The same day that Canton threw off its allegiance, the Governor-General, having
realised the futility of resistance, fled to the British concession at Shameen, whence he
was shipped later in the day to Hong Kong in His Majesty's ship " Handy."
    On the 11th November Mr. Jamieson telegraphed that affairs were becoming worse,
as armed bandits, to the number of about 7,000, were in the city clamouring for money,
of which there was none, and respectable Chinese were taking their departure.

81

At a meeting held on the 13th November the diplomatic body decided to send instructions to the consular body at Canton similar to those which were sent to the consuls at Hankow, regarding their relations with the rebel Government.

On the 9th November several hundred revolutionaries arrived at Swatow by steamer from Canton and took possession of all the Government offices as well as the telegraph and the railway stations. On the 11th November the revolutionaries took Chao Chow. There was no resistance or disturbance at either place.

Fukien (Foochow and Amoy).—This example was immediately followed by the neighbouring province of Fukien. Brief telegraphic reports from His Majesty's consul at Foochow state that the city was captured after sharp fighting ; that the Viceroy committed suicide and the Tartar general was beheaded. Sun, the revolutionary leader then assumed control. At Amoy the taotai and other officials took refuge on a Chinese cruiser and left the revolutionaries a clear field.

Kwangsi simultaneously declared its independence, with the governor as president of the military administration. The provincial assembly has been converted into a Parliament. Customs and *li-kin* revenues are to be collected as usual; treaties recognised ; and foreign merchants and missions strictly protected.

Chekiang.—The province of Chekiang, represented by Hangchow, Ningpo, and Wenchow, exchanged the old allegiance with the new without trouble. The process at Hangchow is described in the accompanying despatch from Mr. Savage.

Kiangsu.—At Nanking a situation has arisen of considerable moment to British interests. I am addressing a separate despatch to you on the subject.*

At Chinkiang the white flag of the rebels was run up over the forts on the 6th November, and on the 8th November Mr. Pitzipios handed an official despatch from the sub-prefect of the new military Government. Although there was a momentary panic, the situation never became critical, as the Manchus handed up their rifles without a struggle. Mr. Pitzipios further reports that since the inauguration of the new Government the customs revenues have been paid to the local agents of the Hong Kong and Shanghai Bank. I may mention that this is a procedure which Mr. Aglen has wisely established wherever the rebel Governments have agreed to it. The revenues are held to his account, pending their ultimate allocation to the foreign loans and indemnity payments, for which they are hypothecated. This subject is also being treated separately from my general reports on the revolutionary movement.

Yünnan.—There has been no further news from Yünnan-fu, and it may be assumed that matters there remain quiet. When Tengyueh, unexpectedly, declared for the revolutionary cause, His Majesty's consul, Mr. Smith, was in Burma, consulting the authorities on frontier matters. On receipt of the news he returned at once to his post on the 14th November and found everything quiet. All foreigners had left for Burma, and their property was guarded. He telegraphs, however, that he has no news of the missionaries at Talifu, which is still Imperialist ; and I have authorised him, if he considers it necessary and safe, to proceed thither and ascertain how matters stand.

Szechuan.—I have received no very recent telegraphic news from Szechuan, but I gather from Mr. Wilkinson's despatches that the situation at Chengtu is not alarming. The news, not usually very reliable, which filters through indicates that fighting still continues in various parts of the province. The mission stations have sustained no harm.

Shantung.—Shantung has now joined the majority. On the 2nd November His Majesty's consul at Tsinanfu reported that 2,000 troops of the 5th Division were being moved to the front and 2,000 more had been warned to hold themselves in readiness. Whether they will get there seems doubtful. The Peking Government has again made a public exhibition of its utter weakness in at once acceding to a number of revolutionary demands made by the students at Tsinan. The provincial reply was the declaration of independence, the governor being elected President of the Republic of Shantung, and the general commanding the 5th Division Vice-President. The troops were placed at the disposal of General Li Yuan-hung, the revolutionary commander-in-chief at Wuchang.

Chefoo has also set up its military Government. The letter from General Li to the people of Shantung, enclosed in Mr. Porter's despatch of the 5th November, is interesting as a specimen of the appeals which are being made to revolutionary sentiment in the provinces. They all allude to the sufferings endured by the Chinese at the coming of the Manchus and to the tyranny they have borne for nearly three hundred years. Mr. Porter's despatch and the enclosure are transmitted herewith.

* See No. 120.

[335]   G

20th Division.—The attitude of the metropolitan province is still one of expectation. For the moment the authority of the Emperor runs in the capital and at Tien-tsin. General Chang, the commander of the notorious 20th Division at Lanchow, has arrived at Tien-tsin. The division itself has left Lanchow for Yungpingfu, and I am informed that trains have been ordered to convey it south of the Yellow River; Chengchow is mentioned as the destination.

Shansi (Taiyuanfu).—The importance of the rebel position on the Shansi Railway, from which they were able to threaten, if they did not at one time intercept the communications with Peking from the south over the Peking-Hankow Railway, is fully realised by the Government. There are in fact indications that a force is being concentrated at Shih Chia Chuang to oust the rebel troops. On the 8th November the acting consul-general at Tien-tsin had reliable information that all the foreigners in Taiyuanfu were safe.

Manchuria.—The acting consul-general at Mukden states that there can be little doubt that educated opinion in Manchuria is in full sympathy with the general desire to rid the country of the dominating Manchu influence, though the racial distinctions between Manchus and Chinese, which have so embittered the struggle elsewhere, scarcely exist in Manchuria. Telegraphing on the 11th November Mr. Willis reported that revolutionary emissaries had been active in Mukden for the past few days, but that both the Viceroy Chao Erh-hsun and the revolutionary party were anxious to avoid any disturbance, for fear of foreign intervention. The attitude of the 2nd Mixed Brigade under the command of General Lan gave some cause for anxiety, but there was dissension within the camp and the provincial assembly of Fengtien succeeded in forming a peace society, under presidency of the Viceroy.

I have, &c.
J. N. JORDAN.

Enclosure 1 in No. 100.

Acting Consul-General Goffe to Sir J. Jordan.

Sir, '   *Hankow, October 26, 1911.*
SINCE the 21st instant, the date of my last despatch, little worth recording has occurred in connection with the revolutionary movement.

On the morning of the 24th the Imperialist forces advanced and drove the rebels back to Kilometre 10, where they are now entrenched, and it would appear that the Imperialists are awaiting the arrival of reinforcements before continuing the attack. So far as I can learn the railway bridges are intact, the rebels having left them so in order, they say, to facilitate their march on Peking. A fleet of eighteen gun-boats under Admiral Sah is reported to be anchored in various places between Kiukiang and Hankow.

Yesterday afternoon Messrs. Butterfield and Swire's agent reported to me that some rebel soldiers had boarded the steam-ship "Tatung," lying at the company's wharf just outside the concession, for the purpose of arresting some Manchus who had just arrived from Ching Chou and had taken passage on the ship. I at once saw the admiral, who despatched an armed guard and brought the Manchus (one man and two women) to the consulate, where they remained the night. They were shipped off to Shanghai this morning by a British steamer, an armed guard escorting them on board and remaining until the vessel left.

Yesterday evening a disreputable-looking Chinaman in foreign clothes came to me and commenced speaking about some "Manchu rebels" whom I had in the compound; but I declined to listen to him and sent him away. In view of this I asked the admiral to increase the consulate guard last night, which he did; and at 10 o'clock it was reported to me that a rebel soldier had been seen lurking about the compound and on being challenged had fled.

By indirect means I am to-day bringing the matter to the notice of General Li, and pointing out to him that his troops cannot board British steamers, and that we will not surrender political offenders. I at the same time expressed my astonishment at this continued hunting down of Manchus, a policy which could not fail to alienate the sympathies of foreigners from the revolutionaries and their cause.

I have, &c.
H. GOFFE.

83

Enclosure 2 in No. 100.

Acting Consul-General Goffe to Sir J. Jordan.

Sir,   *Hankow, October* 29, 1911.
THE commander-in-chief's telegrams will have kept you informed of the course
of the military operations here, and I will confine my remarks to the general situation.
    For the past two days not a few buildings in the concession have been struck by
shells and shrapnel, and bullets have been whizzing about the streets. Some people
in the concessions have been wounded, two or three fatally. At the present moment
(11 A.M.) the Imperialist troops with guns are on the Hupeh road, the western
boundary of the concession, from which they are shelling the rebels in the Chinese city
beyond. The boundaries of the concessions are strongly guarded by bluejackets and
volunteers, and in many instances they have been exposed to considerable danger
from the bullets flying around. The streets are all barricaded, and both sides are being
kept out of the concessions. The heavy fire to which they have been subjected has
damped the ardour of the rebel troops, who were mostly raw recruits, and for the last
sixteen hours they have been fleeing to Wuchang as fast as they can. The hospitals
in the concessions are full of wounded rebels, as are also the American cathedral, the
post-office, and other buildings which have been devoted to this purpose. It is
estimated that there must be well over 500 wounded men in the concession and they
are still pouring in.
    On the afternoon of the 27th, Admiral Sah notified Vice-Admiral Sir A. L. Winsloe
that he would commence to bombard Wuchang the following day at 3 P.M. Accordingly
at noon yesterday all the merchant-ships in port dropped down river about 10 miles,
where they remain anchored. Foreign firms have only been able to keep their
native staffs together by undertaking that in the event of serious trouble they would
be placed on the hulks and towed to a place of safety. When the bombardment was
notified all the Chinese demanded to go on the hulks, which have consequently been
towed away, and there is now not a single hulk alongside the British bund. Many
people have been left without a single servant, and have to provide for themselves as
best they can.
    The rebels insisted on having the telegraph office moved into the native city, and
the result is that the foreign superintendent and all the operators have left. This
means that there is now no telegraphic communication with Hankow from anywhere.
and we are not likely to have steamers arriving or leaving until the bombardment of
Wuchang is concluded. Judging from Admiral Sah's ill-success yesterday, this is likely
to be a matter of days.

                                                            I have, &c.
                                                            H. GOFFE.

Enclosure 3 in No. 100.

Consul Giles to Sir J. Jordan.

Sir,   *Changsha, November* 2, 1911.
    I HAVE the honour to report on the revolutionary movement in Hunan as
follows :—

    The first inkling of trouble in Hupei was when 300 soldiers were sent on board
the "Kian." on the night of the 10th October to be taken down to Hankow, the
Chinese gun-boat "Ch'ut'ai" leaving with a further contingent on the following day.
    I subsequently had to protest against a notification by the Customs taotai that he
proposed to send a posse of soldiers on board British steamers arriving in Changsha to
search them for munitions of war. However, no British steamers arrived here again
until after the establishment of the Provisional Government, having in the meantime
all been chartered by Chinese at Hankow to take them down to Shanghai.
    On the 16th October, when I telegraphed in answer to you, the troubles in Hupei
had apparently awakened no echo in Changsha, although the people were much excited
over the developments in Hankow. However, the same evening a Japanese steamer
arrived with over 1,000 passengers on board, among whom were said to be a large
number of revolutionary leaders, who had come to start the movement here ; and the
following day a distinct change in the situation was perceptible. It was rumoured that
the police intendant, a Mongol, had disappeared, as also a Manchu colonel.
    [335]   G 2

The ammunition of the regular troops, who were known to be in sympathy with the movement, was withdrawn from them and deposited in the adjacent arsenal. The gendarmerie, on the other hand, who were said to be loyal and who had been promised large rewards, were fully armed. Their garrisons in the outlying districts were gradually brought into Changsha, while the regular troops were drafted away in small companies and distributed over the province.

In the afternoon of the 17th October I was informed that a rising had been planned for the night of the 18th October, and the following morning I received confirmatory reports to that effect. I thereupon issued a notice to the foreign community informing them of the signals which, with the permission of the Commissioner of Customs, were to be made at the custom-house in the event of its being considered necessary for them to leave the city. The same afternoon the signals were hoisted, and the bulk of the foreigners crossed the river and established themselves on the island, chiefly at the commissioner's house, which had been provisioned in advance, while a few remained at this consulate outside the North Gate.

An attempt was actually made that night by the regulars, whose barracks are situated outside the East Gate, to enter the city. They set fire to the straw stored in their stables, in the anticipation that the city gates would be opened for the fire-engines; but the gendarmerie, who preserved a neutral attitude throughout, did nothing. In the confusion, however, the regulars managed to recover some 20,000 rounds of ammunition from the arsenal. These the Customs taotai tried to get back the next day, but the general declined to give them up, and further refused to allow any more of his soldiers to be drafted away from Changsha.

As stated above, no British steamers were running at this time, but communication with Hankow was kept up by the two Japanese steamers, which are fortunately under mail contract with their Government. Moreover, at my request, the Japanese consul agreed to detain each of them until the other one had arrived, so that there was always a steamer in port.

On the 20th October, everything seemed so peaceful that I allowed foreigners to return to the city. On Sunday, the 22nd October, at 8·30 A.M., I received a report to the effect that the utmost quiet prevailed everywhere. At 9·30 A.M. the ex-consulate writer, Mr. Li, rushed round to inform me that a number of the regular troops had entered the city, where they had been joined by certain representative revolutionaries, and had proceeded to the governor's yamên. Their commander, General Hsiao, finding he could not control them, had simply disappeared; the gendarmerie, adhering to their policy of neutrality, had refused to close the city gates; and the governor's bodyguard, already won over, offered no resistance. By 2 P.M. the whole city was in the hands of the revolutionaries without a shot having been fired; the white flag was flying everywhere, guards with white badges on their sleeves were patrolling the streets to keep order, and the excitement of the morning subsided as quickly as it had arisen. Once the movement had become a *fait accompli*, the gendarmerie also donned the white badge, and helped to preserve order.

In the meantime, as a precautionary measure, I had given the signal, and the foreigners in the city had again crossed over to the island, while those in the vicinity of the North Gate assembled at this consulate.

Later in the day I received a communication from the revolutionaries, notifying the establishment of a Provisional Government, guaranteeing the protection of foreign life and property and the recognition of loans and indemnities, and requesting the observance of neutrality on the part of British subjects.

I subsequently learnt that the general of the gendarmerie, Huang Chung-hao, had been murdered by the regular troops as having been instrumental in having their ammunition withdrawn from them; the industrial intendant and the Changsha magistrate were also killed for refusing to surrender their seals and papers. The head of the last-named was exhibited over the Little West Gate, an act which caused no little indignation among the people, with all classes of whom the late magistrate had been very popular. The Changsha prefect, the governor, the financial commissioner, the police intendant, and the Customs taotai, all managed to make their escape.

One of the first steps taken by the revolutionaries was to close the city gates and levy contributions, either forced or voluntary, from all the principal gentry and other wealthy residents. Those especially marked out for extortion were the families of men who had rendered conspicuous service to the Manchu dynasty in the past, such as the descendants of Tsêng Kue-fan, of Tse Tsung-t'ang, and others. The former is said to have had to pay 500,000 taels. Indeed, many of them feared for their lives for some time, as also all the Manchu officials stationed in the province. Through the timely

85

intervention of T'an Yen-k'ai, however, who threatened to commit suicide, a massacre was averted.

On the 24th October, the President of the Board for Foreign Relations called on me in a quite informal manner to announce his appointment and to repeat the assurances given in the despatch of the Provisional Government. I noted the undertaking to protect foreign life and property, and seized the opportunity to complain of the obstacles put by the telegraph office in the way of my sending cypher telegrams. Mr. Ch'ên assured me that there would be no difficulty for the future.

On the 25th October I received a second visit from Mr. Ch'ên, who requested me to keep foreigners out of the city altogether, as a temporary measure ; but he gave no satisfactory answer when I enquired the reason for such a request. Later on, however, I learnt from other sources of the dissensions prevailing between the two factions of the republican party in the city, chiefly due to the intrigues of the deputy governor, which threatened at any moment to break out in open fighting. I therefore thought it advisable to enforce once more the rule that foreigners were not to go into the city at all without referring to me.

The trouble came to a head on the night of the 26th October, when revolvers were drawn and bayonets were fixed in anticipation of a fight. The crisis, however, was averted at the last moment by the resignation of the deputy governor, in consideration of a douceur of 10,000 taels. The situation thereupon improved considerably, while the opportune arrival of the German gun-boat " Vaterland " further reassured the foreign residents.

As a matter of fact, the deputy governor eventually failed to carry out his under-taking to resign. On the other hand, the governor, who appears to have acted with moderation throughout, made a further effort to compose the strife by the issue of a proclamation stating that, the Provisional Government having been firmly established, he proposed to resign, and that steps would be taken to elect a successor. On the 31st October, however, the governor and the deputy governor were both shot down by the regular troops, and the city was once again plunged in turmoil. T'an Yen-k'ai was elected governor by the soldiery. He has, however, no military experience, and it is understood that a general of the gendarmerie, Chao Ch'un-t'ing, will be made commander-in-chief. He is not likely to have much, if any, influence with the regulars, though he is said to be liked by his own troops.

The present situation may fairly be described as critical. I have not been able to ascertain definitely why the two generals were murdered by the troops, but it is not unreasonable to assume that the same fate may eventually overtake T'an Yen-k'ai if he fails to please them, in which case anarchy is bound to ensue. The followers of the two murdered men are also expected to endeavour to wreak vengeance, and soldiers are now being posted all round the city in anticipation of such an attempt. The regular troops are hopelessly under-officered ; discipline is tending to disappear ; some 20,000 additional men have already been recruited locally, chiefly from among the loafer element, and if looting starts they will be the first to take a hand in it. The recapture of the Han cities by the Imperial troops and an advance by them on Changsha would also suffice to precipitate an outbreak, in which case the position of the foreign community would be decidedly precarious. In view of the uncertainties of the situation and the probability of a very unsettled winter, I am making arrangements for the women and children to leave Changsha and Siangtan, and to go down to Hankow before the river falls and steam navigation closes. As regards those residing in the remoter places, it is impossible for me to say whether it would be safer for them to stay where they are or to come down to Changsha. I have therefore left it to the discretion of the heads of the individual mission stations to act as they deem best for the safety of the foreigners.

The state of affairs is undoubtedly getting worse. Several members of the Provisional Government have already disappeared, and I received yesterday a despatch from the new governor, asking that foreigners be confined to the island for the present. There is a Japanese gun-boat here, but in the event of trouble she would be chiefly employed in looking after the Japanese community, who number as many as all the other foreign residents put together. The " Vaterland " left here on the 29th October, after a forty-eight hours' stay, under the instructions originally received from the German admiral, no actual disturbance being in progress here at the time. I therefore venture to express the opinion that there can be no reasonable security for the foreign community without the presence of another gun-boat.

I have made arrangements to move over to the island in case I should be finally compelled to leave the consulate. This appears not unlikely, as the news of the
[335]   G 3

recapture of the Han cities by the Imperial troops is now universally credited, and the
house is directly on the line of route which would be followed by the retreating
revolutionaries, and also in the line of fire in the event of an engagement.

I have, &c.

BERTRAM GILES.

Enclosure 4 in No. 100.

Consul Savage to Sir J. Jordan.

Sir,   *Hangchow, November* 6, 1911.

I HAVE the honour to report that the city of Hangchow was taken possession of
by the revolutionary party yesterday, at 2 o'clock in the morning, without any fighting
except an exchange of rifle shots with the Manchus in the Tartar city later in the day,
which appears to have done very little damage to either side. The Lu Chün troops
were led into the city from the neighbouring camps during the night; the governor,
Tsêng Yün, was made a prisoner, and his yamên, set fire to by bombs, was completely
destroyed.

All the Government offices, with the exception of the post-offices and customs,
were immediately occupied by the revolutionaries, as also the railway, telegraph, and
telephone stations and the Government banks.

I attempted twice to telegraph the facts to you yesterday, but my cypher messages
were returned to me, although one I addressed to His Majesty's consul-general at
Shanghai appears to have been allowed through in the afternoon. Otherwise communications have hardly been interrupted, with the exception of the telephone, the wires of
which have been cut in a number of places. Launches and trains ran as usual during
the day.

On Saturday evening a guard of soldiers belonging to the T'ai Chow Gendarmerie
recently drafted to Hangchow was sent to protect the consulate and settlement, under
the command of a major of the staff and a subaltern, both very smart young officers.
At daybreak on Sunday these men and their officers, together with the local police and
the personnel of a couple of armed launches, all appeared wearing the white band
round their left arm.

The revolutionary plan had evidently been carefully laid and worked out with a
minimum of resistance. The local officials were obviously given a few hours' warning.
The judge, Ch'i Yueh, elected to remain in his yamên and take his chance. He was
slightly wounded, probably by a stray shot. The Customs taotai, Hsi Ku, also a
Manchu, appears to have escaped. The Tartar-general had shut himself up with the
Manchus in the Tartar city and at first refused to surrender, although they were
promised immunity if they would give up their arms.

The foreign affairs commissioner, Wang Fêg Kao, availing himself of a plausible
pretext, left the city in the afternoon and called upon me to inform me that he thought
the foreign ladies and children should leave the city. It was too late to do so then, as
the gates were shut; but I telephoned to Dr. Main and telegraphed to Shanghai to
warn other consuls concerned. I had previously asked the governor to send me word
as soon as he considered he could no longer guarantee the protection of foreigners in
the city.

Although it had been evident for some time that the sympathies of the local
Chinese were with the revolutionary party, nothing had transpired until the last
moment to reveal the imminence of the fall of Hangchow. My own impression, as
well as that of some well-informed Chinese, was that nothing definite would take place
here until the fate of the revolution at Wu Ch'ang was decided.

Wild rumours and alarms had, no doubt, been rife for some time, and a panic had
set in which caused more than half the population of Hangchow city to desert their
homes and seek safety elsewhere. But there seemed to be no serious foundation for
the prevailing anxieties.

Here, as elsewhere, the revolution was outwardly purely military; but it would
appear from the native press that it had been assisted and organised by T'ang Shou-ch'ien
and the provincial assembly. The regulars had been deprived of ammunition, quantities
of which were served out to the Manchus. But the high military officers were all
disaffected, and among them was one who had control of the ammunition store and
magazine in the city. A machine-gun in possession of the Manchus was tampered with
by a clever Chinese mechanic, who was called upon recently to put it in order. A

week ago the French missionaries wrote to the Commissioner of Customs, Mr. Destelan, that the auxiliary troops were daily asking their officers whether the time had not yet come to assume the white badge.

The panic among the inhabitants of the city was, in fact, due very largely to the fear that the Manchus would show fight. The few casualties that did occur were mostly caused by the wild firing of rifles from the Tartar city. The Manchus also shot the first messenger sent to open negotiations with them. The revolutionaries then mounted guns on neighbouring hills and fired blank charges at the Tartar city during the day, while communications were established by telephone with the Tartar general. The threat of a real bombardment during the night, and the offer of their lives and a temporary subsidy to the Manchus on their agreeing to give up their arms, prevailed at last, and a horrible massacre was thus avoided.

T'ang Shou-ch'ien, who was at Shanghai, was telegraphed for and arrived on Sunday evening. He refused at first to accept the direction of affairs, although proclamations had already been issued in his name. But owing to the lack of any other prominent leader and to the bickerings which have already manifested themselves among the members of the provincial assembly, who have assumed the control of the various branches of the administration, he has accepted the task temporarily. There is much uncertainty as to the permanence of the appointments which have been made so far to public offices.

The maritime customs are functioning as usual. The commissioner retains charge of the duties collected, but has arranged for most of them to be paid at Shanghai. If, as is said to be contemplated by the insurgents, all *li-kin* dues are to be abolished, the utility of the customs station here will cease to exist. This will, of course, apply to most inland ports.

The commissioner has refused to raise the white or the republican flag. He revived the late inspector-general's green and yellow flag, and explained to the revolutionary deputation which called upon him to discuss the matter that the customs must remain neutral.

The republican or "Kuang Fu" flag is red, with a white square in the right hand top corner, in which is inset a sun outlined in blue.

The revolutionary officers have so far shown the greatest courtesy to foreigners, and much better arrangements for their protection are in force now than a few days ago under the old officials. Better order prevails generally, and confidence is beginning to revive.

I have, &c.
V. L. SAVAGE.

Enclosure 5 in No. 100.

Acting Consul Porter to Sir J. Jordan.

Sir, *Chefoo, November 5,* 1911.

I HAVE the honour to enclose a translation of a letter from General Li Yuan-hung to the people of Shantung, calling upon them to come to the help of the revolutionaries in Hupei.

The letter, which is in somewhat classical style, is obviously meant to appeal more to the educated classes than to the masses. It had for some days been circulated among the cadets and sailors of the naval college, and I was endeavouring to obtain a copy of it, when it was on Friday last published in the local Chinese newspaper, an act of temerity which has passed unnoticed by the Chinese officials.

The newspaper naïvely avoids direct reference to the Manchus in almost every case by substituting blanks for the words whenever they occur.

No effect seems to have been produced in Chefoo by the receipt of this letter as yet, although some of the more fiery spirits among the naval cadets are reported to have amputated a finger or so as a manifestation of their patriotism.

In the opinion of those best qualified to judge there is little likelihood of any disturbance here for the present, but the taotai, in order to be on the safe side, has sent for 500 soldiers from the Tengchow command with a view to the preservation of order in case the lower elements of the population should endeavour to take advantage of the condition of affairs to create disturbance.

A company of these men has already arrived, and a quantity of ammunition for them was landed from the steam-ship "Kraetke" some days ago.

[335] G 4

Placards, of which the following is a translation, were yesterday posted on walls in conspicuous places in the town :—

" Tell our brethren to hasten to raise the patriotic flag and help the people's army to drive out the Manchu Government."

The police promptly removed these, and there has been no attempt to replace them.

The taotai wrote to the foreign consuls yesterday to request them to notify their nationals not to import any arms or ammunition or sell them to Chinese during the existing state of suspense.

As the importation of arms and ammunition is already sufficiently safeguarded against by the existing regulations, I did not feel called upon to do more than send a formal acknowledgment of the letter, which, the Commissioner of Customs informs me, was all that the taotai expected.

An unconfirmed rumour this morning reports the mutiny of troops at Chinan Fu, with the connivance of the provincial assembly, resulting in the capture of the arsenal at Techow, but it is impossible to verify any particular one among the many rumours which circulate freely through the port.

I have, &c.
H. PORTER.

Enclosure 6 in No. 100.

Extract from " Po Hai Pao" of November 4, 1911.

LETTER FROM LI YUAN-HUNG TO SHANTUNG.

(Translation.)

THE Eastern Lu (Shantung) was the earliest to adopt civilisation and in the forefront of culture. Favoured by nature in its mountains and rivers, it has produced generations of sages and worthies. It is noted for the bravery and fighting quality of its inhabitants, who were made use of in turn by Tai Kung and Hsiao Po in the establishment of their kingdoms. Their glorious history is a constant theme. But in the Ming dynasty the downfall of the Government came. For various reasons San Kuei invited the . . . . from every direction into the country with the result that the . . . . from the black waters became rulers over the Celestial Empire. Your province, being adjacent to the metropolitan province, was the first to experience their passage, and the direful slaughter and savage treatment you experienced were no lighter than that meted out to Chin Ting and Yang Chou. These are occurrences of no distant date, and reflection over them brings grief to men's hearts to-day. Indeed, these people could be no kin of yours; their hearts must have been of a different nature. These Manchu chings . . . . in time past encroached upon our cultured civilisation. At heart conscious of their own deficiencies, they sought to maintain undisputed control by blocking every form of progress. Their haughty commands and fierce methods of government have been enforced to an intolerable degree for 300 years, until to-day they have reached an unendurable point. Their daily talk is of a constitution, but all the while they strengthen their autocratic rule. Daily they talk of uniting Han and Manchu, but their obstruction to the Han grows ever greater. Babes still reeking of their mothers' milk are put into high military command. Moribund greybeards are placed in positions of supreme control. Even then they are not satisfied that they have succeeded in reducing us to the point of death, so they impose heavy taxes the proceeds of which go to pay for their extravagances. Railways are sold and mines surrendered in order to curry favour with foreigners. Our protests are met with the cry of rebellion, and the order is, " Kill; do not reason ! " Alas! Alas! Is there one among you devoid of spirit? Is there one dead to the sense of shame? Can you allow this beautiful land to be overrun with hordes of wild savages? Shall polite and cultured people become their slaves? Will they not try to sweep out these . . . . , and clear the country of this disgrace? I, too, am a devoted Han, cherishing deeply the feud. Once the standard was raised Wuchang and Hankow returned to us, while Hunan, Kuangtung, Nanking, Kiangsi stood by and applauded. The south-eastern district has once again seen the light of day.

The eastern kingdom (Shantung) gave birth to the doctrine of Confucius. In your hearts has the great purpose of thrusting back the savage hordes been longest cherished.

Why not take this opportunity of joining in the great cause, so as to continue once more the Yen Emperor's interrupted line and fulfil the genuine Confucian doctrine?

Moreover, the . . . . constantly contemplate handing over the country by choice to foreign nations, from which it is clear that they care nothing for our welfare. By the lease of Kiaochow and the cession of Wei-hai Wei, we have become the slaves of slaves. I think all our brethren of Ch'ing-chou, Yen-chou, Tainan, and Taishan must be filled with shame and bitterness. Again, a feud of nine generations' duration is a great matter, says the "Spring and Autumn." Seize this opportunity and hasten to unfurl the patriotic banner! Befriend our Hupei army. Send to Linching in the west so as to throttle the connection between north and south. In the north, proceed by sea and attack the vital point of Tangku. Let the navy unite in the advance and proceed to the Manchu dens. When the Hans are once more in control, let us establish a united republic. Our ancestral spirits will come from Heaven to aid us. Ah! To unfurl the Han flag on the peaks of Taishan! to wash away the . . . . in the waters of the Yellow River! There should be many valiant spirits amongst you men of Shantung. I ask you to be the very first to lead the van; do not incur the odium of being the laggards in the rear.

No. 101.

Sir J. Jordan to Sir Edward Grey.—(Received December 4.)

Sir,   *Peking, November 16, 1911.*

AS the future of this country is likely to be largely influenced by the financial question, it is interesting to note that the Palace treasure hoarded by the late Empress Dowager, of which so much has been heard and so little really known, is at last being used for defraying the current expenses of the Government. About a week ago 33 boxes of gold bars, representing some 3 million taels, or, say, 400,000*l.*, were handed over by the Palace to the Ministry of Finance, and deposited by the latter in the local branch of the Hong Kong and Shanghai Bank. Nearly a third of the total amount has already been sold and remitted to the War Office for the purchase of ammunition and the payment of the troops.

Nothing could more forcibly illustrate the dire financial straits of the situation than does this unprecedented use of Palace money for the needs of the Government. Much of this treasure bears marks which show that it has been lying unused for over 40 years, and neither the Boxer indemnity nor any of the other pressing demands of recent years ever made any encroachment upon it. It is believed that the sum now withdrawn only represents a small proportion of the total amount left by the late Empress, but inquiries on this point fail to elicit any accurate information.

As a reflection upon the financial methods of Peking, it is permissible to compare the situation as it is with what it might have been had all this money been properly invested, and been made to yield a sum three or four times as large as it now is.

Foreign loans continue to be met for the moment from money lying to the credit of the Chinese Government in London. The Shanghai-Ningpo and the Shanghai-Nanking railway loans were both paid to-day in this way, the latter being, I understand, supplemented by the earnings of the line, but the day is not far distant when there must be foreign supervision of Chinese finances.

I have, &c.
J. N. JORDAN.

No. 102.

Sir J. Jordan to Sir Edward Grey.—(Received December 4.)

Sir,   *Peking, November 17, 1911.*

FOR some time past it has been felt that some notice should be taken by the diplomatic body of the lamentable excesses which are attending the present civil war in this country, and at a meeting which was held at this legation on the 13th instant the view was generally expressed that the Chinese Government should be warned that outrages of the kind which had occurred at Wuchang, Hankow, and other places were regarded with abhorrence by the civilised world, and that the foreign representatives looked to the constituted authorities to do all in their power to prevent a repetition of such atrocities.

A note in this sense, copy of which I have the honour to enclose, was forwarded by me on behalf of my colleagues to the Wai-wu Pu on the 16th instant, and on the same day I transmitted an identic telegram (copy enclosed) to the senior consuls at Shanghai and Hankow, informing them of the action taken by the diplomatic body and instructing them to take similar steps to bring home to the *de facto* authorities at those places the grave responsibility which would rest on them in the event of any recurrence of these massacres.

It is to be feared that Nanking must now be added to the list of places in which the struggle between Manchus and Chinese has been marked by these barbarities.

I have, &c.
J. N. JORDAN.

Enclosure 1 in No. 102.

Note communicated to the Chinese Government by Sir J. Jordan.

LE sentiment de mansuétude qui a dicté l'édit du 11 de ce mois répond trop bien aux idées de tolérance et d'humanité, qui font la gloire de la civilisation moderne, pour que le corps diplomatique accrédité à Pékin ne se fasse un devoir de témoigner sa satisfaction à cette occasion.

Les représentants des Puissances étrangères se plaisent à espérer que le Gouvernement et le peuple de cet Empire auront à cœur d'éviter dans l'avenir la répétition de massacres semblables à ceux qui ont eu Outchang, Hankéou et Taïyouanfou dernièrement pour théâtre, et dont l'horreur a soulevé la réprobation du monde entier.

Dans ces conditions le corps diplomatique a le droit et le devoir d'attirer l'attention des autorités constituées sur la nécessité de prendre d'urgence toutes les mesures en leur pouvoir à l'effet d'empêcher le retour d'atrocités pareilles.

Le corps diplomatique estime que les autorités commettraient une faute inexcusable en se soustrayant à ce devoir essentiel.

Pékin, le 16 novembre, 1911.

(Translation.)

THE spirit of clemency which dictated the edict of the 11th of this month is so fully in harmony with the ideas of tolerance and humanity which are the glory of modern civilisation, that the diplomatic body accredited to Peking consider it their duty to give expression to their satisfaction on this occasion.

The representatives of the foreign Powers cherish the hope that the Government and the people of this Empire will earnestly endeavour to avoid a repetition in the future of massacres similar to those which have recently taken place at Wuchang, Hankow, and Tai-yuan-fu, the horror of which has called forth the condemnation of the entire world.

It is, in these circumstances, the right and duty of the diplomatic body to call the attention of the constituted authorities to the urgent need for every possible measure to be taken to prevent the recurrence of similar atrocities.

The diplomatic body consider that failure to perform this essential duty would constitute an unpardonable fault on the part of the authorities.

Peking, November 16, 1911.

Enclosure 2 in No. 102.

Sir J. Jordan to the Senior Consuls at Shanghai and Hankow.

(Télégraphique.)   *Pékin, le 16 novembre,* 1911.

LE corps diplomatique a fait des représentations très sévères au Gouvernement chinois au sujet des massacres de foules innocentes qui se vérifient en plusieurs parties de l'Empire, et l'a averti que des faits pareils soulèvent l'indignation du monde civilise.

91

Ces massacres étant exécrables de quelque côté qu'ils viennent, le corps diplomatique vous charge de faire une communication analogue aux autorités qui détiennent le pouvoir à Changhaï en leur rappelant les graves responsabilités qui pourraient retomber sur elles.

(Translation.)

(Telegraphic.)   Peking, November 16, 1911.
THE diplomatic body have made the strongest representations to the Chinese Government concerning the massacres of numbers of innocent people which are taking place in various parts of the Empire, and they have warned them that such acts arouse the indignation of the civilised world. As such massacres are execrable, whoever perpetrates them, the diplomatic body instruct you to make a communication in similar terms to the authorities holding power at Shanghai recalling to them the grave responsibilities which they might incur.

No. 103.

Sir J. Jordan to Sir Edward Grey.—(Received December 4.)

Sir,   Peking, November 17, 1911.
YUAN SHIH-KAI, who arrived in the capital on the 13th, has not been long in forming the new Cabinet, for the Regent yesterday issued a decree appointing as Ministers of State the men whom the new Premier had recommended as heads of the various Ministries when he was received in audience the same day. A further decree was issued at the same time appointing Vice-Ministers to each Ministry.

I have the honour to enclose a complete list of the members of the Cabinet, together with the names of the various Vice-Ministers and of those acting as Vice-Ministers *ad interim.* In this list in each case the province of origin has been added.

Liang Tun-yen is reappointed to the Foreign Office. Until Liang arrives, Hu Wei-tê, who has had long experience abroad, is to act for him.

One of Yuan's particular associates, Chao Ping-chün, is confirmed in the post of Minister of the Interior, while the appointment of Yang Shih-ch'i as Acting Minister of Posts and Communications leaves the way open for T'ang Shao-yi to return and take up the substantive post to which he was recently gazetted on the fall of Sheng Hsuan-huai.

As regards the Ministry of Finance, the appointment of Yen Hsiu is likely to give rise to some criticism, for his experience in administrative work has hitherto been confined to the Ministry of Education, of which he has been vice-president. He will, however, be ably assisted by the new Vice-Minister, Ch'en Chin-t'ao, at present the vice-president of the Ta Ch'ing Bank, and who has recently attended the Monetary Conference with the four groups at Berlin as the representative of the Ministry of Finance. He is one of the most prominent of the students returned from America, and is considered a man of real capacity.

The former Minister of Education, T'ang Ching-ch'ung, has been retained in his post, while the portfolio of Minister of Justice has been given to Shen Chia-pen. The latter, who is a member of the Hanlin, is a great authority on Chinese law, and is also one of the scholar members of the Senate. He further acted as vice-president of the Senate during its first session last year.

The new Minister of War, Wang Shih-chen, is a trusted friend of Yuan Shih-kai's, and was the commander-in-chief in Kiangpei previous to his appointment the other day as Acting Governor-General of Hukwang. Admiral Sah returns to the Admiralty, and will be assisted by Vice-Admiral T'an Hsüeh-heng, his former colleague.

An interesting appointment is that of Chang Ch'ien to the Ministry of Agriculture, Works, and Commerce. He was an optimus in the Imperial examinations, and is the president of the Chinese Educational Association. His selection should be popular in the provinces, for he is regarded as a pioneer in the development of industries, but his acceptance of the post is doubtful. The Minister for the Colonies, Ta Shou, a Manchu, formerly filled the position of vice-president of that Ministry, Yang Shih-ch'i, who is only made Acting Minister of the Ministry of Posts and Communications, has been director of the Nanyang College at Shanghai, director of the China Merchants' Steam Navigation Company, and lately commissioner to the

Nanking Exhibition. The Vice-Minister of Posts and Communications, Liang Ju-hao, better known as M. T. Liang, was educated in America, and has held the post of customs taotai both at Tien-tsin and Shanghai.

The most striking appointment of all is perhaps that of Liang Ch'i-ch'ao as Vice-Minister of Justice. He is the well-known colleague of K'ang Yu-wei, and just managed to escape from the country at the time of the *coup d'État* of 1898. Since then he has lived mainly in Japan, and has written many books, especially on legal subjects.

Another Kwangtung man in the shape of Liang Shih-yi returns to power as Acting Vice-Minister of Posts and Communications.

I have, &c.

J. N. JORDAN.

Enclosure 1 in No. 103.

List of Members of Chinese Cabinet.

Ministry.	Minister of State.	Province.
Foreign Affairs	Liang Tun-yen.. ..	Kwangtung.
	Hu Wei-tê (Acting) ..	Chekiang.
Interior ..	Chao Ping-chun ..	Honan.
Finance ..	Yen Hsiu	Chihli.
	Shao-Ying (Acting) ..	Manchu.
Education .	T'ang Ching-ch'ung ..	Kwangsi.
War	Wang Shih-chen ..	Chihli.
	Shou Hsün (Acting) .	Mongol.
Navy	Sa Chen-ping	Fuhkien.
	T'an Hsüeh-heng (Acting)	Kwangtung.
Justice..	Shen Chia-pen	Chekiang.
Agriculture, Works, and	Chang Chien ..	Kiangsu.
Commerce	Hsi Yen (Acting) ..	Manchu.
Posts and Communications	Yang Shih-ch'i (Acting)..	Anhui.
Colonies	Ta Shou	Manchu.

Enclosure 2 in No. 103.

List of Vice-Ministers of the Ministries.

Ministry.	Vice-Minister.	Province.
Foreign Affairs	Hu Wei-tê	Chekiang.
	Ts'ao Ju-lin (Acting) ..	Kiangsu.
Interior	Wu Chen	Chinese Bannerman.
Finance	Ch'en Chin-t'ao.. ..	Kwangtung.
Education	Yang Tu	Hunan.
War	T'ien Wen-lieh..	
Navy	T'an Hsüeh-hong ..	Kwangtung.
Justice	Liang Ch'i-ch'ao ..	Ditto.
	Ting Ch'eng (Acting) ..	Manchu.
Agriculture, Works, and	Hsi Yen	Ditto.
Commerce		
Posts and Communications	Liang Ju-hao	Kwangtung.
	Liang Shih-yi (Acting) ..	
Colonies	Jung Hsün	Manchu.
	Chu Ying-yüan (Acting)..	Chihli.

No. 104.

Sir E. Goschen to Sir Edward Grey.—(Received December 4.)

Sir,   *Berlin, November 30, 1911.*

THE "Norddeutsche Allgemeine Zeitung" announces this evening that the Government of the Kiaochow protectorate has been instructed to send a detachment of 200 men to Tien-tsin immediately. The paper states that these troops form in the first instance a military reserve in the province of Pechili, which can be called up in case of emergency. In order to maintain the strength of the garrison of the protectorate, the full complement of Government troops will be made up at once by men from the main marine battalion. They will be attached to the regular relief transport of the Protectorate Field Battery, which leaves Hamburg to-day on the steam ship "Goeben."

I have, &c.

W. E. GOSCHEN.

No. 105.

Sir J. Jordan to Sir Edward Grey.—(Received December 4.)

(Telegraphic.)   *Peking, December 4,* 1911.

PEACE negotiations. Yuan Shih-kai's terms.

I have to-day sent following telegram to acting consul-general at Hankow :—

"In consultation to-day with Tong Shao-yi, Yuan Shih-kai drew up the following basis of an arrangement. You have my authority to exert your good offices in securing the acceptance of the terms, which have been telegraphed to General Feng :—

"1. An extension for fifteen days of the present armistice on its expiration.

"2. Troops shall not be sent to the south by the northern army; nor shall any proceed to the north from the southern army. (This is intended to apply no less to Nanking than to Wuchang.)

"3. Men from the various provinces, who are now in North China, will be appointed by the Prime Minister in order that representatives of the various provinces appointed by the southern army may discuss with them the general situation.

"4. Prime Minister will nominate Tong Shao-yi as his representative to discuss the situation with General Li Yuan-hung or his representative.

"It is expected that Tong Shao-yi will reach Hankow within five days, and the hope is earnestly expressed that the importance, in the interests of their country, of reconciling their differences and attaining an amicable settlement will be realised by both parties."

No. 106.

Sir Edward Grey to Sir J. Jordan.

(Telegraphic.)   *Foreign Office, December 4,* 1911.

MY telegram of 2nd December.

The troops, to number of 160 all told, leave Hong Kong to-morrow.

No. 107.

Mr. Lew Yuk Lin to Sir Edward Grey.—(Received December 5.)

THE Chinese Minister presents his compliments to His Britannic Majesty's Principal Secretary of State for Foreign Affairs, and has the honour to enclose, for his information, copy of a telegram just received from the Wai-wu Pu, to the closing sentence of which he would beg to call his Excellency's attention.

Chinese Legation, December 4, 1911.

Enclosure in No. 107.

Translation of a Telegram from the Wai-wu Pu, dated December 1, 1911.

IN 1901, when the official constitution of this board was reorganised, it was arranged that the controller must be a Prince and one of the presidents of the board a member of the "Chün-Chi-Chu" (Council of State). A responsible Cabinet having now been established, in accordance with the universal law of constitutional government, no noble of the blood will be allowed to exercise Government authority, and the Ministers will at the same time hold the office of "Kuo-Wu-Ta-Chen" (Ministers of State), as is the rule in all nations. The "Kuo-Wu-Ta-Chen" exercise the same functions as the "Chün-Chi" of former times, the title being changed, but the authority being exactly the same, and therefore there is no inconsistency with the former arrangement.

Hereafter this board in communicating with foreign Ministers will use the title of "Wai-Wu-Ta-Chen" (Minister for Foreign Affairs). Please inform the British Foreign Office, and request them to notify the matter to the British Minister in Peking.

No. 108.

Sir F. Bertie to Sir Edward Grey.—(Received December 7.)

Sir,   *Paris, December 5, 1911.*

WITH reference to your despatch of the 24th ultimo, I have the honour to transmit to you herewith copy of a memorandum which I left with M. de Selves on the 29th ultimo, requesting him to keep His Majesty's Government informed of any news which the French Government might receive from China.

I have received from the French Ministry of Foreign Affairs a memorandum, copy of which I enclose herein, stating that the situation in Yünnan is reported to have improved.

I have, &c.
FRANCIS BERTIE.

Enclosure 1 in No. 108.

Memorandum communicated to M. de Selves.

HIS Majesty's consul-general at Yünnan-fu has reported to His Majesty's Government on the disturbances in the province of Yünnan.

Sir Francis Bertie has been desired by Sir Edward Grey to request M. de Selves to be good enough to keep His Majesty's Government informed of any news which the French Government may receive from China.

The intention of His Majesty's Government is to restrict their own action to the protection of the lives and property of British subjects and of foreign subjects who may be unprotected, and not to impair the integrity of China, which they wish to see preserved.

Paris, November 29, 1911.

Enclosure 2 in No. 108.

Memorandum communicated to Sir F. Bertie.

PAR sa note du 29 novembre dernier, l'Ambassade de Sa Majesté britannique a bien voulu entretenir de la situation du Yunnun le Ministère des Affaires Étrangères et lui exprimer le désir de Sir Edward Grey d'avoir communication des nouvelles de Chine que recevrait le Gouvernement français.

L'ambassade ajoutait que le Gouvernement britannique, soucieux de maintenir l'intégrité de la Chine, avait l'intention de restreindre son action à la protection des sujets anglais, de leurs biens et des étrangers isolés.

Le Gouvernement de la République, également désireux de préserver l'intégrité de la Chine, s'est borné à préparer les mesures strictement nécessaires pour assurer la protection des intérêts français là où ils sont menacés.

La situation du Yunnun a dû le préoccuper d'une façon particulière en raison du chemin de fer construit par ses soins, et dont la destruction entraînerait des conséquences graves pour la sécurité de tous les Européens dans cette province, sans parler des pertes matérielles qu'elle amènerait.

Mais les dernières nouvelles reçues de l'agent français à Yunnan-fou et datées du

27 novembre montrent la situation sous un jour plus satisfaisant. La vie normale reprendrait, et le soulèvement militaire, qui paraissait à craindre, ne s'est pas produit.

Les troupes françaises n'ont pas eu à pénétrer sur le territoire chinois — mesure que le Gouvernement de la république prendrait seulement à la dernière extrémité.

Paris, le 4 décembre, 1911.

(Translation.)

HIS Britannic Majesty's Embassy have by their note of the 29th November last been good enough to keep the Ministry of Foreign Affairs informed of the situation in Yünnan, and to express Sir Edward Grey's desire that any reports received by the French Government from China should be communicated to him.

The embassy added that the British Government, in their anxiety to maintain the integrity of China, intended to limit their action to the protection of British subjects and property and of isolated foreigners.

The Government of the republic, equally desirous of preserving the integrity of China, confined themselves to preparation for those measures which are strictly necessary to ensure the protection of French interests where threatened.

The situation in Yünnan has necessarily occupied the attention of the French Government in a special manner on account of the railway constructed under their auspices, the destruction of which would seriously affect the safety of all Europeans in this province, apart from the material losses which would attend it.

But the latest reports from the French agent at Yünnan-fu, dated the 27th November, give a more satisfactory account of the situation. It would appear that ordinary life has been resumed, and the military rising which was at one time to be feared has not occurred.

It has not been necessary for French troops to enter Chinese territory—a measure to which the Government of the republic would only have resort in the last extremity.

Paris, December 4, 1911.

No. 109.

Sir J. Jordan to Sir Edward Grey.—(Received December 7.)

(Telegraphic.) *Peking, December 6, 1911.*
EDICT issued to-night by Empress Dowager grants request of Prince Chun to be relieved of Regency. Premier and Ministers of State are to be responsible for conduct of Government, while Shih Hsu, a Manchu, and Hsu Shih-Chang, a Chinese, are appointed guardians of the Emperor. Audiences will be granted by the Empress Dowager and Emperor together, while all edicts will bear latter's seal.

No. 110.

Sir J. Jordan to Sir Edward Grey.—(Received December 8.)

Sir, *Peking, November 18, 1911.*
I HAVE the honour to transmit herewith copy of a despatch from His Majesty's consul-general at Chengtu regarding the rising in Szechuan. Mr. Wilkinson's despatch is, I venture to think, interesting, as it shows the situation in Szechuan in a broad aspect, and forecasts the effect that will be produced locally as soon as the news of the Hupeh rising becomes generally known.

For some time now it has been very difficult to obtain reliable information of the progress and devolopment of the movement in Szechuan that started in the form of a widespread agitation against the railway policy of the Imperial Government, and in spite of the fact that His Majesty's consular officers have reported at length all that they have been able to ascertain, it has been practically impossible to verify their information, which is to a large extent gathered from native sources, while they themselves have been much hampered by the state of communications with the various local centres, which have throughout the present trouble been constantly interrupted and always precarious.

The situation is, broadly, that the province to the south and west of Chengtu is overrun by rebels and brigands, against whom the modern-drilled troops have made some spasmodic headway; while to the north and east of the provincial capital the authority of the Government, roughly speaking, still runs.

It is gratifying to add that both Mr. Wilkinson and Mr. Brown, the acting vice-consul at Chungking, have displayed great energy and resource in endeavouring to keep in communication with British subjects in the outlying districts, and to ensure their safety as far as humanly possible, but their task has been one of considerable difficulty and anxiety.

I have, &c.
J. N. JORDAN.

Enclosure in No. 110.

Consul-General Wilkinson to Sir J. Jordan.

Sir,   *Chengtu, October* 15, 1911.
ON the evening of the 13th instant T'ang Yuan-shu, whose visiting card describes him as "Director, Imperial Telegraph College, Szechuan and Thibet; Assistant Director, Imperial Telegraphic Administration, Szechuan and Thibet; Foreign Secretary to Viceroy of Szechuan," called at this consulate with a verbal message from the Governor-General. His Excellency did not wish to put any impediment in the way of the receipt and dispatch of telegrams by the consuls, but he was anxious that any news these last might obtain should not go beyond official circles, lest it should eventually come to the ears of the insurgents.

The same evening I received a telegram from the acting British consul-general at Hankow, in which he informed me that Hankow, Hanyang, and Wuchang are entirely in the hands of the revolutionaries, but that foreigners are safe.

The reason of T'ang's mission and of the anxiety he and Chao chiht'ai displayed on the 13th was now clear. It is evident that the news of the revolution at Wuchang had by that time reached his Excellency, and knowing that I had received some telegrams he sent T'ang round to learn whether I, too, was aware of it, and if I could supply any details. The Governor-General is naturally desirous of holding back this information as long as possible, so as to gain time in making his preparations. I imagine that he is stopping all telegrams but those for or from the consulates. The sinister news must, however, shortly be known throughout Szechuan, when an exceedingly grave situation may arise that can hardly fail to affect the scattered foreign residents.

As long as the revolutionary movement is controlled by responsible leaders, I do not think that foreigners will be menaced; but a large proportion of the insurgents now under arms consists of brigands and other outlaws, who are not likely to be restrained by political considerations. If the revolution succeeds in Hupeh, it is almost certain to be followed by a general rising in Szechuan. The 4,000 Hukuang troops that should be by now within the borders of this province may make common cause with the insurgents, or they may, as the Szechuan Lu-chun have so far done, remain true to their salt. What is to be hoped is that the Szechuan gentry, though they may sympathise with the revolution, will think first and foremost of what they themselves stand to lose by a state of anarchy, and will form local committees of public safety to maintain order in their respective localities.

I am encouraged in this hope by observing what has actually been done in several towns, notably in the north of the province. Here there have been many instances where the min-t'uan, or train-bands under popular control, have dealt energetically with disorderly characters who have attempted to take advantage of the present movement to commit robberies. The magistrates at such towns exist on sufferance; the real power is in the hands of the citizens themselves.

Here at Chengtu the city is still dominated by the constituted authorities, and will continue so to be as long as the troops are sufficient in number and remain loyal. T'ang assured me that the garrison still comprises three ying, which he estimated at 1,500 men. Tuanfang (who reached Fuchou on the 14th instant and should be now at Chungking) brought in his wake a piao, or 2,500 men. Two ying of these marched from Wan Hsien to Shun-ch'ing, where they were due a few days ago. These are intended to furnish garrisons in the north of the province. A number of others are marching overland through Shih-nan Fu, in western Hupeh, to Fuchou; the remainder accompany Tuan tach'en.

Meanwhile, detachments of hsünfang have been moved to Chengtu from Chiating in the one direction and from Chungking in the other. Some of these (said in to-day's paper to amount to two ying) have already arrived; others are on the road. The troops from Kueichow province, T'ang informed me, will be distributed on garrison duty at Sui Fu and other places in the Ch'uan-nan circuit. Those from Shensi will not cross the Szechuan border, but will maintain order on the frontier. He admitted that Hsinching had not fallen on the 11th October, but assured me that General Chu had since occupied it. The rebel leaders at Wenchiang had surrendered.

On the other hand, I am informed by Mr. Ritchie that yesterday's courier to P'eng Hsien was unable to get beyond Hsin Fang, and that the mail to Mienchu Hsien of the 14th instant was rifled by the insurgents.

The situation here, therefore, gives in many respects hardly less cause for anxiety than it did a month ago, and at any time we may again find ourselves cut off from communication with the outside world.

I have, &c.
W. H. WILKINSON.

No. 111.

Admiralty to Foreign Office.—(Received December 8.)

Sir, *Admiralty, December 8, 1911.*
I AM commanded by my Lords Commissioners of the Admiralty to transmit, for the information of the Secretary of State for Foreign Affairs, copy of a telegram, dated the 7th instant, from the commander-in-chief on the China Station relating to the Chinese rebellion.

I am, &c.
W. GRAHAM GREENE.

Enclosure in No. 111.

Commander-in-chief, China, to Admiralty.
(Telegraphic.) *December 7, 1911.*
ARMISTICE arranged till 10th December, and peace proposals will be discussed at Wuchang-fu during this period.

No. 112.

Sir J. Jordan to Sir Edward Grey.—(Received December 8.)

(Telegraphic.) *Peking, December 8, 1911.*
PROPOSED peace conference.
I have telegraphed to-day to acting consul-general at Hankow as follows:—

"Departure of Tong Shao-yi for Hankow, where he is to confer with General Li or his representatives, is fixed for early to-morrow morning."

No. 113.

Sir Edward Grey to Sir J. Jordan.

Sir, *Foreign Office, December 8, 1911.*
I HAVE received your despatch of the 12th ultimo, relative to the steps which have been taken to secure the safety of the British residents in Peking who live outside the legation quarter.
I approve the action taken by you as reported in your above-mentioned despatch.
I am, &c.
E. GREY.

No. 114.

Mr. Lew Yuk-Lin to Sir F. Campbell.—(Received December 9.)

Dear Sir Francis Campbell,   *Chinese Legation, December 8, 1911.*
I BEG to enclose, for the information of your Office, translation of a telegram just received from the Wai-wu Pu regarding the retirement of the Regent and the appointment of Shih-hsu and Hsu Shih-chang as guardians of the Emperor.

Yours sincerely,
LEW YUK-LIN.

Enclosure in No. 114.

Translation of a Telegram from the Wai-wu Pu, dated December 7, 1911.

AN edict was issued to-day by the Empress-Dowager as follows :—

" In compliance with the request contained in the verbal memorial of the Regent begging permission to resign the regency, let the Regent retire into his own palace and resume his former title of Prince Chun. Hereafter the Cabinet Ministers will be responsible for all appointments and Government Acts ; while in the promulgation of edicts requiring the Imperial seal and at Imperial audience I shall be associated with the Emperor.

" Shih-hsu and Hsu Shih-chang are appointed as guardians of the Emperor."

Chinese Legation, December 8, 1911.

No. 115.

Colonial Office to Foreign Office.—(Received December 9.)

Sir,   *Downing Street, December 8, 1911.*
WITH reference to the letter from this department of the 22nd November, I am directed by Mr. Secretary Harcourt to transmit to you, to be laid before Secretary Sir Edward Grey, the accompanying copies of despatches from the Commissioner of Wei-hai Wei, from which it will be seen that Sir J. Lockhart considers it desirable that a man-of-war should be stationed in that part of China.

2. A letter in similar terms has been addressed to the Admiralty.

I am, &c.
G. V. FIDDES.

Enclosure 1 in No. 115.

Commissioner of Wei-hai Wei to Mr. Harcourt.

Sir,   *Wei-hai Wei, November 11, 1911*
I HAVE the honour to inform you that I received a telegram last night from the acting British consul at Chefoo, informing me that His Majesty's consul at Tsinanfu, the capital of the province of Shantung, had telegraphed to him that that province had declared its independence. This seems to imply that the province has declared itself no longer subject to the orders of the Emperor of China, and has joined the revolutionary party.

2. Since the outbreak of the revolution in China, there has been no sign of trouble in this territory or its immediate neighbourhood, and the acting consul reports that Chefoo, distant from Wei-hai Wei 40 miles by sea and 60 by land, and its neighbourhood are at present quiet, though he is desirous of having a man-of-war in that port in case of the occurrence of any unforeseen disturbance, and has applied for one.

3. In view of the manner in which other parts of China have quietly surrendered to the revolutionary party without a blow having been struck, there seems no reason to anticipate that the surrender of the province of Shantung as a whole, and that of Chefoo in particular, will be attended by any disturbances of a serious nature. At the

same time, I agree with the acting consul in thinking that the presence of a man-of-war in this part of China at the present time is desirable as a precautionary measure, though it may perhaps be impossible to spare one now in view of the more pressing requirements of other places in China affected by the revolution.

4. If a Government is established in Shantung by the revolutionary party, and desires to be recognised by this Government, I will apply to you for instructions.

I have, &c.

J. H. STEWART LOCKHART.

Enclosure 2 in No. 115.

Commissioner of Wei-hai Wei to Mr. Harcourt.

Sir,   *Wei-hai Wei, November 14, 1911.*

WITH reference to my despatch of the 11th instant, reporting that the province of Shantung had joined the revolutionary party, I have the honour to inform you that I yesterday received a telegram from the acting British consul at Chefoo, stating that at midnight of the 12th instant the revolutionaries occupied the taotai's yamên and the east fort at Chefoo; that the taotai escaped to a Chinese steamer, and subsequently obtained a temporary asylum in the house of the Commissioner of Customs.

2. To-day I received a communication from the sub-district deputy magistrate of the city of Wei-hai Wei, a translation of which is enclosed. From this communication it will be observed that, acting on the telegraphic instructions of the military department of the Republic at Chefoo, the city of Wei-hai Wei has joined the revolutionary party. A white flag is now hanging outside the yamên of the city magistrate, with characters on it to the effect that the magistrate has been appointed by the military department of the Republic at Chefoo.

3. Immediately on receipt of the above communication I telegraphed to you informing you of its contents, and requesting instructions as to the recognition of and my official relations with the city magistrate and other officials of the revolutionary Government in the province of Shantung.

4. I am glad to be able to report that no trouble of any kind has occurred either here or at Chefoo. The population in this territory has shown no signs of unrest, and is carrying on its occupations as usual. The only fear is that there may be an influx of Chinese from other parts of China where famine and other troubles exist. I have stationed a guard of police at a point on the frontier to prevent so far as possible undesirable characters coming into the territory. As regards Chefoo, I learn from the acting British consul there that a Japanese cruiser had arrived at that port yesterday, and that an American transport was expected to arrive to-day.

I have, &c.

J. H. STEWART LOCKHART.

Enclosure 3 in No. 115.

Sub-District Deputy Magistrate, Wei-hai Wei, to Commissioner of Wei-hai Wei.

(Translation.)

CHAO YU-T'ING, sub-district deputy magistrate of the city of Wei-hai Wei, begs respectfully to state that his yamên having received a telegram from the military department of the Republic (at Chefoo), stating that no public opposition or resistance of any kind had been offered, the city of Wei-hai Wei declared its independence commencing from yesterday, the 13th November. He, therefore, deems it right to inform your Honour, and to express his wishes for your welfare.

His official card is separately enclosed.

November 14, 1911.

100

No. 116.

Sir J. Jordan to Sir Edward Grey.—(Received December 9.)

(Telegraphic.) *Peking, December 9, 1911.*
MISSIONARIES at Hsian-fu.
Acting Consul-General at Hankow telegraphs to-day as follows:—

" A letter, dated the 11th November, has to-day reached me from a British missionary at Hsian-fu, Mr. Shorrock. Letter states that serious injuries were inflicted on Mr. and Mrs. Smith, and that on the first night of the outbreak the following were killed by a mob: Mr. Watne, Mrs. Beckman, and six children belonging to four different families. Protection has been promised to British subjects in the city, all of whom are safe; owing to the insecurity of travelling they prefer to stay there. The Manchus at Hsian-fu have been practically wiped out."

No. 117.

Sir J. Jordan to Sir Edward Grey.—(Received December 10.)

(Telegraphic.) *Peking, December 10, 1911.*
FIFTEEN days' armistice was signed at Hankow 9th December. It provided for cessation of military operations everywhere, except in Szechuan, Shensi, and Shansi, where terms cannot be made known owing to telegraph being interrupted. Reinforcements are only to be sent to those provinces. Tong Shao-yi is appointed Yuan Shih-kai's representative, and will reach Hankow this afternoon.

No. 118.

Sir Edward Grey to Sir J. Jordan.

(Telegraphic.) *Foreign Office, December 11, 1911.*
YOUR telegram of 9th December : Massacre at Hsian-fu.
I leave it to your judgment to decide whether it would not be well to instruct the acting consul-general at Hankow, in concert with his colleagues, to call the attention of the rebel leader to the deplorable effect of this massacre and to the necessity of preventing a recurrence.

No. 119.

Sir J. Jordan to Sir Edward Grey.—(Received December 12.)

Sir, *Peking, November 21, 1911.*
WITH reference to my despatch of the 17th instant, I have the honour to enclose copy of the Wai-wu Pu's reply to the note from the diplomatic body of the 16th instant in regard to the misconduct of the Imperial troops at Hankow and elsewhere.

I have, &c.
J. N. JORDAN.

Enclosure in No. 119.

Wai-wu Pu to Dean of the Diplomatic Corps.

(Translation.)
Sir, *Peking, November 19, 1911.*
WE have the honour to acknowledge the receipt of your Excellency's note of the 16th instant expressing the satisfaction of the diplomatic body with the sentiments which dictated the edict of November 10th, and stating that it is most urgent that every possible step should be taken to prevent the recurrence of further atrocities.

From the above it is evident that all the nations of the world are equally moved by the spirit of humanity and benevolence. My Government entirely shares the view taken by your Excellency and your honourable colleagues, and is extremely grateful for the sincere interest taken in the matter.

With various provinces at present in a state of revolution, the Throne has been compelled to have recourse to employing troops. Proclamations have been frequently issued ordering that discrimination should be exercised in the measures of pacification, for the Throne could never bear that the innocent and law-abiding should suffer equally with the guilty.

The Chinese Government thoroughly appreciates the friendly spirit shown by the diplomatic body, and they have from first to last kept the aforesaid object in view. They have accepted full responsibility for the protection of Chinese and foreigners without distinction. Strict instructions have further been issued to the troops that, apart from actual military operations, there must be no killing or wounding of any kind.

We have, &c.
WAI-WU PU.

No. 120.

Sir J. Jordan to Sir Edward Grey.—(Received December 12.)

Sir,   *Peking, November 23*, 1911.

IN my despatch of the 5th November I stated that the city of Nanking still remained in the hands of the Imperialists, and that on the 30th October His Majesty's consul had telegraphed that there was an improvement in the situation owing to the withdrawal from the city of the modern troops. Mr. Wilkinson's despatch of the 29th October, copy of which is enclosed, explains the position at that date.

Whatever hopes may have been entertained of a peaceful solution of the problem were speedily shattered by the attitude of the Tartar General, Tieh Liang, who was Minister of War before Yin Chang. His Excellency refused to credit the edict of the Throne forbidding the Viceroy to oppose the revolutionaries if they should deliver an attack. He entrenched himself with his 2,000 Manchu troops in the Manchu city, mined the approaches, and awaited events. The remaining troops of various classes, exclusive of the 5,500 new troops who had moved out, amounted on the 7th November to about 7,500 men, all of whom were expected to assist the rebel cause. Mr. Wilkinson's despatch of the 7th November, copy of which I have the honour to enclose, is interesting as showing the situation immediately before the outbreak.

The following day, the 8th November, an attempt was made to win the city, but it failed, chiefly because the old troops under the command of General Chang Hsun stood aloof, and thus neutralised the disparity in numbers. It was now evident that a fierce struggle was ahead. Most of the women and children were got out of the city, and only about a dozen British subjects, including two women and three children, remained. There were, however, still some 200 other foreigners within the walls, nearly all of whom were Americans or Japanese, but two days later all the women and children had safely departed. Bluejackets were landed from the British, German, and Japanese ships to guard the consulates. The situation at this stage is described in Mr. Wilkinson's despatch of the 8th November.

On the 9th November an attack was delivered upon the city by the new troops from Molingkuan, which was repulsed with some loss. General Chang, whose greater force of character had completely eclipsed the Viceroy and the Tartar General, had now inaugurated a reign of terror. Every man who was suspected of being a rebel was put to death ; the possession of money or absence of a queue was sufficient proof ; 100 men of the Viceroy's own bodyguard were decapitated. Information to the above effect, which is contained in Mr. Wilkinson's despatch of the 10th November (copy enclosed), is corroborated by a British engineer of the Shanghai–Nanking Railway. In a letter to Mr. Pope, the general manager, he states that on the night of the 8th November the Imperial soldiers made a house-to-house visitation, beheaded men on the slightest suspicion, and hung the heads over the house doors to a total of 400. This ghastly sight was seen by the postmaster. The engineer also says that they raped women and looted and committed other horrible outrages. They appear to be well supplied with arms and ammunition, but short of food supplies, and accordingly the gates were opened for a short time on the 10th November, and 17,000 inhabitants driven from their homes.

As reported in my telegram of the 18th instant, I remonstrated strongly

[335]   H 3

with Yuan Shih-kai against these atrocities, and urged him to exert all the means in his power to have them stopped. His Excellency did not appear to be aware of the true state of things, but ordered Hu Wei-te, the Acting Foreign Minister, to give the matter his immediate attention. I fear there can be no doubt that these hideous scenes were prolonged for some days.

In the meantime, both sides had acquired reinforcements. The numbers of the Imperial soldiers had swelled to 12,000, and the rebel force had been strengthened by two additional infantry regiments, lately quartered at Chinkiang, and by some artillery and cavalry, all belonging to the 9th division. It may be noted that the rebel Government, in their desire to respect our wish to maintain the neutral character of the Shanghai–Nanking Railway, marched the infantry from Chinkiang instead of railing, as would have been done but for the protest of the railway authorities. It is probable that the rebels have received further reinforcements, both from up-river and from Shanghai. On the 11th November they were reported to have made a slight breach in the south wall, but, telegraphing four or five days later, His Majesty's consul stated that there was not likely to be serious fighting for some days, but that the looting and killing of suspects continued.

On the 15th November His Majesty's consul-general at Shanghai telegraphed that Mr. Pope had received a message from Nanking, stating that the engineers Bourne, Hearne, and Ridgway and their families were besieged by bandits and others at Chuchow and Linhaikuan, on the Tien-tsin–Pukow Railway. Chuchow appears to be about 20 miles north of Pukow, and Linhaikuan some 70 miles north of that. Mr. Fraser added that the railway property had been smashed up and a train badly derailed. He had requested the rebel authorities to do what they could to protect them, but he feared that the places in question might not be under their control. A message dispatched by Mr. Wilkinson, apparently about the same time as that received by Mr. Pope, stated that a revolutionary force had reached Chuchow, that the railway was cut, and the engineers were fleeing. There was no possibility of sending any assistance from Tien-tsin in time, and I can only hope that they succeeded in reaching a place of safety.

I have, &c.
J. N. JORDAN.

Enclosure 1 in No. 120.

Consul Wilkinson to Sir J. Jordan.

Sir,   *Nanking, October 29, 1911.*

I HAD the honour to telegraph to you yesterday that the situation at Nanking had become more critical, and that it was feared that the Manchu troops, who had become almost desperate with suspense, might in a panic precipitate an outbreak.

Since I addressed you on the 27th instant information has come into my possession from a trustworthy source, which shows that certain statements made in my despatch, for which I had as I thought excellent authority, were not altogether correct. In the first place, it appears that the ammunition promised to the new troops by the Viceroy had not actually been handed to them, but was to be given to them on the day I wrote. The Tartar general, however, backed up, I understand, by the provincial treasurer, objected so strongly to the idea, that in the end the Viceroy gave way, and no ammunition was handed out. As a result there was very nearly a mutiny amongst the men the same evening, but they were finally pacified by the efforts of their general and the treasurer, and a compromise arrived at under which, if they moved out of the city within the next two days, the ammunition would be handed to them at their new camps. This morning the remnants of the 33rd and 34th regiments, sadly depleted by desertion, marched out of Nanking. It appears that the men were in terror of the Manchus more than ot the old troops.

Before the Tartar general was able to persuade the Viceroy, high words, I am told, passed between them, in which the former threatened, on any sign of a rising, to bombard the city with his guns, of which he has several, and do as much destruction as he could. As to-night at 8 o'clock is the time, according to the latest report, which the revolutionaries have fixed for their outbreak, the Tartar general's threat, exaggerated to include a general massacre of foreigners as well as Chinese, has caused an indescribable panic. Yesterday and especially to-day literally thousands and thousands of people have been fleeing from the city. The tables have been turned with a vengeance.

It is the Manchus now who are to be the slayers, the Chinese the victims. The situation is, perhaps, really dangerous, because, while an organised rising is, I think, out of the question, the tension is so great that almost anything might happen.

In view of this state of affairs, and because my colleagues and the foreign community generally are convinced of the imminence of an outbreak, I have already taken certain precautions to ensure, as far as possible, the safety of the British subjects living in the city. The men have been warned at the first sign of trouble to send their wives and children to the consulate, and to follow themselves if they consider that they are in any personal danger. I have also two signalmen from H.M.S. "Newcastle" keeping watch night and day at the consulate, who, in the event of the gates of the city being closed, can communicate from a hill near the consulate directly with the ship, and I have arranged with the captain to land twelve men under an officer to act as a consulate guard and, if necessary, escort the women and children. The British community within the city walls consists of about a dozen men and some twenty-five women and children.

Other events which show the apprehensions evidently felt by the officials are the sudden flight to Shanghai with his family of the Commissioner for Foreign Affairs, who only four days ago assured me that any trouble was most unlikely, and the arrival here of a British steamer, the "Pei Ching," specially chartered by the Shanghai taotai to be at the disposal of the Viceroy.

In conclusion, I may mention that the commander of one of the old army battalions recently moved into the city, informed me yesterday that the Manchu garrison had been increased lately to 2,000 men, and under Tieh Liang had been brought to a high state of efficiency. They have fortified themselves in the Manchu city, the approaches of which are mined. In the opinion of the same officer the river defence army, of which there are ten (not eight) battalions in the city, are undoubtedly loyal, but he was not so sure of the other old troops, of whose fighting capacity he seemed to think very little. While he anticipated disturbances in the city he thought the river defence troops, without any assistance from the Manchus, would make short work of the new troops and revolutionaries combined.

I have, &c.
F. E. WILKINSON.

Enclosure 2 in No. 120.

Consul Wilkinson to Sir J. Jordan.

Sir, *Nanking, November 7, 1911.*

I HAD the honour to telegraph to you yesterday that the Viceroy had been ordered by the Throne to offer no opposition to the revolutionaries should they attack Nanking. I understand that his Excellency had previously telegraphed to Peking explaining that the situation in this province was a hopeless one for the Government, and practically recommending this course as the only means of preventing severe bloodshed and the probable destruction of the entire city. No doubt the Throne has also been influenced by the fate which, if fighting should break out here, must be in store for the Manchus living in Nanking, but, if this is so, its motives have been misunderstood by his Excellency Tieh Liang, the Tartar general, who refuses to accept the edict as genuine, and has announced his intention of holding out against the revolutionaries to the bitter end. It is possible, of course, that this is mere bluster on his part, intended to save his face, but, if so, it has been very seriously taken both by the officials and gentry in this city, who are greatly alarmed at the turn the situation has suddenly taken.

Arrangements were actually made yesterday for the establishment at Nanking of a Provisional Government, of which either the president of the provincial assembly, Mr. Chang Chien, or the provincial treasurer, his Excellency Fan Tseng Hsiang, was to be the head, both having been offered and for the time being declined the post, and, as far as I can learn, it has only been the failure so far of any representatives of the revolutionary party to turn up from Shanghai that has delayed the actual handing over of the city to the revolutionaries. The general impression now is that, unless Tieh Liang changes his mind within the next twenty-four hours, by which time a revolutionary force is expected to have arrived, hostilities will break out, and, as he can expect no other help but that of his Manchus, it should not take very long to wipe his garrison out. I can hardly believe, however, that things are likely to reach such a pass.

The military situation in Nanking at present is as follows :—

The new troops, all of whom were moved out of the city last week, are now stationed at Molingkuan, a camp about 15 miles south-west of Nanking. They were without ammunition when they left, and it is generally believed that none has been issued to them since. Before the outbreak, they numbered 5,500 men in all, but their ranks have been greatly depleted by desertion. In Nanking city itself, it is estimated that there are about 3,500 troops belonging to the river defence army, an excellent body of men, mostly natives of Shantung, Honan, and Chihli, about 1,500 provincial troops, mostly Hunanese, some 500 garrison troops, and 2,000 recruits from the north of the province and Anhui, who have been brought into Nanking within the last week. These troops, it is assumed, will all of them assist the revolutionaries in an attack on the Manchus. Against them Tieh Liang can bring 2,000 Manchus, of whom, probably, not more than half are efficient soldiers, but his men are together, and their position well defended.

I have, &c.
F. E. WILKINSON.

Enclosure 3 in No. 120.

Consul Wilkinson to Sir J. Jordan.

Sir,   *Nanking, November 8, 1911.*
SINCE I addressed you yesterday events in Nanking have taken another unexpected turn. General Chang Hsun, the commander-in-chief of the old troops in this city, instead of supporting the Viceroy, as it was expected he would do, in his decision to abstain from fighting and hand over the city to the revolutionaries, has thrown in his lot with the Tartar general, and agreed to assist him in resisting any attempt on the part of the revolutionaries to take the place. There appears to be some question as to whether the Imperial edict ordering the Viceroy to lay down arms either had that meaning, or, if so, whether it was genuine. That his Excellency had no doubts about it is evident from the fact that he informed Mr. Pitzipios at Chinkiang that he had been instructed that there was to be no fighting, and I was personally told that he had received such orders by the Commissioner for Foreign Affairs. In any case, it is on the ground that the Viceroy has been deceived on the point that the Tartar general and General Chang justify their present attitude.

The first intimation that everything was not right came to me at 2 P.M. yesterday from the Commissioner for Foreign Affairs, who told me of Tieh Liang's determination, but added that he thought it was bluster, and even if he meant what he said, he could not hold out very long. The panic, however, amongst the Chinese that afternoon was so very great that it was evident that the situation had suddenly become very serious. At my suggestion the United States consul, who is also senior consul, called on the Viceroy at 5 P.M. to inquire if there was any danger for foreign women and children. His Excellency in reply advised their prompt removal from the city, and gave his consent without demur to the bringing in of armed guards from the ships to protect the consulates. I at once warned all British subjects to prepare to send their wives and families away this morning, and I signalled to Captain Hunt, of H.M.S. "Newcastle," to make arrangements for the landing at short notice of the guard of twelve men upon which we had previously agreed. The same night at 9 o'clock the Commissioner for Foreign Affairs telephoned to me that the situation was very critical, and Mr. Yang Cheng, one of the Viceroy's secretaries, sent a similar message to the Commissioner of Customs. Fighting began at 4 A.M. to-day. What really happened is still uncertain. A band of revolutionaries some 200 strong appears to have entered the city through the South Gate, gone at once to the gaol and released the prisoners, and then attempted an attack on the Viceroy's yamên. In any case, the outbreak was totally unsuccessful. The revolutionaries were not joined by the old troops, and after some fighting, in which about 100 lives were lost, they dispersed and the trouble ended. This morning all the gates of the city were shut, and no one, foreigner or Chinese, was allowed in or out under any pretext whatsoever. By 9 A.M. practically all the British subjects in Nanking had collected at the consulate. As it was important to get the women and children away at once, for the situation still seemed serious, I telephoned to General Chang asking to let them pass out of the gates. He complied with my request by sending an officer to escort them through, and by 2 P.M. all who were going were got out safely. In the meanwhile, the guards from the different ships had entered the city through the Railway Gate, the German, Japanese, und our own consisting of twelve men, and an officer each, and the American of 110 men, of whom thirty have since been sent back to their ship. They found the gate closed, but, after some discussion, were allowed in and made their way to the consulates. The number of British subjects now in the city, leaving the guards out, is about a dozen, including two women and three children, of whom half are at the consulate with me. The other foreigners still remaining number about 200, almost all Americans and Japanese.

What the exact position of affairs in the city now is is not easy to discover or to conjecture accurately. I am informed by Chinese who should be in a position to know that until yesterday morning everything seemed to indicate a peaceful handing over of the city to the revolutionists, for Tieh Liang's bluster was not taken seriously. The Viceroy and practically all the other officials in the city were in favour of surrender, the only point at issue being General Chang's price for the withdrawal of his troops from the city. He is said to have stipulated for 800,000 taels, and the Viceroy, on behalf, it would seem, of the Nanking gentry, would only give him 400,000 taels. This was too little, and the general, therefore, threw in his lot with Tieh Liang. To-day, whether the Viceroy still holds his post or is even alive seems to be doubtful. The ruler of the city is General Chang. My attempts to communicate with the Viceroy have been unsuccessful, and my requests to him have been referred to the general. It is expected that there will be fighting again to-night, for large numbers of revolutionaries are known to be in the city, and many of the old troops are believed to be wavering in their allegiance. The future would seem to depend to a great extent on General Chang. His opposition to a surrender may yet be bought off, in which case there should be no more serious fighting. If he still persists in supporting the Tartar general it seems certain that Nanking will have to stand a siege, but it is doubtful whether the revolutionaries will be in a position to make an effective attack on the city for another fortnight. They appear to be quite confident that the whole of the 9th Division at Molingkuan and elsewhere will join them in the attempt, in which case it is quite possible that it may be successful, for they have many friends within the walls.

I have, &c.
F. E. WILKINSON.

Enclosure 4 in No. 120.

Consul Wilkinson to Sir J. Jordan.

Sir,   *Nanking, November 10, 1911.*

THE hope which I expressed in my despatch of the 8th instant that hostilities at Nanking might yet be averted by an arrangement between General Chang and the revolutionaries does not seem likely to be realised. On the day that I addressed you it was reported to me that the advance-guard of the revolutionary army was approaching Nanking from the direction of Molingkuan, the camp to which the new troops were recently banished from this city. The news proved to be true, for at 2 A.M. on the following morning an attack lasting until dawn was made on the Yü Hua Tai fort, which is situated about half-a-mile outside the South Gate. The attack was not successful, and the revolutionaries were forced to retire, leaving on the field some 200 dead and wounded, whose uniforms proved them to belong to the 34th Regiment of the 9th Division. Their dead bodies were subsequently seen by a foreigner set out in rows outside the South Gate, to which they had evidently been transported, no doubt as a warning to waverers amongst the Imperial troops. From information obtained from a wounded Imperial officer, it would appear that the heavy loss sustained by the revolutionaries was due to misplaced confidence in the disloyalty of the garrison of the fort, for they advanced on it, not firing, but waving their arms and calling on the defenders to join them, as they were all brothers, and it was only after a succession of volleys had shown them their mistake that the few survivors left threw themselves down and returned the fire. The number of casualties amongst the Government troops is not known, but they were comparatively few. Last night there was again heavy firing in the direction of Yü Hua Tai, which is reported, probably without foundation, to have been captured. In any case, it would seem that heavy fighting is again expected in the neighbourhood, as six ying marched out of the South Gate to-day in the direction of the fort, and three Chinese gun-boats, flying the dragon flag, were shelling the hills near Yü Hua Tai this afternoon. In addition to the regiments from

Molingkuan, large bodies of the revolutionary troops have been seen marching towards this city from Chinkiang, and another large force is said to be coming down the Tien-tsin–Pukow Railway, so it is probable that in the near future Nanking wil be seriously attacked.

Within the city the last three days have been days of terror for the unfortunate population. By order of General Chang all persons caught robbing or suspected of being revolutionaries have been summarily dealt with. It is estimated that since Wednesday over 500 people, most of them innocent, have been shot or executed. The absence of a queue or the possession of money, especially the latter, is regarded as positive proof that a man is a rebel. Forty heads were seen by one of my colleagues impaled round General Chang's yamên, and similar sights may be seen in numerous other places. Among the victims have been some 100 men belonging to the Viceroy's own body-guard, whose loyalty was doubtful. The Viceroy himself is still alive, but, after the émeute of Wednesday, he abandoned his yamên and went with the Tartar general to live in a fortified temple on a hill on the east side of the city, whence, however, they returned to their yamêns last night. Both they and the general are in terror of bombs. Every other civil official in the city has fled, and their example has been followed by as many of the inhabitants as have been able to pass through Yi Feng Gate during the short and uncertain period each day for which it is opened. This morning, during the one hour traffic through was allowed, 10,000 people left the city, and another 10,000, forming a queue 2 miles long, were shut in.

With the exception of a few Japanese, who are to leave to-morrow, there are now no foreign women and children in the city. The men are remaining to protect their property, for the police have entirely disappeared from the streets and their servants have deserted them.

From accounts received here, it would appear that the revolutionary forces which are attacking, or about to attack, Nanking consist of the 33rd and 34th Regiments of the 9th Division, lately quartered in this city, the 35th and 36th quartered at Chinkiang, together with the artillery and cavalry regiments of the same division. No doubt there are many volunteers also with them. The whole army is under the command of General Hsü Tung Chih. Of the forces coming down from the north no details are yet available. No serious attack is likely to be made on the city until some large guns which are expected from Chinkiang and Kiangyin have reached them. General Hsü seems to base his hopes of victory rather upon the disaffection amongst the old troops and the scarcity of ammunition in the town than on the effect of any bombardment. There seems to be good reason to believe that the troops in the city are short of ammunition, for large supplies were recently sent for from Kiangnan Arsenal, which, owing to the capture of the arsenal by the revolutionaries, were never received. Work has since been started at the local arsenal, but its capacity is small, and it has been closed so long that the machinery can hardly be in good order.

Of the forces within the town General Chang is the supreme commander. Neither the Viceroy nor the Tartar general have any say in the matter. He appears to have considerably more confidence in the loyalty of his troops than other people have, for he is personally extremely unpopular with them, and they make no secret of their opinion of him. They, however, share his dislike for the new army, which may explain their willingness to fight. Being a warrior of the old school who has risen to his present position entirely through Palace influence, his wife being a favourite maid of honour of the late Empress-Dowager, he professes the greatest contempt for General Hsü, who has a Japanese training. Whether he has any ability himself or not he has yet to show, but he is undoubtedly a man of strong character and has his men well under control. His garrison has been increased within the last few days by another 2.000 recruits, who are to be paid and victualled by the Tartar general, and 600 trained troops from Pukow. The recruits who have not yet been given arms but are being drilled, unless their appearance greatly belies them, are anything but a desirable acquisition to the city, at any rate from the point of view of the inhabitants, and their arrival has caused more uneasiness amongst foreigners than the possibility of a bombardment from outside. The total amount that the general has been able to collect to meet the expenses of the defence is said to be 600,000 taels, in which is included the dollars and sycee found in the mint. Some 2,000,000 dollars were removed from the mint to Shanghai on the 5th instant, whether with or without the knowledge of the Viceroy I am unable to say, and it was also looted on the night of the 7th, so that its contents were probably a disappointment to the general.

As it is impossible at present to send telegrams from the city, and there is also very little reliable news to be got as to the situation outside, I have arranged with the captain of H.M.S. "Newcastle" to send him every day a short report on the state of affairs during the previous twenty-four hours, from which he is to select any items worth retailing, and send them to Shanghai by wireless for transmission to yourself. He will add to his message any information he is able to get himself.

I have, &c.
F. E. WILKINSON.

No. 121.

Sir J. Jordan to Sir Edward Grey.—(Received December 12.)

Sir,   *Peking, November 23, 1911.*
AMONG the subsidiary questions raised by the progress of the revolutionary movement in China, one that has engaged, and continues to engage, my close attention is that of the disposal of the customs revenue collected at the ports, so as to maintain it intact for the service of the foreign debt, for which it is pledged.

Under the system hitherto existing these revenues have been paid into Chinese Government banks and disposed of by the Chinese superintendents of customs at the ports, the Imperial Maritime Customs Service having no responsibility beyond that of verifying and filing the bank receipts in proof of payment of duties. As soon as the administration of a city which was a treaty port passed out of the hands of the Imperial Government into the hands of the revolutionaries, the funds collected were at the mercy of the latter, and there was a serious risk of their being diverted to support military operations or meet other pressing necessities of the rebel Government. The first place where this danger had to be faced was Changsha, the capital of Hunan. Hearing on the 26th October that the commissioner of customs there had been notified by the rebel Government that he might continue to function under their orders, I consulted with the inspector-general of customs, and sent telegraphic instructions to His Majesty's consul to co-operate with the commissioner of customs and assist him in the endeavour to arrange that the revenue should be held as a temporary measure to the order of the inspector-general or of the consular body. I pointed out that the argument to be used was that this revenue was really the property of the foreign bondholders, and that complications with foreign Powers might arise if it were appropriated by the revolutionaries.

The same question arose almost simultaneously at Hankow, where the rebels appointed a superintendent of customs of their own party after the Imperialist authorities had fled. At both places the commissioners of customs appear to have exercised much tact in the negotiations which they were able to enter upon with the rebel leaders, though at Hankow, at least, their representations were doubtless assisted by the presence of the large foreign naval force then lying in the river. Even the small German gun-boat at Changsha had a moral effect which those who have not lived in the interior of China can with difficulty appreciate. The result was eventually an arrangement under which the duties collected were deposited with the Hong Kong and Shanghai Bank in the name of the inspector-general of customs, and this arrangement was followed in each port that passed into rebel hands.

When Shanghai went over in the beginning of this month, the commissioner of customs approached the consular body on the subject, proposing that the revenue collected there should be paid to the account of the inspector-general at the Hong Kong and Shanghai Bank and utilised for current expenses and for the service of the foreign debt. The consular body replied that they had no objection to this as a temporary measure, but advised the commissioner to telegraph to the inspector-general with a view to the diplomatic body being consulted in the matter.

A telegram to the above effect from the senior consul at Shanghai, dated the 6th November, was received by me in my capacity as dean of the diplomatic body on the 7th instant, and in circulating this telegram to the foreign representatives, I adopted a suggestion made to me that the already existing machinery of the Indemnity Commission of Bankers should be substituted for the Hong Kong and Shanghai Bank and utilised for the purpose of holding the customs revenue, and I proposed that, if my colleagues approved the Shanghai suggestion with that modification, I should instruct the consular body to request the rebel authorities to allow this procedure as a temporary expedient, and should ask Mr. Aglen to instruct the commissioner of customs to co-operate in this sense.

The circular was generally approved by the diplomatic body, but with certain reservations ; in view of which I considered it desirable to consult Mr. Aglen in order to ascertain whether he was prepared, so far as the commissioner of customs was concerned, to accept responsibility for the proposed method of dealing with the customs revenue. The result of the exchange of views which thus took place with the inspector-general of customs was to disclose certain objections to the suggested procedure. A memorandum on the subject was drawn up by Mr. Aglen explaining the system under which the revenue was collected prior to the outbreak and the instructions given to the commissioners of customs, with the approval of the Chinese Government, in order to secure the revenues. Mr. Aglen pointed out that these revenues are definitely pledged for the service of certain loans in regular order of priority, and suggested that a special commission of the bankers interested in those loans should be formed to receive the total revenue collected.

I deemed it my duty to lay these considerations before my colleagues, and in a circular issued on the 11th instant I proposed that, in lieu of the arrangement previously outlined, a special commission of the bankers interested in the loans contracted prior to 1900 might be formed and empowered to receive from the inspector-general the total revenue collected, less the customs charge for cost of collection, at such times and in such proportions as the service and order of their respective loans might require. On this commission would rest the responsibility of seeing that the loan payments were regularly met so far as funds permitted, and the commission would decide in what banks the moneys made over were to be lodged. I pointed out that the merits of this proposal lay in the fact that the customs revenues would be entrusted to banks who are responsible to the bondholders for the due service of loans which are secured by a first charge upon those revenues, and that for this reason it was preferable to the alternative previously suggested of paying them into the Indemnity Commission of Bankers, whose services had largely fallen into abeyance. I concluded by inviting my colleagues to a meeting on the 13th to consider the above proposal.

At this meeting I read Mr. Aglen's memorandum and explained the position of the loans prior to 1900 and of the subsequent indemnity of 1901. The former amounted to a nominal capital of 54,455,000l., of which only some 15,500,000l. principal had been repaid, and, while almost all the Powers had become creditors of China since 1900, only Great Britain, Germany, France, and Russia were interested in the loans prior to that date. These four Powers had thus a first mortgage on the customs revenues, while the Governments signatory to the protocol of 1901 had only a second mortgage. It was not therefore natural that the Indemnity Commission of Bankers should have the sole charge of dealing with the receipts from the customs, and I thought that a special commission should be appointed to secure the service of the loans prior to 1900 and to hand over any balance to the Indemnity Commission.

It was agreed, after some discussion, that the banks should be consulted, and an identic telegram was dispatched on the 21st instant to the managers at Shanghai of the banks which are connected with the obligations secured by the customs revenues. The managers of those banks, being regarded as the most suitable persons to decide upon the composition of the proposed commission, were invited to consult together with a view to a joint scheme being submitted by such commission to the diplomatic body at Peking.

On the 20th instant the agent of the Hong Kong and Shanghai Banking Corporation at Peking communicated to me the contents of a telegram from his Shanghai branch, stating that the monthly instalment of interest and sinking fund on the Chinese Imperial Government 5 per cent. gold loan of 1896, amounting to 80,579l., due the same day, had not been paid. The telegram further stated that, in accordance with article 5 of the loan agreement, exchange had been fixed at 2s. 5⅜d. per Shanghai tael for the above amount, being the rate of exchange of the day for telegraphic transfer on London.

I immediately addressed a memorandum to the Wai-wu Pu informing them of this default, reminding them that the loan is secured by the revenue of the Imperial maritime customs, and insisting that steps should be taken to place under the control of the inspector-general the whole revenue, not only of the ports which have been lost to the Government, but also of those which are still controlled by the Government.

It may be explained here that the only ports still under Government control are the Manchurian ports, Tien-tsin, and the leased territory ports, Kiaochow and Dairen. Nanking has not yet seceded, but it may be left out of account, the taotai having gone away. The commissioner of customs is believed to be in control of the revenue there. Mr. Aglen has explained to me that, of the ports mentioned above, the Manchurian ports, viz., Harbin, Hunchun, Antung, and Newchwang, are still on the old footing—that is to say, the revenues collected by the Customs are controlled by the Chinese superintendents of customs, who can dispose of them without reference to the commissioner or the inspector-general. At Tien-tsin the revenue is held to the order of the inspector-general, but as it was so deposited at the express request of the Imperial Government, Mr. Aglen does not hold himself responsible for it, and considers that he would have to remit it if called upon by the Government to do so. At Kiaochow and Dairen the revenue accounts in the banks have always been in the names of the commissioners of customs, but they cannot move them without instructions from the inspector-general, such instructions having hitherto been issued under orders from the Wai-wu Pu.

I handed in the above-mentioned memorandum to the Wai-wu Pu on the 21st instant, and was informed, in reply, that the course I proposed in regard to the customs revenue at the ports still in the hands of the Government had already been recommended to Yuan Kung-pao, and would be carried out. I informed my colleagues at a meeting held to-day of the action I had taken in the matter.

For facility of reference, and in order to give a clear idea of the position as regards the service of the loans in question, I have the honour to forward herewith two lists of the seven loans which are secured on the revenue of the Imperial maritime customs. Table (A) shows the nationality and particulars of the loan, and the total amount of principal outstanding on the 20th November, 1911, the date of the first default. Table (B) shows the amounts due for service of each loan in order of priority during the next twelve months, and a note gives the average revenue of the customs during the last four years. Owing to the fluctuations in exchange such calculations are very uncertain, but they indicate roughly that, on the basis of the last four years, there should be a surplus available for one year's indemnity payments of less than 1,250,000*l*. When it is considered that the service of the indemnity for the year 1912 according to the protocol of 1901—that is, assuming that the payments due for 1911 shall have been met—requires the sum of 2,984,894*l*. (amortisation and interest), it will be apparent that the indemnity bankers have but a remote interest in the customs revenue, and will have to look to the other securities provided—namely, the native customs and the salt gabelle.

I have, &c.
J. N. JORDAN.

Enclosure in No. 121.

STATEMENT respecting Foreign Debt of China secured on Imperial Maritime Customs.

(A.)—The following foreign loans of China are secured on the revenues of the Imperial maritime customs :—

No.	Name and Particulars of Loan.	Principal Outstanding Nov. 20, 1911.	Repayable in
1	Chinese Imperial Government 7 per cent. silver loan of 1894 : 10,900,000 Shanghai taels at 3*s*. = 1,635,000*l*. (Hong Kong and Shanghai Bank.)	2,180,000 Shanghai taels (say) at 2*s*. 6*d*. = £ 272,500	Nov. 1914
2	Chinese Imperial Government 6 per cent. gold loan of 1895 : 3,000,000*l*. (Hong Kong and Shanghai Bank.)	800,000	Dec. 1914
3	Chinese Imperial Government 6 per cent. gold loan of April 1895 (Cassel loan): 1,000,000*l*. (Chartered Bank of India.)	266,700	July 1915
4	Chinese Imperial Government 5 per cent. loan of 1895 (Arnhold Karberg and Co. Nanking loan): 1,000,000*l*.. (Three German banks.)	266,700	June 1915
	Carried forward	1,605,900	

No.	Name and Particulars of Loan.	Principal Outstanding Nov. 20, 1911.	Repayable in
	Brought forward	£ 1,605,900	
5	Chinese Imperial Government 4 per cent. gold loan of 1895 (Russian loan of 1895): 400,000,000 fr. = 15,280,000l. (Issued by French group, Paris, and guaranteed by Russian Government.)	11,367,473	1931
6	Chinese Imperial Government 5 per cent. gold loan of 1896 (Anglo-German loan of 1896): 16,000,000l. (Divided equally between England and Germany.)	12,397,425	1932
7	Chinese Imperial Government 4½ per cent. gold loan of 1898 (Anglo-German loan of 1898): 16,000,000l. (Hong Kong and Shanghai Bank and Deutsch-Asiatische Bank.)	14,022,625	1943
	Total .. .. (approximately)	39,393,423	

(B.)—Payments due for twelve months from November 20, 1911, for service of loans secured by customs revenue in order of priority.

No.	Instalment.	Interest.	Total.	Total for 12 Months.	Date Due.
1	Dollars. .. 1,090,000	Dollars. 76,300 76,300	Dollars. 76,300 1,166,300	Dollars. .. .. 1,242,600 (say) £ 155,325	May 1, 1912. Nov. 1, „
	£	£	£		
2	200,000	24,000 18,000	224,000 18,000	 242,000	Dec. 10, 1911. June 10, 1912.
3	.. 66,700	8,001 8,001	8,001 74,001	 82,700	Jan. 1, „ July 1, „
4	66,700	8,001 6,001	74,701 6,001	 80,701	Jan. 2, „ July 1, „
5	.. 381,971	227,350 227,350	227,350 609,321	 836,671	Jan. 1, „ July 1, „
6	Interest and sinking fund 80,579l. × 12 =			966,948	20th of each month.
7	„ „ „ „ 69,603l. × 12 =			835,236	20th of each month.
	Total for 12 months (approximately) ..			3,199,583	

NOTE 1.—The customs revenue for the four years 1907-10 averaged 137,875,036 Haikuan taels, or, at the average exchange for each year, 4,826,554l. The fixed charge for cost of collection has been 3,000,000 Haikuan taels.

NOTE 2.—The approximate percentage due to each nationality of the total payments due in the next twelve months is as follows: British, 43 per cent.; German, 31 per cent.; French and Russian (loan 5), 26 per cent.

111

No. 122.

Sir J. Jordan to Sir Edward Grey.—(Received December 12.)

(Telegraphic.)   *Peking, December* 12, 1911.
PEACE negotiations.
Consul-general at Shanghai telegraphed yesterday as follows :—

"Letter dated to-day from Wu Ting-fang runs :—

"'General Li Yuan-hung and the eleven provinces have, as I have informed you, elected me to represent them in the negotiations with Tong Shao-yi, a task which I am perfectly willing to undertake. But in the first place, because my departure is not desired by a great many friends in Shanghai, and secondly, since my attention is demanded here by a multitude of duties, I find it practically impossible to go to Wuchang. Arrangements for the conference to take place at Hankow had, I understand, been made with General Li Yuan-hung and the delegates in that city of the eleven provinces by your colleague, Mr. Goffe. Those delegates, of whom many have since left Wuchang, are in agreement with me that in view of its greater suitability it is advisable that Shanghai should, owing to present circumstances, be the meeting place.

"'I should be much obliged if you would kindly move your Minister by telegraph to request that instructions to come to Shanghai to consult with us be sent by Yuan Shih-kai to Tong Shao-yi.'"

I have to-day sent the following telegraphic reply to Mr. Fraser :—

"Instructions to proceed to Shanghai for the conference have been sent to Tong Shao-yi, and stringent orders to observe strictly the armistice have been issued to the Generals in the northern provinces."

No. 123.

Sir J. Jordan to Sir Edward Grey.—(Received December 12.)

(Telegraphic.)   *Peking, December* 12, 1911.
YOUR telegram of 11th December.
After careful consideration of the matter, representatives of Japan, America, Germany, France, and myself had an interview with Yuan Shih-kai on 10th December and endeavoured to arrange for sending relief party under safe escort to Hsian-fu. Yuan Shih-kai is in telegraphic communication with military commander at Tatungkuan, and will let us know whether project is feasible.

No. 124.

Sir Edward Grey to Sir J. Jordan.

Sir,   *Foreign Office, December* 14, 1911.
I HAVE received your despatch of the 16th ultimo, reporting on the progress of the revolutionary movement in China.
I should be glad if you would convey to His Majesty's consular officers at Changsha and Hankow my approval of the action taken by them as reported in this despatch, and my appreciation of their efforts to ensure the safety of British subjects at those ports.

I am, &c.
E. GREY.

112

No. 125.

Sir J. Jordan to Sir Edward Grey.—(Received December 15.)

Sir,   *Peking, November 24, 1911.*

THE present revolutionary movement in China is causing considerable anxiety for the safety of missionaries and other foreign residents in the interior, especially in the country districts of the remoter provinces, such as Shansi, Shensi, Honan, and Szechuan, where anarchy prevails and law and order are for the time being in abeyance. While the revolutionists have up to the present been careful to avoid interfering with or molesting foreigners, the revolution itself has driven forth bands of armed men who are taking advantage of the present lawlessness to terrorise the country and rob and plunder the whole countryside. Nor have foreigners been exempt from their attacks, for a party of Swedish missionaries, in alliance with the China Inland Mission, finding the condition of affairs so menacing round their station at Yün-ch'eng, in the south-west of the province of Shansi, left that place on the 8th instant, and set out for the city of Honan-fu in the province of Honan and the present western rail-head of the Pien-Lo (Kai-feng–Honan-fu) Railway. They had arrived within a few miles of the city of Honan-fu when they were attacked and robbed by a band of mounted and armed men, who not only robbed them of their money and valuables, but inflicted serious injuries on Mr. and Mrs. Blöm, the latter an English lady by birth. After a three days' rest at Honan-fu, where Mr. and Mrs. Blöm's injuries were attended to, the whole party, joined by other Swedish missionaries from Honan-fu and numbering nineteen in all, started by train for Peking and Tien-tsin, and arrived here on the night of the 22nd instant.

Last night another party of Swedish missionaries, twelve in number, from T'ung-chou-fu, also in the south of the province of Shansi, passed through Peking for Tien-tsin.

The city of T'ai-yüan-fu fell on the 23rd ultimo, when the revolutionists proceeded to the official residence of the Governor Lu Chung-ch'i, who, in answer to his questioners, stated that he declined to sever his allegiance to the present dynasty, and told his assailants that he preferred death to surrender. He was thereupon shot, and one of my informants from T'ai-yüan-fu, who afterwards examined the body, saw two bullet wounds in the governor's breast. His wife and son shared the same fate and his official residence was later burned to the ground, whereupon the greater part of the city was given up to pillage and flames and to indiscriminate slaughter. Care, however, was taken that foreigners should be unharmed, and during their enforced confinement they were supplied with food by the revolutionists.

On the 21st instant I received a telegram from His Majesty's consul-general at Yünnan-fu, to the effect that the province of Szechuan is in a state of chaos, that brigands and independent Lolos have started war upon the Chinese, that a French missionary had been killed in the prefecture of Ning-yüan in the south of that province, and that a French mission in the same region had been attacked on the 25th October, when one Annamite was killed and two French officers wounded. Mr. O'Brien-Butler further stated that dissensions had broken out among the leaders of the revolutionists in Yünnan-fu, and that he and the French consul had strongly recommended outlying missionaries to concentrate at the provincial capital, and that all foreigners who could do so should withdraw gradually to Tonquin.

On the same day I received a further telegram from Mr. O'Brien-Butler, stating that the city of Yünnan-fu is in a state of panic, that revolutionary leaders had approached the railway company regarding arrangements for flight, that all foreign women and children had been ordered to leave, and that the ex-Viceroy had arrived at Hanoi. On the 22nd instant he further informed me that a mutiny of the troops in the city, planned for the 18th November, had been frustrated by the vigilance of the revolutionary leader.

Permits to travel by rail have been obtained from the Board of Posts and Communications and forwarded to British missionaries and others who may find it necessary to leave their stations, and I have issued a circular to His Majesty's consuls instructing them to keep in close touch with missionaries within their jurisdictions, and, having regard to local conditions and safety of travel, warn them, especially women and children, of the advisability of proceeding to the nearest port or other centre where protection can more easily be afforded.

I have, &c.
J. N. JORDAN.

No. 126.

Sir J. Jordan to Sir Edward Grey.—(Received December 15.)

Sir,   *Peking, November* 28, 1911.

IN my despatch of the 8th instant I mentioned, amongst other matters incidental to the rights and properties of British subjects in connection with the revolution, the fact that there had been some interference with British shipping on the part of the rebel forces.

The accompanying despatches from His Majesty's consular officers at Kiukiang and Hankow contain such information on this subject as has been brought to my notice. It will be observed that blank shots were fired by the forts at Kiukiang at the steam-ship "Taisang," belonging to Messrs. Jardine, Matheson, and Co. The vessel was passing up in the dark and, paying no attention to the signal, reached her destination. At Hankow another ship, the "Tung Ting," belonging to the same firm, was fired at by the rebels from both sides of the river with live shot. Mr. Goffe sent the vice-consul to see the rebel general, who received him politely and informed him that the occurrence would not be repeated if the ships only passed the forts during the hours of daylight. I have had no complaints from British ship-owners and I conclude that this attitude of the rebel Government is regarded generally as not unreasonable. In the present abnormal circumstances I think that we should concede the rebels such latitude as is demanded by moderate precautions such as these which are based solely on the principle of strict impartiality and carried out with the minimum of disturbance to British trade.

In his despatch of the 9th November Mr. Goffe encloses a despatch from the officer commanding the rebel forces at Kiukiang stating that in order to prevent foreign steam-ships from smuggling munitions of war for the Imperialist forces, vessels would be examined and cleared by a special officer and would only be allowed to proceed during daylight. After consultation with the commander-in-chief Mr. Goffe issued a notification merely stating that he had received such a despatch. I am of opinion that this was a proper manner of dealing with the communication. British subjects could not, of course, have been directed to obey the order, but they are aware of the risk they run in contravening it. I should, however, add that, as far as I know, the consuls at Hankow have never published any proclamation of neutrality such as General Li mentions in his despatch to Mr. Goffe of the 31st October (Enclosure No. 3), although the neutral attitude of the foreign Governments towards the struggle is of course well known.

I have, &c.

J. N. JORDAN.

Enclosure 1 in No. 126.

Consul King to Sir J. Jordan.

Sir,   *Kiukiang, October* 31, 1911.

I HAVE the honour to report that, during the week in which they have now been in possession of Kiukiang city, the rebels have continued to maintain order, and to efficiently protect the lives and properties of the native inhabitants and of those foreign missionaries who are at present resident in the city.

The following is a list of the latter :—

British : Miss Johnston and Miss H. Johnston.

American : Dr. Kupfer, Mrs. Kupfer, Miss E. Kupfer, Miss Tracy, Miss Begg, Miss Woodruff, Mrs. Walley, Dr. Alice Stone, Rev. F. Brown, Rev. C. Goodwin.

Swedish : Rev. C. F. Lindstrom.

There are also some members of the Roman Catholic Mission, including several sisters.

The rebel leader Ma continues to send despatches and letters to me, and I have replied to some of these through my office writer.

Ma's chief anxiety appears to be that the forts, by mistake, may fire upon and damage merchant-vessels passing after dark, and he has requested me to instruct all such vessels not to navigate at night. I have replied that I cannot, of course, comply with his request, and have urged upon him the necessity of exercising great caution if he wishes to avoid complications with the foreign Powers

[335]   I

At the same time, however, I have suggested to our naval authorities at Hankow and Tatung the advisability of warning British ships coming down or going up river.

On two occasions during the past two nights the forts have fired some rounds of blank ammunition to cause merchant-ships to heave to.

The first ship, the "Taisang," belonging to Messrs. Jardine, Matheson, and Co. (Limited), paid no attention to the firing, but came on up to Kiukiang and reported to me.

Last night, however, a ship, said to be under the Chinese flag, thought it advisable to anchor when the firing took place and not to proceed until daylight.

The rebels have enlisted numbers of recruits here, but at present they have not sufficient rifles to arm them all.

I have, &c.

H. KING.

Enclosure 2 in No. 126.

Acting Consul-General Goffe to Sir J. Jordan.

Sir,   *Hankow, November* 3, 1911.

ON the morning of the 31st ultimo, on the arrival of Messrs. Butterfield and Swire's steam-ship "Tung Ting" from Ichang, the master reported to the naval authorities and to myself that when passing Wuchang his ship had been fired on from both sides of the river. After consultation with the commander-in-chief, I sent Mr. Vice-Consul Kirke to Wuchang in His Majesty's ship "Nightingale" to hand the general officer commanding a letter of protest. Mr. Kirke, who was in full uniform and accompanied by two naval officers, was politely received, and General Li expressed his regrets for the occurrence and promised that it should not be repeated if the ships only passed the forts during the hours of daylight. He intimated his intention of sending me a reply, which duly reached me on the evening of the 1st instant, and of which I enclose a translation.

Since that date rifle shots have been fired at one or two British ships and the Red Cross launch has been also fired upon ; but the revolutionaries are now being hard pressed by the Imperial forces and these occurrences are probably due to the rebel soldiers being in such an excited state that they have got beyond the control of their officers.

I have, &c.

H. GOFFE.

Enclosure 3 in No. 126.

General Li to Acting Consul-General Goffe.

(Translation.)

Sir,   *October* 31, 1911.

I HAVE the honour to acknowledge the receipt of your despatch of to-day's date.

[Quotes in full.]

As I have already had the honour to inform you, immediately after the publication of the proclamation of neutrality, which you and the consuls of the various Powers were good enough to issue on the outbreak of hostilities, I gave strict instructions to the officers and men of my army to use every endeavour to protect the foreign concessions and the lives and property of foreigners, and I am happy to say that both officers and men have borne these instructions in mind and have exerted themselves in every way to afford the necessary protection.

This morning the bombardment by the enemy's guns was unusually heavy, and in replying thereto my guns caused some alarm to a British ship, for which occurrence I beg to express my sincere regrets. The military situation, however, is most pressing, and the circumstances such that the possibility of untoward incidents arising can scarcely be avoided, and should such incidents take place, I trust that you will have the goodness to make all due allowances. I shall be extremely grateful if you will instruct British merchant-ships to proceed only by daylight, while I for my part will again issue strict

orders to the officers and men under my command to take every precaution to avoid
alarming foreign merchant-ships, and the commandant at Kiukiang will give similar
instructions to his subordinates in token of our appreciation of the correct attitude of
the Powers in preserving neutrality, and in complying with the requirements of international law.

There is another matter on which I now venture to address you. In times of war
and disturbance it is hardly to be expected that the administration of public affairs can
be carried on as it should be ; but I solemnly undertake, on the cessation of hostilities,
to eradicate the manifold abuses of the Manchu régime, to increase the prosperity of
all foreign residents in China, and to confer on my country the same measure of
peace and prosperity as is enjoyed by every other civilised State. I have every
confidence that I shall be able to accomplish what I have set out to do, and it is this
confidence which constrains me to inform you of my plans beforehand.

I now have the honour to assure you that I shall repeat my orders to the officers
and men under my command and to the commandant of the forts at Kiukiang that they
must on no account open fire on or alarm foreign merchant-ships without cause, and I
trust that you will convey to the master of the " Tung Ting " the expression of my regret
for the occurrence of which he has complained.

I avail, &c.

(Seal of the Commander-in-chief of the Army
of Hupeh of the Republic of China.)

Enclosure 4 in No. 126.

Acting Consul-General Goffe to Sir J. Jordan.

Sir, *Hankow, November 9, 1911.*

I HAVE the honour to transmit herewith a translation of a despatch which I
received yesterday from the general officer commanding the revolutionary troops at
Kiukiang, notifying me that all vessels would be searched there for munitions of war
and supplies destined for the Imperial forces. After consultation with the commander-
in-chief, I have issued a notification simply stating that I was in receipt of such a
despatch.

I have, &c.
H. GOFFE.

Enclosure 5 in No. 126.

Officer Commanding the Republican Forces at Kiukiang to Acting Consul-General Goffe.

(Translation.)
Gentlemen, *Kiukiang, November 3, 1911.*

I HAVE the honour to inform you, that, in order to prevent foreign steam-ships
during the hostilities now existing from smuggling munitions of war for the assistance
of the forces from the north, it is necessary to examine them carefully, and I have
accordingly appointed a special officer to examine and clear such ships. They will not
be allowed to proceed before 7 A.M., and must anchor at 5 P.M., and I have the honour
to request that they may be instructed accordingly.

I have addressed a similar request to the British and Russian consuls at
Kiukiang, and I now have the honour to request you to issue the necessary
instructions.

I avail, &c.
(Seal of the Officer Commanding the
Republican forces at Kiukiang.)

116

No. 127.

Sir J. Jordan to Sir Edward Grey.—(Received December 15.)

(Telegraphic.) *Peking, December 15, 1911.*
FOLLOWING are proposals made to Tong Shao-yi by Revolutionary Government at Wuchang :—

1. Overthrow of Manchu dynasty.
2. Liberal treatment to Imperial family.
3. Considerate treatment of Manchus generally.
4. A united China.

Tong Shao-yi will reach Shanghai on 17th December, and the situation will then demand most serious consideration.

No. 128.

Sir J. Jordan to Sir Edward Grey.—(Received December 15.)

(Telegraphic.) *Peking, December 15, 1911.*
JAPANESE, American, German, French, Russian, and British representatives decided at meeting to-day to request sanction of their Governments to present simultaneously through their consuls at Shanghai following communication to commissioners of the peace conference at Shanghai :—

" Legation of Great Britain, &c., at Peking has been instructed by its Government to make following unofficial representation to commissioners whose task it is to negotiate conditions for restoration of peace in China.

" Government of Great Britain, &c., considers that continuation of present struggle in China exposes not only country itself, but also material interests and security of foreigners, to grave danger.

" Maintaining attitude of absolute neutrality which it has hitherto adopted, Government of Great Britain, &c., deems it its duty unofficially to call the attention of the two delegations to necessity of arriving as soon as possible at an understanding calculated to put an end to present conflict, being persuaded that this view is in accordance with wishes of the two parties concerned."

Conference meets at Shanghai on 18th December, and it was felt that communication, to be effective, should be made before it formally opens.

It was also agreed that no communication should be made unless all the Governments approved.

No. 129.

Sir Edward Grey to Sir J. Jordan.

(Telegraphic.) *Foreign Office, December 16, 1911.*
YOUR telegram of 15th December : Peace Conference at Shanghai.
You should take action proposed as soon as your colleagues receive similar instructions.

No. 130.

Sir J. Jordan to Sir Edward Grey.—(Received December 18.)

Sir, *Peking, November 30, 1911.*
I HAVE the honour to transmit herewith copy of a telegram sent by the revolutionary Government of Kwangtung, informing the diplomatic body at Peking of the establishment of " The Military Government of Kwangtung."
The telegram further states that foreigners are being protected, and that the

district is as quiet as usual, expresses a pious wish for the consolidation of friendly relations, and concludes with a request that the contents of the telegram may be brought to the notice of the various foreign Governments.

The state of the Canton and West Rivers, where piracy is so rampant as to have necessitated the temporary suspension of the steamer service from Hong Kong and the patrolling of the West River by His Majesty's ships (see my telegram of the 29th November), does not confirm the assurance that the region is quiet.

I have, &c.

J. N. JORDAN.

Enclosure in No. 130.

Translation of Telegram addressed to the Diplomatic Body from Canton.

November 21, 1911.

THE military Government of Kwangtung has now been established and every possible protection is being extended to the subjects of all nations residing in the province. The district is as quiet as usual. We are very anxious to consolidate friendly relations and that we should all equally enjoy the blessings of peace. We pray that the various foreign Governments may be informed in the above sense. —Hu Han-Ming, *Military Governor (Tu Tu) of Kwangtung.*

No. 131.

Sir J. Jordan to Sir Edward Grey.—(Received December 18.)

Sir, *Peking, December* 1, 1911.

WITH reference to my despatch of the 23rd ultimo relative to the situation at Nanking, I had the honour to telegraph to you on the 27th November the fact of Mr. Wilkinson's safe exit from that city. This news was received through wireless telegraphy between His Majesty's ship "Newcastle" and Shanghai. Since then communication has been even more precarious than before. His Majesty's consul-general telegraphed yesterday that he had received no information at all from the British authorities at Nanking for two days since the hulks and men-of-war moved away at the request of the revolutionary general so as to facilitate the bombardment of the city by the rebel fleet. I should add that I believe Mr. Wilkinson to be on board one of the hulks.

Mr. Fraser also states that a British subject who left Nanking on the 29th November reports that the city is surrounded on three sides by the revolutionary forces, and that Wu Ting-fang confirms the statement that half the troops at Lion Hill, the strategic point occupied by General Chang Hsun within the city, are sworn revolutionaries, so that their fire is harmless. Doctor Wu said that it was desired to do as little damage as possible, hence the slowness of the rebel operations; but it was expected to take the city very shortly, apparently by assault viâ Hsia Kuan. The Viceroy and the Tartar general are reported to have taken refuge with the Japanese consul, who is now the only consul left in Nanking.

The keenest interest is taken here in the fate of Nanking, which is likely to prove one of the determining factors in the political situation.

I have, &c.

J. N. JORDAN.

No. 132.

Sir J. Jordan to Sir Edward Grey.—(Received December 18.)

(Telegraphic.) *Peking, December* 18, 1911.

YOUR telegram of 16th December.

All six Powers having agreed, instructions have been sent to consuls at Shanghai to-day to make communication as soon as possible.

No. 133.

Sir J. Jordan to Sir Edward Grey.—(Received December 20.)

(Telegraphic.)   *Peking, December* 20, 1911.
MY telegram of 18th December.
I have to-day received the following telegram from His Majesty's consul-general at Shanghai :—

" In accordance with your instructions, the six consuls presented this morning identic notes in English and Chinese to the peace commissioners.
" Tong Shao-yi replied that a second meeting will take place this afternoon, and that strict orders have been given for fighting to cease.
" Wu Ting-fang made a speech to the effect that as this was a struggle for freedom a permanent peace on sound lines must be established, and that a worse revolution would result from a patched-up peace. He himself was a man of peace.
" He wished reporters to be present, but this we objected to.
" Both Tong Shao-yi and Wu Ting-fang asked that their thanks might be conveyed to the Powers."

No. 134.

Colonial Office to Foreign Office.—(Received December 21.)

Sir,   *Downing Street, December* 20, 1911.
I AM directed by the Secretary of State for the Colonies to transmit to you, with reference to letter from the Colonial Office of the 8th December, copies of despatches from and to the Commissioner of Wei-hai Wei on the subject of the revolutionary movement in China.

I am, &c.
JOHN ANDERSON.

Enclosure 1 in No. 134.

Commissioner of Wei-hai Wei to Mr. Harcourt.

Government House, Port Edward, Wei-hai Wei,
Sir,   *November* 20, 1911.
WITH reference to my despatches of the 11th and 14th instant, I have the honour to enclose herewith a translation of a despatch which I received on the 19th instant from the Governor of Shantung, his Excellency Sun Pao-chi.
2. In my despatch of the 11th instant, I informed you that His Majesty's consul at Chinan had telegraphed to the acting British consul at Chefoo that the province of Shantung had declared its independence. The despatch which I have now received from the governor is so skilfully worded in the original that it would be very difficult, if not impossible, for anyone who read it and who was not acquainted with the actual position of affairs to realise that it emanated from the head of a Government that had declared its independence. In addition to the equivocal nature of the language employed in the despatch, it is sealed with the official seal used by the Governor of Shantung in communications addressed to this Government before the declaration of the independence of the province, and is dated the third year of the reign of the present Emperor of China. In these respects it differs from the official communications of the Revolutionary party in other parts of China, which are sealed with a seal that indicates clearly that the authority issuing the communication belongs to the Revolutionary party, and are dated the year of the Emperor Huang Ti, 4609. But the despatch also differs in these and other respects from the communications addressed by the governor to his own subordinates, as will be seen from the enclosed copy of a translation, forwarded by the acting British consul at Chefoo, of a despatch from Captain Wang, chief executive officer of the Provisional Government at Chefoo. In that translation it will be observed that Captain Wang refers to the " president," and dates this despatch the year 4609, whilst the governor signs himself " president," though in his despatch to me he styles himself " governor."

It would, therefore, appear that in addressing foreigners the governor adopts a title and mode of address different from those which he employs in communicating with the Revolutionary authorities subject to his orders.

3. I do not propose to send any acknowledgment of the despatch from the governor until I have received instructions.

4. All is quiet and peaceable in this territory and its neighbourhood at present. White flags, a sign of having joined the Revolutionary party, have been displayed in front of most of the shops in the city of Wei-hai Wei. The Chinese magistrates of the Wêntêng and Jung ch'êng districts which border on this territory have not received any instructions regarding the declaration of the independence of the province of Shantung, and are communicating and acting with this Government as usual.

I have, &c.
J. H. STEWART LOCKHART.

Enclosure 2 in No. 134.

Governor Sun to Commissioner of Wei-hai Wei.

(Translation.)

THE present state of affairs presents many difficulties, and the people's minds are restless and disturbed. In view of these circumstances, the gentry, merchants, and scholars of the province have submitted a petition in which they have requested me to devise some means of dealing with the situation.

As it is my duty as governor to protect and guard the welfare of the territory which I govern, I felt constrained at a time of such danger and difficulty to adopt some temporary expedient for the protection of the general weal. A memorial has therefore been submitted to the throne, stating that a provisional government has been established for the province of Shantung. By it I am empowered to make appointments, carry on the general administration, levy troops, and exercise control over finances, and in the discharge of such duties to act as circumstances dictate, irrespective of precedent or established usage. At the same time, the gentry, merchants, and scholars have been instructed to co-operate with those of the same views as themselves in establishing a deliberative Assembly. It is hoped that the whole province, inclusive of officials and gentry, and the entire civil and military population, will earnestly co-operate with one another in the maintenance of peace and good order, and so ensure the safety and protection of life and property. All the officials, merchants, and missionaries of foreign nationalities residing in the province of Shantung will be most carefully protected. As your Honour has always been most sincere in your political relations and thoroughly understands the present situation, it is certain that you will lend your co-operation and show your sympathy. In addition, therefore, to issuing the necessary instructions for the information of the officials, merchants, and the civil and military population generally of the province, I have deemed it right to address this despatch to your Honour, the contents of which it is requested you will note and communicate to those under your authority for their information and guidance.

Dated 3rd year of Hsuan T'ung, 9th moon, 21st day (11th November, 1911).
Sealed with the seal of the Governor of Shantung.

Enclosure 3 in No. 134.

Captain Wang to Acting Consul Porter.

(Translation.)
Sir, Chefoo, November 16, 1911.
WITH reference to my despatch informing you of the glorious return of this military Government to Chefoo, I have the honour to inform you that I received yesterday a telegram from President Sun of Tsinanfu, instructing this branch Government to preserve order.

I have, therefore, the honour to enclose herewith copy of the telegram for your information.

I have, &c.
WANG.

Dated the 4,609th year, 9th moon, 26th day of the dynasty of Huang Ti.

Enclosure 4 in No. 134.

President Sun to Captain Wang.

(Telegraphic.)   *Tsinan-fu, November* 15, 1911.
TELEGRAM from Wang, executive officer of branch military Government.
Received and read. Thanks for congratulations. Chefoo is attracting attention of
Chinese and foreigners. Reliance is placed on you to maintain order, so as to preserve
peace locally. I am sending an official to aid you in all matters.
                                                                           SUN.

Enclosure 5 in No. 134.

Commissioner of Wei-hai Wei to Mr. Harcourt.

                                        Government House, Port Edward, Wei-hai Wei,
Sir,   *November* 21, 1911.
    WITH reference to my despatch of the 20th instant, I have the honour
to acknowledge the receipt to-day of your telegram of the 20th instant, in which
you inform me that I should communicate with the revolutionary authorities only so
far as is strictly necessary, and should avoid any action implying formal recognition of
the Revolutionary Government.
    2. In accordance with your instructions, I do not propose to send any official
acknowledgment of the receipt of the communication from the magistrate of the city of
Wei-hai Wei and the governor of the province of Shantung, translations of which are
enclosed in my despatches of the 14th and 20th instant.
                                    I have, &c.
                                            J. H. STEWART LOCKHART.

No. 135.

Sir Edward Grey to Sir J. Jordan.

(Telegraphic.)   *Foreign Office, December* 23, 1911.
    ORDERS have been given for eighty British infantry from Hong Kong to relieve
marine guard at Canton.

No. 136.

Sir J. Jordan to Sir Edward Grey.—(Received December 25.)

(Telegraphic.)   *Peking, December* 24, 1911.
    PRINCE CH'ING and Yuan Shih-kai asked to see me to-day. They produced a
draft telegram which they proposed to send to Tong Shao-yi authorising him to leave
decision as to future form of Government to a national assembly composed of
representatives from all the provinces to be elected during the next three months
on conditions mutually arranged beforehand.

No. 137.

Sir Edward Grey to Sir J. Jordan.

(Telegraphic.)   *Foreign Office, December* 26, 1911.
    YOUR telegram of 24th December.
    We desire to see a strong and united China under whatever form of Government
the Chinese people wish.

121

No. 138.

Sir J. Jordan to Sir Edward Grey.—(Received December 29.)

Sir, *Peking, December 6, 1911.*
IN continuation of my despatch of the 18th ultimo, I have the honour to report that from despatches which I have received from His Majesty's consular officers at Chengtu and Chungking, it would appear that the disturbances in Szechuan show unmistakable signs of increasing, and that the movement is rapidly changing its character. The anti-railway agitators, by forcing the Government to deplete the neighbouring provinces of troops, gave the Wuchang revolutionaries the opportunity for which they had been waiting, and now the Wuchang rising has converted the Szechuan one into a frankly anti-dynastic outbreak, aggravated by unfounded rumours of the supposed approach of British troops and by threats of intervention which His Majesty's Legation is represented as having made to the Chinese Government.

Telegraphic communication with Chungking as with Chengtu is only possible by indirect and uncertain routes, but a message which has come through from Mr. Brown viâ Yünnan-fu states that the revolution was effected in Chungking on the 22nd November, that all the foreigners were safe, and the town was quiet.

Mr. Wilkinson informs me that the mission stations north of Chengtu are now in the thick of the disturbances, but the missions and their occupants have so far, almost miraculously, escaped molestation. Mr. Brown reports, however, that Mr. and Mrs. Glanville, of the China Inland Mission, were robbed by a band of armed brigands on the road from Kuei Yang to Chungking.

I have, &c.
J. N. JORDAN.

No. 139.

Sir J. Jordan to Sir Edward Grey.—(Received December 27.)

Sir, *Peking, December 8, 1911.*
I HAVE the honour to transmit to you herewith a copy of a note from the Wai-wu Pu, enclosing a copy of an edict which has been issued by the Empress-Dowager, announcing the formal abdication of the Regent and appointing two high officials, one Manchu and one Chinese, to be guardians of the Emperor. The conduct of the Government is to be carried on by the Prime Minister and the Ministers of the Cabinet, while the Empress-Dowager and the Emperor will preside at audiences and ceremonial functions.

It remains to be seen whether this step will reconcile the country to the acceptance of constitutional Government under an attenuated Manchu sovereignty, or whether the extreme party in the south, regarding it as a further sign of weakness, will insist upon the removal of the Manchus and the establishment of a republican form of Government.

I have, &c.
J. N. JORDAN.

Enclosure 1 in No. 139.

Wai-wu Pu to Sir J. Jordan.

Sir, *December 8, 1911.*
I HAVE the honour to inform your Excellency that on the 6th instant the Cabinet received the following Decree [here follows Decree regarding the abdication of the Regent] and to ask that you will communicate the same to His Majesty's Government.

I avail, &c.
WAI-WU PU.

Enclosure 2 in No. 139.

Extract from the "Gazette" of December 6, 1911.

IMPERIAL EDICT.

(Translation.)
THE Prince Regent has received the following verbal instructions from the Empress-Dowager:—

The Prince Regent has presented a verbal memorial to the effect that during the three years of his regency his employment of officials and his administration of the Government have met with public disfavour. The establishment of a constitution was no more than empty talk, and corruption and malpractices were being carried on to such an extent that the minds of the people had gradually been alienated and the Empire dismembered. Through the mismanagement of one man the whole nation had been thrown into the most grievous distress. It was too late for him to show his repentance by pangs of heart and aches of head, for if he clung to his high office and did not resign he would cease to have the confidence of the people, and though he continued to administer the Government, his commands would be of no effect. What improvement was to be expected under such circumstances? He therefore humbly prayed to be allowed to resign the Regency and to have no further part in the affairs of the State. His statement is most earnest and sincere.

We have been living in retreat in our Palace and have been ignorant of the Government's policy. But the thought of the rising in Wuchang followed by that in other provinces, the dire effects of the warfare which meet our eyes on every side, and its disastrous result on the commerce of friendly nations—the thought of all this keeps us awake at night and robs us of our appetite. It is therefore most important that all the circumstances should be at once investigated and a scheme adopted for pacifying the Empire.

The Prince Regent is of a liberal, honest, and conscientious disposition, but, though most earnest in administration, he lacks the ability to cope with the present situation; he has allowed himself to be befooled, and the whole nation has suffered as the result. His prayer to be allowed to resign should therefore be granted. We hereby command that his seal of regency be given up and destroyed, and that he retire to his own Palace as Prince Ch'un and take no other part in the Government. We further command that he be awarded an annual pension of 50,000 taels, to be paid out of the Civil List. In future, the Prime Minister and the Ministers of the Cabinet shall be responsible for the employment of officials and the whole administration of the Government. All orders shall before promulgation be sealed with the Imperial seal, and we shall perform the ceremonial of audiences, together with the Emperor. As the Emperor is still of tender age some persons should be responsible for his personal safety. We therefore appoint Shih Hsü and Hsü Shih-Ch'ang grand guardians, and charge them with the duty of carefully guarding the Emperor.

In view of the calamities which have occurred in every quarter, and the dangers which beset the Empire, the princes, dukes, and others, who are intimately related to us, and who share our fortunes, should each and all endeavour to cope with the present crisis, observing strictly the regulations of our clan, and not overstepping the bounds.

The Ministers of State, being entrusted with heavy responsibilities, should show themselves all the more loyal and devoted; they should purify their hearts and endeavour to put a stop to corrupt practices, so as to promote the welfare of the country and the prosperity of the people.

All our subjects should understand that we are not keeping the sovereign power for ourselves, but are making a genuine reform in the interests of the people, who must on their part maintain good order and peacefully pursue their occupations, so that the evils arising from conflict and partition of territory may be avoided, and that a glorious and harmonious Government may be instituted. This is our sincere hope.

No. 140.

Sir J. Jordan to Sir Edward Grey.—(Received December 28.)

(Telegraphic.) *Peking, December 28, 1911.*
WITH the approval of the Imperial clan, a decree will be issued this evening ordering the convocation of a national assembly to decide the future form of Government, and recommending a complete cessation of hostilities until the question is settled. It states that the matter is a vital one, which closely affects the internal and external relations of China, and that it must be decided, not by the court or any particular section of the country, but by the collective opinion of the nation.
The language is dignified and conciliatory.

No. 141.

Sir J. Jordan to Sir Edward Grey.—(Received December 29.)

Sir, *Peking, December 8, 1911.*
IN continuation of my despatch of the 16th November, I have the honour to report that hostilities at Hankow, which for some time had been of a desultory nature, were renewed in earnest on the 19th November. Mr. Goffe telegraphed that many shells had fallen in the concessions from the rebel guns at Hanyang, and, as a result of the bombardment of the railway bridge by Admiral Sah's cruisers, which had returned under the revolutionary flag, the Standard Oil Company's installation had caught fire. The concessions do not otherwise appear to have suffered serious damage. On the 27th November the fighting, which had been kept up with great vigour some distance away on the Han River, culminated in the recapture of Hanyang by the Imperialists, and the rebels fled in disorder across the Yang-tsze, abandoning their guns and everything.
General Li has made another attempt to persuade the consuls to recognise his Government, but this is, of course, out of the question. His position is materially weakened by his late defeat, and he has himself been relegated to the post of second in command under General Huang Hsing by the rebel authorities at Shanghai, who pose as the "Provisional Government of the United States of China."
The situation at Ichang is not without danger, owing principally to the proximity of large numbers of railway coolies. I have made representations on this subject to the Chinese Government, and I understand that batches of them have since been shipped to the north. The commander-in-chief has arranged that a gun-boat shall visit Ichang and Changsha at frequent intervals.
The whole of Hunan is in the hands of the revolutionaries, and the dissensions between the military and the gentry seem likely to lead to another upheaval. I have specially drawn the commander-in-chief's attention to the claims which Changsha, owing to its isolated position, has to the protection of a gun-boat during the winter.
The whole of Admiral Sah's squadron has now definitely embraced the rebel cause. The admiral himself remained loyal, and his position was consequently one of some danger. He was given refuge on board one of His Majesty's ships, and he spent the night at His Majesty's consulate at Kiukiang, whence he left in disguise in a merchantman and reached Shanghai in safety.
The city of Canton itself remains quiet, in spite of the warring elements present. It is policed by some 30,000 outlaws under Lu Lan-ch'ing, a celebrated robber chief. General Lung and Admiral Li, the only officials under the late Government who have remained, have promised to co-operate with the new Government in maintaining peace, the chief danger to which is the financial problem. On the other hand, robbery has been general in all quarters of the province, and, as reported in my telegram of the 29th November, piracy on the West River has become so bad as to necessitate the patrol of the river by His Majesty's ships in order to enable the British steam-ship companies to resume the service temporarily suspended.
At the request of the Board of Communications, the Governor of Hong Kong agreed to the suspension of the ordinary train service on the Kanton-Kowloon Railway from the 7th November in order to facilitate the dispatch of troops to the disturbed areas. The Board based their request on the strength of the draft working agreement, and guaranteed indemnity to the British section for the loss of earnings. The

124

provincial administration having furnished an adequate guard, the train service was resumed on the Chinese section between Canton and Sheklung on the 28th November. Since the date of my last report piracy and clan-fighting have been rife at Amoy, and the concession is practically policed by His Majesty's ship "Monmouth." The officials are all quarrelling amongst themselves, and not one of them has a mandate from the Central Government at Foochow. The interior of the province has not escaped a share of the troubles, but wherever a change of government has occurred, even when accompanied by disturbance, the most scrupulous care has been taken not to molest foreigners or converts.

The latest news from Yünnanfu, which is dated the 5th December, indicates that more trouble is feared in the city. The treasury and the customs revenues have been looted at Mengtze, and the establishments of a German and Greek firm attacked and pillaged. Disturbances have taken place elsewhere on the railway, but have not apparently resulted in the death of any foreigners.

In Western Yünnan a rebellion has also been started by Mahommedan and native chiefs.

Chapels in the region of Anshun, Kweichow province, have been burnt, and the missionaries have left.

The Viceroy of India has been good enough to repeat to me the telegrams which he has received from the British trade agents at Gyangtse and Yatung and the political officer in Sikkim, and they indicate that a revolt has broken out in Thibet as widespread as that in China. It is perhaps too early to predict under what auspices authority will eventually be re-established, but the flight and subsequent capture of the amban and the reported intention of the mutinous troops to return to China constitute a damaging blow to Chinese suzerainty, and appear for the present to have shattered the hopes built on Chao Erh-feng's campaigns.

His Majesty's consul at Tsinanfu reports that Shantung first gained autonomy under the Manchu Government and then complete separation from that Government and incorporation in the Chinese Republic from the 13th November. This consummation was brought about by the revolutionary element of a representative assembly formed ad hoc, and assisted by the passive resistance of part of the 5th division. On the 1st December Mr. Tebbitt telegraphed that the province had reverted to Imperial administration, but I have no particulars to explain how this came about. It appears, at any rate, to have been acquiesced in by the troops, as 1,000 men of the 5th division left for Tsaochowfu, in the south-west of the province, on the 5th December, to suppress robbery. At Hsüchowfu, a town just south of Shantung on the Tien-tsin-Pukow Railway, looting was said to be imminent, and the British engineers, Bourne and Hearne, with their families, were virtually held up. A special train, however, brought the families up to Tsinan on the 28th November. The engineers themselves have apparently remained at Hsüchowfu, which was reported to be all quiet on the 6th December.

The railway authorities had received the most urgent instructions from the Central Government to make every effort to establish through communication to Pukow, doubtless in order that troops might be sent to assist in the defence of Nanking, but the junction was effected too late to save the city, and, at my instance, Yuan Shih-kai has agreed not to use the line for military purposes. It is to be hoped that the rebel leaders will equally abstain, but if the present armistice at Hankow should terminate in a failure of the negotiations about to be entered on, it is hardly to be expected that military considerations will be subordinated to the commercial interests of the railway, and the preservation of the line from further damage would again become a matter of great difficulty.

I have not heard how the return of Shantung to its allegiance is regarded at Chefoo, but I have no doubt that the latter port will acquiesce in any arrangements made by the provincial capital. Order has been maintained in the port.

There is no change to report in regard to the state of affairs in Shansi. The rebels hold Taiyuanfu and the Shansi Railway, and the Imperialists remain in occupation of Shihchiachuang, near the junction with the main line to Hankow.

Authentic news of the tragedy at Sianfu, capital of Shensi, has at last reached Peking. The slaughter of Manchus and the destruction of their city was wholesale. Mrs. Beckman, Mr. Watne and six children, apparently all Swedish subjects attached to American missions, were killed by the mob the first day of the outbreak. Three British subjects, namely, Mr. and Mrs. Smith and Mr. Manners, were wounded, but all other British subjects are reported to be unharmed and to be remaining at Sianfu, where they have been promised protection by the rebel usurpers.

125

The acting consul at Harbin reports that there have been no disturbances in the north of Manchuria, and that at Kirin a peace society has been formed similar to that at Mukden.

Mr. Clennell reports that matters are equally peaceful at Newchang, and that the port is more concerned with the preservation of order than with the propagation of revolution.

I have, &c.
J. N. JORDAN.

No. 142.

Sir J. Jordan to Sir Edward Grey.—(Received December 30.)

(Telegraphic.) *Peking, December 30, 1911.*
ON 29th December His Majesty's consul-general at Shanghai telegraphed as follows :—

"A further suspension of hostilities till 5th January was arranged this afternoon at a meeting between Wu Ting-fang and Tong Shao-yi. Order is to be maintained in the town by military police. Hankow and other places are to be evacuated by the Imperial troops, who are to retire 100 *li.* Places evacuated are not to be occupied by revolutionary troops, who are to remain in their present positions. The composition and election of the National Assembly are to be discussed to-morrow afternoon. Pending the meeting of the assembly no foreign loans are to be negotiated."

No. 143.

Sir J. Jordan to Sir Edward Grey.—(Received December 31.)

(Telegraphic.) *Peking, December 31, 1911.*
I HAVE received the following telegram from Shanghai, dated 30th December :—

"The constitution of the National Assembly has been settled to-day. There will be twenty-four sections—Turkestan, the three eastern provinces, Mongolia, Thibet, and the eighteen provinces. Eighteen sections are to form a quorum. Three votes are accorded to each section to be cast by not more than three delegates. Peking will notify Chihli and the first five sections of these arrangements ; both Peking and Nanking will notify Shantung, Honan, and Thibet. The date of assembly is to be fixed before notification is made. The conference will resume discussion to-morrow on this point and on the system of election."

CHINA. No. 1 (1912).

CORRESPONDENCE respecting the Affairs
of China.

Presented to both Houses of Parliament by Command of His Majesty. May 1912.

CHINA. No. 3 (1913).

FURTHER CORRESPONDENCE

RESPECTING THE

AFFAIRS OF CHINA.

[In continuation of " China, No. 3 (1912) " : Cd. 6447.]

Presented to both Houses of Parliament by Command of His Majesty.
August 1913.

LONDON:
PRINTED UNDER THE AUTHORITY OF HIS MAJESTY'S STATIONERY OFFICE
BY HARRISON AND SONS, 45-47, ST. MARTIN'S LANE, W.C.,
PRINTERS IN ORDINARY TO HIS MAJESTY.

To be purchased, either directly or through any Bookseller, from
WYMAN AND SONS, LTD., FETTER LANE, E.C., and 32, ABINGDON STREET, S.W.,
and 54, ST. MARY STREET, CARDIFF; or
H.M. STATIONERY OFFICE (SCOTTISH BRANCH), 23, FORTH STREET, EDINBURGH; or
E. PONSONBY, LTD., 116, GRAFTON STREET, DUBLIN ;
or from the Agencies in the British Colonies and Dependencies,
the United States of America, the Continent of Europe and Abroad of
T. FISHER UNWIN, LONDON, W.C.

1913.

[Cd. 7054.] *Price 9d*

TABLE OF CONTENTS.

Further Correspondence respecting the Affairs of China.

[In continuation of " China, No. 3 (1912) " : Cd. 6447.]

No. 1.

Consul-General O'Brien-Butler to Sir Edward Grey.—(Received April 1.)

Sir,   *Yünnan-fu, February* 18, 1912.

I HAVE the honour to forward to you herewith copy of a report which I have sent to His Majesty's Minister at Peking on the situation in Yünnan province during the half-quarter ended 15th February, 1912.

I have, &c.
(For His Majesty's Consul-General),
H. W. GAMMON.

Enclosure in No. 1.

Report by Consul-General O'Brien-Butler on the Situation in Yünnan Province for Half-Quarter ending February 15, 1912.

SINCE the opening of the New Year, the dominating note in Yünnan-fu has been the activity of the Provisional Government in getting its administrative machinery into thorough working order and in seeking a satisfactory solution to the urgent question of public funds. With the military coercion of the refractory revolutionary party in Tengyueh and the installation of a taotai appointed from Yünnan-fu, the last discordant element in the unity of the province has been removed, and the influence of General Ts'ai remains paramount. The antagonism of certain powerful Yünnanese to the military governor owing to his Hunan birth, which threatened at one time to lead to serious trouble, and the expressed intention of Ts'ai himself to leave Yünnan-fu for his native province, happily did not materialise. He remains the autocrat of Yünnan, and under his direction the provinces of Szechuan and Kueichou are being brought into a state of vassalage to the local capital.

The money question has throughout been recognised as the supreme test of the stability of the Provisional Government, and it has generally been supposed, both among Chinese and Europeans, that the supply of silver could not last beyond the end of February or the middle of March at the longest. A request for voluntary contributions met with no great success and a sum of about 300,000 dollars was all that was realised by this means. The proposal to issue Yünnan currency notes to the value of 1,000,000 taels has fallen through, and the flotation of a public loan, which found considerable favour when the idea was first mooted, has been abandoned owing to the strong opposition of the commissioner of finance, who is in favour of foreign loans, and thinks that he can carry on until the recognition of the republic, when he is confident of obtaining a loan from foreign sources. I am told that the governments in Nanking and Canton were asked for money; the former refused on the grounds that all available funds were required for the campaign against Peking, and Canton was willing for a business transaction at a rate of interest which the local government would not listen to. Under the Imperial Government large sums were received annually from the two provinces of Hupei and Szechuan to meet current expenses of administration which Yünnan was unable to bear unaided. As a last resource, therefore, attention was turned to Szechuan, where internal dissensions are greatly facilitating the execution of a plan which was speedily formed to bring money at all costs to Yünnan-fu. The Yünnan troops, numbering in all over 12,000, are, I am told by the Commissioner of Foreign Affairs, in possession of Sui-fu and Luchow, and have seized the famous salt-wells of

[1270]   B

Tzu-liu-ching, said to have yielded to the Szechuan Government a revenue of 7,000,000 to 8,000,000 taels a-year. An arrangement has been made whereby 300,000 taels a-month from the revenue of the salt-wells are to be paid to the Yünnan Government, and I believe that a first instalment is now on its way to Yünnan-fu. I am unable to obtain confirmation of these statements from His Majesty's consul at Chungking as telegraphic communication is not yet restored. These troops are being paid with Szechuan money and the local treasury is thus relieved of one drain upon its meagre resources.

The province of Kueichou has been giving much anxiety to the Government here. The "Ko Lao Hui" are all-powerful under the leadership of an ex-sergeant of Luchün who is now military governor, and the whole province is said to be seething with unrest. On the 3rd February, the Commissioner of Foreign Affairs, who is a native of Kueichou, left Yünnan-fu with an "army of pacification" of 3,500 men. He is not expected to reach Kueiyang without fighting, and on entering the capital he will make himself military governor, as deputy of the Yünnan Government. He took with him a sum of 200,000 dollars, all in notes, as being the only sum available to replenish a treasury which to all accounts is absolutely depleted. The expressed intention of General Ts'ai is to annex Szechuan (or at least the southern half) and Kueichou, and to form one large province governed from Yünnan-fu, Szechuan to supply the major portion of the money required for the government. There has been some talk of an independent State, but it is scarcely credible that a man of General Ts'ai's ability and foresight will embark on a course so fraught with peril and one which would only result in bringing down on to Yünnan the wrath of republican China: moreover, it remains to be seen what Szechuan will have to say to this arrangement when that province has recovered from its present state of anarchy and chaos.

On the 5th January General Ts'ai invited the consular body and the principal foreign residents in the town to an informal picnic at Heilungt'an, a temple about 8 miles from the city, and his hospitality has since been returned, again unofficially, by the two consulates.

On the 10th appeared a proclamation announcing the adoption of the Western calendar and fixing the 15th January as New Year's Day. Officially the festival was celebrated, but, beyond a general parading of the five-colour flag in every doorway, no notice was taken of the change by the people, and business went on as usual. Great preparations are now being made for the observance of the old-style New Year, but a proclamation has been issued forbidding crackers.

The reinforced railway guards were withdrawn about the middle of January, and this was the sign for a fresh outbreak of petty robberies, and a foreigner's compound (a Montenegrin) near Iliang was attacked and looted. This is the only case of violence against foreigners or their property to be reported since the raids of early December.

The restoration of peace and order throughout the province justified the return of those who had been ordered away from Yünnan-fu, and most of the foreigners are back in the town.

On the 5th February Mr. O'Brien-Butler gave permission for missionaries (men only) to return to Tungch'uan, Chüch'ing, Sapushan, six, five, and three days respectively from the capital, the Chinese having expressed their willingness and recognised their responsibility for protection in Yünnan province only, and laying stress on the necessity of no foreigners going into either Szechuan or Kueichou for the present. Permission for the missionaries to return to Chaotung, a fortnight's journey from Yünnan-fu and near the Szechuan border, has not yet been granted, and so far none have returned to Tali.

No. 2.

India Office to Foreign Office.—(Received April 1, 1912.)

THE Under-Secretary of State for India presents his compliments to the Under-Secretary of State for Foreign Affairs, and forwards herewith, for the information of the Secretary of State, an account of a journey from Peking to Kashgar by Lieutenant-Colonel George Pereira which has been received, through the Government of India, from His Majesty's consul-general at Kashgar.

India Office, March 28, 1912.

3

Enclosure in No. 2.

Major Pereira's Journey from Zaisan to Kashgar.

Mongolia and Chinese Turkistan (Hsin-chiang) to Kuldja.

(Extract.)

1. *Zaisan to Sharasumé.*— Crossing, on the 19th May, 1911, the stream forming the Russo-Chinese boundary, we reached two dirty Kazak "yurtas," standing as an outpost of the Chinese Empire. These "yurtas" are Mongol circular tents of woodwork, covered over with pieces of felt. The Kazaks, called Ha-sa by the Chinese and Hassack by the Mongols, are closely allied to the Kirghiz tribes, leading a nomadic life, living in "yurtas," and tending large flocks of sheep and ponies, besides camels, goats, and bullocks. Only very rarely do they go in for cultivation. They are the original Cossacks. Many of the tribes on the Russian side of the border are also Kazaks, but the Russians always call them Kirghiz and only recognise their own Cossacks. The Chinese Kazaks of the Altai extend from the border to the eastern slopes of the Altai, and have a duke ("kung-yeh") and twelve chiefs ("tsung-kuan"), all of whom are under the Amban at Sharasumé. The duke lives at Tai-li-obo, two days west of that city, whilst the two most powerful chiefs are Ma-mi, who lives north of Sharasumé, and Sugurbuy, who lives south-east of the Dain Nor (lake), on the east side of the Altai. A consul informed me that the latter is very intelligent and the Chinese have given him a red button. Below the chiefs are headmen, whilst important cases are settled by the Amban. The Kazaks are a listless race, who appear to have no interests in life beyond tending their flocks. Even the unenterprising Mongol is bright in comparison.

The country from Zaisan to Sharasumé consists mostly of barren hills and plains, very sparsely inhabited, the Kazaks being found by the few streams, where there are also a few trees.

The black Irtish is crossed by ferry 112¾ miles east of Zaisan ; other streams are forded, excepting the Kran River, near Sharasumé, which divides into two channels, where wooden bridges cross shallow torrents.

Mosquitoes are a great plague, especially on the Irtish in the month of July, driving the inhabitants from the plains into the hills.

2. *Sharasumé,* the local Mongol pronunciation of Sharasumu, meaning "yellow temple." The living Buddha, who used to inhabit it, has now moved further south. The Chinese call it Ch'eng-hua-ssu ("receive and transform temple"). On maps it is erroneously called Tulta, really a district 3 miles further south. It has 1,800 inhabitants, chiefly Chinese from Urumtchi, Tien-tsin, and the north-west provinces, and Sarts. Sart is a Russian word derived from the Persian, and is a good word to describe the various Turki races found chiefly from the T'ien Shan to Kashgar and Yarkand in Chinese territory, and from Tashkent and Andijan in Russia. The Chinese call them Ch'an-t'ou, from the turbans they wind round their heads ! In the cities they are merchants, competing with the Chinese at Sharasumé, outnumbering them at Tarbagatai and Kuldja, and swamping them in Aksu, Uch-Turfan, and Kashgar. They are also farmers in the fertile plains and larger valleys, as, for instance, around Kuldja, where they are known as Taranchi, or tillers of the soil, and around all the big cities south of the T'ien Shan from Aksu to Kashgar. They seem to have more energy at Sharasumé than south of T'ien Shan, where they appear to be as listless and unenterprising as the Kirghiz, and utterly devoid of all patriotism and powers of combination. In fact, I was much struck by seeing their apparent indifference to being ruled over by a mere handful of Chinese. This indifference is partly caused by their natural sloth, and partly, no doubt, by a feeling that the Chinese are preferable as rulers to any other nation. The Sarts, unlike the Kazaks—who, though Mahommedans, appear to be devoid of religion—have a good many mosques south of the T'ien Shan, and appear to be of a fairly pious frame of mind. There are no Russian subjects among the Sart merchants of Sharasumé. Sharasumé is quite a modern city, consisting of two streets, one mostly Chinese, the other Sart. The houses are of mud, with flat roofs. Wages are high, coolies getting 8 mace (a mace is about 3d.), plus 3 mace for food a-day, as the cost of living is dear ; but this only lasts during the summer, as in winter coolies are not wanted. It is not therefore surprising that there is difficulty in getting soldiers at a little over 2 mace a-day.

The Amban ("ts'an-ts'an-ta-ch'en"), commonly spoken of as the Ch'in-ch'ai, or Imperial Commissioner, reports direct to Peking, unlike the three Ambans of Mongolia

[1270   B 2 and the one at Tarbagatai, who are dependent on Tartar generals. At the time of writing all these Ambans must be bannermen, and are therefore mostly Manchus. His jurisdiction extends from the eastern slopes of the Altai, on the east, where he touches the Kobdo district, to the Saure Hills, on the west, where the Tarbagatai district begins. Besides the population (Chinese and Sart) of Sharasumé, he rules over Kazaks and certain Mongol Turgat princes further south.

Both here and at Tarbagatai there is a Chino-Russian bureau (" chung-o-shih-wu-chu "), which corresponds to the usual foreign bureau (" chiao-shih-chu ") of Chinese provincial cities. The director is an energetic young Hunanese, named Hsiung-en-ti.

3. *The Altai Shan.*—We followed the main road to Kobdo through the mountains, crossing several passes, the chief ones being the Wu-hsi-ling (8,850 feet), 25¼ miles east of Sharasumé, the Hashilik Pass (8,920 feet) and the watershed at the Urmogaitu Pass (10,100 feet) at 60¼ miles. On the 7th June, the latter two passes were much blocked by snow drifts, and we had some difficulty in getting through, but on our return on the 27th June the passes were open to traffic and caravans were passing freely between Sharasumé and Kobdo, whilst Kazak " yurtas " and flocks were plentiful in the valleys. The Chinese say the Urmogaitu Pass is closed by snow about the 20th of the 8th moon (*i.e.*, 13th October). I estimated the peaks on the main range of the Altai as between 11,000 and 12,500 feet, and these were covered with snow. The weather was usually mild in the daytime, varying between 50 and 60 degrees (Fahrenheit), excepting from the 21st to the 23rd June, when there was a heavy fall of snow, and the thermometer in my tent fell to 36 degrees at noon.

Sheep cost 4 to 4½ roubles (8s. 8d. to 9s. 9d.) apiece, and milk 10 to 20 kopeks (2½d. to 5d.) a bottle, but the Kazaks do not keep fowls.

Chinese and Sart traders travel about among the Kazaks, whilst we also met three Russian traders living in "yurtas" on the eastern side of the Altai, selling tea, boots, and piece goods, &c. They come from Bi'isk annually and remain about six months.

4. *Money used in Mongolia and the Hsin-chiang* is Chinese, viz., taels and cash. In Sharasumé they have silver taels (a tael equals about 2s. 6d.), very similar to the Chinese dollars, and half tael pieces. We, however, used Russian money (notes and silver) all the way from Zaisan to Kashgar. Generally speaking the rouble equals three-quarters of a tael. A tael is called locally " seer," and is divided by the Sarts into 16 tangas, though there are no tanga coins. Paper taels are also used, but they vary in value. For instance at Kuldja they are issued by the Tartar General of Ili, but as he got into financial difficulties, especially over a leather factory speculation at Kuldja, he flooded the market with notes, with the result that a silver tael is worth 1·3 Kuldja paper taels. Both the ordinary Chinese cash and a special cash, called " Hung-chien " or red cash, are used. The latter is coined at Urumtchi, and 330 red cash = 1,000 ordinary cash.

At Kashgar 400 red cash equal a tael. I found silver lumps at Sharasumé weighed exactly the same as the Kung-fa tael, which is the tael used by the Hong Kong and Shanghai Bank at Peking.

5. *Sharasumé to Tarbagatai.*—We retraced our steps to the Irtish ferry on the Zaisan road, and then turned to the south-west. The country consists of great barren plains, bordered by bare hills, which are occasionally crossed, with very few streams, and practically uninhabited, up to the Saure Hills. Here we entered the district governed by the Amban of Tarbagatai; these hills are mostly covered with grass, affording good pasture to the flocks of Turgut Mongols, who are mixed up with Hassack tribes.

The Saure Hills and country to the south is ruled over by five Turgut Princes, who are under different Ambans. We met the Hobuk-Sali Prince (so-called from the Hobuk River and the Sali or Saure Hills) ; his Chinese name is Chin, and in Mongol O-lo-la-ma-cha-pu, a childless and bashful youth of 24, who has to go annually to Tarbagatai to kotow before the Amban. He was in an encampment of 50 " yurtas," containing some 300 lamas, useless beings, and the chief cause of the present decay of the Mongol race.

This Prince leads a nomadic life, though he has built a yamên at O-wa-te, a day further south. Maps sometimes wrongly show his residence as Wang (Russian " Van "), the Chinese word for " Prince." He was encamped on the Wu-tu-la-sin stream, about 168¼ miles from Sharasumé, and 58½ miles east of where the road enters and traverses for 8¼ miles Russian territory, which is the limit of his principality. Nearing the border we came across some Russian Kazaks. Passing through the strip of Russian territory, we had to show our passports to the Russian officer, who has a post of thirty men, furnished by the Cossack regiment at Zaisan. Leaving the border, we followed a hilly country for 25 miles till we reached the great Tarbagatai Plain, roughly some 70 miles square. It is mostly barren, with dried up grass and weeds, but there are occasional plots of cultivation with Chinese or Tungan colonies or farms. Wheat, millet, and oats are grown, but no opium.

These Tungans are Mohammedans, but I did not come across many of them on this journey. They are found mostly further east in Chinese Turkistan, and are scattered about in Kan-su and Shen-si provinces. Though dressing like and speaking Chinese, they belong to an alien race, but nobody seems to be certain of their origin or even the meaning of the word "Tungan." They were ruthlessly suppressed by the Chinese in two great rebellions, the last one in Kan-su in 1895, and when I was in Kan-su in 1910 the missionaries told me they still bore a strong antipathy to the Chinese, and openly spoke of a day of revenge, but they were so crushed after the last rebellion, it will take them a long time to recover.

6. *Tarbagatai*, so-called from the number of marmots ("tarabagan") found on a hill to the west of the city. It is also called Chuguchak, the name commonly used by the Russians and Sarts, and Ta-ch'eng-t'ing, the Chinese official name. When the country was first conquered by the Chinese in the twenty-fifth and twenty-sixth years of the reign of the Emperor Chien-lung, the Amban at first fixed his residence at Uriar, some 100 miles to the north-west. As the Chinese could not pronounce Uriar they called him the Pei-ya Amban. Finding Uriar too cold he moved to the present site, and the name of Pei-ya is still often used (wrongly) by the Chinese peasants for the present city. The country was formerly occupied by Kalmuks, Mongols, who are called either Olotu (Eleuth) Mongols or Jungar (Zungar) Mongols. Their country extended southwards to Ili, and was called Jungaria (Zungaria), a term now obsolete, but still shown on maps further east. (N.B.—Jungaria is divided into two parts: (i) extending from Tarbagatai to Ili; (ii) the country north of Urumtchi.) At present the Kalmuks are a very decadent race, and I only came across them in the hills south of the Ili Valley and in the Tekes Valley. Tarbagatai consists of two small mud-walled cities connected by a street with all the inns and shops. The eastern city is occupied by a colony of So-lun Manchus (from the Hei-lung chiang province), who also occupy some farms in the plain. The colony was planted when the country was conquered. The small western Chinese city is filled up by two or three yamêns. The population of Tarbagatai is about 4,000, of whom nearly half are Sarts, whilst the rest are Chinese from Tien-tsin and the north-west provinces, or Kazaks. The Chinese are under the T'ing-Kuan, who is responsible to the Governor at Urumtchi. There is also an Amban, who is dependent on the Ili Tartar General, and who rules over the local Manchus, 1,000 families of Kazaks, the fourteen temples of the Turgut Mongol Prince Chin (mentioned in Section 5), and fourteen temples of Kalmuks. This divided rule over Western Mongolia and Chinese Turkistan between the Ili Tartar General, and the Governor of Hsin-chiang at Urumtchi must be a source of increased weakness to the Chinese. Their jurisdiction is constantly overlapping. To the north of the Chinese city there is a regular Russian settlement. The present consul, Mr. Dolbezhe, was formerly in Urumtchi and Ulia-ssutai, speaks Mongol, is very intelligent and well posted in all that is going on. He has two assistants and a Cossack guard. There is also a Russian post-office. The Russian subjects are nearly all Sarts.

7. *Tarbagatai to Kuldja.*—We followed the main road with telegraph for the first 60¾ miles across the great Tarbagatai plain. There are patches of crops with Manchu farms near the city, beyond that the country is mostly barren, with only an occasional village or stage with posts of about half-a-dozen Chinese soldiers, almost the only Chinese we met till reaching Sui-ting Hsien.

About ½ mile beyond Lao-feng-k'ou we left the main road, and turned south-west across a more deserted plain, thinly inhabited by Kazaks. For a short way up to the Mai-le Hills there is more pasture and Kazak encampments. We then entered a very desolate country through the Usum-bulak Hills, across a barren plain, west of the Ebi Nor (lake) with an altitude of only 1,700 feet, and through the Hoy-tush Hills, which mark the boundary between the district of the Tarbagatai Amban and the Province of Hsin-chiang. For 74½ miles we only passed three small springs of brackish water, and did not meet a soul. Borotala, in Chinese "Ta-ying-p'an" (great camp), is 204 miles from Tarbagatai. It has over 200 Sarts and 40 or 50 Chinese, with a colony of Cha-ha Mongols (from near Kalgan) brought here they say in the reign of the Emperor Hsien-feng, but probably much earlier. They furnish some so-called soldiers. I saw one party, whom I mistook for ordinary coolies. At Borotala there is a belt of cultivation about a mile wide, running down the centre of the valley. The crops are wheat, millet, and maize.

Leaving this belt, another desolate stretch is reached, the swift Borotala River being crossed 3 miles further on by a good wooden bridge. Then we ascended through the Kirk-terak Hills, with good pasture, eventually rejoining the main road and telegraph at 247¾ miles from Tarbagatai in the desolate Ssu-t'ai plain. Here, again, we met a few Chinese soldiers ("Hsün-fang-tui," from Suiting-Hsien) at each of the stages. A good road leads round the Sairam Nur (lake), altitude 7,020 feet, to the beautiful Talki gorge (in Chinese "Kuo-tzu-koü"), with a steady descent through steep hills, 800 feet high, fairly well wooded, with undergrowth and wild flowers, the valley affording pasture to Kazak flocks. The road follows near a stream, often crossing it by small wooden bridges in good repair. After 18 miles through the gorge the great Ili plain is reached. It is partly cultivated by Sarts in these parts. The town of Lu-ts'ao-kou has forty or fifty Chinese and Sart mud-houses.

Five and a half miles from Sui-ting Hsien, the road is joined by the one from Djarkent and the Russian telegraph. I did not see any opium. There is a good deal of traffic on the main road.

8. *Sui-ting Hsien or Ili Fu*, erroneously called "Suidun" by Russians. It is the residence of the prefect ("Chih-fu") and magistrate ("Chih-hsien"). There is no north suburb. There are over 2,000 families in the city and suburbs. In the walled city they are mostly Chinese, chiefly from Tien-tsin, whilst in the suburbs and surrounding country they are practically all Sarts. The Belgian Catholic Mission have one resident priest (Père Steinemann), but both here and at Kuldja they find it almost impossible to get converts among the Mahommedans.

9. *Hsin-ch'eng*, 4½ miles south-east of Sui-ting Hsien, is built on the site of Huai-yüan-ch'eng, destroyed in the time of the rebellion, and is called Kura by the Sarts. It is the residence of the Ili Tartar General ("Chiang-chün"). Since Hsin-chiang was turned into a province, under a Governor at Urumtchi, some ten years ago, the powers of the Tartar General have been considerably reduced. The Chinese and Sarts are under the civil provincial Government, whilst the Manchus and local Mongol and Kazak tribes are under the Tartar General. Under him there is a Major-General ("Fu-tu-t'ung"). The present man is Nieh-ko-tai, of course a Manchu, who has charge of the local Hsi-po Manchu colony, who live in Hsin-ch'eng or have colonies in the neighbouring plain. These Hsi-po were originally a tribe from Kirin, who were only incorporated with the Manchus 100 or 200 years ago. Many of them were killed in the last rebellion.

The Tartar General also nominates three brigadiers ("Ling-tui"), all bannermen (and probably Manchus), who usually live in Hsin-cheng; at present they are :—

(1.) Mu-an-chun, in charge of Kalmuks.
(2.) Kuei, in charge of the Cha-ha Mongols on the Borotala plain.
(3.) Fu-shan, in charge of—

(a.) The Alban Kazaks in the Tekes Valley.
(b.) Several tribes of Kazai Kazaks around Kuldja.
(c.) A small tribe of Kirghiz in the Tekes Valley.

10. *The Leather Factory* is about a mile north-north-west of Kuldja. It was started in 1909 by the Tartar general and a rich Sart. The machinery is German, the mechanician a Russian. At first an Austrian foreman was employed, and he turned out excellent leather, but later he had the usual trouble with the officials and returned home, and since then the leather has been of poor quality. The Belgian priest thinks the factory will soon fail, unless they quickly get a competent European manager. It is now being run at a loss, and the Tartar general has flooded the market with tael notes in attempting to relieve his financial embarrassments.

Kuldja to Kashgar.

Kuldja is the Sart name meaning "wild sheep"; in Chinese it is officially called Ning-yüan Hsien, but commonly Chin-ting-ssu (= gold ball temple); altitude 2,420 feet. It is the residence of the Ili Tao-tai, whose jurisdiction extends to the T'ing-kuan at Tarbagatai. The remaining three tao-tais of the province are at Urumtchi, Yangi-shahr near Aksu, and Kashgar. There is a foreign bureau ("Chiao-shih-chu") formerly called the Chino–Russian bureau. Kuldja consists of a small mud-walled city with large suburbs, containing the shops and business quarters. The population is under

30,000, mostly Sarts, with a few Chinese and a large colony of Russian subjects, viz., No-hai, Tartars from Kasan, besides Russian Sarts and a few Russians.

The Russian consul-general has a guard of 1 officer and 80 men. There is also a Russian post office, Russian telegraph office, and a branch of the Russo-Asiatic Bank.

The tao-tai has jurisdiction over Chinese and Sarts, the Kazaks, &c., being under the Tartar general.

There is one resident Belgian priest (Père Raemdonck). Curiously enough, from Mongolia to the T'ien-Shan, the Kazak language is the general language of intercourse. It is very similar to the Sart, and a Chinese-speaking Sart told me about half the words were the same in both languages. South of the T'ien-Shan, Sart is the *lingua franca*.

1. *Kuldja to the Tekes Valley.*—Leaving Kuldja the fertile Ili plain is followed, going easterly for 15 miles and crossing the Ili River by ferry. This and the ferry boat over the Irtish were the only boats we saw during the journey, though some Chinese timber merchants in the Tekes Valley float the wood in rafts to Kuldja. The total absence of boats on lakes or big rivers is another example of the entire lack of interest in progress displayed by Sarts, Kazaks, and Mongols.

Leaving the ferry, we turned southerly across the Ili plain, partly cultivated by Sart peasants ("taranchi") and partly barren, till at 26¾ miles we entered the hills, mostly barren and thinly inhabited by Kalmuks (Jungar Mongols); at 46¾ miles we crossed the Chap-chal Pass (8,950 feet), the watershed of the Sua-su Range, and descending among grass hills, reached the small town of Ot-nin-ta-gai on the Tekes River, 77 miles from Kuldja. It has some 50 Sart mud-houses with two or three shops, besides a few Kalmuk "yurtas." Here we left the main road to Kashgar, which crosses the Tekes by a wooden bridge.

2. *The Tekes Valley.*—We turned easterly down the Tekes Valley, crossing the river 16 miles further on by a very primitive bridge with alarming gradients and inequalities. It is a private speculation kept by a Kan-su Chinese and three or four Chinese assistants, with no fixed toll. These, with a colony of twenty Hu-pei men, who earn a living as carpenters and timber merchants lower down the Tekes Valley, besides one farmer in the Jirgalan Valley, were the only Chinese I met between Kuldja and Aksu on the southern side of the T'ien-Shan. The Tekes is really the main branch of the Ili River; but, as in China, rivers have different names every few miles. The Tekes is mostly pasture, and is divided among the tribes, the Kalmuks occupying the eastern part to the Kok-su. They are under a chief ("tsung-kuan") named Sogata, who lives at Bahachuk, in the hills to the north. The Tekes Valley between the Kok-su and the Kok-terek streams is the winter quarters of the Alban Kazaks, who come down from the Karajun plateau in the hills to the south. They are under a head chief ("bolus") with three lesser chiefs ("tsun-kuan"). The "bolus," Jan-see-it, is directly under Fu-shan, brigadier, in charge of Kazaks at Hsin-ch'eng, and rules over 734 families. We had ocular demonstration of their lack of discipline, as a Kazak was brought before the three lesser chiefs, charged with swindling one of the Sart merchants who go about trading among the Kazaks. The court of justice eventually became the battle ground between the party of the chief and the friends of the accused; the senior chief receiving a black eye and various bruises in the struggle, after which the culprit allowed them to send him as a prisoner to be dealt with by the Chinese at Kuldja. This same chief afterwards attempted to swindle us over the hire of some ponies and a "yurta."

On the right (east) bank of the Kok-terek, there is a colony of eighty Kirghiz families, who, with a small party in the Muzart Pass, are the only Kirghiz north of the T'ien Shan. They are practically the same race as the Kazaks, living like them a pastoral life in "yurtas," and under a chief ("tsung-kuan"); the present man, named Ti-liu-ber-dee, is appointed for life by Fu-shan. Like the Kazak chiefs, he has the minor powers of beating and fining, but important cases are settled by Fu-shan.

From the left bank of the Kok-terek along the Tekes Valley as far as the Ariaz River, the people are Kazai Kazaks under a chief ("bolus"), by name, Yusup, with nine minor chiefs ("tsung-kuan"), who have charge of a varying number of families, for instance Ya-pa-lak, whom we met had charge of sixty families. From the Ariaz to the Muzart Pass, the people are Kalmuks, under two chiefs, a "cheng-tsung-kuan" (first class chief) and a "Fu-tsung-kuan" (second class chief), assisted by five sub-chiefs ("tso-ling"), of whom four live north of the Tekes River, and Bo-wa, the fifth at Shata-ama at the mouth of the Muzart, where he has charge of ten quite untrained Kalmuk soldiers and a subaltern of about 60. There is another post of ten men living in "yurtas" at Aidungai 10 miles higher up the valley. There are colonies of Russian

Kazaks on the Chinese side of the Tekes Valley and at Kordai Mong-yun to the south of the Tekes Valley. In addition to the tribes, there are a few Sart mud store houses scattered about in the Tekes Valley.

There is a third bridge over the Tekes further east, where the road runs from Kuldja to the Jirgalan. The Tekes Valley is from 6 to 12 miles wide, bordered by barren ranges on the north and by foot hills on the south, which gradually increase in height up to the snow-clad peaks of the main range of the T'ien Shan.

3. *The T'ien Shan.*—We followed a short way up the swift flowing Kok-su River, which is crossed by a wooden bridge seven miles south of the Tekes River Bridge. We then turned westwards, ascending some grass downs, to Kara-jun, the summer headquarters of the Alban Kazaks, who leave it for the Tekes Valley in September. Proceeding further west and south to the Kok-su River, we passed along grass valleys between grassy and barren hills. In the autumn this part of the country is uninhabited, but the Turgut Mongols from the Yulduz River move here in the winter. Later, turning northwards to the streams flowing into the Jirgalan Valley, we came across another lot of Kazai Kazaks, numbering 900 families, and ruled over by a chief ("bolus"), named Bu-lun-chi, with three lesser chiefs ("tsung-kuan").

Kazai Kazaks are also found on the Kash River further north under five chiefs ("bolos"), and also to the north of Kuldja under five other chiefs.

South of the Jirgalan, the hills are covered by forests of fine spruce trees, some of them between 200 and 300 feet in height.

Going further west and following the Jirgalan, which is crossed by a bridge near the Tekes River, we found another colony of Alban Kazaks, besides a few Sarts, living in mud houses and surrounded by some cultivation. Descending the Tekes Valley, we found the Ariaz River, which is uninhabited by the Kazaks in the autumn.

4. *The Muzart Pass.*—I made the total length from the Tekes Valley to where it comes out on the Aksu Plain, 100¾ miles. There is an easy ascent up it by the Muzart stream, which is crossed by eight bridges in different places, the road running mostly through spruce forests between high hills. At Kuprur (20¼ miles from Shata-ama), I found about 20 Kirghiz "yurtas" in the snow. A climb of about 1,000 feet in the snow takes one to the summit of the Muzart Pass, 37¾ miles from the entrance, with an altitude of 11,480 feet. There is a difficult descent across and down two glaciers, at the worst part there is a hut with four or five Sarts, who cut steps in the ice, and help down the ponies. Leaving this glacier (the Muz Dawan) there is an easy descent for the rest of the way down stony valleys between high bare hills, occasionally passing a small Sart village, till reaching Koneshahr, a Chinese "likin" station at the mouth of the pass.

5. *The Aksu Plain.*—Leaving the pass, a desolate plain, intersected by an occasional range of bare hills with a few small Sart villages, is crossed for 46 miles to Jam, on the great road from Kashgar to Urumtchi. There are seventy or eighty Sart shops with only two Chinese inhabitants. From Jam to Aksu, 23 miles, the plain is fairly fertile, and dotted with Sart farms. The plain stretches away to the south and west, gradually narrowing and becoming less fertile and ascending the Taushkan River Valley.

6. *Aksu.*—Called Koneshahr ("old city"), and officially Wen-hsiu Hsien. It has 40,000 or 50,000 inhabitants, who are all Sarts with the exception of about 1,500 Chinese and 1,000 or probably less, Tungans. There are about 300 Russian Sarts. The Chinese magistrate ("chih-hsien") lives in a yamên in the small walled city on the west of the large dusty business town. To the south and west there is a very fertile plain, covered with Sart farms, where rice, &c., are grown.

Yangi Shahr ("new city"), officially Wen-hsiu Fu, is about 8 miles to the south-south-east of Aksu and the residence of the Tao-tai, Prefect ("chih-fu"), and Major-General ("Chen-t'ai). In Yangi Shahr there are only about 1,000 Chinese, the rest of the people in the city and those in the surrounding country being Sarts.

7. *Uch Turfan.*—Is 63¼ miles west of Aksu, across a fertile plain with Sart farms. These farms pay a tribute in grain to the Aksu magistrate. They and the city Sarts are directly under three chiefs ("Shang-yu") who live in Aksu, and decide small troubles, whilst more important affairs go before the magistrate. The Sart Prince at Aksu has no authority; he receives a small pension (they told me 900 taels = 112*l*. a year) from the Chinese Emperor.

Uch Turfan has 1,840 families, nearly all Sarts. They told me there were only about 180 Chinese and 1,000 Tungans. The magistrate ("t'ing-kuan") lives in a small walled city on the west side of the business city.

8. *Uch-Turfan to Kashgar.*—Leaving the city the plain gradually becomes less fertile, and Sarts are not found after the first stage (Bash-yakman), 22 miles to the west, where there is a Chinese post.

Following up the Taushkan Valley to Sum-tash, the country is inhabited by Kirghiz, who live in mud houses instead of the usual "yurta." At Sum-tash, 63¼ miles from Uch Turfan, the Taushkan Valley is left and the path rises along stony valleys among barren hills, passing one small Kirghiz village. The Kuldja-wash Pass (10,800 feet) 13¼ miles from Sum-tash, and the Arba-chochuk Pass (11,280) feet at 24 miles, are crossed, and then the road descends for 21¼ miles down stony valleys till it crosses the barren Keklik plain with only one Kirghiz village for 28½ miles, to Pi-chan, where there is a headman ("t'ou-mu") and some twenty Kirghiz "yurtas." Continuing westerly across another plain with about half a dozen Kirghiz "yurta" villages scattered about and passing north of a lake, the road turns south after 64 miles, and descends among barren hills to Soghun-Karaoul on the small Torasu stream, where there is a Chinese "likin" station, and some six Sart houses. The country is now again inhabited by Sarts ; 8 miles further south the hills are finally left and a great plain is crossed westerly up to Kashgar, stretching away out of sight to the south. At first the farms are few and scattered, but for the last 15 miles the country passed through is very fertile, and covered with farms, trees and cultivation.

Summary.

I was surprised to find that the Chinese in Chinese Turkistan were so few in number. Excepting in the big cities, occasionally in a bigger village and very rarely on the road, I never came across them in large numbers. They are vastly outnumbered by the native races (Mongol), Sart, Kazak, and Kirghiz, but the latter are so effete, that the Chinese have no need to fear them, for they appear to be entirely lacking in public spirit, patriotism, desire of progress and powers of combination. The Kazak and Kirghiz, living in "yurtas," do not appear to have progressed at all since the time of Abraham. The Chinese look down on the races subject to them, openly showing their contempt for them, and this show of superiority impresses the abject races of these parts. The Chinese are also assisted by the antipathy which exists, for instance between Mongols and Kazaks.

The Chinese have a set of the most ancient officials I have ever met, and it must be remembered that a Chinese official never takes any active exercise, and is, to all intents and purposes, ten years older than a British official of the same age. The following gives the ages of the eleven chief officials I met on the journey :—

Name—		Age.
Altai Amban at Sharasumé	over	60
Director of Military Board (" Ying-wu Ch'u ")	„	64
Amban at Tarbagatai	„	58
T'ing-kuan at Tarbagatai ..	„	60
Brigadier at Tarbagatai ..	„	62
Ili Tartar General	„	68
Aksu Magistrate (" Chih-hsien ") ..	„	60
Aksu Taotai	„	64
Uch Turfan Magistrate (" T'ing-kwan")	„	70
Manchu Ling-tui (in charge of Kalmuks in Tekes Valley)	„	68
Kashgar Tao-tai..	„	71
Total for eleven officials ..	„	700 years.

In fact the only active ones I met were the brigadier of the Ili Lu-chün, aged 36, the directors of the Foreign or Russo-Chinese bureau at Sharasumé, Tarbagatai and Kuldja, and the magistrate at Kashgar.

GEORGE PEREIRA, *formerly Military Attaché at His Majesty's Legation, Peking.*

Kashgar, December 6, 1911.

No. 3.

Sir E. Goschen to Sir Edward Grey.—(Received April 1.)

Sir,   *Berlin, March 28, 1912.*

I HAVE the honour to transmit herewith précis of a report by the Imperial Admiralty on the development of the protectorate of Kiaochow from October 1910 to October 1911, which has been published in the "North German Gazette."

I have, &c.

W. E. GOSCHEN.

10

Enclosure in No. 3.

Précis of Report by the German Admiralty on the Development of Kiaochow from October 1910 to October 1911.

AT the beginning of the year under review the colony was still suffering from the East Asiatic economic crisis, from which it began to recover in the last few months of 1910 ; the development was again checked in December 1910 by the outbreak of plague, from which several thousand persons died in the neighbouring province of Shantung alone, although the measures taken by the authorities to keep the colony free from infection were entirely successful. In spite, however, of these adverse circumstances, the economic development was very favourable. In the autumn of 1911 the political revolution broke out and paralysed the commerce of the entire Empire. Thanks to the policy adopted since the occupation of Kiaochow, the colony suffered less from the revolution than most other districts, and since the beginning of 1912 the trade of Tsingtau has again shown a considerable increase, which bids fair to be of a durable nature.

The following were the receipts of the Chinese Maritime Customs Office in Tsingtau in the last three years in marks and Haikwan taels :—

Year.	Marks.	Haikwan Taels.
1908–9	3,077,978	1,099,278
1909–10	3,340,459	1,193,021
1910–11	3,658,256	1,306,520

The value of the imports of goods that were not of Chinese origin, with the exception of duty-free materials for railways and mining, rose from 25·9 million dollars (about 51·8 million marks) in the previous year to 28·7 million dollars (about 57·4 million marks) ; while the imports of Chinese goods amounted to 4·8 million dollars (about 16·8 million marks). The exports increased from 29·3 million dollars (about 58·6 million marks) in 1909–10 to 32.3 million dollars (about 64·6 million marks). The total trade therefore, in the year under review amounted to. 69·4 million dollars (138·8 million marks), as against 64·2 million dollars (128·6 million marks) in the previous year.

Until the present year there had been no statistics as to the imports of German goods, and it had been often stated that the German imports bore a comparatively small proportion to those from England, Japan, and America. This statement is now disproved by the present statistics, according to which German goods were imported with a value of 6·8 million Haikwan taels (19 million marks) in the year from the 1st July, 1910, to the 1st July, 1911. The principal imports from Germany were needles, cement, and aniline dyes. Germany also supplies the majority of the railway construction materials for the Tien-tsin–Pukow Railway, which is now approaching completion.

The most important exports in 1909–10 and 1910–11 were :—

	1909–10. Marks.	1910–11. Marks.
Straw Plaiting	22,200,000	14,400,000
Ground nuts	9,000,000	11,400,000
Ground nut oil	3,800,000	4,000,000
Shantung pongees	5,600,000	6,000,000
Yellow silk	4,400,000	4,400,000
Raw cotton	..	3,600,000
Bean oil	1,600,000	3,600,000

The revenue of the colony increased from 4,190,665 marks to 5,325,313 marks ; of this increase 797,303 marks are accounted for by the receipts from the dockyard, so that an increase of about 335,000 marks is due to economic development.

The educational institutions, to which the Marine Administration attaches special importance, again showed a favourable development ; the Government school for German children was attended by 162 scholars ; the German-Chinese high school, which was opened in October 1909, has developed so rapidly that a second building has been constructed ; in the autumn of 1911 the high school was attended by 212 students.

In the Tsingtau dockyard six small steamers, one lighter, and four boilers were constructed for private persons ; the orders from the cruiser squadron were more numerous than in the previous year.

The German authorities have always attached considerable importance to forestry ; the efforts in this direction have met with great success, not only in the colony itself, but in the interest which has been awakened in this industry iu the hinterland of Shantung. This is, the report concludes, a typical instance of the general influence exercised by German industry in the Far East.

No. 4.

Mr. Lew Yuk-Lin to Sir Edward Grey.—(Received April 2.)

Your Excellency,   *Chinese Legation, London, April* 1, 1912.

I HAVE the honour to enclose, for your Excellency's information, a translation of a telegram received from the Wai-wu Pu, giving the names of the members of the first Cabinet of the Chinese Republic in addition to the Prime Minister (Tang Shao-yi).

I have, &c.
LEW YUK-LIN.

Enclosure in No. 4.

Translation of a Telegram from the Wai-wu Pu, dated March 30, 1912.

List of New Cabinet.

Minister of Foreign Affairs, Lu Cheng-hsiang. (Until he comes to take up the post Hu Wei-te will be Minister of Foreign Affairs.)
Minister of Interior, Chao Ping-chün.
Minister of Finance, Hsiung Hsi-ling.
Minister of War, Tuan Ch'i-jui.
Minister of the Navy, Liu Kuan-hsiung.
Minister of Education, Ts'ai Yuan-pei.
Minister of Justice, Wang Chung-hui.
Minister of Agriculture and Forestry, Sung Chiao-jen.
Minister of Industry and Commerce, Chen Chi-mei.
Minister of Communications, the post is held by the Prime Minister.
Chief of the General Staff, Huang-hsing.

Chinese Legation, London, April 1, 1912.

No. 5.

Sir J. Jordan to Sir Edward Grey.—(Received April 5.)

(Telegraphic.)   *Peking, April* 5, 1912.

COMMANDER-IN-CHIEF and consul-general at Shanghai suggest that if an Indian Marine transport can be spared, her presence at Hong Kong during next few months would ensure prompt conveyance of troops to Shanghai if needed.

Suggestion seems to me to be a wise precaution in view of the increasing uncertainty of the situation in Central China. Consul at Nanking telegraphs that there is considerable anxiety there owing to ex-President and Premier having left without paying troops, who are becoming mutinous.

12

No. 6.

Sir J. Jordan to Sir Edward Grey.—(Received April 6.)

Sir, Peking, March 20, 1912.

I HAVE the honour to report that on the 13th March I received a telegram from His Majesty's consul-general at Canton, from which it appears that there was fighting in the city from the 9th to 12th March. The parties chiefly engaged were the so-called "People's Army" and the regular troops. The cause is not very clear, but by the 13th March the local Government had gained the upper hand, and as the disbandment of troops had been almost completed, Mr. Jamieson did not anticipate any further trouble. It is to be hoped therefore that the prolonged tension at Canton has found a safety-valve in this ebullition.

His Majesty's consul-general added that neither foreign life nor property had been injured, and he expected to be able to reduce the military detachment on Shameen before the end of the month.

On the 18th instant Vice-Admiral Sir A. Winsloe telegraphed from Shanghai that the military authorities at Hong Kong considered there was no longer danger of an organised attack by a combination of pirates and troops on Shameen, and submitted that it would be safe to reduce the garrison, retaining only 170 Indian riflemen. A naval reinforcement would be kept there ready to land in case of necessity.

I telegraphed to Admiral Winsloe yesterday that I saw no objection to the proposed reduction.

I have, &c.
J. N. JORDAN.

No. 7.

Sir J. Jordan to Sir Edward Grey.—(Received April 9.)

Sir, Peking, March 21, 1912.

WITH reference to my despatch of the 12th March,* I have the honour to enclose copy of a despatch from His Majesty's consul-general at Chengtu on the relations between the provincial Government of Szechuan and the Yünnanese military contingent. The mutual recriminations exchanged between the two parties would seem likely to lead to warfare of a more serious kind, but as the need for a northern expedition no longer exists, Mr. Wilkinson states his belief that the negotiations which have been opened will eventually end in the Yünnanese troops returning to their own province. Both Yünnan and Szechuan are practically independent of all central control, and the raid which the Yünnan troops have made into Szechuan is probably explained to some extent by the fact that the latter province is a rich one, which in normal times contributes a portion of its surplus revenue towards the support of Yünnan.

I have, &c.
J. N. JORDAN.

Enclosure in No. 7.

Consul-General Wilkinson to Sir J. Jordan.

Sir, Chengtu, February 21, 1912.

THE Chengtu Government received the evening of the 15th instant a telegram despatched from Tzu Chou by their envoys, Hu Ching-yun and others, sent to negotiate with the leaders of the Yünnan contingent. This telegram, which was published yesterday, is to the following effect :—

"After our arrival at Tzu-liu-ching we held several conferences with Han, commander-in-chief of the Yünnan troops, Hsieh and Li, commanders of the two columns, and Huang, commander of the detached corps. An agreement was signed to-day, the 16th February. Tzu-liu-ching and Kungching will be evacuated by the Yünnan troops on the 22nd February, the Ch'ien-wei Salt Works on the 27th February. In conjunction

* See "China, No. 3 (1912)," No. 157.

with the troops at Sui Fu, Lu Chou, and elsewhere they will go down east, and will proceed viâ Hsiang-yang to operate against the north.

"The body of infantry earlier sent under Liu Chi-chih towards Chengtu is to leave at once for Lu Chou. Please ask (Liu) Chi-chih to take with him all his equipment so as to avoid delay.

"We start to-morrow by forced marches for Chengtu, to report in detail."

This morning the "Szechuan Kung Pao" has issued an express, printed on red paper, giving the text of a telegram received by the Chengtu Government on the 19th February from Sun Wen (Sun Yat Sen) at Nanking :—

"The Ch'ing Emperor has abdicated and the republic is united. In honour of this unity of the republic there will be a grand celebration on the 15th February."

Since the latter date had gone by before the news could reach Chengtu, the local Government proposes, says the editor, to commemorate the great event on the 15th of this, the first moon, that is to say, on the 3rd March.

It might be presumed that the Yünnan contingent, having at last consented to evacuate Szechuan, will now return to Yünnan, since the necessity for a northern expedition has ceased with the abdication of the Emperor ; but before pronouncing on this point it would be as well to await the detailed report of the negotiations that is promised by the envoys sent to Tzu-liu-ching. Relations between the Yünnan contingent and the Chengtu Government were dangerously strained at the beginning of this month, when (about the 8th February) the presidents issued a lengthy circular, combatting certain accusations brought against them by the Yünnanese. These accusations, which were telegraphed to all parts of China, were to the effect that :—

1. "The masonic government" (Ko-hui Cheng-fu) of Chengtu is pursuing a policy of exclusivism in regard to men of other provinces and of rapacity in general.

2. Lo Lun (the vice-president) is making the Chengtu Government a mere instrument in the hands of the masonic bodies. Protection of life and property is only granted in exchange for large contributions to masonic funds. Men (the names are given) have been executed or imprisoned because they had no money to purchase masonic rank.

"No more benighted or ruthless monstrosity than this exists nowadays in the world," declared the Yünnanese, and in announcing to China at large the crimes of Chengtu, they state that a grand army from Yünnan, Kueichou, Hupei, and Hunan "is prepared to exterminate these lawless rebels and to construct a new Government for the Szechuanese."

On the other hand, the Chengtu presidents accuse the Yünnan troops of enriching themselves at the expense of those parts of Szechuan of which they are in occupation. "They have increased the excise on salterns everywhere ; from Lu Chou they have seized and sent to Yünnan over 200,000 taels of the duties deposited there." The presidents quote from a telegram addressed by the contingent to Yünnan (it does not appear how this fell into their hands) asking for 100 rifles and 40,000 cartridges, but saying that "Yünnan need not trouble to pay for them." Szechuan, they add, is of all the provinces the most distracted, and they, Yün and Lo, had not the heart to force the inhabitants to contribute towards military expenses ; yet these Yünnanese, void of conscience, are fleecing men everywhere. They call on the Central Government to order the Yünnan contingent either to at once return home or to take immediate part in the northern campaign. A refusal will prove that the Yünnanese either harbour intentions against the integrity of Szechuan, or are the secret agents of the Manchu Ch'ing—public enemies, whose object it is to hamper the operations against Peking. By their "insatiable savagery" the Yünnan troops are provoking an internecine war, and to them must the blame be imputed if foreigners seize the opportunity to intervene, as they did in the case of Hung Hsiu-ch'uan (the Taiping chief).

It may be, of course, that now that the common danger from the north has been withdrawn, opponents who have attacked each other with such bitterness before all China will no longer be restrained from coming to blows, even by the fear of foreign intervention ; but, on the whole, I am inclined to think that the mutual insults will be swallowed, and that the Yünnan contingent will now return to its province.

I have, &c.

W. H. WILKINSON.

No. 8.

Sir J. Jordan to Sir Edward Grey.—(Received April 12.)

Sir,   *Peking, March 26, 1912.*

WHILE events at Peking in the north and at Canton in the south were demonstrating the utter collapse of military discipline following on the proclamation of a Republican Government for the whole of China, with equal rights for all men, an episode was being enacted at Swatow which proved the absolute lack of cohesion and unanimity in the civil administration of the new régime, and which has since led to more serious disturbances.

The trouble originated in January last on the arrival at Swatow of one Ch'en Hung-ê, who had been deputed by the new Tu-tu of Canton to take over the supreme command of the Swatow district with a view to uniting the rival Cantonese and Hakka factions of the new republican administration. Instead, however, of effecting this desirable object, Ch'en Hung-ê seems to have only succeeded in rendering himself personally unpopular with both sides, whose leaders he had expelled to Canton. A rumour soon spread about that Ch'en Hung-ê was to be superseded by a certain Lin Chi-chên, who was chartering a steamer for the purpose of conveying troops from Canton to Swatow.

The receipt of this news caused great excitement amongst the merchants and people of Swatow, who at once threw in their lot with Ch'en Hung-ê sooner than admit yet another administrator from Canton, and expressed their determination to adopt every means in their power to prevent the landing of Lin Chi-chên and his "piratical expedition."

On the 14th February confirmation was received from Canton of the pending departure of Lin Chi-chên with 1,200 troops for Swatow on board the British steamer "Kumchow," a vessel of 1,450 tons, which had been specially chartered for the purpose. Ch'en Hung-ê gathered together a fighting force of some 4,000 men to resist the landing, and ordered the forts to fire should the ship endeavour to effect an entry into the harbour.

Early in the morning of the 15th, His Majesty's consul received a visit from members of the Chamber of Commerce, imploring him to do something to relieve the situation. Mr. Tours replied that he was not concerned with any differences between Lin Chi-chên and the people of Swatow : that all that might concern him in the matter was the nationality of the vessel, and that he would take whatever measures he considered advisable. When the "Kumchow" was signalled that afternoon, His Majesty's consul accordingly steamed out on board His Majesty's ship "Janus" to meet her. Mr. Tours boarded the "Kumchow" and informed the master of the state of affairs, and told him that unless a peaceful landing could be arranged he would be compelled to order the ship away. Mr. Tours then sent for Lin Chi-chên and explained the matter fully to him, and warned him that he could not allow any risk to be run by a vessel flying the British flag. Lin Chi-chên expressed surprise on learning the warmth of the reception which was being prepared for him at Swatow, and suggested that if the nationality of the vessel was the only ground for the intervention of His Majesty's consul, that difficulty might be overcome by the substitution of the new republican flag for the red ensign. While declining the latter proposal, Mr. Tours offered to assist in effecting a reconciliation, and at his request Lin deputed two subordinates to accompany him back to Swatow and endeavour to negotiate with Ch'en Hung-ê.

The following morning Lin's two deputies having failed to report, as they promised, to His Majesty's consul, the latter sent a messenger to enquire of Ch'en Hung-ê, who replied to the effect that he had definitely informed them that he would resist any attempt at landing on the part of Lin Chi-chên and his troops. This determination being further confirmed by the local Chamber of Commerce, Mr. Tours accordingly signalled to the "Kumchow" to leave the port.

I have expressed to Mr. Tours my approval of the judicious manner in which he dealt with this incident.

Frustrated in his attempt to land at Swatow, Lin Chi-chên ordered the master of the "Kumchow" to put him on shore at Hie Chi Chin Bay, some 85 miles to the south-west, in the Hui-chow prefecture, to which it appears that he was actually appointed. But being himself a Hakka, Lin Chi-chên was not content with remaining in that district, and on the 11th March Mr. Tours telegraphed to the effect that serious fighting was in progress between him and Ch'en Hung-ê's party 10 miles from Swatow, and that the latter were being driven back. On the 20th March His Majesty's consul again telegraphed that after further fighting in Swatow itself, Lin's Hakka troops had defeated Ch'en's party, who were, however, still strong in Chao Chow Fu. Fortunately no foreigners were hurt during the promiscuous firing, but many foreign houses were damaged by bullets.

On hearing that another 1,000 troops were to be dispatched from Canton, the consular body telegraphed to the provisional authorities at that port warning them of the danger such a course would involve. But Canton, which, like many other places, has also been suffering from an excess of soldiers, will probably be only too glad of the opportunity of transporting a portion of them to another port. In these circumstances, I have requested the commander-in-chief to retain a gun-boat within call of Swatow for the present.

I have, &c.
J. N. JORDAN.

No. 9.

Sir J. Jordan to Sir Edward Grey.—(Received April 15.)

Sir,   *Peking, March 29, 1912.*

THE accompanying despatch from His Majesty's consul at Nanking describes a state of things which constitutes a wide-spread danger at the present time. Everywhere there are bands of turbulent troops clamouring for arrears of pay, and one district is transferring the danger to another only to find that it, in turn, receives a similar contribution from somewhere else. Canton has shipped its pirates and hardened ruffians to Shanghai and Nanking; they are passed on thence to Chefoo, and the latter port is clamouring to get rid of them with the least possible delay. Every week I send in to the President urgent appeals from consuls for the disbandment of those turbulent visitors, but lack of money prevents him from affording much relief, and the situation goes from bad to worse.

The difficulties connected with the formation of a Government are not yet at an end, and the return of Tong Shao-yi and his Cabinet is still somewhat uncertain. Altogether, the outlook for the moment is decidedly gloomy.

I have, &c.
J. N. JORDAN.

Enclosure in No. 9.

Consul Wilkinson to Sir J. Jordan.

Sir,   *Nanking, March 19, 1912.*

I HAD the honour to telegraph to you yesterday that the large number of unpaid troops in Nanking was causing considerable anxiety to the Chinese community here, who fear that riots similar to those in Peking may break out at any time in this city. As far as I can learn, the Cantonese contingents are the only ones which have been paid up to date. The other troops stationed in Nanking, which include regiments from Chekiang, Kiangsi, and Hunan, as well as local levies, have all of them between two and four months' pay owing to them, and their dissatisfaction has been in no way diminished by the preference shown to their fellow-countrymen from South China. On the 17th instant there were two small mutinies—one amongst the Kiangsi troops, who killed two of their officers, and the other amongst the President's own bodyguard, which consists of Kiangsu men—both of which were suppressed by a cash payment on account to the soldiers, which is merely an incentive to other unpaid troops to follow their example. The delay in paying the men is apparently due to a hitch in the loan negotiations at Peking, which has prevented Yuan Shih-kai from remitting to Nanking the portion of the loan funds promised by him to the Government here. The total number of troops in Nanking and across the river at Pukow is estimated at 20,000 men, of whom between 3,000 and 4,000 are Cantonese.

The list of Ministers nominated by Yuan Shih-kai for his Cabinet was received at Nanking at the beginning of last week. Several of the selections are not regarded as satisfactory by the Assembly, which has decided, however, to wait until Tang Shao-yi's arrival before coming to any definite decision on the subject. In the meanwhile, it has passed a resolution reducing the number of Ministries from twelve, the number advocated by Yuan Shih-kai, to ten, the Ministry of Posts and Telegraphs being abolished, and those of Industry and Commerce merged into one.

The nomination which will probably cause most discussion in the Assembly is that of General Tuan Chi Jui, as Minister of War. At a meeting of army officers held last week in Nanking, a protest against General Tuan's appointment was drawn up and presented to the Assembly. No name was suggested in his place, but it is understood that the army here is in favour of the retention of Huang Hsing.

Pending the arrival of Tang Shao-yi and the final appointment of the Cabinet, Dr. Sun still continues to act as President and issue mandates in that capacity, so that China is now in the position of having two Presidents, as well as an Emperor in the background. There seems a possibility too that the country may continue for some time yet to have two capitals, for the opposition to the removal of the Government to Peking is growing both inside and outside the Assembly, and an effort will undoubtedly be made to retain the capital in Nanking, though no objection will be raised to the President, and possibly the Minister for Foreign Affairs, making Peking their head-quarters.

The struggle between Dr. Sun Wen and the Nanking Prefectural Assembly over the appointment of the prefect here has ended in the complete defeat of the ex-President, who has not only been compelled to accept Mr. Fang Chien's resignation, but to appoint as his successor a nominee of the Assembly. Dr. Sun has now come to loggerheads with the Provincial Assembly at Soochow, which has elected Mr. Chuang Yun Kuan, the acting military governor of Nanking and Soochow, to the substantive post, notwithstanding a strong intimation from the Government here that his appointment would not be acceptable to them. Mr. Chuang has offered to resign, but the Assembly not only insists on his retention, but has asked that he be appointed governor-general of the province, a post to which Huang Hsing is said to aspire, and for which General Hsü Shao Chen, the present warden of Nanking, is the candidate favoured by the gentry and merchants of this city, who believe that he is the only person capable of maintaining order in Nanking should the Government be moved north. General Hsü, I should explain, was the general in command of the 9th division, formerly stationed at Nanking. He is a man of no particular ability, but as he has always been very popular with his troops, it is assumed that he will be better able to keep them under control than anyone else.

I have, &c.
F. E. WILKINSON.

No. 10.

Sir J. Jordan to Sir Edward Grey.—(Received April 15.)

Sir, Peking, March 30, 1912.

IN my despatch of the 14th February last,* mention was made of the recent piratical attacks on British vessels and the general state of lawlessness prevalent on the West River.

I have the honour to forward to you copies of a despatch and enclosures from Vice-Admiral Sir A. Winsloe on this subject, from which it will be seen that the Chinese patrol is utterly useless whenever it is a question of taking action against the robbers.

In a communication to Yuan Shih-kai's secretary, copy of which is also enclosed, I have requested that instructions be sent to Canton to take proper steps to remedy this state of things. I fear, however, that the Peking Government exercise at present but little control in the south, and that any telegrams Yuan Shih-kai may send to the provincial authorities will not materially improve this deplorable state of affairs. His Majesty's consul-general at Canton states in a recent report that some ten cases of piratical attacks on British launches and licensed junks in the vicinity of Hong Kong have already been brought to the notice of the local authorities since the beginning of the year. In most of these cases the attack would seem to have been directed as much from the shore as from native junks, and to come rather under the head of "brigandage" than "piracy."

I have, &c.
J. N. JORDAN.

P.S.—Since writing the above despatch I have received from Captain Ts'ai T'ing-kan copy of a telegram sent by Yuan Shih-kai to the Tu-Tu at Canton on the 30th March, translation of which I have the honour to enclose.

J. N. J.

---

* See "China, No. 3 (1912)," No. 130.

Enclosure 1 in No. 10.

Vice-Admiral Sir A. Winsloe to Sir J. Jordan.

Sir,   *"Flora," at Shanghai, March 16, 1912.*
I HAVE the honour to forward a letter for your Excellency's perusal, describing
the action of the ships of the Chinese patrol on the West River. I would call your
attention specially to the covering note of the commodore's.

I have every torpedo-boat destroyer and river gunboat available on this patrol,
and shall be glad if the new Government could be pressed to improve matters.

It would appear that the term "brigandage" is more applicable than "piracy"
to what is now going on in the West River, and I am of opinion that some reliable
troops stationed on the banks of the river at certain spots would at once check this
trouble.

I have had all my vessels on this patrol now for over three months, and think it
quite time the Chinese put a stop to this trouble.

I have, &c.
A. WINSLOE.

Enclosure 2 in No. 10.

Commodore Eyres to Vice-Admiral Sir A. Winsloe.

Sir,   *March 9, 1912.*
THIS report shows the present value of the Chinese patrol. They invariably are
met steaming as fast as possible away from any disturbance.

I have, &c.
C. J. EYRES.

Enclosure 3 in No. 10.

Lieutenant Upcher to Senior Naval Officer, Canton.

Sir,   *H.M.T.B. "035," Kong Moon, March 3, 1912.*
I HAVE the honour to report the following occurrence.

On Thursday evening, the 29th February, her cargo having arrived early, the
steam-ship "Tai On" sailed at 6 p.m. for Hong Kong with the large Chinese gunboat
as escort.

The steam-ship "On Lee's" cargo did not arrive till late, so I followed with her
at 7 p.m. On nearing Junction Channel I met several tows, the Chinese gunboat and
torpedo-boat, and the "Tai On" returning, and on passing me the captain of the "Tai
On" informed me that there were a large number of pirates off the town of Sailam and
he had been made to turn back, the gunboat doing the same, but he had not
been hit.

I then told him to follow me, and steamed slowly down between the steamers and
switched my searchlight on the bank, but could see nothing and nobody about.

Everything was quiet when we passed on the return trip.

The following is the account I got from the "Tai On" yesterday.

When nearing Sailam, they saw a tow ahead and a large number of men following
her along the bank and firing at her, who, on the approach of the "Tai On," fired two
or three shots at her.

The torpedo-boat which always lies at anchor off the town, then came down at full
speed and shouted to them to turn round as she passed, telling the gunboat the
same. This they both did, and the gunboat, turning first, fired two salvoes with a
machine-gun as she steamed back.

On reaching Junction Channel again, the gunboat suggested that the "Tai On"
should again turn and go past them, but the pilot refused and the captain waited
for me.

As far as can be ascertained, the torpedo-boat ran without firing a shot directly
the firing started, while the gunboat did not seem inclined to go on at first, although
she did open fire.

I have, &c.
S. W. UPCHER.

18

Enclosure 4 in No. 10.

Memorandum.

HIS Majesty's Minister is in receipt of a despatch from the British Admiral, complaining that acts of piracy and brigandage are frequently recurring on the West River above Canton, and that the measures taken by the Chinese authorities for their repression are inadequate and ineffective.

The British senior naval officer on the West River station reports that on several occasions when British shipping has been held up by pirates, the Chinese gunboats charged with the duty of patrolling these waters, instead of rendering assistance, have been seen steaming away at full speed from the scene of disturbance. The Admiral adds that brigands on shore take as prominent a share in these lawless acts as the pirates on the river, and suggests that bodies of reliable soldiery stationed along the banks of the river might put a stop to these outrages.

Sir John Jordan hopes that telegraphic instructions may be sent to the Canton provincial authorities to take proper steps to remedy without delay this serious state of affairs.

Peking, March 30, 1912.

Enclosure 5 in No. 10.

Telegram from Yuan Shih-kai to Canton Tu-Tu, Ch'en.

(Translation.)   *March* 30, 1912.

STATEMENT just received from British Minister to the effect that he is in receipt of a despatch from the British Admiral stating that acts of piracy and brigandage are frequently recurring on the West River above Canton, and that the measures taken by the Chinese authorities for their repression are very ineffective.

British senior naval officer on the West River station reports that British vessels have been harassed by pirates on several occasions, but that Chinese gunboats patrolling the river render no assistance, and are only seen steaming away at full speed from the scene of the disturbance and that brigands on shore act in as lawless a way as the pirates.

He hopes that reliable troops may be stationed at various points along the river to put a stop to these outrages.

Such a state of affairs there is dangerous in the extreme. If pirates and brigands are allowed to commit lawless acts at will, and our troops are powerless to intervene and restore order, I fear that the ultimate result involved will be the creation of a very serious situation.

I earnestly trust that you will dispatch troops to the spot to take effective action. Please reply by telegraph.

No. 11.

Sir J. Jordan to Sir Edward Grey.—(Received April 15.)

Sir,   *Peking, March* 31, 1912.

WITH reference to my despatch of the 14th February,* I have the honour to transmit herewith a summary by Sir S. Head of events in the provinces during the past month which have not been otherwise reported to you.

I have, &c.
J. N. JORDAN.

Enclosure in No. 11.

Summary by Sir S. Head.

THE general state of unrest pervading the whole country, owing to the large numbers of undisciplined troops awaiting disbandment and the lack of funds for their

* See " China, No. 3 (1912)," No. 130.

pay, has been already reported in separate despatches respecting the different localities concerned. There remain, however, a few events which may be briefly summarised here.

The chief of these was the firing on the British ship "Shasi" between Chêng-ling-chi and Yochow, which is at the junction of the Yang-tsze River and Lake Tung Ting. Some eighty shots are said to have been fired at this vessel during her hour's run between these two places, but fortunately no harm was done, and the local authorities at once expressed their regret and took prompt action on receiving the protest of His Majesty's consul. In this, as in the very few other cases which have so far occurred of foreigners being molested, there would still seem to be no sign of xenophobe feeling. A dangerous state of affairs, however, undoubtedly exists owing to the collapse of all discipline among the troops.

Mr. King writes from Kiukiang that the general feeling of uncertainty as to the future has resulted in a very considerable stoppage of trade, and has created in the minds of the people a sense of anxiety and nervousness which easily develops into panic whenever there are rumours of the approach of troops from other districts. The local Government lacks stability, and the local officials do not possess in any measure the confidence of the people.

In a despatch from Wuchow His Majesty's consul states that brigandage and lawlessness is general throughout the Wuchow, Hsunchow, and Liuchow prefectures to a much greater extent than during the rebellion of 1905. The principal acts of pillage have been the raiding of the towns of Ho Hsien and T'eng Hsien and of four other market centres, as well as the murder of the magistrate of Jung Hsien in a fight at that place. In the case of Ho Hsien the brigands were assisted by the complicity of neighbouring officials. Mr. Coales adds that the local administration, while making itself unpopular by the barbarous and arbitrary manner in which it treats prisoners and suspects, is also earning general contempt by its weakness in dealing with the situation. On the river the native junks pay a regular toll to the brigands, proportionate to their cargo, to ensure safe passage, the rates on outward goods being 2½ dollars per 100 piculs of general cargo and 5 dollars for the same quantity of rice.

One of the most distracted provinces at the present time appears to be Shantung, which the authorities have made the dumping-ground for mutinous troops both from the north and the south. His Majesty's consul at Chefoo reports that there are some 10,000 miscellaneous troops in the north of that province, and that the authorities are at a loss for funds wherewith to pay them. Towards the end of the month the situation became so serious that steps were taken by the consular body at Chefoo to protest against the large number of Chinese soldiers in the foreign settlement, whose reckless handling of firearms was a source of considerable alarm to the community. Sir John Jordan also brought the matter to the notice of Yuan Shih-kai on the 24th March, urging the withdrawal of these troops from the foreign area. There are now two American men-of-war and a transport at Chefoo, whose presence has so far prevented an actual outbreak, and His Majesty's ship "Pegasus" has been ordered to pay occasional visits there from Wei-hai Wei.

No. 12.

Sir J. Jordan to Sir Edward Grey.—(Received April 22.)

Sir,   *Peking, April 3, 1912.*

I HAVE the honour to enclose copy of a despatch from His Majesty's consul at Nanking, forwarding, in translation, the text of the provisional constitution of the Chinese Republic which has been passed by the advisory council at Nanking. This constitution is to do duty until it is replaced by a permanent one to be drawn up by the national convention, which it is hoped will be elected in due course on a properly regulated suffrage.

The advisory council at Nanking is incurring much popular criticism as not being entitled to be considered a representative body, and there is an urgent demand for the summoning of the Deliberative Assembly mentioned in article 3 of the provisional constitution. This Deliberative Assembly is to arrange the organisation and method of election of a national convention, which is to meet within ten months from the date of the promulgation of the provisional constitution, and will then proceed to draw up the permanent constitution of the Republic of China.

Great changes in the government of nations have, no doubt, been often the work of a few leading men acting in advance of the standard of intelligence amongst the mass of their countrymen, but it is hard to believe in the adaptation of republican institutions, as outlined in the provisional constitution, to the needs of Mongols, Tibetans, and the vast majority of the people of China. The contrast between the doctrinaire theories of the Nanking council and their actual performance is sufficiently marked to cause serious misgiving as to the ability of the new men to govern China. For the moment, presidential decrees are the only enactments which have any force.

I have, &c.

J. N. JORDAN.

Enclosure 1 in No. 12.

Consul Wilkinson to Sir J. Jordan.

Sir,   *Nanking, March* 21, 1912.

I HAVE the honour to enclose a translation of the provisional constitution of the Chinese Republic as passed by the National Assembly, which has been kindly furnished to me by the Foreign Office here, and which may be regarded, therefore, as semi-official. The powers of the President, the Ministry, and the Assembly, are all very loosely defined in the constitution, and will probably be a source of frequent dispute in the future. The Assembly, for instance, has already taken exception to the fact that the new Cabinet has been selected by President Yuan and not by the Premier on whom, according to the Assembly's reading of the constitution, the duty properly devolves. Fault has also been found with the President for increasing the number of Ministries to twelve after the Assembly had decided that ten was enough. These are differences which will no doubt be easily settled, but it is only too probable that they are but a prelude to others of a graver nature which are bound to ensue as the struggle for supremacy between the President, the Ministry, and the Assembly develops.

Since I last addressed you there has been no further trouble with the army, but as no funds have yet arrived from Peking, the situation is still somewhat critical. From what I can learn the soldiers have been persuaded to wait for their pay until the arrival of Tang Shao Yi, who, they have been told, is bringing enough money with him to satisfy all their demands. It is to be hoped that a disappointment is not in store for them. The number of troops in the city has been increased during the last few days by the arrival of some 2,000 men from Kuangsi and Kueichow under the command of General Wang Chih Hsiang, the ex-fantai and tutu of the former province. General Wang, who, though a civil official, has a great reputation as a soldier, being one of the generals who suppressed the Kuangsi rebellion of 1905, is talked of as the future Governor-General of Chihli, of which province he is a native. There is a possibility, too, that he may be Minister of War as he appears to be the only high official of any reputation possessing the necessary qualifications for the post, who might possibly be acceptable to both north and south.

The Tien-tsin–Pukow Railway are now running two trains daily along the whole length of the line, that is, from Pukow to the point where it joins the German section. The line is still badly in want of rolling-stock as General Chang Hsün, notwithstanding the protests of the Government here, has not yet returned the cars and trucks which he took away with him. A new managing director of the name of Tao Hsün has been recently appointed.

I have, &c.

F. E. WILKINSON.

Enclosure 2 in No. 12.

The Provisional Constitution of the Republic of China.

ARTICLE 1.—*General Provisions.*

THE Republic of China is established by the people of China.

2. The sovereignty of the Republic of China resides in the people.

3. The territory of the Republic of China consists of twenty-two provinces, Inner Mongolia, Outer Mongolia, Thibet, and Kokonor.

4. The Government of the Republic of China shall be composed of the Deliberative Assembly, the Provisional President, the Ministers of State, and the courts of justice.

ARTICLE 2.—*Citizens.*

5. The citizens of the Republic of China shall be equal, irrespective of race, class, or religion.

6. The citizens shall enjoy the following rights and liberties :—

(1.) No person shall be arrested, detained, tried, or punished without due process of the law.

(2.) No house shall be broken into or searched without due process of the law.

(3.) Every citizen shall have the right to own property and follow his occupation.

(4.) Every citizen shall enjoy the liberty of speech, writing, publication, calling meetings, and forming societies.

(5.) Every citizen shall enjoy the right of privacy in correspondence.

(6.) Every citizen shall have the right to reside or remove at pleasure.

(7.) Every citizen shall enjoy the liberty of religious belief.

7. Citizens shall have the right to petition Provincial Assemblies.

8. Citizens shall have the right to petition the administrative offices.

9. Citizens shall have the right to sue, and to be tried at the courts of justice.

10. Citizens shall have the right to appeal to the administrative court, when officials of the Government have illegally infringed their rights.

11. Citizens shall have the right to compete in Government service examinations.

12. Citizens shall have the right to elect and to be elected.

13. Citizens shall pay taxes as prescribed by law.

14. Citizens shall serve in the army as prescribed by law.

15. The rights and liberties of citizens specified in this article may, in the interest of the public, or for the maintenance of order and peace, or in case of any other urgent necessity, be curtailed by due process of law.

ARTICLE 3.—*The Deliberative Assembly.*

16. The legislative power of the Republic of China shall be vested in the Deliberative Assembly.

17. The Deliberative Assembly shall be constituted by representatives returned from various territories as specified in section 18.

18. Five representatives shall be returned to the Assembly from each province, Inner Mongolia, Outer Mongolia, and Thibet ; and one from Kokonor. The method of election shall be left to the decision of the electoral territory, and each representative of the Assembly shall be entitled to only one vote in session.

19. The duties and powers of the Deliberative Assembly shall be :—

(1.) To make all laws.

(2.) To pass the budget of the Provisional Government.

(3.) To establish a system of national taxation, currency, and uniform weights and measures.

(4.) To decide the making of public loans and such other arrangements as pertain to the National Treasury.

(5.) To ratify all matters specified in sections 34, 35, and 40.

(6.) To reply to questions sent by the Provisional Government.

(7.) To attend to petitions of citizens.

(8.) To express and present views to the Government regarding law and other matters.

(9.) To question Ministers of State and demand their presence at the Assembly to give reply.

(10.) To request the Government to punish officials guilty of receiving bribes, or otherwise acting contrary to law.

(11.) To impeach the Provisional President, if he be recognised as having acted as a traitor, provided there is a quorum of four-fifths of the whole number of members, of whom two-thirds vote in favour.

(12.) To impeach any Minister of State, if he be recognised as having failed to carry out his duties, or having acted contrary to law, provided there is a quorum of three-fourths of the whole number of members, of whom two-thirds vote in favour.

21. The Deliberate Assembly shall itself convene the meeting, and decide the opening and closing of the sessions.

21. All meetings of the Deliberative Assembly shall be public, but may be held in camera, if any Minister of State so request, or the majority of the members so decide.

22. The matters decided by the Deliberative Assembly shall be promulgated and carried out by the Provisional President.

23. If the Provisional President vetoes any Bill passed by the Deliberative Assembly he shall state his objections within ten days after it has been presented to him, and the matter shall be placed before the Assembly for reconsideration. If two-thirds of the members reaffirm their decision the same shall be carried out as prescribed in section 22.

24. The Speaker of the Deliberative Assembly shall be elected by ballot, and shall be declared elected if the ballot returns one-half of the total votes cast.

25. The members of the Deliberative Assembly shall bear no responsibility to outsiders for their speeches and decisions made in the Assembly.

26. Except for crimes committed during the session, and for others involving internal disturbance or external complication, the members of the Deliberative Assembly shall not be arrested during such session without the consent of the Assembly.

27. The standing rules of the Deliberative Assembly shall be made by the Assembly itself.

28. The Deliberative Assembly shall be dissolved as soon as the National Convention meets which shall succeed to all its rights and powers.

ARTICLE 4.—*The Provisional President and Vice-President.*

29. The Provisional President and Vice-President shall be elected by the Deliberative Assembly by a vote of two-thirds of the members at a quorum of three-fourths of the whole number.

30. The Provisional President shall represent the Provisional Government, control political affairs, and promulgate laws.

31. The Provisional President shall execute the laws and promulgate such orders as are authorised by the law.

32. The Provisional President shall be Commander-in-chief of the army and navy.

33. The Provisional President shall make all Government service rules and regulations, subject to the approval of the Deliberative Assembly.

34. The Provisional President shall have power to appoint and dismiss all civil and military officials, except Ambassadors and Ministers, whose appointment and dismissal shall be approved by the Deliberative Assembly.

35. The Provisional President shall have power, with the consent of the Deliberative Assembly, to declare war, conclude peace, and make treaties.

36. The Provisional President shall have power to declare martial law as authorised by the law.

37. The Provisional President, as representative of the whole nation, shall receive foreign Ambassadors and other public Ministers.

38. The Provisional President shall have power to recommend measures to the Deliberative Assembly for consideration.

39. The Provisional President shall have power to confer decorations and other honorary distinctions.

40. The Provisional President shall have power to grant general amnesty, special amnesty, commutation and rehabilitation ; but the granting of a general amnesty shall have the approval of the Deliberative Assembly.

41. In case of the impeachment of the Provisional President by the Deliberative Assembly, the judges of the highest court of justice shall elect nine judges to constitute a special tribunal for that purpose.

42. The Provisional Vice-President shall act for the President in case he resigns or is otherwise unable to attend to his duties.

ARTICLE 5.—*Ministers of State.*

43. The Prime Minister and the Ministers of the Boards shall be called Ministers of State.

44. The Ministers of State shall assist the Provisional President and share his responsibility.

45. The Ministers of State shall countersign all bills proposed, laws promulgated and orders issued by the Provisional President.

46. The Ministers of State and their deputies shall have the privilege to attend and speak in the Assembly.

47. A Minister of State on impeachment by the Deliberative Assembly shall be removed from office by the Provisional President, but at the request of the President the case may be reconsidered by the Assembly.

ARTICLE 6.—*The Courts of Justice.*

48. The courts of justice shall consist of judges appointed by the Provisional President and the Minister of Justice. The organisation of the courts and the qualification of the judges shall be prescribed by law.

49. The courts of justice, as authorised by the law, shall have power to try all civil and criminal cases, except those involving administrative matters and of a special nature which shall be tried by a different procedure.

50. All trials in the courts of justice shall be open to the public, except those affecting peace and order which shall be tried in secret session.

51. Judges, in the discharge of their duties, shall be independent and not be interfered with by their superiors.

52. During the tenure of office, the salaries of judges shall not be diminished, nor their services transferred ; and, except when in conformity with the law, they deserve punishment, or retirement from office, they shall not be removed. Regulations for the removal of judges shall be prescribed by a special law.

ARTICLE 7.—*Supplementary Provisions.*

53. Within ten months after the promulgation of the present constitution, the Provisional President shall call the National Convention whose organisation and method of election shall be decided by the Deliberative Assembly.

54. The constitution of the Republic of China shall be drawn up by the National Assembly, and until it comes into effect the provisional constitution shall have the same force as the aforesaid constitution.

55. The present constitution may be amended by a vote of two-thirds of the members of the Assembly, or on the recommendation of the Provisional President with the approval of three-fourths of the members out of a quorum of four-fifths of the number present.

56. The present constitution shall take effect from the date of its promulgation, and all enactments heretofore passed for the organisation of the Provisional Government shall from the said date become null and void.

No. 13.

Sir J. Jordan to Sir Edward Grey.—(Received April 20.)

Sir,   *Peking, April 4, 1912.*

I HAVE the honour to report, with reference to your despatch of the 6th February,* that in due course the proposed modification in the composition of the Wai-wu Pu, whereby the President can in future be other than an Imperial Prince, met with the assent of all the treaty Powers.

I may here mention that the Wai-wu Pu has recently changed its name to Wai-chiao Pu (Ministry of Foreign Affairs).

I have, &c.

J. N. JORDAN.

---

* See "China, No. 3 (1912)," No. 91.

No. 14.

War Office to Foreign Office.—(Received April 23.)

Sir,   *War Office, Whitehall, April 23*, 1912.

I AM commanded by the Army Council to address you with reference to a telegraphic despatch, dated the 5th April, 1912, from His Majesty's Minister at Peking, in which he puts forward the suggestion that an Indian marine transport should be retained at Hong Kong to enable troops to be conveyed on an emergency to Shanghai.

2. I am to inform you that the council have consulted the India Office on the subject, and it has been ascertained that the cost of retaining an Indian marine transport in chinese waters would amount to at least 3,600*l*. per mensem, in addition to the cost of the coal expended on the voyage from and back to India.

3. The Admiralty was then consulted as to the time required to charter shipping at Hong Kong for the conveyance of a force such as might reasonably be dispatched to Shanghai in case of emergency. The commodore at Hong Kong has replied to the Admiralty enquiry on this subject to the effect that such arrangements could be made in two or three days.

4. I am to enquire whether under these circumstances the Secretary of State for Foreign Affairs considers that it is necessary to give effect to the suggestion of Sir John Jordan as regards the retention at Hong Kong of an Indian marine transport.

I am, &c.
E. W. D. WARD.

No. 15.

Sir Edward Grey to Sir J. Jordan.

(Telegraphic.)   *Foreign Office, April* 23, 1912.
YOUR telegram of 5th April.

War Office suggest that, in place of retaining Indian Marine transport at Hong Kong, which would cost 3,600*l*. a month, exclusive of coal, shipping should be hired locally in case of emergency.

The commodore at Hong Kong reports that sufficient shipping could be obtained in two or three days.

Please ascertain the views of the commander-in-chief and his Majesty's consul-general at Shanghai on this proposal, and inform me by telegraph.

No. 16.

Sir J. Jordan to Sir Edward Grey.—(Received April 26.)

Sir,   *Peking, April* 8, 1912.
I HAVE the honour to transmit herewith, in translation, three communications addressed to me by the Ministry of Foreign Affairs, announcing respectively the composition of the new Cabinet, the appointment of Mr. Hu Wei-tê to be Foreign Minister *ad interim*, and the change of the Chinese designation of the Ministry of Foreign Affairs from Wai-wu Pu to Wai-chiao Pu.

Of this last it is sufficient to say that from a literary point of view it is a change for the better, the substitution of the combination wai-chiao ("foreign relations") for wai-wu ("foreign things") removing any lack of dignity which may have attached to the latter phrase.

The Cabinet whose formation was announced on the 30th March represents an attempt to combine the nominees of north and south, and its selection has been delayed by much wrangling between the various parties. It is even now quite uncertain whether all the persons designated will accept office, but it was felt that the announcement could not be further postponed without grave risk of weakening the already precarious position of the Provisional Government.

As regards the number of the Ministries, it will be noted that the former Ministry of Commerce has been divided into a Ministry of Agriculture and Forests and a Ministry of Industry and Commerce, while the Ministry of Dependencies has been eliminated altogether. The latter change is significant as denoting the intention of making Mongolia and Thibet integral parts of the republic.

Only the Ministers of Internal Affairs and of War are at present in Peking. The Premier is expected to arrive shortly, and the remainder in about a fortnight, but how long it will be before they are able to form a harmonious executive remains to be seen. It is true that Sun Yat-sen formally laid down his office as Provisional President on the evening of the 29th March, as soon as the Cabinet had been finally agreed upon, but the same willingness to subordinate his personal ambitions to the public welfare has not been manifested by the republican generalissimo, Huang Hsing, whose attitude at the present time is likely to have an important bearing on the fortunes of the Coalition Government.

It will be observed that Huang's name appears in the note of the 30th March as Chief of the General Staff. This appointment seems to have been in the nature of a sop to his disappointment at being rejected for the Secretaryship of State for War in favour of the northern general, Tuan Ch'i-jui, and a presidential order of the same date urged him in flattering terms to devote himself especially to the military affairs of the Liang Kiang provinces.

This was evidently not sufficient to appease this firebrand of the south, for a further presidential order on the next day appoints Huang to be Resident General of Nanking, and to remain in full command of the southern armies, the post of Chief of the General Staff being given to another nominee, who immediately declined it, and it is still vacant.

This would seem to indicate that, whatever show of approaching unity there may be in the civil administration of the country, the amalgamation under one head of the northern and southern armies is for the time being impracticable, and as the military element still controls the situation, this acknowledgment of a military dictator in the southern capital may be fraught with serious consequences.

I have, &c.

J. N. JORDAN.

Enclosure 1 in No. 16.

Wai-wu Pu to Sir J. Jordan.

(Translation.)

Sir, March 30, 1912.

ON the 13th March the orders of the Provisional President were received specially appointing T'ang Shao-yi to be Prime Minister.

. Also on the 30th March the orders of the Provisional President have been received commanding Lu Cheng-hsiang to be Secretary of State for Foreign Affairs, Chao Ping-chün to be Secretary of State for Internal Affairs, Hsiung Hsi-ling to be Secretary of State for Finance, Tuan Ch'i-jui to be Secretary of State for War, Liu Kuan-hsiung to be Secretary of State for the Navy, Ts'ai Yüan-p'ei to be Secretary of State for Education, Wang Ch'ung-hui to be Secretary of State for Justice, Sung Chiao-jên to be Secretary of State for Agriculture and Forests, and Ch'ên Chi-mei to be Secretary of State for Industry and Commerce. The appointment of Secretary of State for Communications is to be held, in addition to his other duties, by the Premier, T'ang Shao-yi.

Also, on this same day, the orders of the Provisional President have been received commanding Huang Hsiug to be Chief of the General Staff.

We have the honour to notify you officially of the above for communication to His Majesty's Government.

We avail, &c.

(Seal of the Wai-wu Pu.)

Enclosure 2 in No. 16.

Wai-wu Pu to Sir J. Jordan.

(Translation.)

Sir,   March 30, 1912.

ON the 30th March the orders of the Provisional President have been received as follows :—

"Lu Cheng-hsiang being now on a mission abroad, pending his arrival to take up his appointment, Hu Wei-tê is commanded to act as Secretary of State for Foreign Affairs."

We have the honour to notify you officially of the above.

We avail, &c.

(Seal of the Wai-wu Pu.)

Enclosure 3 in No. 16.

Wai-wu Pu to Sir J. Jordan.

(Translation.)

Sir,   April 1, 1912.

THE orders of the Provisional President of the 30th March, appointing the Secretaries of State for the various Ministries, have already been communicated to you.

We have now the honour to inform you that in future the title to be given to this Ministry is "Ministry of Foreign Affairs."

We avail, &c.

(Seal of the Wai-wu Pu.)

No. 17.

Sir J. Jordan to Sir Edward Grey.—(Received April 26.)

Sir,   *Peking, April 11, 1912.*

WITH reference to my despatch of the 8th instant reporting on the formation of the new republican Cabinet, I have the honour to transmit herewith a despatch from His Majesty's consul at Nanking on the same subject.

Mr. Wilkinson alludes to the difficulties which arose over the appointment to the Ministry of War and over that of General Huang Hsing to the post of generalissimo of the Nanking army.

Huang Hsing, a native of Hunan, has been connected with the revolutionary movement since the time of his leaving school, and concerned in revolutionary plots for the past dozen years or more, and was one of the leading spirits among Chinese students in Japan who formed a league to resist Russian aggression in Manchuria. On his return to China he became president of a young progressive party, called in Hunan "China Awake," and has been connected with Sun Yan-sen in the organisation of the revolutionary party. Altogether Huang, who is 39 years of age, is a man of action, and his present career at Nanking will be followed with anxiety.

I have, &c.

J. N. JORDAN.

Enclosure in No. 17.

Consul Wilkinson to Sir J. Jordan.

Sir,   *Nanking, April 1, 1912.*

IN accordance with the arrangement made between President Yuan and the Nanking Government, the Premier, Mr. Tang Shao Yi, arrived in Nanking on the 24th ultimo to discuss the proposed coalition Cabinet with the authorities here and obtain for it the approval of the Assembly. The names of the new Ministers had been previously telegraphed to President Sun by President Yuan, but as several of the appointments were regarded in Nanking with disfavour and two of the names had to be struck off the list owing to the reduction by the Assembly of the number of ministries from twelve to ten, it was not until the 29th instant that a Cabinet was finally arranged by Mr. Tang Shao Yi to which both President Yuan and the Nanking

Government were agreeable. As I ventured to anticipate in my despatch of the 19th ultimo, keen contention arose over the appointment to the Ministry of War. The opposition to General Tuan Chi Jui on the part of the military element here was so strong that his chances of getting the appointment seemed very small. It was overcome, however, by the argument that the services of General Huang Hsing, the ex-Minister of War and alternative candidate, were indispensable at Nanking if order was to be maintained amongst the troops. and that therefore, even if he got the appointment, it would be impossible for him to go up to Peking. To compensate General Huang Hsing for his disappointment he has been made chief of the staff and generalissimo of the Nanking army. The naval element in Nanking strongly objected to General Lan Tien Wei's appointment as Minister of Marine as he was not a naval officer. The post was then offered to Admiral Sah, but refused by him, and was finally given to Captain Liu Kuan Hsiung.

The names of the new Ministers were submitted to the National Assembly for approval at a special session held for the purpose on the evening of the 29th ultimo, when, with the exception of Mr. Liang Ju Hao as Minister of Communications, all the candidates were approved by the Assembly. What the objections to Mr. Liang were I have not heard, but I am told that the Premier was very much hurt at his rejection. Until another selection is made for the post Mr. Tang Shao Yi will combine the duties of Minister of Communications with the Premiership.

It is admitted by everyone here that the new Cabinet is a triumph for President Yuan. All the more important posts in it—the Premiership, the Ministries of War, Finance, the Interior, and Foreign Affairs—are all held by nominees of his own. The explanation given me is that the destinies of the country having been placed in Yuan's hands, it was only fair to allow him the choice of the men who were to be his chief instruments in carrying out his policy. Of the capabilities of the various Ministers there are very different views held in Nanking. No one regards the Cabinet as ideal, but it is held to be as satisfactory as could have been expected under the circumstances. The general opinion, however, is that the composition of the present Cabinet is of little importance, for it can only have a brief existence during which it will be dominated by the personality of the President, who is the only member of the Government who has the confidence of the people behind him.

No decision has yet been arrived at on the question of the removal of the Cabinet and Assembly to Peking, which is to be discussed at a special meeting of the Assembly to be held this week. The opposition to their departure is still very strong, though no one seems to doubt that, in view of the absolute necessity for having a single centre of authority, the whole of the Government must in the end go north. In that event, General Huang Hsing will remain in Nanking as the supreme military authority, while a tutu will be appointed to take charge of the civil affairs of the province. For the post of tutu there are now three candidates : General Hsu Kuo Chen, the warden of Nanking ; Mr. Cheng Te Chuan, the ex-Minister of the Interior and former Governor of of Soochow ; and Mr. Chuang Yun Kuan, the present tutu of Kiangsu. The first two have been recommended for the post by President Sun, while the last named is the candidate recommended by the Provincial Assembly.

In his speech to the Assembly announcing the names of the Cabinet Ministers, Mr. Tang Shao Yi also referred, though only very briefly and without going into any particulars, to the financial difficulties of the Government, which made it necessary for them to borrow capital from abroad.

The number of troops in Nanking has been increased during the past week by the return of several more thousand Canton and Chekiang soldiers from the north. Arrangements are, however, being made to send all the Cantonese troops, about 9,000 men, back to their province during the next few days. Yesterday 2,000 of them left and to-day a similar number are to go, two of Messrs. Butterfield and Swire's boats having been specially chartered to convey them. Unfortunately, owing to lack of funds with which to pay them, it has been found impossible either to disband or to send away any of the other troops.

President Sun is to hand over the President's seal of office to Mr. Tang Shao Yi to-day. He has postponed his departure to the middle of the week. I understood that Mr. Sun proposes to spend the next few months lecturing all over China on republicanism, after which the probabilities are that he will return to political life.

I have, &c.
W. H. WILKINSON.

28

No. 18.

Sir J. Jordan to Sir Edward Grey.—(Received April 26.)

Sir,								Peking, April 11, 1912.
	I HAVE the honour to transmit herewith copy of a report which has been
addressed to me by the military attaché at His Majesty's Legation respecting recent
mutinous outbreaks among the Chinese troops.
							I have, &c.
							J. N. JORDAN.

Enclosure in No. 18.

Report by Lieutenant-Colonel Willoughby.

	FROM all quarters of the republic in quick succession reports have been received
during the past month of mutinies, looting, and unruliness on the part of the troops.
The principal cases are briefly enumerated below :—

	At Chin-kiang (Kiang-su) His Majesty's consul reported on the 1st March that a
corps of mixed provincials, the "Chin Hsing Tui," were out of control and giving
trouble.
	At Chinan-fu (Shantung) the troops of the 5th division and provincial troops,
who had been very unruly since the China New Year, robbing, assaulting women, and
generally disregarding orders, continued misbehaving till the 2nd March, when General
Ma Lung Piao arrived to command the 5th division.
	At Chungking (Szechuan), at the beginning of March, some 2,000 to 3,000 Yünnan
troops arrived. As their progress had been marked by pillage and misbehaviour ever
since they entered the province the city gates were shut against them, and they were
bought off with a sum of 300,000 taels.
	At Pao-ting-fu (Chih-li), on the 2nd March, a mutiny broke out among the
regulars of the 2nd and 6th divisions, and looting and burning began. All classes of
the troops, new and old, and even the police seem to have caught the infection. A
large proportion of the revolted soldiers of the 2nd division scattered in bands over the
countryside plundering.
	At Shih-chia-chang (Chih-li), on the night of the 2nd March, troops of the
3rd division and the bodyguard of the late Governor Chang, of Shan-si, broke out and
looted the place, including some foreign property.
	At Tien-tsin (Chih-li), about 10 P.M. on the 2nd March, looting and burning started
in the city, the work of deserters of the 3rd division from Peking joined by the
Tien-tsin fire brigades and local militia guards and a mob of the lowest classes. The
disturbances continued throughout the night. There was much firing in the air to
intimidate, but little loss of life ; loot, not violence, evidently being the aim. The
German doctor, Schreyer, was shot dead in the city while on rescue work. It is
noteworthy that the gentry appealed for the aid of foreign troops.
	At Kiukiang (Kiang-si) on the 4th March trouble broke out among the troops
owing to dissensions along the local revolutionary leaders, but very little looting or
rioting actually took place.
	At Canton, on the 5th March, some troops at Heung Shan refused to disband.
	On the 8th March fighting ensued over the disbandment of the "Ao Battalion."
	On the 9th March serious fighting began between the "Luchun" (regulars) and
the "people's army," and lasted till the 12th March. Some 1,200 to 1,500 people were
said to have been killed, two-thirds of them being civilians.
	Again on the 19th and 20th March fighting occurred between mutineers and
Government troops at the Whampoa and Bogue Forts. Piracy has been rife in the
Delta.
	At Tai-an-fu, Yen-chou, and Han-chuang (Shantung), on the line of the Tien-tsin–
Pu-kou Railway, General Chang Hsun's troops (who, it will be remembered, came up
from Nanking and Hsu-chou-fu), were reported by His Majesty's consul at Chinan-fu
to have been thoroughly disorganising the railway traffic, being especially unruly at
Tai-an. Brigandage was also said to be rampant in south-west Shantung.

Ichou (Chih-li), near the Western Imperial Mausolea, was reported to have been looted by "provincial troops" on the 9th March.

At Yangchou (Kiang-su), on the Grand Canal near Chinkiang, His Majesty's consul at the latter place reported on the 12th March that General Hsu and his men (mostly old "provincial troops "), numbering some 10,000 men, were openly mutinous.

In Thibet, on the 16th March, fighting took place at Pemajong (between Gyantse and Shigatse) between Thibetan and Chinese troops, in which the latter were worsted.

On the 28th March fighting again took place near Gyantse, between Thibetan and Chinese troops, resulting in the surrender and disarmament of the Chinese.

At Shanghai, on the 18th March, revolutionary troops (of Canton and Shantung), sent there for disbandment from Nanking, were reported by Admiral Winsloe to be giving trouble in the native city. Other troops were brought out against them and fired upon them, killing three before they surrendered.

At Swatow (Kuang-tung), on the 20th March, the pillage of Swatow native city by troops from Canton was reported.

At Ching-chou (Shantung), on the 23rd March, regulars and provincial troops started looting and burning. They robbed the post office and some fifty banks, shops, &c. There was no violence to persons however. The Manchu and other troops were used against the looters, but appear to have had some compact with them, as only one man was killed.

At Hsian-fu (Shen-si), on the 23rd March, a mutiny occurred among the troops sent from Peking. 2,000 were said to be plundering the adjacent villages. Foreigners were safe in the city. The gates were closed.

At Soochow (Kiang-su), on the 27th March, soldiers started burning and looting in the city. The gates were closed. The officers are said to have hidden themselves.

On the 30th March His Majesty's consul-general at Shanghai reported that only 100 of the cavalry regiment remained, all the rest having dispersed with their loot. He added that only the failure of the mutineers to obtain gun ammunition to blow in the gates saved the city.

At Chefoo (Shantung) throughout the month the presence of a large number of undisciplined and unruly troops (some 10,000) from the south, and their insolent behaviour towards foreigners, combined with their reckless handling of firearms have been a constant menace to the peace of the place. The military governor openly proclaimed that unless funds could be raised to pay them, there would be a mutiny and looting in Chefoo. The soldiers in hospital moreover were said to be always talking of the good time coming when the looting started.

Kan-su. A telegraphic report from Hsian-fu, dated the 3rd April, speaks of "serious disturbances in Kan-su."

From Nanking, on the 4th April, His Majesty's consul telegraphed that there was great anxiety owing to the departure of the Premier and ex-President Sun, and that the troops were getting mutinous ; and that they were still unpaid.

It will be noticed that all the above-mentioned instances of indiscipline have occurred since the outbreak in Peking on the 29th February. Many others have been reported during the few preceding weeks, e.g., the dissensions and fighting between the Yünnan, Kuei-chou, and Szechuan troops, the revolt of the Chinese regular troops in the "Thibetan marches," the looting of towns by the Kuang-si troops, and lawlessness and brigandage everywhere. The sacking of Ning-hsia-fu (Kan-su) and the troubles and fighting in the New Dominion must also be mentioned.

Amid all this lawlessness and turbulence one remarkable fact stands out, and that is the almost universal respect that has been shown for foreign life and property, and the general absence of anti-foreign feeling. There have, it is true, been regrettable exceptions to this general rule, but in the main it may be said that revolutionary and imperialist alike have shown an almost surprising degree of deference for the foreigner.

M. E. WILLOUGHBY, *Military Attaché.*

Peking, April 6, 1912.

No. 19.

Admiralty to Foreign Office.—(Received April 26.)

Sir, *Admiralty, April 26, 1912.*

I AM commanded by my Lords Commissioners of the Admiralty to transmit, for the information of the Secretary of State for Foreign Affairs, copy of a telegram, dated the 26th instant, from the commander-in-chief on the China station, relative to the British military force at Hankow.

Copy has been sent to the War Office.

I am, &c.
W. GRAHAM GREENE.

Enclosure in No. 19.

Commander-in-Chief, China, to Admiralty.

(Telegraphic.) *Shanghai, April 25, 1912.*

WITH regard to military force at Hankow, have ordered back Royal Engineers and Royal Artillery to Hong Kong, leaving only 100 rifles. Have consulted His Majesty's Minister at Peking.

No. 20.

Sir J. Jordan to Sir Edward Grey.—(Received April 26.)

(Telegraphic.) *Peking, April 26, 1912.*

TRANSPORT at Hong Kong. Your telegram of 23rd April.

Following from His Majesty's consul-general at Shanghai:—

"Commander-in-chief agrees, in view of the expense mentioned, proposal must be abandoned. He suggests that commodore be instructed to arrange that vessel be always available for immediate charter in case of need.

"In my opinion local trouble, if it came, would come without much warning, and we should have to rely on the local forces; of other trouble there should be ample warning."

No. 21.

Foreign Office to War Office.

Sir, *Foreign Office, April 27, 1912.*

WITH reference to your letter of the 23rd instant, relative to the proposed retention of an Indian Marine Transport at Hong Kong to convey troops to Shanghai on an emergency, I am directed by Secretary Sir E. Grey to inform you that, in view of the opinions expressed in the telegram of the 26th instant from His Majesty's Minister at Peking, a copy of which has already been sent to you, he does not consider that it will be necessary to give effect to the proposals contained in Sir J. Jordan's telegram of the 5th instant.

Sir E. Grey hopes, however, that the commander-in-chief's proposal that he should be authorised to make arrangements for a vessel to be always available at Hong Kong for the transport of troops will be approved.

Copy of this letter is being sent to the Admiralty.

I am, &c.
W. LANGLEY.

No. 22.

Sir J. Jordan to Sir Edward Grey.—(Received April 29.)

Sir, *Peking, April 11, 1912.*

I HAVE the honour to enclose copy of a despatch from His Majesty's consul at Nanking, giving a summary of the Premier's speech to the National Assembly at Nanking when he announced the names of the Cabinet selected to form the new coalition Government. It will be seen that Tong Shao-yi estimates that a sum of 215,000,000 taels (nearly 30,000,000*l.*) will be required to meet the expenditure of the present year in connection with undertakings, none of which is of a productive nature. This is equivalent to nearly half of the Boxer indemnity, the payment of which has severely taxed the resources of the country during the last ten years, and which China has now ceased to meet altogether. The warmest well-wishers of China cannot view the financial outlook without serious misgiving, and I fully share the opinion of one of my colleagues, who told me the other day that if he were an enemy of China he would advise her to go on borrowing indiscriminately, but that as a sincere friend he felt bound to see that the expenditure of foreign money was surrounded with necessary safeguards.

The only statesman who seems to appreciate the situation is the President Yuan Shih-kai. I never see him but he dwells upon the cry for money which reaches him from all the provinces. Yesterday he again referred to the question, and admitted quite frankly that no revenue is being collected in the greater part of the country.

I have, &c.
J. N. JORDAN.

Enclosure in No. 22.

Consul Wilkinson to Sir J. Jordan.

Sir, *Nanking, April 4, 1912.*

SINCE I addressed you on the 1st instant the Chinese newspapers have published the text of the Premier's speech at the meeting of the National Assembly held on the 29th ultimo, when he announced to them the names of the Cabinet Ministers selected by President Yuan to form the new Coalition Government. The following is a summary of it.

The Premier begins by referring to the disturbed state of the country. The first duty, he says, of the new Government will be to restore order; the second, to carry out the reforms mentioned in the treaties entered into by China since 1900, the most important being the abolition of *li-kin* in return for an increase in the customs duties; the third, to foster and develop agriculture, commerce, and industry, for which purpose experts would be placed at the head of the Ministries which had special charge of such matters.

He then refers to the financial needs of the country which made it necessary for them to borrow money from abroad. In the budget for the last Chinese year the income of China was estimated at 297,000,000 taels, the expenditure at 350,000,000 taels. The deficit, therefore, was 54,000,000 taels, to which must be added the sum of 24,000,000 taels, additional expenditure incurred during the year, but not allowed for in the estimates, making a total deficit of 78,000,000 taels. Then there was the interest on the loan of 200,000,000 taels raised in June last year for currency reform and the construction of the Canton–Hankow Railway, which would amount to 10,000,000 taels, and also the interest due, but not paid since the revolution broke out, on China's other loans and indemnities, which totalled up to date 20,000,000 taels. They had to reckon, too, the cost of maintaining the troops raised since October last, eighty divisions in all, of which, say, twenty could be disbanded, leaving sixty to be provided for until the end of the year. As each division involved an expenditure of 120,000 taels a-month, the total cost would be 80,000,000 taels. They needed further 10,000,000 taels to repair the damage done to buildings, 10,000,000 taels for gratuities, &c., to the families of soldiers and civilians killed, and something for compensation that would be claimed by foreigners. Finally, there was the cost of running the Provisional Government up to date, 7,000,000 taels. The total amount, therefore, for which special provision would have to be made before the end of the year would be between 214,000,000 taels and 215,000,000 taels.

The speech concludes with the announcement of the names of the Ministers selected, for each of whom Mr. Tang Shao-yi has a good word to say, though he is compelled to admit that neither Mr. Chen Chi Mei nor Mr. Sung Chiao Jen, the Ministers respectively of Industry and Commerce and of Agriculture, are experts in the matters committed to their charge.

On the 2nd instant another special meeting of the Assembly was held to decide whether or not the Government should be transferred to Peking, and although the result was a foregone conclusion, the debate was a very lengthy and acrimonious one. In the end the resolution to go north was carried by twenty votes to six.

Both ex-President Sun and Mr. Tang Shao-yi left Nanking yesterday for Shanghai. The latter's departure was a surprise, and has considerably alarmed the population of Nanking, who fear that the troops, having been disappointed in their hopes that the Premier had brought with him the necessary funds to pay off the arrears of pay due to them, may break out at any moment into mutiny and sack the town. Extraordinary precautions are, however, being taken to prevent an outbreak. A regiment of Cantonese soldiers, which had been embarked on a transport preparing to leaving for the south, has been landed again, and is assisting General Hsü Shao Chen's soldiers to patrol the streets.

General Hsü Shao Chen, I should mention, has been appointed chief of the staff in succession, apparently, to General Huang Hsing. He appears, however, to be very reluctant indeed to accept the post.

I have, &c.
F. E. WILKINSON.

No. 23.

Sir J. Jordan to Sir Edward Grey.—(Received May 3.)

Sir,
Peking, April 18, 1912.
I HAVE the honour to enclose copies in translation of two telegrams from Li Yuan-hung which have appeared in the vernacular press and have produced a considerable impression upon public opinion.

The first is addressed to Yuan Shih-kai, who recently gave me to understand that he welcomed its receipt as expressing views with which he was in complete agreement.

After pointing out that a President without a Cabinet is not in a position to carry on a Government, the writer dwells on the dangers of the situation, at the head of which he places the possibility of foreign intervention after the manner of the allied expedition of 1900. He then describes the lawless state of the country arising from the hordes of undisciplined men under arms, which the revolution brought into being. He admits frankly, what all foreigners have long felt, that the disbandment of these so-called troops is a question with which China is powerless to deal unless she is able to raise foreign money for the purpose, and patriotism obliges him to regard this as a painful operation. It may be so, but it is one to which China will have eventually to submit, and if foreign money is to be used for securing the pacification of this distracted country it is earnestly to be hoped that its expenditure will be carefully safeguarded.

Yuan Shih-kai estimates that there are over a million of men under arms in China, and considers that the only hope for the country is that means should be found for enabling the majority of them to return to some form of settled life. But Chinese statesmanship is not fertile in practical suggestions for converting this marauding population into peaceful citizens of the republic. Yuan himself thinks that a considerable number might find useful employment in building the Hukuang Railway, and that conservancy works in the Yang-tsze valley, which has this year suffered from one of the worst floods on record, might absorb an appreciable portion of the Yang-tsze contingent, but there would still be a large residue for whom no livelihood would be available in the present state of China's productive development. Visionaries like Sun Yat Sen talk airily of bridging the Yang-tsze, but if the ex-President returns to Canton he will find the disposal of the pirates and brigands who have been running the province during the last few months a problem sufficient to absorb all his energies.

Perhaps the most noticeable point in this telegram is the reflection it makes on the moral condition of China and the want of any religious system. China is as nearly destitute of religion as any country can be, and there is a growing feeling among reflecting men that education without religion will not produce the necessary element of stability. The adoption of Christianity as the national religion can hardly be regarded as a serious proposal, but the mere fact that such an idea is occasionally mooted shows the wonderful change public opinion has undergone in recent years.

The telegram which forms enclosure No. 2 in this dispatch is an almost despairing appeal to the various leaders to sink their personal views and lose no time in forming a coalition Government for the union of the north and south. It was mainly in deference to this pointed remonstrance that the dangerous experiment of bringing up a southern army to Peking was abandoned, and the forcible hint that Li would not allow " the great Yü's wide domain " to go to ruin evidently hastened the decision of the Nanking leaders to start for Peking, where they are expected to-morrow.

I have, &c.
J. N. JORDAN.

Enclosure 1 in No. 23.

Circular Telegram from Li Yuan-hung to the President, Huang Hsing, and the Tu-Tus for communication to the Premier and Cabinet.

HE complains that his previous telegrams urging prompt formation of the Government, despite the earnest entreaty in which they were couched, met with contemptuous silence. He goes on : " Time flies, and the Cabinet has still not started north. Who is to blame for the calamities which are impending from all sides ? Are patriots to retire in disgust while the widow sits sadly at her loom ? " *

From the aspect of foreign aggression : " Peking and Tien-tsin are crowded with foreign troops. Treaties have been jointly entered into for the bringing up of reinforcements. Recently attempts have been made to sow dissension in our army, and to disturb public opinion by means of *ballons d'essai*. The fisherman gets the profit as he contentedly surveys the prospect. This vast expanse of our territory is destined to be without a single plot of undesecrated soil."

From the point of view of internal anarchy : " Disturbances have broken out in Soochow and Canton ; the situation in Shensi and Kansu displays uncertainty and confusion. Trouble in Shantung is scarcely over when Anhui and North Kiangsu become the scenes of conflict.

" It seems as if there was to be no end of calamity. Surely this, if ever, is the time to hasten the union of the country ; yet those in power are harbouring mutual suspicions, while proclaiming their honest intentions aloud. They seem indifferent to the fast crumbling nation, like a chess-board losing piece after piece. Alas ! I have been born in an unlucky age and must deplore the ruin which approaches, as in my extremity I turn sadly to heaven. Now that a republic is ours, no one must allow his private ambition to make him the object of criticism. Each should earnestly co-operate with the other, and even if perchance the policy proposed may not be suitable, Parliament will be able to adjust existing differences, and in the last resort the people's will must prevail. If you desire the prosperity of the nation, why should you allow suspicion to be engendered ? Further delay at Nanking or Shanghai, and the suggestion to add to your dignity by bringing up a large force of troops will render it easy for others to take advantage just as ghosts haunt a lonesome house, or wolves are attracted by a deserted valley. Suppose the Northern army should misunderstand and mutiny against the administration ; there is also a danger lest the Dynastic Society might suddenly cause a revolution at one's very elbows. The least lack of precaution makes the prospect appalling indeed. This suspicious tendency is clearly sufficient to ruin the country. While the Government is still not resting on secure foundations and the people's minds are distraught, even the humblest has a desire to sustain the fortunes of the State. When Confucius left his native region, he looked sadly towards Tortoise Hill ; when C'hu Yuan left Ch'u, he threw himself into the waters of the Hunan stream. Surely your knowledge of antiquity and observation of existing facts must make you, worthy patriots as you all are, unwilling to sit in indifference ? Even if your ability be incapable of dealing with the task ahead, you ought at least to persevere till something is accomplished, and then it will not be too late to retire when opportunity offers. Which is the more important, individual reputation or the country's fate ? If you deem it an honourable thing to seek the solitude of your native place, while

---

* Classical allusion to a woman who complained of the rottenness of the Government, when men acquiesced in it.

D

disaster daily approaches nearer, and the country's destiny is in the balance, you too will perish in the disaster just as the patriots who starved themselves on Shouyang Mountain rather than submit to the new dynasty. Hence retirement is useless in your own interests. I repeat, you must all combine at this perilous juncture; even so, success is far from sure. If even one Cabinet office is not filled, collective responsibility is impossible to enforce. How much more so when the whole Government is still waiting for its respective heads! If you are satisfied to let our race suffer extermination, and deem the destruction of China a worthy achievement, then I have no more to say, and will await death with folded arms. If, on the other hand, you pity your fellow-countrymen, and are alive to the interests of your posterity, eager to restore men's vanishing affection, and to sustain this new-born republic's life, I ask you to act as I previously advised, that is, to let the Ministers already in Peking arrange for the administration, and to let those who are in Nanking start forthwith for the north with a light escort. If any of you incur danger through your hardihood in venturing on the journey, pray mete out punishment to me as a just atonement. If, through your insistence in taking up troops for your protection, disaster results, you gentlemen will then deserve punishment in order to make atonement to the nation. If, after one week's time, you still delay, you are wilfully letting your country go to ruin. I will not allow the great Yü's wide domain, with its unfortunate inhabitants, to share the ruin which will then await each one of you; I shall ask the President to appoint other Ministers to act in your places, in order to redeem the position. My breath catches as I utter these words, and pent-up feelings compel me to pause. I gaze in spirit towards the Chihli sky, and respectfully await a telegram from you in response."

Kuo Kuang Hsin Wen, April 12, 1912.

Enclosure 2 in No. 23.

Li Yuan-hung's Lament on the Situation.

THE following message was yesterday received by Yuan Shih-kai from the vice-president Li, in connection with the delay in forming the Government, and the jeopardy ensuing therefrom :—

" I previously expounded my views of the need for settling the site of the capital, and had the satisfaction of seeing them acted upon. Although many days have elapsed since the inauguration of the President, the Cabinet is still unformed. Without a Government a State cannot exist ; a Government cannot be formed without a Cabinet. A President with an empty title, and without heads of departments to assist him, is like an embryo which has never come to birth, or like an undeveloped infant. The condition is undistinguishable from having no Government at all. At a time like this, when our fortunes hang upon a thread, and when even the greatest display of energy by no means secures us from the reproach of being too late, every day which passes but enhances the danger, and further procrastination can mean nothing less than ruin.

" I beg to lay before yourself and others my opinions regarding the crisis which confronts us. Firstly, the danger from foreign relations : Since the righteous crusade started in the south and east, the losses to foreign trade have been enormous, but, having no pretext for intervention, the Powers have had to submit in silence. Now that the mutiny in Peking and neighbourhood has occurred, and has even extended to Tien-tsin and Paotingfu, prosperous thoroughfares and centres of trade have become a desert. If one Power brings up troops, another follows in its wake ; sites are settled for barracks and detachments parade the streets. No protest is possible against their liberty of action. While ostensibly they are protecting their trade, in reality they are destroying our independence. We are once again face to face with a disaster like the allied expedition of 1900.

" Secondly, the danger from the military : When the civil war began, troops were enlisted throughout last autumn and winter ; they were without discipline and regarded crime as a title to merit, and anarchy as duty. To them mob law spelled equality and browbeating coercion was freedom ; their general's prestige afforded them a talisman on which to trade, and honourable names became material for party catchwords. The example spread from above, and if one went under, another took his place. Rewards and punishments were not distributed with impartiality, commands ceased to carry weight :

each province assumed independence of action, and each army acted like masters in their own house. The tendency was acted upon as when an echo reverberates, until what began as a spark ended as a prairie-consuming conflagration. What cared they for the dismemberment or disintegration of China? In the Yang-tsze Valley the new Government is handicapped by the prevalence of lawlessness; the flag of the dispossessed dynasty is still the rallying ground for bandit spirits. The least procrastination may well end in internecine strife.

"Thirdly, the danger from the financial situation: In the last days of the Manchu dynasty various reforms were set on foot, while the poverty of the country had reached a zenith. Thus, the construction of railways and the raising of loans became a source of calamity. Recently the number of troops in the south has been enormously increased; even in Wuchang and its environs alone there is a force of nearly 100,000 men, while there is not a province but has received vast accessions to its normal strength. Meantime there is a complete dearth of arms and funds; the position is equally embarrassing to the State and to the individual. Disbandment is scarcely practicable owing to the danger of mutiny; retention of the troops is difficult owing to want of money to pay them. It is as if a pyramid of eggs were on the verge of toppling! Further, in every department of Government a constructive policy has to be carried out in manifold directions, and success is impossible without ample supplies of money. A policy of raising loans remains the only course, even as if one cured an ulcer by cutting the flesh away. Railways and mines have to be pledged as security, while each plays for his own hand. The Powers are hungrily watching for the opportunity to gain monopoly of loans and to control their expenditure; if the slightest mistake is made, they exercise a deadly coercion. The warning of the Yin dynasty is not far off; Poland affords an apt example.

"Fourthly, the danger from the condition of the population: Floods have been raging up and down the Yang-tsze Valley, and whole families are starving or perishing by the roadside. The recent war has made many homeless, and the advancing spring finds them without a roof over their heads. The river has risen over ten feet; the fields are inundated and the dykes cannot be repaired. No relief has been feasible, and they are visited with an appalling calamity. The weak die under the struggle, while the strong take to marauding. Disease stalks through the land and corpses lie in heaps, so that the population is rapidly becoming decimated.

"Fifthly, the danger on the educational side: Of all classes of the people, the literati are the most difficult to govern. Of old time, the Tang and the Sung dynasty made use of the then prevailing examination systems as a means to attract scholars to the Government service, and thus bind them by strong ties to the dynasty. But since the war began the schools have had to close, and myriads of teachers and pupils are congregated in the provincial capitals. Being without a livelihood, they take to random disputations, and rally round them kindred spirits. Strife of factions and party spirit inevitably ensue; each tries to overthrow the other, until an honourable calling is disgraced, and all bounds of restraint are infringed. The waves of clamour are continually rising, and the bulwarks of society are shaken to their foundations. Even men of high character are not ashamed to follow such guides. If a nation is destitute of a system of morals, all bonds and principles must fall to the ground; if literary men throw over all restraint, no civilisation can endure. The Tartar sovereignty exists no longer, but that race still retains its religious worship; India is a nation in bondage, but reverence for the Buddha remains. Is our ancient and noble race to sink lower than such as they? If we force the flower of our people to degenerate into demagogues, woe betide us hereafter! 'If the gem is injured in the casket, who but its custodian is to blame?' The above points stand out as most salient in their bearing on our future fortunes. The situation is fraught with other dangers which cannot all be gone into now, but the important question to note is that the dispute about the site of the capital, followed as it has been by obstinate dissension in regard to the formation of the Cabinet, and the resultant ill-feeling to which it gives rise, practically involves treating the millions of our people as sport of the dice. Reflection on matters like these makes one's blood run cold. All of you, my worthy friends, have encountered, without flinching, the most deadly perils for the general good, and have been actuated by no mere motives of vulgar ambition. The noble purity of your purpose has been long evident, both to God and men. Sun Yat Sen has for nearly twenty years led the movement from his foreign exile, yet at the moment of success he finely withdraws into retirement without a smirch on his good name. His good example should make the timid stand firm, and inspire self-seekers with integrity. But I need not dwell on what each one of our party admits.

" When first the banner of the revolution was raised, the people's rights were the rallying point on which all currents of opinion converged. The object was as plain as the sun or the moon. Advocates of a constitution came over to our side in favour of this new policy, while the representatives of the army secretly sympathised with our cause. Now that the republic is an accomplished fact, and union has been effected between north and south, it is impossible to appraise exactly to whom belongs the larger measure of desert, whether to those who initiated the design and made its accomplishment practicable, or to those who rendered secret aid. In my opinion, while the work of destruction may demand talent different in scope from that of construction, each is none the less dependent on the other's co-operation. Hence, at a dire crisis like the present, the Cabinet ought to be formed of persons who combine knowledge and experience to an unusual degree, irrespective of whether they represent the conservative or reform party, and whether they hail from north or south. All should stand together in order to assure the formation of the Cabinet becoming an accomplished fact. Even though, perchance, perfection cannot be attained in a small proportion of Cabinet posts, due regard must be paid to the exigencies of the situation with a view to compromise. You ought not to allow the stability of the whole structure to be shaken through a slight defect in detail. If one Ministry is not represented by the right man, harm can only accrue to one department ; if delay in forming the Cabinet continues, imminent ruin confronts the country. The consequences involved are obvious to the meanest comprehension. Moreover, Parliament is vested with the prerogative of impeachment. Hence, is it not better to leave possible improvements to a future day, than to sacrifice everything on the instant? I cannot but believe that men of your ability will appreciate the needs of the times, and will decide this vital question with rapidity and resolution. Further evasion and postponement will bring ruin daily nearer ; ten days from now the situation will have become even less favourable than it is at this moment. It was the fisherman who secured the profit when the oyster-catcher's beak stuck fast in the oyster's shell. When that day comes, we may, as miserable captives and slaves, deplore the result of fratricidal strife, but with the destruction of our race repentance will be too late.

" As long as breath remains in my body, I shall be faithful to my pristine purpose, and after profound consideration of these kaleidoscopic changes feel strengthened in my resolve. It is because I cannot endure that our glorious country shall incur dismemberment that I feel forced to speak of what I conceive to be the danger which impends. Did not Duke Chuang of the Chu State once admonish his fellow-men : 'Woe is at hand ' ? So Tou Lien warned the Prime Minister, Chu Yuan : ' Harmony is the first need in a State.' How much more is this true of a moment like the present, when the peril is so much greater ! I am told that the Manchus and Mongols appreciate the position, and are ready to send representatives to the Assembly. Their loyal patriotism is deserving of all praise. If, then, we Chinese persist in delay, we shall be failing both in our duty to the homeless multitudes as also in the respect which we owe to the heroes who have died.

" I therefore humbly entreat you to urge a speedy settlement, so that the Government can be constituted without further delay. Only when the machinery of the administration is in full working order will it be possible to boast that stability exists. This is not the time to wrangle, to apportion reward to the deserving, or punishment to the guilty. When the country once more enjoys an orderly Government, and we have recovered our sovereign rights, it will be time enough to hold thanksgiving services and bestow honour on whom it is due. Then, even though I incur punishment for having spoken presumptuously, I, Li Yuan-hung, shall be able to close my eyes in peace. My heart is too full for utterance, and I know not what I say.".

No. 24.

Sir J. Jordan to Sir Edward Grey.—(Received May 6.)

Sir,   *Peking, April 20, 1912.*
IN my despatch of the 30th January last* I had the honour to report that a Bankers' Commission had been formed at Shanghai for the purpose of receiving and disposing of the customs revenues for the service of the foreign debt.

* See " China, No. 3 (1912)," No. 113.

Under the terms of reference agreed upon by the foreign representatives for the guidance of the commission, the native customs revenue collected by the Maritime Customs was treated in the same manner as the maritime customs revenue proper, and was divided amongst the three banks interested in the loans contracted prior to 1900, namely, the Hong Kong and Shanghai Bank, the Deutsch-Asiatische Bank, and the Russo-Asiatic Bank.

On the 13th March the Bankers' Commission addressed to me as dean a letter, copy of which is enclosed, stating that the Yokohama Specie Bank had requested that the native customs revenue might be divided amongst all the banks interested in the indemnity. The commission had no objection to this being done, and I was requested to obtain the sanction of the diplomatic body to the change.

In circulating the commission's letter amongst my colleagues, I took occasion to observe that there appeared to me to be no objection to the proposal, except that it would involve dividing a relatively small amount of revenue among what would seem to be an unnecessary number of bank accounts, and would entail a readjustment of the arrangement so recently concluded with the Chinese authorities.

As I expected, however, those foreign representatives whose banks would benefit by the proposal approved the change, and accordingly on the 12th instant I was empowered to address a memorandum to the Wai-chiao Pu informing them that the suggestion had received the approval of the diplomatic body on the ground that this native customs revenue was assigned as one of the securities for the indemnity under the protocol of 1901, and requesting them to give the necessary instructions to the inspector-general of customs ; at the same time the Bankers' Commission were notified of the action taken. I have the honour to enclose copies of both these communications.

I have, &c.

J. N. JORDAN.

Enclosure 1 in No. 24.

International Bankers' Commission to Sir J. Jordan.

Sir, *Shanghai, March* 13, 1912.
THE native customs revenue collected by the Imperial Maritime Customs is now being deposited with the Hong Kong and Shanghai Bank here, who, under instructions from the inspector-general of customs, divides it weekly with the Deutsch-Asiatische Bank and the Russo-Asiatic Bank. The Yokohama Specie Bank, however, requests that the money be divided up amongst the various banks interested in the indemnity.

The Bankers' Commission have no objection to this being done, and I am therefore directed by them to refer the matter to you, requesting you to kindly lay the same before the diplomatic body at Peking, and obtain their sanction thereto.

It is suggested that the money should be deposited in accordance with the proportion of each bank's share of the indemnity, which, on the basis of past collections of native customs revenue of about 30 lacs of taels a-year, works out roughly as follows :—

—		—	Monthly.	Quarterly.
		Per cent.	Taels.	Taels.
Hong and Shanghai Bank	.. ..	11	27,500	82,500
Banque de l'Indo-Chine	.. ..	16	40,000	120,000
Deutsch-Asiatische Bank	.. ..	21	52,500	157,500
Banque Sino-Belge ..	.. ..	8	20,000	60,000
International Banking Corporation	..	7	17,500	52,500
Yokohama Specie Bank (Limited)	..	8	20,000	60,000
Russo-Asiatic Bank ..	.. .	29	72,500	217,500
		100	250,000	750,000

I have, &c.
H. M. S. MAN, *Secretary,*
International Bankers' Commission.

38

Enclosure 2 in No. 24.

Memorandum communicated to Wai-chiao Pu.

IN his memorandum of the 30th July, 1911,* the dean had the honour to inform the Wai-wu Pu that instructions had been issued by the foreign representatives at Peking to the managers of their respective banks at Shanghai to adopt the scheme in eight articles prepared by the inspector-general of customs for devoting the customs revenue at all the ports to the service of the foreign loans and the indemnity.

Under this scheme the native customs revenue collected by the Maritime Customs, and accumulated at Shanghai, is treated in the same manner as the maritime customs revenue, and divided amongst the three banks interested in the loans contracted prior to 1900, viz., the Hong Kong and Shanghai, the Deutsch-Asiatische, and the Russo-Asiatic Banks.

The Bankers' Commission has now suggested that the native customs revenue should be divided amongst the various banks interested in the indemnity in accordance with each bank's share thereof, instead of amongst the three banks mentioned above.

The diplomatic body approve this suggestion in view of the fact that, under article 6 of the protocol of 1901, this native customs revenue is one of the revenues assigned as security for payment of the indemnity.

The dean is accordingly requested by the diplomatic body to ask that instructions in this sense may be issued to the inspector-general of customs for transmission to the commissioner of customs at Shanghai.

Peking, April 12, 1912.

Enclosure 3 in No. 24.

Sir J. Jordan to the International Bankers' Commission.

Sir,   *Shanghai, April 12, 1912.*

YOUR letter of the 13th ultimo regarding the division of the native customs revenue between the various banks interested in the indemnity was duly laid before the diplomatic body, and I am now desired by my colleagues to inform you that they approve the suggestion therein contained, namely, that the native customs revenue collected by the Maritime Customs should be deposited in accordance with each bank's share of the indemnity.

I have to-day addressed a communication in this sense to the Chinese Government, requesting that the necessary instructions may be given to the inspector-general of customs accordingly.

I am, &c.
J. N. JORDAN.

No. 25.

Sir Edward Grey to Sir J. Jordan.

Sir,   *Foreign Office, May 11, 1912.*

I HAVE received your despatch of the 20th ultimo, reporting an arrangement which has been come to for the distribution of the native customs revenue amongst the banks interested in the Boxer indemnity.

Among the terms of reference agreed on by the foreign representatives at Peking for the guidance of the Bankers' Commission, it is stipulated that, if normal conditions are not restored by the end of 1912, then at that time an account shall be taken of the surplus of the maritime customs revenue available for the indemnity, and such account shall be sent to the diplomatic body for their decision as to its disposal.

I should be glad to learn whether this arrangement still holds good, or whether it has been in any way affected by the recent decision as to the distribution of the native customs revenue.

I am, &c.
E. GREY.

---

* Not received at Foreign Office.

No. 26.

War Office to Foreign Office.—(Received May 15.)

Sir,   *War Office, May 15, 1912.*
I AM commanded by the Army Council to acknowledge the receipt of your letter
dated the 27th April, 1912, and to inform you that they have consulted the Admiralty
with a view to giving effect to the suggestion of the Secretary of State for Foreign
Affairs contained in the last paragraph as regards arrangements being made for a
vessel to be always available at Hong Kong for the transport of troops.
2. I am to state for the information of Secretary Sir E. Grey that the Admiralty
are of opinion that reliance may be placed on a suitable vessel being available at any
time at Hong Kong for transport, and I am to enquire whether, in the circumstances,
it is considered necessary actually to charter and fit out a transport, thereby saving
a delay which it is estimated will not exceed two or three days in the actual dispatch
of the troops on an emergency.

I am, &c.
E. W. D. WARD.

No. 27.

Foreign Office to War Office.

Sir,   *Foreign Office, May 18, 1912.*
WITH reference to your letter of the 15th instant, relative to the question of
holding a transport in readiness at Hong Kong for the purpose of reinforcing the
British troops at Shanghai in the event of a sudden emergency, I am directed by
Secretary Sir E. Grey to inform you that, in view of the opinion expressed in the last
paragraph of the telegram of the 26th April from His Majesty's Minister at Peking
(of which a copy has already been sent to you), he does not consider that it will be
necessary to incur the expense of actually chartering and fitting out a transport,
provided that the local naval authorities are satisfied that a suitable vessel will always
be available at short notice.

I am, &c.
W. LANGLEY.

No. 28.

Sir J. Jordan to Sir Edward Grey.—(Received May 22.)

Sir,   *Peking, May 3, 1912.*
I HAVE the honour to transmit to you herewith a copy of the address which the
President, Yuan Shih-kai, delivered at the opening of the so-called National Council on
the 29th ultimo, and which gives an outline of the measures which the new Government
proposes to carry out.
The President rightly places the financial question in the forefront of his
programme, and candidly admits the necessity of a recourse to foreign capital for
meeting the needs of the administration. The temporary issue of Treasury bonds and
the eventual negotiation of a large loan are considered to be the only feasible means of
dealing with the situation. An increase of the customs duties and the reform of the
salt gabelle are the two sources from which the fresh obligations of the country are to be
chiefly met. The annual receipts of the former will, it is estimated, yield an additional
16,000,000 taels, and the increase of the salt gabelle is given as 50,000,000 taels. These
figures have evidently been supplied by the Premier, Tong Shao-yi, who cannot,
however, claim to have any special acquaintance with the subject.
Improvement in the sytem of land taxation and the reform of the currency are
other measures promised by the Republican Government, whose President dwells
significantly upon the necessity of having foreign financial expert advice.
The disbandment of the heterogeneous masses of troops, on which the maintenance of any form of stable government depends, receives less attention than it
deserves, although it is admitted that the burden they impose upon the resources

of the country is greater than it can bear. The problem of their disbandment is the burning question of the moment, and its solution will require not only money, but other qualities of which China stands sadly in need at present.

I have, &c.
J. N. JORDAN.

Enclosure in No. 28.

Extract from the " Peking Daily News " of April 30, 1912.

OPENING OF THE NATIONAL COUNCIL: PRESIDENT YUAN'S ADDRESS.

I, YUAN SHIH-KAI, having been elected to the present position by the people, am labouring day and night under the apprehension that I may not discharge my duties satisfactorily. I now, with sincerity and candidness, express the following to our people.

Those who entertain high ideals and aims will, no doubt, expect that what I am going to say at the beginning of my presidential career will be far-reaching in its effect and full of novelty, but, under the present circumstances, I can hardly dare to entertain such an expectation.

The principle of government, both in ancient and modern times, consists in the establishment and maintenance of public order and in the clear definition and promulgation of legal systems, so that externally there shall be good and friendly relationship, and internally there shall be peace between the weak and the strong. It is with the realisation of these ideals that the country can have her foundation well laid and her existence in the world perfectly secure. Recently, owing to the outbreak of the revolution, the people have lost their usual trade, and the Government, as well as private individuals, is now confronted with great difficulties. Moreover, the soldiers are, generally speaking, ignorant of the precept of obedience, and the people are seldom mindful of the public welfare. Among those who resort to empty discussions many would neglect the practical side of the question, and among those who have their private interests to further, many would not for a moment cast aside their selfish aims. If such a state of affairs is allowed to exist without any effort being made to reform it, public order will be disturbed and legal institutions will be destroyed. It would indeed be difficult to secure the proper protection of life and property of the people, and it would be entirely out of the question to speak of the country as being in the best of trim.

I have heretofore entertained the policy of progressive reform, and have not, in spite of many obstacles, been willingly conservative. I have tried hard to realise my object for the past several tens of years, and my efforts, I believe, are well known and appreciated by our people. Especially at the present moment, when the country has just passed through the revolution, order should be speedily restored, so that the economic condition of the people may be ameliorated, reconstruction work should be carried out with due care and energy, and all measures should be adopted with due regard to their practical value. For instance, in the construction of an edifice its foundation should be carefully selected and well laid, and labour and material should be properly chosen. All its layers should be solidly laid one over the other. Attention should not be devoted solely to the outward appearance of the edifice by taking particular pains in plaster work and adornment. The edifice when built after this fashion will be durable, but if built crudely and negligently it is to be feared that before the four walls are erected the building will be already showing some signs of tumbling down. The damage thus sustained would indeed be great. Hence, it is absolutely necessary that there should be a solid foundation on which the construction work is to be carried out with speed and resolution, so that good results may be attained.

The important question of reconstruction is that regarding finance. Last year the budget, though showing a deficit balance on the expenditure side, nevertheless indicated an estimated revenue of over 260,000,000 taels. During the preceding semester trade has been paralysed, and there has been a marked decrease of the national revenue. Our indebtedness to foreign countries has not for the time being been discharged. Now we have to carry out political reforms, and in doing so we must import foreign capital. Consequently, it is necessary to decide on the essential features of our financial reform in order to augment our national credit. The sum of money annually required to repay our loan debts and indemnities with interest is about 50,000,000 taels. Our foreign

loans have been generally secured by pledging the customs revenue and others by the
li-kin duties. The indemnity loans have been secured by pledging the customs and the
salt revenues.

We shall immediately negotiate with the treaty Powers for the increase of our
customs duty. On the other hand, the *li-kin* taxes will be abolished and the export
duties decreased. The annual receipt of the maritime and native customs may thus be
increased from 44,000,000 taels to over 60,000,000 taels, which will be more than sufficient to meet the repayment of the above-mentioned loans. As to railway and other
loans, they will be paid by railway and other receipts, any deficit to be made up from
the salt revenue.

There are yet foreign loans contracted by the different provinces amounting to
over 10,000,000 taels. The amount of the Boxer indemnity which fell due last winter,
and not yet paid, is over 12,000,000 taels. Both of these will be immediately paid up
out of the big loan which will be secured by the new Government.

For meeting the needs of the Government administration, an estimate will be
immediately made in order to fix a schedule for spending the big loan properly. For
the present, short period Treasury bonds will first be issued in order to meet the present
and urgent needs. These bonds will be redeemed by the proceeds of the big loan.
This step is the only feasible one for augmenting our national credit.

The salt gabelle will be reformed after western methods, and its revenue will thus
be increased to another 50,000,000 taels.

Land taxation will be improved. The evils practised by the former yamen runners
will be eradicated, and the heavy burden on the people will be lightened. The lands
hitherto unsurveyed will be surveyed by professional men properly selected, and a scale
of taxation will be fixed.

The reform of the currency consists in the unification of the coinage system, and,
being the most important part of our financial reforms, it will be put into effect without
delay.

There are at present very few who are cognisant of financial matters in our
country, and such as we have are lacking in experience. Hereafter, in the inauguration
of the various political institutions, it will be necessary to employ talent from other lands
for their guidance and expert advice.

At the beginning of our republic the industrial development of our country must
first be looked into. Hence, there have been established the Department of Agriculture
and Forestry and the Department of Industry and Commerce, in order to work out the
idea of subsidy and encouragement. Students in the different schools will also be
specially trained in industrial pursuits, so as to consolidate the foundation of the
country. The industry of the country is still in its infancy. In brief, China is really
an agricultural country. The reclamation of waste lands, forestry, pasturage, fishery,
tea and mulberry industries are riches hidden in the soil, and are resources waiting to
be developed. I wish our people would not look up to the air to gain their livelihood,
but should concentrate their attention to what is underneath their feet. Take the
mineral resources, for instance. It is especially necessary that all mining regulations
should be revised without delay, with the primary object of giving the people themselves
facilities for developing the resources of the country. A liberal policy will be adopted
in order to secure its general acceptance by the masses. Moreover, commercial laws,
uniform weights and measures should be speedily adopted and enforced.

At present there are multitudinous and heterogeneous troops. Their number is far
larger than is usual, and the expense for their maintenance is unusually great. It is
too heavy a burden for the country to bear. The Department of Finance and the
Department of War have already been instructed to devise and enforce measures to
provide for the soldiery.

In view of the religious liberty of the people, all religions will be regarded as being
on the same footing, and there will be no discrimination against any particular one.
There should be mutual respect and avoidance of mutual distrust among the people
irrespective of whether they practise any particular religion or not, or whatever faith
they may embrace, so that they may all share in the enjoyment of public peace and
happiness.

The Chinese people have their customs and traditions to maintain, and it is difficult
to effect, within a short time, the unification of usages and practice. Education is not
yet universal in its application, and reform still meets with obstruction and doubt by the
people. *Esprit de corps* is still lacking among the soldiery, and their training must be
directed toward the improvement of their morale. As the legal system is not yet
completely established, some of the people still waive their legal rights. The means of

communication are not yet perfected, and local prejudice still prevails. With regard to all these matters the Secretaries of State will consult together from time to time to effect improvement.

During recent years the foreign Powers have generally adopted a peaceful and just attitude towards us, demonstrating their friendly intention to assist and co-operate with us. This, without doubt, testifies to the present state of civilisation, and we must feel grateful for their friendly spirit. Our people should therefore clearly understand this idea, and should consider as of the first importance that we should treat with them frankly and sincerely with a view to consolidating our international relationship. All the treaties concluded heretofore will be observed implicitly, and those international engagements which have not been performed will be promptly taken in hand.

The people may indeed be very joyful over the adoption of a republican régime after having been for thousands of years under the rule of despotism, but I am greatly concerned over the fact that they have not progressed. I sincerely hope that our people may constantly realise that there is room for much improvement, and not entertain a feeling of self-sufficiency. I profoundly wish that they may regard each other with justice and good faith, and not eye each other with mutual distrust. The country can only be strong when the 400,000,000 people entertain but one mind.

The Premier, Mr. Tang, and the Secretaries of State, specially appointed, are all talented men, who are well able to cope with the changed condition. I, Shih-kai, am relying on their co-operation in furthering the good weal of the country, and hope that the people will place their full confidence in them and give them their support.

No. 29.

Sir J. Jordan to Sir Edward Grey.—(Received May 22.)

Sir,   *Peking, May 4,* 1912.

I HAVE the honour to transmit herewith some notes on the native press of Peking for the first quarter of this year compiled by the Chinese Secretary.

I have, &c.

J. N. JORDAN.

Enclosure in No. 29.

Note on the Peking Press for First Quarter of 1912.

IN the first days of the year there was a strong Manchu element among the journals of the capital; the "Tiching Hsinwen" was openly in favour of the dynasty's continuance in the form recommended by Chang Shao-tseng last October. The "Cheng Pao" went even further, and seemed to advocate a responsible Cabinet from which princes of the blood would not necessarily be excluded. The "Ai Kuo Pao," the paper enjoying by far the largest circulation of any in Peking, was distinctly anti-Chinese, but this fact is not remarkable when one recalls that its founder was an Imperial clansman and brother of Duke Heng. The "Ti Kuo Pao" was against the republic, but recommended the exclusion of the princes from Peking and the marriage of the ex-Emperor, when of age, to a Chinese of good family. The "Peiching Jih Pao," which is the most influential of any Chinese journal and represents moderate Cantonese sentiment, had been frankly against any dynastic change, on the ground that the house of Gioro, though far from being a great ruling family, was not inferior to the Mings, and that it was better to put up with it, if clipped of its power, than to revert to the houses of Chu or Chou, representing the Ming and Sung dynasties. The "Kuang Hua Jih Pao" was pro-Manchu at the beginning of January and appeared to be subsidised by Prince Ch'ing, as it never lost an opportunity of eulogising him. It was against the Cantonese clique, and attacked the then Premier for his subservience to T'ang Shao-yi and his comrades. It, however, went over to the republican idea in the middle of January, and warned the Manchu Sovereigns of the fate of Louis XVI and Charles I.

The "Kuo Feng Pao," which was started in the middle of last year with the object of furthering the impending revolution, fixed originally to break out in May of this year, was the only Peking paper which openly urged the overthrow of the Manchus and the deprivation of the Imperial title for the dispossessed Emperor. Its strong pro-republican views soon brought it into conflict with the police, and it was compelled temporarily to moderate its tone.

Such was the position when the Premier's life was threatened by what is believed by many to have been a Manchu plot, the bomb outrage of January. From that date the tone of the press completely changed ; every newspaper advocated abdication as the only solution, and both the " Cheng Pao " and the " Ti Ching Hsin " became anti-dynastic. It would appear as if a campaign had been organised by the Premier's Cantonese party to further the idea of a republic ; journals which had ridiculed its practicability for China now became enthusiastic for its adoption. The " Peiching Jih Pao," which, though Cantonese, may fairly be called impartial, and which never hesitated to condemn some of the more glaring faults of the late dynasty, e.g., the appointment of incompetent and corrupt princes to command of the army and navy, now took the view that in no case must Yuan Shih-kai accept the presidency of the proposed republic. With this reservation it was prepared to recommend the new Government being given a fair trial. The other papers, with the exception of the " Kuo Feng Pao," which has been consistently against Yuan and openly regretted the failure of the plot to assassinate him, seemed for the moment to have come over to his side and to hail him as the saviour of the country.

Upon the abdication becoming an accomplished fact on the 12th February, every journal wrote glowingly of the prospects of the new régime ; Yuan's election to the provisional presidency was warmly approved by nearly all, and even the " Peiching Jih Pao " said that, if he would give a pledge in no circumstances to be candidate for the first President, there was no grave objection to his holding the provisional position. The " Kuo Feng Pao," while regretting his election on the ground that his antecedents render him unworthy of trust, was willing to suspend judgment for a time, and spoke of the opportunity which was now given to him to mend his ways. Since that date, however, the President has been the object of criticism and condemnation on the part of every paper without exception. His appointments have come in for strong disapproval ; his presidential utterances have been accused of lacking authority ; his personal character has been attacked ; he has been called a nervous weakling who does not know his own mind from day to day, and from whom all unpleasant news must be concealed. The best which has been said of him is that he is fit to hold office under others, but quite unworthy of the highest command.

Naturally the mutiny of the 29th February was taken by the press as a sign of the President's complete incompetence : " If," they said, " he cannot even prevent his own troops from rebelling against his authority, what possible claim can he have to the position which he holds ? " His leniency to the undisciplined hordes which constitute the army of China has evoked the most violent condemnation. Even papers which are supposed to be Government organs, such as the " Ting Yi Pao " or the " Min Shih Pao," avoid bestowing compliments on Yuan, though they are comparatively hopeful of the future of the republic. Several journals publish cartoons of the President as a monkey (a play on his name being intended), which are evidently meant to bring him into contempt. The " Kuo Min Kung Pao " has a picture of a monkey playing a fiddle with the legend " Luan T'an," i.e., " He touches the strings at random," and by play on the words " He talks rubbish." The " Kuo Feng Pao " openly threatens to throw a bomb at him unless he amends. He is represented by nearly all the press as an intensely ambitious, cruel, and unscrupulous man, who is without governing capacity, and who would be comparable to the great traitors and villains of Chinese history, if not for his inferior attainments.

The new régime finds scant favour in the columns of the metropolitan press ; writers confess themselves bitterly disappointed, and declare that with a weak President and an arbitrary but incompetent Advisory Council the outlook is black in the extreme. The Premier is spoken of as scarcely fit to be comprador of a foreign hong by the " Kuo Min Kung Pao ; " another paper, the " Ya Hsi Ya Pao," which is controlled by Fukienese, says that China has rid herself of the Manchu despotism and obtained in exchange a Cantonese autocracy. Although one or two spasmodic articles have appeared in the " Kuo Min Kung Pao " which might lead the reader to suppose that the restoration of the dispossessed dynasty was advocated, there are so far no signs that the return of the Manchus is considered as conceivable or to be desired. It is said that a new journal will shortly appear with the avowed object of furthering the cause of the Mings. It is only right to end by saying that Sun Yat Sen is warmly applauded for his disinterested laying-down of the provisional presidency by every journal ; comparisons are made between him and Yuan greatly to the latter's disadvantage. Sun is spoken of as the hero of the revolution ; the one man who has been consistent from first to last.

No. 30.

Sir J. Jordan to Sir Edward Grey.—(Received May 28.)

Sir,   *Peking, May* 6, 1912.

WITH reference to my despatch of the 31st March last, I have the honour to forward herewith a summary by Sir Somerville Head of events in the provinces during the past month.

I have, &c.
J. N. JORDAN.

Enclosure in No. 30.

Summary of Events in the Provinces up to April 30, 1912.

THOUGH the country is still in an administratively chaotic condition, and the southern provinces continue to disregard the Government at Peking, recent reports from His Majesty's consular officers reflect, on the whole, a more peaceful state of affairs.

With regard to the recent attack on American missionaries at Wushan on the Yang-tsze River between Ichang and Chungking, Mr. Hewlett reports as follows :—

" On the 22nd March I received a telegram from Mr. Lu, who is an instructor in the Chengtu schools, and was sent down to escort three American teachers to Chengtu, dated Wushan 8 A.M., asking for help, as the three teachers, Messrs. Sheldon, Hofmann, and Hicks, had been attacked by pirates and badly hurt. I telegraphed this information to the United States consuls at Hankow and Chungking and at once arranged for a foreign doctor, a missionary interpreter, and two Red Cross boats to go to their assistance. The survivors of the party eventually arrived here in safety on the evening of the 25th.

" The attack was made about five miles from Wushan at 3 A.M. in the morning of the 22nd. The so-called robbers came on to the boat armed with swords, and not one of the twenty-four boatmen made any attempt whatever to assist the foreigners. Mr. Hofmann only received one slight wound in the neck ; Mr. Sheldon received no fewer than thirty-five sword cuts, all of which required dressing ; Mr. Hicks was stabbed by a thrust through the lung, delivered apparently as he was stooping to get his revolver out of his suit case. The whole attack lasted only some five minutes, and the booty secured was comparatively small. Fortunately for the wounded, a Chinese doctor, attached either to the Yünnan troops coming down or to the Szechuan troops going up river, was close at hand and dressed the wounds with such skill that a French doctor who arrived on the scene during the day did not feel that it was necessary to alter the dressings.

" The so-called pirates were armed with military swords, dressed in a close-fitting uniform, and not the loose garments of the ordinary coolie, and all wore black turbans —a uniform used by the retainers of the Yünnan troops. 200 of whom arrived in Ichang a few days afterwards. That they were an organised band admits of no doubt whatever, and their attack seems to have been as well planned as it was deliberate."

The United States vice consul at Hankow is making an enquiry into this attack. On the same day at the same spot a boat containing twelve Chinese passengers was attacked and eight persons killed. It is therefore not yet proved that this case furnished any evidence of actual anti-foreign feeling, but it certainly shows that the consequences of murdering a foreigner are no longer taken into serious account, probably because the bandits are now aware that there is no authority capable of enforcing punishment, and that they are therefore free to attack with impunity any travellers, whether Chinese or foreigners.

The idea of " China for the Chinese " would seem to be gaining ground. Students returning from Japan, America, and England all share the ardent desire to control the settlements and concessions in China and abolish extra-territoriality. They complain of the treatment of Chinese by foreigners at Shanghai and other treaty ports, and wish to keep in their own control the finances, railways, and other enterprises of China.

His Majesty's consul-general at Hankow reports that conditions throughout Hupeh province have somewhat improved, but that the situation at Wuchang still gives cause for anxiety. In addition to the dissension amongst the prominent men in the

Republican party and the general dissatisfaction with the distribution of the spoils of office, there is very little money available either for paying off the troops or providing them with the means of returning to their homes. The receipt, however, of a portion of the Belgian loan has slightly relieved matters, and a gradual disbandment of the Wuchang army is being effected.

The situation of Honan is still far from satisfactory. The discipline of the troops is conspicuous by its absence, and looting and rioting are matters of frequent occurrence. Shensi has shown signs of improvement, and for the moment all is quiet at Sianfu.

With the coming of spring and the drifting away of the more enterprising robbers to Kuangtung and other wealthier provinces, there has been a great improvement in the state of affairs on the West River. Chartered junks from Nanning to Wuchow continue to be convoyed by guard boats, while those from intermediate ports are furnished with guards. Li Li-t'ing, the ex-pirate in charge of the river as far as Hsunchou-fu, is reported to have done good work in keeping the river free, but on account of insufficient remuneration is threatening to resign.

It is satisfactory to record a considerable improvement during the past month in the situation in North Shantung, where a serious attempt is being made to reduce the number of troops scattered over this region. On the 13th April two Chinese cruisers left Chefoo for Shanghai, with General Lan Tien Wei and about 700 troops on board, and on the 16th another 1,000 troops were despatched south to Shanghai and Foochow. This leaves about 4,000 men of all arms in Chefoo, practically none of whom now remain in the foreign quarter. There are nevertheless some 8,000 or 9,000 men still in the neighbourhood, but it is the intention of the Tutu to continue the process of reduction and disbandment until there remain 4,000 men distributed round Chefoo, Tengchow, Jung Ch'eng, and Wen Tung, which number he considers the minimum required to preserve order in this part of Shantung. The behaviour of the troops has been on the whole good. The Tu-tu seems to have been provided with ample funds, and has even manifested his good-will towards the foreign community by presenting them, as an *amende honorable* for their previous discomfort, with the sum of 3,000 dollars towards the purchase of a steam-roller.

The Tu-tu has now come to Peking to confer with Yuan Shih-kai in regard to the question of placing Chefoo once more under the control of the provincial authorities at Tsinan-fu. Some anxiety is felt in the south of the province owing to the independent attitude adopted by General Chang Hsun, who still maintains a considerable body of men along the Tien-tsin–Pukow Railway and refuses to deliver up the rolling-stock in his possession, except on the understanding that it is not used for the transport of "revolutionary" troops. It will be remembered that Chang Hsun was the general in command of the Imperial troops at Nanking when that city was captured by the revolutionary forces. He has been sitting astride the Tien-tsin–Pukow Railway ever since, and he is stated to have recruited fresh levies to such an extent that his force now amounts to 20,000 men.

S. H.

No. 31.

Sir J. Jordan to Sir Edward Grey.—(Received May 28.)

Sir,   *Peking, May 7, 1912.*
WITH reference to my despatch of the 20th ultimo, I have the honour to report that I have received a reply from the Wai-chiao Pu to the request made to them on the 12th April on behalf of the diplomatic body and the Bankers' Commission to the effect that the inspector-general of customs has issued instructions to the Shanghai commissioner to transfer for deposit in the various banks concerned, in proportion to their respective shares in the indemnity, all the funds placed to the credit of the inspector-general's native customs account.

I beg to enclose translation of the Wai-chiao Pu's memorandum.
                                                                I have, &c.
                                                                J. N. JORDAN.

Enclosure in No. 31.

Memorandum communicated to Sir J. Jordan by Wai-chiao Pu, May 3, 1912.

(Translation.)
WITH reference to the dean's memorandum, stating that, under the scheme prepared last year by the inspector-general of customs for the repayment of the foreign loans and the indemnity, the native customs revenue collected by the Maritime Customs and accumulated at Shanghai is divided amongst the three banks interested in the loans contracted prior to 1900, viz., the Hong Kong and Shanghai, the Deutsch-Asiatische and the Russo-Asiatic Banks, and that the Bankers' Commission had now suggested that it should be divided amongst the various banks interested in the indemnity in accordance with the proportion of each bank's share thereof, the Wai-chiao Pu approached the Revenue Council with a request to take such action as they might see fit.

A reply has now been received stating that in regard to this matter the inspector-general of customs has issued instructions to the Shanghai commissioner to transfer for deposit in the various banks, in proportion to the amounts of their respective concern in the 1901 indemnity, all the funds deposited to the credit of the inspector-general's native customs account.

No. 32.

War Office to Foreign Office.—(Received June 4.)

Sir,   *Whitehall, June 3, 1912.*
  · I AM commanded by the Army Council to address you on the subject of the detachment of British troops which was dispatched from the South China command to Hankow in response to the request of the Foreign Office.

2. It will be remembered that last month the naval commander-in-chief, with the concurrence of His Majesty's Minister at Peking, reduced this detachment by sending back to Hong Kong the Royal Artillery and Royal Engineer details, amounting to sixty-two all ranks, leaving the detachment at the present strength of 100 infantry.

In view of the fact that, according to reports received, no attacks on the foreign concessions at Hankow have been threatened for some time past, I am to enquire whether, in the opinion of the Secretary of State for Foreign Affairs, the continued retention of a military force at Hankow is necessary.

A copy of this letter has been forwarded to the Admiralty.

I am, &c.
E. W. D. WARD.

No. 33.

Admiralty to Foreign Office.—(Received June 5.)   ·

Sir,   *Admiralty, June 4, 1912.*
  I AM commanded by my Lords Commissioners of the Admiralty to acquaint you, for the information of the Secretary of State for Foreign Affairs, that the commander-in-chief, China, reports in a telegram, dated the 29th May, that the troops are being withdrawn from Canton. His Majesty's Minister Peking has concurred.

His Majesty's ship " Clio " remains there for the present.
I am, &c.
W. GRAHAM GREENE.

No. 34.

Sir J. Jordan to Sir Edward Grey.—(Received June 8.)

Sir,   Peking, May 17, 1912.
    I HAVE the honour to transmit to you herewith an account which I have received
from Major George Pereira, formerly military attaché at His Majesty's Legation,
of his journey from Kashgar to Lan-chou Fu.

                                                            I have, &c.
                                                            J. N. JORDAN.

                            _____

Enclosure in No. 34.

Major Pereira's Journey from Kashgar to Lan-chou Fu.

                            _____

1. *The Journey.*

    I LEFT Kashgar on the 15th December, 1911, with two big carts, each drawn
by four horses and mules, and reached Lan-chou Fu, a distance of 2,437¾ miles, on the
15th April, 1912.
    The chief cities passed are :—Ak su Yangi-shahr, or Wen-hsiu Fu, at 342¼ miles.
This is the Chinese official city of Ak-su, with some 1,000 Chinese in the city, and
about 700 Sarts in the suburbs. Kuchar or K'u-ch'ê Chou, at 534 miles is surrounded
by trees and orchards, with a population, the magistrate informed me, of over 90,000
inhabitants in the two cities and surrounding country, all of whom are Sarts, with the
the exception of 3,000 Tungan, and 600 or 700 Chinese. Karashahr or Yen-ch'i Fu
has nearly 6,000 families (on an average five can be allowed to a family), they are
mostly Tungans, with many Chinese and only a few Sarts. It is 773 miles from
Kashgar. It is 3,190 feet above sea level, whilst Kashgar is 3,730 feet. There is a
big drop, descending among rocky hills to the Turfan plain, to Toksun at 943¾ miles,
only 130 feet above the sea level. From it the road ascends, passing over the Ta-pan
Shan pass, 3,610 feet, at 998¾ miles, to Urumchi (in Chinese Ti-hua Fu, or more commonly known as Hung-miao-tzu from a red temple north of the city). Its altitude is
2,740 feet, and the population of the city and suburbs with the thinly populated
country in the vicinity is reckoned at 60,000 or 70,000 inhabitants, of whom the
majority are Chinese with many Tungans, and about 5,000 Sarts. It is 1,063½ miles
(reckoned as 4,140 *li* by the Chinese) from Kashgar. From Urumchi I took the
southern route, as the more common road, viâ Ku-ch'eng, has a difficult pass, liable to
be blocked by snow in winter. The road recrosses the Ta-pan Shan pass, and drops to
Turfan or T'u-lu-fau T'ing (320 feet) at 125¼ miles. It consists of two walled cities,
about 1¼ miles apart ; as is usual in the Hsin-Chiang, one is the Chinese official city, and
the other is the Sart city. The total population of the two cities is put at 1,000 Sart
families, 900 Tungan, and 300 Chinese families. The road again ascends, and making a big
bend to the north, reaches Ha-mi T'ing with a Sart city of Kumul ½ mile to the south
at 427¼ miles from Urumchi (+ 2,340 feet). Population of the two cities, 700 or 800
Chinese and Tungan families, mostly Chinese, and 500 Sarts. The most important of
the six or seven Sart Princes of the Hsin-Chiang lives at Ku-mul. He is always very
friendly to British travellers in grateful remembrance of the Indian Government sending
back some of his stranded subjects, free of charge. This Prince—Sha-mu-hu-so-shih by
name—has a certain amount of influence among the Sarts, but the majority of these
Princes have been deprived of all power, and are subsidised by the Chinese. The
boundary between the provinces of Hsin-Chiang and Kansu in 573½ miles from Ha-mi.
The Su-lo Ho, a difficult river to cross when the ice is breaking in February, as there is
no bridge, flows north of An-hsi Chou (+ 3,530 feet), distant 675½ miles from
Urumchi. It is a poor city with over 300 families, or 900 including the adjacent
country. Su Chou (+ 4,700 feet) at 862½ miles, has some 15,000 inhabitants, with
30,000 including surroundings. It has lost much of its importance since the Mahommedan rebellion. Kan-chou Fu (+ 5,020 feet) at 1,019¼ miles has 40,000 inhabitants.
The name of the province is derived from this city and Su Chou. Liang-chou Fu
(+ 5,020 feet) at 1,188¾ miles has 27,500 inhabitants. Lan-chou Fu (+ 5,120 feet) is
1,374¼ miles from Urumchi, with a population which experts put at anything from

75,000 to 200,000 inhabitants; I should think that 100,000 would be about a correct estimate. The telegraph keeps near the road all the way from Kashgar to Lan-chou Fu.

2. *The Country.*

(a.) *Hsin-Chiang.*—From Kashgar to Ha-mi the country is mostly desert with low scrub, fertile oases only being found round the cities, with some cultivation round the villages, but the land is thinly populated, and I think an estimate of 2,000,000 for the whole of the Hsin-Chiang is too high. The most fertile places are the Kashgar plain and the Ili valley, and in the lesser degree the Ak-su and Kuchar plains, whilst the dreary Go-bi desert stretches from 6½ miles east of Hami to the Su-lo Ho, a distance of 239½ miles by road.

(b.) *Kansu.*—From An-hsi Chou to Kan-chou Fu the road mostly crosses thinly populated plains of grass or gravel and sand with occasional Chinese farms. After Kan-chou Fu the country still remains thinly populated for the most part, gradually rising to 9,420 feet at the watershed Ting-ch'iang-miao, 72 miles from Kan-chou Fu, and then descending to a fairly fertile plain around Liang-chou Fu. It then rises again for 67 miles to the Wu-shai-ling, 10,370 feet, where the watershed of the Huang Ho is reached. After following down alongside and crossing the P'ing-fan River it leaves it 47¾ miles from Lan-chou Fu, and winds up and down among barren hills, till reaching the fertile Huang Ho valley 10½ miles from Lan-chou Fu. Kansu is probably the poorest of the eighteen provinces of China. Père Richard, in his book on the geography of China, estimates the population of the province as 10,386,000, but Mgr. Otto, who has lived for many years and travelled a good deal in the province, thinks the estimates are too high. On the other hand, considering the great extent of Kansu with populous valleys along the Huang Ho, especially round Ning-hsia Fu and Lan-chou Fu, and the amount of cultivation on the roads between Lan-chou Fu and Hsi-ning Fu and between Lan-chou Fu and Ch'in Chou, I have come to the opinion that Père Richard's figures are underestimated. The provinces of Hsin-Chiang and Kansu are run at an annual loss to the Government, and the deficit has to be made up by contributions from the richer provinces such as Szechuan. The Hsin-Chiang appears to be a useless burden to China in every way; the Chinese soldiers, who garrison it, are the worst I have seen in all my travels, undisciplined and untrained, and quite unequal to the task of offering any resistance to an attack, whilst the population consists of a mixture of effete races with a total lack of any powers of combination, and apparently uninspired by the slightest patriotism, ambition, or desire to improve.

3. *Population of the Hsin-Chiang.*

1. *The Chinese* form a very small percentage, and are only numerically superior in the city of Urumchi and two or three of the Chinese cities, such as Ak-su Yangi-shahr and Kashgar Yang-shahr. They mostly consist of bad characters who have found it advisable to leave their own provinces.

2. *The Sarts or Ch'an-t'ou* form the large bulk of the population from Kashgar to Karashahr, in the Turfan valley, and from Turfan to Ha-mi. Their chief aim in life appears to be to lead a peaceful life under the foreign masters who will give them the least trouble. They are Mahommedans.

3. *The Tungans or Tungarns* are Mahommedans, whose origin is unknown, and even the meaning of the word Tungan is uncertain. They are probably allied to the Mahommedans of Kansu and Shensi. They speak and dress like the Chinese, but they consider themselves as a different race, and differ from them in appearance, having rounder eyes, &c. They are, however, greatly inferior in numbers to the Sarts, and are so scattered and apparently without powers of combination as to afford no danger. They form the bulk of the population at Karashahr, and in the thinly populated country along the road from that city to the Turfan valley, and from north of the Turfan valley to Urumchi, where the Chinese predominate. Owing to lack of soldiers the governor had to enlist some of them during the recent troubles, and as they are totally lacking in discipline, this step was viewed with some anxiety by the few Europeans who reside in Urumchi. The governor even had to have recourse to assistance from the Sart soldiers of the Ha-mi princes. The Chinese have made attempts in the past to enlist Sart soldiers, but they have always proved useless—a fortunate thing for the Chinese, as, if they were of any value, they would have no difficulty in expelling them from the land.

49

4. *The Manchus.*—There was formerly a Manchu city near Urumchi, but it is now deserted. There is a colony of So-lun Manchus near Tarbagatai, and colonies of Hsi-po Manchus in the Ili Valley. On the road I passed a troop of seventy Hsi-po Manchus, sent from Ha-mi to swell the rabble collected by the governor at Urumchi—a ragged lot, with antique single-loading carbines, lances, and banners.

5. *Mongols.*—I met a few Turgut Mongols from the Yulduz Valley around Karashahr, whilst Kalmuks or Zungar Mongols are occasionally seen at Urumchi. They occupy a tract of land to the north of Urumchi, and are also scattered about in the hills from Tarbagatai to the T'ien Shan. Other tribes of Mongols are mixed up with Kazaks in the hills north of the road I followed from Urumchi to Ha-mi. They also extend along the country to the north of Kansu, and some colonies are mixed up with Thibetans to the south of An-hsi Chou and Su-Chou. Mgr. Otto told me they were ruled over by some 300 princes, and these are much divided among themselves, and also often separated from princes of the same tribes by tribes of Kazaks, who have no love for Mongols. They are not a source of danger. Like the Sarts and Thibetans, they are also lacking in initiative and powers of combination.

6. *The Kazaks or Hassacks.*—During this journey I only met a few at Urumchi. They are the most effete of all the degenerate races I came across in Central Asia.

4. The Revolution in Hsin-Chiang.

This was caused by the new Tartar general discovering that the Prefect of Ili Fu and Brigadier-General Yang-tsuan-hsü, commanding the Ili brigade of "lu-chün," were considerably out in their accounts. To get out of the difficulty they declared a republic at Ili, murdered the Tartar general, and forced the former Tartar general, by giving him the alternative of losing his head, to become President. About the same time some of the provincial troops ("hsün-fang-tui"), mostly men from Hunan and Szechuan, mutinied at Urumchi, but they were surrounded by the local brigade of "lu-chün" and over 100 were killed or afterwards executed; and at the end of January, when approaching Urumchi, I passed batches of forty sent down nominally to guard the passes leading to Ak-su, but really to get them out of the way. When I reached Urumchi, on the 1st February, everything appeared to have quieted down, business was being carried on as usual, and all the "lu-chün" and available troops had been dispatched to the north-west to resist the advance of the Ili republicans. Owing to the usual lack of foresight on the part of the officials the men were insufficiently provided with clothes for the inclement weather, and many suffered from frostbite. As an example of the inefficiency of the Urumchi "lu-chün," only one officer was acquainted with the manner of working the guns, and as he happened to have been one of the few men killed in putting down the revolt the artillery was rendered useless. The governor, Yuan-ta-hua, an Anhui man, aged 57, had become very unpopular owing to the cruelty with which he put down the mutiny; and additional annoyance was felt against him after my departure by his insisting on carrying on the contest long after the news had been received of the Manchu abdication, prompted either by the ambition of becoming dictator of the province or by a feeling that therein only lay his chance of personal safety. Judging from what I saw and heard of the troops engaged on either side they appear to have been afraid of coming to close quarters, and the fighting dwindled down to three small skirmishes, in one of which the troops of the governor were successful, and in the other two victory remained with the Ili troops. Governor Yuan has the reputation of being very anti-foreign, though personally I found him very friendly when I called on him.

5. The Revolution in Kansu.

After travelling in every one of the eighteen provinces, I have come to the conclusion that the people of Kansu are the least troublesome and anti-foreign. This is probably due to their being of a less excitable temperament, and also to their having come less in contact with low types of Europeans. The chief cause of anxiety was the danger of a Mahommedan rebellion. Their two great risings, the last one in 1894, were put down by the Chinese with the greatest cruelty, but so effectively that the Mahommedans have since realise their weakness, whilst cherishing a hatred of their conquerors. In the cities of Kansu they are only allowed to live in the suburbs. Their great centre is Ho Chou, three days' journey to the south-west of Lan-chou Fu, which I am on the point of visiting. Nearly every Mahommedan family in China has the name of Ma, and their leader is General Ma-an-liang, aged 60, a silent and strong-willed man, whom I

[1270]

E

recently visited. When the troubles broke out the governor decided to rely on the Mahommedans, and the very effete brigade of "lu-chün" near Lan-chou Fu, which I inspected twenty-one months ago, was disbanded. A band of Mahommedan soldiers was sent up to Ninghsia Fu in the north-east of the province, and behaved with great cruelty, their chief object being loot. General Ma-an-liang was sent down to fight the Shensi republicans at Hsi-an Fu, each of his men taking one or two extra men to bring back the loot. In the actual fighting they were defeated, though they returned with a good deal of plunder. On his return to Lan-chou Fu, General Ma, instead of being tried by court-martial for his failure, had the calm audacity to demand 200 taels (25l.) indemnity for every one of his men who had been killed, and refused to return the rifles and to take his men back to Ho Chou. Some arrangement has now been come to, and he leaves for that city about the 2nd May. The Chinese troops here consist of two or three battalions of provincial troops ("hsün-fang-tui") and the bodyguard of the "tu-tu" (the new name for the governor, since the abolition of the post of Viceroy). These troops, known as "wei-tui," are 1,300 strong, and divided into five battalions. One of them told me they only received 2,300 cash (1,400 cash is one tael, or 2s. 6d.) a-month, so it is not surprising that they are quite untrained and useless. About 1,000 men were camped on the city wall. They were armed mostly with Tower muskets but had some Mausers. They relied, however, chiefly on piles of stones, and an arrangement to let down a lamp to identify their enemies at night-time, a system of warfare out of date at the time of the patriarchs. They now propose to restart the Lu-chün brigade. The probability is that P'eng-ying-chia, recently appointed treasurer ("fan-t'ai") of the province will be made governor ("tu-tu"), in place of the present man who is only acting. He is a Chinese from Mukden, aged 46, an active man, and very well disposed to foreigners. In 1901 he was magistrate of the city of Tung-an Hsien, near Peking, and under orders to be shot. However, I represented his case to our general at Tien-tsin, and he was handed over to us and released, so he now cherishes a very friendly feeling to the British.

6. Manchu Colonies in Kansu.

The small Manchu city, 2 miles to the south-west of Lan-chou Fu, has long been deserted by the Manchus on account of the difficulty of getting water, and is now occupied by ninety Chinese families. There is a Manchu colony of 200 families at Chuang-lang, 2 miles south of P'ing-fan Hsien, another near Liang-chou Fu, another near Ning-hsia Fu, and I believe one at Chung-wei Hsien on the Huang Ho, to the south-south-west of Ning Hsia Fu.

7. Miscellaneous.

In Kansu one is struck by the number of ruined houses and villages, especially on the road from An-hsi Chou to Lan-chou Fu, and the walled farms and villages, relics of the Mahommedan rebellions. As I have previously remarked, the occupation of the Hsin Chiang is a source of weakness to the Chinese, and they would be much better off if they withdrew behind the Gobi desert and fixed the boundary at the Su-lo Ho, not going beyond An-hsi Chou, and the fertile country round Sa-chou (or Tun-huang) further west. For the same reason any idea of occupying or reoccupying Thibet should be abandoned.

As an example of the military state of Kansu, the garrison of Su Chou was 2,350 on paper, but when the troubles broke out it was found that the garrison was actually under 300, the pay for the remainder finding its way into the pockets of the officials, so when the Viceroy at Lanchou Fu telegraphed for reinforcements, they were only able to send him twenty men! Before my arrival at Su Chou there had been a mild attempt at revolt by a small party of Hunanese and Szechuan men, who had egged on the ignorant and unarmed peasants so that even the reduced garrison was strong enough to suppress them without difficulty, and some harmless peasants paid the penalty for their folly by having their heads chopped off. Kansu is the poorest province in China, and the large bulk of the population are peasants, who lead a life with a perpetual risk of starvation, if the crops should fail. Mgr. Otto took me to some farms near his house at Sung-shu Chuang, 7¼ miles west of Liang Chou Fu, to show me the state of the people. The people were nearly destitute, and he told me they had not enough money to buy clothes for their children, who run about naked or with only one small garment. Fortunately the Chinese are a patient and long-enduring race, always cheerful and making the best of their existence. Unluckily they are a most improvident race, and never put by anything for a rainy day. If they wish to do so they would find it difficult, as they have no place to keep their money, and would be in perpetual danger of being robbed. It is not therefore surprising to find that they are anxious to grow opium, which is their only means of increasing their scanty earnings. The greatest boon that could be conferred on them would be to send an expert into the country to examine the soil and recommend some paying crop to replace opium. Practical assistance of this sort, backed up by Chinese official assistance, would be the greatest blessing that foreigners could confer on the Chinese.

8. Coinage.

There should be a uniform system throughout the Chinese dominions. At present everything is chaos. The tael, at present generally worth about half-a-crown, is supposed to be the unit, but it varies in value not only in every province, but even in every city. The difficulty is increased by lumps of silver, called sycee, being used, of every sort of size and shape, so that each piece has to be weighed, and the difficulty and chances of robbery are increased from the fact that nearly every pair of scales has a different weight. Apart from a lot of the silver being bad, it varies in quality in each province, and the silver which is used in Hsin Chiang will often not be taken in Szechuan. To add to the confusion silver coins, generally dollars—sometimes as in Hsin Chiang half taels—are coined by the provincial authorities, but these are only accepted in the provinces or often only parts of the province in which they are coined. Even worse than the silver are the copper coins, and on account of the weight they are very difficult to carry about. In some provinces they use the "T'ung tzu'rh," roughly 100 go to a dollar, but the usual money is the "cash," with a hole in the centre, usually made up in strings of nominally 500 coins. The number of these that go to a tael vary again in every city and village, and in addition they change from day to day. For instance in three days at Lan-chou Fu the tael was worth 1,410, 1,405, and 1,370 cash. To add to the confusion of the traveller a few coins are always short on every string; for instance, in one city on one day 90 cash represent a nominal 100, whilst on another day it is 92 and in another place 94. I was told at Kuei-hua Cheng in Northern Shansi that the strings there had the full 500 coins, and out of curiosity I counted two strings and found they were correct, but this is a unique experience in my wanderings of thirteen years throughout the Chinese Empire.

In some cities the officials issue notes, but these are generally only accepted in the city and its immediate vicinity. They are usually for a tael, half a tael, 1,000 cash or 500 cash—notes for all of which are current in Lan-chou Fu, and accepted at their proper value—but often, as in the case of those issued by the Tartar general at Ili, who flooded the market so as to increase his income, they are only accepted locally, and then only at a large discount. Unfortunately in a poverty-stricken country like China, where I suppose 90 per cent. of the population are constantly faced with the danger of starvation, a coin of very small value like the cash is an absolute necessity, but there is no reason why the silver coinage should not be completely overhauled, and a uniform system adopted. It would, of course, meet with great opposition from the officials, who would lose a great opportunity for "squeeze," and also by the bankers and money-changers. Under the present system everybody is busily engaged in robbing his neighbour, and being robbed in his turn, and probably an industrious robber is no better off at the end of his life than if he had been perfectly honest all his existence, and surrounded by honest neighbours.

9. The Revolution in China.

When I left Urumchi on the 9th February, I was assured by the timid that Kansu was on the verge of breaking out into a state of anarchy, but luckily this proved to be unfounded, and I everywhere found perfect peace. This was in a great measure due to the courage and firmness displayed by the late Viceroy Ch'ang, who though deserted by most of the higher officials, who resigned in panic, faced the difficulty like a man, and weathered the storm. As a reward for his services he is now living in retirement at Kuei-hua Ch'eng. The only signs of past troubles I met with were a head hanging from a tree near the North Gate of Su Chou, but this is not a very rare spectacle, and the order by the officials to keep the gates of Su Chou and Chia-yü Kuan closed. The only outward signs of a change of government are the abolition of the post of Viceroy, the nominal adoption of the Gregorian calendar, and the display of the new flag with its five colours, red on the top for the Chinese, yellow for the Manchus, blue for Mongolia, white for the Mahommedans, and black for Thibet. I do not suppose it makes the slightest difference to over 90 per cent. of the population whether the Government is Imperial or Republican. It cannot, at any rate for a long time, affect the lives of the peasant, who forms the large bulk of the population, the coolie, or the carter. An upheaval, however, gives a grand opportunity to brigands, and they are the great source of danger. Corruption is an evil that has entered so largely into Chinese life that I doubt if it can be eradicated for a century. A really honest man would find life almost unbearable, and would generally run the risk of ending his life in destitution.

GEORGE PEREIRA.

Lan-chou Fu, Province of Kansu,
North-West China, April 29, 1912.

No. 35.

War Office to Foreign Office.—(Received June 10.)

Sir,   *Whitehall, June 8, 1912.*
I AM commanded by the Army Council to address you with reference to the continued retention in North China of an additional battalion of British infantry surplus to the authorised establishment of that command.

2. It will be remembered that the 1st Battalion Royal Inniskilling Fusiliers, which was due to proceed to India on relief by the Somersetshire Light Infantry, was retained in North China at the request of the Foreign Office.

3. This regiment is still being retained in that command in excess of the normal garrison, and the establishment of infantry for home defence remains proportionately depleted.

4. In this connection I am to point out that, at the request of the Foreign Office, the garrison at Hong Kong was also reinforced last February by two Indian infantry battalions and one Indian mountain battery, which still remain there as a reserve to meet eventualities in China.

5. Under these circumstances I am to enquire whether in the opinion of the Secretary of State for Foreign Affairs the condition of affairs in China is such as to warrant the withdrawal of the Royal Inniskilling Fusiliers in the ordinary course without relief by another battalion, about November next; and, since the arrangements for this withdrawal have to be fitted in with the general programme of Indian and colonial reliefs, now being completed, I am to ask that you will kindly favour the council with a reply at the earliest possible date.

I am, &c.
E. W. D. WARD.

No. 36.

Sir Edward Grey to Sir J. Jordan.

(Telegraphic.)   *Foreign Office, June 15, 1912.*
PLEASE let me have your views as to the withdrawal of the Inniskillings about November. In the event of an emergency arising, the War Office point out that troops are available at Hong Kong.

No. 37.

Sir J. Jordan to Sir Edward Grey.—(Received June 17.)

Sir,   *Peking, May 29, 1912.*
WITH reference to my despatch of the 27th February last* and previous correspondence, I have the honour to forward herewith, for your information, copy of the first report from the International Bankers' Commission at Shanghai, showing the total amount of customs revenue received and expended from the 1st January to 30th April, 1912, on account of the service of the loans secured by that revenue. The report also shows the total amount of revenue collected for account of the indemnity of

*. See " China, No. 3 (1912);" No. 148.

1901—that is to say, the native customs revenue received up to the 30th April, 1912.
I do not consider it necessary to trouble you with the various statements and accounts
enclosed in the report, which are summarised in the report itself; but it is satisfactory
to note that the commission has been able to pay all instalments of principal as well as
interest due on the various loans secured by the customs revenue.

These documents have been forwarded to me as dean of the diplomatic body
through the senior consul at Shanghai, and are being circulated for the information of
my colleagues.

It will be noticed that no payments have been made yet on account of the
indemnity; but this is because the sum available for this purpose, amounting to less
than 640,000 taels, is as yet too small to begin appropriating. The arrears of indemnity
due for seven months (the last payment having been made on the 30th September,
1911) amount, without interest, to 1,741,187l., requiring approximately from 11,600,000
to 13,900,000 taels, according as exchange varies from 3s. to 2s. 6d. Apart from the
arrangement under which the service of the indemnity is postponed to the end of the
year, the sum of 1,800,000 taels odd which is shown to credit of the loan service
account would not have been available for indemnity payments, inasmuch as it is all,
and more, required to maintain the service of the loans. Indeed, on account of the
specially heavy payments due in June and July, the loan service is not unlikely to fall
into arrears for a time, but at the end of the year, if trade goes on as at present, it is
probable that there will be not only sufficient revenue in hand to meet the first loan
payments due in January 1913, but a surplus balance available for transference to
indemnity account. Any such balance, however, can do but little to help the service
of the indemnity, on which, unless it is otherwise provided for, the sum of 3,701,115l.
(not counting interest on arrears) will be due on the 31st December.

I trust that the present report will make it clear that the unsatisfactory position
of the indemnity account, so far as payments-from the customs revenue are concerned,
is due entirely to the insufficiency of that revenue, and not to any defect in the
arrangement for utilising it for the service of the loans and indemnity. It is perhaps
unnecessary to add that the customs receipts formed the only source of revenue
available at the time, and that even still, six months later, the Central Government
is not in a position to enforce the collection of any appreciable amount of revenue from
the provinces.

I have, &c.
J. N. JORDAN.

Enclosure in No. 37.

International Bankers' Commission to Sir J. Jordan.

Sir, *Shanghai, May* 13, 1912.
IN accordance with clause 7 of the resolutions approved of by the diplomatic
body at Peking last January, in which it is stated that the "International Bankers'
Commission shall furnish to the diplomatic body, through the consuls at Shanghai, a
quarterly report showing the appropriation of the revenue received by the Imperial
Maritime Customs," I have the honour to forward you herewith* :—

1. Statement showing the total amount of revenue received and expended from
the 1st January to 30th April, 1912, on account of Chinese loan service.
2. Copy of Inspector-General of Customs' "Foreign Revenue" account to the
30th April last at the Hong Kong and Shanghai Bank.
3. Copy of the Commissioner of Customs', Shanghai, "Chinese Loan Service
Account" to the 30th April last at the Hong Kong and Shanghai Bank, together with
certificate of balance.
4. Copy of the Commissioner of Customs', Shanghai, "Chinese Loan Service
Account" to the 30th April last at the Deutsch-Asiatische Bank, together with
certificate of balance.
5. Copy of the Commissioner of Customs', Shanghai, "Chinese Loan Service
Account" to the 30th April last at the Russo-Asiatic Bank.
6. List of instalments of principal and interest on Chinese loans paid, up to and
including the 30th April, through the Hong Kong and Shanghai Bank.

* Not received at Foreign Office

[1270] E 3

54

7. List of instalments of principal and interest on Chinese loans paid, up to and including the 30th April, through the Deutsch-Asiatische Bank.
8. List of instalments of principal and interest on Chinese loans paid, up to and including the 30th April, through the Russo-Asiatic Bank.
9. List of instalments of principal and interest on Chinese loans paid, up to and including the 30th April, through the Chartered Bank of India, Australia, and China.

From these statements you will observe that the total revenue received since the 1st January, 1912, to 30th ultimo amounted to 12,308,828·36 taels. From this amount 10,435,720·34 taels have been taken to pay for all the instalments of principal and interest due on the various loans up to and including the 30th ultimo, and which are secured by the customs revenue. In addition to this sum 61,031·19 taels have been paid for interest charged by the banks on the overdue payments of their instalments. The net balance on hand, amounting to 1,813,719·34 taels, lies at the credit of the Commissioner of Customs' account as follows :—

		Taels.
With the Hong Kong Bank, to the extent of	..	604,025·62
„ Deutsch-Asiatishe Bank, to the extent of	..	604,025·60
„ Russo-Asiatic Bank, to the extent of ..	..	605,668·12

I also have the honour to send you herewith :—

1. Statement showing total amount of revenue collected for account of " Chinese Indemnity."
• 2. Copy of Commissioner of Customs', Shanghai, " Chinese Indemnity Account " to the 30th April with the Hong Kong and Shanghai Bank, together with certificate of balance.
3. Copy of Commissioner of Customs', Shanghai, " Chinese Indemnity Account " to the 30th April with the Deutsch-Asiatische Bank, together with certificate of balance.
4. Copy of Commissioner of Customs', Shanghai, " Chinese Indemnity Account " to the 30th April with the Russo-Asiatic Bank, together with certificate of balance.

There have been no moneys paid out from this account, and the total revenue received amounts to 638,255·35 taels, which lies at the credit of the Commissioner of Customs' " Indemnity Account " as follows :—

		Taels.
With the Hong Kong and Shanghai Bank, to the extent of	..	212,717·88
„ Deutsch-Asiatische Bank, to the extent of	..	212,717·88
„ Russo-Asiatic Bank, to the extent of ..	..	212,819·59

I further enclose copy of the Inspector-General of Customs' " Native Customs Revenue Account " to the 30th ultimo with the Hong Kong and Shanghai Bank, showing a balance in his favour of 1,002·60 taels.
This letter is being forwarded to you through the senior consul here, and I am also sending a copy of same to each consul interested, together with the statements showing total amounts received and expended on account of " China Loan Service " and " Indemnity " accounts.

I have, &c.
H. M. S. MAN, Secretary,
International Bankers' Commission.

No. 38.

Admiralty to Foreign Office.—(Received June 19.)

Sir, Admiralty, June 19, 1912.
I AM commanded by my Lords Commissioners of the Admiralty to transmit, for the information of the Secretary of State for Foreign Affairs, copy of a telegram dated to-day from the Commander-in-chief, China.
I am, &c.
W. GRAHAM GREENE.

Enclosure in No. 38.

Commander-in-chief, China, to Admiralty.

(Telegraphic.)   *Wei-hai Wei, June* 19, 1912.
IN consequence of revolutionary forces having seized British property, Kashing, near Shanghai, am sending " Newcastle " there.

No. 39.

Sir Edward Grey to Sir J. Jordan.

(Telegraphic.)   *Foreign Office, June* 20, 1912.
BRITISH troops at Hankow.
Do you consider the continued retention of the detachment of 100 infantry necessary? The War Office have approached me on the subject. They point out that for some time past the foreign concessions have not been threatened.

No. 40.

Sir J. Jordan to Sir Edward Grey.—(Received June 21.)

Sir,   *Peking, June* 4, 1912.
I HAVE the honour to acknowledge the receipt of your despatch of the 11th ultimo, enquiring whether the arrangement for the disposal of the surplus of the maritime customs revenue at the end of 1912 for the service of the indemnity has been in any way affected by the recent decision as to the distribution of the native customs revenue.

The recent decision referred to concerns only the question of the custody of the funds transferred from the inspector-general's native customs revenue account, pending their appropriation to the service of the indemnity for which this small revenue is primarily pledged. The decision has no bearing on the question of the surplus of the maritime customs revenue.

My despatch of the 31st ultimo, forwarding a quarterly statement by the bankers' commission, which has crossed your despatch under acknowledgment, will serve to explain the position in regard to the service of the indemnity, which is entirely unaffected by the distribution of the native customs revenue (as opposed to the maritime customs revenue) between eight or nine banking accounts instead of between three.

I have, &c.
J. N. JORDAN.

No. 41.

Sir J. Jordan to Sir Edward Grey.—(Received June 21.)

(Telegraphic.)   *Peking, June* 21, 1912.
YOUR telegram of 15th June: Withdrawal of British troops from North China.
It is impossible to foresee what situation may be in November, but outlook points to pessimism rather than hopefulness, and does not, in my opinion, warrant any hope of withdrawal or reduction in near future.

No. 42.

Sir Edward Grey to Sir J. Jordan.

(Telegraphic.) *Foreign Office, June 22, 1912.*
TELEGRAM has been received from General Officer Commanding, South China, reporting that, owing to raids on villages within Hong Kong frontier, six companies of Indian infantry will be sent out on 25th June to patrol frontier and occupy points.

No. 43.

Sir J. Jordan to Sir Edward Grey.—(Received June 24.)

Sir, *Peking, June 7, 1912.*
WITH reference to my despatch of the 6th ultimo, I have the honour to forward herewith a summary by Sir Somerville Head of events in the provinces during the past month.

I have, &c.
J. N. JORDAN.

Enclosure in No. 43.

Summary of Events in the Provinces during the month of May, 1912.

IT cannot be said that there has been any improvement in the state of affairs in the provinces during the past month. Szechuan especially has been prolific in disturbing rumours, and seems to be a happy hunting-ground for the yellow press of China. Stories of British armies advancing on China through Thibet and Assam and of the exacting demands of foreign Shylocks are freely disseminated by agitators and secret societies, and are the cause of a rectudescence of anti-foreign feeling over a large part of the country.

In Shantung Boxers are said to have appeared in several districts round Lin-ch'ing-chou, and the magistrate has applied for troops to suppress them. Brigandage is also rife over the whole of the west of this province. Great difficulty is being experienced in collecting the land tax, though here also the fruitless attempt is being made to collect subscriptions towards the needs of the State as a means of avoiding foreign loans. Chang Hsun is moving from his quarters in a train on the railway line to an official residence in Yenchoufu, which would seem to show that he intends remaining there for the present.

At Nanking the military resident has paid over 100,000 dollars to the chamber of commerce for distribution amongst the sufferers of the mutiny of the 11th April, whose total claims amounted to 210,000 dollars. Those whose losses were under 100 dollars were paid in full, but the rest received a fixed proportion only of their claims, the larger the claim the smaller the percentage paid. It is calculated that by this means very few people could have been seriously out of pocket, especially as most of the booty, which was of no great value, has been recovered. There are indications, however, that Nanking is not yet at the end of its troubles.

His Majesty's consul at Foochow reports that during the first few days of May a state of uneasiness prevailed at that port. It was stated that the Hunanese soldiers, long dissatisfied with their pay, and unfriendly with the Fukienese, contemplated a general massacre of the latter. The rumour caused large numbers of the inhabitants to leave the city, and the state of affairs appeared serious enough to the United States and German consuls to justify them in asking for the presence of gun-boats. The Governor, however, acted with praiseworthy promptitude. A priest who had issued inflammatory leaflets was executed, and his head exposed with that of a soldier who had also been beheaded for disorderly conduct, and eventually quiet was restored.

His Majesty's consul at Swatow reports that by the end of March, the independent Hakka leader, Lin Chi-chen, had driven out Chen Hung-ô, the nominee of the Canton Republican authorities, and had established himself strongly in Swatow. He made no attempt to set up any kind of local Government, but contented himself with efforts to extort money from the Swatow merchants, nominally for the upkeep of his troops. The Canton authorities deputed Wu Hsiang-ta, a former brigadier-general at Chao-chow-fu, to go to Swatow with a sufficient force to turn out Lin Chi-chen and to take over control. When Wu finally arrived on the scene, instead of taking military measures he proceeded to invite Lin to dinner, an invitation which was declined. Thereupon ensued a month's haggling until Lin was persuaded to reduce the price of his departure from 300,000 dollars to 80,000 dollars. The money was handed over to Lin on the understanding that he would leave Swatow with all his men at the earliest possible moment. After a few days it was found that Lin had quietly slipped away to Hong Kong with the money, leaving his troops unpaid behind. The Swatow Chamber of Commerce once more collected funds and gave the soldiers tickets and money to take them to Canton, but the majority of the soldiers converted their tickets into cash and disappeared.

No. 44.

Admiralty to Foreign Office.—(Received June 24.)

Sir, *Admiralty, June 24, 1912.*
I AM commanded by my Lords Commissioners of the Admiralty to transmit, for the information of the Secretary of State for Foreign Affairs, copy of a telegram, dated the 23rd instant, from the Commander-in-chief, China, respecting the unrest in China.

I am, &c.
W. GRAHAM GREENE.

Enclosure in No. 44.

Commander-in-chief, China, to Admiralty.
(Telegraphic.) *June 23, 1912.*
THE general situation over all China is worse than it was a short time ago, and troops have again been dispatched to Canton at the request of the consul-general there.

No. 45.

Sir J. Jordan to Sir Edward Grey.—(Received June 25.)

(Telegraphic.) *Peking, June 25, 1912.*
BRITISH troops at Hankow.
Your telegram of 20th June.
I have carefully considered the matter and cannot recommend withdrawal of garrison at present.*

No. 46.

Sir J. Jordan to Sir Edward Grey.—(Received June 26.)

Sir, *Peking, June 6, 1912.*
I HAVE the honour to report that recent despatches and telegrams from His Majesty's consular officers in Szechuan, Hupei, and other provinces point to a recrudescence of anti-foreign agitation in connection with the proposals for the supervision of foreign loans to China.
In a memorandum, copy of which I have the honour to forward herewith, I have drawn the serious attention of the Central Government to the possible consequences of this agitation, the leading features of which are briefly described therein. The appeal for voluntary subscriptions to the State continues, with some degree of enthusiasm, throughout the provinces, and is supported by misrepresentations of the nature of the loan proposals and by references to the foreign financial control exercised over Turkey

* Copy sent to War Office June 26, 1912.

and Egypt, and to the example of France in paying off the indemnity of the Franco-Prussian war, which display a childish ignorance not only of the rudiments of political economy, but of the simple facts of modern history.

I spoke yesterday to Yuan Shih-kai about this movement, and earnestly impressed upon him the necessity for checking it before it assumed serious proportions. He attributed it to the unreasoning ignorance of the Chinese, and to the wide publicity which the prolonged negotiations in Europe had received. He has sent a telegraphic warning to the provinces to repress the anti-loan agitation, but experience shows that steps of this kind have but little effect in present circumstances.

I have, &c.

J. N. JORDAN.

Enclosure in No. 46.

Memorandum communicated to the Wai-chiao Pu.

HIS Majesty's Minister has the honour to draw the serious attention of the Wai-chiao Pu to the recrudescence of anti-foreign agitation in Szechuan, Hupei, and other provinces of China.

On the '18th March last, at Chia-t'ing, in Szechuan, a placard was posted purporting to be issued by the local authorities, and offering a reward of 1,000 taels for each foreigner's head, while in April last slips of wood, bearing an inscription that for every foreigner taken or killed a reward of 1,000 dollars would be given, were thrown into the River Yangtze, in Szechuan province, and allowed to float down stream until the officials took proper steps to have them extracted and destroyed.

About the same time the "Red Lantern Sect" made its appearance at An Hsien, Ta Yi, Wen Chiang, P'i Hsien, Kuan Hsien, Ta Tsu, and other places. The practices of this society bear features of resemblance to those of the "Boxers" of the year 1900; some of its members have been known to carry on their persons scrolls inscribed, "Adhere to the Ch'ing and wipe out the foreigners."

These and other manifestations of hostility have undoubtedly been fostered by the recent agitation against the contraction by China of foreign loans, and the latter phase has actually been supported, instead of being suppressed, by the local authorities. A telegram of the 1st instant from His Majesty's consul-general at Chengtu states that on the 31st May the financial commissioner issued a proclamation, with the object of hastening taxation, denouncing foreigners for long harbouring designs against China. Such being the attitude of the responsible authorities in the provinces towards a foreign loan, it is not surprising that the native press feels itself free to give vent to still more inflammatory utterances, with the inevitable consequence that the people become imbued with a spirit of avowed hostility, and the public peace is seriously endangered.

Sir John Jordan desires to remind the Wai-chiao Pu that the duty of repressing the present anti-foreign tendency of this agitation is one which not only the provincial authorities, but also the Central Government are bound to use every means in their power to carry into effect.

Peking, June 5, 1912.

No. 47.

Sir J. Jordan to Sir Edward Grey.—(Received June 26.)

Sir,   *Peking, June 8, 1912.*

I HAVE the honour to report that on the 15th May last I received a telegram from the general officer commanding at Hong Kong to the effect that, should it be considered necessary to retain the British troops now stationed in the concession at Canton, he would be prepared to relieve them by a similar number. His Majesty's consul-general at Canton, whose opinion I invited, reported that he considered the present situation would justify the complete withdrawal of the troops early in June.

I also consulted the naval commander-in-chief, and we agreed that, though there was no doubt always a possibility of a counter-revolution, the eventuality was too remote to justify the heavy expense entailed by the relief and retention of the British guard. A British ship-of-war is to be stationed permanently at Canton for the

present, and troops can reach that port in a few hours from Hong Kong in case of need, while the position of the concession on Shameen renders it defensible until relief arrives.
I have accordingly telegraphed to-day to His Majesty's consul-general in this sense, and the troops will doubtless shortly be withdrawn to Hong Kong.

I have, &c.
J. N. JORDAN.

No. 48.

Foreign Office to War Office.

Sir, *Foreign Office, June 26, 1912.*
WITH reference to your letter of the 8th instant, enquiring whether the situation in China would warrant the withdrawal of the 1st Battalion Royal Inniskilling Fusiliers from Peking in November next, I am directed by Secretary Sir E. Grey to transmit to you herewith a copy of a telegram from His Majesty's Minister at Peking,* stating that the outlook does not warrant any hope of withdrawal or reduction in the near future.
Sir E. Grey entirely concurs in the view expressed by Sir J. Jordan in this matter.

I am, &c.
W. LANGLEY.

No. 49.

Sir J. Jordan to Sir Edward Grey.—(Received July 1.)

Sir, *Peking, June 12, 1912.*
IN my despatch of the 6th instant I reported that I had represented to Yuan Shih-kai the serious proportions which the anti-loan agitation was assuming in the provinces, and that he had promised to issue telegraphic instructions explaining the situation and warning the people to refrain from fomenting trouble.
The telegram in which these instructions were conveyed to the authorities of Szechuan, the province chiefly concerned, has been published in the native newspapers, and a copy of it is enclosed herewith.

I have, &c.
J. N. JORDAN.

Enclosure in No. 49.

Extract from the "Cheng Pao" of June 8, 1912.

THE following telegram has been sent by the President, through the Cabinet, to the Szechuan authorities:—

" I learn that owing to misapprehension of the facts, opposition to the loan exists in Szechuan, and that rumours are being disseminated and meetings held, with the result that men's minds are in a ferment. This encouragement of agitation is due to the misconception that China is resorting to a foreign loan under compulsion from alien capitalists, and that the groups' audit of expenditure of the loan funds connotes a foreign supervision of our finances. The situation is said to be more alarming than at the time of the opposition to the railway loan last year, and, in addition, the Red Lantern and other societies are seizing the opportunity to create disturbances, so that a danger of anti-foreign outbreaks exists.
"Ever since last autumn the country has been overrun with troops, and universal distress prevails ; to-day the republic has been formed, but the national foundations are still not firmly established. How, then, should wild and erroneous rumours be permitted to sow a harvest of danger ? When the patriotic crusade started in Wuchang and Hankow the Powers observed a strict neutrality, and subsequently approved of the republic ; this is clear proof of their sympathy for the new Government and of the absence of any hostile feelings in our regard.
"As to the loan, if the national finances were sufficient, why should we seek assistance from foreign capital ? Unfortunately, the sources of revenue have long since

* No. 41.

been dried up in Peking, and perpetual appeals for funds flow in from the provinces. In some cases things have reached a stage where the troops are confined to a diet of gruel, and are still wearing winter garments at the summer's height. If we wait for the national subscription to bring relief, apart from the fact that one is loath to impose fresh exactions on the people in these hard times, the gradual stream of slowly accruing funds would be quite inadequate to meet existing needs. Moreover, the money market would probably be affected and the supply of ready money would dwindle. Hence negotiations have been carried on with the groups for temporary advances to ease the situation. Various conditions were proposed, and after much discussion it was decided that both parties should appoint auditors. Such auditing applies only to the expenditure of the advances, and will cease simultaneously with the cessation of the advances. It thus differs *in toto* from a foreign supervision of finances, and resembles a private arrangement between two parties. *A* borrows money from *B ; B* wishes to know how it is going to be spent, so as to protect his pocket. As soon as *A* has settled his debt, *B*'s rights as lender cease. This procedure is invariable in all joint-stock banking and railway enterprises. Provided China's industry develops and her finances are replenished, there would not be the slightest difficulty in paying off even the load of debt accumulated by the dispossessed Manchu dynasty. The Cabinet has recently decided to ask the Secretary of State for Finance to resume negotiations with the groups with a view to lightening the conditions in a wholly satisfactory way. Does not this do away with all fear of financial supervision ? Huang Hsing's suggestion for initiating a national fund has met with an enthusiastic response all over China, and affords an admirable means of stimulating patriotism. I entertain the highest respect for the idea. But if Szechuan disseminates wild rumours and disturbances ensue, the discrepancy of a single scruple may widen to a ten-thousand-league gulf of error.

"If, peradventure, the rallying cry of patriotism becomes a means for perpetrating anti-foreign outbreaks, the seed of opposition to the loan may bring forth fruits of eternal financial bondage. Recall for a moment the events of 1900 under the dispossessed Manchu dynasty ! Did not the Imperial decrees invariably extol the Boxers as loyal patriots ? Yet the end was that the allied forces entered the capital, our sovereign rights were sacrificed, and an indemnity was paid, until the people were driven in desperation to a hazardous enterprise and the dynasty perished from the earth.

"To-day our infant republic is budding into new life : its case resembles that of a man sick with a wasting malady for whom judicious nursing is essential. If he overtaxes his physical powers and allows his limbs to riot in an excess of effort, an opening is afforded for the invasion of some fresh distemper. What hope will there be for our country remaining whole ? The fate of Poland or of Egypt awaits her. Ever since the days of the southern Sung dynasty China has been ruined by this spirit of inflated arrogance. This was the malady of which both the Sung and the Ming dynasties perished. To-day the Powers are watching us, and protests have already been made about our conduct ; the consequences for our republic are pregnant with fate. A man must outrage his own dignity before he is exposed to outrage from others ; a nation must first destroy itself before others can destroy it. It is written : 'The people's erroneous utterances are verily the steps of catastrophe.' Szechuan occupies a position of strategic importance on the south-west, and abounds in undeveloped resources : why should it work its own undoing by acts involving a load of foreign debt ? The authorities are to issue notices in simple language for the information of all, so that suspicions may be dissipated and incipient disorder may be nipped in the bud. If hesitating procrastination permit disaster to accrue, the Tutu of Szechuan will be held responsible."

No. 50.

Admiralty to Foreign Office.—(Received July 6.)

Sir, *Admiralty, July 6, 1912.*

I AM commanded by my Lords Commissioners of the Admiralty to transmit, for the information of the Secretary of State for Foreign Affairs, copy of a telegram, dated the 6th instant, from the commander-in-chief on the China station relative to the rioting at Wuhu.

I am, &c.
W. GRAHAM GREENE.

Enclosure in No. 50.

Commander-in-chief, China Station, to Admiralty.

(Telegraphic.)   July 6, 1912.
SOLDIERS discharged from Nanking caused grave riot on 4th July at Wuhu.
Rioters looted and burnt large shop.   His Majesty's ships "Bramble" and
"Pegasus" present.   Have reported to Sir J. Jordan.

No. 51.

Sir J. Jordan to Sir Edward Grey.—(Received July 10.)

Sir,   Peking, June 24, 1912.
    I HAVE the honour to transmit herewith copy of a report which has been
addressed to me by the military attaché at His Majesty's Legation respecting the
recent mutinies of Chinese troops.

                                                            I have, &c.
                                                            J. N. JORDAN.

Enclosure in No. 51.

Report by Lieutenant-Colonel Willoughby.

    CERTAIN recent occurrences in the Chinese forces, in widely separated regions,
point to a recrudescence of military unrest, and are symptomatic of the general
relaxation of the bonds of discipline which has resulted from the unsettled state of the
country and the uncertainty in the minds of the troops regarding their pay and their
future.   Among the northern troops rumours of disbandment have been the cause of
a considerable amount of discontent and unrest.
    The following are some of the instances of indiscipline to which I allude :—
    1. At Nanking at the end of last month an extensive mutiny was planned by the
the 34th regiment, but was promptly suppressed.   I have received the following
information as to the situation in Nanking on the 9th June :—
    " The number of soldiers in the city is rather more than 30,000.   About 1,200 of
these are Cantonese, the rest being mostly from Hunan, Anhui, Kiangsu, Kiangsi, and
Shantung.
    " About a month ago all the small-arms ammunition of the troops was withdrawn,
except that of the Ching-pei Chün, a body of military police, 2,400 strong, on whom
Huang Hsing appears to rely in case of trouble.
    " On the 26th May there was an extensive mutiny planned by the 34th regiment,
quartered on the Exhibition Buildings, but the outbreak was suppressed by the
Ching-pei Chün, who surrounded the mutineers and trained machine guns on the
barracks.
    " On the 28th May further trouble was expected, and guards were placed on the
foreign consulates, where they remained for four days.
    " On the same day two emissaries of the pro-Imperialist party were caught in the
city and executed soon after.
    " On the 1st June the head of the Bureau of Foreign Affairs besought the aid of
the foreign consuls.
    " There are roughly 100,000 troops in South Central China who look to Huang
Hsing, and the upper classes in Nanking seem to think that his going away would
mean disaster.
    " On the 6th June there were strong rumours of an uprising by the troops,
instigated by secret agents of the Imperialist party.   On the same day the 16th
and 17th regiments, quartered near the Pei-men Ch'iao, were ordered by Huang Hsing
to disband, and were given one month's pay.   The men demanded twice the amount,
and on this being refused they marched in a body to the arsenal in the south of the
city.   The Ching-pei Chün were again hurriedly turned out and without any serious
conflict put the others to flight.   For some hours the city was in a state of panic,
unprecedented for many years, and all the banks and big shops in the wealthy quarter

62

(south-west) closed their doors. It is noteworthy that this did not happen even at the time of the big outbreak two months ago, so the situation must have been considered unusually serious.

"The condition of the soldiers is much the same as it was two months ago. They now number about 50,000. The main fault is that the men do not have nearly enough to do. Sunday is not the only 'day off' with them, and I understand that the lack of employment and loafing which I noticed all over the north and centre of the city is typical of what goes on always.

"The soldiers' pay varies. I met some who were getting 3½ dollars and others 7½ dollars a-month. With the exception of the Ching-pei Chün (military police) the garrison has not been paid for nearly two months. This is certain, as is also the fact that there is no money available in Nanking for the purpose. The present state of the populace is decidedly panicky. A few days ago an unexpected and quite harmless noise caused a street full of shops to close their doors.

"The return of Chang Hsün is an ever-present bogy, threatening the coming of a counter-revolution. There has been no sign whatever of any anti-foreign feeling in Nanking. After dark the city is under martial law, and all the main roads are heavily patrolled by the military police."

2. In Soochow an outbreak was planned for the 1st June, but failed owing to its premature disclosure to the authorities. His Majesty's Minister has received the following account of the affair through His Majesty's consul-general at Shanghai :—

"About a month ago Niu Chêng Nieh (a Soochow man), who had been for three months acting military governor of Shantung, returned to Soochow and began to secretly preach sedition among the troops, claiming to be leader of the counter-revolution, aiming at exterminating the tu-tu and other officials, and putting himself at head of affairs. His adherents were K'uai (of the tu-tu's yamên) and several officers, including Colonel Chü of the Hsien Fêng Regiment and the majors commanding the 1st and 2nd battalions of it, whose men are mostly Kiangsu men, and ready to follow their officers. The 3rd battalion of it (Anhui men) and the 45th and 46th regiments, comprising the bulk of the rest of the garrison, refused to have anything to do with Niu. The outbreak was planned for noon, 1st June, but on the 31st May the major commanding the 3rd battalion of the Hsien Fêng Regiment reported the whole affair to the authorities. The tu-tu sent troops of body-guard with a battery to Hu Ch'ui barracks of the two battalions of mutineers, about 2 miles north-west of the city, and forced them to surrender about 10 P.M. on the 31st May, and give up their arms and equipment. K'uai and two of his brothers were arrested. Niu escaped, but Colonel Chü and three of his subordinates were caught next day (1st June), and K'uai, his brothers, and two of the subordinates were shot. On the 2nd June Colonel Chü and the two battalion commanders were tried by court martial, and it was said that one of them was to be shot on the 3rd. The men of the two mutinous battalions were each given 9 dollars and disbanded, and the loyal 3rd battalion of the Hsien Fêng Regiment was tranferred to the 45th regiment.

"The 600 troops sent up from Wu Sung-on the 2nd June were detrained at Wai Kua Tang, 10 miles north-east of Soochow, as the trouble was over, and their services were not required.

"I gathered the impression that if the outbreak had occurred as planned, and the tu-tu been slain, probably there would have been a general rising of the troops all over this part of the country."

His Majesty's consul-general at Shanghai, in forwarding this report, remarks on the similarity of the circumstances to those that ushered in the revolution at Hankow, and adds that the worst feature in the case is the paying off without punishment of some 1,000 disaffected soldiers, who will probably take to brigandage in the creeks near Shanghai.

3. At Chefoo the attitude of the Chinese soldiery appears to have been growing increasingly anti-foreign.

The senior consul, in forwarding, on the 10th June, to the British Minister, as dean of the diplomatic body, a letter from the Chefoo Chamber of Commerce regarding the ill effect on the trade of the port, due to the quartering of 8,000 soldiers on the inhabitants, remarks, inter alia, "We also regret to notice a rapidly growing hostile feeling towards foreigners on the part of these men, who are raw recruits, and a danger to friend and foe alike."

His Majesty's consul at Chefoo on the 11th June, speaks of the "anxiety" that was "once more beginning to be felt owing to the continued presence of the troops, whose numbers had been increased, and the lack of adequate funds with which to pay them."

He further mentions that acts of insolence " such as elaborate expectoration when a foreigner passes, and the sudden bursting forth into songs of an anti-foreign character on the part of troops meeting foreigners when on the march, or when passing foreign dwellings, are of fairly frequent occurrence. Chinese merchants," he adds, " fearing an eventual mutiny, are again, as they have already twice before done, sending their valuables, and in some cases their families, to Dairen or Tsingtau for safety. The silk and lace-producing centres in the interior are being overrun by bands of brigands and armed deserters."

4. At Chinan Fu a serious mutiny of provincial troops took place on the 13th and 14th June. The report of His Majesty's consul there of the affair is to the following effect :—

" It appears that some dissatisfaction has existed recently among the provincial troops (Hsün Fang Tui) stationed here, partly on account of a change in the general commanding, partly on account of a rumour in the native press, that the corps was to be disbanded.

" Stories are also abroad that agents for the restoration of the Monarchy have been trying to create sedition among the Hsün Fang Tui. Yet another report states that soldiers recently disbanded in Tien-tsin, hoping to share in the looting that would follow, had induced the Hsün Fang Tui to mutiny by representing that the latter would soon be thrown out of occupation too.

" In any case, early in the night of the 13th–14th June a large portion of the Hsün Fang Tui—a number, it seems, refused to join in the mutiny—left their barracks outside the east suburb and went to the arsenal, a couple of miles to the north of the city. Here they parleyed with the arsenal guard, also Hsün Fang Tui, the majority of whom joined the mutineers, and allowed them to provide themselves with arms and ammunition.

" They then returned and broke into the city by the east gate about 4 A.M., making use of a machine-gun in the course of their operations. By this time heavy guards of Luchün were already on the settlement, which lies to the west of the city. The latter fired—a foreigner who saw them says only in the air—on a number of mutineers who skirted the settlement to try and enter the city on the West. No looting was attempted on the settlement, and this seems to have been all the firing that occurred there.

" Meanwhile the looters had got into the city and proceeded to loot the main streets. I was not awakened until about 5, when considerable rifle firing could be heard inside the city, about a mile and a-half from the consulate. This continued till about 7 A M. A large fire also broke out which burnt all the houses for a distance of some 300 yards along the main street and for a considerable distance back on either side. Most of the disturbance was in the Hsi Ta Ch'ieh, the one big street of the city where all the wealthy business houses are. Good shops were, however, also looted in other parts ; very little looting went on in the suburbs.

" The post office, all the native banks, and practically all the big shops have been looted. I have heard no estimate of losses yet, but the amount must be considerable.

" The majority of the looters were, of course, Hsün Fang Tui, but it is said that a few of the ordinary police, the constabulary (Ching Wei Tui) and Luchün in the city could not resist the temptation to join in when they saw looting going on under their eyes. A number of the riffraff also joined in.

" A portion of the 94th regiment of Luchün was in the city and, except in a few cases, remained faithful. I do not know how far they really tried to quell the outbreak. The firing was heavy for three hours, but the loss of life has been very small, and it is said that the soldiers only fired in the air.

" About 7 A.M. the looters began to leave the city, making coolies carry their booty before them. They went to the hills to the south and out into the surrounding country. Nothing appears to have been done to stop them.

" Desultory firing, which gradually became less and less and finally resolved itself into occasional single shots, continued till noon. About 2 P.M. a heavy downfall of rain, lasting for an hour, did much to restore order and quench smouldering fires.

" As soon as I was awakened I telephoned to the governor, who personally told me that 1,000 men had mutinied.

" I heard afterwards that he had sent his own wife and family to the Roman Catholic Mission, the only foreigners in the actual city itself, which is not very far from his yamên.

" I may mention here that before 7 A.M. sixty Chinese ladies and children, all belonging to the families of officials, a number of whom live in this neighbourhood, had come to the English mission for refuge.

"Going to the yamên I passed through the streets where most of the damage had been done; I saw no dead bodies about; fires were still smouldering, and there was evidence of a great deal of damage. Everything was quite quiet, and I had no difficulty in getting along. It was quite suspected at this time that a number of Hsün Fang Tui were still in the city, and that some who had gone out with loot in the morning had returned to engage in further rioting during the night. How the Luchün would behave was also a matter of surmise. Some anxiety was felt, but the night passed quiet quietly. The streets of the city were cleared by Luchün at 7 P.M., and no one was allowed in them after that time.

"The following afternoon the governor sent a messenger to the German consul to say that the governor guaranteed the safety of all foreigners, and that they would be protected by the Luchün, whom he considered reliable.

"I do not think there is any cause for alarm in the present situation : everything depends on the attitude of the Luchün (the 5th division of regulars). General Ma has considerable personal influence with his troops, and is believed to have them well in hand. The fact that they have not broken out in the first two nights after the mutiny is a good sign for the future."

This report of Consul Smith disposes of the rumours of the governor having sought safety in flight to the Roman Catholic Mission. He appears, on the other hand, to have shown commendable courage and to have personally accompanied the troops.

5. At Mukden the 3rd regiment of the 2nd Manchurian Mixed Brigade mutinied at 10 P.M. on the night of the 19th June. Captain Cardew, R.E., a language student residing there, briefly telegraphed me information of the occurrence on the 20th inst. Subsequent information published by Reuter's agency here states that indiscriminate shooting occurred until daylight. The Bank of Communications in the north suburb outside the city was looted and burnt, as were several other banks and jewellers' shops. Loss of life was slight. Foreigners were not interferred with in any way. Foreign women and children sought refuge in the British consulate-general. About 100 houses were burned, but by noon the fires were extinguished.

Captain Cardew's message states that the mutineers failed to enter the city.

It is noteworthy that this outbreak occurred in quite one of the best bodies of troops in the Chinese army. The 2nd Manchurian Mixed Brigade was a special body of troops formed from the Pei-yang divisions of the Luchün, and lent to Manchuria, pending the formation of local divisions in the three eastern provinces. These Pei-yang divisions, the 2nd and 4th, were the only two divisions left under the control of Yuan Shih-kai (then Viceroy of Chih-li), when the remaining metropolitan divisions were placed directly under the War Office. I would further recall the fact that this 2nd Manchurian Mixed Brigade was staunchly loyalist at the time of the revolution, and refused to be seduced from its allegiance by its commander, Lan Tien Wei, who left his brigade and subsequently commanded a body of revolutionary troops which came up from Shanghai to Chefoo for the Northern Punitive Expedition.

6. Shanghai.—At Shanghai, on the 19th June, according to Reuter's agency, an outbreak occurred in the afternoon in the Chinese city in connection with the soldier's· pay. One soldier was killed and a few others were injured ; but the affair otherwise was not serious.

A telegram from Shanghai, dated the 17th June, and published in the "Peking Daily News" of the 18th June, mentioned that the wages of the arsenal troops had been duly paid, but not that of the Chapei troops. General Li had offered to pay the latter one dollar each in advance, which they had refused. The reason why their pay had not been issued was not known.

7. At Cho-chou, between Peking and Pao-ting Fu, trouble occurred among the troops of the 3rd division some days ago. Colonel I-tung-ts'ai, of the 9th infantry regiment, was killed by his own men.

8. At Pai K'ou Ho (near Liu-li Ho), some 30 miles south-west of Peking, the 5th and 6th Yings (camps or battalions), of the Huai Chün (Chih-li provincial troops) are reported to have deserted with their arms within the last few days.

9. At Hai-tien, the barracks of the Guards alongside the Summer Palace, there has undoubtedly been of late some considerable unrest in that corps. It appears that there has been an intention to send considerable Manchu detachments of the Guards to the eastern and western Imperial Mausolea, the Chinese portion of the Guards being left at Hai-tien. This separation of the corps gave rise to suspicion of early disbandment.

It is difficult to obtain information, as the Chinese authorities are very reticent about the matter; but it seems, at any rate, certain that there has been some serious unrest, and that some executions have taken place (it is said, even of officers).

10. *Foochow.*—His Majesty's consul, writing on the 15th May, says: "During the first few days of May a state of comparative uneasiness existed. It was stated that the Hunanese soldiers, long dissatisfied with their pay and unfriendly to the Fukienese, contemplated a general massacre of the latter. Large numbers of the inhabitants left the city. Enigmatic leaflets were distributed with the object of exciting the people, and the United States and German consuls asked for gunboats, which were sent. The decapitation of a disorderly soldier resulted in his comrades wrecking the Shen-pang-ting (court of justice), but quiet was restored by a body of soldiers sent by the orders of the military governor.

12. *Hsin-yang Chou.*—According to the "Peking Daily News" of the 18th June, a military uprising is reported. Discontented soldiers, aided by local ruffians and disbanded troops, are stated to have started an uprising, which began with the machine-gun company, which left barracks without leave on the 30th May. Soldiers stationed at Chu-chia Chai, Hsin-tien, Kuang-shui, and Liu-ying joined in the mutiny. The trouble was at its height between the 12th and 14th June. The mutineers were induced to surrender their arms and be disbanded, officers with two months' pay, soldiers with half a month's pay. Except for officers and men arrested before then, the mutineers were given a general amnesty. Those arrested are awaiting trial by court-martial. The country in the neighbourhood is now said to be quiet. (Hsin-yang Chou is on the Peking–Hankow line near the southern border of Ho-nan.)

13. *Lanchow Fu (Kan Su).*—According to an East Asiatic Lloyd telegram, dated Shanghai, the 18th June, a mutiny occurred in the artillery there owing to their pay not having been issued. After a considerable amount of firing the riot was suppressed.

14. *Canton.*—According to Reuter's correspondent at Hong Kong, telegrams from Shameen state that firing occurred on the night of the 14th June opposite the foreign concessions (Shameen), where soldiers pursuing rebels kept up an erratic fusillade for ten minutes, whereby several passers-by were killed or wounded, including a Chinese doctor.

An unsatisfactory feature of these occurrences is the timidity or the powerlessness of the authorities to punish military indiscipline, which can only grow worse with continued impunity. That the situation at the capital is regarded as not altogether satisfactory by the Central Government is indicated by orders issued to the traffic department of the Peking–Mukden Railway for certain important movements of troops from the neighbourhood of Ching-wang-tao to Peking between the 18th and 23rd June. The amount of rolling-stock indented for to convey troops from Tang-ho (near Ching-wang-tao), Pei-tai-ho, and Liu-shou-ying (near Pei-tai-ho) was: 9 first-class, 53 third-class, 10 ballast cars, and 37 covered cars, which would suffice for the carriage of a mixed brigade of 4,000–5,000 men. A telegram, however, received from the officer commanding the British post at Fengt'ai at 11 P.M. to-night, informs me that the movement is in abeyance, *i.e.*, that the traffic department have been informed that they need not now send the rolling-stock. The orders given in the first instance, nevertheless, are a significant sign of the times.

M. E. WILLOUGHBY, *Lieutenant-Colonel, Military Attaché.*

Peking, July 20, 1912.

No. 52.

Sir J. Jordan to Sir Edward Grey.—(Received July 11.)

Sir, *Peking, June 24, 1912.*

I HAVE the honour to state that I have received the following information from His Majesty's consul-general at Kashgar dealing with the progress of the revolutionary movement in the New Dominion:—

Differences between the conservative Governor of Urumtchi and the republican leader in possession of Ili led to active hostilities on the 1st April, resulting in the defeat of Governor Yuan with a loss of 1,000 men. On the 13th April the Ko Ming Tang made a disturbance at Aksu and killed both the taotai and the prefect. The news of this event created a profound impression at Kashgar. The taotai promptly cut off his queue, advising the Chinese to do likewise. He further had a scroll hung up in his yamên with the words "Long live the Chinese Republic." Some of the officials, however, including Chiao Titai, the military governor, refused to commit themselves, and retained their queues.

Towards the end of April the taotai and the titai (military governor) of Kashgar composed their differences, the latter having unfeignedly declared in favour of the republic and shorn his queue. The tension between Ili and Urumtchi also relaxed owing to the Governor of Urumtchi realising the hopelessness of his position and tendering his resignation. Mr. Macartney states that the Kashgar population remained peaceful, looking upon the struggle as one of purely Chinese concern.

In May the disturbances were renewed by the murder, on the 5th, of the Prefect of Kucha, and, on the 7th, of Yuen Taotai, who had accepted the post of republican governor, and of the district magistrate of Kashgar. The titai proclaimed himself governor and the city was panic-stricken. The assassins, however, elected other officials to the vacancies and tore down the republican flags. Nevertheless the coup did not appear to have been made by anti-republicans so much as by disbanded soldiers and vagabonds. To satisfy these latter the titai organised them into a new regiment, and since that date Kashgar has practically been at their mercy. The civil and military officials are only able to guide them by following them. On the 20th May Mr. Macartney telegraphed that this gang now numbered 500 strong, and was levying blackmail on the authorities. The taotai elected by them was in a state of terror and acted under their orders. By the end of the month, however, the ringleaders had already begun to quarrel amongst themselves. Foreigners have not been interfered with.

I have, &c.
J. N. JORDAN.

No. 53.

Sir J. Jordan to Sir Edward Grey.—(Received July 15.)

Sir,   *Peking, June 28, 1912.*
THE sudden departure of Tong Shao-yi for Tien-tsin and his subsequent resignation of the post of Premier have caused considerable interest and speculation in Peking, and have generally been regarded as an indication that the Cantonese element of which Tong is the most prominent representative is discontented with the policy of Yuan Shih-kai and his Government. There has been a perceptible and growing estrangement between the President and the Premier for some time past, and it has been evident that their old friendship would no longer bear the strain of acute political differences. As negotiator between the north and the south at the Shanghai Conference, Tong claimed to be the founder of the republic, and was inclined to arrogate to himself a larger share of authority than the President was disposed to yield. Tong belonged to the extreme faction of the republican party, and had behind him the influence of Sun Yat-sen, Huang-hsing, and other leaders in the south. The President, on the other hand, stood for the nation as a whole, and eschewed all connection with the numerous political parties which the revolutionary changes have called into existence. The resignation of their chief led to the withdrawal of several other members of the Cabinet, and for a time it looked as if the President would find it difficult to carry on a Government. As it is, the new appointments are not likely to strengthen his position in the country. The Foreign Minister, Lu Chêng-hsiang, who has taken over the duties of Premier, has spent all his official life abroad, and has no knowledge or experience of his own country. He is extremely amiable and agreeable, but has none of the qualifications of a leader of men, and his health will probably prove a bar to his remaining in office for any length of time. The President remains the only strong man in the country, and seems undeterred by the desertion of his friends or the calumnies of his enemies. The latter recently spread a rumour that he was aiming at the Throne. To meet this, he issued a manifesto (copy enclosed), in which he asked the world to believe that he had been a convert to republican ideas long before the revolution broke out, and took high heaven to witness that he would never be false to the charge the nation had confided to him.

I have, &c.
J. N. JORDAN.

67

Enclosure in No. 53.

Yuan Shih-kai to Li Yuan-hung and the Provincial Tu-Tus.

(Telegraphic.) *Peiching Jih Pao, June 26, 1912.*
FROM my student days I, Yuan Shih-kai, have admired the example of the Emperors Yao and Shun who treated the Empire as a public trust, and considered that the record of a dynasty in history for good or ill is inseparably bound up with the public spirit or self-seeking by which it has been animated. On attaining middle age I grew more familiar with foreign affairs, was struck by the admirable republican systems in France and America, and felt that they were a true embodiment of the democratic precepts of the ancients. When last year the patriotic crusade started in Wuchang its echoes went forth into all the provinces, with the result that this ancient nation with its 2,000 years of despotism adopted with one bound the republican system of government. It was my good fortune to see this glorious day at my life's late eve ; I cherished the hope that I might dwell in the seclusion of my own home and participate in the blessings of an age of peace. But once again my fellow-country-men honoured me with the pressing request that I should again assume a heavy burden, and on the day on which the republic was proclaimed I announced to the whole nation that never again shall a monarchy be permitted in China. At my inauguration I again took this solemn oath in the sight of heaven above and earth beneath. Yet of late ignorant persons in the provinces have fabricated wild rumours to delude men's minds, and have adduced the career of the First Napoleon on which to base their erroneous speculations. It were best not to enquire as to their motives ; in some cases misconception may be the cause, in others deliberate malice. The republic has now been proclaimed for six months ; so far there is no prospect of recognition from the Powers, while order is far from being restored in the provinces. Our fate hangs upon a hair ; the slightest negligence may forfeit all. I, who bear this arduous responsibility, feel it my bounden duty to stand at the helm in the hope of successfully breasting the wild waves. But while those in office are striving with all their might to effect a satisfactory solution, spectators seem to find a difficulty in maintaining a generous forbearance. They forget that I, who have received this charge from my countrymen, cannot possible look dispassionately on when the fate of the nation is in the balance. If I were aware that the task was impossible and played a part of easy acquiescence, so that the future of the republic might become irreparable, others might not reproach me, but my own conscience would never leave me alone. My thoughts are manifest in the sight of high heaven. But at this season of construction and dire crisis how shall these mutual suspicions find a place ? Once more I issue this announcement ; if you, my fellow-countrymen, do indeed place the safety of China before all other considerations, it behoves you to be large-minded. Beware of lightly heeding the plausible voice of calumny, and of thus furnishing a medium for fostering anarchy. If evilly-disposed persons, who are bent on destruction, seize the excuse for sowing dissension to the jeopardy of the situation, I, Yuan Shih-kai, shall follow the behest of my fellow-countrymen in placing such men beyond the pale of humanity. A vital issue is involved. It is my duty to lay before you my inmost thought so that suspicion may be dissipated. "Those who know have the right to impose their censure." It is for public opinion to judge. Such is my announcement, and I ask you to take due note.

No. 54.

Sir J. Jordan to Sir Edward Grey.—(Received July 22.)

Sir, *Peking, July 5, 1912.*
THE accompanying report on the Postal Service, which has been unanimously adopted by the National Council, is a significant illustration of the attitude which responsible authorities in this country are adopting towards all institutions of a foreign character. It is proposed that the French Postmaster-General, M. Piry, shall be relieved of all administrative powers, and be reduced to the position of "a first-class

[1270] F 2

68

adviser," who is not to concern himself as to whether his advice is accepted or not. The other foreigners in the service are to be placed on the same footing as Chinese employés, and are to be dismissed if they disobey the Chinese chief of the Postal Department.

I have, &c.
J. N. JORDAN.

Enclosure in No. 54.

Report on the Petition to recover the Administration of the Postal Service.

THE Postal Service was handed over to the Ministry of Communications under the late régime, but there have been constant complaints, and the real control of the service has not yet passed over to the board.

The articles contained in the petition, after careful investigation, are found to be true, and the three suggestions offered by the petitioners are practicable. Therefore, it is hoped that the Government be requested to put them into effect.

Tseng Yu Lan (Kiangsi), the chairman of the committee, reported the result of the meeting. He said that there were many grievances set forth in Hung Nung's petition.

1.—(1.) The Postmaster-General Piry's usurpation of authority :—

(a.) His refusal to acknowledge the late Director-General, Yuan Chang Kwan.

(b.) His insistence upon taking over control of the postal college, and appointing foreign postal officers there as teachers.

(c.) Disparaging the worth of graduates of the postal college and those studying postal systems abroad.

(d.) Giving undue promotions to foreigners.

(2.) Ambiguity in the postal accounts :—

(a.) Though the service is progressing each year, yet there are deficits.

(b.) The sale of Hsuan Tung commemoration stamps and the profit made in the increase of postage from 2 to 3 cents were both intended to make up the advances obtained from the customs ; but these were appropriated for the general promotion of the foreign staff.

(c.) Increasing the number of head offices, in order to give promotion to some foreigners and make them district postmasters, having no regard to their heavy cost.

(3.) Partiality in the treatment of the native and foreign staffs :—

(a.) Responsible positions of postmasters, accountants, inspectors, and postal officers are exclusively occupied by foreigners.

(b.) Promotions for foreigners are quick and easy, but those for Chinese are exceedingly slow.

(c.) With Chinese there are no allowances, but with foreigners there are allowances of all sorts.

(d.) Foreigners absconding with official funds are as a rule excused, but Chinese absconding are sent to prison.

(e.) During the last revolt of soldiers the letter carriers never deserted, and when they asked for half a-month's extra pay it was refused, on the ground that the service lacked funds. But at the same time, for the luxury of the foreign staff, a large amount was spent in building a stable.

The following are suggestions regarding the treatment of Mr. Piry :—

(1.) Promote him to be a first-class adviser.

(2.) He should advise the Minister, Vice-Minister, and the councillor.

(3.) He should be relieved of all administrative powers.

(4.) His salary should remain the same.

(5.) A contract should be made with him.

(6.) He may in future make suggestions, but it shall not concern him whether they are accepted or not.

2. The foreign staff:—

(1.) Until the promulgation of the official postal system they are to remain the same; but when the system has been promulgated their positions shall be defined.

(2.) They shall obey the chief of the postal department of the board, or be dismissed.

(3.) The pay of both foreign and Chinese staffs shall be similar, with the exception of a special allowance to the former.

(4.) They shall receive a letter of engagement from the board, and all other documents of that nature shall be cancelled.

(5.) They are only entitled to pay and allowance, and no other expenses.

3. How to improve the service :—

(1.) Fix an official system.
(2.) There should be two accountants in every head office.
(3.) One accountant should be a Chinese.
(4.) The service should use the Chinese language, and when dealing with foreigners use French.
(5.) Hereafter, should any new foreigner be employed, he should undergo an entrance examination, and be promoted in the same way as his Chinese colleagues.
(6.) The head post-office in the board should be abolished.
(7.) After the head office in the board has been abolished, all the foreigners there should receive suitable posts from the board.

As these suggestions of the petitioners seem practicable, the chairman is of opinion that the Government should be requested to take the necessary measures.

The speaker then put the report to vote, which was passed. It was also agreed to dispense with the second and third readings.

No. 55.

Sir J. Jordan to Sir Edward Grey.—(Received July 22.)

Sir,   Peking, July 6, 1912.
WITH reference to my despatch of the 7th ultimo, I have the honour to forward herewith a summary by Sir S. Head of events in the provinces during the month of June.

I have, &c.
J. N. JORDAN.

Enclosure in No. 55.

Summary of Events in the Provinces during the month of June, 1912.

THE past month has been chiefly characterised by sporadic outbreaks amongst the troops at Mukden, Tsinanfu, and other centres. This aspect of the situation has been fully reported upon by the military attaché. The object in all cases seems to have been the same, namely loot, and foreigners have not been molested. At Mukden the soldiers are said to have been paid up to the end of May, but so many deductions were made for food, uniform, and other necessaries, as well as for an enforced contribution towards the national funds, that the actual amount received by them was very small. They were accordingly much discontented and resolved to make up their arrears in what has now almost become the recognised way. The severe punishment meted out to the chief offenders has in no wise diminished their ill-feeling.

The situation at Chefoo which was showing signs of improvement in April has again given cause for serious anxiety, and the consular body have urged that steps should be taken for the immediate disbandment of the large number of troops (about 8,000) quartered round the city. The Central Government have decided to devote 400,000 taels out of the recent advance of 3,000,000 taels to the pay and disbandment of the troops in North Shantung, and 300,000 taels are said to have been already remitted to Chefoo for that purpose. General Chu Tung-fang was sent by

Yuan Shih-kai to superintend the disbandment, but on his arrival he found that no arrangements had yet been made ; and the situation there is still described as critical. Szechuan continues to apply to daily life the tenets of the revolutionary agitators. Mr. Brown reports from Chungking that it may be assumed without exaggeration that general insecurity of life and property exist everywhere throughout that part of the province except within the walls of the larger towns ; while the smaller towns are given over to the joys of anarchical government. Tales of peculation of public funds pour in from all sides ; the war notes are no longer accepted, except under compulsion, by the merchants, and there is every indication of approaching bankruptcy. Nevertheless this same part of the province would appear to be taking the lead in the matter of the national subscription, over which it is displaying great enthusiasm. It is said that 500,000 taels have been already remitted to Peking, and that another 1,200,000 taels will shortly follow. The promoters of the agitation actually mention 100,000,000 taels as the most conservative estimate of the amount which will be eventually forthcoming, but it will be a matter for general surprise if they should realise anything approaching this large sum. Meetings are held and lectures given for this purpose ; the officers are said to have announced their intention of giving one month's pay, and the men from 60 to 70 per cent. of a month's pay towards the cause. A bureau with an executive of six has been established to forward the movement and supervise the collection of the funds, and all the guilds have undertaken to urge their members to contribute. The anti-foreign feeling roused by the loan proposals would seem to have largely subsided on their nature being explained to the people at the instance of Yuan Shih-kai. The Chungking native press have addressed a letter to the acting consul couched in friendly terms, assuring him that the subscription movement is a purely patriotic one, and has no anti-foreign bias.

In contrast to Szechuan, His Majesty's consul at Chinkiang reports that there is no trace of any anti-loan agitation in that district. The interests of the Chinkiang people seem to be chiefly local, and ideas as to the future of the republic do not go beyond those interests. There is a lukewarm attempt at raising contributions to the national fund, but this is associated in the minds of the people with a kind of census which is being taken with a view to the levying of a poll-tax.

His Majesty's consul at Nanking reports that unrest in the army is on the increase both at Nanking and elsewhere in the province of Kiangsu. The 3rd Brigade has been bribed into submission by the payment in the case of the soldiers of 12 dollars and travelling expenses for each man, and in the case of officers of two months' pay, in return for which they have agreed to forfeit all arrears due and disband quietly. There has been trouble, however, since with other regiments, notably at Linhuaikan, where the townspeople have only been able to purchase immunity from looting by a payment in cash of 3,000 dollars, a bargain which they have been told only holds good for a week. On the 3rd July a serious outbreak with the usual looting and burning took place at Wuhu.

General Chang Hsün, having moved into his new building at Yenchoufu, as mentioned in last month's summary, has now been induced to return the rolling-stock held by him to the Tien-tsin–Pukow Railway. Traffic on this line is developing rapidly ; but it is threatened with a check by the proposed establishment at the Pukow terminus of a *li-kin* station from which it has hitherto been free.

On the 14th June, Cheng Te Chuan, the military governor of Kiangsu, arrived at Nanking from Soochow, and General Huang Hsing left for Shanghai the same night.

From information supplied to the acting consul-general at Hankow, the general situation in Honan is at present practically normal and gives no cause for anxiety.

At Foochow a general state of nervousness and unrest still prevails, and that part of the country cannot be said to be turning to any good account the practical independence which it at present enjoys.

Beyond the detention of the British motor-launch " Chit On " at the end of May, there have been very few acts of piracy on the West River. Brigandage on land, however, continues to be prevalent in the Wuchow district. Small robber bands of ten or twelve rove around pillaging isolated houses. The Government lives from hand to mouth, while indulging in a fruitless dispute regarding the proposal to remove the provincial capital to Nanning. The gentry are split up into factions and quarrelling amongst themselves, and it is calculated that there are not sufficient funds to pay the troops beyond a month.

S. H.

No. 56.

War Office to Foreign Office.—(Received July 26.)

Sir,   *War Office, July 25, 1912.*

I AM commanded by the Army Council to inform you, with reference to your letter dated the 26th June, 1912, that, in view of the opinions expressed by the Secretary of State for Foreign Affairs, they have decided to replace the Royal Inniskilling Fusiliers —due to leave North China during the coming trooping season—by another battalion of British infantry.

2. The relief will be carried out early in November.

I am, &c.
E. W. D. WARD.

No. 57.

Sir J. Jordan to Sir Edward Grey.—(Received August 2.)

(Telegraphic.)   *Peking, August 2, 1912.*

AN agreement was signed yesterday appointing Dr. Morrison as political adviser to the Chinese Government for five years.

No. 58.

Sir J. Jordan to Sir Edward Grey.—(Received August 26.)

Sir,   *Peking, August 5, 1912.*

I HAVE the honour to enclose the translation of a note which I have received from the Wai-chiao Pu, reaffirming, in the case of provincial railways, the principle laid down that loans contracted with foreigners will not be considered valid unless they have been previously sanctioned by the Chinese Government.

I have issued circular instructions to His Majesty's consular officers requesting them to bring the contents of this communication to the notice of British subjects residing in their several districts.

I have, &c.
J. N. JORDAN.

Enclosure in No. 58.

Wai-chiao Pu to Sir J. Jordan.

Sir,   *July 25, 1912.*

IN former times if provincial officials had recourse to foreign loans to meet urgent public requirements, they were invariably obliged to report the matter beforehand to the throne, and, the consent of the Central Government having been given, by way of recording and authenticating the transaction, an official communication on the subject was addressed to the Minister in Peking of the country concerned. The foreign merchant making the loan was also required to report the matter in the first instance to his Minister in Peking and ascertain through the latter from the Central Government that a memorial on the subject had been submitted to the throne, before he undertook to make the loan. If there were no record of the Imperial sanction having been thus obtained, and the foreigner lent the money simply on his own authority, the State, irrespective of any contract which might have been made, did not recognise the trans-action at all, and, in the event of complications ensuing, took no steps on behalf of the lender for the recovery of the money.

The above conditions were notified by the then Tsungli Yamên in an official com-munication, dated the 4th December, 1891, to the Foreign Ministers at Peking, who were desired to convey the information to the merchants of their respective countries; there have been constant instances of the adoption of the procedure therein laid down.

Several cases have recently come to the knowledge of the Wai-chiao Pu in which railways in the provinces under commercial management have had recourse to foreign loans without reporting to, or requesting the consent of, the Central Government, and have, on their own authority, concluded the terms of the loan with foreign merchants or other persons direct.

In order, therefore, to guard against possible abuses, it is necessary to reaffirm the existing stipulation and to state definitely that in future no foreign loan contracted by any railway in the provinces, even though under commercial management, can be valid unless it has been submitted to, and allowed by, the Central Government, and also that foreign merchants, before concluding the terms of any loan, must report to the Minister of their nationality at Peking and request him to ascertain definitely whether Government has given its sanction to the transaction, before undertaking to make the loan, with a view to securing satisfactory safeguards.

I have the honour to communicate the above information to your Excellency for notification to the British mercantile community throughout the country.

I avail, &c.

(Seal of the Wai-chiao Pu).

No. 59.

Sir J. Jordan to Sir Edward Grey.—(Received August 21.)

Sir,
Peking, August 6, 1912.

WITH reference to my despatch of the 6th ultimo, I have the honour to forward herewith a summary by Sir S. Head of events in the provinces during the month of July.

I have, &c.
J. N. JORDAN.

Enclosure in No. 59.

Summary of Events in the Provinces during the month of July 1912.

THOUGH the state of affairs throughout the country still leaves much to be desired, the past month shows a certain improvement of a negative nature. There have been no serious outbreaks amongst the troops ; disbandment is being gradually effected ; the people are wearying of politics and returning to their harvests ; and the agitation in connection with the national subscription shows signs of dying out through lack of serious support.

His Majesty's consul at Tsinan-fu reports that affairs there are resuming a normal aspect after the mutiny of the previous month. Steps are being taken for the disbandment of the central division, which it is hoped to effect within three months. The governor himself inspects the troops every week or two and dismisses them in small batches of about 200 at a time.

General Ch'u T'ung-feng, who had been sent to superintend the disbandment of the troops at Chefoo, was at first under some difficulty owing to the lack of proper instructions from Peking to the local authorities ; but he has now drawn up a scheme which should prove satisfactory if only the necessary funds are forthcoming. Towards the middle of the month the situation at Chefoo again became critical owing to an outburst of queue-cutting mania on the part of soldiers and rowdies. Gangs of men armed with rifles and shears paraded the streets and removed the queues of all with whom they came in contact. This lasted for two days, causing a general panic amongst all classes of the population ; shops were closed and the streets deserted. A serious feature of the campaign was the complete indifference shown towards the rights of foreigners. One gang burst into a foreign shop and cut off the queues of all the Chinese staff. Meeting a messenger attached to a consulate, in uniform and carrying an official despatch, they docked his queue without the slightest hesitation. They also tried to enter Messrs. Cornabe, Eckford, and Co.'s offices and were only prevented by a show of force. They succeeded in getting into the compound of Messrs. Toche and Co., a French firm, but were ejected without difficulty. A lady in a ricksha was stopped and made to wait while the coolie was operated on ; and a small child, 8 years old, who had strayed from the Anglican Mission compound, was caught and seriously cut in the course of its struggles. The consular body protested strongly to the acting governor, and finally General Lien, in command of the majority of the troops, himself paraded the streets, revolver in hand, to restore order. The local authorities subsequently expressed their regret to the consular body for the disregard shown by the soldiers towards foreign property; at the instance of the acting British consul, General Lien posted up a notice threatening severe punishment for any repetition of this offence. General Lien has now been placed in command of all the troops at Chefoo and is endeavouring to co-operate with General Ch'u in the disbandment.

At Nanking His Majesty's consul reports that confidence is rapidly reviving amongst all classes under the energetic rule of Governor Cheng. Although Peking only remitted to Cheng 200,000 taels out of the 2,000,000 promised, they have allowed him to intercept 250,000 taels out of the contribution of 500,000 taels made by Szechuan province to the National Loan Fund; but of this latter sum only 100,000 taels has actually reached him. The governor has used this money to disband some 2,000 to 3,000 miscellaneous soldiers from different regiments. All that these latter have received over and above their pay has been 8½ dollars for travelling expenses; but unfortunately it has transpired that large numbers of them have spent the money in riotous living in the city and are now wandering about destitute, to the alarm of the more peaceful inhabitants. Cheng Te Chuan is proving equally active in the reform of the civil administration and is rapidly evolving order out of the chaos left by General Huang Hsing, but he has great difficulty in obtaining sufficient funds even for current expenses.

The province of Kiangsi is reported to be gradually resuming its normal conditions, and the disbandment of troops is being effected there without trouble. A similar state of affairs is reported from Hupeh, where General Li claims now to have only some 60,000 men under his command—about one-half the number he had a few months ago.

In Hunan, Shensi, Kansuh, and Honan matters are still very unsettled, though there is said to be no danger whatever to foreigners, and brigandage and terrorism still prevail. At Honan-fu there was a mutiny accompanied by looting on the 10th July. At Kaifeng a body of some thirty armed men entered the provincial Parliament on the 27th July and cleared out the members, wounding some ten or twenty of them. The assailants were dressed in civilian clothes, but they are said to have been soldiers whose object was to overawe the Assembly, which had been recently criticising their action. Dr. Gray, of His Majesty's Legation, has gone to Kaifeng at the request of the Chinese authorities to render medical assistance to the wounded members. Fortunately the harvest prospects in Honan are exceptionally good, and it is hoped, therefore, that this may induce large numbers of the men to return to their homes.

Szechuan remains disturbed by dissensions between the high officials, but it is hoped that the dispatch of the more rowdy elements of the population on the expedition to Thibet may remove the immediate cause of unrest. The anti-foreign agitation in connection with the loan proposals would seem to have collapsed, though the movement for a national subscription continues, but is no longer received with the same enthusiasm. A large number of the higher subscriptions are said to have been paid in the military notes issued last year by the provincial Governments and which are now practically unnegotiable. The total amounts received up to date at Peking, or on their way, have been published by the Ministry of Finance as follows :—

					Taels.
Hunan	..	..	..	..	300,000 received.
Honan	..	..	..	..	300,000 not received.
Shen-ching	..	..	..	..	500,000 received.
Kirin	..	..	..	..	800,000 not received.
Heilung-chiang	..	..	..	..	150,000 received.
Chengtu	..	..	..	..	500,000 received.
Chungking	..	..	..	..	1,000,000 on the way.
Nanchang	..	..	..	..	200,000; only 100,000 taels received.
Kwangtung	..	..	..	..	1,000,000; only 360,000 taels received.
Kwangtung Chamber of Commerce	..	..			380,000 all received.
Yunnan	..	..	..	..	200,000 all received.
Kueilin	..	..	..	..	200,000 received.

Total, 5,530,000 taels (about 730,000*l.*), of which 2,690,000 taels (about 370,000*l.*) has been received.

In addition to the above, contributions have been sent by Chinese in the Straits Settlements, Philippines, &c. On the other hand, it must be remembered that Peking is not receiving any of the usual revenues from provincial taxation, but is, on the contrary, being urged from all sides with requests for money.

The southern provinces of Kuangsi, Kuangtung, and Fukien remain practically independent of control from Peking. The acting British consul at Wuchow reports that not a single civil official holds his appointment with the active concurrence of the Central Government, while the military officers are appointed and transferred by the sole authority of the tutu. In the only matter in which the Central Government attempted to interfere, namely, in regard to the transfer of the provincial capital to Nanning, it was compelled to yield to local wishes. The local authorities are doing their best to suppress the brigandage which still prevails in this province. Over 500 robbers have been beheaded at Wuchow alone during the past six months, and executions are said to have been carried out on the same scale in other parts of Kuangsi.

S. H.

No. 60.

Sir J. Jordan to Sir Edward Grey.—(Received September 5.)

(Telegraphic.)   *Peking, September 5, 1912.*
A WIDESPREAD military revolt appears to be imminent in the south and west of Yünnan, which it is suspected has been engineered by General Li Ken Yuan with the idea of restoring his prestige.

His Majesty's consul at Tengyueh considers a critical situation has arisen, and I have authorised him to use his discretion in withdrawing, if need be, to Burmah with other British subjects and missionaries at Talifu. He may apply to the Government of Burmah for an escort, should the Chinese refuse to supply it, and if, as seems possible, withdrawal cannot be effected without one.

No. 61.

Sir J. Jordan to Sir Edward Grey.—(Received September 14.)

Sir,   *Peking, August 28, 1912.*
THE execution of Chang Chen-wu and Fang-wei outside the walls of Peking in the early hours of Friday morning the 16th instant, by the orders of the President, after summary trial by court-martial, has evoked a good deal of criticism from those who fondly imagine that China has reached a stage of constitutional development when drastic measures of the kind are unnecessary and abhorrent in a republican country.

Chang Chen-wu, the better-known man of the two, was a teacher in a primary school at Wuchang, but threw in his lot with the revolution as a soldier, and rose rapidly to the post of vice-chief of the Bureau of Military Affairs. He appears to have rendered good service to the cause and to have earned the approbation of his chief, General Li Yuan-hung, which, however, he forfeited by his subsequent conduct. The indictment against him was contained in telegrams from the general to President Yuan, the Cabinet, and the Advisory Council, which have been given wide publicity. Some of the charges are of a rather vague nature, but he was accused, and doubtless justly, of having misappropriated funds and falsified accounts on a large scale, and of planning a military rising for the purpose of overthrowing the present Government. There is said to be evidence, though it has not been published, that his schemes included the assassination of the President and Vice-President, and the accession to power of Chen Chi-mei, late Tu-tu of Kiangsu, Huang-hsing, who was for a time Minister of War in the Provisional Government of Nanking, and himself—as President, Vice-President, and generalissimo, respectively. When he first became suspect Chang was offered a special appointment in Mongolia, with the double object of giving him an opportunity to reform and of removing him from the sphere of his activities, but he made impossible conditions and returned to Wuchang to renew his mischief-making. General Li thereupon persuaded him on some pretext to come to Peking again, where he could be disposed of with less risk of disturbance. He and his accomplice dined at an hotel in the Legation Quarter, and on repairing to their lodgings in the Chinese city were seized in the small hours of the morning and executed.

75

The Advisory Council at once demanded an explanation from the Government, and after some demur this was given by the Minister of War on the 23rd instant. The Government's defence, which I think can scarcely be disputed, was briefly that they had ample evidence of guilt, and that the safety of the State rendered the step they had taken imperative. Although the Hupeh members of the council accepted the President's explanations in a private interview, a large section of that body hold that the Government's defence does not justify what they regard as a breach of the constitution, and they have since been clamouring for the impeachment of the Premier and the Minister of War, but the necessary quorum has not hitherto been obtained. In spite of protests from various quarters, it is noticeable that at Wuchang, where the President's action might be expected to have provoked most criticism, it is upheld by the Chinese guilds. It does not, moreover, appear to have in any way retarded the growth of the mutual understanding which, from all accounts, is being established between President Yuan and Dr. Sun Yat-sen, and in which the hopes of a reconciliation between north and south are centred.

I have, &c.
J. N. JORDAN.

No. 62.

Sir J. Jordan to Sir Edward Grey.—(Received September 23.)

Sir,   *Peking, September 6, 1912.*
WITH reference to my despatch of the 6th ultimo, I have the honour to forward herewith a summary by Sir Somerville Head of events in the provinces during the month of August.

I have, &c.
J. N. JORDAN.

Enclosure in No. 62.

Summary of Events in the Provinces during the month of August.

AT the beginning of the month a mutiny broke out at Pukow owing to the delay in paying the troops, who had received nothing except a few cents on account since March, although funds had recently been handed over to the military authorities for the purpose. The outbreak extended to Hsuchow-fu about 40 miles up the Tien-tsin-Pukow Railway. Order was quickly restored by General Po Wei with two regiments from Nanking; but the large majority of the mutineers are said to have escaped with their booty—which still seems to be the most effective method of disbandment employed in the Chinese army. At Nanking itself the work of paying off the troops continues slowly as far as funds permit. Unfortunately, it has not been found possible to disband the officers as well as the men, and the former have been given temporary commissions as military aides-de-camp to the governor. About 300 such commissions have already been issued. The same difficulty with the officers has been experienced in Shantung, where disbandment is also slowly proceeding.

Some excitement was caused at the end of July by the account published in the papers of the execution at Sian-fu of a Roman Catholic native priest on a trumped up charge. The state of affairs throughout Shensi is still very unsettled, and it has not yet been found possible to permit lady missionaries to return to that province.

In Szechuan and other central provinces the harvest has been good, but the scarcity of silver and general lack of confidence has prevented any return to normal conditions of prosperity. The national subscription movement no longer finds any supporters, the people being now completely disillusioned as to the possibility of reorganising the country by this means. In reply to an enquiry from the lieutenant-commander of His Majesty's ship "Snipe," His Majesty's consul at Ichang informed him on the 13th August that there was nothing in the present situation at that port to render the constant presence of a ship necessary, and it is probable that the "Snipe" has now moved lower down the river.

A critical state of affairs is reported from Yünnan-fu and Tengyueh. There would appear to be much disaffection amongst the troops in this province. Tsai, the Military Governor of Yünnan-fu, has left in some haste for Mengtse; while the notorious General Li Ken Yuan is still paramount in the west, and is said to be stirring up trouble.

There is nothing to add to the previous report respecting the situation in the remaining provinces. Mongolia and the New Dominion in the north and Kuangtung in the south would seem to be going from bad to worse.

S. H.

No. 63.

Sir J. Jordan to Sir Edward Grey.—(Received September 23.)

Sir,   *Peking, September 6, 1912.*

WITH reference to my despatch of the 29th May last, I have the honour to enclose herewith copy of the second quarterly report from the International Bankers' Commission at Shanghai, showing the appropriation of the customs revenue during the three months ended the 31st July, 1912.

The report shows that all instalments of principal and interest due up to the end of July on the loans secured by the customs revenue have been paid off, and that the balance in hand on the 31st July was 3,447,474 taels.

No payments were made during the quarter on account of the indemnity of 1901, and the balance at credit of the indemnity account was 1,348,116 taels. It may be noted here that as no payments on account of the indemnity have been made since the 30th September last, the amount due on the 31st July, 1912, was 2,487,412*l.*, exclusive of interest on arrears.

The enclosures in the report are summarised in the report itself, and I forward herewith only the last, a letter from the Deputy Commissioner of Customs at Shanghai, remitting 152,000 taels as a contribution from the *li-kin* revenue towards the service of the 4½ per Cent. Gold Loan of 1898. This loan is specially secured on certain *li-kin* revenues, and until January last it never formed a charge on the general customs revenue. The loan is, however, also secured on the general customs revenue, and the *li-kin* collection having been disorganised by the revolution, the service of the loan, which requires over 500,000 taels a-month, has had to be met since the beginning of this year entirely from the general revenue, with the exception of the comparatively small sum now remitted from *li-kin*.

I have, &c.
J. N. JORDAN.

Enclosure 1 in No. 63.

Secretary, International Bankers' Commission, to Sir J. Jordan.

Sir,   *Shanghai, August 13, 1912.*

WITH reference to your despatch of the 30th January last,* in which it is stated that the International Bankers' Commission shall furnish to the Diplomatic Body at Peking a quarterly report showing the appropriation of the customs revenue, I have the honour to hand you herewith† :—

1. Statement showing the total amount of revenue received and expended on account of Chinese Loan Service for quarter ended the 31st ultimo.

2. Copy of Inspector-General of Customs " Foreign Revenue Account " with the Hong Kong and Shanghai Bank from the 30th April to the 31st July.

3. Copy of the Commissioner of Customs, Shanghai, "Chinese Loan Service Account" with the Hong Kong and Shanghai Bank from the 30th April to the 31st July, together with certificate of balance.

4. Copy of the Commissioner of Customs, Shanghai, "Chinese Loan Service Account" with the Deutsch-Asiatische Bank, together with certificate of balance.

* See " China, No. 3 (1912)," No. 113.   † Not received at Foreign Office.

5. Copy of the Commissioner of Customs, Shanghai, "Chinese Loan Service Account" with the Russo-Asiatic Bank from the 30th April to the 31st July, together with certificate of balance.

6. List of instalments of principal and interest on Chinese loans paid through the Hong Kong and Shanghai Bank from the 30th April to the 31st July.

7. List of instalments of principal and interest on Chinese loans paid through the Deutsch-Asiatische Bank.

8. List of instalments of principal and interest on Chinese loans paid through the Russo-Asiatic Bank.

9. List of instalments of principal and interest on Chinese loans paid through the Chartered Bank of India, Australia, and China.

10. Copy of letter dated the 1st July from the Deputy Commissioner of Customs, Shanghai, forwarding 152,000 taels from the *li-kin* revenue account as remittance towards 4½ per Cent. Loan instalment, due the 5th idem.

From these statements it will be noticed that the total revenue collected from the 30th April to the 31st July amounted to 10,011,524·73 taels against 12,308,828·36 taels collected during first quarter.

Payments of loan instalment of principal and interest total 8,539,960·54 taels against 10,435,720·34 taels for the quarter ended the 30th April.

Interest on overdue instalments amounted to only 617·17 taels against 61,031·19 taels paid for the previous three months.

Credit interest amounting to 10,807·85 taels has been allowed by the three custodian banks at the rate of 2 per cent. on the account standing in their books.

All instalments of principal and interest due up to and including the 31st July have been paid off, and the balance on hand on that date, amounting to 3,447,474·21 taels is divided up amongst the three custodian banks as follows :—

				Taels.
Hong Kong and Shanghai Bank	..	..	..	1,149,364·88
Deutsch Asiatische Bank	..	..	..	1,149,068·54
Russo-Asiatic Bank ..	..	..	..	1,149,040·79

I also have the honour to hand you herewith :—

1. Statement showing total amount of revenue collected for account of "Chinese Indemnity."

2. Copy of Commissioner of Customs, Shanghai, "Chinese Indemnity account" to the 31st July with the Hong Kong and Shanghai Bank, together with certificate of balance.

3. Copy of Commissioner of Customs, Shanghai, "Chinese Indemnity account" to the 31st July with the Deutsch-Asiatische Bank.

4. Copy of Commissioner of Customs, Shanghai, "Chinese Indemnity account" to the 31st July with the Russo-Asiatic Bank.

5. Copy of Commissioner of Customs, Shanghai, "Chinese Indemnity account" to the 31st July with the Yokohama Specie Bank.

6. Copy of Commissioner of Customs, Shanghai, "Chinese Indemnity account" to the 31st July with the Banque de l'Indo-Chine.

7. Copy of Commissioner of Customs, Shanghai, "Chinese Indemnity account" to the 31st July with the International Banking Corporation.

8. Copy of Commissioner of Customs, Shanghai, "Chinese Indemnity account" to the 31st July with the Banque Sino-Belge.

There have been no payments made during the past three months on account of the indemnity, and the amount collected during the period, viz., 705,856·94 taels, together with balance brought forward from the 30th April, viz., 638,255·35 taels, appears at the credit of the Commissioner of Customs Indemnity account as follows :—

			Taels.
With the Hong Kong and Shanghai Bank to the extent of	..	..	148,664·12
„ Deutsch-Asiatische Bank to the extent of ..	..	..	283,316·09
„ Russo-Asiatic Bank to the extent of	..	..	391,027·69
„ Yokohama Specie Bank to the extent of ..	..	..	107,687·16
„ Banque de l'Indo-Chine to the extent of ..	..	..	215,442·20
„ International Bank to the extent of	..	..	94,258·47
„ Banque Sino-Belge to the extent of	..	..	107,721·06

The banks have also allowed credit interest at 2 per cent. on the account in their books, which amounts to 4,004·50 taels, and which is included in the above balances.

78.

I further enclose copy of the Inspector-General of Customs " Native Customs Revenue Account " to the 31st July with the Hong Kong and Shanghai Bank. This letter is sent you through the senior consul here, and a copy is being forwarded to each consul interested.

I have, &c.
H. M. S. MAN, *Secretary*,
International Bankers' Commission.

Enclosure 2 in No. 63.

Deputy Commissioner, Shanghai, to Secretary, International Bankers' Commission.

Dear Sir, *Custom-house, Shanghai, July 1, 1912.*
I HAVE received from the Inspector-General of Customs two orders on his *li-kin* revenue account, each for 76,000 Shanghai taels, and made out, respectively, to the order of the Hong Kong and Shanghai Bank and the Deutsch-Asiatische Bank. I should be obliged if you would kindly forward these two orders to the banks concerned, at the same time informing them that they represent what the inspector-general can furnish as the *li-kin* proceeds quota towards the monthly instalment of the 4½ per Cent. Loan of 1898 due on the 5th July, 1912.

In this connection I am directed by the inspector-general to say that *li-kin* remittances from the collectorates concerned have been practically suspended since the completion of the instalment due the 5th December, 1911, and that the funds from this source now forthcoming represent quota received on account at irregular intervals from two collectorates, Soochow and Hangchow, only, with a very small addition of Ichang salt *li-kin.*

I am, &c.
ALEX. W. CROSS,
Deputy Commissioner in charge.

No. 64.

Admiralty to Foreign Office.—(Received September 30.)

Sir, *Admiralty, September 30, 1912.*
I AM commanded by my Lords Commissioners of the Admiralty to transmit, for the information of the Secretary of State for Foreign Affairs, copy of a telegram, dated the 30th instant, from the commander-in-chief on the China station respecting the return of troops from Hankow.

I am, &c.
W. GRAHAM GREENE.

Enclosure in No. 64.

Commander-in-chief, China, to Admiralty.

(Telegraphic.) *September 30, 1912.*
TROOPS at Hankow.
I am arranging for the return of the detachment to Hong Kong, their presence at Hankow being no longer necessary. His Majesty's Minister at Peking has concurred in their withdrawal.

No. 65.

Sir J. Jordan to Sir Edward Grey.—(Received October 5.)

Sir, *Peking, September 18, 1912.*
WITH reference to my despatch of the 5th ultimo, I have the honour to transmit herewith, in translation, a note which I have received from the Wai-chiao Pu, stating that no foreign loan or mortgage in respect of mining property can be

recognised as valid unless the transaction has received the previous assent of the Chinese Government.

This communication was discussed at a meeting of the foreign representatives on the 16th instant, and it was decided not to reply to it, but I am circulating it to His Majesty's consular officers for their information and guidance.

I have, &c.
J. N. JORDAN.

Enclosure in No. 65.

Wai-chiao Pu to Sir J. Jordan.

(Translation.)

Sir,   *Peking, August 3, 1912.*
WE have received the following communication from the Ministry of Industry and Commerce :—

"This Ministry has general charge of the administration of mines, and all sales, purchases, and transfers of, as well as loans and mortgages on, mining property by mine-owners must be notified and formally sanctioned before they can be put into effect. It is reported, however, that in various places mine-owners are constantly engaging in private loan or mortgage transactions, and it has even happened that agreements have been made with foreigners without the previous consent of a majority of the shareholders. It is of the utmost importance, therefore, that it should be made clear that any mortgage, under whatsoever name or title made, for foreign money, on any mine managed by Chinese merchants, can have no valid effect unless it has received the sanction of the Ministry."

On the 25th ultimo I addressed a note to your Excellency, stating that no foreign loan contracted by any railway under commercial management in the provinces could be valid unless submitted to, and allowed by, the Central Government. The question of mining affairs is on the same footing and should be treated in the same manner. In future the borrowing of foreign capital by mine-owners, to be effective, must have received the sanction of the Central Government, while the foreign lending merchant must request his Minister to ascertain whether the formal sanction of the Chinese Government has actually been given ; then only can the loan be made and satisfactory safeguard be ensured.

I have the honour to communicate the above information to your Excellency for notification to the British mercantile community throughout the country.

I avail, &c.
(Seal of Wai-chiao Pu.)

No. 66.

Sir J. Jordan to Sir Edward Grey.—(Received October 9.)

Sir,   *Peking, September 24, 1912.*
I HAVE the honour to report that on the 15th instant Mr. Lu Cheng-hsiang, whose ill-health had for some weeks previously incapacitated him for the transaction of public business, handed over the portfolio of Minister for Foreign Affairs to Mr. Liang Ju-hao, better known to foreigners in this country as M. T. Liang, his "style" being Liang Meng-t'ing.

The new Minister, who is a native of Canton province, and was educated in America, has previously held office as Director of Northern Railways, as taotai at Newchwang, customs taotai at Tien-tsin in 1907 during the viceroyalty of Yuan Shih-kai, and for a brief period as Shanghai taotai. During his tenure of office as President of the Board of Foreign Affairs, Yuan brought him up to Peking as a secretary in that department, and he subsequently joined Tang Shao-yi at Mukhden as secretary to the Provincial Administration.

Mr. Liang has a fluent command of English, a pleasant manner, and considerable experience in dealings with foreigners.

It will be remembered that Mr. Liang was nominated by the President as candidate for the Ministry of Communications in the first Coalition Cabinet, but was vetoed by the Nanking Assembly ; his acceptance by the National Council as Minister

for Foreign Affairs is consequently another sign of Yuan Shih-kai's steadily increasing influence.
On the 22nd instant Mr. Lu Cheng-hsiang's resignation of the office of Premier was likewise accepted. His successor has not yet been appointed, but will probably be Mr. Chao Ping-chün, the Minister of the Interior, another staunch henchman of Yuan Shih-kai's, who has been acting as head of the Cabinet during Mr. Lu's illness.
I have, &c.
J. N. JORDAN.

No. 67.

Sir J. Jordan to Sir Edward Grey.—(Received October 21.)

Sir,
Peking, October 6, 1912.
WITH reference to my despatch of the 6th September, I have the honour to forward herewith a summary by Sir Somerville Head of events in the provinces during the month of September.
I have, &c.
J. N. JORDAN.

Enclosure in No. 67.

Summary of Events in the Provinces for the month of September 1912.

THE visit of Dr. Sun Yat Sen and other southern leaders to Peking, and the complete adherence they have now expressed to the policy of his Excellency Yuan Shih-kai, has given a great stimulus towards the unity of the country, and strengthened the administration of the Central Government. Dr. Sun Yat Sen has been commissioned to study the question of railway development, General Huang Hsing that of mines while General Chen Chi Mei is being sent abroad to investigate political constitutions. However visionary and unpractical the schemes advocated by Dr. Sun may appear, they at least have had the merit of diverting the attention of the people from politics to the more important question of economic development, and to the necessity for improving the means of communication in China, even if foreign capital has to be employed for the purpose. Schemes for improved methods of sericulture, agriculture and afforestation, are also being discussed in the provinces, and there seems little doubt that, once order and confidence are restored, questions of economic development will be pushed forward with energy.
Unfortunately these desirable conditions are lacking. Brigandage and lawlessness are still reported from all sides. His Majesty's consul at Nanking reports that some 3,000 disbanded soldiers are preying upon the neighbourhood of Hsuchowfu, and that an equal number of troops have been sent up from Nanking to deal with them. According to a telegram in the newspapers, the regular troops have been defeated. At Wuchang a serious mutiny at the end of the month was fortunately frustrated by General Li, who obtained information of the impending rising in time to arrest the ring-leaders ; but the situation at that port is still very unsettled. There have been smaller military riots at Shasi, further up the Yang-tsze, and in the Province of Kueichow to the south-west, where 200 soldiers were surrounded and killed by armed bandits. The condition of Shensi is still very unsettled, though here, as elsewhere, foreigners are not molested in any way.
The Province of Fukien remains in a state of nervous unrest. In the middle of September there was an outbreak at Hsing Hua on the coast south of the Foochow prefecture, and it became necessary to call in all foreign missionaries from that district. By the end of the month, however, the local troops inflicted a severe defeat on the rebels, and missionaries have since been permitted to return. The action of P'eng, the assistant governor, who had gathered round him a considerable force in opposition to the local Government, gave rise to some anxiety, and at one time serious fighting between the opposing troops appeared imminent. A solution of the difficulty, however, has now been found in the established process of summoning P'eng to Peking to receive a further appointment on account of his eminent services to the Republican cause ; but it is not yet certain whether he will avail himself of the invitation.

In a despatch from Chungking, His Majesty's consul reviews the critical situation of the finances of the Province of Szechuan, which, seriously impaired by the railway rising of last year, have suffered still more from the subsequent disorders in the interior. Local defence and other needs have diverted from Chentu and Chungking a large portion of the normal revenue, which has been still further diminished by evasion of *li-kin* and other tax payments. The Treasury is admittedly empty, and no satisfactory scheme of raising funds has yet been evolved. Meanwhile, there is a large decrease of silver and an increase of heavily depreciated paper currency.

General Hsiung, commander of the 5th army division at Chungking, has been displaying great energy in suppressing various risings all over the province. He has succeeded in defeating and executing the rebel leader Li-Shao-yi, who for months past had been carrying on brigandage on an extensive scale with a force of some 20,000 outlaws in the Ta Chu district. General Hsiung is now occupied in pursuing the remnants of this scattered band. The politicians of Chengtu and Chungking continue their fruitless rivalry for the leadership of Szechuan.

The Government of Canton remains in the hands of a band of inexperienced young revolutionaries, and order is only maintained by the energy of the chief of the police. Money is very scarce, and there is a general lack of confidence in the present administration.

At a meeting held at Yunnanfu on the 15th September, after the return of Tutu Tsai from his sudden visit to Mengtse, the Tung-men-hui and Kung-yi-ho-tang parties agreed to unite their forces, and elected General Li Ken Yuan, now the most powerful man in the province, as their president. General Li Ken Yuan made his triumphal entry into Yunnanfu on the 3rd October.

S. H.

No. 68.

Sir J. Jordan to Sir Edward Grey.—(Received November 18.)

Sir, Peking, October 31, 1912.

I HAVE the honour to enclose herewith an extract from the "Official Gazette" of the 22nd instant, showing that commissioners are to be sent from the Ministry of Finance to the provinces to investigate financial conditions with a view to restoring the impoverished condition of the Central Government.

I have, &c
J. N. JORDAN.

Enclosure in No. 68.

Extract from the "Gazette" of October 22, 1912.

PETITION from Chou Hsueh-hsi to the President. In view of the financial straits of the country, I propose to send commissioners to every province to study the financial conditions there. My purpose is to find out the position of each individual province as regards finance, and how it compares with the others. The commissioners will make investigations as to the division of administrative expenditure and draw up schemes for estimates, and I hope, while putting the Central Government in possession of accurate information as to the condition financially of the provinces, also to bring to the consciousness of the provinces the impoverished condition of the Central Government. At present the ordinary administrative expenditure of the Central Government is at the very least 4,000,000 taels a-month, and to meet this we are forced to have recourse to foreign loans. The commissioners will be empowered to draw up schemes with the concurrence of the tutus for the raising of revenue to meet the expenses of administration, and for the enforcing of the national taxes. I have to ask your approval of the attached list of commissioners* who will investigate conditions in the provinces specified. (The President has signified his approval.) .

---

* Not received at the Foreign Office.

[1270] G

82

No. 69.

War Office to Foreign Office.—(Received November 22.)

Sir, *War Office, November 21, 1912.*

I AM commanded by the Army Council to address you again on the subject of the temporary additions which were made last year to the garrisons in North and South China.

In view of the necessity for the immediate preparation of the estimates in connection with movements of troops during 1913–14, I am to request that you will ascertain whether in the opinion of Secretary Sir E. Grey the presence of all or any of the following units may be dispensed with during the trooping season September 1913—March 1914 :—

In Hong Kong (South China command): The 25th and 26th Punjabis, and two infantry battalions from India ; the 24th Hazara mountain battery from India.

In Peking and Tien-tsin (North China command): The second British infantry battalion serving there.

All the above are in excess of the normal peace garrisons of the commands named.

I am, &c.

E. W. D. WARD.

───────────────────────

No. 70.

Sir Edward Grey to Sir J. Jordan.

(Telegraphic.) *Foreign Office, December 5, 1912.*

IN view of immediate preparation of estimates in connection with movements of troops 1913–14, War Office enquire whether the presence of all or any of the following additional troops may be dispensed with during the trooping season September 1913–March 1914 :—

In South China Command : The two extra native infantry battalions and the mountain battery from India.

In the North China Command : The second British infantry battalion.

Please telegraph your views.

───────────────────────

No. 71.

Sir J. Jordan to Sir Edward Grey.—(Received December 6.)

(Telegraphic.) *Peking, December 6, 1912.*

YOUR telegram of 5th December.

I do not think that it would be safe to dispense with any of the additional troops mentioned.

───────────────────────

No. 72.

Foreign Office to War Office.

Sir, *Foreign Office, December 10, 1912.*

WITH reference to your letter of the 21st ultimo, with regard to the withdrawal of the additional troops from the North and South China commands during the trooping season of 1913–14, I am directed by Secretary Sir E. Grey to inform you that, in view of the opinion expressed by His Majesty's Minister at Peking in his telegram of the 6th December, copy of which was forwarded to you by this department on the 7th instant, he considers that it will be impossible for the present to dispense with the presence of these troops.

I am, &c.

W. LANGLEY.

No. 73.

Sir J. Jordan to Sir Edward Grey.—(Received December 23.)

Sir,   *Peking, December 6, 1912.*
WITH reference to my despatch of the 6th September last, forwarding a copy of the second quarterly report from the International Bankers' Commission for the three months ended the 31st July, 1912, I have the honour to enclose a further report from the bankers dealing with the appropriation of customs revenue for the quarter ended the 31st October, 1912.

As shown in the report, all instalments of principal and interest on the loans secured by the customs revenues have been paid off up to the 31st October, and the balance in hand on that date amounted to 9,486,626 taels.

The indemnity instalment due in October 1911, representing 2,070,187 taels, for which exchange was actually settled, has also been paid during the past quarter. As the available revenues were insufficient to meet the charge by the sum of 39,656 taels, the balance was provided for through the Hong Kong and Shanghai Bank by an overdraft from the "Native Customs Revenue Account," which has subsequently been paid off by means of the remittances from the ports.

I have, &c.
J. N. JORDAN.

Enclosure in No. 73.

Chartered Bank of India, Australia, and China to Sir J. Jordan.

Sir,   *Shanghai, November 22, 1912.*
IN compliance with the instructions contained in your despatch of the 30th January, I am directed to hand you herewith* :—

1. Statement showing the net amount of the Maritime Customs Revenue received and expended on account of the Chinese Loan Service for quarter ending the 31st October.

2. Copy of Inspector-General of Customs "Foreign Revenue" account with the Hong Kong and Shanghai Bank, Shanghai, from the 31st July to the 31st October.

3. Copy of the Commissioner of Customs, Shanghai, "Chinese Loan Service Account" with the Hong Kong and Shanghai Bank, Shanghai, from the 31st July to the 31st October, together with certificate of balance.

4. Copy of the Commissioner of Customs, Shanghai, "Chinese Loan Service Account" with the Deutsch-Asiatische Bank, Shanghai, together with certificate of balance.

5. Copy of the Commissioner of Customs, Shanghai, "Chinese Loan Service Account" with the Russo-Asiatic Bank, Shanghai, together with certificate of balance.

6. List of instalments of principal and interest on Chinese loans paid through the Hong Kong and Shanghai Bank from the 31st July to the 31st October.

7. List of instalments of principal and interest on Chinese loans paid through Deutsch-Asiatische Bank.

From these statements it will be observed that the net revenue collected from the 31st July to the 31st ultimo amounted to 10,567,935·66 taels against 10,011,524·73 taels for the previous quarter, and 12,308,828·36 taels for the first quarter.

Payments of loan instalments of principal and interest amounted to 4,444,450·24 taels, and all instalments due up to and including the 31st ultimo have been paid off, leaving a balance on hand on that date of 9,486,626·60 taels, which is divided up amongst the three custodian banks as follows :—

	Taels.
Hong Kong and Shanghai Bank	.. 3,162,208·87
Deutsch-Asiatische Bank ..	.. 3,162,208·87
Russo-Asiatic Bank ..	.. 3,162,208·86
Total	.. 9,486,626·60

* Not received at the Foreign Office.

                                                         H

I am further directed to forward you :—

1. Statement showing net amount of Native Customs Revenue collected for account of Chinese indemnity for quarter ended the 31st October last.

2. Copy of the Commissioner of Customs, Shanghai, "Chinese Indemnity Account," from the 31st July to the 31st ultimo, with the Hong Kong and Shanghai Bank, Shanghai.

3. Copy of the Commissioner of Customs, Shanghai, "Chinese Indemnity Account," from the 31st July to the 31st ultimo, with the Deutsch-Asiatische Bank.

4. Copy of the Commissioner of Customs, Shanghai, "Chinese Indemnity Account," from the 31st July to the 31st ultimo, with the Russo-Asiatic Bank.

5. Copy of the Commissioner of Customs, Shanghai, "Chinese Indemnity Account," from the 31st July to the 31st ultimo, with the Yokohama Specie Bank.

6. Copy of the Commissioner of Customs, Shanghai, "Chinese Indemnity Account," from the 31st July to the 31st ultimo, with the Banque de l'Indo-Chine.

7. Copy of the Commissioner of Customs, Shanghai, "Chinese Indemnity Account," from the 31st July to the 31st ultimo, with the International Banking Corporation.

8. Copy of the Commissioner of Customs, Shanghai, "Chinese Indemnity Account," from the 31st July to the 31st ultimo, with the Banque Sino-Belge.

The indemnity instalment, due in October 1911, was paid during the past quarter, the equivalent of which amounted to 2,070,187·63 taels; the total receipts, however, amounted to only 2,045,827·87 taels, leaving a shortage of 39,656·64 taels after paying sundry cheques issued by the inspector-general amounting to 15,306·88 taels. This shortage, it was agreed, should be advanced by the Hong Kong and Shanghai Bank by means of an overdraft on the Inspector-General "Native Customs Revenue Account." All remittances from the ports of Native Customs Revenue, as they are received, will be applied to the reduction of this overdraft.

A copy of the Inspector-General's "Native Customs Revenue Account" to the 31st October, showing a debit balance of 39,656·64 taels, is also enclosed for your guidance. The overdraft has, however, since been paid off.

This letter is sent you as usual through the senior consul here, and a copy is being forwarded to each consul interested.

I have, &c.

H. M. S. MAN, *Secretary,*
International Bankers' Commission.